KARL MARX

Theories of Surplus Value

PART I

LAWRENCE & WISHART LONDON

Translated by Emile Burns

SBN 85315 212 8

Karl Marx

KARL MARX

THEORIES OF SURPLUS-VALUE

(Volume IV of Capital)

PART I

PROGRESS PUBLISHERS

Moscow

TRANSLATED BY EMILE BURNS
EDITED BY S. RYAZANSKAYA

К. МАРКС

ТЕОРИИ ПРИБАВОЧНОЙ СТОИМОСТИ

(IV том «Капитала»)

Часть I

На английском языке

First printing 1963
Second printing 1969
Third printing 1975
Fourth printing 1978

М $\frac{10101-287}{014(01)-78}$ без объявл.

PUBLISHER'S NOTE

This translation has been made from Karl Marx, *Theorien über den Mehrwert,* Teil 1, Dietz Verlag, Berlin, 1956. The arrangement of the material and the notes correspond on the whole to the Russian edition of Marx-Engels, *Collected Works,* Vol. 26, Part I, Moscow, 1962, prepared by the Institute of Marxism-Leninism in Moscow, where the manuscript of the work is kept.

It has been attempted to keep the translation as closely as possible to the original. When, for the sake of clarity, it has been found necessary to insert a few words these are enclosed in square brackets. In order to avoid confusion, the square brackets occasionally used by Marx in the manuscript have been replaced either by pointed brackets ⟨ ⟩ or, when the passages enclosed were longer, by braces { }.

Quotations from French, German and Italian authors are given in English in the text and are reproduced in the original language in the Appendix. In the case of British writers cited by Marx from a French source, the original English version appears in the text and the French translation used by Marx in the Appendix. Where an omission in a passage quoted has not been indicated by Marx, the ellipsis is enclosed in square brackets. Other discrepancies between the quotations as recorded by Marx and as they appear in the original source, are mentioned in footnotes. Words underlined by Marx, both in his own writing and in the extracts quoted by him, are set in italics, as are also titles of publications and foreign words customarily italicised. Chapter and section headings correspond in general to those of the Russian edition. Headings set in square brackets have been provided by the Institute of Marxism-Leninism in Moscow on the basis of formulations used by Marx in the chapter or section in question.

The numbers of Marx's notebooks are indicated by Roman numerals, those of the manuscript pages by Arabic numerals, which are separated from the text by vertical lines. As a rule these numbers are printed only at the beginning of the relevant portion of the manuscript, but where passages have been transposed the number of the manuscript page (and, when there is a change to another notebook, also the number of the notebook) is shown both at the beginning of the passage (e.g. ||XII-659|) and also at the end (e.g. |XII-659||).

CONTENTS

PREFACE 13

[CONTENTS OF THE MANUSCRIPT *THEORIES OF SURPLUS-VALUE*] 37

[GENERAL OBSERVATION] 40

[*CHAPTER I*] SIR JAMES STEUART [Distinction between "Profit upon Alienation" and the Positive Increase of Wealth] 41

[*CHAPTER II*] THE PHYSIOCRATS 44

[1. Transfer of the Inquiry into the Origin of Surplus-Value from the Sphere of Circulation into the Sphere of Direct Production. Conception of Rent as the Sole Form of Surplus-Value] 44

[2. Contradictions in the System of the Physiocrats: the Feudal Shell of the System and Its Bourgeois Essence; the Twofold Treatment of Surplus-Value] 49

[3. Quesnay on the Three Classes in Society. Further Development of Physiocratic Theory with Turgot: Elements of a Deeper Analysis of Capitalist Relations] 54

[4. Confusion of Value with Material Substance (Paoletti)] 60

[5. Elements of Physiocratic Theory in Adam Smith] 60

[6. The Physiocrats as Partisans of Large-Scale Capitalist Agriculture] 64

[7. Contradictions in the Political Views of the Physiocrats. The Physiocrats and the French Revolution] 65

[8. Vulgarisation of the Physiocratic Doctrine by the Prussian Reactionary Schmalz] 67

[9. An Early Critique of the Superstition of the Physiocrats in the Question of Agriculture (Verri)] 67

[*CHAPTER III*] ADAM SMITH 69

[1. Smith's Two Different Definitions of Value; the Determination of Value by the Quantity of Labour Expended Which Is Contained in a Commodity, and Its Determination by the Quantity of Living Labour Which Can Be Bought in Exchange for This Commodity] 69

[2. Smith's General Conception of Surplus-Value. The Notion of Profit, Rent and Interest as Deductions from the Product of the Worker's Labour] 77

[3. Adam Smith's Extension of the Idea of Surplus-Value to All Spheres of Social Labour] 85

[4. Smith's Failure to Grasp the Specific Way in Which the Law of Value Operates in the Exchange between Capital and Wage-Labour] 86

[5. Smith's Identification of Surplus-Value with Profit. The Vulgar Element in Smith's Theory] 89

[6. Smith's Erroneous View of Profit, Rent of Land and Wages as Sources of Value] 92

[7. Smith's Dual View of the Relationship between Value and Revenue. The Vicious Circle of Smith's Conception of "Natural Price" as the Sum of Wages, Profit and Rent] 95

[8. Smith's Error in Resolving the Total Value of the Social Product into Revenue. Contradictions in His Views on Gross and Net Revenue] 97

[9. Say as Vulgariser of Smith's Theory. Say's Identification of the Social Gross Product with the Social Revenue. Attempts to Draw a Distinction between Them by Storch and Ramsay] 103

[10. Inquiry into How It Is Possible for the Annual Profit and Wages to Buy the Annual Commodities, Which Besides Profit and Wages Also Contain Constant Capital] 107

[(a) Impossibility of the Replacement of the Constant Capital of the Producers of Consumption Goods through Exchange between These Producers] 107

[(b) Impossibility of Replacing the Whole Constant Capital of Society by Means of Exchange between the Producers of Articles of Consumption and the Producers of Means of Production] . . 125

[(c) Exchange of Capital for Capital between the Producers of Means of Production. Annual Product of Labour and the Product of Labour Newly Added Annually] 138

[11. Additional Points: Smith's Confusion on the Question of the Measure of Value. General Character of the Contradictions in Smith] 150

[*CHAPTER IV*] THEORIES OF PRODUCTIVE AND UNPRODUCTIVE LABOUR 152

[1. Productive Labour from the Standpoint of Capitalist Production: Labour Which Produces Surplus-Value] 152

[2. Views of the Physiocrats and Mercantilists on Productive Labour] 153

[3. The Duality in Smith's Conception of Productive Labour. His First Explanation: the View of Productive Labour as Labour Exchanged for Capital] 155

[4. Adam Smith's Second Explanation: the View of Productive Labour as Labour Which Is Realised in Commodity] 160

[5. Vulgarisation of Bourgeois Political Economy in the Definition of Productive Labour] 174

[6. Advocates of Smith's Views on Productive Labour. On the History of the Subject] 176

[(a) Advocates of the First View: Ricardo, Sismondi] 176

[(b) Early Attempts to Distinguish between Productive and Unproductive Labour (D'Avenant, Petty)] 178

[(c) John Stuart Mill, an Adherent of Smith's Second View of Productive Labour] 182

[7.] Germain Garnier. [Vulgarisation of the Theories Put Forward by Smith and the Physiocrats] 183

[(a) Confusion of Labour Which Is Exchanged against Capital with Labour Exchanged against Revenue. The False Conception that the Total Capital Is Replaced through the Revenue of the Consumers] 183

[(b) Replacement of the Constant Capital by Means of the Exchange of Capital against Capital] 187

[(c) Vulgar Assumptions of Garnier's Polemics against Smith. Garnier's Relapse into Physiocratic Ideas. The View of the Unproductive Labourer's Consumption as the Source of Production—a Step Backwards as Compared with the Physiocrats] 198

[8.] Charles Ganilh [Mercantilist Conception of Exchange and Exchange-Value. Inclusion of All Paid Labour in the Concept of Productive Labour] 203

[9. Ganilh and Ricardo on Net Revenue. Ganilh as Advocate of a Diminution of the Productive Population; Ricardo as Advocate of the Accumulation of Capital and the Growth of Productive Forces] 213

[10.] Exchange of Revenue and Capital [Replacement of the Total Amount of the Annual Product: (a) Exchange of Revenue for Revenue; (b) Exchange of Revenue for Capital; (c) Exchange of Capital for Capital] 230

[11.] Ferrier [Protectionist Character of Ferrier's Polemics against Smith's Theory of Productive Labour and the Accumulation of Capital. Smith's Confusion on the Question of Accumulation. The Vulgar Element in Smith's View of "Productive Labourers"] . . . 252

[12.] Earl of Lauderdale [Apologetic Conception of the Ruling Classes as Representatives of the Most Important Kinds of Productive Labour] 264

[13. Say's Conception of "Immaterial Products". Vindication of an Unrestrained Growth of Unproductive Labour] 266

[14.] Count Destutt de Tracy [Vulgar Conception of the Origin of Profit. Proclamation of the "Industrial Capitalist" as the Sole Productive Labourer] 269

[15. General Nature of the Polemics Against Smith's Distinction between Productive and Unproductive Labour. Apologetic Conception of Unproductive Consumption as a Necessary Spur to Production] 281

[16.] Henri Storch [Unhistorical Approach to the Problems of the Interaction between Material and Spiritual Production. Conception of "Immaterial Labour" Performed by the Ruling Class] 284

[17.] Nassau Senior [Proclamation of All Functions Useful to the Bourgeoisie as Productive. Toadyism to the Bourgeoisie and the Bourgeois State] 287

[18.] Pellegrino Rossi [Disregard of the Social Form of Economic Phenomena. Vulgar Conception of "Labour-Saving" by Unproductive Labourers] 292

[19. Apologia for the Prodigality of the Rich by the Malthusian Chalmers] 299

[20. Concluding Observations on Adam Smith and His Views on Productive and Unproductive Labour] 300

[*CHAPTER V*] NECKER [Attempt to Present the Antagonism of Classes in Capitalism as the Antithesis between Poverty and Wealth] 305

[*CHAPTER VI*] QUESNAY'S TABLEAU ÉCONOMIQUE (Digression) 308

[1. Quesnay's Attempt to Show the Process of Reproduction and Circulation of the Total Capital] 308

[2. Circulation between Farmers and Landowners. The Return Circuit of Money to the Farmers, Which Does Not Express Reproduction] 308

[3. On the Circulation of Money between Capitalist and Labourer] 314

[(a) The Absurdity of Speaking of Wages as an Advance by the Capitalist to the Labourer. Bourgeois Conception of Profit as Reward for Risk] 314

[(b) Commodities Which the Labourer Buys from the Capitalist. A Return Flow of the Money Which Does Not Indicate Reproduction] 321

[4. Circulation between Farmer and Manufacturer According to the Tableau Économique] 328

[5. Circulation of Commodities and Circulation of Money in the Tableau Économique. Different Cases in Which the Money Flows Back to Its Starting-Point] 333

[6. Significance of the Tableau Économique in the History of Political Economy] 343

[*CHAPTER VII*] LINGUET [Early Critique of the Bourgeois-Liberal View of the "Freedom" of the Labourer] 345

ADDENDA

[1. Hobbes on Labour, on Value and on the Economic Role of Science] 353

[2.] Historical: Petty [Negative Attitude to Unproductive Occupations. Germs of the Labour Theory of Value. Attempt to Explain Wages, Rent of Land, the Price of Land and Interest on the Basis of the Theory of Value] 354

[3.] Petty, Sir Didley North, Locke 364

[4.] Locke [Treatment of Rent and Interest from the Standpoint of the Bourgeois Theory of Natural Law] 365

[5.] North [Money as Capital. The Growth of Trade as the Cause of the Fall in the Rate of Interest] 368

[6. Berkeley on Industry as the Source of Wealth] 372

[7.] Hume and Massie 373

[(a) Massie and Hume on Interest] 373

[(b) Hume. Fall of Profit and Interest Dependent on the Growth of Trade and Industry] 373

[(c) Massie. Interest as Part of Profit. The Level of Interest Explained by the Rate of Profit] 375

[(d) Conclusion] 377

[8. Addendum to the Chapters on the Physiocrats] 378

[(a) Supplementary Note on the Tableau Économique. Quesnay's False Assumptions] 378

[(b) Partial Reversion of Individual Physiocrats to Mercantilist Ideas. Demand of the Physiocrats for Freedom of Competition] 379

[(c) Original Formulation of Why It Is Impossible to Increase Value in Exchange] 380

[9. Glorification of the Landed Aristocracy by Buat, an Epigone of the Physiocrats] 381

[10. Polemics against the Landed Aristocracy from the Standpoint of the Physiocrats (an Anonymous English Author)] 382

[11. Apologist Conception of the Productivity of All Professions] 387

[12.] Productivity of Capital. Productive and Unproductive Labour 389

[(a) Productivity of Capital as the Capitalist Expression of the Productive Power of Social Labour] 389

[(b)Productive Labour in the System of Capitalist Production] 393

[(c) Two Essentially Different Phases in the Exchange between Capital and Labour] 397

[(d) The Specific Use-Value of Productive Labour for Capital] 399

[(e) Unproductive Labour as Labour Which Performs Services; Purchase of Services under Conditions of Capitalism. Vulgar

Conception of the Relation between Capital and Labour as an Exchange of Services] 401
[(f) The Labour of Handicraftsmen and Peasants in Capitalist Society] 407
[(g) Supplementary Definition of Productive Labour as Labour Which Is Realised in Material Wealth] 409
[(h) Manifestations of Capitalism in the Sphere of Immaterial Production] 410
[(i) The Problem of Productive Labour from the Standpoint of the Total Process of Material Production] 411
[(j) The Transport Industry as a Branch of Material Production. Productive Labour in the Transport Industry] 412
[13. Draft Plans for Parts I and III of *Capital*] 414
[(a) Plan for Part I or Section I of *Capital*] 414
[(b) Plan for Part III or Section III of *Capital*] 414
[(c) Plan for Chapter II of Part III of *Capital*] 415

APPENDICES

Quotations in French, German and Italian 419
Notes 473
Index of Authorities 492
Name Index 500

PREFACE

Theories of Surplus-Value was written by Marx between January 1862 and July 1863. This work is part of the voluminous manuscript of 1861-63, entitled by Marx *Zur Kritik der Politischen Oekonomie* (*A Contribution to the Critique of Political Economy*) and written by him as the immediate sequel to the first part of *A Contribution to the Critique of Political Economy* published in 1859. The 1861-63 manuscript consists of 23 notebooks (the pages numbered consecutively from 1 to 1472) running to some 200 printed sheets in length: it is the first systematically worked out draft—though still only rough and incomplete—of all four volumes of *Capital*. *Theories of Surplus-Value* forms the longest (about 110 printed sheets) and most fully elaborated part of this manuscript and is *the first and only draft of the fourth, concluding volume of "Capital"*. Marx called this volume, as distinguished from the three theoretical volumes, the *historical*, *historico-critical*, or *historico-literary* part of his work.

Marx began to write *Theories of Surplus-Value* within the framework of the original plan of his *Critique of Political Economy* as he had projected in 1858-62. On the basis of what Marx says of the structure of his work in his introduction to the first part of *A Contribution to the Critique of Political Economy*, in his letters of 1858-62 and in the 1861-63 manuscript itself, this plan can be presented in the following schematic form:

PLAN OF THE CRITIQUE OF POLITICAL ECONOMY
AS PROJECTED BY MARX IN 1858-62

- I. Capital:
  - [introduction: Commodity and Money]
  - (a) Capital in general:
    - 1. The production process of capital:
      - 1. Transformation of money into capital
      - 2. Absolute surplus-value
      - 3. Relative surplus-value
      - 4. The combination of both
      - 5. Theories of surplus-value
    - 2. The circulation process of capital
    - 3. The unity of the two, or capital and profit
  - (b) The competition of capitals
  - (c) Credit
  - (d) Share capital
- II. Landed property
- III. Wage-labour
- IV. The state
- V. Foreign trade
- VI. The world-market

It can be seen from this plan that *Theories of Surplus-Value* was originally conceived by Marx as a historical excursus to that section of his theoretical study of "capital in general" which was devoted to the problem of the production process of capital. This historical excursus was to conclude the section on the production process of capital, in the same way as in the first part of *A Contribution to the Critique of Political Economy* the chapter on commodities was concluded by the historical excursus "On the History of the Theory of Commodities" and the chapter on money by the historical excursus "Theories of the Medium of Circulation and of Money".

That was Marx's original plan. But in the process of working it out the historical excursus on theories of surplus-value went far beyond the limits of this plan. The subject-matter of the theories to be investigated and criticised by Marx itself demanded an extension of the limits of the inquiry. The critical analysis of the views of bourgeois economists on surplus-value was unavoidably interwoven for Marx with the analysis of their ideas of profit; and in so far as these ideas were bound up with erroneous conceptions of ground-rent, it was necessary also to examine the theory of rent—and so on. On the other hand, in order to make the criticism of erroneous theories comprehensive and exhaustive, Marx counterposed to them one or another positive part of the nev economic theory created by Marx himself—a theory that represents the greatest revolutionary transformation in the whole of economic science.

To grasp fully the character of the material and structure of *Theories of Surplus-Value* it is necessary to bear in mind also the following. At the time when Marx began his work on the *Theories*, of the theoretical parts of *Capital* only the first—"The Production Process of Capital"—had been more or less worked out in writing, and even that not fully (this question is examined in the first five notebooks of the 1861-63 manuscript). The second and third parts—to be more exact, certain sections of them—existed only in the form of preliminary sketches in the manuscript of 1857-58. In writing the historical part, therefore, Marx could not simply make reference to certain pages of his theoretical work, but was obliged to undertake a positive elaboration of those theoretical questions which came up in the critical analysis of all previous political economy.

All this led to the historical excursus *Theories of Surplus-Value* assuming immense proportions. In the voluminous manuscript of 1861-63 the historical, or historico-critical, part fills notebooks VI to XV inclusive, plus XVIII, and a number of separate historical essays in notebooks XX to XXIII.

The main text of *Theories of Surplus-Value* is contained in notebooks VI to XV and XVIII, written in the period from January 1862 to January 1863 inclusive. The table of contents compiled by Marx and written on the covers of notebooks VI to XV refers also to this text. This table of contents is of great importance for an understanding of the general structure of Marx's work, its component parts and its plan. In the present edition it is printed at the very beginning of the first part (pp. 37-39). The historico-critical essays and notes contained in the last notebooks of the manuscript, and written in the spring and summer of 1863, are supplementary to the main text.

In the course of his work on *Theories of Surplus-Value* the range of problems examined by Marx was constantly extending. And in the end this led Marx to the idea that it was necessary to separate off the whole of the historico-critical material to form a special, fourth volume of *Capital*. In the process of Marx's work on *Capital* the decisive significance of the division into three parts (1. The Production Process of Capital, 2. The Circulation Process of Capital, 3. The Unity of the Two), which Marx originally had in mind only for the section "Capital in General", became more and more apparent. This division into three parts proved to be so important and so profound that gradually even those subjects which, according to the original plan, were not among the complex of questions allocated by Marx to the section "Capital in General", came to be included in it (for example, the competition of capitals, credit, rent). Parallel with this process of working out the three theoretical parts of *Capital*, which gradually incorporated all the theoretical problems of the political economy of capitalism, Marx became more and more strongly convinced that the historico-critical inquiry should be presented in the form of a separate book—as the fourth volume of *Capital*.

About a month after finishing his work on the 1861-63 manuscript Marx (in a letter dated August 15, 1863) wrote to Engels about this manuscript of his: "... I look at this compilation now and see how I have had to turn everything upside-down and how I had to create even the *historical* part out of material of which some was quite unknown...." By "the historical part" Marx meant the *Theories of Surplus-Value*, which he was therefore already considering as a separate, special part of his work; whereas as late as January 1863 he was proposing to distribute this historico-critical material among the theoretical sections of his inquiry into "Capital in General", as is evident from the plans he drew up for the first and the third parts of *Capital* (see pp. 414-16 of the present volume).

Marx's intention to carry through a critical examination of the history of political economy, starting from the middle of the seventeenth century, is shown by his detailed historico-critical essay on Petty, contained in notebook XXII of the manuscript, written in May 1863; it has the characteristic heading "Historical: Petty". This essay, which has no internal connection with either the preceding or following text, was clearly intended by Marx for the historico-critical part of his work. Petty's views on value, wages, rent, the price of land, interest, etc., are analysed in the essay. Such a wide treatment of Petty's economic views shows that already in May 1863 Marx had conceived the idea which four years later (April 30, 1867) he explicitly set out in a letter to Siegfried Meyer, when he wrote regarding the structure of his *Capital*: "*Volume I* comprises the '*Process of Capitalist Production*' ... *Volume II* gives the continuation and conclusion of the theories, *Volume III the history of political economy from the middle of the seventeenth century*" (Marx at that time proposed to issue the second and third books of *Capital* in *one* volume).

We find the first direct reference to the fourth, "historico-literary", book of *Capital* in Marx's letter to Engels of July 31, 1865. Marx wrote to Engels about how he is getting on with his *Capital*: "There are still three chapters to write in order to complete the theoretical part (the first three books). Then there is still the fourth book, the historico-literary one, to write, which is relatively the easiest part to me as all the problems have been solved in the first three books and this last is therefore more of a repetition in historical form." Here the question may arise why Marx says that he still has "to write" the fourth book of *Capital*, although in the letter of August 15, 1863 quoted above he speaks of "the historical part" as of something already written. The difference in the formulations of 1863 and of 1865 is to be explained by the fact that in the intervening period, in the course of 1864-65, Marx recast and rewrote all three theoretical parts of his work, but the fourth part— "the historico-literary"—was still in the original form as it had been written in 1862-63, and therefore had to be worked over again in conformity with his re-editing of the first three volumes of *Capital*.

From Marx's letter of November 3, 1877 to Siegmund Schott it appears that Marx also later on regarded the historical part of *Capital* as in some degree already written. In this letter Marx says of his work on *Capital*: "In fact I myself began *Capital*, precisely in the reverse order (beginning with the third historical part) from that in which it is presented to the public, with the qualification, however, that the first volume, which was the last to be taken in hand, was prepared for the press straightway while the two others still remained in the raw form that every inquiry originally assumes." Here the historical part is called the third for the reason that Marx, as already mentioned, intended to issue the second and third books of *Capital* in one volume, as Volume II, and the fourth book, "History of the Theory", as the third volume.

These statements by Marx entitle us to regard *Theories of Surplus-Value* (with the supplementary historical sketches and notes from notebooks XX-XXIII) as the original and only draft of the fourth book—or fourth volume—of *Capital*. Engels and Lenin called *Theories of Surplus-Value* the fourth volume of *Capital*.

For these reasons, the words "Volume IV of *Capital*" have, in the present volume, been added in round brackets to the title

Theories of Surplus-Value given by Marx in his 1861-63 manuscript.

* * *

Engels first refers to the manuscript *Theories of Surplus-Value* in his letters to Kautsky of February 16, and March 24, 1884. In the second letter Engels sends word of the agreement reached with Meissner, the publisher of *Capital*, as to the sequence in which the second and then the third book of *Capital*, and *Theories of Surplus-Value* as the concluding part of the whole work, were to be published.

In his letter to Bernstein, written in August 1884, Engels speaks in greater detail of this concluding part of *Capital*. Here we find: "... 'History of the Theory', between ourselves, is in the main written. The manuscript of *A Contribution to the Critique of Political Economy* ... contains, as I believe I showed you here, about 500 quarto pages of *Theories of Surplus-Value*, in which it is true there is a good deal to be cut out, as since then it has been worked up in a different way, but there is still enough."

Engels's preface (dated May 5, 1885) to Volume II of *Capital* gives the most detailed information about the manuscript *Theories of Surplus-Value* and the form in which Engels intended to publish it. He points out that *Theories of Surplus-Value* makes up the main body of the lengthy manuscript *A Contribution to the Critique of Political Economy*, written in 1861-63, and continues: "This section contains a detailed critical history of the pith and marrow of Political Economy, the theory of surplus-value, and develops parallel with it, in polemics against predecessors, most of the points later investigated separately and in their logical connection in the manuscript for Books II and III. After eliminating the numerous passages covered by Books II and III I intend to publish the critical part of this manuscript as *Capital*, Book IV. Valuable as this manuscript is, it could not be used for the present edition of Book II."

In his letters of the late eighties and early nineties Engels repeatedly mentions his intention of proceeding with the preparation of the fourth volume, *Theories of Surplus-Value*, after the publication of Volume III of *Capital*. He however already speaks far less categorically about eliminating the theoretical passages contained in the manuscript of the *Theories*.

The last mention by Engels of the manuscript *Theories of Sur-*

plus-Value is in his letter to Stephan Bauer dated April 10, 1895. As this letter shows, Engels was still hoping in 1895 that he would succeed in publishing this work of Marx's. But Engels did not manage to prepare the concluding volume of *Capital* for the printer; he died barely four months after this letter was written.

From Engels's statements quoted above it is clear that he attributed great importance to the manuscript *Theories of Surplus-Value*, and regarded it as Volume IV of *Capital*. But it is also evident that in 1884-85 Engels intended to remove from the text of this manuscript "numerous passages covered by Books II and III".

Here the question naturally comes up: what should be our attitude with regard to this proposal or intention of Engels?

Only Engels, the great companion and comrade-in-arms of Marx, and in a certain sense the co-author of *Capital*, could have removed from the manuscript *Theories of Surplus-Value* a whole series of passages. In order that the parts of the manuscript that remained after the elimination of these passages should not appear as disconnected fragments, it would have been necessary to work them over to a considerable extent and to link them together with specially written interpolations. And only Engels had the right to work over Marx's text in such a way.

There is one more reason in favour of keeping in the text of *Theories of Surplus-Value* the "numerous passages" mentioned above. Engels's intention to cut out these passages was only his *original* intention, formed before he had begun a detailed study of the manuscript *Theories of Surplus-Value*. And we know from Engels's preface to Volume III of *Capital* that, in the course of his actual work on the preparation of Marx's manuscripts for the printer, he sometimes revised his original intentions and plans. Thus, Engels originally wanted to recast Part V of Volume III of *Capital*, as this part of Marx's manuscript was still in unfinished form. Engels says in his preface that he had tried at least three times to make a fundamental recasting of this part, but in the end abandoned this idea and decided to confine himself "to as orderly an arrangement of available matter as possible, and to making only the most indispensable additions". By analogy with this, it may be presumed that if Engels had actually come to prepare the manuscript *Theories of Surplus-Value* for the press, he would have kept the theoretical digressions contained in it. This presumption is all the more probable because among the digressions are some in which Marx presents very important theoretical analyses, essentially supplementing the exposition, for example, in Volume III of *Capital*—particularly the section on rent.

Lenin had an extremely high regard for the theoretical analyses contained in the manuscript *Theories of Surplus-Value*. He often referred in his writings to *Theories of Surplus-Value*, expressing equally great esteem for both the historico-critical and the purely theoretical content of this work of Marx. He valued particularly highly the sections in which Marx developed his own views on the nature of rent (see V. I. Lenin, *The Agrarian Question and the "Critics of Marx"*, Eng. ed., Moscow, 1954, pp. 29 and 158; *The Agrarian Programme of Social-Democracy in the First Russian Revolution, 1905-1907*, Eng. ed., Moscow, 1954, pp. 101, 140, 143). Lenin refers to "Marx's remarkable passages in his *Theories of Surplus-Value*, where the revolutionary significance—in the bourgeois-democratic sense—of land nationalisation is explained with particular clarity" (*The Proletarian Revolution and the Renegade Kautsky*, Eng. ed., Moscow, 1952, p. 152; see *The Agrarian Programme of Social-Democracy in the First Russian Revolution, 1905-1907*, Eng. ed., Moscow, 1954, pp. 145, 175-76; *Works*, 4th Russ. ed., Vol. 15, p. 148, and Vol. 16, p. 104, etc.). He cited from *Theories of Surplus-Value* Marx's principal theses on absolute rent, and stated that they confirmed the correctness of his own treatment of this problem made some years before the publication of the *Theories*, in his work *The Agrarian Question and the "Critics of Marx"* (see Eng. ed., Moscow, 1954, p. 29).

* * *

Theories of Surplus-Value was first published by Kautsky in 1905-10, and since then has been more than once republished in this Kautsky edition both in German and in other languages; it has been published several times in Russian.

The Kautsky edition has many radical defects. Setting out from the totally false assumption that the manuscript *Theories of Surplus-Value* was devoid of any harmonious plan and was something of a "chaos", Kautsky subjected it to an arbitrary "adaptation", revising the most important principles of revolutionary Marxism.

First of all Kautsky crudely violated the arrangement of the material set forth by Marx in the table of contents which he compiled and in fact adhered to in his work. Kautsky completely ignored this table of contents in preparing his edition, and did not even include it in the book.

The material in Marx's manuscript is arranged consistently and in definite logical sequence. Analysing the attempts of bourgeois economists to resolve the basic problems of political economy, Marx reveals the class limitations that characterised even classical bourgeois political economy, the inability of the bourgeois economists to provide any internally consistent and scientifically grounded solution of the questions they dealt with, and above all of the central problem—the problem of surplus-value. Marx's manuscript reveals that the development of bourgeois political economy was a process full of contradictions; thus in examining the theories of Smith and Ricardo, Marx shows that in certain respects they brought science forward in comparison with the Physiocrats, but in other respects they repeated the mistakes of the Physiocrats and even took a step backwards. Kautsky distorted this deeply dialectical survey of Marx; he tried to subordinate the whole material of the manuscript to an external, purely chronological sequence, and to present the course of development of bourgeois political economy as a smooth evolutionary process.

Following his chronological plan, Kautsky placed at the very beginning of his edition not the characterisation of the views of James Steuart, which in Marx's manuscript forms the introduction to the chapter on the Physiocrats, but four short fragments (on Petty, D'Avenant, North and Locke, Hume and Massie), taken for the most part from notebooks XX and XXII. Kautsky mechanically transferred these fragments (as also certain others) to the first chapter of the first volume, and by so doing jumbled together the connected exposition of notebooks VI-XVIII (from James Steuart to Richard Jones) with the supplementary essays in notebooks XX-XXIII.

In Marx's manuscript the analysis of Quesnay's theory on the reproduction and circulation of the total capital came after the analysis of Smith's theories; in the Kautsky edition this part of the manuscript precedes the chapter on Smith, and is given in a form rehashed by Kautsky, who arbitrarily removed nine-tenths of this section from the main text and put it into an appendix printed in small type and wedged into the main text.

Kautsky also put the theoretical digressions in which Marx sets out his own view of the reproduction of the social capital into a separate appendix printed in small type and inserted in the text of the book. Kautsky tore them out from various places in the manuscript, grossly violating the inner connection between the historico-critical and the theoretical studies of Marx.

Kautsky was also responsible for obvious departures from the arrangement of the material given in Marx's manuscript, in the second volume of his edition. Marx began this part of the manuscript with a critique of Rodbertus's theory of rent; the Kautsky edition starts with the chapter "Surplus-Value and Profit", dealing with Ricardo, and the critique of Rodbertus's theory comes only after this chapter. In Marx's manuscript the analysis of Ricardo's views on surplus-value and on the process of the changing rate of profit is placed after the critique of the Ricardian theory of rent; in the Kautsky edition it is in the chapter "Surplus-Value and Profit" which begins the volume. Here also Kautsky, by departing from the sequence of the material in the manuscript, obscures important points of principle in Marx's work, in particular, Marx's idea that Ricardo's errors in the theory of rent had left their stamp on the Ricardian doctrine of profit.

As a result of all these arbitrary rearrangements which he made in the manuscript, problems that are organically connected are torn apart in the Kautsky edition. For example, the chapter "Ricardo's Theory of Profit" in Marx's manuscript contains a critique of Ricardo's views on the process of the formation of the average rate of profit and of his views on the causes of its fall. In the Kautsky edition these two parts of one and the same chapter of Marx's manuscript are separated from each other by 350 pages of the text.

All the material in the manuscript is given by Kautsky in a form which obscures the questions of the class struggle, and the deep connection between economic theories and the social and political environment in which they are developed. Thus for example, in the second volume of the Kautsky edition there is a section headed by Kautsky "Anderson and Malthus. Roscher". In the corresponding passage of the manuscript Marx shows that Anderson's views on rent were distorted by Malthus in the interest of the most reactionary elements of the ruling classes, while Ricardo's conclusions were directed against the landowning aristocracy. After this, Marx dwells on the vulgar economist Roscher, who crudely distorted the whole history of the question. The clear, politically sharp content of this section of the manuscript, which is a model of profound class analysis of the history of political economy, has been unsystematically lumped together by Kautsky under one general and quite colourless title which is a mere enumeration of names.

This type of editorial titling is extremely characteristic of the Kautsky edition. Almost all the titles which Kautsky furnished for the chapters and paragraphs of his edition bear an objectivist, neutral character. This applies, for example, to titles such as: "Adam Smith and the Concept of Productive Labour", "Ricardo's Conception of Value", "Riçardo's Idea of Surplus-Value", "The Rate of Profit", "Value and Surplus-Value", "Variable Capital and Accumulation", and so on. Kautsky's titles have nowhere set off Smith's two different definitions of value, the twofold nature of Smith's views on the relations between value and revenue, Ricardo's inability to connect the law of the average rate of profit with the law of value, etc., which Marx had brought to light. In his titling Kautsky also glosses over the vulgar element in the views of Smith and Ricardo: and he supplies the chapters on Ramsay, Cherbuliez and Richard Jones with titles calculated to give the reader the entirely false impression that some elements of Marxist political economy were to be found already in the works of these bourgeois economists.

Kautsky's distortions and revisions of Marx's text are shown in their crudest and most overt form in the numerous cuts that he made. Kautsky omitted, in his edition, not only individual words and sentences, but also whole passages, some of which fill three, four or more pages of the manuscript, in Marx's compact writing. Among the parts of the manuscript Kautsky omitted there is even a whole chapter, which appears in Marx's table of contents under the title: "Bray as Adversary of the Economists". Kautsky also omitted, among many others, the passage in the manuscript in which Marx speaks of the economic preconditions of the absolute impoverishment of the working class under capitalism. Having started on the path of falsification, the revisionist Kautsky, who denied the absolute impoverishment of the working class, did not hesitate to conceal from the reader Marx's arguments on this important question of principle.

In "editing" Marx's manuscript, Kautsky tried to tone down the annihilating criticism to which Marx subjected the views of the bourgeois economists, and to substitute "decorous" sleek expressions for the angry, passionate, caustic language used by Marx in his merciless criticism of the apologists of the bourgeoisie. Thus Kautsky in all passages removed from Marx's characterisation of bourgeois economists such epithets as "asses", "dogs", "canaille".

Finally, characteristic of the entire Kautsky edition are the numerous and sometimes extremely crude mistakes in deciphering the text of the manuscript, inaccurate and in a number of cases obviously incorrect translations of English and French expressions occurring in the text, arbitrary editorial interpolations inconsistent with the movement of Marx's thought, the absolutely impermissible substitution of some of Marx's terms by others, and so on.

The complete disregard of Marx's table of contents, the arbitrary and incorrect arrangement of the manuscript material, the objectivist titles which avoid the class essence of the conceptions criticised by Marx, the obscuring of the fundamental antithesis between Marx's economic teaching and the whole bourgeois political economy, the removal of a number of passages containing important theses of revolutionary Marxism, from which Kautsky more and more departed—all this suggests that what we have here is not only gross violations of the elementary requirements of a scientific edition, but also the direct falsification of Marxism.

* * *

The present edition contains in full both the main text of *Theories of Surplus-Value*—to which the table of contents compiled by Marx refers and which gives a connected exposition of the "history of the theory" from James Steuart to Richard Jones—and the digressions supplementing this main text which are in notebooks V, XV, XX, XXI, XXII and XXIII. These supplementary sections are put in the form of appendices, in order not to interfere with the sequence of the exposition given in the main text.

The length of all this material (about 110 printed sheets) makes it necessary to divide the book into three parts. The appendices are distributed among these three parts in such a way that each part concludes with those supplementary digressions and notes which directly refer to its contents.

The arrangement of the main text follows exactly the table of contents which Marx compiled. Only those few changes which Marx himself indicated have been made in the order of the text in some of the manuscript books. Thus, for example, in notebook

VII Marx, in dealing with Smith's conception of productive labour, and referring in this connection to the vulgarisation of Smith's views by Germain Garnier, makes a long digression about John Stuart Mill. This begins with these words: "Before dealing with Garnier, something incidentally here [by way of a digression] on the above-mentioned *Mill junior*. What is to be said here really belongs later in this section, where the Ricardian theory of surplus-value is to be discussed; therefore not here, where we are still concerned with Adam Smith." In accordance with this indication and with the table of contents of notebook XIV, later compiled by Marx, the excursus on John Stuart Mill has been placed in the present edition in the third part of *Theories*, in the chapter on the decline of the Ricardian school, where Marx allocates a special section to John Stuart Mill. Another example of transposition: notebook X contains a short chapter on the English socialist Bray (pp. 441-44 of the manuscript); in the later compiled plan of the contents of the last chapters of *Theories of Surplus-Value* (on the cover of notebook XIV) Marx however assigned the section "Bray as Adversary of the Economists" to the chapter "Adversaries of the Economists"; following this indication by Marx, in the present edition pages 441-44 have also been transferred to the third part of the work.

The division of the text into chapters follows Marx's directions in the table of contents he compiled and in various places in the manuscript itself. For the titles given to the separate parts of the manuscript, use has been made of (1) the titles from Marx's table of contents; (2) the titles from Marx's draft plans for Parts I and III of *Capital*, which have reference to certain sections of the manuscript of *Theories*; (3) the few headings in the text of *Theories* itself. All these taken together, however, form only a comparatively small part of the titles that had to be provided for the sections and subsections of the manuscript. The rest of the titles—the majority—have been drawn up by the editors on the basis of the text of corresponding parts of the manuscript, with the fullest possible use of Marx's own terminology and formulations. The titles given by the editors—as in general all that the editors are responsible for—have been put in square brackets, so that they can be easily distinguished from titles given by Marx.

Obvious slips of the pen occurring in the manuscript have been corrected as a rule without being expressly mentioned in footnotes. A few obvious slips of the pen in the text of notebooks

VI and X were corrected by Engels's own hand, in the manuscript itself. Specific terms used by Marx in the 1861-63 manuscript are explained in notes. The titles of books cited and mentioned by Marx are given in the text of this edition in the language of the original.

* * *

In spite of the fact that *Theories of Surplus-Value* was left in a form that had not prepared for the press, this work gives a connected and complete picture of that "History of the Theory" which Marx intended to form the final, fourth volume of *Capital.* In it Marx sets forth the whole course of evolution of bourgeois political economy from the time of its birth up to its "grave", as vulgar political economy was called by Marx.

As already mentioned, in the present edition all the material of *Theories of Surplus-Value* and the supplementary sections relating to it have been divided into three parts. The content of the manuscript itself determines the way in which the material is divided.

The first part consists of seven chapters of the main text (notebooks VI-X) and thirteen supplementary sections. This part is devoted in the main to a critical analysis of the views of the Physiocrats (chapters II and VI) and of Adam Smith (chapters III and IV). Chapter I ("Sir James Steuart"), characterising Steuart's hopeless attempt to give a rational form to the monetary and mercantile system, serves as an introduction to the analysis of Physiocratic theory. By contrasting the Physiocrats with Steuart Marx was able to bring out more sharply the role of the Physiocrats and their significance in the development of political economy—namely, that they transferred the origin of surplus-value from the sphere of circulation to the sphere of production.

Analysing the economic views of the Physiocrats, Marx shows the contradictions in their system, the dual nature of their conception of surplus-value, which is presented in their works sometimes as a pure gift of nature, at other times as the result of the special productivity of agricultural labour appropriated by the owner of the land. It is this that gives the key to an understanding of the further evolution of the Physiocratic school. Marx shows the battle of ideas within this school, and traces the vulgarisation of Physiocratic theory by its epigones. His analysis of the ideological struggle within the Physiocratic school is inseparably linked with his characterisation of the class essence of the Physiocrats' views.

Marx also reveals the contradictions and inconsistencies in the treatment of the most important economic categories in Adam Smith's theory (Chapter III). Subjecting Smith's theory to a critical analysis, Marx brings out the vulgar element it contains. This contrast between the scientific and the vulgar element in Smith's doctrine provides the necessary basis for understanding the further evolution of bourgeois political economy, which, as Marx shows, took on a more and more vulgar character as the class struggle between the proletariat and the bourgeoisie grew sharper.

In Chapter III, in connection with the criticism of Smith's dogma which resolves the entire value of the social product into revenue, Marx gives a theoretical analysis of the reproduction of the total social capital, and deals particularly fully with the problem of the replacement of constant capital. In addition to its general theoretical significance, this excursus (the longest of the theoretical digressions in the first part) is of great importance also because it shows how Marx arrived at his theory of the two departments of social production.

Chapter IV deals with Smith's views on productive and unproductive labour. Along with this it gives an analysis of the struggle that flared up in connection with Smith's views, and describes the vulgarisation of bourgeois political economy in handling the question of productive and unproductive labour. Marx traces the process of vulgarisation not only of Smith's views on this question, but also of the views of the Physiocrats. Many of the vulgar conceptions here criticised by Marx are widely held also in contemporary bourgeois political economy, which has degenerated into open apologetics of capitalism.

Chapter VI ("Quesnay's Tableau économique") takes us back to the Physiocrats. There was good reason for this arrangement of the material. Though Adam Smith's theory, as Marx's comprehensive analysis shows, represented as a whole a considerable step forward in the development of bourgeois political economy, in his analysis of the process of reproduction Smith takes a step backwards in comparison with the Physiocrats. Marx's arrangement of the material indicates the zigzag course of development of classical bourgeois political economy, its forward movement in the treatment of particular questions and its backward movement in the treatment of others.

Two short chapters on Necker and Linguet give an analysis of two early attempts to portray the antagonistic nature of the two classes under capitalism.

The appendices to Part I contain the historico-critical essays and notes from notebooks V, XX, XXI, XXII, XXIII and the cover of XIII. Appendices 1-7 contain characterisations of the economic views of Hobbes, Petty, Locke, North, Berkeley, Hume and Massie. In these views Marx discerns the rudiments of the labour theory of value, and of the doctrine of capital and of interest. Appendices 8-10 give supplementary material on the Physiocratic school. Appendix 11 contains a critique of the apologetic conception of the productiveness of all trades—a conception that is widespread in contemporary bourgeois political economy. Appendix 12 is a lengthy theoretical essay from notebook XXI of the manuscript, in which Marx elaborates his own view—which is the only scientific view—of the problems of productive and unproductive labour. This theoretical essay as it were draws the general conclusions from the historico-critical analysis of the problem of productive labour given by Marx in the lengthy Chapter IV of the main text. Finally, we print in Appendix 13 the draft plans for Parts I and III of *Capital*. They are very important for an understanding of the history of how *Capital* took shape; moreover, they contain formulations of certain themes which relate to its historico-critical part.

In the second part of *Theories of Surplus-Value* (chapters VIII-XVIII, notebooks X-XIII) the critical analysis of Ricardo's doctrine holds the central place. Along with this there is an analysis of Adam Smith's theory of cost-price and of rent. In his analysis of Ricardo's system, Marx shows that it contains a number of faulty premises which owed their origin to Smith. In this connection, Marx subjects the corresponding views of Smith to special scrutiny.

In conformity with the arrangement of the material in Marx's manuscript, the second part begins with the lengthy "excursus" dealing with Rodbertus's theory of rent (Chapter VIII). The fact that the concept of absolute rent was altogether missing in Ricardo's theory of rent constituted in Marx's view its principal defect. Marx therefore prefaces his analysis of Ricardo's theory with an extensive examination of Rodbertus's attempts to develop this concept. In this connection, Marx substantiates his own theory of absolute rent.

The second "excursus" (Chapter IX) is a compressed historical sketch of the development of views on differential rent. Marx here lays bare the class roots of the various theories on this question. In addition, Marx gives in this chapter a profound analysis of the basic premises of the theory of rent, and reveals the close connection between the theory of rent and the theory of value, showing how errors in the theory of value lead to erroneous conclusions in the theory of rent.

These two "digressions" in this way prepare the ground for the thorough-going analysis of Ricardo's theory contained in chapters X-XVIII.

While stressing Ricardo's great theoretical merits, Marx at the same time underlines the defects of his method in principle—Ricardo's inability to link the law of the average rate of profit with the law of value, the presence of vulgar elements in his theory of profit, his confusion of the process of formation of market value with the process of equalisation of the average rate of profit, his confusion of the laws of surplus-value with the laws of profit, and so on. All these defects, as Marx shows, are also evident in Ricardo's theory of rent. Criticising this theory, Marx develops his own theory of rent, embracing both the theory of absolute rent and the theory of differential rent.

Chapters XV, XVI and XVII contain a critical analysis of Ricardo's views on surplus-value, profit and accumulation. In Chapter XVII Marx counterposes the genuinely scientific understanding of crises as a necessary outcome of the internal contradictions of capitalism to Ricardo's mistaken views regarding the nature of crises. Chapter XVIII is a critique of Ricardo's views on the question of gross and net revenue, and also of his views on the economic consequences of the introduction of machinery.

Thus the critical analysis of Ricardo's doctrine which Marx makes in the second part of *Theories of Surplus-Value* embraces all aspects of Ricardo's system, showing his scientific merits and at the same time bringing out the theoretical errors and class limitations of his views.

Marx's short supplementary notes, written on the covers of notebooks XI and XIII, are given as appendices to Part II. They contain brief observations by Marx on particular historical questions connected with the theory of capital and of rent.

Part III of *Theories of Surplus-Value* (chapters XIX-XXIV, notebooks XIII-XV and XVIII) deals in the main with the dissolution of the Ricardian school and the economic views of the

English socialists whom Marx spoke of as "the proletarian opposition based on Ricardo".

In Parts I and II Marx demonstrated how bourgeois political economy was vulgarised in relation only to particular questions; in Part III, however, he shows how, with the sharpening of the class struggle between the bourgeoisie and the proletariat, the process of vulgarisation lays hold of the very foundations of political economy, its initial principles, its essential categories.

In the lengthy chapter on Malthus (Chapter XIX) Marx exposes the absurdity and profoundly reactionary character of the Malthusian defence of extravagance by the unproductive classes which he glorifies as a means of avoiding overproduction. In this chapter, as in other places in his work, Marx brands Malthus as "a shameless sycophant of the ruling classes", who falsified science in the interests of the landed aristocracy and the most reactionary elements of the bourgeoisie.

Marx shows that Ricardo's successors also took a step backward on the basic questions of political economy; they in fact more and more openly renounced all the valuable elements in Ricardo's system (Chapter XX). He points to the denial by Torrens that the labour theory of value is applicable to capitalist economy, and shows that James Mill returned to the vulgar conception of supply and demand in the question of wages. Marx exposes the return to this conception also in the case of Wakefield and Stirling.

This process of dissolution of the Ricardian school reaches its completion with McCulloch, whose cynical apologetics for the capitalist mode of production were most closely linked with "unscrupulous eclecticism" in the sphere of theory. Marx shows that the distortion of the concept of labour by McCulloch, who extended it to natural processes, meant in fact the complete abandonment of the labour theory of value.

Marx detects deeply reactionary features also in the polemical essays against Ricardo written by English bourgeois economists of the 1820s, in their denial of the objective character of the laws of political economy, their confusion of value with price, and their abandonment of even the category of value.

In Chapter XXI Marx analyses the economic views put forward by the "proletarian opposition based on Ricardo" (Ravenstone, Hodgskin and others). Their merit, Marx points out, was that they strongly emphasised the capitalist exploitation of the workers, their view that profit, rent and interest were the surplus-labour of the workers, their polemics against the apologetic theory that capital was productive and against the conception that the capitalists accumulated means of subsistence for the workers.

Along with this, Marx traced the theoretical errors in the economic views of the socialist adherents of Ricardo: their underestimation of the significance of materialised, past labour; their incorrect idea of the process of reproduction in capitalist society; their lack of comprehension of the inner connection between the fetishisation of capital and the real relations which of necessity give birth to this fetishisation, and so on. Marx shows that these socialist adherents of Ricardo were unable to pass beyond the bourgeois premises of Ricardo's theory, to reconstruct its very foundations.

Chapters XXII, XXIII and XXIV are devoted to a critical analysis of the ideas of Ramsay, Cherbuliez and Richard Jones. Marx notes that they attempt to differentiate between constant and variable capital and that in this connection they conjecture on the significance of the organic composition of capital. In his critical analysis of their views Marx shows how the limits of their bourgeois horizon made it impossible for these economists to develop the germs of correct ideas which in their minds were combined with vulgar conceptions of capital and the rate of profit.

The main text of *Theories of Surplus-Value* ends with the analysis of the views of Jones. In the plan or table of contents written by Marx on the cover of notebook XIV, after the chapter "Richard Jones" come the words "(End of this Part 5)" (see p. 38 of the present volume).

There is a long appendix to Part III of *Theories of Surplus-Value*, entitled "Revenue and Its Sources. Vulgar Political Economy". The main theme of this section, which fills the second half of notebook XV, is the problem of revenue and its sources. But along with this Marx also lays bare the class and gnosiological roots of vulgar political economy, which clings to the outward semblance of the fetishised forms of revenue and its sources, and builds on them its apologetic "theories". Marx brings out the essential difference between classical and vulgar political economy. In passing, Marx criticises also the economic views of representatives of vulgar socialism. This section, therefore, although written by Marx not so much from the historical as from the theoretical point of view, bears a direct relation to the historico-critical studies in Part III of *Theories of Surplus-Value*, and so must be included in it as an appendix to Part III. Later on Marx wrote that the last, historico-critical volume of *Capital* would contain a special and comprehensive chapter on the representatives of vulgar political economy (see Marx's letter to Kugelmann, July 11, 1868).

* * *

Marx formulated the essential conclusions from his deep and comprehensive analysis of the history of bourgeois political economy, in concise and generalised form, in the Afterward to the second edition of Volume I of *Capital* (January 1873): In so far as it is bourgeois "Political Economy can remain a science only so long as the class struggle is latent or manifests itself only in isolated phenomena." He wrote of classical bourgeois political economy in England that it "belongs to the period in which the class struggle was as yet undeveloped". With the development of the class struggle between the bourgeoisie and the proletariat the character of bourgeois political economy undergoes a sharp change. From the time of the conquest of political power by the bourgeoisie in France and England "the class struggle, practically as well as theoretically, took on more and more outspoken and threatening forms. It sounded the knell of scientific bourgeois economy.... In place of disinterested inquiries, there were hired prize-fighters; in place of genuine scientific research, the bad conscience and the evil intent of apologetic".

Against the background of this general degradation of bourgeois political economy the figures of a few economists stood out, who tried, as Marx says, "to harmonise the political economy of capital with the claims, no longer to be ignored, of the proletariat". Such an attempt to "reconcile the irreconcilable" was made by John Stuart Mill. Marx notes the complete hopelessness of such attempts, which remained wholly within the bounds of bourgeois political economy and bore witness to its decay and bankruptcy. In this connection Marx strongly emphasises the outstanding significance of "the great Russian scholar and critic" N. G. Chernyshevsky, who in his *Outlines of Political Economy According to Mill*, as Marx says, "has thrown the light of a master mind" on the bankruptcy of bourgeois political economy.

Chernyshevsky wrote his critical analysis of John Stuart Mill's book in 1860-61, that is, almost at the same time as Marx was at work on his *Theories*.

Through all of Chernyshevsky's writings runs the idea of the need to create a new political economy, which, as opposed to former political economy which he characterised as "the theory of the capitalists", he called quite explicitly "the theory of the working people".

To create a new, genuinely scientific political economy, involving a radical revolutionary upheaval in economic science, was possible only for the leader and teacher of the revolutionary proletariat—Karl Marx. And only Marx, constructing the magnificent edifice of *Capital* on radically new principles, could build up that scientific history of all bourgeois political economy which he presented in the historico-critical part of his work of genius—*Theories of Surplus-Value*.

* * *

In the imperialist epoch all the contradictions of the capitalist system reach their greatest intensity, and the class struggle grows extremely sharp. This is reflected in the most acute form also in the economic fabrications of the latest apologists of capitalism. In their efforts to defend the decaying social system of the exploiters which is doomed to destruction, contemporary bourgeois economists and the pseudo-socialists who echo their views cling fast to the most reactionary of the vulgar conceptions which were put forward by their predecessors in the pre-monopoly epoch of capitalism and were subjected to annihilating criticism in Marx's *Theories of Surplus-Value*.

Thus in contemporary bourgeois literature the old hackneyed thesis, that every increase in wages leads inevitably to higher prices, still runs its course. This thesis, the vulgar and anti-scientific nature of which Marx emphasised again and again in *Theories of Surplus-Value*, is now used to justify the bourgeoisie's attack on the living standards of the working class.

Contemporary bourgeois economists (as for example Keynes, who made a sensation with his "anti-crisis" projects, and his followers) shamelessly repeat the reactionary idea of Malthus, exposed by Marx, of the salutary role of the unlimited growth of unproductive consumption as a means to fight economic crises. Praise for wasteful unproductive consumption in the conditions of today sounds particularly ominous: it brings to the fore that form of unproductive consumption which is linked with the preparation of a new world war and which consumes an ever-growing share of the budgets of capitalist states. Present-day bourgeois literature, especially American, preaches in every way the "theory" that only increased armaments orders, and in the final account war itself, can avert economic crises of overproduction.

Malthus's population theory—routed by Marx in *Theories of Surplus-Value* and in other works—is also used to justify imperialist wars. Contemporary American and British Malthusians (for example, Vogt in the U.S.A. and Huxley in England) preach the cannibal "doctrine" that only a war of annihilation can establish the appropriate "balance" between the number of people on the earth and the means of subsistence at their disposal. They declare that a high death-rate is a salutary factor for civilisation, and hold up as an example to all nations those countries where the death-rate reaches particularly high proportions.

In fashioning their reactionary anti-scientific conceptions bourgeois economists of today rely on the outworn theories, long since exposed by Marxism, of the old vulgar political economy fabricated in the first half of the nineteenth century. They also reject the labour theory of value, and strive to replace it with vulgar "theories" of utility, demand and supply, costs of production, and so on. They also take their stand on the famous "trinitarian formula", according to which rent is determined by nature, interest by capital, and wages by labour. Like all preachers of a "general harmony" in capitalist society who preceded them, they too deny the inevitability of capitalist crises, which are the necessary outcome of the internal contradictions of capitalism.

In *Theories of Surplus-Value* Marx subjected all these apologist subterfuges of vulgar political economy to devastating criticism. This great work of Marx has for that reason outstanding importance not only for understanding the history of bourgeois political economy, but also for the struggle against the present-day representatives of bourgeois reaction, who try to revive long-routed pseudo-scientific conceptions in order to use them in their dirty trade of justifying and defending the inhuman system of imperialism, that last stage of the capitalist system which has outlived its time.

Institute of Marxism-Leninism,
C.C. C.P.S.U.

KARL MARX

THEORIES OF SURPLUS-VALUE

(Volume IV of *Capital*)

[CONTENTS OF THE MANUSCRIPT *THEORIES OF SURPLUS-VALUE*][1]

|| VI—219b|Contents of notebook VI:

5. Theories of Surplus-Value[2]

(a) Sir James Steuart

(b) The Physiocrats

(c) Adam Smith |VI—219b||

|| VII—272b| [Contents of notebook VII]

5. Theories of Surplus-Value

(c) Adam Smith (continuation)

(Inquiry into how it is possible for the annual profit and wages to buy the annual commodities, which besides profit and wages also contain constant capital) |VII—272||

|| VIII—331 b| [Contents of notebook VIII]

5. Theories of Surplus-Value

(c) Adam Smith (conclusion)[3] | VIII—331b||

|| IX—376b | [Contents of notebook IX]

5. Theories of Surplus-Value

(c) Adam Smith. Conclusion

(d) Necker | IX—376b ||

|| X—421c | [Contents of notebook X]

5. Theories of Surplus-Value

Digression. Quesnay's Tableau économique

(e) Linguet

(f) Bray

(g) Herr Rodbertus. Digression. New theory of rent: |X—421c ||

||XI—490a | [Contents of notebook XI]

5. Theories of Surplus-Value
   (g) Rodbertus
   Digression. Note on the history of the discovery of the so-called Ricardian law
   (h) Ricardo
   Ricardo's and Adam Smith's theory of cost-price (refutation)
   Ricardo's theory of rent
   Tables, with elucidation, of differential rent | XI—490||

||XII—580b | [Contents of notebook XII]

5. Theories of Surplus-Value
   (h) Ricardo
   Table, with elucidation, of differential rent
   (Observations on the influence of the change in value of means of subsistence and raw material — therefore also in the value of machinery—on the organic composition of capital)
   Ricardo's theory of rent
   Adam Smith's theory of rent
   Ricardo's theory of surplus-value
   Ricardo's theory of profit | XII—580b ||

||XIII—670a | [Contents of notebook XIII]

5. Theories of Surplus-Value, etc.
   (h) Ricardo
   Ricardo's theory of profit
   Ricardo's theory of accumulation. Critique of this (development of crises from the basic form of capital)
   Ricardo's Miscellanea. Conclusion of Ricardo (John Barton)
   (i) Malthus |XIII—670a ||

||XIV—771a | [Contents of notebook XIV and plan of further chapters of *Theories of Surplus-Value*]

5. Theories of Surplus-Value
   (i) Malthus
   (k) Decline of the Ricardian school (Torrens, James Mill, Prevost, polemical writings, McCulloch, Wakefield, Stirling, John Stuart Mill)
   (l) Adversaries of the economists[4]
   (Bray as adversary of the economists)[5]
   (m) Ramsay
   (n) Cherbuliez

(o) Richard Jones[6]. (End of this Part 5)
Episode: Revenue and its sources[7] | XIV—771a ||
||XV—862a | [Contents of notebook XV]
5. Theories of Surplus-Value
1. Proletarian opposition on the basis of Ricardo
2. Ravenstone. Conclusion[8]
3. [and] 4. Hodgskin[9]
So-called amassment as a mere phenomenon of circulation
(Stocks, etc.—circulation reservoirs)
(Compound interest; fall in the rate of profit based on this)
Vulgar political economy[10]
(Interest-bearing capital. Existing wealth in relation to the movement of production)
(Interest-bearing capital and commercial capital in relation to industrial capital. Older forms. Derivative forms)
(Development of interest-bearing capital on the basis of capitalist production)
(Usury. Luther, etc.)[11]. |XV—862a ||

[GENERAL OBSERVATION]

||VI—220| All economists share the error of examining surplus-value not as such, in its pure form, but in the particular forms of profit and rent. What theoretical errors must necessarily arise from this will be shown more fully in Chapter III,[12] in the analysis of the greatly changed form which surplus-value assumes as profit.

[C H A P T E R I]

SIR JAMES STEUART

[DISTINCTION BETWEEN "PROFIT UPON ALIENATION" AND THE POSITIVE INCREASE OF WEALTH]

Before the Physiocrats, surplus-value—that is, profit in the form of profit—was explained purely from *exchange*, the sale of the commodity above its value. Sir James Steuart on the whole did not get beyond this restricted view; he must rather be regarded as the man who reproduced it in scientific form. I say "in scientific form". For Steuart does not share the illusion that the surplus-value which accrues to the individual capitalist from selling the commodity above its value is a creation of new wealth. He distinguishes therefore between *positive* profit and *relative* profit.

"*Positive profit*, implies no loss to any body; it results from an *augmentation* of labour, industry, or ingenuity, and has the effect of swelling or augmenting the *public good*.... *Relative profit*, is what implies a loss to some body; it marks a vibration of the balance of wealth between parties, but implies *no addition to the general stock* ... the *compound* is easily understood; it is that species of profit... which is partly *relative*, and partly *positive* ... both kinds may subsist inseparably in the same transaction." (*Principles of Political Economy, Vol.* I, *The Works of Sir James Steuart, etc.*, ed. by General Sir James Steuart, his son, etc., in 6 vols., London, 1805, pp. 275-76.)

Positive profit arises from "augmentation of labour, industry and ingenuity". *How* it arises from this Steuart makes no attempt to explain. The further statement that the effect of this profit is to augment and swell "*the public good*" seems to indicate that Steuart means by it nothing but the greater mass of use-values produced in consequence of the development of the productive powers of labour, and that he thinks of this positive profit as quite distinct from capitalists' profit—which always presupposes an increase of exchange-value. This interpretation is fully confirmed by his further exposition. He says to wit:

"In the *price* of goods, I consider two things as really existing, and *quite different* from [...] another; [...] the *real value* of the commodity, and the *profit upon alienation*" (l. c., p. 244).

The price of goods therefore comprises two elements that are completely different from each other; firstly their *real value*, secondly, the *profit upon alienation*, the profit realised through their transfer to another person, their sale.

||221| This *profit upon alienation* therefore arises from the price of the goods being greater than their real value, or from the goods being sold *above* their value. Gain on the one side therefore always involves loss on the other. No addition to the general stock is created. Profit, that is, surplus-value, is relative and resolves itself into "a vibration of the balance of wealth between parties". Steuart himself rejects the idea that surplus-value can be explained in this way. His theory of "vibration of the balance of wealth between parties", however little it touches the nature and origin of surplus-value itself, remains important in considering the distribution of surplus-value among different classes and among different categories such as profit, interest and rent.

That Steuart limits all profit of the individual capitalist to this "relative profit", profit upon alienation, is shown by the following:

The "real value", he says, is determined by the "quantity" of labour, which "upon an average, a workman of the country in general may perform... in a day, a week, a month". Secondly: "the value of the workman's subsistence and necessary expense, both for supplying his personal wants, and... the instruments belonging to his profession, which must [...] taken upon [...] average as above. ..." Thirdly: "... the values of the materials ..." (l. c., pp. 244-45). "These three articles being known, the price of manufacture is determined. It cannot be lower than the amount of all the three, that is, than the *real value*; *whatever is higher*, *is the manufacturer's profit*. This will [...] be in proportion to *demand*, and therefore will fluctuate according to circumstances" (l. c., p. 245). "Hence appears the necessity of a great demand, in order to promote flourishing manufactures ... the industrious [...] regulate their living and expense according to their certain profit" (l. c., p. 246).

From this it is clear that: The profit of the "manufacturer", of the individual capitalist, is always relative profit, always profit upon alienation, always derived from the excess of the price of the commodity over its real value, *from its sale above its value*. If therefore all commodities were sold at their *value*, no profit would exist.

Steuart wrote a special chapter on this; he examines in detail:

"How profits consolidate into prime cost" (l.c., Vol. III, p. 11sq.).

Steuart on the one hand rejects the conception of the Monetary and Mercantile systems, according to which the sale of commodities above their value, and the profit resulting therefrom, creates surplus-value, a positive increase of wealth.* On the other hand he holds to their view that the profit of the individual capital is nothing but this excess of the price over the ||222| value, the profit upon alienation. This however according to him is only *relative*, the gain on the one side being compensated by the loss on the other, and consequently this movement is nothing more than "a vibration of the balance of wealth between parties".

In this respect Steuart is therefore the *rational* expression of the Monetary and Mercantile systems.

His service to the theory of capital is that he shows how the process of separation takes place between the conditions of production, as the property of a definite class, and labour-power.[13] He gives a great deal of attention to this *genesis* of capital—without as yet seeing it directly as the genesis of capital, although he sees it as a condition for large-scale industry. He examines the process particularly in agriculture; and he rightly considers that manufacturing industry proper only came into being through this process of separation in agriculture. In Adam Smith's writings this process of separation is assumed to be already completed.

(Steuart's book [appeared] *1767* in London, *Turgot's* [*Réflexions sur la formation et la distribution des richesses* was written in] *1766*, Adam Smith's [*An Inquiry into the Nature and Causes of the Wealth of Nations*] *1775*.)

---

* Even the Monetary system, however, thinks of this profit as arising not within a country, but only in exchange with other countries. In this it remains stuck in the Mercantile system [which assumed] that this value takes the form of money (gold and silver) and the surplus-value is therefore expressed in the balance of trade, which is settled with money.

[CHAPTER II]

THE PHYSIOCRATS

[1. Transfer of the Inquiry into the Origin of Surplus-Value from the Sphere of Circulation into the Sphere of Direct Production. Conception of Rent as the Sole Form of Surplus-Value]

The analysis of *capital*, within the bourgeois horizon, is essentially the work of the Physiocrats. It is this service that makes them the true fathers of modern political economy. In the first place, the analysis of the various *material components* in which capital exists and into which it resolves itself in the course of the labour-process. It is not a reproach to the Physiocrats that, like all their successors, they thought of these material forms of existence—such as tools, raw materials, etc.—as capital, in isolation from the social conditions in which they appear in capitalist production; in a word, in the form in which they are elements of the labour-process in general, independently of its social form—and thereby made of the capitalist form of production an eternal, natural form of production. For them the bourgeois forms of production necessarily appeared as natural forms. It was their great merit that they conceived these forms as physiological forms of society: as forms arising from the natural necessity of production itself, forms that are independent of anyone's will or of politics, etc. They are material laws, the error is only that the material law of a definite historical social stage is conceived as an abstract law governing equally all forms of society.

In addition to this analysis of the material elements of which capital consists within the labour-process, the Physiocrats established the forms which capital assumes in circulation (fixed capital, circulating capital, even though as yet they give them other names), and in general the connection between the process of circulation and the reproduction process of capital. We shall come back to this in the chapter on circulation.[14]

In these two principal points Adam Smith inherited the legacy of the Physiocrats. His service—in this connection—is limited to fixing the abstract categories, to the greater consistency of the baptismal names which he gave to the distinctions made by the Physiocrats in their analysis.

||223| As we have seen,[15] the basis for the development of capitalist production is, in general, that *labour-power*, as the *commodity* belonging to the workers, confronts the conditions of labour as commodities maintained in the form of capital and existing independently of the workers. The determination of the *value* of labour-power, as a commodity, is of vital importance. This value is equal to the labour-time required to produce the means of subsistence necessary for the reproduction of labour-power, or to the price of the means of subsistence necessary for the existence of the worker as a worker. It is only on this basis that the difference arises between the *value* of labour-power and the *value which that* labour-power *creates*—a difference which exists with no other commodity, since there is no other commodity whose use-value, and therefore also the use of it, can increase its *exchange-value* or the exchange-values resulting from it.

Therefore the foundation of modern political economy, whose business is the analysis of capitalist production, is the conception of the *value of labour-power* as something fixed, as a given magnitude—as indeed it is in practice in each particular case. The *minimum of wages* therefore correctly forms the pivotal point of Physiocratic theory. They were able to establish this although they had not yet recognised the nature of value itself, because this *value of labour-power* is manifested in the price of the necessary means of subsistence, hence in a sum of definite use-values. Consequently, without being in any way clear as to the nature of value, they could conceive the value of labour-power, so far as it was necessary to their inquiry, as a definite magnitude. If moreover they made the mistake of conceiving this *minimum* as an unchangeable magnitude—which in their view is determined entirely by nature and not by the stage of historical development, which is itself a magnitude subject to fluctuations—this in no way affects the abstract correctness of their conclusions, since the difference between the value of labour-power and the value it creates does not at all depend on whether the value is assumed to be great or small.

The Physiocrats transferred the inquiry into the origin of surplus-value from the sphere of circulation into the sphere of direct production, and thereby laid the foundation for the analysis of capitalist production.

Quite correctly they lay down the fundamental principle that only that labour is *productive* which creates a *surplus-value*, in whose product therefore a higher value is contained than the sum of the values consumed during the production of this product. Since the value of raw and other materials is given, while the value of the labour-power is equal to the minimum of wages, this surplus-value can clearly only consist in the excess of labour which the labourer returns to the capitalist over and above the quantity of labour that he receives in his wage. But it does not appear in this form with the Physiocrats, because they have not yet reduced value in general to its simple substance—the quantity of labour or labour-time.

||224| Their method of exposition is, of course, necessarily governed by their general view of the nature of value, which to them is not a definite social mode of existence of human activity (labour), but consists of material things—land, nature, and the various modifications of these material things.

The difference between the *value* of labour-power and *the value created* by it—that is, the surplus-value which the purchase of labour-power secures for the user of labour-power—appears most palpably, most incontrovertibly, of all *branches of production*, in *agriculture*, the primary branch of production. The sum total of the means of subsistence which the labourer consumes from one year to another, or the mass of material substance which he consumes, is smaller than the sum total of the means of subsistence which he produces. In manufacture the workman is not generally seen directly producing either his means of subsistence or the surplus in excess of his means of subsistence. The process is mediated through purchase and sale, through the various acts of circulation, and the analysis of value in general is necessary for it to be understood. In agriculture it shows itself directly in the surplus of use-values produced over use-values consumed by the labourer, and can therefore be grasped without an analysis of value in general, without a clear understanding of the nature of value. Therefore also when value is reduced to use-value, and the latter to material substance in general. Hence for the Physiocrats agricultural labour is the only *productive labour*, because it is the only labour that *produces a surplus-value*, and *rent* is the *only form of surplus-value* which they know. The workman in industry does not increase the material substance; he only alters its form. The material—the mass of material substance—is given to him by agriculture. It is true that he adds value to the substance, not through his labour, but through the costs of production of his labour: through the total means of subsistence which he consumes during his labour, equivalent to the minimum of wages, which he receives from agriculture. Because agricultural labour is conceived as the only productive labour, the form of surplus-value which distinguishes agricultural labour from industrial labour, *rent*, is conceived as the only form of surplus-value.

Profit on capital in the true sense, of which rent itself is only an offshoot, therefore does not exist for the Physiocrats. Profit is seen by them as only a kind of higher wages paid by the landowners, which the capitalists consume as revenue (and which therefore enters into their costs of production in the same way as the minimum wages of the ordinary workmen); this increases the value of the raw material, because it enters into the consumption costs which the capitalist, [the] industrialist, consumes while he is producing the product, transforming the raw material into a new product.

Surplus-value in the form of *interest on money*—another branch of profit—is consequently declared by one section of the Physiocrats, such as Mirabeau the elder, to be usury and contrary to nature. Turgot on the other hand derives his justification of it from the fact that the money capitalist could buy land, that is, rent, and that therefore his money capital must bring him in as much surplus-value as he would receive if he converted it into landed property. This means therefore that interest too is not newly created value, not surplus-value; it only explains why a part of the surplus-value gained by the landowners finds its way to the money capitalists in the form of interest, just as it is explained on other grounds ||225| why a part of this surplus-value finds its way to the industrial capitalist in the form of profit. Because *agricultural labour* is the only productive labour, the only labour that creates surplus-value, the *form of surplus-value* which distinguishes agricultural labour from all other branches of labour, *rent*, is the *general form of surplus-value*. Industrial profit and interest are merely different categories into which rent is divided and, in certain portions, passes from the hands of the landowners into the hands of other classes. This is the direct opposite to the view held by later economists beginning with Adam Smith, because they rightly consider *industrial profit* to be the *form* in which surplus-value is *originally* appropriated by capital, hence as the original general form of surplus-value—

they present interest and rent as mere offshoots of industrial profit, which is distributed by the industrial capitalists to various classes, who are co-owners of surplus-value.

In addition to the reason already stated—that agricultural labour is the labour in which the creation of surplus-value appears in material and tangible form, and apart from the process of circulation—there were a number of other considerations which explain the standpoint of the Physiocrats.

First, because in agriculture rent appears as a third element, as a form of surplus-value which is not found in industry or merely has a transient existence. It was surplus-value over and above surplus-value (profit), and so the most palpable and most conspicuous form of surplus-value, surplus-value raised to the second power.

"By means of agriculture," as *Karl Arnd*, the home-bred economist, says in *Die naturgemässe Volkswirtschaft, etc.* (Hanau, 1845, pp. 461-62), "a value is created—in the rent of land—which is not to be met with in industry and trade; a value which remains over when the labour and capital employed have been completely replaced."

Secondly: leaving foreign trade out of account—as the Physiocrats rightly did and had to do in an abstract study of bourgeois society—it is clear that the number of workmen engaged in manufacture, etc., and completely detached from agriculture—the "free hands", as Steuart calls them—is determined by the mass of agricultural products which the farm labourers produce in excess of their own consumption.

"It is obvious, that the relative numbers of those persons who can be maintained without agricultural labour, must be measured wholly by the productive powers of the cultivators" (Richard Jones, *On the Distribution of Wealth*, London, 1831, pp. 159-60).

As agricultural labour thus forms the natural basis (on this, see an earlier notebook[16]) not only for surplus-labour in its own sphere, but also for the independent existence of all other branches of labour, and therefore also for the surplus-value created in them, it is clear that it was bound to be considered the creator of surplus-value, so long as the substance of value was regarded as definite, concrete labour, and not abstract labour with its measure, labour-time.

||226| *Thirdly*. All surplus-value, not only relative but absolute, depends on a given productivity of labour. If the productivity of labour had reached only such a stage of development that a man's labour-time no more than sufficed to keep him alive,

to produce and reproduce his own means of subsistence, then there would be no surplus-labour and no surplus-value, and there would be no difference at all between the value of labour-power and the value which it creates. The possibility of surplus-labour and of surplus-value therefore arises from a given productivity of labour, a productivity which enables labour-power to create more than its own value, to produce more than the needs dictated by its life process. And indeed this productivity, this level of productivity which is presupposed as the starting-point, must first—as we saw in the *second* point above—make its appearance in agricultural labour. It appears therefore as *a gift of nature, a productive power of nature.* Here, in agriculture, from the very beginning there is a large measure of co-operation of the forces of nature—the increase of human labour-power through the use and exploitation of the forces of nature working automatically. This utilisation of the forces of nature on a large scale appears in manufacture only with the development of large-scale industry. A definite stage in the development of agriculture, whether in the country concerned or in other countries, forms the basis for the development of capital. Up to this point absolute surplus-value coincides with relative. (*Buchanan*—a great adversary of the Physiocrats—makes this point even against Adam Smith, when he tries to show that agricultural development preceded the emergence of modern town industry).

Fourthly. Since it is the great and specific contribution of the Physiocrats that they derive value and surplus-value not from circulation but from production, they necessarily begin, in contrast to the Monetary and Mercantile system, with that branch of production which can be thought of in complete separation from and independently of circulation, of exchange; and which presupposes exchange not between man and man but only between man and nature.

[2. Contradictions in the System of the Physiocrats: the Feudal Shell of the System and Its Bourgeois Essence; the Twofold Treatment of Surplus-Value]

Hence the contradictions in the Physiocratic system.

It is in fact the first system which analyses capitalist production, and presents the conditions within which capital is produced, and within which capital produces, as eternal natural laws of production. On the other hand, it has rather the character of a bourgeois reproduction of the feudal system, of the dominion of landed property; and the industrial spheres within which capital first develops independently are presented as "unproductive" branches of labour, mere appendages of agriculture. The first condition for the development of capital is the separation of landed property from labour—the emergence of land, the primary condition of labour, as an independent force, a force in the hands of a separate class, confronting the free labourer. The Physiocrats therefore present the landowner as the true capitalist, that is, the appropriator of surplus-labour. Feudalism is thus portrayed and explained from the viewpoint of bourgeois production; agriculture is treated as the branch of production in which capitalist production—that is, the production of surplus-value—exclusively appears. While feudalism is thus made bourgeois, bourgeois society is given a feudal semblance.

This semblance deceived Dr. Quesnay's adherents among the nobility, such as the crotchety and patriarchal *Mirabeau* the elder. Among the later representatives ||227| of the Physiocrats, especially *Turgot*, this illusion disappears completely, and the Physiocratic system is presented as the new capitalist society prevailing within the framework of feudal society. This therefore corresponds to bourgeois society in the epoch when the latter breaks its way out of the feudal order. Consequently, the starting-point is in France, in a predominantly agricultural country, and not in England, a predominantly industrial, commercial and seafaring country. In the latter country attention was naturally concentrated on circulation, on the fact that the product acquires value, becomes a commodity only when it becomes the expression of general social labour, money. In so far, therefore, as the question concerned not the form of value, but the amount of value and the increase of value, *profit upon expropriation*—that is, relative profit as Steuart describes it—is what catches the eye. But if the creation of surplus-value in the sphere of production itself is what has to be established, it is necessary first of all to go back to that branch of production in which surplus-value is found independently of circulation—that is, agriculture. The initiative was therefore taken in a predominantly agricultural country. Ideas related to those of the Physiocrats are to be found in fragmentary form in older writers who preceded them, partly in France herself, for example, Boisguillebert. But it is only with the Physiocrats that these ideas develop into an epoch-making system.

The agricultural labourer, depending on the minimum of wages, the *strict nécessaire*,* reproduces more than this *strict necessaire*, and this more is rent, *surplus-value*, which is appropriated by the owners of the fundamental condition of labour—nature. So what they say is not: the labourer works more than the labour-time required for the reproduction of his labour-power; the value which he creates is therefore greater than the value of his labour-power; or the labour which he gives in return is greater than the quantity of labour which he receives in the form of wages. But what they say is: the amount of use-values which he consumes during the period of production is smaller than the amount of use-values which he creates, and so a surplus of use-values is left over.—Were he to work only for the time required to reproduce his own labour-power, there would be nothing over. But the Physiocrats only stuck to the point that the productivity of the earth enables the labourer, in his day's labour, which is assumed to be a fixed quantity, to produce more than he needs to consume in order to continue to exist. The surplus-value appears therefore as a *gift of nature*, through whose co-operation a definite quantity of organic matter—plant seeds, a number of animals—enables labour to transform more inorganic matter into organic.

On the other hand, it is taken for granted that the landowner confronts the labourer as a capitalist. He pays for the labour-power, which the labourer offers to him as a commodity, and he receives in return not only an equivalent, but appropriates for himself the enlarged value arising from the use of this labour-power. The alienation of the material condition of labour from labour-power itself is presupposed in this exchange. The starting-point is the feudal landowner, but he comes on to the stage as a capitalist, as a mere owner of commodities, who makes profitable use of the goods exchanged by him for labour, and gets back not only their equivalent, but a surplus over this equivalent, because he pays for the labour-power only as a commodity. He confronts the free labourer as an owner of commodities. In other words, this landowner is in essence a capitalist. In this respect too the Physiocratic system hits the mark, inasmuch as the separation of the labourer from the soil and from the ownership of land is a fundamental condition ||228| for capitalist production and the production of capital.

Hence the contradictions in this system: it was the first to explain *surplus-value* by the appropriation of the labour of oth-

* The most indispensable, the absolutely necessary.—*Ed.*

ers, and in fact to explain this appropriation on the basis of the exchange of commodities; but it did not see that value in general is a form of social labour and that surplus-value is surplus-labour. On the contrary, it conceived value merely as use-value, merely as material substance, and surplus-value as a mere gift of nature, which returns to labour, in place of a given quantity of organic material, a greater quantity. On the one hand, it stripped rent—that is, the true economic form of landed property—of its feudal wrapping, and reduced it to mere surplus-value in excess of the labourer's wage. On the other hand, this surplus-value is explained again in a feudal way, as derived from nature and not from society; from man's relation to the soil, not from his social relations. Value itself is resolved into mere use-value, and therefore into material substance. But again what interests [the Physiocrats] in this material substance is its quantity—the excess of the use-values produced over those consumed; that is, the purely quantitative relation of the use-values to each other, their mere exchange-value, which in the last resort comes down to labour-time.

All these are contradictions of capitalist production as it works its way out of feudal society, and interprets feudal society itself only in a bourgeois way, but has not yet discovered its own peculiar form—somewhat as philosophy first builds itself up within the religious form of consciousness, and in so doing on the one hand destroys religion as such, while on the other hand, in its positive content, it still moves only within this religious sphere, idealised and reduced to terms of thought.

Hence also, in the conclusions which the Physiocrats themselves draw, the ostensible veneration of landed property becomes transformed into the economic negation of it and the affirmation of capitalist production. On the one hand, all taxes are put on rent, or in other words, landed property is in part confiscated, which is what the legislation of the French Revolution sought to carry through and which is the final conclusion of the fully developed Ricardian modern political economy. By placing the burden of tax entirely on rent, because it alone is surplus-value—and consequently any taxation of other forms of income ultimately falls on landed property, but in a roundabout way, and therefore in an economically harmful way, that hinders production—taxation and along with it all forms of State intervention, are removed from industry itself, and the latter is thus freed from all intervention by the State. This is ostensibly done for the benefit of landed property, not in the interests of industry but in the interests of landed property.

Connected with this is *laissez faire, laissez aller**; unhampered free competition, the removal from industry of all interference by the State, monopolies, etc. Since industry [as the Physiocrats see it] creates nothing, but only transforms values given it by agriculture into another form; since it adds no new value to them, but returns the values supplied to it, though in altered form, as an equivalent; it is naturally desirable that this process of transformation should proceed without interruptions and in the cheapest way; and this is only realised through free competition, by leaving capitalist production to its own devices. The emancipation of bourgeois society from the absolute monarchy set up on the ruins of feudal society thus takes place only in the interests of the feudal landowner transformed into a capitalist ||229| and bent solely on enrichment. The capitalists are only capitalists in the interests of the landowner, just as political economy in its later development would have them be capitalists only in the interests of the working class.

It can be seen therefore how little the modern economists, [such as] Herr Eugène Daire (who published the works of the Physiocrats together with his prize essay on them), have understood the Physiocrats when they treat their specific theories—of the exclusive productivity of agricultural labour, of rent as the only surplus-value, and of the landowners' pre-eminent status in the system of production—as if they had no connection and were only fortuitously associated with their proclamation of free competition, the principle of large-scale industry, of capitalist production. At the same time it is understandable how the feudal semblance of this system, in the same way as the aristocratic tone of the Enlightenment, was bound to win a number of feudal lords as enthusiastic supporters and propagandists of a system which, in its essence, proclaimed the rise of the bourgeois system of production on the ruins of the feudal.

---

* Lit.: let go, let act (let people act as they choose); demanding that the Government should not interfere in the economic life of the country. —*Ed.*

[3. Quesnay on the Three Classes in Society. Further Development of Physiocratic Theory with Turgot: Elements of a Deeper Analysis of Capitalist Relations]

We will now examine a number of passages, partly to elucidate and partly in support of the theses advanced above.

With *Quesnay* himself, in the *Analyse du Tableau économique*, the nation consists of three classes of citizens:

> "*the productive class*" (agricultural labourers), "*the class of landowners* and the *sterile class*" ("all the citizens occupied with other services and with other labours than those of agriculture") (*Physiocrates, etc.*, édition Eugène Daire, Paris, 1846, 1 partie, p. 58).

Only the agricultural labourers, not the landowners, appear as a productive class, as a class which creates surplus-value. The importance of this class of landowners, which is not "sterile", because it is the representative of "surplus-value", does not rest on its being the creator of surplus-value, but exclusively on the fact that it appropriates surplus-value.

[With] *Turgot* [the Physiocratic system is] most fully developed. In some passages in his writings the pure gift of nature is presented as *surplus-labour*, and on the other hand the necessity for the labourer to yield up what there is in excess of his necessary wage [is explained] by the separation of the labourer from the conditions of labour, and their confronting him as the property of a class which uses them to trade with.

The first reason why agricultural labour alone is productive is that it is the natural basis and pre-condition for the independent pursuit of all other forms of labour.

> "His" (the husbandman's) "labour, in the sequence of the labours divided among the different members of the society, retains the same primacy ... as the labour which provided his own food had among the different kinds of labour which, when he worked alone, he was obliged to devote to his different kinds of wants. We have here neither a primacy of honour nor of dignity; it is one of *physical necessity*.... What his labour causes the land to produce beyond his personal wants is the only fund for the wages which all the other members of the society receive in exchange for their labour. The latter, in making use of the price of this exchange to buy in their turn the products of the husbandman, only return to him"(as matter) "exactly what they have received from him. We have here a very essential difference ||230| between these two kinds of labour" (*Réflexions sur la formation et la distribution des richesses* (1766). Turgot, *Oeuvres*, édition Daire, t. I, Paris, 1844, pp. 9-10).

How then does surplus-value arise? It does not arise from circulation, but it is realised in circulation. The product is sold at its value, not *above* its value. There is no excess of price over value. But because it is sold at its value, the seller realises a surplus-value. This is only possible because he has not himself paid in full for the value which he sells, that is, because the product contains a portion of value which has not been paid for by the seller, which he has not offset by an equivalent. And this is the case with agricultural labour. The seller sells what he has not bought. Turgot at first presents this unbought element as a *pure gift of nature*. We shall see, however, that in his writings this pure gift of nature becomes imperceptibly transformed into the surplus-labour of the labourer which the landowner has not bought, but which he sells in the products of agriculture.

"As soon as the labour of the husbandman *produces more than* his wants, he can with this superfluity *that nature accords him as a pure gift* over and above the wages of his toil, buy the labour of the other members of the society. The latter, in selling it to him gain only their livelihood; but the husbandman gathers, beyond his subsistence, a wealth which is independent and disposable, *which he has not bought and which he sells*. He is, therefore, the sole source of the riches, which, by their circulation, animate all the labours of the society, *because he is the only one whose labour produces over and above the wages of labour*" (l.c., p. 11).

In this first conception we have, to begin with, the essence of surplus-value—that it is value realised in sale, without the seller having given an equivalent for it, without his having bought it. *Unpaid value*. But in the second place this is conceived as a pure gift of nature, this excess over the *wage of labour*; because after all it is a gift of nature, it depends on the productivity of nature that the labourer is able to produce in his day's labour more than is necessary for the reproduction of his labour-power, more than the amount of his wages. In this first conception the total product is still appropriated by the labourer himself.... And this total product is divided into two parts. The first forms his wages; he is presented as his own wage-labourer, who pays himself the part of the product that is necessary for the reproduction of his labour-power, for his subsistence. The second part, which is the excess over the first, is *a gift of nature* and forms surplus-value. The nature of this surplus-value, of this pure gift of nature, will however take clearer shape, when the premise of the proprietor who cultivates his land is abandoned and the two parts of the product, wages and surplus-value, accrue to different classes, the one to the wage-worker, the other to the landowner.

The formation of a class of wage-labourers, whether in manufacture or in agriculture itself—at first all *manufacturiers** appear only as *stipendiés,*** wage-labourers of the cultivating proprietor—requires the separation of the conditions of labour from labour-power, and the basis for this separation is that the land itself becomes the private property of one part of society, so that the other part is cut off from this objective condition for making use of its labour.

"In the early stages there was no need to distinguish the proprietor from the cultivator.... In this early time, as every industrious man would find as much land as he ||231| wished, he could not be tempted *to work for others*.... But in the end all land found its master, and those who could not have properties had at first no other resource than that of *exchanging the labour of their arms*, in the employment of the *stipendiary* class" (i.e., the class of artisans, of all non-agricultural labourers) "for the superfluous portion of the produce of the cultivating proprietor" (l.c., p. 12).

The cultivating proprietor with the considerable surplus which the land gave to his labour, could "pay men to cultivate his land; and for men who live on wages, it was as good to earn them in this business as in any other. *Thus ownership of land had to be separated from the labour of cultivation, and soon it was*.... The landowners began to shift the labour of cultivating the soil on to the wage-labourers" (l.c., p. 13).

In this way, therefore, the relation between capital and wage-labour arises in agriculture itself. It first arises when a number of people find themselves cut off from ownership of the conditions of labour—above all from the land—and have nothing to sell but their labour itself.

For the wage-labourer, however, who can no longer produce commodities, but must sell his labour itself, the *minimum* of wages, the equivalent of the necessary means of subsistence, necessarily becomes the law which governs his exchange with the owner of the conditions of labour.

"The mere workman who has only his arms and his industry, has nothing unless he succeeds in selling his labour to others.... In every kind of work it cannot fail to happen, and as a matter of fact it does happen, that the wages of the workman are limited to what is necessary to procure him his subsistence" (l.c., p. 10).

Then as soon as wage-labour has arisen, "the produce of land is divided into two parts: the one includes the subsistence and the profits of the husbandman, which are the reward of his labour and the condition upon which he undertakes to cultivate the field of the proprietor. What remains is that independent and disposable part which the *land gives as pure gifts to him who cultivates it*, over and above his advances and the wages of his trouble; and this is the portion of the proprietor, or the revenue with which the latter can live without labour and which he uses as he will" (l.c., p. 14).

---

* Manufacturers.—*Ed.*

** Those who are paid (wages or a salary).—*Ed.*

This pure gift of the land, however, is now already defined as a gift which it gives to him "who cultivates it", and thus as a gift which it makes to labour; as the productive power of labour applied to the land, a productive power which labour possesses through using the productive power of nature and which it thus derives from the land—but it derives it from the land only as labour. In the hands of the landowner, therefore, the surplus appears no longer as a "gift of nature", but as the appropriation—without an equivalent—of another's labour, which through the productivity of nature is enabled to produce means of subsistence in excess of its own needs, but which, because it is wage-labour, is restricted to appropriating for itself, out of the product of the labour, only "what is necessary to procure him" [i. e., the worker] "his subsistence".

> "The *cultivator* produces *his own wages*, and, in addition, the revenue which serves to pay the whole class of artisans and other stipendiaries.... *The proprietor has nothing except through the labour of the cultivator*" (therefore not through a pure gift of nature); "he receives from him his ||232| subsistence and that wherewith he pays the labours of other stipendiaries ... the cultivator has need of the proprietor only by virtue of conventions and laws ..." (l.c., p. 15).

Thus in this passage surplus-value is explicitly stated to be the part of the cultivator's labour which the proprietor appropriates to himself without giving any equivalent, and he sells the product of his labour, therefore, without having bought it. Only what Turgot has in mind is not exchange-value as such, the labour-time itself, but the surplus of products which the cultivator's labour supplies to the proprietor over and above his own wages; which surplus of products, however, is only the embodiment of the amount of time which he works gratis for the proprietor in addition to the time which he works for the reproduction of his wages.

We see thus how, *within the limits of agricultural labour*, the Physiocrats have a correct grasp of surplus-value; they see it as a product of the wage-labourer's labour, although they in turn conceive this labour in the concrete forms in which it appears in use-values.

The capitalist exploitation of agriculture—"leasing or letting of land"—is, it may be noted in passing, described by Turgot as "the most advantageous method of all, but it presupposes a land that is already rich" (l. c., p. 21).

<In considering surplus-value it is necessary to turn from the sphere of circulation to the sphere of production. That is to say, to

deduce surplus-value not simply from the exchange of commodity for commodity, but from exchange as it occurs within production, between the owners of the conditions of labour and the labourers themselves. These too confront each other as owners of commodities, and consequently there is no assumption here of production independent of exchange.>

<In the Physiocratic system the proprietors [landowners] are the *salariants*,* labourers and manufacturers in all other branches of industry being wage-labourers or stipendiaries. Consequently also the governing and the governed.>

Turgot analyses the conditions of labour as follows:

"In every craft, it is necessary that the workman should have tools in advance, that he should have a sufficient quantity of the materials upon which he has to labour; it is necessary that he should subsist while waiting for the sale of his finished goods" (l.c., p. 34).

All these advances, these conditions on which alone labour can be performed, which are therefore *preconditions* of the labour-process, are originally provided gratis by the land:

It is the land which "has provided the first fund of advances prior to all cultivation", in fruits, fish, game, etc., in tools such as tree branches, stones, in domestic animals, which multiply through the process of procreation, and moreover each year yield products in "milk, fleeces, hides and other materials, which, with the wood obtained in the forests, have formed the first fund for the works of industry" (l.c., p. 34).

Now these conditions of labour, these advances to labour become *capital* as soon as they have to be advanced to the labourer by a third person, and this is the case from the moment when the labourer owns nothing but his labour-power itself.

"*When* a large part of the society had *only their arms to maintain them*, it was necessary that those who thus lived on wages should begin by having *something in advance*, either to procure the materials upon which to labour or to maintain them while waiting for the payment of their wages" (l.c., pp. 37-38).

||233| Turgot defines "*capitals*" as "accumulated movable values" (l. c., p. 38). Originally the proprietor or cultivator pays wages directly each day and supplies the material, for example, to the spinner of flax. As industry develops, larger advances and continuity of the process of production are necessary. This is then undertaken by the possessor of capital. In the price of his products he must recover all his *advances* and a profit equal to

* The payers of wages.—*Ed.*

"what his money would have been worth to him if he had employed it in the purchase of an estate", besides his wages, "for doubtless, if the profit were the same, he would have preferred to live without any exertion on the revenue of the land he could have acquired with the same capital" (l.c., pp. 38-39).

The "stipendiary industrial class" is itself subdivided "into capitalists, entrepreneurs and simple workers", etc. (p. 39). Agricultural entrepreneurs are in the same position as these [industrial] entrepreneurs. They must similarly get all their advances replaced, along with the profit as shown above.

"All this must first be deducted from the price of the products of the earth; the *surplus* serves the cultivator for payment the proprietor for the permission he has given him to make use of his field for setting his enterprise on foot. This is the price of the lease, the revenue of the proprietor. the *net produce*; for all the land produces, up to the amount that replaces the advances of every kind and the profits of the person who has made the advances, cannot be regarded as a revenue, but only as *the return of the expenses of cultivation*; when one considers that, if the cultivator did not get them back, he would take care not to employ his resources and his toil in cultivating the field of another" (l.c., p. 40).

Finally:

"Although capitals are partly formed by saving from the profits of the working classes, yet, as these profits always come from the earth—inasmuch as they are all paid either from the revenue, or as part of the expenditure which serves to produce the revenue—it is evident the capitals come from the land just as much as the revenue does; or, rather, that they are nothing but the accumulation of the part of the values produced by the land that the proprietors of the revenue, or those who share it with them, can lay by every year without using it for the satisfaction of their wants" (l.c., p. 66).

It is quite right, that if rent is the only surplus-value, accumulation takes place only from rent. What the capitalists accumulate apart from rent, they pinch from their wages (their revenue, destined for their consumption—since this is how profit is defined).

As profit, like wages, is reckoned in with the costs of cultivation, and only the surplus forms the revenue of the proprietor, the latter—in spite of the honourable status given him—is in fact excluded from the costs of cultivation (and thereby from being an agent of production), just as with the Ricardians.

The emergence of the Physiocrats was connected both with the opposition to Colbertism and, in particular, with the hullabaloo over the John Law system.

[4. Confusion of Value with Material Substance (Paoletti)]

||234| The confusion of value with material substance, or rather the equating of value with it, and the connection between this view and the whole outlook of the Physiocrats, comes clearly to light in the following extracts from *Ferdinando Paoletti*: *I veri mezzi di render felici le società* (in part directed against Verri, who in his *Meditazioni sulla Economia politica* (1771), had attacked the Physiocrats). (Paoletti of Toscana, op. cit., t. XX, [published by] Custodi, Parte moderna.)

"Such a *multiplication of matter*" as are the products of the earth "has certainly never taken place through industry, nor is it possible. This gives matter only form, it only modifies it; consequently nothing is created by industry. But, the objection may be raised, industry gives matter form, and consequently it is productive; even if this is not a production of matter, it is nevertheless one of form. Very well, then, I won't contest this. But *that is not creation of wealth*; *on the contrary, it is nothing but an expense*.... Political economy presupposes, and takes as the object of its investigation, material and real production, which is found only in agriculture, since this alone multiplies the substances and products which form wealth.... Industry buys raw materials from agriculture, in order to work them up; its labour—as we have already said—gives these raw materials only a form, but it adds nothing to them and does not multiply them" (pp. 196-97). "Give the cook a measure of peas, with which he is to prepare your dinner; he will put them on the table for you well cooked and well dished up, but in the same quantity as he was given, but on the other hand give the same quantity to the gardener for him to put into the ground; he will return to you, when the right time has come, at least fourfold the quantity that he had been given. This is the true and only production" (p. 197). "Things receive value through the needs of men. Therefore the value or the increase of value of commodities is not the result of industrial labour, but of the labourers' outlays" (p. 198). "Hardly has a new manufacture of any kind made its appearance, but it immediately spreads within and outside the country; and see! *very soon* competition from other industrialists and merchants brings the price down to its correct level, which ... is determined by the value of the raw material and the costs of the labourers' maintenance" (pp. 204-05).

[5. Elements of Physiocratic Theory in Adam Smith]

Agriculture is the first of all branches of industry to use the forces of nature on a considerable scale. Their use in manufacturing industry becomes apparent only at a higher stage of industrial development. The following quotation shows how, in this connection, Adam Smith still reflects the prehistory of large-scale industry and for this reason upholds the Physiocratic point of view, and how Ricardo answers him from the standpoint of modern industry.

‖235| In Book II, Ch. V [of his *An Inquiry into the Nature and Causes of the Wealth of Nations*], Adam Smith says with reference to the rent of land:

"It is the work of nature which remains after deducting or compensating every thing which can be regarded as the work of man. It is seldom less than a fourth, and frequently more than a third of the whole produce. No equal quantity of productive labour employed in manufactures can ever occasion so great a reproduction. *In them nature does nothing*; *man does all*; and the reproduction must always be in proportion to the strength of the agents that occasion it" [Adam Smith, *An Inquiry into the Nature and Causes of the Wealth of Nations*.... By J. R. McCulloch, Vol. II, Edinburgh, 1828, p. 147.]

On which Ricardo comments [in his *On the Principles of Political Economy, and Taxation*], 2nd edition, 1819, note to pp. 61-62:

"Does nature nothing for man in manufactures? Are the powers of wind and water, which move our machinery, and assist navigation, nothing? The pressure of the atmosphere and the elasticity of steam, which enable us to work the most stupendous engines—are they not the gifts of nature? to say nothing of the effects of the matter of heat in softening and melting metals, of the decomposition of the atmosphere in the process of dyeing and fermentation. There is not a manufacture which can be mentioned, in which nature does not give her assistance to man, and give it too, generously and gratuitously."

[An anonymous author emphasises] that the Physiocrats regarded profit as only a deduction from rent:

For instance, "say they,* of the price of a piece of lace, one part merely replaces what the labourer consumed, and the other part is only transferred from one man's pocket <i.e., that of the landlord> to another's" (*An Inquiry into those Principles, respecting the Nature of Demand and the Necessity of Consumption, lately advocated by Mr. Malthus, etc.*, London, 1821, p. 96).

The view of Adam Smith and his followers that the accumulation of capital is due to personal stinting and saving and self-denial of the capitalists also originates from the view of the Physiocrats that profit (including interest) is merely revenue for the consumption of the capitalists. They could say this because they only regarded land rent as the true economic, so to speak legitimate, source of accumulation.

* In the manuscript: "The Physiocrats say f. i."—*Ed.*

"He," says Turgot, i.e., the husbandman, "is the only one whose labour produces *over and above the wages of labour*" (Turgot, l.c., p. 11).

Here the entire profit is thus reckoned in with the wages of labour.

||236| "The cultivator creates over and above that restitution" (of his own wages) "the revenue of the proprietor; and the artisan creates no revenue, either for himself or for others" (l.c., p. 16). "All the land produces up to the amount that replaces the advances of every kind and the profits of the person who has made the advances, *cannot be regarded as a revenue*, but only as *the return of the expenses of cultivation*" (l.c., p. 40).

Adolphe Blanqui, *Histoire de l'économie politique*, Brussels. 1839, says [of the Physiocrats] on p. 139:

[They were of the opinion that] "Labour applied to the cultivation of the soil produced not only the wherewithal to maintain the labourer throughout the entire duration of the task, but also *an excess of value*" (surplus-value) "which could be added to the mass of already existing wealth. They called this excess the *net product*". (Thus they conceive surplus-value in the form of the use-values in which it appears) "The net product had necessarily to belong to the owner of the land and constituted in his hands a revenue fully at his disposal. What then was the net product of the other industries? ... Manufacturers, merchants, workmen, all were the employees, *the stipendiaries* of agriculture, sovereign creator and dispenser of all wealth. The products of the labour of these latter represented in the system of the *Economists*[17] only the equivalent of what they had consumed during the task, so that after their work was completed, the sum total of wealth was absolutely the same as before, *unless the workmen or the masters had placed in reserve*, that is to say *s a v e d, what they had the right to consume*. Thus, then, labour applied to the soil was the only labour productive of wealth, and labour in other industries was regarded as *s t e r i l e*, because *no increase in the general capital resulted from it*."

<Thus the Physiocrats saw the production of surplus-value as the essence of capitalist production. It was this phenomenon that they had to explain. And it remained the problem, after they had eliminated the profit upon alienation of the Mercantile system.

"In order to acquire money," says *Mercier de la Rivière*, "one must buy it, and, after this purchase, one is no richer than one was before; one has simply received in money the same value that one has given in commodities" (Mercier de la Rivière, *L'Ordre naturel et essentiel des sociétés politiques*, t. II, p. 338).

This holds good both for ||237| purchase and for sale, as also for the whole metamorphosis of the commodity, or for the result of the exchange of different commodities at their value, that is, the exchange of equivalents. Whence, therefore, comes surplus-value? That is, whence comes capital? That was the problem for the Physiocrats. Their error was that they confused the *increase of material substance*, which because of the natural processes of vegetation and generation distinguishes agriculture and stock-raising from manufacture, with the *increase of exchange-value*. Use-value was their starting-point. And the use-value of all commodities, reduced, as the scholastics say, to a universal, was the material substance of nature as such, whose increase in the same form occurs only in agriculture. >

Germain Garnier, the translator of Adam Smith and himself a Physiocrat, correctly expounds their *theory of savings*, etc. First he says that manufacture, as the Mercantilists maintained of all production, can *only* produce surplus-value through the profit of expropriation, by selling commodities above their value, so that only a new distribution of values created takes place, but no new addition to the created values.

"The labour of artisans and manufacturers, opening no new source of wealth, *can only be profitable through advantageous exchanges*, and has only a purely relative value, a value which will not be repeated if there is no longer the opportunity to *gain on the exchanges*" (his translation *Recherches sur la nature et les causes de la richesse des nations*, t. V, Paris, 1802, p. 266[18]). Or the savings which they make, the values which they secure over and above those which they expend, must be stinted from their own consumption. "The labour of artisans and manufacturers, though only able to add to the general amount of the wealth of society the savings made by the wage-labourers and the capitalists, may well tend by these means to enrich society" (l.c., p. 266).

And in greater detail: "The labourers in agriculture enrich the State by the very product of their labour: labourers in manufactures and commerce, on the contrary, cannot enrich it otherwise than through *savings on their own consumption*. This assertion of the Economists is a consequence of the distinction which they have established, and appears to be quite incontestable. Indeed, the labour of artisans and manufacturers cannot add anything else to the value of the material than the value of their own labour, that is to say, the value of the wages and profits which this labour should have earned, at the rates actually current in the country ||238| for the one and the other. For these wages, whether they be small or large, are the reward of labour; they are what the labourer has the right to consume and is presumed to consume; because it is only in consuming them that he can enjoy the fruits of his labour, and this enjoyment is all that in reality constitutes his reward. Similarly profits, whether they be high or low, are also regarded as the daily and continuous consumption of the capitalist, who is naturally presumed to proportion his enjoyments to the revenue that his capital gives him. Thus unless the workman curtails a part of the comforts to which he has the right in accordance with the current rate of wages assigned *to his labour*; unless the capitalist resigns himself to saving a part of the revenue which his capital brings him, both the one and the other will consume, in proportion as the piece of work is completed, the whole value resulting from this work. The total quantity of the wealth of society will then be, after their labour is over, the same as it was before, *unless they have saved* a part of what they had the right to consume and what they could consume without being charged with wasting; in which case the total quantity of the wealth of society will have been increased *by the whole value of these savings*. Consequently it is correct to say that the agents of manufacture and commerce can *only add to the total quantity of wealth existing in society by their privations alone*" (l.c., pp. 263-64).

Garnier is also quite correct in noting that Adam Smith's theory of accumulation through savings rests on this Physiocratic foundation. (Adam Smith was strongly infected by the Physiocrats, as he nowhere shows more strikingly than in his critique of the Physiocrats). Garnier says:

"Finally, if the Economists have maintained that manufacturing and commercial industry can only add to the national wealth by privations, Smith has likewise said that industry would be practised in vain, and the capital of a country would never grow larger, unless the economy augmented it by its savings" (Book II, Ch 3). "Smith is therefore in full agreement with the Economists" and so on (l.c., p. 270).

[6. The Physiocrats as Partisans of Large-Scale Capitalist Agriculture]

||239| Among the immediate historical circumstances which facilitated the spread of Physiocratic theory and even its emergence, Adolphe Blanqui, in the work already mentioned, adduces:

"Of all the values which shot up in the feverish atmosphere of the *system*" (Law's), "nothing remained except ruin, desolation and bankruptcy. *Landed property alone* did not go under in the storm." <For this reason Herr Proudhon, in *Philosophie de la Misère*, puts landed property only after credit.> "It even improved its position by changing hands and by being *subdivided on a large scale*, perhaps for *the first time* since feudalism" (l.c., p. 138). In particular, "The innumerable changes of ownership which were effected under the influence of the system, began the process of parcelling out property.... Landed property arose for the first time from the condition of torpor in which the feudal system had kept it for so long. This was a real awakening for agriculture.... It" (the land) "passed now from out of a condition of mortmain and came into circulation" (l.c., pp. 137-38).

Turgot as well as *Quesnay* and his other adherents also want *capitalist* production in agriculture. Thus Turgot:

"The leasing or letting of land ... this latter method" (large-scale agriculture, based on the modern system of leases) "is the most advantageous of all, but it presupposes a country that is already rich" (see Turgot, l.c., p. 21).

And Quesnay in his *Maximes générales du gouvernement économique d'un royaume agricole*:

"The pieces of land which are employed in growing grain should as far as possible be joined together in large-scale farms which can be managed by rich farmers" (i.e., capitalists) "since the expenses for the maintenance and repair of the buildings are smaller and therefore the costs are correspondingly much lower and the net product much greater in the case of large agricultural undertakings than in the case of small."

In the same passage Quesnay admits that the increased productivity of agricultural labour accrues to the "net revenue", and therefore in the first place to the landowner, i. e., the owner of surplus-value, and that the relative increase of the latter arises not from the land but from the social and other arrangements for raising the productivity of labour. ||240| For he says in the same place:

"Every advantageous" <i.e., advantageous to the net product> "economy in labour which can be accomplished with the aid of animals, machines, water-power and so on, will be of benefit to the population," etc.

At the same time Mercier de la Rivière (l. c., t. II, p.407) has an inkling that surplus-value at least in manufacture has something to do with the manufacturing workers themselves. (Turgot extended this to all production, as already mentioned.) In the passage cited he exclaims:

"Moderate your enthusiasm, ye blind admirers of the false products of industry. Before ye extol its miracles, open your eyes and see how many live in poverty or at least, in need, among those producers who understand the art of converting 20 sous into the value of a thousand écus. *Who then benefits by this enormous increase in value? What do you say! Comforts are unknown to those through whose hands it is accomplished. Take warning then by this contrast!*"

[7. Contradictions in the Political Views of the Physiocrats. The Physiocrats and the French Revolution]

[There were] contradictions in the system of the Economists, taken as a whole. Among others, Quesnay was for the absolute monarchy.

"There must be only one supreme power.... The system of opposing forces in a government is ruinous. It merely indicates discord among the great and the suppression of the small people" (in the above-mentioned *Maximes générales*, etc.).

Mercier de la Rivière [says]:

By the very fact "that man is intended to live in a community, he is intended to live under a despotism" ([*L'Ordre naturel et essentiel des sociétés politiques*], t. I, p. 281).

And to crown all the "Friend of the People",[19] the Marquis de Mirabeau—Mirabeau the Elder! It was precisely this school, with its *laissez faire, laissez aller*, that overthrew Colbertism and all forms of government interference in the activities of bourgeois society. It allowed the State to live on only in the pores of this society, as Epicurus placed his gods in the pores of the world! The glorification of landed property in practice turns into the demand that taxes should be put exclusively on ground-rent, [and this implies] the virtual confiscation of landed property by the State, just as with the radical section of the Ricardians. The French Revolution, in spite of the protests of Roederer and others, accepted this taxation theory.

Turgot himself [was] the radical bourgeois minister who prepared the way for the French Revolution. For all their sham feudal pretences the Physiocrats were working hand in hand with the Encyclopaedists! |240||

||241| Turgot sought to anticipate the measures of the French Revolution. By the edict of *February 1776* he abolished the guilds. (This edict was revoked three months after it was promulgated.) Similarly he annulled the road-making *corvée des paysans*.* He tried to introduce the single tax on rent of land.[20]

||241| We shall come back again later to the great service rendered by the Physiocrats respecting the analysis of capital.[21]

Meanwhile just this point: surplus-value (according to them) is due to the productivity of a special kind of labour, agricultural labour. And on the whole this special productivity is due to nature itself.

In the Mercantile system, surplus-value is only relative—what one wins, the other loses: profit upon alienation or oscillation of wealth between different parties. So that within a country, if we consider the total capital, no creation of surplus-value in fact takes place. It can only arise in the relations between one nation and other nations. And the surplus realised by one nation as against the other takes the form of money (the balance of trade), because it is precisely money that is the direct and independent form of exchange-value. In opposition to this—for the Mercantile system in fact denies the creation of absolute surplus-value—the Physiocrats seek to explain absolute surplus-value: the *net product*. And since the net product is fixed in their minds as use-value, agriculture [is for them] *the sole creator of it*.

---

* Compulsory labour exacted of the peasants.—*Ed.*

[8. Vulgarisation of the Physiocratic Doctrine by the Prussian Reactionary Schmalz]

One of the most naïve representatives of Physiocratic theory—how far removed he is from Turgot!—is the old smeller-out of demagogues[22] and royal Prussian Privy Councillor Schmalz. For instance:

"If nature pays him" (the lessor of the land, the landowner) "*even double the legal interests*, on what plausible ground could anyone dare to deprive him of it?" (*Économie politique*, traduit par Henri Jouffroy, etc., t. I. Paris, 1826, p. 90.[23])

The minimum of wages is so formulated by the Physiocrats that the consumption (or expenditure) of the labourers is equal to the wage *that they receive*. Or as Herr Schmalz puts it in a general way:

"The average wage in a trade is equal to the average of what a man in this trade consumes during the time of his labour" (l.c., p. 120).

"*Rent of land* is the one and only element of the national revenue; ||242| and interest on capitals employed and the wages of all kinds of labours only make the product of this rent pass and circulate through everyone's hands" (l.c., pp. 309-10).

"The utilisation of the land, its faculty, its capacity for the annual reproduction of rent, is all that constitutes the national wealth" (l.c., p. 310). "If we go back to the foundations, to the first elements of the *value* of all objects, whatsoever they may be, we are forced to recognise that this value is nothing other than that of the simple products of nature; that is to say, although labour may have given a new value to these objects and raised their price, this new value, or this price, is only made up nevertheless of the total values put together of all the natural products which, because of the new form that labour has given them, have been destroyed, consumed, or used by the labourer in one way or another" (l.c., p. 313).

"This kind of labour" (agriculture proper) "being the only labour that contributes to the production of *new bodies*, it is therefore the only labour that can, up to a certain point, be considered productive. As for labours in working up material or in industry ... they simply give a new form to bodies which nature has produced" (l.c., pp. 15-16).

[9. An Early Critique of the Superstition of the Physiocrats in the Question of Agriculture (Verri)]

Against the superstition of the Physiocrats.

Verri (Pietro): *Meditazioni sulla Economia politica.* (First printed 1771), t. XV. [Published by] Custodi, Parte moderna.

"All the phenomena of the universe, whether produced by the hand of man or through the universal laws of physics, are not actual *new creations*, but merely a *modification* of matter. *Joining together* and *separating* are the only elements which the human mind always finds on analysing the concept of *reproduction*; and it is just the same with the *reproduction of value* and of *wealth*, when earth, air and water in the fields are transformed into corn, or when the hand of man transforms the secretions of an insect into silk, or some pieces of metal are arranged to make the mechanism of a watch" (pp. 21-22). Further: The Physiocrats call "the class of manufacturing labourers *sterile*, because in their view *the value of manufactured products is equal to the raw material* plus *the means of subsistence which the manufacturing labourers consume during the time of manufacture*" (l.c., p. 25).

||243| On the other hand, Verri calls attention to the constant poverty of the agricultural population in contrast to the progressive enrichment of the artisans, and then goes on to say:

"This proves that the artisan, in the price which he receives, gets not only the *replacement of his outlay on consumption, but a certain sum over and above that; and this sum is a new quantity of value created* in the annual production" (l.c., p. 26). "The newly-created value is therefore that part of the price of the agricultural or industrial products which they *yield over and above the original value* of the materials and the necessary outlays on consumption while they are being worked up. In agriculture the seed and the consumption of the husbandman must be deducted, as in manufacture the raw material and the consumption of the industrial workman; and every year *new value* is created, *to the amount of the balance that remains*" (l.c., pp. 26-27).

[CHAPTER III]

ADAM SMITH

[1. Smith's Two Different Definitions of Value; the Determination of Value by the Quantity of Labour Expended Which Is Contained in a Commodity, and Its Determination by the Quantity of Living Labour Which Can Be Bought in Exchange for This Commodity]

Adam Smith, like all economists worth speaking of, takes over from the Physiocrats the conception of the average wage, which he calls the natural price of wages.

"A man must always live by his work, and his wages must at least be sufficient to maintain him. They must even upon most occasions be somewhat more, otherwise it would be impossible for him to bring up a family, and the race of such workmen could not last beyond the first generation." ([Adam Smith, *Wealth of Nations*, Oxford University Press, London, 1928, Vol. I, p. 75, Garnier] t. 1, l. I, ch. VIII, p. 136.*)

Adam Smith expressly states that the development of the productive powers of labour does not benefit the labourer himself. He says (l. I, ch. VIII [*An Inquiry into the Nature and Causes of the Wealth of Nations*] edit. McCulloch, London, 1828):

"The produce of labour constitntes the natural recompense or wages of labour. In that original state of things, which precedes both the *appropriation of land* and the *accumulation of stock*, the whole produce of labour belongs to the labourer. He has neither landlord nor master to share with him. Had this state continued, the wages of labour *would have augmented with all those improvements in its productive powers*, to which the *division of labour* gives occasion. All things would gradually have become cheaper." < At any rate all those things requiring a smaller quantity of labour for their reproduction, but they "would" not only have become cheaper; they have, in point of fact, become cheaper.> "They would have been produced

* Marx refers to Garnier's French translation of Adam Smith's work from which he takes the quotation. All excerpts from Smith's *Wealth of Nations* quoted by Marx in French in the manuscript are printed in this edition in English as given in Adam Smith, *An Inquiry into the Nature and Causes of the Wealth of Nations*, Oxford University Press (O.U.P) (The World's Classics), London 1928. In two volumes. Those passages which Marx has taken from Garnier's French translation are marked in the text "Garnier". The French extracts used by Marx are printed in the Appendix. —*Ed.*

by a smaller quantity of labour; and as the commodities produced by equal quantities of labour would naturally in this state of things be exchanged for one another, they would have been purchased likewise with ||244| the produce of a smaller quantity [...] But this original state of things, in which the labourer enjoyed the whole produce of his own labour, *could not last beyond the first introduction of the appropriation of land and the accumulation of stock.* It was at an end, therefore, long before the most considerable improvements were made in the productive powers of labour, and it would be to no purpose to trace further what might have been its effects upon the recompense or wages of labour" (Vol. I, pp. 107-09).

Here Adam Smith very acutely notes that the really great development of the productive power of labour starts only from the moment when it is transformed into wage-labour, and the conditions of labour confront it on the one hand as landed property and on the other as capital. The development of the productive power of labour thus begins only under conditions in which the labourer himself can no longer appropriate its result. It is therefore quite useless to investigate how this growth of productive powers might have influenced or would influence "wages", taken here as equal to the product of labour, on the hypothesis that the product of labour (or the value of this product) belonged to the labourer himself.

Adam Smith is very copiously infected with the conceptions of the Physiocrats, and often whole strata run through his work which belong to the Physiocrats and are in complete contradiction with the views specifically advanced by him. This is so, for example, in the theory of rent, etc. For our present purpose we can completely disregard these passages in his writings, which are not characteristic of himself, but in which he is a mere Physiocrat.[24]

In the first part of this work, when dealing with the analysis of the commodity, I have already pointed out[25] Adam Smith's inconsistency in his treatment of how exchange-value is determined. In particular, [I have shown] how he sometimes confuses, and at other times substitutes, the determination of the value of *commodities* by the quantity of labour required for their production, with its determination by the quantity of living labour with which commodities can be bought, or, what is the same thing, the quantity of commodities with which a definite quantity of living labour can be bought. Here he makes the *exchange-value* of labour the measure for the value of commodities. In fact, he makes *wages* the measure; for wages are equal to the quantity of commodities bought with a definite quantity of living labour, or to the quantity of labour that can be bought by a definite quantity of commodities. The value of labour, or rather of labour-power, changes, like that of any other commodity, and is in no way specifically different from the value of other commodities. Here value is made the measuring rod and the basis for the explanation of value—so we have a vicious circle.

From the exposition that follows, however, it will be seen that this vacillation and this jumbling up of completely heterogeneous determinations of value do not affect Smith's investigations into the nature and origin of surplus-value, because in fact, without even being aware of it, whenever he examines this question, he keeps firmly to the correct determination of the exchange-value of commodities—that is, its determination by the quantity of labour or the labour-time expended on them. |244||

||VII—283a | <Many examples can be given to show how often in the course of his work, when he is explaining actual facts, Smith treats the quantity of labour contained in the product as value and determining value. Some of these are quoted by Ricardo.[26] His whole doctrine of the influence of the division of labour and improved machinery on the price of commodities is based on it. Here one passage will be enough to cite. In ch. XI, l. I Adam Smith speaks of the cheapening of many manufactured goods in his time, as compared with earlier centuries, and he concludes with the words:

> "It cost a greater quantity of labour ||283b| to bring the goods to market. When they were brought thither, therefore, they must have purchased, or exchanged for the price, of a greater quantity." ([*Wealth of Nations*, O.U.P. edition, Vol. I, p. 284], [Garnier] t. II, p. 156).> |VII—283b||

||VI—245| Secondly, however, this contradiction in Adam Smith and his passing from one kind of explanation to another is based upon something deeper, which Ricardo, in exposing this contradiction, overlooked or did not rightly appreciate, and therefore also did not solve. Let us assume that all workers are producers of commodities, and not only produce their commodities but also sell them. The value of these commodities is determined by the necessary labour-time contained in them. If therefore the commodities are sold at their value, the labourer buys with one commodity, which is the product of twelve hours' labour-time, another twelve hours' labour-time in the form of another commodity, that is to say, twelve hours' labour-time which is embodied in another use-value. The value of his labour is therefore equal to the value of his commodity; that is, it is equal

to the product of twelve hours' labour-time. The selling and buying again, in a word, the whole process of exchange, the metamorphosis of the commodity, alters nothing in this. It alters only the form of the use-value in which this twelve hours' labour-time appears. The value of labour is therefore equal to the value of the product of labour. In the first place, equal quantities of materialised labour are exchanged in the commodities—in so far as they are exchanged at their value. Secondly, however, a certain quantity of living labour is exchanged for an equal quantity of materialised labour, because, firstly, the living labour is materialised in a product, a commodity, which belongs to the labourer, and secondly, this commodity is in turn exchanged for another commodity which contains an equally large quantity of labour. In fact, therefore, a certain quantity of living labour is exchanged for an equal amount of materialised labour. Thus it is not only commodity exchanging for commodity in the proportion in which they represent an equal quantity of materialised labour-time, but a quantity of living labour exchanging for a commodity which represents the same quantity of labour materialised.

On this assumption the value of labour (the quantity of commodities which can be bought with a given quantity of labour, or the quantity of labour which can be bought with a given quantity [of commodities]) could serve as the measure of the value of a commodity just as well as the quantity of labour contained in it, since the value of labour always represents the same quantity of materialised labour as the living labour requires for the production of this commodity; in other words, a definite quantity of living labour-time would always command a quantity of commodities which represents an equal amount of materialised labour-time. But in all modes of production—and particularly in the capitalist mode of production—in which the material conditions of labour belong to one or several classes, while on the other hand nothing but labour-power belongs to another class, the working class, what takes place is the opposite of this. The product or the value of the product of labour does not belong to the labourer. A definite quantity of living labour does not command the same quantity of materialised labour, or a definite quantity of labour materialised in a commodity commands a greater quantity of living labour than is contained in the commodity itself.

But as Adam Smith quite correctly takes as his starting-point the commodity and the exchange of commodities, and thus the producers initially confront each other only as possessors of commodities, sellers of commodities and buyers of commodities, he therefore discovers (so it seems to him) that in the exchange between capital and wage-labour, ||246| materialised labour and living labour, the general law at once ceases to apply, and commodities (for labour too is a commodity in so far as it is bought and sold) do not exchange in proportion to the quantities of labour which they represent. *Hence* he concludes that labour-time is no longer the immanent measure which regulates the exchange-value of commodities, from the moment when the conditions of labour confront the wage-labourer in the form of landed property and capital. He should on the contrary, as Ricardo rightly points out, have drawn the opposite conclusion, that the expressions "quantity of labour" and "value of labour" are now no longer identical, and that therefore the relative value of commodities, although determined by the labour-time contained in them, is not determined by the value of labour, since that was only correct so long as the latter expression remained identical with the former. Later on, when we deal with Malthus,[27] we can show how wrong and absurd it would be, even when the labourer appropriated his own product, i. e., the value of his own product, to make this value or the value of labour the measure of value, in the same sense in which labour-time or labour itself is the measure of value and the value-creating element. For even in that case the labour which can be bought with a commodity cannot serve as a measure in the same sense as the labour contained in it. One would be merely an index to the other.

In any case Adam Smith feels the difficulty of deducing the exchange between capital and labour from the law that determines the exchange of commodities, since the former apparently rests on quite opposite and contradictory principles. And indeed the contradiction could not be solved so long as capital was set directly against labour instead of against labour-power. Adam Smith was well aware that the labour-time expended on the reproduction and maintenance of labour-power is very different from the labour which it [i. e., labour-power] itself can perform. Thus he himself quotes from Cantillon's *Essai sur la nature du commerce*:

> "The labour of an able-bodied slave, the same author adds, is computed to be worth double his maintenance; and that of the meanest labourer, he thinks, cannot be worth less than that of an able-bodied slave" ([*Wealth of Nations*, O.U.P. edition, Vol. I, p. 75], [Garnier] t. I, l.I, ch. VIII, p. 137).

On the other hand it is strange that Adam Smith did not grasp how little the objection he raises has to do with the law that determines the exchange of commodities for each other. That commodities A and B exchange in proportion to the labour-time contained in them is in no way upset by the proportions in which the producers A or B divide the products A and B, or rather their value, between themselves. If a part of A goes to the landowner, another to the capitalist, and a third part to the labourer, no matter what the share of each may be, this does not alter the fact that A itself exchanges with B according to its value. The relation between the labour-time contained in commodities A and B is in no way affected by how the labour-time contained in A and B is appropriated by various persons. "When the exchange of broadcloth for linen has been accomplished, the producers of broadcloth will share in the linen in a proportion equal to that in which they previously shared in the broadcloth" ([Karl Marx], *Misère de la Philosophie*, p. 29).[28] It is this, too, that later the Ricardians rightly maintained against ||247| Adam Smith. Thus the Malthusian John Cazenove says:

"... Interchange and Distribution distinct from each other. ...* The circumstances which affect the one do not always affect the other. For instance, a reduction in the cost of producing any particular commodity will alter its relation to all others; but it will not necessarily alter its own distribution, nor will it in any way affect theirs. Again, a general reduction in the value of commodities affecting them *all alike* will not alter their relation to each other. It might or might not affect their distribution" (John Cazenove: Preface to his edition of Malthus's *Definitions in Political Economy*, London, 1853, [p. VI]).

But since the "distribution" of the value of the product between capitalist and worker is itself based on an exchange between commodities—commodities and labour-power—Adam Smith is justifiably startled. The fact that he had also made the value of labour, or the extent to which a commodity (or money) can purchase labour, the measure of value, has a disturbing effect on Smith's argument when he comes to the theory of prices, shows the influence of competition on the rate of profit, etc.; it deprives his work of all unity, and even excludes a number of essential questions from his inquiry. As we shall soon see, however, it did not affect his exposition of *surplus-value in general*, because here

* The manuscript reads: "Interchange of commodities and distribution must be kept distinct each other."—*Ed.*

he keeps consistently to the correct determination of value by the labour-time expended in different commodities.

So now to his treatment of the question.

But first we must mention one other circumstance. Adam Smith mixes up different things. First he states in Book I, Ch. V:

> "Every man is rich or poor according to the degree in which he can afford to enjoy the necessaries, conveniences and amusements of human life. But after the division of labour has once thoroughly taken place, it is but a very small part of these with which a man's own labour can supply him. The far greater part of them he must derive from the *labour of other people*, and he must be rich or poor *according to the quantity of that labour which he can command, or which he can afford to purchase. The value of any commodity*, therefore, to the person who possesses it, and who means not to use or consume it, himself, but *to exchange it for other commodities, is equal to the quantity of labour* which *it enables him to purchase or command*. Labour, therefore, is the *real* measure of the *exchangeable value* of all commodities" ([*Wealth of Nations*, O.U.P. edition, Vol. I, pp. 32-33], [Garnier] t. I, pp. 59 to 60).

> Further: "*They*" (the goods) "contain *the value of a certain quantity of labour, which we exchange* ||248| for what *is supposed at the time to contain the value of an equal quantity*.... It was not by gold or by silver, but by labour, that all the wealth of the world was originally purchased; and its value, to those who possess it, and who want to exchange it for some new productions, is precisely equal to the quantity of labour which it can enable them to purchase or command" ([ibid., p. 33], [Garnier] l. I, ch. V, pp. 60-61).

> Finally: "*Wealth*, as Mr. Hobbes says, is *power*. But the person who either acquires, or succeeds to a great fortune, does not necessarily acquire or succeed to any political power, either civil or military.... The power which that possession immediately and directly conveys to him, is the power of purchasing a certain command over *all the labour, or over all the produce of labour which is then in the market*" ([Ibid.], [Garnier] l.c., p. 61).

It can be seen that in all these passages Adam Smith confuses *the labour of other people* with the *produce of this labour*. The exchange-value of the commodity which anyone possesses consists—after the division of labour—in the commodities belonging to someone else which he can buy, i. e., in the quantity of someone else's labour which is contained in them, the quantity of someone else's materialised labour. And this quantity of the labour of others is equal to the quantity of labour that is contained in his own commodity. As he expressly says:

> "They" (the goods) "contain the value of a certain quantity of labour, which we exchange for what is supposed at the time to contain *the value of an equal quantity*."

The emphasis here is on the change brought about by the *di-*

vision of labour: that is to say, that wealth no longer consists in the product of one's own labour, but in the quantity of the labour of others which this product commands, the social labour which it can buy, the quantity of which is determined by the quantity of labour it itself contains. In fact, only the concept of exchange-value is here involved—that my labour now counts only as social labour, and consequently its product determines my wealth by its command over an equal quantity of social labour. My commodity, which contains a definite quantity of necessary labour-time, gives me command over all other commodities of equal value, and therefore over an equal quantity of the labour of others realised in other use-values. The emphasis here lies on the equalisation, brought about through the division of labour and exchange-value, of *my* labour with the labour of *others*, in other words, with social labour (the fact that *my* labour too, or the labour contained in my commodities, is already *socially* determined, and has fundamentally changed its character, escapes Adam), and not at all on the difference between *materialised* labour and *living* labour, and the specific laws of their exchange. In fact, Adam Smith is here saying nothing more than that the value of commodities is determined by the labour-time contained in them, and that the wealth of the owner of commodities consists in the quantity of social labour at his disposal.

However, the equating here of *labour* and *product of labour* ||249| in fact provides the first occasion for the confusion between the determination of the value of commodities by the quantity of labour contained in them, and the determination of their value by the quantity of living labour that they can buy, in other words, their determination by the value of labour. When Adam Smith says:

> "His fortune is greater or less, precisely in proportion to the extent of this power, or to the quantity of either of other men's labour, or, *what is the same thing*" (here is the false identification) "*of the produce of other men's labour*, which it enables him to purchase". ([*Wealth of Nations*, O.U.P. edition, Vol. I, p. 33], [Garnier] l.c., p. 61.)

He might just as well have said: it is in proportion to the quantity of social labour contained in his own commodity or fortune; as indeed he also says:

> "They" (the goods) "contain the value of a certain quantity of labour, which we exchange for what is supposed at the time [to contain] the value of *an equal quantity*."

(The word *value* is here superfluous and meaningless.) The false conclusion emerges already in this Chapter V, when for example he says:

"Labour alone, therefore, never varying in its *own value*, is alone the ultimate and real standard by which the value of all commodities can at all times and places be estimated and compared" ([ibid., p. 36], [Garnier] l.c., p. 66).

What is true of labour itself and consequently of its measure, labour-time—that the value of commodities is always proportionate to the labour-time realised in them, no matter how the *value of labour* may change—is here claimed for this changing value of labour itself.

Here Adam Smith is examining only commodity exchange in general: the nature of exchange-value, of the division of labour and of money. The parties to the exchange still confront each other only as owners of commodities. They buy the labour of others in the form of a commodity, just as their own labour appears in the form of a commodity. The quantity of social labour which they command is therefore equal to the quantity of labour contained in the commodity with which they themselves make the purchase. But when in the following chapters he comes to the exchange between materialised labour and living labour, between capitalist and worker, and then *stresses* that the value of the commodity is now no longer determined by the quantity of labour it itself contains, but by the quantity—which is different from this—of living labour of others which it can command, i. e., buy, he is not in fact saying by this that commodities themselves no longer exchange in proportion to the labour-time they contain; but that the *increase of wealth*, the increase of the value contained in the commodity, and the extent of this increase, depends upon the greater or less quantity of living labour which the materialised labour sets in motion. And put in this way it is correct. Smith, however, remains unclear on this point.

[2. Smith's General Conception of Surplus-Value. The Notion of Profit, Rent and Interest as Deductions from the Product of the Worker's Labour]

||250| In Chapter VI of Book I Adam Smith passes on from those relations in which it is assumed that the producers confront one another only as sellers and possessors of commodities to the relations of exchange between those who possess the conditions of labour and those who possess labour-power alone.

"In that early and rude state of society which *precedes both the accumulation of stock and the appropriation of land, the proportion between the quantities of labour necessary for acquiring different objects*, seems to be the only circumstance which can afford any rule for exchanging them for one another.... It is natural that what is usually the produce of two days' or two hours' labour, should be worth double of what is usually the produce of one day's or one hour's labour" ([ibid., p. 52] t. I, ch. VI, pp. 94-95, Garnier).

That is to say, the labour-time necessary to produce different commodities determines the proportion in which they exchange for one another, or their *exchange-value*.

"In this state of things, the whole produce of labour belongs to the labourer; and the quantity of labour commonly employed in acquiring or producing any commodity, is the only circumstance which can regulate the quantity of labour which it ought commonly to purchase, command, or exchange for" ([ibid., p. 53], [Garnier] l. c., p. 96).

Consequently, on this assumption the labourer is a mere seller of commodities, and one commands the labour of another only in so far as he buys the other's commodity with his commodity. He thus commands with his commodity only so much of the other's labour as is contained in his own commodity, since both exchange only commodities against each other, and the exchange-value of the commodities is determined by the labour-time or quantity of labour they contain.

But, Adam continues:

"As soon as *stock has accumulated in the hands of particular persons*, some of them will naturally employ it in setting to work industrious people, whom they will supply with materials and subsistence, *in order to make a profit by the sale of their work, or by what their labour adds to the value of the materials*" ([ibid., p. 53], [Garnier] l.c., p. 96).

Stop, before we follow the passage further. In the first place, whence come the "industrious people" who possess neither means of subsistence nor materials of labour—people who are hanging in mid air? If we strip Smith's statement of its naïve phrasing, it means nothing more than: capitalist production begins from the moment when the conditions of labour belong to one class, and another class has at its disposal only labour-power. This separation of labour from the conditions of labour is the precondition of capitalist production.

Secondly, however, what does Adam Smith mean when he says that the employers of labour set labourers to work "*in order to make a profit by the sale of their work*, or by what their labour ||251| adds to the value of the materials"?

Does he mean by this that the profit comes from the *sale*, that the commodity is sold *above* its value—that is, what Steuart calls profit upon alienation, which is nothing but a vibration of wealth between parties?* Let him answer for himself.

"In exchanging *the complete manufacture* either for money, *for labour*," (here again is a source of new error) "or for other goods. over and above what may be sufficient to pay the price of the materials, and the wages of the workmen, *something must be given* for the profits of the undertaker of the work, who hazards his stock in this adventure" ([ibid., p. 53], [Garnier], l.c.).

We shall return to this "hazarding" later (see notebook VII, p. 173) in the chapter on the apologetic accounts of profit.[29] This something given for the *profits* of the undertaker, when the complete work is exchanged, does it come from the sale of the commodity above its value, is it Steuart's profit upon alienation?

"The *value*," Adam continues immediately, "*which the workmen add to the materials*, therefore, resolves itself *in this case*" (when capitalist production has begun) "*into two parts, of which the one pays their wages, the other the profits of their employer upon the whole stock of materials and wages which he advanced*" ([ibid., p. 53], [Garnier] l.c., pp. 96-97).

Here therefore Adam Smith explicitly states: the profit which is made on the sale of the complete manufacture originates not from *the sale* itself, not from the sale of the commodity *above* its value, is not profit upon alienation. The value, that is, the quantity of labour which the workmen add to the material, falls rather into two parts. One pays their wages or is paid for through their wages. By this transaction the workmen give in return only as much labour as they have received in the form of wages. The other part forms the profit of the capitalist, that is, it is a quantity of labour which he sells without having paid for it. If therefore he sells the commodity at its value, that is, for the labour-time contained in it, in other words if he exchanges it for other commodities in accordance with the law of value, then his profit originates from the fact that he has not *paid for* a part of the labour contained in the commodity, but has nevertheless *sold* it. Adam Smith has thereby himself refuted the idea that the circumstance that the whole product of his labour no longer belongs to the labourer, that he is obliged to share it or its value with the owner of capital, invalidates the law that the proportion in which commodities exchange for each other, or their exchange-value, is

* See pp. 41-42 of the present volume.—*Ed.*

determined by the quantity of labour-time materialised in them. Indeed, on the contrary, he traces the profit of the capitalist precisely to the fact that he has not paid for a part of the labour added to the commodity, and it is from this that his profit on the sale of the commodity arises. We shall see how further on Adam Smith even more explicitly derives profit from the labour performed by the workman over and above the quantity of labour with which he *pays for* his wages, that is to say, replaces it by an equivalent. Thereby he has recognised the true origin of surplus-value. At the same time he has expressly stated that it does not arise from the ||252| advanced funds, whose value—however useful they may be in the real labour-process—merely reappears in the product; but that it arises exclusively from the new labour which the workmen *add to the materials* in the new process of production, in which those funds figure as means of labour or instruments of labour.

On the other hand, the phrase "in exchanging the complete manufacture either for money, *for labour*, or for other goods . . ." is wrong (and arises from the confusion mentioned earlier).

If he exchanges the commodity for money or for a commodity, his profit arises from his selling more labour than he has paid for, from the fact that he does not exchange an equal quantity of materialised labour for an equal quantity of living labour. Adam Smith therefore must not put the exchange either for money or for other goods on the same footing as the exchange of the complete manufacture for labour. For in the first exchange the surplus-value originates from the fact that the commodities are exchanged at their value, for the labour-time contained in them, which however is in part *unpaid for*. Here it is assumed that the capitalist does not exchange an equal quantity of past labour for an equal quantity of living labour; that the quantity of living labour appropriated by him is greater than the quantity of living labour he has paid for. Otherwise the workman's wage would be equal to the value of his product. The profit on the exchange of the complete manufacture for money or commodities, if they are exchanged at their value, arises therefore from the fact that the exchange between the complete manufacture and the living labour is subject to other laws; that no equivalents are exchanged here. These cases, therefore, must not be lumped together.

Profit is consequently nothing but a deduction from the value which the workmen have added to the material of labour. They add to the material, however, nothing but a new quantity of labour. The workman's labour-time therefore resolves itself into two parts: one for which he has received an equivalent, his wages, from the capitalist; the other which he gives to him gratis and which constitutes the *profit*. Adam Smith rightly points out that only the part of the labour (value) which the workman newly adds to the material resolves itself into wages and profit, that is to say, the newly-created surplus-value in itself has nothing to do with the part of the capital which has been advanced (as materials and instruments).

Adam Smith, who has thus reduced profit to the appropriation of the unpaid labour of others, at once goes on to say:

"The profits of stock, it may perhaps be thought, are only a different name for the wages of a particular sort of labour, the labour of inspection and direction" ([ibid., p. 53], [Garnier] p. 97).

And he refutes this false view of the labour of superintendence. We shall return to this later, in another chapter.[30] Here it is only important to stress that Adam Smith very clearly recognises, brings out and expressly emphasises the contradistinction between his view of the origin of profit and this apologist view. After pointing out this contradistinction he proceeds:

||253| "In this state of things the whole produce of labour does not always belong to the labourer. He must in most cases share it with the *owner of the stock* which employs him. Neither is the quantity of labour commonly employed in acquiring or producing any commodity, the only circumstance which can regulate the quantity which it ought commonly to purchase, command or exchange for. An *additional quantity*, it is evident, must be due for the profits of the stock which advanced the wages and furnished the materials of that labour" ([ibid., pp. 54-55], [Garnier] l.c., p. 99).

This is quite correct. Given capitalist production, materialised labour—in the form of money or commodity—always purchases, besides the quantity of labour which it itself contains, an "additional quantity" of living labour "for the profits of the stock"; which however in other words means nothing but that it appropriates for nothing, appropriates without paying for it, a part of the living labour. Adam Smith is superior to Ricardo in that he so strongly emphasises how this change begins with capitalist production. On the other hand, he is inferior to Ricardo in that he is never able to free himself from the viewpoint—though it is one he himself refuted by his own analysis—that through this changed relation between materialised labour and living labour a change takes place in the determination of the relative value of commodities, which in relation to each other represent nothing but materialised labour, given quantities of realised labour.

After thus presenting surplus-value in the one form, the form of profit, as part of the labour which the worker performs over and above the part of the labour which pays his wages, he does the same with the other form of surplus-value, *rent of land*. One of the objective conditions of labour alienated from labour, and therefore confronting it as other men's property, is *capital*; the other is the *land* itself, the land as *landed property*. Therefore after dealing with the *owner of capital*, Adam Smith continues:

> "As soon as the land of any country has all become private property, the landlords, like *all other men*, love to reap where they never sowed, and demand a *rent* even for its natural produce.... He" (the labourer) "must give up to the landlord *a portion of what his labour either collects or produces*. This portion, or, what comes to the same thing, the price of this portion, constitutes the *rent of land*" ([ibid., p. 55], [Garnier], l.c., pp. 99-100).

Like industrial profit proper, rent of land is only a part of the labour which is added by the labourer to the materials and *which he gives up*, hands over to the owner of the land without being paid for it; hence, only a part of the surplus-labour performed by him over and above the part of the labour-time which he works to pay his wages or to return an equivalent for the labour-time contained in his wages.

Thus Adam Smith conceives *surplus-value*—that is, surplus-labour, the excess of labour performed and realised in the commodity *over and above* the paid labour, the labour which has received its equivalent in the wages—as the *general category*, ||254| of which profit in the strict sense and rent of land are merely branches. Nevertheless, he does not distinguish surplus-value as such as a category on its own, distinct from the specific forms it assumes in profit and rent. This is the source of much error and inadequacy in his inquiry, and of even more in the work of Ricardo.

Another form in which surplus-value appears is *interest on capital*, interest on money. But this "*interest on money is always*", Adam Smith says in the same chapter, "*a derivative revenue*, which, if it is not paid from the *profit* which is made by the use of the money, must be paid from some other source of revenue" (therefore either rent or wages. In the latter case, assuming the average wage, it does not originate from surplus-value but is a deduction from the wage itself or—and in this form, as we shall later have occasion to see, it appears in undeveloped capitalist production—it is only another form of profit[31]) "unless perhaps the borrower is a spendthrift, who contracts a second debt in order to pay the interest of the first" ([ibid., p. 58], [Garnier], l. c., pp. 105-06). Interest is therefore either a part of the *profit* made with the capital lent; in this case it is only a secondary form of profit itself, a branch of profit, and thus only a further division between different persons of the surplus-value appropriated in the form of profit. Or it is paid out of rent. In which case the same holds good. Or the borrower pays the interest out of his own or someone else's capital. In which case it in no way constitutes surplus-value, but is merely a different distribution of existing wealth, vibration of the balance of wealth between parties, as in profit upon alienation. Excluding the latter case, when interest is not in any way a form of surplus-value (and excluding the case where it is a deduction from the wage or itself a form of profit; Adam Smith does not mention this latter case), interest is therefore only a secondary form of surplus-value, a mere part of profit or of rent (affecting merely their distribution), and therefore also is nothing but a part of unpaid surplus-labour.

"The stock which is lent at interest is always *considered* as a capital by the lender. He expects that in due time it is to be restored to him, and that in the meantime the borrower is to pay him a certain annual rent for the use of it. The borrower may use it either as a *capital*, or as a *stock reserved for immediate consumption*. If he uses it as a capital, he employs it in the maintenance of productive labourers, *who reproduce the value with a profit*. He can, in this case, both restore the capital and pay the interest without alienating or encroaching upon any other source of revenue. If he uses it as a stock reserved for immediate consumption, he acts the part of a prodigal, and dissipates in the maintenance of the idle, what was destined for the support of the industrious. He can, in this case, neither restore the capital nor pay the interest, without either alienating or encroaching upon some other source of revenue, such as the property or [...] rent of land" (Vol. II, b. II, ch. IV, p. 127, edit. McCulloch).

||255| Thus whoever borrows money, which here means capital, either uses it himself as capital, and makes a profit with it. In this case the interest which he pays to the lender is nothing but a part of the profit under a *special name*. Or he consumes the borrowed money. Then he increases the wealth of the lender by reducing his own. What takes place is only a different distribution of the wealth that passes from the hand of the spendthrift into that of the lender, but there is no generation of surplus-value. In so far therefore as interest in any way represents surplus-value, it is nothing but a part of profit, which itself is nothing but a definite form of surplus-value, that is, unpaid labour.

Finally, Adam Smith observes that in the same way all incomes of persons who live on the proceeds of taxes are paid either from wages, and are therefore a deduction from wages themselves; or have their source in profit and rent, thus representing only claims whereby various social strata share in the consumption of profit and rent, which themselves are nothing but different forms of surplus-value.

"All taxes, and all the revenue which is founded upon them, all salaries, pensions, and annuities of every kind, are ultimately derived from some one or other of those three original sources of revenue, and are paid either immediately or mediately from the wages of labour, the profits of stock, or the rent of land ([*Wealth of Nations*, O.U.P. edition, p. 58], [Garnier] l. I, ch. VI, p. 106).

Thus interest on money, along with taxes or revenues derived from taxes—in so far as they are not deductions from wages themselves—are merely shares in profit and rent, which are themselves in turn reducible to surplus-value, that is, unpaid labour-time.

This is Adam Smith's general theory of surplus-value.

In yet another passage Adam Smith sums up his views on the whole question, making it all the more clear how far he is from even attempting in any way to prove that the value added by the labourer to the product (after deducting the costs of production, the value of raw materials and of the instruments of labour) is no longer determined by the labour-time contained in the product, because the labourer does not himself appropriate this value in full, but has to share it—the value or the product—with the capitalist and the landowner. The way in which the value of a commodity is distributed among the producers of this commodity naturally alters nothing in the nature of this value or in the relative value of commodities to one another.

"As soon as land becomes private property, the landlord demands a share of almost all the produce which the labourer can either raise, or collect from it. *His rent makes the first deduction from the produce of the labour which is employed upon land.* It seldom happens that the person who tills the ground has wherewithal to maintain himself till he reaps the harvest. His maintenance is generally advanced to him from the stock of a master, the farmer who employs him, and who would have no interest to employ him, unless he was to share in the produce of his labour, or unless his stock was to be replaced to him with a profit. *This profit makes a second deduction* ||256| *from the* [...] *labour which is employed upon land.* The produce of almost all other labour is liable *to the like deduction of profit.* In all arts and manufactures the greater part of the workmen stand in need of a master to advance them the materials of their work, and their wages and maintenance till it be completed. *He shares in the produce of their labour, or in the value which it adds to the materials upon which it is bestowed; and in this share consists his profit*" ([McCulloch edition] Vol. I, b. I, ch. VIII, pp. 109-10).

Here therefore Adam Smith in plain terms describes rent and profit on capital as mere *deductions* from the workman's product or the value of his product, which is equal to the quantity of labour added by him to the material. This deduction however, as Adam Smith has himself previously explained, can only consist of that part of the labour which the workman adds to the materials, over and above the quantity of labour which only pays his wages, or which only provides an equivalent for his wages; that is, the surplus-labour, the unpaid part of his labour. (Therefore, incidentally, profit and rent or capital and landed property can never be a *source of value.*)

[3. Adam Smith's Extension of the Idea of Surplus-Value to All Spheres of Social Labour]

We see the great advance made by Adam Smith beyond the Physiocrats in the analysis of surplus-value and hence of capital. In their view, it is only one definite kind of concrete labour—agricultural labour—that creates surplus-value. Therefore what they examine is the use-value of labour, not labour-time, general social labour, which is the sole source of value. In this special kind of labour, however, it is *nature*, the land, which in fact creates the surplus-value, consisting in an increase of (organic) matter—the excess of the matter produced over the matter consumed. They see it, however, still in quite a restricted form and therefore distorted by fantastic ideas. But to Adam Smith, it is general social labour—no matter in what use-values it manifests itself—the mere quantity of necessary labour, which creates value. Surplus-value, whether it takes the form of profit, rent, or the secondary form of interest, is nothing but a part of this labour, appropriated by the owners of the material conditions of labour in the exchange with living labour. For the Physiocrats, therefore, surplus-value appears only in the form of rent of land. For Adam Smith, rent, profit and interest are only different forms of surplus-value.

When I speak of surplus-value, in relation to the total sum of capital advanced, as *profit on capital*, this is because the capitalist directly engaged in production *directly* appropriates the surplus-labour, no matter under what categories he has subsequently to share this surplus-value with the landowner or with the lender of capital. Thus the farmer pays the landowner directly. And the manufacturer, out of the surplus-value he has appropriated, pays rent to the owner of the land on which the factory stands, and interest to the capitalist who has advanced capital to him.

||257| <There are now still to be examined: 1. Adam Smith's confusion of surplus-value with profit; 2. his views on productive labour; 3. how he makes rent and profit *sources of value*, and his false analysis of the "natural price" of commodities, in which the value of raw materials and instruments is not supposed to have a separate existence, and therefore not to be considered, apart from the price of the three sources of revenue.>

[4. Smith's Failure to Grasp the Specific Way in Which the Law of Value Operates in the Exchange between Capital and Wage-Labour]

Wages or the equivalent with which the capitalist buys the temporary disposal of labour-power are not a commodity in its immediate form, but the commodity metamorphosed, money, the commodity in its independent form as exchange-value, as the direct materialisation of social labour, of labour-time in general. With this money the labourer naturally buys commodities at the same price as any other possessor of money <disregarding here such details as, for example, that he buys on less favourable conditions and in worse circumstances, etc.>. He faces the seller of commodities as does every other possessor of money—as a buyer. He enters commodity circulation itself not as a labourer, but as pole Money facing pole Commodity, as possessor of commodity in its general, always exchangeable form. His money is once more transformed into commodities, which are to serve him as use-values, and in this process he buys commodities at the current market-price—generally speaking, at their value. In this transaction he carries through only the act M—C, which indicates a change of form, but, as a general rule, by no means a change in magnitude of value. Since however, by his labour materialised in the product, he has added not only as much labour-time as was contained in the money he received, he has paid not only an equivalent but has given surplus-labour gratis—which is precisely the source of the profit—he has thus *in fact* (the mediating process, the sale of his labour-power, is not relevant when we are dealing with the result) given a higher value than the value of the sum of money which forms his wages. In return, he has bought with more labour-time the quantity of labour realised in the money which comes to him as wages. It can therefore be said that in the same way he has indirectly bought all the commodities into which the money (which is only the independent expression of a definite quantity of social labour-time) he received is converted with more labour-time than they contain, although he buys them at the same price as any other buyer or possessor of a commodity in its first transformation. Conversely, the money with which the capitalist buys labour contains a smaller quantity of labour, less labour-time, than the quantity of labour or labour-time of the workman contained in the commodity produced by him. Besides the quantity of labour contained in this sum of money which forms the wage, the capitalist buys an additional quantity of labour for which he does not pay, an excess over the quantity of labour contained in the money he pays out. And it is precisely this additional quantity of labour which constitutes the surplus-value created by capital.

But as the money ||258| with which the capitalist buys labour (in the actual result, even though mediated through exchange not with labour directly, but with labour-power) is nothing other than the transmuted form *of all other commodities*, their independent existence as exchange-value, it can equally well be said that all commodities in exchange with living labour buy more labour than they contain. It is precisely this more that constitutes surplus-value.

It is Adam Smith's great merit that it is just in the chapters of Book I (chapters VI, VII, VIII) where he passes from simple commodity exchange and its law of value to exchange between materialised and living labour, to exchange between capital and wage-labour, to the consideration of profit and rent in general—in short, to the origin of surplus-value—that he feels some flaw has emerged. He senses that somehow—whatever the cause may be, and he does not grasp what it is—in the actual result the law is suspended: more labour is exchanged for less labour (from the labourer's standpoint), less labour is exchanged for more labour (from the capitalist's standpoint). His merit is that he emphasises—and it obviously perplexes him—that with the *accumulation of capital* and the *appearance of property in land*—that is, when the conditions of labour assume an independent existence over against labour itself—something new occurs, apparently (and actually, in the result) the law of value changes into its opposite. It is his theoretical strength that he feels and stresses this contradiction, just as it is his theoretical weakness that the contradiction shakes his confidence in the general law, even for simple commodity exchange; that he does not perceive how this contradiction arises, through labour-power itself becoming a commodity, and that in the case of this specific commodity its use-value—which therefore has nothing to do with its exchange-value—is precisely the energy which creates exchange-value. Ricardo is ahead of Adam Smith in that these apparent contradictions—in their result real contradictions—do not confuse him. But he is behind Adam Smith in that he does not even suspect that this presents a problem, and therefore the *specific* development which the law of value undergoes with the formation of capital does not for a moment puzzle him or even attract his attention. We shall see later how what was a stroke of genius with Adam Smith becomes reactionary with Malthus as against Ricardo's standpoint.[32]

Naturally, however, it is at the same time this deep insight of Adam Smith's that makes him irresolute and uncertain, cuts the firm ground from under his feet, and prevents him—in contrast to Ricardo—from reaching a consistent and comprehensive theoretical view of the abstract, general foundations of the bourgeois system.

||259| The above-quoted statement by Adam Smith that the commodity buys more labour than it contains, or that labour pays a higher value for the commodity than the latter contains, is thus formulated by Hodgskin:

> "*Natural* or *necessary price** means [...] the whole *quantity of labour* nature requires from man, that he may produce any commodity.... Labour was the original, is now and ever will be the only purchase money in dealing with nature.... Whatever quantity of labour may be requisite to produce any commodity, the labourer must always, in the present state of society, give a great deal more labour to acquire and possess it than is requisite to buy it from nature. Natural price thus** increased to the labourer is *social price* ... we must always attend to the difference *between natural and social price****" (Thomas Hodgskin, *Popular Political Economy*, etc., London, 1827, pp. 219-20).

In this presentation Hodgskin reproduces both what is correct and what is confused and confusing in Adam Smith's view.

* In the manuscript: "The *natural* price (or *necessary* price)".—*Ed.*

** In the manuscript: "so".—*Ed.*

*** In the manuscript: "Man muss immer zwischen den beiden unterscheiden."—*Ed.*

[5. Smith's Identification of Surplus-Value with Profit. The Vulgar Element in Smith's Theory]

We have seen how Adam Smith explains *surplus-value* in general, of which the rent of land and profit are only different forms and component parts. As he presents it, the part of capital which consists of raw material and means of production has nothing directly to do with the creation of surplus-value. The latter arises exclusively from the additional quantity of labour which the labourer gives *over and above* the part of his labour which forms only the equivalent for his wages. Therefore it is only that part of the capital advanced which consists in wages from which surplus-value directly arises, since it is the only part of capital which not only reproduces itself but produces an overplus. In profit, on the other hand, the surplus-value is calculated on the total amount of capital advanced, and besides this modification other new complications arise through the equalisation of profits in the various spheres of production of capital.

Because Adam makes what is in substance an analysis of surplus-value, but does not present it explicitly in the form of a definite category, distinct from its special forms; he subsequently mixes it up directly with the further developed form, profit. This error persists with Ricardo and all his disciples. Hence arise (particularly with Ricardo, all the more strikingly because he works out the fundamental law of value in more systematic unity and consistency, so that the inconsistencies and contradictions stand out more strikingly) a series of inconsistencies, unresolved contradictions and fatuities, which the Ricardians (as we shall see later in the section on profit) attempt to solve with phrases in a scholastic way.[33] Crass empiricism turns into false metaphysics, scholasticism, which toils painfully to deduce undeniable empirical phenomena by simple formal abstraction directly from the general law, or to show by cunning argument that they are in accordance with that law. At this point where we discuss Adam Smith we will give an example, because the confusion creeps in immediately not when he is dealing specifically with profit or rent—those particular forms of surplus-value—but where he is thinking of them only as forms of surplus-value in general, as *deductions* from the labour bestowed by the labourers upon the materials.

||260| After Adam Smith has said, in Book I, Chapter VI, "The value which the workmen *add* to the materials, therefore, resolves itself in this

case into two parts, of which the one pays their wages, the other the profits of their employer upon the whole stock of materials and wages which he advanced", he continues: "He" (the entrepreneur) "could have no interest to employ them, unless he expected from the sale of their work something more than what was sufficient to replace his stock to him; and he could have no interest to employ a great stock rather than a small one, unless his profits were to bear some proportion to the extent of his stock" [ibid., p. 53].

We note first: surplus-value, the overplus which the entrepreneur makes over and above the amount of value required to replace his stock, is reduced by Adam Smith to that part of the labour which the workmen add to the materials over and above the quantity that pays their wages—thus making this overplus arise purely from the part of the capital which is laid out in wages. Then, however, he immediately conceives this overplus in the form of profit—that is, he thinks of it not in relation to the part of the capital from which it arises, but as an overplus over the total value of the capital advanced, "upon the whole stock of materials and wages which he advanced". (It is oversight that the means of production are here left out of account). He therefore conceives surplus-value directly in the form of profit. Hence the difficulties that soon appear.

The capitalist, Adam Smith says, "could have no interest to employ them, unless he expected from the sale of their work *something more* than what was sufficient to replace his stock to him".

Once capitalist relations are assumed, this is quite correct. The capitalist does not produce in order to satisfy his needs with the product; he produces with absolutely no direct regard for consumption. He produces in order to produce surplus-value. But this premise—which amounts to no more than that, capitalist production being assumed, the capitalist produces for the sake of surplus-value—is not made use of by Adam Smith to *explain surplus-value*, as some of his silly disciples subsequently did; that is to say, he does not explain the existence of surplus-value by the interests of the capitalist, by his desire for surplus-value. On the contrary, he has already derived surplus-value from the value which the workmen add to the materials over and above the value which they add in exchange for the wages they have received. But then he goes on at once: the capitalist would have no interest to employ a great stock rather than a small one, unless his profits were to bear some proportion to the extent of the stock advanced. Here profit is no longer explained by the nature of surplus-value, but by the "interest" of the capitalist. Which is downright silly.

Adam Smith does not sense that, by thus directly confusing surplus-value with profit and profit with surplus-value, he is upsetting the law of the origin of surplus-value which he has just established. ||261| If surplus-value is only the part of the value (or of the quantity of labour) *added* by the workman *in excess* of the part that he adds to the materials to replace the wages, why should that second part grow as the direct result of the value of the capital advanced being in one case greater than in the other? The contradiction becomes even clearer in the example which Adam Smith himself gives immediately following on this, in order to refute the view that profit is wages for the so-called labour of superintendence.

For he says:

"They" (the profits of stock) "are, however, altogether different" (from wages), "are regulated by quite different principles, and bear no proportion to the quantity, the hardship, or the ingenuity of this supposed labour of inspection and direction. *They are regulated altogether by the value of the stock employed*, and are greater or smaller in proportion to the extent of this stock. Let us suppose, for example, that in some particular place, where *the common annual profits* of manufacturing stock *are ten per cent* there are two different manufactures, in each of which twenty workmen are employed, at the rate of fifteen pounds a year each, or at the expense of three hundred a year in each manufactory. Let us suppose, too, that the coarse materials annually wrought up in the one cost only seven hundred pounds, while the finer materials in the other cost seven thousand. The capital annually employed in the one will, in this case, amount only to one thousand pounds; whereas that employed in the other will amount to seven thousand three hundred pounds. At the rate of ten per cent, therefore, the undertaker of the one will expect a yearly profit of about one hundred pounds only; while that of the other will expect about seven hundred and thirty pounds. But though their profits are so very different, their labour of inspection and direction may be either altogether or very nearly the same" ([ibid., pp. 53-54], [Garnier] l.c.).

From surplus-value in its general form we come straight to a general rate of profit, which has nothing directly to do with it. But let us pass on! In both manufactories twenty workmen are employed; in both their wages are the same, £ 300. Proof therefore that it is not perhaps a case of a higher kind of labour being employed in one as compared with the other, so that one hour's labour and therefore also one hour's surplus-labour would in one be equal to several hours' surplus-labour in the other. On the contrary, the same average labour is assumed in both, as the equality of their wages shows. How then can the surplus-labour which the workers add, beyond the price of their wages, be worth seven times as much in one factory as in the other? Or why should the workers in one factory, because the materials they work up in it are seven times as costly as in the other, provide seven times as much surplus-labour as in the other, although in both factories they receive the same wages, and therefore work the same time to reproduce ||262| their wages?

The seven times greater profit in the one manufactory as compared with the other—or in general the law of profit, that it is in proportion to the magnitude of the capital advanced—thus *prima facie* contradicts the law of surplus-value or of profit (since Adam Smith treats the two as identical) that it consists purely of the unpaid surplus-labour of the workmen. Adam Smith puts this down with quite naïve thoughtlessness, without the faintest suspicion of the contradiction it presents. All his disciples—since none of them considers surplus-value in general, as distinct from its determinate forms—followed him faithfully in this. With Ricardo, as already noted, it merely comes out even more strikingly.

As Adam Smith resolves surplus-value not only into profit but also into the rent of land—two particular kinds of surplus-value, whose movement is determined by quite different laws—he should certainly have seen from this that he ought not to treat general abstract form as directly identical with any of its particular forms. With all later bourgeois economists, as with Adam Smith, lack of theoretical understanding needed to distinguish the different forms of the economic relations remains the rule in their coarse grabbing at and interest in the empirically available material. Hence also their inability to form a correct conception of money, in which what is in question is only various changes in the form of exchange-value, while the magnitude of value remains unchanged.

[6. Smith's Erroneous View of Profit, Rent of Land and Wages as Sources of Value]

Lauderdale, in *Recherches sur la nature et l'origine de la richesse publique (traduit par Lagentie de Lavaïsse, Paris*, 1808), raises the objection to Adam Smith's exposition of surplus-value—which he says corresponds with the views already advanced by Locke—that according to it capital is not an original source of wealth, as Smith makes out, but only a derivative source. The relevant passages run:

"Above a century ago, Mr. Locke stated pretty nearly the same opinion" (as Adam Smith).... "'Money', he said, 'is a barren thing and produces nothing; but by compact transfers that profit that was the reward of one man's labour into another man's pocket'" (Lauderdale, p. 116).

"If this, however, was a just and accurate idea of the profit of capital, it would follow that the profit of stock must be a derivative, and not an original source of revenue; and capital could not therefore be considered as a source of wealth, its profit being only a transfer from the pocket of the labourer into that of the proprietor of stock"(pp. 157-58). (l.c., p. 116-17)* [Lauderdale, James Maitland, *An Inquiry into the Nature and Origin of Public Wealth...*, Edinburgh and London, 1804, pp. 157-58].

In so far as the value of the capital reappears in the product, it cannot be called a "source of wealth". Here it is only as accumulated labour, as a definite quantity of materialised labour, that it adds its own value to the product.

Capital is productive of value only as a *relation*, in so far as it is a coercive force on wage-labour, compelling it to perform surplus-labour, or spurring on the productive power of labour to produce relative surplus-value. In both cases it only produces value as ||263| the power of labour's own material conditions over labour when these are alienated from labour; only as one of the forms of wage-labour itself, as a condition of wage-labour. But in the sense commonly used by economists, as stored up labour existing in money or commodities, capital—like all conditions of labour, even the unpaid natural forces—functions productively in the labour-process, in the production of use-values, but it is never a source of value. It creates no new value, and only adds exchange-value to the product at all in so far as it has exchange-value that is to say, only in so far as it itself consists in materialised labour-time, so that labour is the source of its value.

Lauderdale is right in this respect—that Adam Smith, after explaining the nature of surplus-value and of value, wrongly presents capital and land as independent sources of exchange-value. They are sources of revenue for their owners in so far as they are titles to a certain quantity of surplus-labour, which the labourer must perform over and above the labour-time required to replace his wages. Thus Adam Smith says for example:

"*Wages, profit, and rent*, are the *three original sources of* all revenue, *as well as of all exchangeable value*" ([*Wealth of Nations*, O.U.P. edition, p. 57], [Garnier], l.I, ch. VI).

---

* Marx refers to the French translation from which he takes these passages. See Appendix, p. 427—*Ed.*

Just as it is true that they are the three original sources of all revenue, so it is false that they also are the three original sources *of all exchangeable value*, since the value of a commodity is exclusively determined by the labour-time contained in it. After just presenting rent and profit as mere deductions from the value or from the labour added by the workman to the raw material, how can Adam Smith call them original sources of exchangeable value? (They can only be that in the sense that they set in motion the original source, that is to say, that they compel the workman to perform surplus-labour.) In so far as they are titles (conditions) for the appropriation of a part of the value, that is, of the labour materialised in the commodity, they are sources of income for their owners. But the distribution or appropriation of value is certainly not the source of the value that is appropriated. If this appropriation did not take place, and the workman received the whole product of his labour as his wage, the value of the commodities produced would be just the same as before, although it would not be shared with the landowner and the capitalist.

The fact that landed property and capital are sources of income for their owners, that is, give them the power to appropriate a part of the values created by labour, does not make them sources of the value which they appropriate. But it is equally wrong to say that wages are an original source of exchangeable value, although wages, or rather the continuous sale of labour-power, is a source of income for the labourer. It is the labour and not the wages of the labourer that creates value. Wages are only already existing value, or if we consider the whole of production, the part of the value created by the labourer which he himself appropriates; but this appropriation does not create value. His wages can therefore rise or fall without this affecting the value of the commodity produced by him. |263||

||265| <The following quotation should be added to what has been said above in regard to Adam Smith making the categories in which the value of the commodity is appropriated into sources of this value: After he has refuted the view that profit is only another name for the wages of the capitalist, or wages of labour of superintendence, he concludes:

> "In the *price* of commodities, therefore, the *profits* of stock constitute a component part altogether *different* from the wages [of labour], and regulated by quite different principles" ([ibid., p. 54], [Garnier] b. I, ch. VI, p. 99).

Adam Smith has just shown that the value added by the workmen to the materials is divided between them and the capitalists in the form of wages and profit; labour is therefore the only *source of value*, and the price of wages and the price of profits arise, out of this source of value. But these prices themselves are not a *source of value*. > |265||

[7. Smith's Dual View of the Relationship between Value and Revenue. The Vicious Circle of Smith's Conception of "Natural Price" as the Sum of Wages, Profit and Rent]

||263| Here we will leave entirely out of account how far Adam Smith regards rent as a constituent element of the price of commodities. For our present inquiry this question is all the more unimportant because he treats rent just as he treats profit, as a mere part of surplus-value, a deduction from the labour added by the labourer to the raw material, and consequently ||264| in fact also as a deduction from profit, inasmuch as the total unpaid surplus-labour is *directly* appropriated by the capitalist in his relations with labour; it does not matter under what categories he may later have to share this surplus-value with owners of the conditions of production—the landowner or the lender of capital. For the sake of simplicity we shall therefore speak only of wages and profit as the two categories into which newly-created value is divided.

Let us assume that twelve hours of labour-time are materialised in a commodity (*leaving out of account* the value of the raw material and instruments of labour consumed in it.) We can express its value as such only in *money*. Let us therefore assume that twelve hours of labour-time are likewise materialised in five shillings. Thus the value of the commodity is five shillings. By the natural price of commodities Adam Smith understands nothing but their value expressed in money. (The market-price of the commodity, of course, stands either above or below its value. Indeed, as I shall show later, even the average price of commodities is *always different* from their value.[34] Adam Smith, however, does not deal with this in his discussion of natural price. Moreover, neither the market-price nor still less the fluctuations in the average price of commodities can be comprehended except on the basis of an understanding of the nature of value.)

If the surplus-value contained in the commodity is twenty per cent of its total value, or what amounts to the same thing, twenty-five per cent of the necessary labour contained in it, then this value of five shillings, the natural price of the commodity, can be resolved into four shillings wages and one shilling surplus-value (which here we will call profit, following Adam Smith). It would be correct to say that the magnitude of value of the commodity determined independently of wages and profit, or its natural price, can be resolved into four shillings wages (the price of the labour) and one shilling profit (the price of the profit). But it would be wrong to say that the value of the commodity arises from adding together or combining the price of the wages and the price of the profit which are regulated independently of the value of the commodity. If this were the case there would be absolutely no reason why the total value of the commodity should not be 8 shillings, 10 shillings, etc., according to whether one assumes the wages to be 5 shillings and the profit 3 shillings, and so on.

When Adam Smith is examining the "natural rate" of wages or the "natural price" of wages, what guides his investigation? The natural price of he means of subsistence required for the reproduction of labour-power. But by what does he determine the natural price of these means of subsistence? In so far as he determines it at all, he comes back to the correct determination of value, namely, the labour-time required for the production of these means of subsistence. But when he abandons this correct course, he falls into a vicious circle. By what is the natural price of the means of subsistence determined, which determine the natural price of wages? By the natural price of "wages", of "profit", of "rent", which constitute the natural price of those means of subsistence as of all commodities. And so *in infinitum*. The twaddle about the law of demand and supply of course does not help us out of this vicious circle. For the "natural price" or the price corresponding to the value of the commodity is supposed to exist just when demand meets supply, that is, when the price of the commodity does not stand above or below its value as a result of fluctuations in demand and supply; when, in other words, the cost-price[35] of the commodity (or the value of the commodity supplied by the seller) is also the price which the demand pays.

||265| But as we have said: In investigating the natural price of wages Adam Smith in fact falls back—at least in certain passages—on the correct determination of the value of the commodity. On the other hand, in the chapter dealing with the natural rate or the natural price of profit he gets bogged down, so far as the real problem is concerned, in meaningless commonplaces and tautologies. In fact, at first it was the value of the commodity

which he saw as regulating wages and profit and rent. Then however he sets to work the other way round (which was closer to what empirical observation showed and to everyday ideas), and now the natural price of commodities is supposed to be calculated and discovered by adding together the natural prices of wages, profit and rent. It is one of Ricardo's chief merits that he put an end to this confusion. We shall return to this point briefly when we are dealing with him.[36]

Here there is only this further point to be noted: the *given magnitude* of value of the commodity, serving as a fund for the payment of wages and profit, appears empirically to the industrialist in the form that a definite market-price for the commodity holds good for a shorter or longer time, in spite of all fluctuations in wages.

It is necessary therefore to call attention to this peculiar train of thought in Adam Smith's book: first the value of the commodity is examined, and in some passages correctly determined—so correctly determined that he traces out in general form the origin of surplus-value and of its specific forms, hence deriving wages and profit from this value. But then he takes the opposite course, and seeks on the contrary to deduce the value of commodities (from which he has deduced wages and profit) by adding together the natural prices of wages, profit and rent. It is this latter circumstance that is responsible for the fact that he nowhere correctly explains the influence of oscillations of wages, profit, etc., on the price of commodities—since he lacks the basis [for such an explanation] |VI—265||

* * *

|VIII—364|| <*Adam Smith, Value and Its Component Parts.* Smith's erroneous conception, see above, which he [develops] in spite of his originally correct view, is shown also in the following passage:

> "Rent ... enters into the composition of the price of commodities in a different way from wages and profit. High or low wages and profit are the *causes of high or low price; high or low rent is the effect of it*" (*Wealth of Nations*, b. I, ch. XI, [O.U.P. edition, p. 165]).[37]> |VIII—364||

[8. Smith's Error in Resolving the Total Value of the Social Product into Revenue. Contradictions in His Views on Gross and Net Revenue]

||VI—265| We come to another point, which is linked with the analysis of the price or value of the commodity (since the two are here still assumed to be identical). Let us assume that

Adam Smith has calculated correctly—that is to say, the value of the commodity being given, he has correctly resolved it into the constituent parts in which this value is distributed among the various agents of production—but has not on the contrary tried to deduce value from the price of these constituent parts. Thus we shall leave this aside and also the one-sided way in which wages and profit are presented only as forms of distribution, and hence both as revenues in the same sense that their owners can consume.-Apart from all this, Adam Smith himself raises a question, and this again shows his superiority over Ricardo—not that he finds the right solution to the question he raises, but that he raises it at all. ||266| What Adam Smith says is:

"These three parts" (wages, profit and rent) "seem either immediately or ultimately to make up the *whole* price of corn."

(Of all commodities, Adam Smith here takes corn, because in some commodities rent does not enter into the price as a constituent part.)

"A *fourth part*, it may be thought, is necessary for replacing the stock of the farmer, or for compensating the wear and tear of his labouring cattle, and other instruments of husbandry. But it must be considered, that the price of an instrument of husbandry, such as a labouring horse, is itself made up of the same three parts; the rent of the land upon which he is reared, the *labour* of tending and rearing him, and the profits of the farmer, who advances both the rent of this land, and the wages of this labour."

<Here profit appears as the primary form, which also includes rent.>

"Though the price of the corn, therefore, may pay the price as well as the maintenance of the horse, the *whole* price still resolves itself, either immediately or ultimately, into the same three parts of rent, labour and profit" ([*Wealth of Nations*, O.U.P. edition, p. 56], [Garnier] b. I, ch. VI).

(Here it is perfectly preposterous that all of a sudden he says labour instead of wages, while he does not put landed property or capital for rent and profit.)

But was it not equally obviously necessary to consider that just as the farmer included the price of the horse and the plough in the price of the corn, the horse breeder or the plough maker from whom the farmer bought the horse and the plough, would include in the price of the horse and the plough the price of the instruments of production (in the case of the former, perhaps another horse) and of raw materials such as feeding stuffs and iron, whereas the fund from which the horse breeder and plough maker *paid* wages and profit (and rent) consisted only in the new labour which they *added* in their sphere of production to the amount of value present in their constant capital? Since therefore Adam Smith admits, in relation to the farmer, that the price of his corn includes, besides the wages, profit and rent paid by him to himself and others, also *a fourth constituent part which is different from these*—the value of the constant capital he has used up, such as horses, agricultural implements, etc.—this must also hold good for the horse breeder and the manufacturer of agricultural implements; and it is of no avail for Adam Smith to send us from pillar to post. Incidentally, the example of the farmer is peculiarly unhappily chosen for sending us from pillar to post, for in this case the items of constant capital include one that does not at all need to be bought from somebody else, namely the seed; and does this constituent part of the value resolve itself into wages, profit or rent for anybody?

But for the present let us proceed, and see whether Smith sticks to his view that the value of every commodity is resolvable into one or all of the sources of revenue: wages, profit, rent; and can therefore, being destined for consumption, be devoured or at any rate used up in one way or another for personal use (not industrial consumption). First ||267| another preliminary point. In the case for example of gathering berries and such like it can be assumed that their value consists entirely of wages, although here also as a rule some appliances, such as baskets and so on, are required as means of labour. But examples of this kind are quite irrelevant here, where we are dealing with capitalist production.

To start with, once more the repetition of the view expressed in Book I, Chapter VI; *Book II, Chapter II*, (b. II, *Garnier* pp. 212-13) states:

"It has been shown ... *that the price of the greater part of commodities* resolves itself into three parts, of which one pays the wages of the labour, another the profits of the stock, and a third the rent of the land" [*Wealth of Nations*, O.U.P. edition, p. 313].

According to this, the whole value of any commodity resolves itself into revenue, and therefore falls to the share of one or another of the classes which live on this revenue, as a fund for consumption. Now since the total production of a country, each year for example, consists solely of the total of the values of the commodities produced, and since the value of each single one of these commodities is resolved into revenues, so also must their sum, the annual product of labour, the gross revenue, be consumable annually in this form. And so immediately after this passage Smith himself raises the point:

"Since this is the case, it has been observed, with regard to every particular commodity, taken separately, it must be so with regard to *all* the commodities which compose the whole annual produce of the land and labour of every country, taken complexly. *The whole price or exchangeable value* of the annual produce, must resolve itself into the same three parts, and be parcelled out among the different inhabitants of the country, either as the wages of their labour, the profits of their stock, or the rent of their land" ([ibid., p. 313], [Garnier] l.c., p. 213).

This is in fact the necessary consequence. What is true of the individual commodity is necessarily true of the total sum of commodities. But *quod non*,* says Adam. He goes on:

"But though the whole value of the annual produce of the land and labour of every country is thus divided among, and constitutes a revenue to, its different inhabitants; yet, as in the rent of a private estate, we distinguish between the *gross rent* and the *neat rent*, so may we likewise in the revenue of *all the inhabitants* of a great country" ([ibid., p. 313], [Garnier] l.c., p. 213).

(But stop! Above he told us the direct opposite: in the case of the individual farmer we can distinguish a fourth part into which the value of his wheat for example resolves itself, namely the part which merely replaces the constant capital used up. This is *directly* true for the individual farmer. But when we go further into it, what is constant capital for him resolves itself at an earlier point, in another person's hand before it became capital in his, into wages, profit, etc., in a word, into revenue. Therefore if it is true that commodities, considered in the hands of an individual producer, contain one part of the value which does not form revenue, then it is untrue for "all the inhabitants of a great country", because what in one person's hand is constant capital derives its value from the fact that it came from another person's hand as the aggregate price of wages, profit and rent. Now he says the direct opposite.)

Adam Smith continues:

||268| "The *gross* rent of a private estate comprehends whatever is paid by the farmer; the *neat rent*, what remains free *to the landlord*, after deducting the expense of management, of repairs, and all other *necessary charges*; or what, without hurting his estate, he can afford to place in his stock reserved for immediate consumption, or to spend upon his table," etc. ... "His real wealth is in proportion, not to his *gross*, but to his *neat* rent" [ibid., pp. 313-14].

* Not so.—*Ed.*

(In the first place, Smith brings in here something improper. What the farmer pays as rent to the landowner, just as what he pays as wages to the labourers, is like his own profit, part of the value or price of the commodity, which resolves itself into revenue. The question is however whether the commodity contains yet another constituent part of its value. He admits this here, as he should admit it in the case of the farmer, but that should not prevent the latter's corn (i.e., the price *or* exchange-value of his corn) from being resolvable merely into revenue. Secondly, a note in passing. The real wealth of which an individual farmer, considered as a *farmer*, can dispose, depends on his profit. But on the other hand, as owner of commodities he can sell the whole farm, or if the land does not belong to him, he can sell all constant capital there is on it such as draught cattle, agricultural implements, etc. The value which he can realise in this way, therefore the wealth at his disposal, is conditioned by the value, that is the size of the constant capital belonging to him. However, he can only sell this again to another farmer, in whose hands it is not disposable wealth but constant capital. So we are still just where we were.)

"The *gross* revenue of all the inhabitants of a great country comprehends the *whole* annual produce of their land and labour" (previously we were told that this total—that is its value—resolves itself into wages, profits and rents, nothing but different forms of net revenue); "the *neat* revenue, what remains free to them, after deducting the expense of maintaining, first, their *fixed*, and, secondly, their *circulating capital*"; (so he now deducts instruments of labour and raw materials); "or what, without encroaching upon their capital, they can place in their *stock reserved for immediate consumption*." (So now we learn that the price or exchangeable value of the total stock of commodities, just as in the case of the individual capitalist, so also for the whole country, is resolvable into a fourth part which does not form a revenue for anyone and cannot be resolved into wages, profit or rent.)

"The whole expense of maintaining the *fixed capital* must evidently be excluded from the neat revenue of the society. Neither the *materials necessary* for supporting their useful machines and instruments of trade, their profitable buildings, etc., nor *the produce of the labour necessary* for fashioning those materials into the proper form, can ever make any part of *it*. The *price of that labour* may indeed make a part of it; as the workmen so employed may place *the whole value* ||269| *of their wages in their stock reserved for immediate consumption*. But in other sorts of labour, *both the price and the produce go to this stock*; the price to that of the workmen, the produce to that of other people, whose subsistence, conveniences, and amusements, are augmented by the labour of those workmen" ([*Wealth of Nations*, O.U.P. edition, p. 314], [Garnier] l.c., pp. 214-15).*

Here Adam Smith once more shies away from the question which he has to answer—the question concerning the fourth part of the total price of the commodity, which is not resolved into either wages, profit or rent. First something that is quite wrong: with makers of machinery, as with all other industrial capitalists, the labour which fashions the raw materials of the machine, etc., into the proper form in fact consists of necessary and surplus-labour, and therefore resolves itself not only into the wages of the workmen, but also into the profit of the capitalist. But the value of the materials and the value of the instruments with which they are fashioned by the workmen into the proper form, is resolvable into neither the one nor the other. That products which are destined by their nature not for individual consumption but for industrial consumption do not enter into the stock reserved for immediate consumption, has nothing at all to do with it. Seed, for example (that portion of the corn which serves for sowing), by its nature could also enter into the stock for consumption; but by its economic function it must enter into the stock for production. But furthermore it is quite wrong to say with regard to the products destined for individual consumption that both the full price and the product enter into the *stock for consumption*. Linen, for example, when not used for sail-cloth or other productive purposes, all goes as a product into consumption. But not its price, for one part of this price replaces the linen yarn, another part looms and so on, and only a part of the price of the linen is converted into revenue of any kind.

Just now Adam told us that the materials necessary for machines, profitable buildings, etc. "can never make any part of this *neat* revenue", any more than the machines and so on fashioned from them can; presumably, therefore, they form a part of the gross revenue. Shortly afterwards, [Garnier] l. c., Chapter II of Book II, p. 220, he says on the contrary:

"The machines and instruments of trade, etc., which compose the *fixed capital* either of an individual or of a society, make no part *either of the gross or of the neat revenue* of either; so *money*..." [ibid., p. 317].

---

* All the same, nearer the right view than the others. [This was added by Marx in pencil.]—*Ed.*

Adam's twistings and turnings, his contradictions and wanderings from the point, prove that, once he had made wages, profit and rent the constituent component parts of exchangeable value or of the total price of the product, he had got himself stuck in the mud and had to get stuck.

[9. Say as Vulgariser of Smith's Theory. Say's Identification of the Social Gross Product with the Social Revenue. Attempts to Draw a Distinction between Them by Storch and Ramsay]

Say, who tries to hide his dull superficiality by repeating in absolute general phrases Smith's inconsistencies and blunders, says:

"If we consider a nation as a whole, it has no net product; for since the *products* have only a value equal to the *costs* of their production, when these *costs* are deducted, the whole *value* of the *products* is deducted.... The *annual revenue* is the *gross revenue*" [Jean-Baptiste Say]. (*Traité d'économie politique...*, Troisième édition, Paris, 1817, t. II, p. 469.)

The value of the total annual products is equal to the quantity of labour-time materialised in them. ||270| If this aggregate value is deducted from the annual product, then in fact, so far as value is concerned, there remains no value, and by this deduction both the net revenue and the gross revenue have come to a final end. But Say thinks that the annually produced values are annually consumed. Hence for the whole nation there is no net product, but only a gross product. In the first place, it is not true that the annually produced values are annually consumed. This is not the case for a large part of the fixed capital. A large part of the annually produced values enters into the labour-process without entering into the process of the formation of value, that is to say, without their total value being annually consumed. But in the second place: a part of the annual consumption of values consists of values that are used not as the stock for consumption, but as means of production, and which are returned to production (either in the same form or in the form of an equivalent), just as they originated in production. The second part consists of the values which can enter into individual consumption over and above the first part. These form the net product.

Storch says of this trash of Say's:

"It is [...] evident that the value of the annual product is divided partly into capital and partly into profits, and that each *of these parts of the value of the annual product goes regularly to purchase the product needed by the nation*, as much for the purpose of preserving its capital as for renewing its consumable stock" (Storch, *Cours d'économie politique*, t. V: *Considérations sur la nature du revenu national*, Paris, 1824, pp. 134-35). "Let us then imagine a family which through its own labour is self-sufficing in all its needs, such as there are so many examples of in Russia ... is the *revenue* of such a family equal to the gross product coming from its land, its capital and its industry? Can it live in its barns or its stables, eat its seed and forage, clothe itself with its labouring cattle, amuse itself with its agricultural implements? According to Mr. Say's thesis, all these questions would have to be answered in the affirmative" (l.c., pp. 135-36). "Mr. Say [...] regards the gross product as the revenue of society; and from this he concludes that society can consume a value equal to this product" (l.c., p. 145). "The (net) revenue of a nation is not the excess of values produced *over the totality of values consumed* (as Say, the author, imagines it to be). but only [the excess of values produced] over the *values consumed in order to produce*." Therefore, "if a nation consumes all this excess in the year it is produced, it consumes all its (net) revenue" (l.c., p. 146). "If it is admitted that the revenue of a nation is equal to its gross product, so that no *capital* is to be deducted, then it must also be admitted that this nation may consume unproductively the entire value of its annual product, without in the least reducing its future revenue" (l.c., p. 147). "... *the products which represent the* [constant] *capital of a nation are not consumable*" (l.c., p. 150).

Ramsay (George)—*An Essay on the Distribution of Wealth* (Edinburgh, 1836)—remarks on the same subject, namely, Adam Smith's fourth part of the total price, or what I call constant capital as distinct from the capital laid out in wages:

||271| "Mr Ricardo," he says, "[... seems to...] consider the whole produce as divided between wages and profits, forgetting the part necessary for replacing fixed capital" (p. 174, note).

By "fixed capital" Ramsay in fact means not only instruments of production, etc., but also the raw material—in short, what I call constant capital within each sphere of production. When Ricardo speaks of the division of the product into profit and wages, he always assumes that the capital advanced to production itself and consumed in it has been deducted. Nevertheless, on the main issue Ramsay is right. Because Ricardo does not make any further examination at all of the constant part of capital, and pays no attention to it, he makes gross errors and in particular confuses profit with surplus-value, besides errors in investigating oscillations in the rate of profit and so on.

Let us hear now what Ramsay himself says:

"In what manner is a comparison to be instituted between the product and* the stock expended upon it?...** With regard to a whole nation ... it is evident that all the various elements of the stock expended must be reproduced in some employment or another, otherwise the industry of the country could not go on as formerly. The raw material of manufactures, the implements used in them, as also in agriculture, the extensive machinery engaged in the former, the buildings necessary for fabricating or storing the produce, must all be parts of the total return of a country, as well as of the advances of*** [...] its master-capitalists. Therefore, the quantity of the former may be compared with that of the latter, each article being supposed placed as it were beside that of a similar kind" (l.c., pp. 137-39). Now as regards the individual capitalist, since he does not *replace* his outgoings in kind, "by far the greater number must be obtained by exchange, a certain portion of the product being necessary for this purpose. Hence each individual master-capitalist comes to look much more to the exchangeable value of his**** product than to its quantity" (l.c., pp. 145-46). "The more the *value of the product* exceeds the *value of the capital* advanced, the greater will be his**** profit. Thus, then, will he estimate it, by comparing value with value, not quantity with quantity.... Profit [...] must rise or fall exactly as the proportion of the gross produce, or of its *value*, required to *replace necessary advances*, falls or rises [...] the rate of profit must depend immediately upon two circumstances*****; first, the proportion of the whole produce which goes to the labourers; secondly, the proportion which must be set apart for replacing, either in kind or by exchange, the fixed capital" (l.c., pp. 146-48, passim).

< What Ramsay here says on the rate of profit has to be considered in Chapter III, on profit. [38] It is important that he rightly lays stress on this element. On the one hand what Ricardo says is correct—that the cheapening of commodities which form constant capital (which Ramsay calls fixed capital) always depreciates a part of the existing capital. This is especially true of fixed capital proper—machinery, etc. It is of no advantage to the individual capitalist that the surplus-value rises in relation to the total capital, if the rise in this rate has been due to a fall in the total value of his constant capital (which he already had before the depreciation). But this is true only to a very small extent for that part of the capital which consists of raw materials or completed commodities (which do not form part of the fixed capital). The existing amount of these that

* The beginning of the sentence has been translated by Marx into German and shortened as follows: "Wie Vergleichen das Produkt und".—*Ed.*

** In the manuscript. "In".—*Ed.*

*** In the manuscript: "all".—*Ed.*

**** In the manuscript: "the".—*Ed.*

***** In the manuscript: "Also upon two circumstances hängt die rate of profit ab".—*Ed.*

can be depreciated in this way is always only an insignificant magnitude compared with the total production. It holds good for each capitalist only to a slight extent for that part of his capital expended as circulating capital. On the other hand—since the profit is equal to the proportion of the surplus-value to the total advanced capital, and since the quantity of labour that can be absorbed depends not on the value but on the quantity of raw materials and on the efficiency of the means of production—not on their exchange-value but on their use-value—it is clear that the greater the productivity of industry in the branches whose ||272| product enters into the formation of constant capital, the smaller the outlay of constant capital required to produce a given quantity of surplus-value; consequently the greater the proportion of this surplus-value to the whole advanced capital, and therefore the higher the rate of profit for a given amount of surplus-value.>

(What Ramsay considers doubly—replacement of product by product in the process of reproduction for the whole country, and replacement of value by value for the individual capitalist—are two aspects, both of which, in relation to the individual capital, must be taken into account in the *circulation process of capital, which is at the same time its reproduction process.*)

Ramsay did not solve the real difficulty which occupied Adam Smith's attention and entangled him in all kinds of contradictions. Put plainly, it is this: The whole capital (as value) resolves itself into labour, is nothing but a certain quantity of materialised labour. The paid labour, however, is equal to the wages of the labourers, the unpaid labour is equal to the capitalists' profit. So the whole capital must be resolvable, directly or indirectly, into wages and profit. Or is labour somewhere performed which consists neither of wages nor profit, and merely has the purpose of replacing the values used up in production which are, however, the conditions of reproduction? But who performs this labour, since all labour performed by the labourer is resolved into two quantities, one which maintains his own power to produce, and the otner which forms the profit of capital?

[10. Inquiry into How It Is Possible for the Annual Profit and Wages to Buy the Annual Commodities, Which Besides Profit and Wages Also Contain Constant Capital][39]

[(a) Impossibility of the Replacement of the Constant Capital of the Producers of Consumption Goods through Exchange between These Producers]

To rid the problem of any spurious admixture, there is one more point to mention at the outset. When the capitalist transforms a part of his profit, of his revenue, into capital—into means of labour and materials of labour—both are paid for by that part of the labour which the labourer has performed gratis for the capitalist. Here we have a new quantity of labour forming the equivalent for a new quantity of commodities, commodities which as use-values consist of means of labour and materials of labour. This therefore enters into the accumulation of capital and presents no difficulty; we have here the growth of the constant capital beyond its previous limits, or the formation of new constant capital in excess of the amount of constant capital that already exists and must be replaced. The difficulty is the reproduction of the *existing* constant capital, not the formation of new constant capital in excess of what has to be reproduced. The new constant capital obviously originates in profit, and has existed for a moment in the form of revenue which is later transformed into capital. This part of the profit consists of *the surplus labour-time, which, even without the existence of capital, must constantly be performed by society, in order to have at its disposal, so to speak, a fund for development, which the very increase of population makes necessary.*

<There is a good explanation of constant capital, but only in so far as concerns its use-value, in Ramsay's work, p. 166, which runs:

> "... be the amount* of the gross return" (of the farmer, for example) "small or great, the quantity of it required for replacing what has been consumed in these different forms, can undergo no alteration whatsoever.** This quantity must be considered as *constant*, so long as production is carried on the same scale.">

So we must first start from the fact: new formation of constant capital—as distinct from the reproduction of the existing constant capital—flows from profit as its source; that is, assuming on the one hand that the wages only suffice for the reproduction of labour-

* In the manuscript: "return"—*Ed.*
** In the manuscript: "whatever".—*Ed.*

power, and on the other that the whole surplus-value is embraced under the category "profit", since it is the industrial capitalist who *directly appropriates* the whole surplus-value, [irrespective of] to whom and where he has to surrender some of it later.

<"... the master* [...] is the general distributor of the national revenue** [...] who undertakes to pay [...] to the labourers, the wages [...]—to the" (moneyed) "capitalist, the interest [...]—to the proprietor, the rent of his land" (Ramsay, [l.c.], pp. 218-19).

In calling the whole surplus-value profit, we regard the capitalist: 1. as the person who immediately appropriates the whole surplus-value created; 2. as the distributor of that surplus-value between himself, the moneyed capitalist, and the proprietor of the soil.>

||VII—273| That this new constant capital arises from profit however means nothing but that it is due to a part of the surplus-labour of the labourers. Just as the savage, in addition to the time he needs for hunting, must necessarily use some time for making his bow; or just as in patriarchal agriculture, the peasant, in addition to the time spent in tilling the soil, must use a certain quantity of labour-time in producing most of his implements.

But the question here is: Who is it that labours in order to replace the equivalent of the constant capital already expended in production? The part of the labour which the labourer performs for himself replaces his wages, or, considered in relation to the whole of production, creates his wages. On the other hand, his surplus-labour which forms the profit is in part a consumption fund for the capitalist, and in part is transformed into additional capital. But the capitalist does not replace the capital already used up in his own production out of this surplus-labour or profit. <Were this the case, the surplus-value would not be a fund for new capital formation, but for the maintenance of the old capital.> But the necessary labour which forms the wages and the surplus-labour which forms the profit make up the whole working-day, and no other labour is performed in addition to these. (The contingency of the capitalist's labour of superintendence is included in wages. In this aspect he is the wage-worker, even though not of another capitalist, yet of his own capital.) What then is the source, the labour, that replaces the constant capital?

The part of the capital expended in wages is replaced (leaving

* In the manuscript: "master-capitalist".—*Ed.*

** In the manuscript: "wealth".—*Ed.*

surplus-labour out of account) by new production. The labourer consumes the wages, but he adds as much new labour as he has destroyed of old labour; and if we consider the whole working class, without allowing the division of labour to confuse us, he reproduces not only the same value but the same use-values, so that, according to the productivity of his labour, the same value, the same quantity of labour, is reproduced in a greater or smaller quantity of these same use-values.

If we take society at any one moment, there exists simultaneously in all spheres of production, even though in very different proportions, a definite constant capital—presupposed as a necessary condition of production—that once for all belongs to production and must be given back to it, as seed must be given back to the land. It is true that the *value* of this constant part can fall or rise, depending on whether the commodities of which it is composed have to be reproduced at less or greater cost. This *change in value*, however, never alters the fact that in the process of production, into which it enters as a condition of production, it is a postulated value which must reappear in the value of the product. Therefore this change of value of the constant capital can here be ignored. In all circumstances it is a definite quantity of *past, materialised labour*, which passes into the value of the product as a determining factor In order to bring out more clearly the nature of the problem, let us therefore assume that the production costs or the value of the constant part of the capital similarly remain unchanged, remain constant. It also makes no difference that for example the whole value of the constant capital may not pass into the products in a single year, but, as is the case with fixed capital, only passes into the aggregate products of a series of years. For the question here centres on that part of the constant capital which is actually consumed within the year, and therefore also must be replaced within the year.

The question of the reproduction of the constant capital clearly belongs to the section on the reproduction process or circulation process of capital—which however is no reason why the kernel of the matter should not be examined here.

||274| Let us first take the labourer's wages. He receives, then, a certain sum of money in which say ten hours' labour are materialised, if he works 12 hours for the capitalist. These wages are converted into means of subsistence. These means of subsistence are all commodities. Assume that the price of these commodities is equal to their value. But in the value of these commodities there

is one component part which covers the value of the raw materials they contain and the means of production used up in them. All the component parts of the value of these commodities taken together, contain, however, like the wages spent by the labourer, only ten hours' labour. Let us assume that two-thirds of the value of these commodities consists of the value of the constant capital they contain, and one-third, on the other hand, of the labour which has finally made the product into a finished article for consumption. Thus the labourer, with his ten hours of living labour, replaces two-thirds of constant capital and one-third of living labour (added to the article in the course of the year). If there were no constant capital in the means of subsistence, the commodities, which he buys, the raw material in them would have cost nothing, and no instrument of labour would have been required to make them. In that case there are two possibilities. Either the commodities, as before, would contain ten hours' labour; then the labourer replaces ten hours' living labour by ten hours' living labour. Or the same quantity of use-values into which his wages are converted and which he needed for the reproduction of his labour-power would have cost only $3\,^1/_3$ hours' labour (with no instrument of labour and no raw material which is itself a product of labour). In this case the labourer has only to perform $3\,^1/_3$ hours' necessary labour, and his wages would in fact fall to $3\,^1/_3$ [hours'] materialised labour-time.

Let us assume that the commodity is linen: 12 yards (the actual price does not matter here)=36 shillings or £1.16.0. Of this, let one-third be labour added, two-thirds for raw material (yarn) and wear and tear of machinery. Let the necessary labour-time=10 hours; the surplus-labour therefore=2. Let one hour's labour, expressed in money,=1 shilling. In this case the 12 hours' labour =12 shillings, wages=10 shillings, profit=2 shillings. Let us assume that labourer and capitalist spent the whole of their wages and profit, that is 12 shillings (the total value that has been added to the raw material and machinery, the whole quantity of new labour-time materialised in the transformation of yarn into linen), on linen itself as a consumption article. (And it is possible that subsequently more than one labour day will be spent on their own product.) A yard of linen costs 3 shillings. With the 12 shillings labourer and capitalist together—adding wages and profit together—can only buy four yards of linen. These four yards of linen contain 12 hours' labour, of which however only 4 are newly-added labour, 8 representing the labour realised in the constant capital. With the 12 hours' labour wages and profit together buy only one-third of their total product, because two-thirds of this total product consist of constant capital. The 12 hours' labour are divisible into 4+8, of which 4 replace themselves, while 8—independently of the labour added in the weaving process—replace such labour as entered into the weaving process in already materialised form, as yarn and machinery.

In regard to that part of the product, of the commodity, which exchanges against or is bought by wages and profit as an article of consumption (or for any other purpose, even reproduction, for the purpose for which the commodity is bought makes no difference to the transaction), it is therefore clear that the part of the value of the product which is formed by the constant capital is paid for from the fund of newly-added labour, which is resolved into wages and profit. How much or how little of constant capital and how much or how little of the labour added in the last production process is bought by wages and profit combined, in what proportions the labour last added and in what proportions the labour realised in constant capital is paid for, depends on the original proportions in which they entered as component parts of value into the finished commodity. To simplify matters we assume the proportion of two-thirds labour realised in constant capital to one-third newly-added labour.

||275| Now two things are clear:

First. The proportion we have assumed in the case of the linen —that is, in the case where labourer and capitalist realise wages and profit in the commodities they have themselves produced, when they buy back a part of their product—this proportion remains the same when they expend the same quantity of value on other products. On the assumption that every commodity contains two-thirds of constant capital and one-third newly-added labour, wages and profit together could always only purchase one-third of the product. The 12 hours' labour=four yards of linen. If these four yards of linen are transformed into money, then they exist as 12 shillings. If these 12 shillings are retransformed into some commodity other than linen, they buy a commodity of the value of 12 hours' labour, of which 4 are newly-added labour, 8 labour realised in constant capital. Consequently, this proportion holds good generally provided the other commodities contain the same original proportion of labour last added and of labour realised in constant capital as linen.

Secondly. If the daily newly-added labour=12 hours, of these

12 hours only 4 replace themselves—that is, the living, newly-added labour; while 8 pay for the labour realised in the constant capital. But who pays for the 8 hours of living labour which are not replaced by living labour? It is precisely the 8 hours of realised labour contained in the constant capital that are exchanged for the 8 hours of living labour.

There is not the slightest doubt, therefore, that the part of the finished commodity which is bought by wages and profit combined—which together however are nothing but the total quantity of labour newly added to the constant capital—is replaced in all its elements: the newly-added labour contained in this part as well as the quantity of labour contained in the constant capital. Further, there is not the slightest doubt that the labour contained in the constant capital has here received its equivalent from the fund of living labour newly added to it.

But now comes the difficulty. The *total product* of the 12 hours of weaving labour—and this product is absolutely different from what this weaving labour has itself produced—is 12 yards of linen, of the value of 36 hours' labour or 36s. But wages and profit together, or the total labour-time of 12 hours can buy back *only* 12 of these 36 hours' labour, or of the total product only 4 yards, not a piece more. What happens to the other 8 yards? (*Forcade, Proudhon.* [40])

First we note that the 8 yards represent nothing but the constant capital advanced. It has however been given a changed form of use-value. It exists as a new product, no longer as yarn, loom, etc., but as linen. These 8 yards of linen, just like the 4 others which have been bought by wages and profit, contain—considered as value—one-third labour added in the weaving process, and two-thirds pre-existing labour materialised in the constant capital. In the case of the 4 yards previously discussed one-third of the newly-added labour covered the weaving labour contained in these 4 yards, that is, covered itself; two-thirds of the weaving labour on the other hand covered the constant capital the 4 yards contained. But now we have it the other way round: in the 8 yards of linen, two-thirds of the constant capital covers the constant capital they contain, and one-third of the constant capital covers the newly-added labour.

What then happens to the 8 yards of linen, which have absorbed the value of the whole constant capital which has been maintained during the 12 hours' weaving labour, or which went into the production process, but is now in the form of a product destined for direct, individual (not industrial) consumption?

The 8 yards belong to the capitalist. Were he to consume them himself, besides the two-thirds of a yard representing his profit, ||276| then he could not reproduce the constant capital contained in the 12 hours' weaving process; in general—with regard to the capital contained in this 12 hours' process—he is no longer able to function as a capitalist. He therefore sells the 8 yards of linen, transforming them into money to the amount of 24 shillings, or 24 hours' labour. But here we come to the difficulty. To whom does he sell them? Into whose money does he transform them? But we shall return to this in a moment. Let us first have a look at the further process.

When he has transformed into money, sold, converted into the form of exchange-value, the 8 yards of linen—that is to say, the part of the value of his product which is equal to the constant capital he advanced—he buys again with it commodities of the same kind (with regard to their use-value) as those which originally composed his constant capital. He buys yarn and looms and so on. He divides the 24 shillings between raw materials and means of production, in the proportions in which these are required for the manufacture of new linen.

His constant capital is therefore, as a use-value, replaced by new products of the same labour as that of which it originally consisted. The capitalist has reproduced the constant capital. This new yarn, looms, etc., however (on the assumption with which we began) likewise consist of two-thirds of constant capital and one-third of newly-added labour. While the first 4 yards of linen (newly-added labour and constant capital) have thus been paid for exclusively by newly-added labour, these 8 yards of linen are replaced by their own newly-produced elements of production, which consist partly of newly-added labour and partly of constant capital. Hence it seems that at least a part of the constant capital exchanges for constant capital in another form. The replacement of the products is real, bacause at the same time as the yarn is being worked up into linen, flax is being worked up into yarn and flax seed into flax; in the same way, while the loom is wearing out, a new loom is being made; and similarly, while the latter is being manufactured, new wood and iron is being produced. The elements are produced in one sphere of production at the same time as they are being worked up in the others. But in all these *simultaneous* processes of production, although each of them represents a higher stage of the product, constant capital is simultaneously being used up in varying proportions.

The value of the finished product, the linen, therefore resolves itself into two parts, of which one repurchases the simultaneously produced elements of constant capital, while the other is expended on articles of consumption. For the sake of simplification no account is here taken of the retransformation of part of the profit into capital; that is, as throughout this inquiry, it is assumed that wages plus profit, or the total of the labour added to the constant capital, are consumed as revenue.

The only question left is: Who buys the part of the total product with whose value the elements of constant capital that have meanwhile been newly produced are again bought? Who buys the 8 yards of linen? We assume, in order to leave no loopholes, that it is a type of linen specially intended for individual consumption, and is not, like perhaps sail-cloth, for industrial consumption. Here also the purely intermediary operations of commerce—so far as they are only mediatory—must be left completely out of account. For example, if the 8 yards of linen were sold to a merchant, and even if they pass through the hands of not one but twenty merchants and are twenty times bought and resold, then at the twentieth time they must at last be sold by the merchant to the actual consumer, who therefore actually pays the producer or the *last,* the twentieth merchant, who as far as the consumer is concerned represents the *first merchant,* that is to say, the actual producer. These intermediary transactions postpone or, if you like, mediate the final transaction, but they do not explain it. The question remains exactly the same whether it is: who buys the 8 yards of linen from the linen manufacturer, or: ||277| who buys them from the twentieth merchant into whose hand they have come through a series of exchanges?

The 8 yards of linen, just as the first 4 yards, must pass into the fund for consumption. That is to say, they can only be paid for out of wages and profit, for these are the only sources of revenue for the producers, who figure here as the only consumers. The 8 yards of linen contain 24 hours' labour. Let us now assume (taking 12 hours as the generally valid normal working-day) that labourer and capitalist in two other branches spend their whole wages and profit on linen, as labourer and capitalist in the weaving industry have done with their whole day's labour (the labourer his 10 hours, the capitalist the 2 hours' surplus-value made on his labourer, that is, on 10 hours). Then the linen weaver would have sold the

8 yards, the *value* of his constant capital for 12 yards would be replaced, and this value could again be spent on the particular commodities of which the constant capital consists, *because* these commodities, yarn, loom, etc., available on the market, have been produced at the same time as yarn and loom were being worked up into linen. *The simultaneous production* of yarn and loom as products alongside the production process into which they enter as products but from which they do not emerge as products, explains how it is that the part of the *value* of the linen equal to the value of the material worked up into it—[such as yarn], loom, etc.—can be again transformed into yarn, loom, etc. If this production of the elements of linen did not proceed simultaneously with the production of the linen itself, the 8 yards of linen, even when they have been sold and transformed into money, could not be retransformed once more from money into the constant elements of linen. *

On the other hand, however, although there may be new yarn, new looms, etc., on the market, and therefore production of new yarn and looms had taken place while finished yarn and finished loom were being transformed into linen—in spite of the simultaneous production of yarn and loom alongside the production of the linen—the 8 yards of linen cannot be retransformed into these material elements of constant capital for the weaving industry before they are sold, before they are converted into money. The continuous real production of the elements of linen, running side by side with the production of linen itself, therefore does not yet explain to us the reproduction of the constant capital, before we know whence comes the fund to buy the 8 yards of linen, to give them back the form of money, of independent exchange-value.

In order to solve this last difficulty we have assumed that B and C—which can stand for shoemaker and butcher—have spent their total wages and profit, that is, the 24 hours' labour-time which they have at their disposal, entirely on linen. And this gets us over our difficulty with A, the linen weaver. His whole product, the 12 yards of linen in which 36 hours' labour is materialised, has been replaced by wages and profit alone—that

* As for example is now the case with the yarn or cloth of the cotton manufacturers, as a result of the American Civil War. The mere sale of their product is no guarantee for them that it will be retransformed, since there is no cotton on the market.

is, by the whole of the labour-time newly added to the constant capital in the spheres of production A, B and C. All the labour-time contained in the linen, both that already existing in its constant capital and that newly added in the weaving process, has been exchanged against labour-time which did not previously exist as constant capital in any sphere of production, but which was added simultaneously to the constant capital in the three production spheres A, B and C, *in the last stage of production*.

Though therefore it is still wrong to say that the original value of the linen was composed of wages and profit alone—since however it was made up of the value equal to the total of wages and profit, 12 hours' weaving, and the 24 hours' labour which, independently of the weaving process, was contained in the yarn, loom, in a word, the constant capital—it would on the other hand be correct to say that the equivalent of the 12 yards of linen, the 36s. for which they have been sold, is composed of wages and profit alone; that is, not only the weaving labour but also the labour contained in yarn and loom are replaced entirely by newly-added labour, namely 12 hours' labour in A, 12 hours in B and 12 hours in C.

The value of the commodity sold is itself divided ||278| into newly-added labour (wages and profit) and pre-existing labour (value of the constant capital); that is the value for the seller (in fact [the value] of the commodity). On the other hand, the purchasing value, the equivalent given by the buyer to the seller, is made up entirely of newly-added labour, wages and profit. But as every commodity, before it is sold, is a commodity for sale and becomes money through a mere change of form, so every commodity, after it has been sold, would be made up of other component parts of value than it is composed of as a buying commodity (as money), which is absurd. Further: the labour performed by society for example in one year would not only cover itself—so that if the total quantity of commodities is divided into two equal parts, one half of the year's labour would form an equivalent for the other half—but the one-third of the labour, which forms the current year's labour in the total labour contained in the annual product, would cover three-thirds of the labour, would be equal to a magnitude three times greater than itself. This is still more absurd.

In the above example we have shifted the difficulty, pushed it on from A to B and C. But this has only increased the difficulty, not made it simpler. *In the first place*, in dealing with A we had the way out that 4 yards, containing as much labour-time as had been added to the yarn, that is, the total wages and profit in A, were consumed in linen itself, in the product of A's own labour. With B and C this is not the case, since they consume the total labour-time added by them, their total wages and profit, in the product of sphere A, in linen, and so not in the product of B or C. They have therefore to sell not only the part of their product representing the 24 hours' labour of constant capital, but also the part of their product which represents the 12 hours' labour newly added to the constant capital. B must sell 36 hours' labour, not only 24 like A. C is in same position as B. *Secondly*, in order to see A's constant capital, to get it off his hands and transform it into money, we need the whole newly-added labour not only of B but also of C. *Thirdly*, B and C cannot sell any part of their product to A, since the whole part of A which constitutes revenue has already been expended in A itself by the producers of A. Nor can they replace the constant part of A by any part of their own product, since on the assumption we have made their products are not production elements for A but commodities which enter into individual consumption. The difficulty increases at each further step.

In order to exchange the 36 hours contained in A's product (that is, two-thirds or 24 hours in constant capital, one-third or 12 hours in newly-added labour) entirely for labour added to constant capital, A's wages and profit—the 12 hours' labour added in A—one-third of the product had to be consumed by A itself. The other two-thirds of the total product=24 hours, represented the value contained in the constant capital. This value was exchanged for the total quantity of wages and profit or newly-added labour in B and C. But in order that B and C should be able, with the 24 hours in their products that make up their wages [and profit], to buy linen, they must sell these 24 hours in the form of their own products—and in addition to replace the constant capital they must sell 48 hours of their own products. They have therefore to sell products of B and C to the amount of 72 hours, in exchange for the total quantity of profit and wages in the other spheres D, E, etc.; and this means (with a normal 12-hour day) that 12×6 hours (=72) or the labour added in six other spheres of production must be realised in the products B and C; ||279| that is, the profit and wages or the total labour added to their respective constant capital in D, E, F, G, H, I.

In these circumstances the value of the total product of B+C would be paid for entirely in newly-added labour, that is, the aggregate wages and profit, in production spheres D, E, F, G, H, I. But in these six spheres the total product would then have to be sold (since no part of these products would be consumed by their producers themselves, as they have already put their whole revenue into products B and C), and no part of it could be accounted for within their own spheres; that is, the product of 6×36 hours' labour=216, of which 144 represent constant capital and 72 (6×12) newly-added labour. Now in order in turn to transform the products of D, etc., similarly into wages and profit, that is, into newly-added labour, all the newly-added labour in the 18 spheres K^1—K^{18}, that is to say, the total sum of wages and profit in these 18 spheres, must be entirely expended on the products of spheres D, E, F, G, H, I. These 18 spheres K^1—K^{18} would have to sell—since they consumed none of their products themselves, but had already spent their entire revenue in the 6 spheres D—I—18×36 hours' labour or 648 hours' labour, of which 18×12 or 216 are in newly-added labour, and 432 in labour contained in the constant capital. In order therefore to transform this total product of K^1—K^{18} into the labour added or total wages and profit in other spheres, the labour added in the spheres L^1—L^{54} would be required; that is to say, 12×54=648 hours' labour. Spheres L^1—L^{54}, in order to exchange their total product which is equal to 1,944 hours (of which 648=12×54 is the newly-added labour and 1,296 hours' labour is the labour contained in the constant capital) for newly-added labour, would have to absorb the newly-added labour of spheres M^1—M^{162}, for 162×12=1,944; these in their turn must absorb the newly-added labour of spheres N^1—N^{486} and so on.

This is the beautiful progression *in infinitum* which we arrive at if all products are resolved into wages and profit, newly-added labour—if not only the labour added in the commodity but also its constant capital have to be paid for by newly-added labour in another sphere of production.

In order to convert the labour-time contained in product A, 36 hours (one-third newly-added labour, two-thirds constant capital), into newly-added labour, that is, to have it paid for by wages and profit, we at first assumed that one-third of the product (whose value is equal to the total of wages and profit) was consumed or bought—which is the same thing—by the producers of A themselves. This was the progress. [41]

1. *Production sphere A*. Product=*36* hours' labour. *24* hours' labour, constant capital. 12 hours' labour, newly added. One-third of the product consumed by the shareholders of the 12 hours, wages and profit, labourer and capitalist. There remain to be sold two-thirds of the product of A, equivalent to the 24 hours' labour contained in the constant capital.

2. *Production spheres B^1—B^2*. Product=*72* hours' labour; of which *24*, labour added, 48, constant capital. They buy with it the two-thirds of A's product, replacing the value of A's constant capital. But they have now to sell the 72 hours' labour, of which the value of their total product consists.

3. *Production spheres C^1—C^6*. Product=*216* hours' labour; of which *72* added labour (wages and profit). They buy with it the entire product of B^1—B^2. But they have now to sell 216, of which 144 are constant capital.

||280| 4. *Production spheres D^1—D^{18}*. Product=648 hours' labour, 216 labour added, and 432 constant capital. With the labour added they buy the total product of production spheres C^1—C^6=216. But they have to sell 648.

5. *Production spheres E^1—E^{54}*. *Product*=1,944 hours' labour; 648 labour added and 1,296 constant capital. They buy the total product of production spheres D^1—D^{18}. But they have to sell 1,944.

6. *Production spheres F^1—F^{162}*. *Product*=5,832, of which 1,944 added labour and 3,888 constant capital. With the 1,944 they buy the product of E^1—E^{54}. They have to sell 5,832.

7. *Production spheres G^1—G^{486}*.

In order to simplify the problem, only one working-day of 12 hours is assumed throughout, in every production sphere, divided between capitalist and labourer. It does not solve the problem to increase the number of working-days, but complicates it needlessly.

So, to get a clearer picture of the law of this series:

1. *A*. *Product*=36 hours. Constant capital=24 hours. *Total of wages and profit* or *newly-added labour*=12 hours. The latter is consumed by capital and labour in the form of the product of A itself. A's product to be sold, equal to its constant capital,=24 hours.

2. *B^1—B^2*. We need here two days' labour, that is, 2 production spheres, to pay for A's 24 hours.

Product=2×36, or 72 hours, of which 24 hours labour and 48 constant capital.

Product of B^1 and B^2 to be sold=72 hours' labour, no part of it consumed in their own spheres.

6. C^1—C^6. We need here 6 days' labour, because 72=12×6, and the total product of B^1—B^2 has to be consumed by the labour added in C^1—C^6. Product=6×36=216 hours' labour, of which 72 newly added, 144 constant capital.

18. D^1—D^{18}. We need here 18 days' labour because 216=12×18 so, since there is two-thirds constant capital per day's labour, 18×36 is the total product=648 (432 constant capital).

And so on.

The figures 1, 2, [etc.] placed at the beginning of paragraphs signify the working-days or the different kinds of labour in different production spheres, as we assumed one working-day in each sphere.

Therefore: 1. *A*. *Product=36 hours.* Added labour *12* hours. *Product to be sold* (constant capital)=24 hours.

Or:

1. *A*. *Product to be sold or constant capital*=24 hours. Total product 36 hours. Labour added *12 hours. Consumed in A itself.*

2. B^1—B^2. Buys with added labour=24 hours A. *Constant capital* 48 hours. *Total product* 72 hours.

6. C^1—C^6. Buys with added labour *72* hours B^1—B^2 (=12×6). *Constant capital* 144, total product=216. Etc.

||281| Therefore:

1. *A*. Product=3 working-days (36 hours). 12 hours added labour. *24 hours* constant capital.

2. B^{1-2}. *Product*=2×3=6 working-days (72 hours). Added labour=*12×2=***24** *hours. Constant capital*=48=2×24 hours.

6. C^{1-6}. *Product*=3×6 working-days=3×72 hours=216 hours' labour. *Added labour*=6×12 hours (=72). *Constant capital*=2×72=144.

18. D^{1-18}. *Product*=3×3×6 working-days=3×18 working-days (=54 working-days)=648 hours' labour. Added labour= =12×18=216. Constant capital=432 hours' labour.

54. E^{1-54}. *Product*=3×54 working-days=162 working-days= =1,944 hours' labour. Added labour=54 working-days=648 hours' labour; 1,296 constant capital.

162. F^{1-162}. *Product*=3×162 working-days (=486)=5,832 hours' labour, of which 162 working-days or 1,944 hours' labour are added labour, and 3,888 constant capital.

486. G^{1-486}. *Product=3×486 working-days*, of which 486 work-

ing-days or 5,832 hours' labour are labour added, and 11,664 constant capital.

Etc.

Here we would already have the goodly total of 1+2+6+18+ +54+162+486 different working-days in different production spheres=729 different production spheres, which already implies a considerably ramified society.

In order to sell the total product of A (where only 12 hours' labour=1 working-day is added to the constant capital of 2 working-days, and wages and profit consume their own product), that is, only the 24 hours' constant capital—and moreover to sell it again entirely for newly-added labour, for wages and profit—we need 2 working-days in B^1 and B^2; which however require a constant capital of 4 working-days, so that the total product of B^{1-2}=6 working-days. These must be *all* sold, because *from here on* it is assumed that each subsequent sphere does not consume any of its own product, but spends its profit and wages only on the product of the preceding spheres. In order to replace these 6 working-days of the product of B^{1-2}, 6 working-days are necessary, which however presuppose a constant capital of 12 working-days. The total product of C^{1-6} therefore=18 working-days. In order to replace these by labour, 18 working-days D^{1-18} are necessary, which however presuppose a constant capital of 36 working-days; so that the product=54 working-days. To replace these, 54 working-days are needed, E^{1-54}, which presuppose a constant capital of 108. Product=162 working-days. Finally, to replace these, 162 working-days are needed, which however presuppose a constant capital of 324 working-days; that is, total product 486 working-days. This is F^{1-162}. Finally, to replace this product of F^{1-162}, we need 486 working-days (G^{1-486}), which however presuppose a constant capital of 972 working-days. So the total product of G^{1-486}=972+486=1,458 working-days.

But now let us assume that with sphere G we reach an end to the shifting; and ||282| our progression would soon bring us to an end in any society. How would the matter stand then? We have a product comprising 1,458 working-days of which 486 newly-added labour and 972 labour realised in constant capital. The 486 working-days can then be spent in the previous sphere F^{1-162}. But what is to buy the 972 working-days contained in the constant capital? Beyond G^{486} there is no new sphere of production and therefore no new sphere of exchange. In the spheres that lie behind it, except for F^{1-162}, there is nothing to be exchanged. Moreover, G^{1-486} has expended all its wages and profit up to the last centime in F^{1-162}. Therefore the 972 working-days realised in the total product of G^{1-486}, which are the equivalent of the constant capital it contains, remain unsaleable. It has thus not helped us at all to shift through nearly 800 branches of production the difficulty of the 8 yards of linen of sphere A, or the 24 hours' labour, the 2 working-days, representing in its product the value of the constant capital.

It is no use imagining that the reckoning would have a different result if perhaps A did not spend its whole wages and profits in linen, but spent a part of it on the product of B and C. The limit of the outlays, the hours of labour added which are contained in A, B, C, can always only command a labour-time equal to themselves. If they buy more of one product, then they buy less of the other. It would only confuse the reckoning, but in no way alter result.

What then is to be done? In the above calculation we find:

	Work-ing days	Labour added	Con-stant capital
A Product =	3	1	2
B " =	6	2	4
C " =	18	6	12
D " =	54	18	36
E " =	162	54	108
F " =	486	162	324
Total:	729	243	486

(one-third of A's product consumed by A itself)

If the last 324 working-days ([F's] constant capital) in this account were equal to the constant capital which the farmer replaces for himself, subtracts from his product and returns to the land—and so has not to be paid for by new labour—then the account would balance. The riddle, however, would only be solved because a part of the constant capital replaces itself.

In fact therefore we have had consumed 243 working-days, corresponding to the newly-added labour. The value of the final product, 486 working-days, is equal to the value of the total constant capital contained in A—F, which is also 486 working-days. In order to account for this, we assume 486 days of new labour in G, from which however the only satisfaction we get is that instead of having to account for a constant capital of 486 days, ||283| we have to account for a constant capital of 972 working-days in G's product, which is equal to 1,458 working-days (972 constant capital+486 labour). If now we want to get out of our difficulty by supposing that G works without constant capital, so that the product is only equal to the 486 days of newly-added labour, the account would of course be cleared; but we would have solved the problem of who pays for the part of the value contained in the product which forms the constant capital, by assuming a case in which the constant capital equals nil and hence forms no part of the value of the product.

In order to sell A's total product entirely for newly-added labour, in order to resolve it into profit and wages, *the whole of the labour added in A, B and C* must be spent on the labour realised in product A.[42] Likewise to sell the total product of B+C, all labour newly added in D^1—D^{18} is needed.[43] Similarly, to buy the total product of D^1—D^{18}, all labour added in E^{1-54}. To buy the total product of E^{1-54}, all labour added in F^{1-162}. And finally, [to buy] the total product of F^{1-162}, the total labour-time added in G^{1-486}. At the end, in these 486 production spheres represented by G^{1-486}, the total labour-time added is equal to the total product of the 162 spheres F, and this total product which is replaced by labour is as large as the constant capital in A, B^{1-2}, C^{1-6}, D^{1-18}, E^{1-54}, F^{1-162}. But the constant capital of sphere G, twice the size of the constant capital used in A—F^{162}, is not replaced and cannot be replaced.

In fact we have found, on our assumption that in all production spheres the proportion of the newly-added to the pre-existing labour is 1 : 2, that always twice [as many] new production spheres [as all preceding ones taken together][44] must use all their new labour to buy the product of the preceding spheres—the labour added of A and B^{1-2}, to buy A's total product; the labour added of 18 D or D^{1-18} (2×9), to buy the product of C^{1-6}, and so on. In short, that twice as much newly-added labour as the product itself contains is always needed, so that there must be twice as much newly-added labour in the last production sphere G as there actually is, in order to buy the total product. In a word, we find in the result of G what was already there in our starting-point A, that the newly-added labour cannot buy any greater quantity of its own product than it itself amounts to and that it *cannot* buy the labour pre-existing in the constant capital.

It is therefore impossible for the value of the revenue to cover the value of the total product. But since, apart from the revenue, *no fund exists from which this product sold by producers to (indi-*

vidual) consumers can be paid for, it is impossible for the value of the total product, minus the value of the revenue, ever to be sold, paid for or (individually) consumed. On the other hand it is necessary for every product to be sold and paid for at its price (on the assumption that price is here equal to value).

For that matter, it might have been foreseen from the outset that introducing the acts of exchange, sales and purchases between different commodities or the products of different production spheres, would not bring us a step forward. In A, the first commodity, the linen, we had one-third or ||283a| 12 hours of newly-added labour and 2×12 or 24 hours of pre-existing labour in the [constant] capital. Wages and profit could only repurchase that part of the product of commodity A—and therefore also of any equivalent of commodity A in any other product—which is equal to 12 hours' labour. They could not buy back their own constant capital of 24 hours, hence they could not repurchase the equivalent of this constant capital in any other commodity either.

It is possible for the relation of added labour to constant capital to be different in commodity B. But however different the proportion may be of constant capital to newly-added labour in the various spheres of production, we can calculate the average, and so say that in the product of the whole society or of the whole capitalist class, in the total product of capital, the newly-added labour is equal to *a*, the labour pre-existing as constant capital is equal to *b*. In other words, the proportion of 1 : 2 which we assumed in A, the linen, is only a symbolical expression of *a* : *b* and is not intended to imply anything more than that a definite and definable relation of some kind or other exists between these two elements—the living labour added in the current year or in any other period selected, and the past labour pre-existing as constant capital. If the 12 hours added to the yarn buy not only linen, but for example linen only to the amount of 4 hours, then they could buy some other product to the amount of 8 hours, but they could never buy more than 12 hours altogether; and if they buy another product to the value of 8 hours, then 32 hours' linen in all must be sold by A. The example A therefore holds good for the total capital of the entire society, and though the problem can be complicated by introducing the exchange of different commodities, the problem itself remains unchanged.

Let us assume that A is the total product of society: then one-third of this total product can be bought by the producers for their own consumption, bought and paid for with the total of their wages and their profits, equal to the total newly-added labour, the amount of their aggregate revenue. They have no fund with which to pay for, to buy and consume, the other two-thirds. Just as the newly-added labour, the one-third which consists of profit and wages, is itself covered by its own product, or withdraws only that part of the value of the product which contains one-third of the total labour, newly-added labour or its equivalent, so must the two-thirds of pre-existing labour be covered by its own product. That is to say, the constant capital remains equal to itself and replaces itself out of that part of the value which represents the constant capital in the total product. The exchange between various commodities, the series of purchases and sales between different spheres of production, brings about a change in form only in the sense that the constant capitals in the various production spheres mutually replace each other in the proportion in which they were originally contained in them.

We must now examine this more closely. |283a||

[(b) Impossibility of Replacing the Whole Constant Capital of Society by Means of Exchange between the Producers of Articles of Consumption and the Producers of Means of Production]

||283b| This view—that the annual product of the country is divided into wages and profits (rents, interest, etc., included in the latter)—is expressed by Adam Smith, Book II, Chapter II, in examining the circulation of money and the credit system (on this, compare later *Tooke*), where he says:

> "The circulation of every country may be considered as divided into two different branches; the circulation of the dealers with one another, and the circulation between the dealers and the consumers." (Garnier explains that by dealers Adam Smith here means "all traders, manufacturers, artisans, and so on; in a word, the agents of the trade and industry of a country"). "Though the same pieces of money, whether paper or metal, may be employed sometimes in the one circulation and sometimes in the other; yet as both are constantly going on at the same time, each requires a certain stock of money, of one kind or another, to carry it on. *The value of the goods circulated between the different dealers never can exceed the value of those circulated between the dealers and the consumers; whatever is bought by the dealers being ultimately destined to be sold to the consumers*" ([*Wealth of Nations*, O.U.P. edition, Vol. I, pp. 358-59], [Garnier] t. II, b. II, ch. II, pp. 292-93).[45]

To this, as well as Tooke, we must come back later.[46]

Let us return to our example. The day's product of A, a linen weaving factory, was equal to 12 yards=36s.=36 hours' labour, of which 12 are newly-added labour divisible into wages and profit, and 24 hours or 2 days equal to the value of the constant capital, which now however, instead of the old form of yarn and loom, exists in the form of linen, but in a quantity of linen equal to 24 hours=24s. In this there is the same quantity of labour as in the yarn and loom which it replaces, and with it therefore the same quantity of yarn and loom can be bought again (on the assumption that the value of yarn and loom has remained the same, that the productivity of labour in these branches of industry has not altered). The spinner and the loom maker must sell the whole of their year's or their day's product (which for our purpose here is the same thing) to the weaver, for he is the only person for whom their commodity has use-value. He is their only consumer.

But if the weaver's constant capital is equal to 2 working-days (his daily consumed constant capital), then for one working-day of the weaver there are two working-days of spinner and machine maker—2 working-days which may themselves be divided in very different proportions into labour added and constant capital. But the total daily product of spinner and machine maker together (assuming that the machine maker makes only looms)—constant capital and added labour together—cannot amount to more than 2 days' labour while that of the weaver, because of the 12 hours' labour newly added by him, amounts to 3 working-days. It is possible that spinner and machine maker consume as much living labour-time as the weaver. Then the labour-time contained in their constant capital must be smaller. However that may be, they can in no case use the same quantity of labour (*summa summarum*) materialised and living, as the weaver. It would be possible for the weaver to use proportionately less living labour-time than the spinner (the latter for example would certainly use less than the flax-grower); in that case the excess of his constant capital over the variable part of his capital must be so much greater.

||284| The weaver's constant capital thus replaces the entire capital of the spinner and the loom maker, not only their own constant capital but the labour newly added in the spinning process and in the manufacture of machines. The new constant capital therefore here replaces other constant capitals completely and, besides that, the total amount of the labour newly added to them. By the sale of their commodities to the weaver, spinner and loom maker have not only replaced their constant

capital, but have received payment for their newly-added labour. His constant capital replaces for them their own constant capital and realises their revenue (wages and profit together). In so far as the weaver's constant capital replaces for them only their own constant capital, which they have handed over to him in the forms of yarn and loom, constant capital in one form has only been exchanged for constant capital in another form. There has in fact been no change of value in the constant capital.

Let us now go further back. The spinner's product is divided into two parts, flax, spindles, coal, etc., in a word his constant capital, and the newly-added labour; similarly for the machine maker's total product. When the spinner replaces his constant capital, he pays not only for the total capital of the spindle manufacturer, etc., but also for that of the flax-grower. His constant capital pays for the one part of their constant capital plus the labour added. Then as for the flax-grower, his constant capital—after deducting agricultural implements, etc.—consists of seed, manure, etc. We will assume—as in agriculture must always be the case, more or less directly—that this part of the farmer's constant capital is an annual deduction from his own product, which he must return each year, out of his own product, to the land—that is, to production itself. Here we find a part of the constant capital which replaces itself and is never sold, and therefore also is never paid for, and is never consumed, never enters into individual consumption. Seed, etc., are the equivalent of so much labour-time. The value of the seed, etc., enters into the value of the total product; but the same value, because it is the same amount of products (on the assumption that the productivity of labour has remained the same), is also deducted again from the total product and returned to production, not entering into circulation.

Here we have at least one part of the constant capital—that which can be regarded as the raw material of agriculture—which replaces itself. Here therefore is an important [branch]—the most important branch in size and in the amount of capital it contains—of the annual production in which an important part of the constant capital, the part which consists of raw materials (apart from artificial fertilisers, etc.), replaces itself and does not enter into circulation, and is therefore not replaced by any form of revenue. Therefore the spinner has not got to repay to the flax-grower this part of the constant capital (the part of the constant capital which is replaced and paid for by the flax-grower himself); nor has the weaver to pay for this to the spinner, nor the buyer of the linen to the weaver.

Let us assume that all those who directly or indirectly participated in the production of the 12 yards of linen (=36 shillings=3 working-days or 36 hours' labour) were paid in linen itself. It is clear in the first place that the producers of the elements of the linen, of the constant capital of the linen, *could not consume their own product*, since these products are produced for production and do not enter into immediate ||285| consumption. They must therefore spend their wages and profits on linen—on the product which finally enters into individual consumption. What they do not consume in linen, they must consume in some other consumable product exchanged for linen. As much (in value) linen is therefore consumed by others as they consume in other consumable products instead of linen. It is the same as if they had themselves consumed it in linen, since as much as they consume in another product is consumed in linen by the producers of other products. The whole problem must therefore be cleared up, without any reference to exchange, by considering how the 12 yards of linen are divided up between all the producers who have taken part in its production or in the production of its elements.

Spinner and loom maker, who we assume also makes spinning machinery, have added one-third in labour, their constant capital amounting to two-thirds of yarn and loom. Of the 8 yards of linen (or 24 hours) or 24s., which replace their total product, they can consequently consume $\frac{8}{3}$ [yards], that is, $2\frac{2}{3}$ [yards] of linen or 8 hours' labour or 8s. Therefore $5\frac{1}{3}$ yards or 16 hours' labour remain to be accounted for.

$5\frac{1}{3}$ yards or 16 hours' labour represent the constant capital of the spinner and of the loom maker. Let us assume that of the spinner's constant capital two-thirds is raw material and is spent on flax; then the flax-grower can consume these two-thirds entirely in linen, since his constant capital <but here we take the wear and tear of his implements of labour, etc., as equal to nil> is not put into circulation at all; he has already deducted it and reserved it for reproduction. He can therefore buy two-thirds of the $5\frac{1}{3}$ yards of linen[47] or 16 hours' labour, which is equal to $3\frac{5}{9}$ yards, or $10\frac{2}{3}$ hours' labour. So there remains to be accounted for only $5\frac{1}{3}$ minus $3\frac{5}{9}$ yards, or $16-10\frac{2}{3}$ hours' labour, that is, $1\frac{7}{9}$ yards or $5\frac{1}{3}$ hours' labour. These $1\frac{7}{9}$ yards or $5\frac{1}{3}$ hours' labour resolve themselves into the constant capital of the loom maker and the total product of the spinning machinery maker, who are assumed to be one person.

‖286| Therefore once again:

	Total product	Constant capital	Weaving labour added	Consumption
Weaver	12 yards linen (36s.) (36 hours' labour)	8 yards (24 hours) (24s.)	12 hours	12 hours 12s.=4 yards

Of the weaver's **constant capital** let $^3/_4$=yarn and $^1/_4$=loom (means of production in general). The weaver thus pays 6 yards or 18 hours to the spinner and 2 yards or 6 hours to the machine maker, etc.

Spinner				Machine maker			
Total product	Constant capital	Spinning labour added	Consumption	Total product	Constant capital	Labour added	Consumption
6 yards 18s. 18 hours	4 yards 12s. 12 hours	2 yards 6s. 6 hours	2 yards 6s.	2 yards 6s. 6 hours	$^4/_3$ yards	$^2/_3$ yard	$^2/_3$ yard

Of the 8 yards which replace the weaver's constant capital, therefore, 2 yards (=6s.=6 hours) are consumed by the spinner, and $^2/_3$of a yard (2s.=2 hours' labour) by the maker of looms, etc.

What remains for us to account for is thus $8-2^2/_3$ yards$=5^1/_3$ yards (=16s.=16 hours' labour). These remaining $5^1/_3$ yards (=16s.=16 hours' labour) are resolved as follows: We assume that in the 4 yards which represent the spinner's constant capital, that is, the elements of his yarn, $^3/_4$ is the equivalent of the flax, and $^1/_4$ of the spinning machine. The elements of the ||287| spinning machine will be reckoned in further on with the constant capital of the loom maker. The two are assumed to be the same person.

Of the 4 yards which replace the spinner's constant capital, $^3/_4$=3 yards are therefore resolved into *flax*. A considerable part of the constant capital in the flax, used in its production, has not however to be replaced; for the flax-grower has already returned it to the land in the form of *seed*, *manure*, *fodder*, *cattle*, etc. Therefore in the part of his product that he sells, only the wear and tear of his instruments of labour, etc., has to be included as constant capital. Here we must rate the labour added at two-thirds at least and the constant capital to be replaced at one-third at the most.

Thus:

	Total product	Constant capital	Farm labour	Consumable
Flax	3 yards 9s. 9 hours' labour	1 yard 3s. 3 hours' labour	2 yards 6s. 6 hours' labour	2 yards 6s. 6 hours' labour

Thus what we have still to account for is:

1 yard (3s., 3 hours' labour), equal to the flax-grower's constant capital;

$1^1/_3$ yards (4s., 4 hours' labour), equal to the constant capital for the loom;

finally 1 yard (3s., 3 hours' labour) for the *total product* contained in the spinning machine.

First what the machine maker can consume for the spinning machine has to be deducted:

	Total product	Constant capital	Engineering labour added	Consumable
Spinning machine	1 yard 3s. 3 hours' labour	$^2/_3$ yard 2s. 2 hours' labour	$^1/_3$ yard 1s. 1 hour's labour	$^1/_3$ yard 1s. 1 hour's labour

Moreover, the *agricultural machinery*, the flax-grower's constant capital, has to be divided into its consumable and other parts:

	Total product	Constant capital	Engineering labour	Consumable
Agricultural machine	1 yard 3s. 3 hours' labour	$^2/_3$ yard 2s. 2 hours' labour	$^1/_3$ yard 1s. 1 hour's labour	$^1/_3$ yard 1s. 1 hour's labour

If therefore we put together that part of the total product which represents machinery, it amounts to 2 yards for the loom, 1 yard for the spinning machine, 1 yard for the agricultural machine, 4 yards in all (12s., 12 hours' labour or $^1/_3$ of the total product, 12 yards of linen). Of these 4 yards, the machine maker can consume $^2/_3$ of a yard for the loom, $^1/_3$ for the spinning machine, ditto $^1/_3$ for the agricultural machinery, in all $1^1/_3$ yards. $2^2/_3$ yards are left, that is, $^4/_3$ constant capital for the loom, $^2/_3$ for the spinning machine, and $^2/_3$ for the agricultural machine$=$ $^8/_3=2^2/_3$ yards ($=$8s.$=$8 hours' labour). This therefore forms the machine builder's constant capital which has to be replaced. Of what now does this constant capital consist? On the one hand, of its raw material, iron, wood, leather belting; and so on. But on the other hand, of that part of the machine he works with (which he may have built himself) which he uses in building machines and which gets worn out. Let us assume that the raw material amounts to two-thirds of the constant capital, and the machine-building machine to one-third. This latter one-third is to be examined later. The two-thirds for wood and iron ||288| amount to two-thirds of the $2^2/_3$ yards (or $2^2/_3$ yards$=$$^8/_3$ yards$=$$^{24}/_9$ yards), $^1/_3$ of this$=$$^8/_9$; therefore $^2/_3$$=$$^{16}/_9$ yards.

Let us then assume that here [in the production of wood and iron] machinery is one-third and added labour two-thirds (since there is nothing for raw material); then two-thirds of the $^{16}/_9$ yards replace labour added, and one-third machinery. Thus what is left again for machinery is $^{16}/_{27}$ yard. The constant capital of the producers of iron and wood, in short, of the extractive industry, consists only of instruments of production—which we here call machinery in general—and not of raw material.

Therefore $^8/_9$ yard for the machine-building machine, $^{16}/_{27}$ yard for the machinery used by the producers of iron and wood. So $^{24}/_{27}+^{16}/_{27}=^{40}/_{27}=1^{13}/_{27}$ yards. This, therefore, has in turn to be put down to the machine builder's account.

Machinery. $^{24}/_{27}$ of a yard forms the replacement for the machine building machine. But this in turn is divided into raw material (iron, wood, etc.), the part of the machinery used up in building the machine-building machine, and labour added. So, if each of the elements is one-third of the total, $^{8}/_{27}$ of a yard would go for the labour added, and $^{16}/_{27}$ of a yard would be left for the *constant capital* to be replaced in the machine-building machine, that is, $^{8}/_{27}$ of a yard for raw material and $^{8}/_{27}$ of a yard to replace the part of the value representing the machinery used up in working up this raw material (together $^{16}/_{27}$ of a yard).

On the other hand the $^{16}/_{27}$ of a yard, which replace the iron and wood producers' machinery, likewise consist of raw material, machinery and labour added. This last is equal to one-third, that is, equal to $\frac{16}{27\times 3}=^{16}/_{81}$ of a yard, and the constant capital in this part of the machinery consists of $^{32}/_{81}$ of a yard, of which $^{16}/_{81}$ is for the raw material, $^{16}/_{81}$ to make good the wear and tear of the machinery.

Thus there remains in the machine builder's hands, as constant capital to make good the wear and tear of his machinery, $^{8}/_{27}$ of a yard, with which he replaces the wear and tear of his machine-building machine, and $^{16}/_{81}$ of a yard for the wear and tear of the iron and wood producers' machinery that has to be replaced.

Apart from this he had, for the replacement of his constant capital, $^{8}/_{27}$ of a yard for the raw material (contained in the machine-building machine) and $^{16}/_{81}$ for the raw material contained in the iron and wood producers' machines. Of this, however, another two-thirds consist of labour added and one-third of machinery used up. Therefore two-thirds of the $^{24}/_{81}+^{16}/_{81}=^{40}/_{81}$ is paid for labour, that is, $\frac{26^2/_3}{81}$. Of this raw material, ||289| $\frac{13^1/_3}{81}$ is again left to replace machinery. This $\frac{13^1/_3}{81}$ of a yard therefore comes back to the machinery manufacturer.

Now there would again be in the hands of the latter: $^{8}/_{27}$ of a yard for the replacement of the wear and tear of the machine-building machine, $^{16}/_{81}$ to replace the wear and tear of the iron, etc., producers' machinery, and $\frac{13^1/_3}{81}$ for the part of the value to replace the machinery in the raw material, iron, etc.

And so we might go on calculating to infinity, with ever smaller fractions, but never able to divide the 12 yards of linen without a remainder.

Let us briefly resume the course of our inquiry up to this point. We said at the start that in the different spheres of production there are different proportions as between the newly-added labour (which partly replaces the variable capital laid out in wages, and partly forms the profit, the unpaid surplus-labour) and the constant capital to which this labour is added. We could however assume an average proportion, for example, *a*—labour added, *b*—constant capital; or we could assume that the proportion of the latter to the former is $2:1 = {}^2/_3 : {}^1/_3$. If this holds good in each production sphere of capital, we went on, then the labour added (wages and profit together) in one particular sphere of production can always only buy one-third of its own product, since wages and profit together form only one-third of the total labour-time realised in the product. But the other two-thirds of the product, which replace his constant capital, also belong to the capitalist. If he wishes to continue production, however, he must replace his constant capital, that is, retransform two-thirds of his product into constant capital. To do this, he must sell the two-thirds.

But to whom? We have already deducted the one-third of the product that can be bought with the total of wages and profit. If this total represents 1 day's labour or 12 hours, then the part of the product whose value is equal to the constant capital represents 2 days' labour or 24 hours. So we assume that [the second] one-third of the product is bought by profit and wages in another branch of production, and the last one-third is bought in turn by profit and wages in a third branch of production. But then we have exchanged the constant capital of Product I for wages and profit exclusively, that is, for newly-added labour, by making the whole labour added to Products II and III be consumed in the form of Product I. Of the six working-days contained in Products II and III, in both newly-added and pre-existing labour, none has been replaced or bought by the labour contained in either Product I or in Products II and III. So we had in turn to make the producers of other products spend all their labour added on Products II and III, and so on. Finally we had to come to a halt at a Product X, in which the labour added was as much as the constant capital of all the earlier products; but its own constant capital two-thirds larger, would be unsaleable. Thus we have not come one step forward with the problem. In the case of Product X, as in the case of Product I, the question remains: to whom is the part of the product sold which replaces the constant capital? Or is the one-third new labour added to the product to replace the one-third new labour plus the two-thirds pre-existing labour contained in the product? Is one-third to be equal to three-thirds?

So from this it became clear that the shifting of the difficulty from Product I to Product II, etc., in a word, merely bringing in to the problem the exchange of commodities, was of no avail.

||290| So we had to pose the question in a different way.

We assumed that the twelve yards of linen (=36s.=36 hours' labour) were a product containing 12 hours' labour or 1 working-day of the weaver (necessary labour and surplus-labour together, that is, the equivalent of the total of profit and wages), while two-thirds represented the value of the constant capital, yarn and machinery, etc., contained in the linen. We further assumed, in order to eliminate any recourse to quibbles and intermediate transactions, that the linen was of a kind destined only for individual consumption, and therefore could not serve in turn as raw material for some new product. By this we assumed that it was a product that had to be paid for from wages and profit, that it must be exchanged for revenue. And finally to simplify things we assume that no part of the profit is reconverted into capital, but that the whole profit is spent as revenue.

As for the first 4 yards, the first one-third of the product, equal to the 12 hours' labour added by the weaver, we soon settled that. They are resolved into wages and profit; their value is the same as the value of the weaver's total profit and wages. They are therefore consumed by him and his workmen themselves. This solution for the four yards is unconditionally valid. For if profit and wages are consumed not in linen but in some other product, this can only happen because the producers of some other product consume the part of it which is consumable by them in linen and not in their own product. If of the 4 yards of linen, for example, only 1 is consumed by the linen weaver himself, and 3 yards in meat, bread, and cloth, then just the same as before, the value of the 4 yards of linen is consumed by the linen weavers themselves; only they have consumed $^{3}/_{4}$

of this value in the form of other commodities, while the producers of these other commodities have consumed in the form of linen the meat, bread and cloth consumable by them as wages and profit. <Here, as throughout this inquiry, it is of course always assumed that the commodity is sold and sold at its value.>

But now comes the real problem. The weaver's constant capital exists now in the form of 8 yards of linen (=24 hours' labour=24s.); if he wants to continue production, he must transform these 8 yards of linen into money, 24s., and with this 24s. he must buy newly-produced commodities, to be found on the market, of which his constant capital consists. To simplify the problem, let it be assumed that he does not replace his machinery within a period of years, but that every day, out of the proceeds of his product, he has to replace in kind the part of the machinery that is equal to the part of the value of the machinery worn out each day. He must replace the part of the product that is equal to the value of the constant capital it contains with the elements of this constant capital, or the material conditions of production for his labour. On the other hand, his product, the linen, does not enter any other sphere of production as a condition of production, but passes into individual consumption. He can therefore replace the part of his product which represents his constant capital only by exchanging it for revenue or for the part of the value of the product of other producers which consists of wages and profit, consequently of newly-added labour. The problem is thus posed in its correct form. The question is only: in what conditions can it be solved?

A difficulty that arose in our first presentation of it has now been partly overcome. Although in each sphere of production the labour added is equal to one-third, the constant capital—on the assumption made—to two-thirds, this one-third labour added—or the total value of the revenue (of wages and profit; as already noted earlier, no account is here taken of the part of the profit which is again transformed into capital)—is only consumable in the products of the branches of industry which work directly for individual consumption. The products of all other branches of industry can only be consumed as capital, can only enter into industrial consumption.

||291| The constant capital represented by the 8 yards (=24 hours=24s.) consists of yarn (raw material) and machinery. Let us say $^3/_4$ raw material and $^1/_4$ machinery. (Under raw material we can here also reckon all auxiliary materials such as oil,

coal, etc. But for the sake of simplicity it is better to disregard these.) The yarn would cost 18s. or 18 hours' labour=6 yards; the machinery 6s.=6 hours' labour=2 yards.

If therefore the weaver uses his 8 yards to buy yarn for 6 yards and machinery for 2 yards, with his constant capital of 8 yards he has covered not only the constant capital of the spinner and the loom manufacturer, but also the labour newly added by them. A part of what appears as the weaver's constant capital therefore represents newly-added labour on the part of the spinner and the machinery manufacturer, and consequently is for them not capital but revenue.

Of the 6 yards of linen, the spinner can himself consume one-third=2 yards (equal to the labour newly added, profit and wages). But 4 yards replace for him only flax and machinery. Say 3 yards for flax, 1 yard for machinery. He must pass on the payment for these. Of the 2 yards the machinery manufacturer can himself consume two-thirds of a yard; but $^4/_3$ only replace for him iron and wood, in a word, raw material, and the machinery used for building the machine. Say, of the $^4/_3$ yards, 1 yard for raw material and $^1/_3$ of a yard for machinery.

Of the 12 yards of linen, we have consumed up to this point: first, 4 for the weaver, second, 2 for the spinner, and third, $^2/_3$ for the machine builder; together $6^2/_3$. So $5^1/_3$ remain to be accounted for. And these $5^1/_3$ are distributed as follows:

The spinner has to replace, out of the value of 4 yards, 3 for flax, 1 for machinery.

The machinery manufacturer has to replace, out of the value of $^4/_3$ yards, 1 for iron, etc., $^1/_3$ for machinery (what he has himself used up in building the machines).

The 3 yards for flax are therefore paid by the spinner to the flax-grower. In the case of the latter, however, there is the special feature that a part of his constant capital (namely, seed, manure, etc., in short all products of the land which he returns to the land) does not enter at all into circulation, and consequently does not need to be deducted from the product that he sells; this product on the contrary expresses only added labour, and consequently consists entirely of wages and profit (except for the part which replaces machinery, artificial fertilisers, etc.). So let us assume as before that one-third of the total product is labour added; then 1 yard of the 3 would come under this category. Taking as before for the 2 other yards that one-quarter is for machinery, that would be $^2/_4$ yard. The other $^6/_4$, on the other hand, would also be for labour added, since in this part of the flax-grower's product there is no constant capital, which he has already deducted earlier. So $2^{2}/_{4}$ yards would go for the flax-grower's wages and profit. What remains is $^{2}/_{4}$ yard for replacement of machinery. <Thus of the $5^{1}/_{3}$ yards which we had to consume, $2^{2}/_{4}$ have gone ($5^{4}/_{12}-2^{6}/_{12}=2^{10}/_{12}=2^{5}/_{6}$ yards).> This last $^{2}/_{4}$ of a yard would therefore be used by the flax-grower to buy machinery.

The machinery manufacturer's account would now stand like this: of the constant capital for the loom he had laid out 1 yard for iron, etc.; $^{1}/_{3}$ of a yard for the wear and tear of the machine-building machine in producing the loom.

In addition, however, the spinner buys from the machinery manufacturer spinning machinery for 1 yard, and the flax-grower buys from him agricultural implements for $^{2}/_{4}$ of a yard. Of these $^{6}/_{4}$ yards, the machinery manufacturer has to consume $^{1}/_{3}$ for labour added, and to expend $^{2}/_{3}$ for the constant capital laid out in the spinning machine and the agricultural implements. $^{6}/_{4}$ however $=^{18}/_{12}$. So the machine builder would have $^{6}/_{12}$ of a yard ||292| again for consumption, $^{12}/_{12}$ or 1 yard to convert into constant capital. (Of the $2^{5}/_{6}$ yards not yet consumed, $^{1}/_{2}$ yard therefore has gone. $^{14}/_{6}$ yards are left, or $2^{2}/_{6}$, or $2^{1}/_{3}$ yards.)

Of this yard the machinery manufacturer would have to expend $^{3}/_{4}$ on raw material, iron and wood, etc., $^{1}/_{4}$ to pay to himself for the replacement of the machine-building machine.

So the total account would now stand like this:

Machinery manufacturer's constant capital	For the loom: 1 yard for raw material, $^{1}/_{2}$ of a yard for wear and tear of his own machinery. For spinning machine and agricultural implements: $^{3}/_{4}$ of a yard for raw material, $^{1}/_{4}$ of a yard for wear and tear of his own machinery.
	Hence equal to $1^{3}/_{4}$ yards for raw material, $^{1}/_{3}+$ $+^{1}/_{4}$ for wear and tear of his own machinery.

The $1^{3}/_{4}$ yards or $^{7}/_{4}$ yards therefore buy from the iron and wood manufacturers iron and wood to this value. $^{7}/_{4}=^{21}/_{12}$. But here a new question arises. In the case of the flax-grower, the raw material which is part of the constant capital did not enter into the product he sold, because it had already been deducted. In this case we must resolve the total product into labour added and machinery. If we even assumed that here the added labour was equal to two-thirds of the product, the machinery one-third, $^{14}/_{12}$ would be consumable. And $^{7}/_{12}$ would remain as constant capital for machinery. This $^{7}/_{12}$ would come back to the machinery manufacturer.

What was left of the 12 yards would then amount to $^{1}/_{3}+^{1}/_{4}$ yard, which the machinery manufacturer would have to pay to himself for the wear and tear of his own machinery, and $^{7}/_{12}$ of a yard, which the iron and wood manufacturers return to him for machinery. Hence $^{1}/_{3}+^{1}/_{4}=^{4}/_{12}+^{3}/_{12}=^{7}/_{12}$. In addition, the $^{7}/_{12}$ returned by the iron and wood manufacturers. (Together $^{14}/_{12}=1^{2}/_{12}=1^{1}/_{6}$.)

The iron and wood manufacturers' machinery and instruments of labour must be bought from the machinery manufacturer, just as those of the weaver, the spinner and the flax-grower. Thus of the $^{7}/_{12}$ of a yard, let one-third, equal to $^{2}/_{12}$, be labour added. This $^{2}/_{12}$ of a yard can therefore also be consumed. The remaining $^{5}/_{12}$ (actually $^{4}/_{12}$ and $\frac{^{2}/_{3}}{12}$, but there's no need to be so exact) represents the constant capital contained in the woodcutter's axe and the iron manufacturer's machinery, $^{3}/_{4}$ pig-iron, wood, etc., and $^{1}/_{4}$ machinery used up. (Of the $^{14}/_{12}$ yards $^{12}/_{12}$ is left, or 1 yard=3 hours' labour=3s.) Therefore of the 1 yard, $^{1}/_{4}$ of a yard for replacement of the machine-building machine and $^{3}/_{4}$ of a yard for wood, iron, etc.

Hence for the wear and tear of the machine-building machine $^{7}/_{12}$ of a yard$+^{1}/_{4}$ of a yard$=^{7}/_{12}+^{3}/_{12}=^{10}/_{12}$ of a yard. On the other hand it would now be quite pointless again to resolve the $^{3}/_{4}$ of a yard for wood and iron into their component parts and to return a part of it once more to the machinery manufacturer, who would return a part of it again to the iron ||293| and wood manufacturers. Something would always be left over and a progression to infinity.

[(c) Exchange of Capital for Capital between the Producers of Means of Production. Annual Product of Labour and the Product of Labour Newly Added Annually]

Let us then take the problem as it now stands.

$^{10}/_{12}$ or $^{5}/_{6}$ of a yard in value has to be replaced by the machinery manufacturer himself in the worn-out machine. $^{3}/_{4}$ or $^{9}/_{12}$ of a yard represents an equal amount of value in wood and iron. The machinery manufacturer has given it to the iron and wood manufacturers, in order to replace his raw material. We have in hand the residuum of $^{19}/_{12}$ or $1^{7}/_{12}$ yards.

The balance of $^{5}/_{6}$ of a yard which the machinery manufacturer keeps for making good his wear and tear$=^{15}/_{6}$ shillings$=^{15}/_{6}$ hours' labour, that is, $2^{3}/_{6}$, or $2^{1}/_{2}$s., or $2^{1}/_{2}$ hours' labour. The machinery manufacturer cannot accept any linen for this value; he would himself have to sell it again, in order with the 2s. 6d. to make good the wear and tear of his machinery, in a word, to make new machine-building machines. But to whom is he to sell it? To producers of other products (other than iron and wood)? But these producers have consumed in linen all that they were able to consume in this form. Only the 4 yards which constitute the weaver's wages and profit are exchangeable for other products (apart from those contained in the constant capital or the labour of which this capital consists). And we have already accounted for these 4 yards. Or is he to pay workers with it? But we have already deducted from his products all that labour has added to them, and we have taken it as all consumed in linen.

To put the matter in another way:

The weaver has to replace for **machinery**	2 yards	= 6s.	= 6 hours' labour
The spinner	1 „	= 3 „	= 3 „ „
The flax-grower	$^{2}/_{4}$ „	= $1^{1}/_{2}$ „	= $1^{1}/_{2}$ „ „
The iron and wood producers	$^{7}/_{12}$ „	= $1^{3}/_{4}$ „	= $1^{3}/_{4}$ „ „
Total yards expended on machinery or the part of the value of the linen which consists of machinery	**$4^{1}/_{12}$ yards**	**$=12^{1}/_{4}$s.**	**$=12^{1}/_{4}$hours' labour**

To simplify the calculation, say 4 yards$=$12s.$=$12 hours labour. Of this, for labour (profit and wages) one-third$=^{4}/_{3}$ yards$=1^{1}/_{3}$ yards.

$2^{2}/_{3}$ remain for constant capital. Of this, $^{3}/_{4}$ for raw material, $^{1}/_{4}$ for wear and tear of machinery. $2^{2}/_{3}=^{8}/_{3}=^{32}/_{12}$. A quarter of this$=^{8}/_{12}$.

This $^{8}/_{12}$ of a yard for wear and tear of machinery is all that the machinery manufacturer is still burdened with. For he pays $^{24}/_{12}$ or 2 yards to the iron and wood manufacturers for raw material.

||294| It is wrong, then, to charge the iron and wood manufacturers again for machinery, since all that they have to re-

place in machinery, namely $^{7}/_{12}$ of a yard, has already been brought into the machinery manufacturer's account. In the latter's item, the whole of the machinery that they need for the production of iron and wood has already been included, and it therefore cannot come a second time into the reckoning. The last two yards for iron and wood (the residuum of $2^{8}/_{12}$) consist therefore entirely of labour, since there is no raw material used, and can therefore be consumed in linen.

Thus the whole residuum is $^{8}/_{12}$ of a yard or $^{2}/_{3}$ of a yard for wear and tear of the machinery used by the machinery manufacturer.

The whole problem was partly solved by the fact that the part of the farmer's *constant capital*, which does not itself consist of labour newly added or in machinery, does not circulate at all, but is already deducted, replaces itself in his own production, and therefore also—apart from the machinery—his whole *circulating* product consists of wages and profit and consequently can be consumed in linen. This was one part of the solution.

The other part was that what appears in one sphere of production as constant capital, in other spheres of production appears as new labour added during the same year. What in the weaver's hand appears as constant capital consists in large part of the revenue of the spinner, machinery manufacturer, flax-grower and iron and wood producers (also of the collier, etc.; but for the sake of simplification this is not brought into it). (This is so clear that, for example, when the same manufacturer both spins and weaves, his constant capital seems to be smaller than that of the weaver and the labour added by him greater, that is to say, the part of his product which consists of labour added, revenue, profit and wages. Thus in the case of the weaver revenue was equal to 4 yards=12s.; constant capital 8 yards=24s. If he both spins and weaves, his revenue is equal to 6 yards. His constant capital also equals 6 yards; that is, 2 yards for loom, 3 yards flax, and 1 yard spinning machinery.)

Thirdly, however, the solution so far found is that all producers who supply only raw material or means of production for the product which finally enters into individual consumption, cannot consume their revenue—profit and wages, the [labour] newly added—in their own product, but they can consume the part of the value of this product which represents revenue only in the consumable product, or, what is the same thing, [they have to exchange it] for a consumable product of other producers containing the same amount of value Their newly-added labour enters into the final product as a component part of the value, but is only consumed in the form of the final product, while as a use-value it is contained in the final product as raw material or machinery used up.

Hence the part of the problem which now remains to be solved is reduced to this: What happens to the $^2/_3$ of a yard for the wear and tear [of the machine-building machine]—not of the machines used in production, for these represent new labour, that is, new labour which gives the raw material (which has itself no raw material that costs anything) the form of new machinery but—[what happens] to the depreciation of the machinery manufacturer's machine-building machine? Or to put it another way: Under what conditions can the machinery manufacturer consume the $^2/_3$ of a yard=2s.=2 hours' labour in linen, and at the same time replace his machinery? That is the real question. This takes place in fact. It necessarily takes place. Hence the problem: how is this phenomenon to be explained?

||295| Here we leave entirely out of account the part of the profit which is transformed into new capital (both circulating and fixed, variable and constant capital). It has nothing to do with our problem, for here new variable capital as well as the new constant capital are created and replaced by *new* labour (a part of the surplus-labour).

So putting this case on one side, the total of labour newly added, in a year for example, is equal to the total of profit and wages, i. e., equal to the total of the annual *revenue* spent on products which enter into individual consumption, such as food, clothing, heating, dwelling-house, furniture, etc.

The total of these products going into consumption is equal in value to the total labour added annually (to the total value of the revenue). This quantity of labour must be equal to the total labour contained in these products, both the added and the pre-existing labour. In these products not only the labour newly added, but also the constant capital they contain, must be paid for. Their value is therefore equal to the total of profit and wages. If we take linen as the example, then the linen represents for us the aggregate of the products entering into individual consumption annually. This linen must not only be equal to the value of all its elements of value, but its whole use-value must be consumable by the various producers who take their share of it. Its whole value must be resolvable into profit and wages, that is, labour newly added each year, although it consists of labour added and constant capital.

This is partly explained, as we have said, by:

First. A part of the constant capital required for the production of the linen does not enter into it, either as use-value or as exchange-value. This is the part of the flax which consists of seed, etc.; the part of the constant capital of the agricultural product which does not enter into circulation, but is directly or indirectly returned to production, to the land. This part replaces itself, so it does not need to be repaid out of the linen. < A peasant may sell his whole harvest, say 120 quarters. But then he must buy from another peasant for example 12 quarters of seed, and the latter has then to use as seed, out of his 120 quarters, 24 quarters instead of 12 quarters, $^{1}/_{5}$ instead of $^{1}/_{10}$ of his product. In both cases 24 quarters of the 240 quarters are given back to the land as seed. Of course, this makes a difference in the circulation. In the first case, where each deducts one-tenth, 216 quarters enter circulation. In the second case 120 quarters of the first and 108 quarters of the second enter circulation, that is, 228 quarters. As in the previous case, 216 quarters reach the actual consumers. Here therefore we have an example of the fact that the total of values as between dealers and dealers is greater than the total of values as between dealers and consumers.[48] > (Moreover there is the same difference in all cases in which a part of the profit is transformed into new capital; moreover, transactions between dealers and dealers extend over many years, etc.)

This part [of the raw material required] for the production of the linen, that is, the consumable products, therefore does not have to replace a considerable part of the constant capital required for its production.

Secondly. A large part of the constant capital required for the linen, that is, for the annual consumable product, appears at one level as constant capital, at another level as labour newly added, and consequently in fact consists of profit and wages, revenue, for one, while the same sum of value appears as capital for another. Thus a part of [the weaver's] constant capital is reducible to the labour of the spinner, etc.

||296| *Thirdly.* In all the intermediate processes that are necessary to produce the consumable product, a large part of the products, apart from the raw material and certain auxiliary

materials, never passes into the use-value, but only enters into the consumable product as a component part of its value—such as machinery, coal, oil, tallow, leather belting, etc. In each of these processes which in fact always only produce the constant capital for the next stage—in so far as, through the division of social labour, they take the form of separate branches of business—the product of each stage is divided into one part representing the newly-added labour (consisting of profit and wages, and, with the proviso[49] made above, forms revenue), and another part which represents the value of the constant capital consumed. It is therefore clear that in each of these spheres of production only that part of the product can be consumed by its own producers which represents wages and profit—only that part which remains over after deducting the quantity of products equal to the value of the constant capital they contain. But none of these producers consumes any part whatever of the products of the previous stage, or of the products, of all the stages, which in fact produce nothing but constant capital for a further stage.

Thus although the final product—the linen, which represents all consumable products—consists of newly-added labour and constant capital, and so the final producers of this consumable product can only consume that part of it which consists of the labour last added, of their total wages and profits, their revenue—nevertheless all the producers of constant capital consume or realise their newly-added labour only in the consumable product. Thus although this consists of labour added and constant capital, its purchase price consists—in addition to that part of the product which is equal to the quantity of labour last added—of the total quantity of all the labour added in the production of its constant capital. They realise all added labour in the consumable product instead of in their own product—so that in this respect it is the same as if the consumable product consisted entirely of wages and profit, of labour added.

From the consumable product, the linen (the exchange of consumable products for each other and the previous transformation of the commodities into money makes no difference), the producers from whose sphere of production it emerges as a finished product themselves deduct the part of the product equal to their revenue—equal to the labour last added by them, equal to the total wages and profit. With the other part of the consumable product they pay the component part of the value due to the producers who have directly supplied them with their constant capital. All of this part of their consumable product therefore covers the value of the revenue and constant capital of the producers of this constant capital in its nearest stage. The latter however keep only the part of the consumable product whose value is equal to their revenue. With the other part they pay in turn the producers of their constant capital, equal to revenue plus constant capital. *The account, however, can only be settled* if it is only revenue, newly-added labour, not constant capital, that has to be replaced by the last part of the linen, the consumable product. For on the assumption we have made the linen enters only into consumption and does not in turn form the constant capital of another phase of production.

This has already been shown to be the case for a part of the product of agriculture.

In general, it is only products that enter as raw materials into the final product of which it can be said that they are consumed as products. Other products enter into the consumable product only as component parts of value. The consumable product is bought by revenue, that is, by wages and profit. Its total value must therefore be resolvable into wages and profit, that is, into the labour added in all its stages. The question now arises: in addition to the part of the product of agriculture which is returned to ||297| production by its producers themselves—seed, cattle, manure, etc.—is there yet another part of the constant capital which does not enter into the consumable product as a component part of value, but is replaced in kind in the process of production itself?

Fixed capital in all its forms can of course only be considered here to the extent that its value enters into production and is consumed.

Apart from agriculture (including cattle-raising and fish farming, and forestry, in which reproduction is artificially organised)—and so apart from all raw materials for clothing, actual means of sustenance and a large part of the products entering into fixed capital in industry, such as sails, rope, belting, etc.—in mining there is the partial replacement of constant capital in kind out of the product, so that the part which enters into circulation does not have to replace this part of the constant capital. For example, in coal production some of the coal is used to work the steam-engine which pumps out water or raises coal.

The value of the annual product is therefore partly equal to the part of the labour pre-existing in coal and consumed in producing the coal, and partly equal to the quantity of labour added (leaving out of account wear and tear of machinery, etc.). Of the total product, however, the part of the constant capital which consists in coal itself is directly deducted and returned to production. No one has to replace this part for the producer, because he replaces it himself. If the productivity of labour has neither fallen nor risen, then too the part of the value which this part of the product represents remains unchanged, and is equal to a definite aliquot part of the quantity of labour existing in the product—partly pre-existing labour, partly labour added during the year. In the other mining industries too there is a partial replacement of the constant capital in kind.

Waste products—as for example cotton waste and so on—are fed to the fields as fertiliser or become raw material for other branches of industry, as for example linen rags [in the production] of paper. In such cases, as in the former case, part of an industry's constant capital may be directly exchanged for the constant capital of another industry. For example, cotton for cotton waste used as fertiliser.

In general, however, there is a cardinal difference between the production of machines and primary production (of raw materials: iron, wood, coal) and the other phases of production: in the latter, there is no interaction between them. Linen cannot be a part of the spinner's constant capital, nor can yarn (as such) be part of the constant capital of the flax-grower or machinery manufacturer. But the raw material of machinery—apart from such agricultural products as leather belting, rope, etc.—is wood, iron and coal, while on the other hand machinery in its turn enters as a means of production into the constant capital of the producers of wood, iron, coal, etc. In fact, therefore, both replace each other a part of their constant capital in kind. Here there is exchange of constant capital for constant capital.

Here it is not merely a question of accounting. The producer of iron debits the machinery manufacturer for the wear and tear of the machinery used up in producing the iron and the machinery manufacturer debits [the producer of iron] for the wear and tear of his machinery in constructing the machines. Let the producers of iron and coal be the same person. First, he himself replaces the coal, as we have seen. Secondly, the value of his total product of iron and coal is equal to the value of the labour added plus the labour pre-existing in the worn-out machinery. After deducting from this total product the quantity of iron that replaces the value of the machinery, the quantity of iron which is left represents the labour added. The latter part forms the raw material of manufacturers of machinery, instruments, etc. The machinery manufacturer pays the iron manufacturer for this latter part in linen. In exchange for the first part, he supplies him with machinery to replace the old.

On the other hand, the part of the machinery manufacturer's constant capital which represents the wear and tear of his machine-building machines, instruments, etc.—and therefore consists neither of raw material (leaving out of account here the machinery used [in coal and iron production] ||298| and the part of the coal which replaces itself) nor of labour added, and so neither of wages or profit—this wear and tear is in fact made good by the machinery manufacturer appropriating for himself one or two of his own machines to serve as machine-building machines. This part of his product merely comes to an excess consumption of raw material. For it does not represent labour newly added, since in the total product of the labour so many machines are equal to the value of the added, so many machines are equal to the value of the raw material, and so many machines are equal to the part of the value that was contained in machine-building machines. It is true that this last part does contain labour added. But in value this is equal to zero, since the labour contained in the raw material and in the machinery used up is not reckoned in the group of machines that represents labour added; and the part which replaces the new labour and machinery is not reckoned in the second group, which replaces the raw material; and consequently in the third part—considered as value—neither labour added nor raw material is contained, but this group of machines represents only the wear and tear of the machinery.

The machinery of the machinery manufacturer himself is not sold. It is replaced in kind, deducted from the total product. Consequently the machines which he sells represent only raw material (which consists only of labour, if he has already been charged for the wear and tear of the raw material producer's machinery) and labour added, and therefore are resolvable into linen for himself and for the raw material producer. As for what specially concerns the relations between the machinery manufacturer and the producer of raw materials, the latter has deducted, in respect of the part of his machinery that has been wasted, a quantity of iron equal to its value. He exchanges this with the machinery manufacturer, so that each of them pays the other in kind, and this process has nothing to do with the division of revenue between them.

So much for this question, to which we shall return in connection with the circulation of capital.[50]

In reality, the constant capital is replaced by being constantly produced anew and in part by reproducing itself. The part of the constant capital which enters into the consumable product is however paid for out of the living labour which enters into the non-consumable products. Because the latter labour is not paid for in its own products, it can resolve the whole consumable product into income. A part of the constant capital, considered as part of the annual product, is only seemingly constant capital. Another part, although it enters into the total product, does not enter into the consumable product either as a component part of its value or as a use-value, but is replaced in kind, remaining always incorporated in production.

Here we have considered how the total consumable product is divided up and resolved into all the component parts of value and conditions of production that have entered into it.

But always there are, simultaneously and side by side, the consumable product (which, in so far as it consists of wages, is equal to the variable part of capital), the production of the consumable product, and the production of all parts of the constant capital required for its production, whether it enters into it or not. In the same way, each capital is always simultaneously divided into constant and variable capital, and although the constant capital, like the variable, is continuously replaced by new products, it is always in existence in the same form, so long as production of the same kind goes on.

||299| The relation between the machinery manufacturer and the primary producers—of iron, wood, etc.—is that they in fact exchange with each other a part of their constant capital (which has nothing in common with the transformation of a part of the constant capital of one into revenue for the other[51]), because their products—although one is a previous stage for the other—on both sides enter as means of production into the constant capital of the other. In return for the machinery which the producer of iron, wood, etc., needs, he gives the machine builder iron, wood, etc., to the value of the machine to be replaced. This part of the machine builder's constant capital is for him just the same as seed is for the peasant. It is part of his annual product

which he replaces in kind for himself and which is not resolved into revenue for him. On the other hand, what is thus replaced for the machine builder in the form of raw material is not only the raw material contained in the iron producer's machine, but also the part of the value of this machine which consists of labour added and wear and tear of his own machinery. Thus it replaces for him not only the wear and tear of his own machinery, but can be regarded as accounting for (replacing) a part of the wear and tear contained in the other machines.

It is true that this [machine sold] to the producer of iron also contains component parts of value equal to the raw material and the labour added. But on the other hand there is correspondingly less wear and tear to be accounted for in the other machines. This part of their constant capital—that is, of the product of their annual labour which replaces only the part of the value of the constant capital representing wear and tear—therefore does not enter into the machines which the machine builder sells to other industrialists. But as regards the wear and tear in these other machines, it is in fact replaced for the machine builder by the above-mentioned two-thirds of a yard of linen, the equivalent of 2 hours' labour. With that, he buys pig-iron, wood, etc., to the same value, and replaces the wear and tear in another form of his constant capital—[in the form] of iron. Thus a part of his raw material replaces for him the value of his wear and tear, in addition to the value of the raw material. This raw material, however, as far as the producer of iron, etc., is concerned, consists only of the labour-time added, as the machinery of these producers of raw materials (iron, wood, coal, etc.) has already been accounted for.

Thus all the elements of the linen are resolved into a sum of quantities of labour equal to the amount of labour newly added, but not equal to the amount of the total labour contained in the constant capital and perpetuated by reproduction.

That the quantity of labour consisting partly of living labour, partly of pre-existing labour, which forms the total of commodities which enter each year into individual consumption, and thus are consumed as revenue, cannot be greater than the labour added annually, is for that matter a tautology. For the revenue is equal to the total of profit and wages, which is equal to the total labour newly added, and is equal to the total of the commodities which contain an equal quantity of labour.

The case of iron producer and machine builder is onlv one

example. Between different spheres of production, where the products of each enter into the other as means of production, an exchange in kind takes place too (even though concealed by a series of money transactions) between the constant capital of the one and that of the other. In so far as this is the case, the consumers of the final product which enters into consumption have not got to replace this constant capital, since it has already been replaced. |299||

||304| <For example: in the manufacture of locomotives, every day the waste amounts to whole wagon-loads of iron filings. These are collected and resold (or charged in account) to the same iron manufacturer who supplied the locomotive manufacturer with his principal raw material. The iron manufacturer again gives them solid form, adding new labour to them. However in the form in which he sends them back to the locomotive manufacturer, these filings represent the part of the value of the product which replaces raw material. In this way not the same filings but constantly a certain quantity of filings, move hither and thither between the two factories. This part forms in turn the raw material for each of the two branches of industry and, considered as value, only wanders from one shop to the other. Consequently it does not enter into the final product, but is a replacement in kind of the constant capital.

In fact, every machine supplied by the machinery manufacturer, from the standpoint of value, is divided into raw material, labour added, and wear and tear of machinery. But the whole total that enters into the production of other spheres can only be equal in value to the total value of the machinery minus the part of the constant capital which is continually passing backwards and forwards between the machinery manufacturer and the iron manufacturer.

One quarter of wheat sold by a peasant is as dear as another, and a quarter of wheat that is sold is no cheaper than one that is returned to the land in the form of seed. Still, if the product equals 6 quarters, and the quarter equals £3—each quarter containing component parts of value for labour added, raw material and machinery—and if he has to use 1 quarter as seeds, he would only sell to consumers 5 quarters, equal to £15. They would therefore not pay for the part of the value contained in the 1 quarter of seed. And this is the point: how can the value of the product sold be equal to all the elements of value contained in it—labour added and constant capital—and how in spite of this does the consumer buy the product and yet not pay for the constant capital? >[52] |304||

||300| <In addition to the foregoing:

The following quotation shows how little the insipid Say even understood what the question was:

"In order fully to understand this subject of revenues, it is necessary to take into account that the entire value of a product is divided into revenues for various persons; for the *total* value of each product is composed of the profits of the landowners, of the capitalists and of the craftsmen who have contributed to bring it into existence. This is why the revenue of society is equal to the *gross value* which has been produced, and not, as the sect of Economists[53] imagines, to the *net product* of the land.... If the only revenues in a nation were the excess of the values produced over the values consumed, this would lead to a truly absurd result: that a nation which had consumed in the year values as great as it had produced would have no [...] revenue." ([Jean-Baptiste Say, *Traité d'économie politique...*, troisième édition], t. II, [Paris, 1817], pp. 63-64.)

In fact, in the year that was past it would have had a revenue, but it would have none the next year. It is not true that *the annual product of labour*, of which *the product of the annual labour* forms only one part, consists of revenue. On the other hand, it is correct that this is the case with the part of the product which each year enters into individual consumption. The revenue, which consists only of added labour, is able to pay for this product, which consists partly of added and partly of pre-existing labour; that is to say, the labour added in these products can pay not only for itself but also for the pre-existing labour, because another part of the product—which also consists of labour added and pre-existing labour—replaces only pre-existing labour, only constant capital.>

[11. Additional Points: Smith's Confusion on the Question of the Measure of Value. General Character of the Contradictions in Smith]

<To the points in Adam Smith's theory just discussed must be added that in his vacillations on the determination of value —in addition to the apparent contradiction in regard to wages[54] —there is also confusion [of idea]: in so far as he confuses the measure of value as the immanent measure which at the same time forms the substance of value, with the measure of value in the sense that money is called a measure of value. With regard to the latter the attempt is then made to square the circle —to find a commodity whose value does not change to serve

as a constant measure for others. On the question of the relation of the measure of value as money to the determination of value by labour-time, see the first part of my work.[55] This confusion is also to be found in Ricardo in certain passages.> |300||

* * *

||299| Adam Smith's contradictions are of significance because they contain problems which it is true he does not solve, but which he reveals by contradicting himself. His correct instinct in this connection is best shown by the fact that his successors take opposing stands based on one aspect of his teaching or the other.[56]

[CHAPTER IV]

THEORIES OF PRODUCTIVE AND UNPRODUCTIVE LABOUR

We come now to the last controversial point in Adam Smith's writings which we have to consider: *the distinction between productive and unproductive labour.*

||300| In Adam Smith's definition of what he calls *productive labour* as distinguished from *unproductive labour*, we find the same two-sided approach as we have found on every question up to now. Jumbled together in his presentation we find two definitions of what he calls productive labour, and to begin with we will examine the first, the correct definition.

[1. Productive Labour from the Standpoint of Capitalist Production: Labour Which Produces Surplus-Value]

Productive labour, in its meaning for capitalist production, is wage-labour which, exchanged against the variable part of capital (the part of the capital that is spent on wages), reproduces not only this part of the capital (or the value of its own labour-power), but in addition produces surplus-value for the capitalist. It is only thereby that commodity or money is transformed into capital, is produced as capital. Only that wage-labour is productive which produces capital. (This is the same as saying that it reproduces on an enlarged scale the sum of value expended on it, or that it gives in return more labour than it receives in the form of wages. Consequently, only that labour-power is productive which produces a value greater than its own.)

The mere existence of a class of capitalists, and therefore of capital, depends on the productivity of labour: not however on its absolute, but on its relative productivity. For example: if a day's labour only sufficed to keep the worker alive, that is, to reproduce his labour-power, ||301| speaking in an absolute sense his labour would be productive because it would be reproductive; that is to say, because it constantly replaced the values (equal to the value of its own labour-power) which it consumed. But in the capitalist sense it would not be productive because it produced no surplus-value. (It produced in fact no new value, but only replaced the old; it would have consumed it—the value—in one form, in order to reproduce it in the other. And in this sense it has been said that a worker is productive whose production is equal to his own consumption, and that a worker is unproductive who consumes more than he reproduces.)

Productivity in the capitalist sense is based on relative productivity—that the worker not only replaces an old value, but creats a new one; that he materialises more labour-time in his product than is materialised in the product that keeps him in existence as a worker. It is this kind of productive wage-labour that is the basis for the existence of capital.

<Assuming, however, that no capital exists, but that the worker appropriates his surplus-labour himself—the excess of values that he has created over the values that he consumes. Then one could say only of this labour that it is truly productive, that is, that it creates new values.>

[2. Views of the Physiocrats and Mercantilists on Productive Labour]

This conception of productive labour follows naturally from Adam Smith's view of the origin of surplus-value, that is, of the nature of capital. In so far as he holds to this conception he is following a course that was taken by the Physiocrats and even by the Mercantilists; he only frees it from misconceptions, and in this way brings out its inner kernel. Though wrong in thinking that only agricultural labour is productive, the Physiocrats put forward the correct view that from the capitalist standpoint only that labour is productive which creates a surplus-value; and in fact a surplus-value not for itself, but for the owner of the conditions of production; labour which produces a net product not for itself, but for the landowner. For the surplus-value or surplus labour-time is materialised in a surplus-produce or net product. (But here again they have a wrong conception of this; in as much as there is, for example, more wheat than labourers and farmers eat; but also in the case of cloth there is more than what the cloth manufacturers—workman and master

—need for their own clothing.) Surplus-value itself is wrongly conceived, because they have a wrong idea of value and reduce it to the use-value of labour, not to labour-time, social, homogeneous labour. Nevertheless, there remains the correct definition that only the wage-labour which creates more value than it costs is productive. Adam Smith frees this definition from the wrong conception with which the Physiocrats linked it.

If we go back from the Physiocrats to the Mercantilists, there too we find one aspect of their theory which contains the same view of productive labour, even though they were not conscious of it. The basis of their theory was the idea that labour is only productive in those branches of production whose products, when sent abroad, bring back more money than they have cost (or than had to be exported in exchange for them); which therefore enabled a country to participate to a greater degree in the products of newly-opened gold and silver mines. They saw that in these countries there was a rapid growth of wealth and of the middle class. What in fact was the source of this influence exerted by gold? Wages did not rise in proportion to the prices of commodities; that is, wages fell, and because of this relative surplus-labour increased and the rate of profit rose—not because the labourer had become more productive, but because the absolute wage (that is to say, the quantity of means of existence which the labourer received) was forced down—in a word, because the position of the workers grew worse. In these countries, therefore, labour was in fact more productive for those who employed it. This fact was linked with the influx of the precious metals; and it was this, though they were only dimly aware of it, which led the Mercantilists to declare that labour employed in such branches of production was alone productive.

||302| "The remarkable increase [of population] which has taken place [...] in almost every European State, during the last fifty or sixty years, has perhaps proceeded chiefly from the increased productiveness of the American mines. An increased abundance of the precious metals" (of course as a result of the fall in their real value) "raises the price of commodities in a greater proportion than the price of labour; it depresses the condition of the labourer, and at the same time increases the gains of his employer, who is thus induced to enlarge his circulating capital to the utmost of his ability, to hire as many hands as he has the means to pay;—and it has been seen that this is precisely the state of things most favourable to the increase of people.... Mr. Malthus observes, that 'the discovery of the mines of America, during the time that it raised the price of corn between three and four times, did not nearly so much as double the price of labour'. ... The price

of commodities intended for home consumption (of corn for instance) does not immediately rise in consequence of an influx of money; but as the rate of profit in agricultural employments is thus depressed below the rate of profit in manufactures, capital will gradually be withdrawn from the former to the latter: thus all capital comes to yield higher profits than formerly, and a rise of profits is always equivalent to a fall of wages" (John Barton, *Observations on the Circumstances which Influence the Condition of the Labouring Classes of Society*, London, 1817, pp. 29 sqq.).*

So, firstly, according to Barton, in the second half of the eighteenth century there was a repetition of the same phenomenon as that which, from the last third of the sixteenth century and in the seventeenth, has given the impulse to the Mercantile system. Secondly, as only exported goods were measured in gold and silver on the basis of its reduced value, while those for home consumption continued to be measured in gold and silver according to its former value (until competition among the capitalists put an end to this measuring by two different standards), labour in the former branches of production appeared to be directly productive, that is, creating surplus-value, through the depression of wages below their former level.

[3. The Duality in Smith's Conception of Productive Labour. His First Explanation: the View of Productive Labour as Labour Exchanged for Capital]

The second, wrong conception of productive labour which Smith develops is so interwoven with the correct one that the two follow each other in rapid succession in the same passage. To illustrate the first conception it is therefore necessary to tear the quotations into separate parts.

"There is one sort of labour which adds to the value of the subject upon which it is bestowed: there is another which has no such effect. The former, as *it produces a value*, may be called *productive*; the latter, *unproductive labour*. Thus the labour of a manufacturer *adds*, generally, to the value of the materials which he works upon, *that of his own maintenance, and of his master's profit*. The labour of a menial servant, on the contrary, adds to the value of nothing. Though the manufacturer has his wages *advanced* to him by his master, he, *in reality, costs him no expense*, the value of those wages being generally restored, *together with a profit*, in the improved value of the subject upon which his labour is bestowed. But the maintenance of a menial servant never is restored. A man *grows rich* by employing a multitude of manufacturers: he grows poor, by maintaining a multitude of menial

* In translating this passage Marx has abridged it somewhat.—*Ed.*

servants" ([Adam Smith, *An Inquiry into the Nature and Causes of the Wealth of Nations,*] b. II, ch. III, Vol. II, ed. McCulloch, pp. 93 and 94).

In this passage—and in its continuation to be quoted later, the contradictory definitions jostle each other even more closely—what is in the main and pre-eminently understood by productive labour is labour which produces a surplus-value—"his master's profit"—in addition to the reproduction of the value of "his" (the labourer's) "own maintenance". Also, the industrialist could not grow *rich* "by employing a multitude of manufacturers" (working men), unless the latter, in addition to the value which their own maintenance costs, added also a surplus-value.

Secondly, however, in this passage Adam Smith treats as productive labour, labour which in general "produces a value". ||303| Leaving this latter statement out of account for the moment, however, we will first cite other passages in which the first conception is partly repeated, partly formulated more sharply, but particularly also further developed.

> "If the quantity of food and clothing, which were ... consumed by unproductive, had been distributed among productive hands, they would have reproduced, *together with a profit*, the full value of their consumption" (l.c., p. 109; b. II, ch. III).

Here the productive labourer is quite explicitly one who not only produces for the capitalist the full value of the means of subsistence contained in his wages, but reproduces it for him "with a profit".

Only labour which produces capital is productive labour. Commodities or money become capital, however, through being exchanged directly for labour-power, and exchanged only in order to be replaced by more labour than they themselves contain. For the use-value of labour-power to the capitalist as a capitalist does not consist in its *actual* use-value, in the usefulness of this particular concrete labour—that it is spinning labour, weaving labour, and so on. He is as little concerned with this as with the use-value of the product of this labour as such, since for the capitalist the product is a commodity (even before its first metamorphosis), not an article of consumption. What interests him in the commodity is that it has more exchange-value than he paid for it; and therefore the use-value of the labour is, for him, that he gets back a greater quantity of labour-time than he has paid out in the form of wages. Included among these productive workers, of course, are all those who contribute in one way or another to the production of the commodity, from the actual operative to the manager or engineer (as distinct from the capitalist). And so even the latest English official report on the factories "*explicitly*" includes in the category of employed wage-labourers all persons employed in the factories and in the offices attached to them, with the exception of the manufacturers themselves (see the wording of the report before the concluding part of this rubbish).

Productive labour is here defined from the standpoint of capitalist production, and Adam Smith here got to the very heart of the matter, hit the nail on the head. This is one of his greatest scientific merits (as Malthus rightly observed, this critical differentiation between productive and unproductive labour remains the basis of all bourgeois political economy) that he defines productive labour as labour *which is directly exchanged with capital*; that is, he defines it by the exchange through which the conditions of production of labour, and value in general, whether money or commodity, are first transformed into capital (and labour into wage-labour in its scientific meaning).

This also establishes absolutely what *unproductive labour* is. It is labour which is not exchanged with capital, but *directly* with revenue, that is, with wages or profit (including of course the various categories of those who share as co-partners in the capitalist's profit, such as interest and rent). Where all labour in part still pays itself (like for example the agricultural labour of the serfs) and in part is directly exchanged for revenue (like the manufacturing labour in the cities of Asia), no capital and no wage-labour exists in the sense of bourgeois political economy. These definitions are therefore not derived from the material characteristics of labour (neither from the nature of its product nor from the particular character of the labour as concrete labour), but from the definite social form, the social relations of production, within which the labour is realised. An actor, for example, or even a clown, according to this definition, is a productive labourer if he works in the service of a capitalist (an entrepreneur) to whom he returns more labour than he receives from him in the form of wages; while a jobbing tailor who comes to the capitalist's house and patches his trousers for him, producing a mere use-value for him, is an unproductive labourer. The former's labour is exchanged with capital, the latter's with revenue. The former's labour produces a surplus-value; in the latter's, revenue is consumed.

Productive and unproductive labour is here throughout conceived from *the standpoint of the possessor of money, from the standpoint of the capitalist*, not from that of the *workman*; hence the nonsense written by Ganilh, etc., who have so little understanding of the matter that they raise the question whether the labour or service or function of the prostitute, flunkey, etc., brings in returns. |303||

||304| A writer is a productive labourer not in so far as he produces ideas, but in so far as he enriches the publisher who publishes his works, or if he is a wage-labourer for a capitalist.

The use-value of the commodity in which the labour of a productive worker is embodied may be of the most futile kind. The material characteristics are in no way linked with its nature which on the contrary is only the expression of a definite social relation of production. It is a definition of labour which is derived not from its content or its result, but from its particular social form.

On the other hand, on the assumption that capital has conquered the whole of production—and that therefore a *commodity* (as distinct from a mere use-value) is no longer produced by any labourer who is himself the owner of the conditions of production for producing this commodity—that therefore only the capitalist is the producer of *commodities* (the sole commodity excepted being labour-power)—then revenue must be exchanged either against commodities which capital alone produces and sells, or against labour, which just like those commodities is bought in order to be consumed; that is, only for the sake of its particular material characteristics, its use-value—for the sake of the *services* which, through its particular material characteristics, it renders to its buyer and consumer. For the producer of these services the services rendered are commodities. They have a definite use-value (imaginary or real) and a definite exchange-value. For the buyer, however, these services are mere use-values, objects in which ||305| he consumes his revenue. These unproductive labourers do not receive their share of revenue (of wages and profits), their co-partnership in the commodities produced by productive labour, gratis: they must buy their share in them; but they have nothing to do with their production.

It is, however, in any case clear: the greater the part of the revenue (wages and profit) that is spent on commodities produced by capital, the less the part that can be spent on the services of unproductive labourers, and vice versa.

The determinate material form of the labour, and therefore of its product, in itself has nothing to do with this distinction between productive and unproductive labour. For example, the cooks and waiters in a public hotel are productive labourers, in so far as their labour is transformed into capital for the proprietor of the hotel. These same persons are unproductive labourers as menial servants, inasmuch as I do not make capital out of their services, but spend revenue on them. In fact, however, these same persons are also for me, the consumer, unproductive labourers in the hotel.

"That part of the annual produce of the land and labour of *any country which replaces a capital*, never is *immediately* employed to maintain any but productive hands. It *pays the wages of productive labour* only. That which is *immediately* destined for constituting a revenue either as profit or as rent, may maintain indifferently either productive or unproductive hands. Whatever part of his stock a man employs as a capital, he always expects it to be replaced to him with a profit. He employs it, therefore, in maintaining *productive hands* only; and after having served in the function of a capital to him, it constitutes a revenue to them. Whenever he employs any part of it *in maintaining unproductive hands* of any kind, that part is, from that moment, withdrawn from his capital, and placed in his stock reserved for immediate consumption" (l.c., p. 98).

To the extent that capital conquers the whole of production, and therefore the home and petty form of industry—in short, industry intended for self-consumption, not producing commodities—disappears, it is clear that the unproductive labourers, those whose services are directly exchanged against revenue, will for the most part be performing only *personal* services, and only an inconsiderable part of them (like cooks, seamstresses, jobbing tailors and so on) will produce material use-values. That they produce no *commodities* follows from the nature of the case. For the commodity as such is never an immediate object of consumption, but a bearer of exchange-value. Consequently only a quite insignificant part of these unproductive labourers can play a direct part in material production once the capitalist mode of production has developed. They participate in it only through the exchange of their services against revenue. This does not prevent, as Adam Smith remarks, the value of the services of these unproductive labourers being determined and determinable in the same (or an analogous) way as that of the productive labourers: that is, by the production costs involved in maintaining or producing them. Other factors also come into play in this connection, but they are not relevant here.

||306| The labour-power of the productive labourer is a commodity for the labourer himself. So is that of the unproductive labourer. But the productive labourer produces commodities for the buyer of his labour-power. The unproductive labourer produces for him a mere use-value, not a commodity; an imaginary or a real use-value. It is characteristic of the unproductive labourer that he produces no commodities for his buyer, but indeed receives commodities from him.

"The labour of some of the most respectable orders in the society is, like that of menial servants, unproductive of any value.... The sovereign, for example, with all the officers both of justice and war who serve under him, the whole army and navy, are unproductive labourers. They are the servants of the public, and are maintained by a part of the annual produce of the industry of other people.... In the same class must be ranked... churchmen, lawyers, physicians, men of letters of all kinds; players, buffoons, musicians, opera-singers, opera-dancers, etc." (l.c., pp. 94-95).

It itself, as has been said, this distinction between productive and unproductive labour has nothing to do either with the particular speciality of the labour or with the particular use-value in which this special labour is incorporated. In the one case the labour is exchanged with capital, in the other with revenue. In the one case the labour is transformed into capital, and creates a profit for the capitalist; in the other case it is an expenditure, one of the articles in which revenue is consumed. For example, the workman employed by a piano maker is a productive labourer. His labour not only replaces the wages that he consumes, but in the product, the piano, the commodity which the piano maker sells, there is a surplus-value over and above the value of the wages. But assume on the contrary that I buy all the materials required for a piano (or for all it matters the labourer himself may possess them), and that instead of buying the piano in a shop I have it made for me in my house. The workman who makes the piano is now an unproductive labourer, because his labour is exchanged directly against my revenue.

[4. Adam Smith's Second Explanation: the View of Productive Labour as Labour Which Is Realised in a Commodity]

It is however clear that in the same measure as capital subjugates to itself the whole of production—that is to say, that all commodities are produced for the market and not for immediate consumption, and the productivity of labour rises in this same measure—there will also develop more and more a material difference between productive and unproductive labourers, inasmuch as the former, apart from minor exceptions, will exclusively produce *commodities*, while the latter, with minor exceptions, will perform only personal services. Hence the former class will produce immediate, material wealth consisting of *commodities*, all commodities except those which consist of labour-power itself. This is one of the aspects which lead Adam Smith to put forward other points of difference, in addition to the first and in principle determining specific difference between productive and unproductive labour. Thus, following through various associations of ideas, he says:

"The labour of a menial servant" (as distinct from that of a manufacturer) "*adds to the value of nothing* ... the maintenance of a menial servant *never is restored*. A man grows rich by employing a multitude of manufacturers: he grows poor, by maintaining a multitude of menial servants. The *labour of the latter*, however, *has its value*, and deserves its reward as well as that of the former. But the labour of the manufacturer *fixes and realises itself in some particular subject or vendible commodity, which lasts for some time at least after that labour is past*. It is, as it were, a certain quantity of labour stocked and stored up to be employed, if necessary, upon some other occasion. That subject, or what is the same thing, the price of that subject, can afterwards, if necessary, put into motion a quantity of labour equal to that which had originally produced it. The labour of the menial servant, ||307| on the contrary, *does not fix or realise itself in any particular subject or vendible commodity*. His *services generally perish in the very instant of their performance*, and *seldom leave any trace or value behind them*, for which an equal quantity of service could *afterwards* be procured. The labour of some of the most respectable orders in the society is, like that of menial servants, *unproductive of* [...] *value*, and *does not fix or realise itself in any permanent subject, or vendible commodity*" (l.c., pp. 93-94 passim).

To define the unproductive labourer we here have the following determinants, which at the same time reveal the links in Adam Smith's train of thought:

It (the labour of the unproductive labourer) is "unproductive of [...] value", "adds to the value of nothing", "the maintenance" (of the unproductive labourer) "never is restored", "[it] does *not fix* or *realise itself in any particular subject or vendible commodity*". On the contrary, "his services generally perish in the very instant of their performance, and seldom leave any trace or value behind them for which an equal quantity of service could *afterwards* be procured". Finally, his labour "does* not fix or realise itself *in any permanent subject or vendible commodity*".

* In the manuscript: "it does".—*Ed.*

Here "productive of value" or "unproductive of value" is used in a different sense from that in which these terms were used originally. The reference is no longer to the production of a surplus-value, which in itself implies the reproduction of an equivalent for the value consumed. But according to this presentation the labour of a labourer is called productive in so far as he replaces the consumed value by an equivalent, by adding to any material, through his labour, a quantity of value equal to that which was contained in his wages. Here the definition by social form, the determination of productive and unproductive labourers by their relation to capitalist production, is abandoned. From Chapter IX of Book IV (where Adam Smith criticises the doctrine of the Physiocrats), it can be seen that he came to make this aberration as a result partly of his opposition to the Physiocrats and partly under their influence. If a labourer merely replaces each year the equivalent of his wages, then for the capitalist he is not a productive labourer. He does indeed replace his wages, the purchase price of his labour. But the transaction is absolutely the same as if this capitalist had bought the commodity which this labourer produces. He pays for the labour contained in the constant capital and in the wages. He possesses the same quantity of labour in the form of the commodity as he had before in the form of money. Its money is not thereby transformed into capital. In this case it is the same as if the labourer himself owned his conditions of production. He must each year deduct the value of the conditions of production from the value of his annual product, in order to replace them. What he consumed or could consume annually would be that portion of the value of his product equal to the new labour added to his constant capital during the year. In this case, therefore, it would not be capitalist production.

The first reason why Adam Smith calls this kind of labour "productive" is that the Physiocrats call it "stérile"* and "non-productive".**

Thus Adam Smith tells us in the chapter referred to:

"First, this class" (namely the industrial classes, who do not carry on agriculture), "it is acknowledged" [by the Physiocrats], "*reproduces annually the value* of its own annual consumption, and *continues, at least, the existence of the stock or capital which*

* Sterile.—*Ed.*

** Unproductive.—*Ed.*

maintains and employs it.... Farmers and country labourers, indeed, over and above the stock which maintains and employs them, reproduce annually a *neat produce*, a free rent to the landlord ... the labour of farmers and country labourers is certainly more productive than that of merchants, artificers, and manufacturers. The superior produce of the one class, however, does not render the other *barren* or *unproductive*" ([*Wealth of Nations* O.U.P. edition, Vol. II, pp. 294-95], [Garnier], l.c., t. III, p. 530).

Here, therefore, Adam Smith falls back into the Physiocratic ||308| standpoint. The real "productive labour", which produces a surplus-value and therefore a "neat produce", is agricultural labour. He abandons his own view of surplus-value and accepts that of the Physiocrats. At the same time he asserts, as against the Physiocrats, that manufacturing (and according to him, also commercial) labour is nevertheless also productive, even if not in this highest sense of the word. He therefore drops the definition by social form, the definition of what a "productive labourer" is from the standpoint of capitalist production; and asserts, in opposition to the Physiocrats, that the non-agricultural, industrial class reproduces its own wages, that is, it does after all produce a value equal to the value it consumes, and thereby "continues, at least, the existence of the stock or capital which employs it". Hence arises, under the influence of and in contradiction to the Physiocrats, his second definition of what is "productive labour".

"Secondly," says Adam Smith, "it seems, on this account, altogether improper to consider artificers, manufacturers, and merchants, in the same light as menial servants. *The labour of menial servants does not continue the existence of the fund which maintains and employs them. Their maintenance and employment is altogether at the expense of their masters, and the work which they perform is not of a nature to repay expense.* That work consists in *services* which *perish generally in the very instant of their performance*, and *does not fix or realise itself in any vendible commodity, which can replace the value of their wages and maintenance*. The labour, on the contrary, of artificers, manufacturers, and merchants, *naturally does fix and realise itself in some such vendible commodity*. It is up on this account that, in the chapter in which I treat of *productive* and *unproductive labour*, I have classed artificers, manufacturers, and merchants among the *productive* labourers, and menial servants among the *barren* or *unproductive*" ([ibid., p. 295], [Garnier], l.c., p. 531).

As soon as capital has mastered the whole of production, revenue, in so far as it is at all exchanged against labour, will not be exchanged directly against labour which produces *commodities*, but against mere *services*. It is exchanged partly against *commodities* which are to serve as use-values, and partly against *services*, which as such are consumed as use-values.

A *commodity*—as distinguished from labour-power itself—is a material thing confronting man, a thing of a certain utility for him, in which a definite quantity of labour is fixed or materialised.

So we come to the definition already in essence contained in point I: a productive labourer is one whose labour *produces commodities*; and indeed such a labourer does not consume more commodities than he produces, than his labour costs. His labour fixes and realises itself "*in some such vendible commodity*", "*in any vendible commodity which can replace the value of their wages and maintenance*"—(that is, of the workers who produced these commodities). By producing commodities the productive worker constantly reproduces the variable capital which he constantly consumes in the form of wages. He constantly produces the fund which pays him, "which maintains and employs him".

In the first place. Adam Smith naturally includes in the labour which fixes or realises itself in a vendible and exchangeable commodity all intellectual labours which are directly consumed in material production. Not only the labourer working directly with his hands or a machine, but overlooker, engineer, manager, clerk, etc.—in a word, the labour of the whole personnel required in a particular sphere of material production to produce a particular commodity, whose joint labour (co-operation) is required for commodity production. In fact they add their aggregate labour to the constant capital, and increase the value of the product by this amount. (How far is this true of bankers, etc.?[57])

||309| *Secondly*, Adam Smith says that on the whole, "generally", this is not the case with the labour of unproductive labourers. Even though capital has conquered material production, and so by and large home industry has disappeared, and the industry of the small craftsman who makes use-values directly for the consumer at his home—even then, Adam Smith knows quite well, a seamstress whom I get to come to my house to sew shirts, or workmen who repair furniture, or the servant who scrubs and cleans the house, etc., or the cook who gives meat and other things their palatable form, fix their labour in a thing and in fact increase the value of these things in exactly the same way as the seamstress who sews in a factory, the engineer who repairs the machine, the labourers who clean the machine, or the cook who cooks in a hotel as the wage-labourer of a capitalist. These use-values are also, potentially, commodities; the shirts may be sent to the pawnshop, the house resold, the furniture put up to

auction, and so on. Thus these persons have potentially also produced commodities and added value to the objects on which they have worked. But this is a very small category among unproductive workers, and does not apply either to the mass of menial servants or to parsons, government officials, soldiers, musicians and so on.

But however large or small the number of these "unproductive labourers" may be, this much at any rate is evident—and is admitted by the limitation expressed in the phrase "services which perish *generally* in the very instant of their performance", etc.—that neither the special kind of labour nor the external form of its product necessarily make it "productive" or "unproductive". The same labour can be productive when I buy it as a capitalist, as a producer, in order to create more value, and unproductive when I buy it as a consumer, a sender of revenue, in order to consume its use-value, no matter whether this use-value perishes with the activity of the labour-power itself or materialises and fixes itself in an object.

The cook in the hotel produces a commodity for the person who as a capitalist has bought her labour—the hotel proprietor; the consumer of the mutton chops has to pay for her labour, and this labour replaces for the hotel proprietor (apart from profit) the fund out of which he continues to pay the cook. On the other hand if I buy the labour of a cook for her to cook meat, etc., for me, not to make use of it as labour in general but to enjoy it, to use it as that particular concrete kind of labour, then her labour is unproductive, in spite of the fact that this labour fixes itself in a material product and could just as well (in its result) be a vendible commodity, as it in fact is for the hotel proprietor. The great difference (the conceptual difference) however remains: the cook does not replace for me (the private person) the fund from which I pay her, because I buy her labour not as a value-creating element but purely for the sake of its use-value. Her labour as little replaces for me the fund with which I pay for it, that is, her wages, as, for example, the dinner I eat in the hotel in itself enables me to buy and eat the same dinner again a second time. This distinction however is also to be found between commodities. The commodity which the capitalist buys to replace his constant capital (for example, cotton material, if he is a cotton printer) replaces its value in the printed cotton. But if on the other hand he buys it in order to consume the cotton itself, then the commodity does not replace his outlay.

The largest part of society, that is to say the working class, must incidentally perform this kind of labour for itself; but it is only able to perform it when it has laboured "productively". It can only cook meat for itself when it has produced a wage with which to pay for the meat; and it can only keep its furniture and dwellings clean, it can only polish its boots, when it has produced the value of furniture, house rent and boots. To this class of productive labourers itself, therefore, the labour which they perform for themselves appears as "unproductive labour". This unproductive labour never enables them ||310| to repeat the same unproductive labour a second time unless they have previously laboured productively.

Thirdly. On the other hand: an entrepreneur of theatres, concerts, brothels, etc., buys the temporary disposal over the labour-power of the actors, musicians, prostitutes, etc.—in fact in a roundabout way that is only of formal economic interest; in its result the process is the same—he buys this so-called "unproductive labour", whose "services perish in the very instant of their performance" and do not fix or realise themselves "any permanent" ("particular" is also used) "subject or vendible commodity" (apart from themselves). The sale of these to the public provides him with wages and profit. And these services which he has thus bought enable him to buy them again; that is to say, they themselves renew the fund from which they are paid for. The same is true for example of the labour of clerks employed by a lawyer in his office—except for the fact that these services as a rule also embody themselves in very bulky "particular subjects" in the form of immense bundles of documents.

It is true that these services are paid for to the entrepreneur out of the revenue of the public. But it is no less true that this holds good of all products in so far as they enter into individual consumption. It is true that the country cannot export these services as such; but it can export those who perform the services. Thus France exports dancing masters, cooks, etc., and Germany schoolmasters. With the export of the dancing master, or the schoolmaster, however, his revenue is also exported, while the export of dancing shoes and books brings a return to the country.

If therefore on the one hand a part of the so-called unproductive labour embodies itself in material use-values which might just as well be commodities (vendible commodities), so on the other hand a part of the services in the strict sense which assume no objective form—which do not receive an existence as things separate from those performing the services, and do not enter into a commodity as a component part of its value—may be bought with capital (by the *immediate* purchaser of the labour), may replace their own wages and yield a profit for him. In short, the production of these services can be in part subsumed under capital, just as a part of the labour which embodies itself in useful things is bought directly by revenue and is not subsumed under capitalist production.

Fourthly. The whole world of "commodities" can be divided into two great parts. First, labour-power; second, commodities as distinct from labour-power itself. As to the purchase of such services as those which train labour-power, maintain or modify it, etc., in a word, give it a specialised form or even only maintain it—thus for example the schoolmaster's service, in so far as it is "industrially necessary" or useful; the doctor's service, in so far as he maintains health and so conserves the source of all values, labour-power itself—these are services which yield in return "a vendible commodity, etc.", namely labour-power itself, into whose costs of production or reproduction these services enter. Adam Smith knew however how little "education" enters into the costs of production of the mass of working men. And in any case the doctor's services belong to the *faux frais** of production. They can be counted as the cost of repairs for labour-power. Let us assume that wages and profit fell simultaneously in total value, from whatever cause (for example, because the nation had grown lazier), and at the same time in use-value (because labour had become less productive owing to bad harvests, etc.), in a word, that the part of the product whose value is equal to the revenue declines, because less new labour has been added in the past year and because the labour added has been less productive. If in such conditions capitalist and workman wanted to consume the same amount of value in material things as they did before, they would have to buy less of the services of the doctor, schoolmaster, etc. And if they were compelled to continue the same outlay for both these services, then they would have to restrict their consumption of other things. It is therefore clear that the labour of the doctor and the schoolmaster does not directly create the fund out of which they are

* Incidental expenses, that is "mere expenses, unproductive expenditure either of living labour or of materialised labour" (Marx).—*Ed.*

paid, although their labours enter into the production costs of the fund which creates all values whatsoever—namely, the production costs of labour-power.

||311| Adam Smith continues:

"Thirdly, it seems, upon every supposition, improper to say, that the labour of artificers, manufacturers, and merchants, does not increase the *real revenue* of the society. Though we should suppose, for example, as it seems to be supposed in this system, that the value of the daily, monthly, and yearly consumption of this class was exactly equal to that of its daily, monthly, and yearly production; yet it would not from thence follow, that its labour added nothing to the real revenue, to the real value of the annual produce of the land and labour of the society. An artificer, for example, who, in the first six months after harvest, executes ten pounds worth of work, though he should, in the same time, consume ten pounds worth of corn, and other necessaries, yet really adds the value of ten pounds to the annual produce of the land and labour of the society. While he has been consuming a half-yearly revenue of ten pounds worth of corn and other necessaries, he has produced an equal value of work, capable of purchasing, either to himself, or to some other person, an equal half-yearly revenue. The value, therefore, of what has been consumed and produced during these six months, is equal, not to ten, but to twenty pounds. It is possible, indeed, that no more than ten pounds worth of this value may ever have existed at any one moment of time. But if the ten pounds worth of corn and other necessaries which were consumed by the artificer, had been consumed by a soldier, or by a menial servant, the value of that part of the annual produce which existed at the end of the six months, would have been ten pounds less than it actually is in consequence of the labour of the artificer. Though the value of what the artificer produces, therefore, should not, at any one moment of time, be supposed greater than the value he consumes, yet, at every moment of time, the actually existing value of goods in the market is, in consequence of what he produces, greater than it otherwise would be" ([*Wealth of Nations*, O.U.P. edition, Vol. II, pp. 295-96], [Garnier], 1.c., t. III, pp. 531-33).

Is not the [total] value of the commodities at any time in the market greater as a result of the "unproductive labour" than it would be without this labour? Are there not at every moment of time in the market, alongside wheat and meat, etc., also prostitutes, lawyers, sermons, concerts, theatres, soldiers, politicians, etc.? These lads or wenches do not get the corn and other necessaries or pleasures for nothing. In return they give or pester us with their services, which as such services have a use-value and because of their production costs also an exchange-value. Reckoned as consumable articles, there is at every moment of time, alongside the consumable articles existing in the form of goods, a quantity of consumable articles in the form of services. The total quantity of consumable articles is therefore at every moment of time greater than it would be without the consumable services. Secondly, however, the value too is greater; for it is equal to the value of the commodities which are given for these services, and is equal to the value of the services themselves. Since here, as in every exchange of commodity for commodity, equal value is given for equal value, the same value is therefore present twice over, once on the buyer's side and once on the seller's.

<Adam Smith goes on to say in reference to the Physiocrats:

"When the patrons of this system assert, that the *consumption* of artificers, manufacturers, and merchants, is *equal to the value of what they produce*, they probably mean no more than that their *revenue*, or *the fund destined for their consumption, is equal to it*" (that is, to the value of what they produce) ([ibid., p. 296], [Garnier] l.c., p. 533).

In this the Physiocrats were right in relation to workmen and employers taken together, rent forming only a special category of the latter's profit.>

||312| <*Adam Smith* notes on the same occasion—that is, in his criticism of the Physiocrats—Book IV, Chapter IX (edit. Garnier, t. III):

"The annual produce of the land and labour of any society can be augmented only in two ways; either, *first*, by some *improvement in the productive powers of the useful labour* actually maintained within it; or, *secondly*, *by some increase in the quantity of that labour.* The improvement in the productive powers of useful labour depends, first, *upon the improvement in the ability of the workman*; and, secondly, *upon that of the machinery with which he works.... The increase in the quantity of useful labour* actually employed within any society must depend altogether upon *the increase of the capital which employs it*; and *the increase of that capital*, again, *must be exactly equal to the amount of the savings* from the revenue, either of the particular persons who manage and direct the employment of that capital, or of some other persons, who lend it to them" ([ibid., p. 297], [Garnier], pp. 534-35).

Here we have a double vicious circle. *First*: the annual product is augmented by greater productivity of labour. All means to augment this productivity (in so far as this is not due to accidents of nature such as a specially favourable season, etc.) require an increase of capital. But in order to increase the capital, the annual product of labour must be increased. First circle. *Secondly*: the annual product can be augmented by an increase in the quantity of labour employed. The quantity of labour employed, however, can only be increased if the capital which employs it is first increased. Second circle. Adam Smith helps himself out of both vicious circles with "*savings*", by which he means in fact the transformation of revenue into capital.

To think of the whole profit as "revenue" for the capitalist is already in itself wrong. The law of capitalist production requires on the contrary that a part of the surplus-labour, of the unpaid labour, performed by the workman should be transformed into capital. When the individual capitalist functions as a capitalist—that is, as a functionary of capital—he himself may think of this as saving; but it also appears to him as a necessary reserve fund. The increase of the quantity of labour does not however depend only on the number of workmen, but also on the length of the working-day. The quantity of labour can therefore be increased without increasing the part of the capital that is converted into wages. Similarly, on this assumption there would be no need to increase the machinery, etc. (although it would wear out more quickly; but this makes no difference). The only thing that would have to be increased is the part of the raw material that resolves itself into seed, etc. And it remains true that, taking a single country (excluding foreign trade), surplus-labour must first be applied to agriculture before it becomes possible in the industries which get their raw materials from agriculture. A part of these raw materials, such as coal, iron, wood, fish, etc. (the last-named for example as manure), in a word, all fertilisers other than animal manures, can be got by merely increasing the labour (the number of labourers remaining the same). There can therefore be no lack of these. On the other hand it has been shown above that the increase of productivity in its origin always presupposes merely the concentration of capital, not the accumulation of capital.[58] Later however each process supplements the other.>

<The reason why the Physiocrats preached *laissez faire, laissez passer*, in short, free competition, is correctly stated in the following passages from Adam Smith:

> "The trade which is carried on between these two different sets of people" (country and town) "consists ultimately in a certain quantity of rude produce exchanged for a certain quantity of manufactured produce. The dearer the latter, therefore, the cheaper the former; and whatever tends in any country to raise the price of manufactured produce, tends to lower that of the rude produce of the land, and thereby to discourage agriculture."

But all fetters and restrictions placed on manufactures and foreign trade make manufactured commodities, etc., dearer. Therefore, etc. (Smith, [ibid., p. 308] [Garnier trans.], l. c., pp. 554-56).

* * *

||313| Smith's second view of "productive" and "unproductive labour"—or rather the view that is interwoven with his other view—therefore amounts to this: that the former is labour which produces *commodities*, and the latter is labour which does not produce "any commodity". He does not deny that the one kind of labour, equally with the other, *is a commodity*. See above*: "The labour of the latter ... has its value, and deserves its reward as well as that of the former" (that is, from the economic standpoint; there is no question of moral or other standpoints in the case of either the one or the other kind of labour). The concept commodity however implies that labour embodies, materialises, realises itself in its product. Labour itself, in its immediate being, in its living existence, cannot be directly conceived as a commodity, but only labour-power, of which labour itself is the temporary manifestation. Just as it is only in this way that wage-labour in the true sense can be explained, so it is with "unproductive labour", which Adam Smith throughout defines by the costs of production required to produce the "unproductive labourer". A *commodity* must therefore be conceived as something different from labour itself. Then, however, the world of commodities is divided into two great categories:

On one side, labour-power.

On the other side, commodities themselves.

The materialisation, etc., of labour is however not to be taken in such a Scottish sense as Adam Smith conceives it. When we speak of the commodity as a materialisation of labour—in the sense of its exchange-value—this itself is only an imaginary, that is to say, a purely social mode of existence of the commodity which has nothing to do with its corporeal reality; it is conceived as a definite quantity of social labour or of money. It may be that the concrete labour whose result it is leaves no trace in it. In manufactured commodities this trace remains in the outward form given to the raw material. In agriculture, etc., although the form given to the commodity, for example wheat or oxen and so on, is also the product of human labour, and indeed of labour transmitted and added to from generation to generation, yet this is not evident in the product. In other forms of industrial labour the purpose of the labour is not at all to alter the form of the thing, but only its position. For example, when a commodity is brought from China to England, etc., no trace of the labour in-

* See p. 161 of the present volume.—*Ed.*

volved can be seen in the thing itself (except for those who call to mind that it is not an English product). Therefore the materialisation of labour in the commodity must not be understood in that way. (The mystification here arises from the fact that a social relation appears in the form of a thing).

It remains true, however, that the commodity appears as past, objectivised labour, and that therefore, if it does not appear in the form of a thing, it can only appear in the form of labour-power itself; but never directly as living labour itself (except only in a roundabout way which in practice seems the same, but whose significance lies in the determination of different rates of wages). Productive labour would therefore be such labour as produces commodities or directly produces, trains, develops, maintains or reproduces labour-power itself. Adam Smith excludes the latter from his category of productive labour; arbitrarily, but with a certain correct instinct—that if he included it, this would open the flood-gates for false pretensions to the title of productive labour.

In so far therefore as we leave labour-power itself out of account, productive labour is labour which produces commodities, material products, whose production has cost a definite quantity of labour or labour-time. These material products include all products of art and science, books, paintings, statues, etc., in so far as they take the form of things. In addition, however, the product of labour must be a *commodity* in the sense of being "some vendible commodity", that is to say, a commodity in its first form, which has still to pass through its metamorphosis. (A manufacturer may himself construct a machine if he cannot get one built anywhere else, not to sell it but to make use of it as a use-value. However, he then wears it out as a part of his constant capital and so sells it piecemeal in the form of the product which it has helped to make.)

||314| Certain labours of menial servants may therefore equally well take the form of (potential) *commodities* and even of the same use-values considered as material objects. But they are not productive labour, because in fact they produce not "commodities" but immediate "*use-values*". As for labours which are productive for their purchaser or employer himself—as for example the actor's labour for the theatrical entrepreneur—the fact that their purchaser cannot sell them to the public in the form of commodities but only in the form of the action itself would show that they are unproductive labours.

Apart from such cases, productive labour is such as produces *commodities*, and *unproductive labour* is such as produces personal services. The former labour is represented in a vendible thing; the latter must be consumed while it is being performed. The former includes (except for that labour which creates labour-power itself) all material and intellectual wealth—meat as well as books—that exists in the form of things; the latter covers all labours which satisfy any imaginary or real need of the individual—or even those which are forced upon the individual against his will.

The *commodity* is the most elementary form of bourgeois wealth. The explanation of "productive labour" as labour which produces "commodities" also corresponds, therefore, to a much more elementary point of view than that which defines productive labour as labour which produces capital.

Adam Smith's opponents have disregarded his first, pertinent definition, and instead have concentrated on the second, pointing out the unavoidable contradictions and inconsistencies to which it gives rise. And their attacks were made all the easier for them by their insistence on the material content of the labour, and particularly the specific requirement that the labour must fix itself in a more or less *permanent* product. We shall see in a moment what it was that particularly gave rise to the polemics.

But first this further point. Adam Smith says of the Physiocratic system that its great merit is that it represented the wealth of nations as consisting

> "not in the unconsumable riches of money, but in the consumable goods annually produced by the labour of the society"([*Wealth of Nations*, O.U.P. edition, p. 299], [Garnier] t. III, l. IV, ch. IX, p. 538).

Here we have a deduction of his second definition of productive labour. The definition of surplus-value naturally depended on the form in which value itself was conceived. In the Monetary and Mercantile systems it is therefore presented as *money*; by the Physiocrats, as the produce of the land, as agricultural product; finally in Adam Smith's writings as *commodity* in general. In so far as the Physiocrats touch on the substance of value, they resolve it entirely into pure use-value (matter, corporeal object), just as the Mercantilists resolve it into the pure form of value, the form in which the product *makes itself manifest* as general social labour: money. With Adam Smith, both conditions of the commodity—use-value and exchange-value—are combined; and so all labour is productive which manifests itself in any use-value, any useful product. That it is labour that manifests itself in the product already implies that the product is equal to a definite quantity of general social labour. As against the Physiocrats, Adam Smith re-establishes the value of the product as the essential basis of bourgeois wealth; but on the other hand he divests value of the purely fantastic form—that of gold and silver—in which it appeared to the Mercantilists. Every commodity is *in itself* money. It must be recognised that at the same time Adam Smith also falls back more or less into the Mercantilist conception of "permanency"—in fact, inconsumability. We can recall the passage in Petty (see my first volume, p. 109,[59] where I quote from Petty's *Political Arithmetick*) where wealth is valued according to the degrees in which it is imperishable, more or less permanent, and finally gold and silver are set above all other things as wealth that is "not perishable".

Adolphe Blanqui (*Histoire de l'économie politique*, Bruxelles, 1839, p. 152) says [of Adam Smith]:

> "In restricting the sphere of *wealth* exclusively to those values which are embodied in material substances, he erased from the book of production the whole boundless mass of immaterial values, daughters of the *moral capital* of civilised nations," etc.

[5. Vulgarisation of Bourgeois Political Economy in the Definition of Productive Labour]

The polemics against Adam Smith's distinction between productive and unproductive labour were for the most part confined to the *dii minorum gentium** (among whom moreover Storch was the most important); they are not to be found in the work of any economist ||315| of significance—of anyone of whom it can be said that he made some discovery in political economy. They are, however, the hobby-horse of the second-rate fellows and especially of the schoolmasterish compilers and writers of compendia, as well as of *dilettanti* with facile pens and vulgarisers in this field. What particularly aroused these polemics against Adam Smith was the following circumstance.

The great mass of so-called "higher grade" workers—such as state officials, military people, artists, doctors, priests, judges, lawyers, etc.—some of whom are not only not productive but in

* Gods of the lesser tribes.—*Ed.*

essence destructive, but who know how to appropriate to themselves a very great part of the "material" wealth partly through the sale of their "immaterial" commodities and partly by forcibly imposing the latter on other people—found it not at all pleasant to be relegated *economically* to the same class as clowns and menial servants and to appear merely as people partaking in the consumption, parasites on the actual producers (or rather agents of production). This was a peculiar profanation precisely of those functions which had hitherto been surrounded with a halo and had enjoyed superstitious veneration. Political economy in its classical period, like the bourgeoisie itself in its *parvenu* period, adopted a severely critical attitude to the machinery of the State, etc. At a later stage it realised and—as was shown too in practice—learnt from experience that the necessity for the inherited social combination of all these classes, which in part were totally unproductive, arose from its own organisation.

In so far as those "unproductive labourers" do not produce entertainment, so that their purchase entirely depends on how the agent of production cares to spend his wages or his profit—in so far on the contrary as they are necessary or make themselves necessary because of physical infirmities (like doctors), or spiritual weakness (like parsons), or because of the conflict between private interests and national interests (like statesmen, all lawyers, police and soldiers)—they are regarded by Adam Smith, as by the industrial capitalists themselves and the working class, as incidental expenses of production, which are therefore to be cut down to the most indispensable minimum and provided as cheaply as possible. Bourgeois society reproduces in its own form everything against which it had fought in feudal or absolutist form. In the first place therefore it becomes a principal task for the sycophants of this society, and especially of the upper classes, to restore in theoretical terms even the purely parasitic section of these "unproductive labourers", or to justify the exaggerated claims of the section which is indispensable. The *dependence* of the ideological, etc., classes on the *capitalists* was in fact proclaimed.

Secondly, however, a section of the agents of production (of material production itself) were declared by one group of economists or another to be "unproductive". For example, the landowner, by those among the economists who represented industrial capital (Ricardo). Others (for example Carey) declared that the merchant in the true sense of the word was an "unproductive" labourer. Then even a third group came along who declared that the "capitalists" themselves were unproductive, or who at least sought to reduce their claims to material wealth to "wages", that is, to the wages of a "productive labourer". Many intellectual workers seemed inclined to share the scepticism in regard to the capitalist. It was therefore time to make a compromise and to recognise the "productivity" of all classes not directly included among the agents of material production. One good turn deserves another; and, as in the *Fable of the Bees*,[60] it had to be established that even from the "productive", economic standpoint, the bourgeois world with all its "unproductive labourers" is the best of all worlds. This was all the more necessary because the "unproductive labourers" on their part were advancing critical observations in regard to the productivity of the classes who in general were "*fruges consumere nati*"*; or in regard to those agents of production, like landowners, who do nothing at all, etc. Both the *do-nothings* and their *parasites* had to be found a place in this best possible order of things.

Thirdly: As the dominion of capital extended, and in fact those spheres of production not directly related to the production of material wealth became also more and more dependent on it—especially when the positive science (natural sciences) were subordinated to it as serving material production—||316| the sycophantic underlings of political economy felt it their duty to glorify and justify every sphere of activity by demonstrating that it was "linked" with the production of material wealth, that it was a means towards it; and they honoured everyone by making him a "productive labourer" in the "primary" sense, namely, a labourer who labours in the service of capital, is useful in one way or another to the enrichment of the capitalist, etc.

In this matter even such people as Malthus are to be preferred, who directly defend the necessity and usefulness of "*unproductive* labourers" and pure parasites.

[6. Advocates of Smith's Views on Productive Labour. On the History of the Subject]

[(a) Advocates of the First View: Ricardo, Sismondi]

It is not worth the trouble to examine in detail the inanities of Germain Garnier (Smith's translator), the Earl of Lauderdale,

* "Born to consume the fruits" (Horace).—*Ed.*

Brougham, Say, Storch, and later Senior, Rossi, and so on, in regard to this question. We shall cite only a few characteristic passages.

But first a passage from *Ricardo*, in which he shows that it is much more advantageous for the "productive labourers" when the owners of surplus-value (profit, rent) consume it in "unproductive labourers" (as menial servants, for instance) than in luxury products produced by the "productive labourers".

<*Sismondi*, *Nouveaux principes*, t. I, p. 148, accepts the correct statement of Smith's distinction (as also of course does Ricardo): the real distinction between productive and unproductive classes is:

"The one always exchanges its labour against the capital of a nation; the other always exchanges it against a part of the national revenue."

Sismondi—likewise following Adam Smith—on surplus-value:

"Although the labourer, by his daily labour, may have produced much more than his daily outlay, after sharing with the landowner and the capitalist what remains for him is seldom much beyond what is strictly necessary for his existence" (Sismondi, *Nouveaux principes*, etc., t. I, p. 87).

Ricardo says:

"If a landlord, or a capitalist, expends his revenue in the manner of an ancient baron, in the support of a great number of retainers, or menial servants, he will give employment to much more labour, than if he expended it on fine clothes, or costly furniture; on carriages, on horses, or in the purchase of any other luxuries. In both cases the net revenue would be the same, and so would be the gross revenue, but the former would be realised in different commodities. If my revenue were 10,000 *l.*, the same quantity nearly of productive labour would be employed, whether I realised it in fine clothes and costly furniture, etc., etc., or in a quantity of food and clothing of the same value. If, however, I realised my revenue in the first set of commodities, no more labour would be *consequently* employed:—I should enjoy my furniture and my clothes, and there would be an end of them; but if I realised my revenue in food and clothing, and my desire was to employ menial servants, all those whom I could so employ with my revenue of 10,000 *l.*, or with the food and clothing which it would purchase, *would be to be added to the former demand for labourers*, and this addition would take place only because I chose this mode of expending my revenue. As the labourers, then, are interested in *the demand for labour*, they must naturally desire that as much of the revenue as possible should be diverted from expenditure on luxuries, to be expended in the support of menial servants" ([David] Ricardo, [*On the*] *Principles* [*of Political Economy, and Taxation*], third edition, [London], 1821, pp. 475-76).

[(b) Early Attempts to Distinguish between Productive and Unproductive Labour (D'Avenant, Petty)]

D'Avenant quotes from an old statistician, Gregory King, a list entitled *Scheme of the Income and Expense of the Several Families of England, calculated for the year 1688.* In this, the erudite King divides the whole nation into two main classes: "*Increasing* the Wealth of the Kingdom—2,675,520 heads", and "*Decreasing* the Wealth of the Kingdom—2,825,000 heads"; thus the former is the "productive" class, the latter the "unproductive". The "*productive*" class consists of Lords, Baronets, Knights, Esquires, Gentlemen, Persons in Office and Places, merchants in oversea trade, Persons in the Law, Clergymen, freeholders, farmers, persons in liberal arts and sciences, shopkeepers and tradesmen, artisans and handicrafts, Naval Officers, Military Officers. As against these, the "*unproductive*" class consists of: common seamen, labouring people and out servants (these are agricultural labourers and day wage-labourers in manufacture), cottagers (who in D'Avenant's time were still a fifth of the total English population), ||317| common soldiers, paupers, gipsies, thieves, beggars and vagrants generally. D'Avenant explains this list of ranks prepared by the learned King as follows:

"By which he means, That the First Class of the People, from Land, Arts and Industry, maintain themselves, and add every Year something to the Nation's General Stock; and besides this, out of their Superfluity, contribute every Year so much to the maintenance of Others. That of the Second Class, some partly maintain themselves by Labour [...] but that the rest, as most of the Wives and Children of these, [...] are nourish'd at the Cost of Others; and are a Yearly Burthen to the Publick, consuming Annually so much as would be otherwise added to the Nation's General Stock" (D'Avenant, *An Essay upon the Probable Methods of Making a People Gainers in the Ballance of Trade*, London, 1699, p. 50).

In addition to this, the following passage from D'Avenant is rather characteristic of the views of the Mercantilists on surplus-value:

It is "... the Exportation of our own Product that must make England rich; to be Gainers in the Ballance of Trade, we must carry out of our own Product, what will purchase the Things of Foreign Growth that are needful for our own Consumption, with some *Overplus* either in Bullion or Goods to be sold in other Countries; *which Overplus* is the *Profit a Nation makes by Trade*, and it is more or less according to the natural Frugality of the People that Export," (a frugality which the Dutch have, but not the English—l.c., pp. 46-47) "or as from the low Price of Labour and Manufacture they can afford the Commodity cheap, and at *a rate not to be under-sold in Foreign Markets*" (D'Avenant, l.c., pp. 45-46).

<"... by what is Consum'd at Home, one loseth only what another gets, and the Nation in General is not at all the Richer; but all Foreign Consumption is a clear and certain Profit" (*An Essay on the East-India Trade*, etc., London, 1697). [In D'Avenant, *Discourses on the Publick Revenues, and on the Trade of England...*, Part II, London, 1698, p. 31.]>

<This work *printed in the form of an appendix* to another work of D'Avenant's, which he tries to defend,[61] is not the same as the *Considerations on the East-India Trade*, 1701, quoted by McCulloch.>

Incidentally, it must not be thought that these Mercantilists were as stupid as they were made out to be by the later Vulgar-Freetraders. In Volume II of his *Discourses on the Publick Revenues, and on the Trade of England*, etc., *London, 1698*, D'Avenant says among other things:

"Gold and Silver are indeed the Measure of Trade, but the Spring and Original of it, in all Nations, is the Natural, or Artificial Product of the Country, that is to say, what their Land, or what their Labour and Industry produces. And this is so true, that a Nation may be suppos'd, by some Accident, quite without the Species of Money, and yet, if the People are numerous, industrious, vers'd in Traffick, skill'd in Sea-Affairs, and if they have good Ports, and a Soil fertile in variety* of Commodities, such a people will have Trade, [...] and, they shall quickly get among 'em, a plenty of Gold and Silver**: So that the real and effective Riches of a Country, is its Native Product" (p. 15). "Gold and Silver are so far from being [...] the only Things that deserve the name of Treasure, or the Riches of a Nation that in truth, Money is at Bottom no more than the Countries with which Men in their dealings have been accustom'd to reckon..." (p. 16). "We understand that to be Wealth which maintains the Prince, and the general Body of his People, in Plenty, Ease and Safety. We esteem that to be Treasure which for the use of Man has been converted from Gold and Silver, into Buildings and Improvements of the Country. As also other Things *convertible* into those Metals, as the Fruits of the Earth, Manufactures or Foreign Commodities and stock of Shipping ... even perishable Goods, may be held the Riches of a Nation, if they are *convertible*, tho' not *converted* into Gold and Silver; and this we believe does not only hold between Man and Man, [...] but between one Country and another" (pp. 60-61). "The Common People being the Stomach of the Body Politick, [...] that Stomach" in Spain did not take the money as it should have done, ||318| and failed to digest it.... "Trade and Manufactures are the only Mediums by which such a digestion and distribution of Gold and Silver can be made, as will be Nutritive to the Body Politick" (pp. 62-63).

Moreover, Petty too had the conception of *productive labourers* (though he also includes soldiers):

* In the manuscript: "in a variety".—*Ed.*
** In the manuscript: "a plenty of silver and gold".—*Ed.*

"Husbandmen, Seamen, Soldiers, Artizans and Merchants, are the very Pillars of any Common-Wealth; all the other great Professions, *do rise out of the infirmities and miscarriages of these*; now the Seaman is three of these four" (navigator, merchant, soldier) ([William Petty,] *Political Arithmetick*, etc. [in *Several Essays in Political Arithmetick*], London, 1699, p. 177). "... the Labour of Seamen, and Freight of Ships, is always of the nature of an Exported Commodity, the *overplus* whereof, above what is Imported, brings home Money, etc." (p. 179).

In this connection Petty also explains the advantages of the division of labour:

"Those who have the command of the Sea-Trade, may Work at easier Freight with more profit, than others at greater:" (higher freight charges) "for a Cloth must be cheaper made, when one" etc., "another" etc. "so those who command the Trade of Shipping, can build" different sorts of vessels for different purposes, "one sort of vessels for the turbulent Sea, another for Inland Waters and Rivers ... one sort for War ... another for Burthen", etc. ... And this "is" the chief of several Reasons, why the Hollanders can go at less Freight than their Neighbours, viz., because they can afford a particular sort of Vessels for each particular Trade"* (l.c., pp. 179-80).

Here too Petty strikes quite a Smithian note when he continues:

If taxes are taken from industrialists, etc., in order to give [money] to those who in general are occupied in ways "which produce *no material thing*, or things of real use and value in the *Commonwealth*: In this case, the Wealth of the Publick will be diminished: Otherwise than as such Exercises, are Recreations and Refreshments of the mind; and which being moderately used, do qualify and dispose Men to what in it self is more considerable" (l.c., p. 198). After computing how many people are needed for industrial work "...The Remainder [...] may safely and without possible prejudice to the Commonwealth, be employed in the Arts and Exercises of Pleasure and Ornament; *the greatest whereof is the Improvement of natural Knowledge*" (l.c., p. 199). "There is much more to be gained by Manufacture than Husbandry; and by Merchandize than Manufacture..." (l.c., p. 172). "... a Seaman is in effect three Husbandmen..." (p. 178). |VII—318||

* * *

||VIII—346| *Petty, Surplus-Value.* In one passage of Petty's there can be seen an anticipation of the nature of *surplus-value*, although he treats it only in the form of rent. Especially when it is put alongside the following passage, in which he determines the relative value of silver and corn by the relative quantities of each that can be produced in the same labour-time.

---

* This passage was translated by Marx into German and slightly shortened.—*Ed.*

"If a man can bring to London an ounce of Silver out of the Earth in Peru, in the same time that he can produce a Bushel of Corn, then one is the natural price of the other; now if by reason of new and more easier Mines a man can get two ounces of Silver as easily as formerly he did one, then Corn will be as cheap at ten shillings the Bushel, as it was before five shillings, *caeteris paribus**."

"... let a hundred men work ten years upon Corn, and the same number of men the same time, upon Silver; I say, that the neat proceed of the Silver is the price of the whole neat proceed of the Corn, and like parts of the one, the price of like parts of the other."

"Corn will be twice as dear where** are two hundred Husbandmen to do the same work which an hundred could perform..." ([William Petty], *On Taxes and Contributions*, 1662) (in the edit. of 1679, pp. 32, 24, 67).

The passages to which I alluded above are the following:

"... as Trades and curious Arts increase; so the Trade of Husbandry will decrease, or else the Wages of Husbandmen must rise, and *consequently* the Rents of Lands must fall" (p. 193).

"... if Trade and Manufacture have increased in England ... if a greater part of the People, apply themselves to those Faculties, than there did heretofore, and if the price of Corn be no greater now, than when Husbandmen were more numerous, and the Tradesmen fewer; it follows from that single reason ... that the Rents of Land must fall: As for Example, suppose the price of Wheat be 5s. or 60d. the Bushel; now if the Rent of the Land whereon it grows be the third Sheaf"; (i.e., part, share) "then of the 60d. 20d. is for the Land, and 40d. for the Husbandman; but if the Husbandman's wages should rise one-eighth part, or from 8d. to 9d. per Diem,*** then the Husbandman's share in the Bushel of Wheat rises from 40d. to 45d. and consequently the Rent of the Land must fall from 20d. to 15d. for we suppose *the price of the Wheat still remains the same*; especially *since we cannot raise it*, for if we did attempt it, Corn would be brought in to us, ||347| (as into Holland) from Foreign Parts, where the State of Husbandry was not changed." ([William Petty], *Political Arithmetick* [in *Several Essays in Political Arithmetick*], London, 1699, pp. 193-94.) |VIII—347||

* * *

||VIII—364| <*Petty*. The following passage, where rent in general is treated as a surplus-value, a net product, should be compared with the one quoted above from Petty:

"Suppose a man could with his own hands plant a certain scope of land with Corn, that is, could Dig, or Plough; Harrow, Weed, Reap, Carry home, Thresh, and Winnow so much as the Husbandry of this Land required [...]. I say, that when this man hath subducted his seed out of the proceed of his Harvest, and also what himself hath both eaten and given to others in ex-

* Other things being equal.—*Ed.*

** In the manuscript: "when there".—*Ed.*

*** Per day.—*Ed.*

change for Clothes, and other Natural necessaries; that the Remainder of Corn is the natural and true Rent of the Land for that year; and the *medium* of seven years, or rather of so many years as makes up the Cycle, within which Dearths and Plenties make their revolution, doth give the ordinary Rent of the Land in Corn. But a further, though collateral question may be, how much *English* money this Corn or Rent is worth; I answer so much as the money, which another single man can save, within the same time, over and above his expense, if he imployed himself wholly to produce and make it; viz. Let another man go travel into a Countrey where is Silver, there Dig it, Refine it, bring it to the same place where the other man planted his Corn; Coyne it, etc. the same person, all the while of his working for Silver, gathering also food for his necessary livelihood, and procuring himself covering, etc. I say, the Silver of the one must be esteemed of equal value with the Corn of the other" (*Traité des taxes,*[62] pp. 23-24). [William Petty, *A Treatise of Taxes, and Contributions...*, London, 1662, pp. 23-24. Marx quotes the passage from Charles Ganilh, *Des Système d'économie politique...*, t. II, Paris, 1821, pp. 36-37.]*> |VIII—364||

[(c) John Stuart Mill, an Adherent of Smith's Second View of Productive Labour]

||VII—318| Mr. *John Stuart Mill*, in *Essays on Some Unsettled Questions of Political Economy*, London, 1844, also struggled with the problem of productive and unproductive labour; but in so doing he in fact added nothing to Smith's (second) definition except that labours which produce labour-power itself are also productive.

"*Sources of enjoyment* may be accumulated and stored up; enjoyment itself cannot. The wealth of a country consists of the sum total of the permanent sources of enjoyment, whether material or immaterial, contained in it; and labour or expenditure which tends to augment or keep up these permanent sources, should, we conceive, be termed *productive*" (l.c., p. 82). "If the mechanic who made the spinning-jenny laboured productively, the spinner also laboured productively when he was learning his trade: and what they both consumed productively, that is to say, its consumption did not tend to diminish, but to increase the sum of the permanent sources of enjoyment in the country, by effecting a new creation of those sources, more than equal to the amount of the consumption" (l.c., p. 83).

* * *

We will now briefly run over the twaddle written against Adam Smith in connection with productive and unproductive labour.

---

* See Appendix, p. 433.—*Ed.*

[7.] Germain Garnier [Vulgarisation of the Theories Put Forward by Smith and the Physiocrats]

||319| The fifth volume [contains Garnier's] Notes to his translation of Smith's *Wealth of Nations* (Paris, 1802).

On "productive labour" in the highest sense Garnier shares the view of the Physiocrats; he only makes it somewhat weaker. He opposes Smith's view that "productive labour ... is that which realises itself in some particular subject or vendible commodity, which lasts for some time at least after that labour is past" ([Garnier] l. c., t. V, p. 169).[63] |VII—319||

[(a) Confusion of Labour Which Is Exchanged Against Capital with Labour Exchanged against Revenue. The False Conception that the Total Capital Is Replaced through the Revenue of the Consumers]

||VIII—347| (*Germain Garnier*). He brings forward various arguments against Adam Smith (which are in part repeated by later authors).

First.

> "This distinction is false, inasmuch as it is based on a difference which does not exist. *All labour is productive* in the sense in which the author uses this word *productive*. The labour of the one as of the other of these two classes is equally productive of some enjoyment, commodity or utility for the person who pays for it, otherwise this labour would not find wages."

<It is therefore productive because it produces some use-value and is sold, has an exchange-value, and is thus itself a commodity.>

In developing this point, however, Garnier cites examples by way of illustration, in which the "unproductive labourers" do *the same thing*, produce the same use-value or the same kind of use-value as the "productive". For example:

> "The servant who is in my service, who lights my fire, who dresses my hair, who cleans and keeps in order my clothes and my furniture, who prepares my food, etc., performs *services absolutely of the same kind* as the laundress or the seamstress who cleans and keeps in order her customers' linen; ... as the eating-house keeper, cook-shop proprietor or publican who carries on his trade of preparing food for persons whom it suits better to come and dine with him; as the barber, the hairdresser" (for Adam Smith, however, most of these fellows are as little reckoned among productive workers as the servants) "who perform immediate services; finally as the mason, the tiler, joiner, the glazier, the stove-setter [...], etc., and the multitude of building labourers who come when they are called to carry out restorations and repairs, and whose annual income depends as much on simple repair and maintenance work as on new construction."

(Adam Smith nowhere says that the labour which fixes itself in a more or less permanent object cannot be equally well repairs as the making of new things.)

"This kind of labour consists less in producing than in maintaining; its aim is less to add to the value of the subjects to which it is applied than to prevent their decay. All these labourers, including the servants, *save the person who pays them the labour of maintaining his own things...*"

(They can therefore be regarded as machines for maintaining value, or rather use-values. *Destutt de Tracy* also asserts this view of the "saving" of labour. See further on. The unproductive labour of one does not become productive by saving the other *unproductive labour*. One of the two performs it. A part of Adam Smith's unproductive labour—but only the part which is absolutely necessary in order to consume things, which so to speak belongs to the *costs of consumption* (and then, too, only when it saves this time for a productive worker)—becomes necessary as a result of the division of labour. But Adam Smith does not deny this "division of labour". If everyone had to perform productive and unproductive labour, and through the dividing up of these kinds of labour between two persons both were better performed, according to Adam Smith this would in no way alter the circumstance that one of these labours is productive and the other unproductive.)

"It is for that and for that alone that they most often labour" (for one person to save the labour of looking after himself, ten have to look after him—a curious way of "saving" labour; besides "unproductive labour" of this kind is most often made use of by those who do nothing); "thus, either they are all *productive*, or none of them is productive" (l.c., p. 172).

||348| *Secondly*. A Frenchman cannot forget the *ponts et chaussées*. * Why, he says, call productive

"the labour of an inspector or director of a private enterprise in trade or manufacture, and *non-productive*, the labour of the government official who, watching over the upkeep of public highways, of navigable canals and ports, of monies and other important instruments destined to enliven commercial activity, watching over the security of transport and communications, the carrying out of conventions, etc., can with justice be regarded as the *inspector of the great social manufacture*? It is labour of absolutely the same nature, though on a vaster scale" (pp. 172-73).

In so far as such a lad takes part in the production (or conservation and reproduction) of material things which *could be sold*

* Lit.: bridges and roads—in France this designated the administration of roads and communications.—*Ed.*

were they not in the hands of the State, Smith might call his labour "productive". "Inspectors of the great social manufacture" are purely French creations.

Thirdly. Here Garnier falls into "moralising". Why should the "manufacturer of perfumery, who flatters my sense of smell", be productive and not the musician, who "enchants my ear"? (p. 173). Smith would reply: because the former supplies a material product and the latter does not. Morals and the "merits" of the two lads have nothing to do with the distinction.

Fourthly. Is it not a contradiction that the "violin maker, the organ builder, the music dealer, the mechanic, etc.", are productive, and the professions for which these labours are only "preparations" are unproductive?

> "All of them have, as the final aim of *their labour, a consumption of the same kind.* If the result which some of them have in view does not deserve to be counted among *the products* of the labour of society, why should one treat more favourably what is nothing but a *means for attaining this result?*" (l.c., p. 173).

On this reasoning, a man who eats corn is just as productive as the man who produces it. For with what aim is corn produced? In order to eat it. So if the labour of eating is not productive, why should the labour of cultivating corn be productive, since it is only a means for attaining this aim? Besides, the man who eats produces brain, muscles, etc., and are these not just as worthy products as barley or wheat?—an indignant friend of humanity might ask Adam Smith.

In the first place, Adam Smith does not deny that the unproductive labourer produces a product of some sort. Otherwise he would not be a labourer at all. Secondly, it may seem strange that the doctor who prescribes pills is not a productive labourer, but the apothecary who makes them up is. Similarly the instrument maker who makes the fiddle, but not the musician who plays it. But that would only show that "productive labourers" produce products which have no purpose except to serve as means of production for unproductive labourers. Which however is no more surprising than that all productive labourers, when all is said and done, produce firstly the means for the payment of unproductive labourers, and secondly, products which are consumed by those who *do not perform any labour.*

Of all these comments, No. II is that of a Frenchman who can't forget his *ponts et chaussées*; No. III amounts only to morals; No. IV either contains the stupidity that consumption is just as productive as production <which is not true in bourgeois society, where one produces and another consumes> or that some productive labour merely produces the material for unproductive labour, which Adam Smith nowhere denies. Only No. I contains the correct point that Adam Smith, by his second definition, calls *the same* kinds of labour ||349| productive and unproductive—or rather that according to his own definition he would have to call a relatively small part of his "unproductive" labour *productive*; a point therefore that does not tell against the *distinction*, but against the *subsumption* of certain activities under the distinction or *the way it is applied*. After making all these comments, the learned Garnier finally comes to the point.

> "The only general difference that can, it seems, be observed between [...] the two classes assumed by Smith, is that in the class which he calls *productive*, there is or *may always be some intermediary person between the maker of the object and the person who consumes it*; whereas in the *labour* that he calls *non-productive*, *there cannot be any intermediary*, and the relation *between the labourer and the consumer is necessarily direct and immediate*. It is evident that there is *necessarily* a direct and immediate relation between the person who uses the experience of the physician, the skill of the surgeon, the knowledge of the lawyer, the talent of the musician or actor, or finally the services of the domestic servant, and each of these different hired workers at the moment of their labour; while in the professions constituting the other class, *the thing to be consumed being material and palpable*, *it can be the subject of many intermediary exchanges* after leaving the person who makes it before it reaches the one who consumes it" (p. 174).

In these last words Garnier shows, in spite of himself, the concealed association of ideas that exists between Smith's first distinction (labour which is exchanged against capital, and labour which is exchanged against revenue) and his second (labour which fixes itself in a material, vendible commodity and labour which does not so fix itself). The latter by its nature *cannot* for the most part be subordinated to the capitalist mode of production; the former can. To say nothing of the fact *that on the basis of capitalist production*, where the great majority of material commodities—material and palpable things—is produced by wage-labourers under the domination of capital, [unproductive] labours (or services, whether those of a prostitute or of the Pope) can only be paid for either out of the wages of the productive labourers, or out of the profits of their employers (and the partners in those profits), quite apart from the circumstances that those productive labourers produce the material basis of the subsistence, and consequently, the existence, of the unproductive labourers. It is however characteristic of this shallow French cur that he, who wants to be an expert in political economy and so an explorer of capitalist production, considers *inessential* the feature which makes this production capitalist—the exchange of capital for wage-labour instead of the direct exchange of revenue for wage-labour or the revenue which the labourer directly pays to himself. By so doing Garnier makes capitalist production itself an inessential form instead of a necessary—though only historically, that is, transiently necessary—form for the development of the social productive powers of labour and the transformation of labour into social labour.

"... it would also always be necessary to deduct from his *productive* class all labourers whose labour consists purely of cleaning, conserving or repairing finished articles, and consequently does not put any new product into circulation" (p. 175).

(Smith nowhere says that the labour or its product must enter into the circulating capital. It can enter directly into fixed capital, like the mechanic's labour repairing a machine in a factory. But in this case its *value* enters into the circulation of the product, the commodity. And the repairers, etc., who do this labour as servants, do not exchange ||350| their labour against capital but against revenue.)

"It is in consequence of this difference that the *non-productive* class, as Smith has observed, subsists only on revenues. In fact, since this class allows of no intermediary between itself and the consumer of its products, that is to say, the person who enjoys its labour, it is paid immediately by the consumer; and *he pays only from revenues.* As against these, the labourers of the *productive* class, being as a rule paid by an *intermediary who intends to make a profit from their labour, are most often paid by capital.* But this capital is always in the end replaced by the revenue of a consumer, otherwise it would not circulate and therefore would not yield any profit to its possessor."

This last "but" is quite childish. In the first place, a part of the capital is replaced by capital and not by revenue, whether this part of the capital circulates or does not circulate (as in the case of seed).

[(b) Replacement of the Constant Capital by Means of the Exchange of Capital against Capital]

When a coal-mine supplies coal to an ironworks and gets from the latter iron which enters into the operations of the coal-mine as means of production, the coal is in this way exchanged for capital to the amount of the value of this iron, and reciprocally the iron, to the amount of its own value, is exchanged as capital for coal. Both (considered as use-values) are products of new labour, although this labour was produced with means of labour that were already in existence. But the value of the product of the year's labour is not the product of the labour [newly added] in the year. It also replaces the value of the past labour which was materialised in the means of production. Therefore the part of the total product which is equal to this value is not a part of the product of the year's labour, but the reproduction of past labour.

Let us take for example the product of the daily labour of a coal-mine, an ironworks, a timber producer and a machine-building factory. Let the constant capital in all these industries be equal to one-third of all the component parts of value in the product: that is, let the proportion of pre-existing labour to living labour be 1 : 2. Then all these industries produce each a daily product of x, x′, x″, x‴. These products are certain quantities of coal, iron, timber and machinery. As such products, they are products of the day's labour (but also of the daily consumed raw materials, fuel, machinery, etc., which have all contributed to the day's production). Let the values of these be equal to z, z′, z″, z‴. These values are not the product of the day's labour, since $\frac{z}{3}, \frac{z'}{3}, \frac{z''}{3}, \frac{z'''}{3}$ are only equal to the value which the constant elements of z, z′, z″, z‴ had before they entered into the day's labour. Therefore also $\frac{x}{3}, \frac{x'}{3}, \frac{x''}{3}, \frac{x'''}{3}$, or a third part of the use-values produced, represent only the value of the pre-existing labour and continually replace it. <The exchange which here takes place between pre-existing labour and the *product* of living labour is of quite a different nature from the exchange between labour-power and the conditions of labour existing as capital.>

x=z; yet z is the value of the total x,[64] but one-third of z is equal to the value of the raw material, etc., contained in the total x. Thus $\frac{x}{3}$ is a part of the day's product of the labour <but not at all the product of the day's labour, but on the contrary of the previous pre-existing labour combined with it> in which the pre-existing labour combined with the day's labour reappears and is replaced. Now it is true that each aliquot part of x, which is simply the quantity of actual products (iron, coal, etc.), represents in its value one-third pre-existing labour and two-thirds labour performed or added the same day. Pre-existing labour and the day's labour enter into the total product in the same proportion as they enter into each separate product of which the total product is made up. But if I divide the total product into two parts, putting one-third on one side and two-thirds on the other, it is the same as if the one-third represents only pre-existing labour and the other two-thirds only the labour of the day. In fact the first one-third represents all past labour which entered into the total product, the full value of the means of production consumed. After deducting this one-third, therefore, the other two-thirds can represent only the product of the day's labour. The two-thirds in fact represent the total amount of the day's labour that was added to the means of production.

The last two-thirds are therefore equal to the producer's revenue (profit and wages). He can consume them, that is, spend them on articles which enter into his individual consumption. Suppose that these two-thirds of the coal produced daily were bought by the consumers or purchasers not with money, but with the commodities which they have previously transformed into money in order to buy coal with it. A part of these two-thirds of the coal will enter into the individual consumption of the coal producers themselves, for heating, etc. This part therefore does not enter into circulation, or if it does first enter into circulation it will be withdrawn again from it ||351| by its own producers. Minus this part of the two-thirds which the producers of coal themselves consume, they must exchange all the rest of it (if they want to consume it) for articles which enter into individual consumption.

In this exchange it is a matter of complete indifference to them whether the sellers of the consumable articles exchange capital or revenue for the coal; that is to say, whether for example the cloth manufacturer exchanges his cloth for coal in order to heat his private dwelling (in this case the coal itself in turn is an article of consumption for him, and he pays for it with revenue, with a quantity of cloth that represents profit); or whether James, the cloth manufacturer's footman, exchanges the cloth he has received as wages for the coal (in this case the latter is once more an article of consumption and exchanged for the revenue of the cloth manufacturer, who in turn however has exchanged his revenue for the unproductive labour of the footman); or whether the cloth manufacturer exchanges cloth for coal in order to replace the coal required in his factory that has been used up. (In the latter case the cloth that the cloth manufacturer exchanges represents for him constant capital, the value of one of his means of production; and the coal represents for him not only the value but his means of production in kind. But for the coal producer the cloth is an article of consumption, and both cloth and coal represent for him revenue; the coal, revenue in its non-realised form; the cloth, revenue in its realised form.)

But as for the last one-third of the coal, the coal producer cannot spend it on articles which enter into his individual consumption; he cannot spend it as revenue. It belongs to the process of production (or reproduction) and must be transformed into iron, timber, machinery—into articles which form the component parts of his constant capital and without which the production of coal cannot be renewed or continued. He could, it is true, exchange also this one-third for articles of consumption (or, what is the same thing, for the money of the producers of these articles), but in fact only on the condition that he exchanges these consumption articles in turn for iron, timber, machinery—that they enter neither into his own consumption nor into the outlay of his revenue, but into the consumption and revenue outlays of the producers of timber, iron and machinery; all of whom, however, in turn find themselves in the position of not being able to expend one-third of their product on articles for individual consumption.

Now let us assume that coal enters into the constant capital of the producers of iron and timber, and of the machine builder. On the other hand iron, timber, and machinery enter into the constant capital of the producer of coal. In so far as these products of theirs enter [into their] mutual [constant capital] to the same amount of value, they replace themselves in kind, and one has to pay the other only the balance for the surplus that he has bought from him in excess of what he has sold to him. In fact, in such a transaction money appears in practice (through the medium of bills of exchange, etc.) only as *means of payment*, not as coin, means of circulation; and only the balance is paid in money. The producer of coal will need a part of this one-third of his coal for his own reproduction, just as he deducted from the product a part of the two-thirds for his own consumption.

The whole quantity of coal, iron, timber and machinery which are reciprocally replaced in this way by the exchange of constant capital for constant capital, of constant capital in one natural form for constant capital in another natural form, has absolutely nothing to do either with the exchange of revenue for constant capital or with the exchange of revenue for revenue. It plays exactly the same role as seed in agriculture or the capital stock of cattle in cattle-rearing. It is a part of the *yearly product of labour*, but it is not a part *of the product of the year's [newly-added] labour* (on the contrary it is a part of the product of the year's labour plus the pre-existing labour), which (conditions of production remaining the same) replaces itself annually as means of production, as constant capital, without entering into any circulation other than that between dealers and dealers and without affecting the *value* of the part of the product which enters into the circulation between dealers and consumers.*

Let us assume that the whole one-third of the coal is thus exchanged in kind for its own elements of production, iron, timber, machinery. <It might be possible for example to exchange the entire amount direct for machinery; but the machine builder in turn would exchange it as constant capital, not only for his own but for that of the producers of iron and timber.> In fact, each hundredweight of the two-thirds of his product in coal ||352| which he exchanged for articles of consumption, exchanged as revenue, would, from the standpoint of value, consist of two parts, as the total product does. One-third of a hundredweight would be equal to the value of the means of production used up in the hundredweight, and two-thirds of the hundredweight would be equal to the labour newly added to this third by the producers of the coal. But if the total product is for example equal to 30,000 hundredweight he exchanges only 20,000 hundredweight as revenue. On the assumption made, the other 10,000 hundredweight would be replaced by iron, timber, machinery, etc., etc.; in a word, the whole value of the means of production used up in the 30,000 hundredweight would be replaced in kind by means of production of the same sort and of equal value.

The buyers of the 20,000 hundredweight thus do not pay a single farthing for the value of the pre-existing labour contained in the 20,000 hundredweight; for the 20,000 represent only two-thirds of the value of the total product in which the newly-added labour is realised. It comes to the same thing, therefore, as if the 20,000 hundredweight represented only labour newly added (during the year, for example) and no pre-existing labour. The buyer therefore pays the whole value of each hundredweight, pre-existing labour plus newly-added labour, and yet he pays only

* See pp. 125 and 139 of the present volume.—*Ed.*

for the newly-added labour; and that is because the quantity he buys is only 20,000 hundredweight, only that quantity of the total product which is equal to the value of all the newly-added labour. Just as little does he pay for the farmer's seed in paying for the wheat which he eats. The producers have mutually replaced this part for each other; therefore they do not need to have it replaced a second time. They have replaced it with the part of their own product which it is true is the year's product of their labour, but is not at all the product of their year's labour, but on the contrary is the part of their annual product that represents the pre-existing labour. Without the new labour the product would not be there; but in the same way it would not be there without the labour materialised in the means of production. If it were merely the product of the new labour, then its value would be less than it now is, and there would be no part of the product to be returned to production. But if the other method of labour [using means of production] were not more productive and did not yield more product in spite of a part of the product having to be returned to production, it would not be used.

Although no part of the value of the one-third of the coal enters into the 20,000 hundredweight of coal sold as revenue, any change in the value of the constant capital which the one-third or 10,000 hundredweight represented would nevertheless bring about a change of value in the other two-thirds which are sold as revenue. Let production in iron, timber, machinery and so on, in a word, in the elements of production of which the one-third of the product is composed, become more costly. Let the productivity of mining labour remain the same. The 30,000 hundredweight are produced with the same quantity of iron, timber, coal, machinery and labour as before. But since iron, timber and machinery have got dearer, cost more labour-time than before, more coal than before must be given for them.

||353| As previously, the product would be equal to 30,000 hundredweight. The coal-mining labour has remained as productive as it was before. With the same quantity of living labour and the same amount of timber, iron, machinery, etc., it produces 30,000 hundredweight as before. The living labour, as before, is represented by the same value, say £20,000 (reckoned in money). On the other hand timber, iron, etc., in a word, the constant capital, now cost £16,000 instead of £10,000; that is to say, the labour-time contained in them has increased by six-tenths, or 60 per cent.

The value of the total product is now equal to £36,000; it was

£30,000 before; it has therefore risen by one-fifth, or 20 per cent. So also every aliquot part of the product costs one-fifth, or 20 per cent, more than before. If a hundredweight cost £1 previously, then now it costs £1 plus one-fifth of £1=£1. 4s. Previously, $^1/_3$ or $^3/_9$ of the total product was equal to constant capital, $^2/_3$ equal to labour added. Now the proportion of the constant capital to the value of the total product is as 16,000 : 36,000= $={}^{16}/_{36}={}^4/_9$. It amounts therefore to one-ninth [of the value of the total product] more than before The part of the product which is equal to the value of the labour added was formerly $^2/_3$ or $^6/_9$ of the product, now it is $^5/_9$.

So we get:

	Constant capital	Labour added
Value = £36,000	£16,000 ($^4/_9$ of the product)	£20,000 (the same value as before = $^5/_9$ of the product)
Product = 30,000 cwt.	13,333 $^1/_3$ cwt.	16,666 $^2/_3$ cwt.

The coal miners' labour would not have become less productive; but the product of their labour plus the pre-existing labour would have become less productive; that is, $^1/_9$ more of the total product would be required to replace the component part of the value ||354| formed by the constant capital. $^1/_9$ less of the product would be equal to the value of the labour added. Now as before the producers of iron, timber, etc., would only pay for 10,000 cwt. of coal. Previously these cost them £10,000. They will now cost them £12,000. A part of the costs of the constant capital would therefore be made good, since they would have to pay the increased price for the part of the coal which they get in replacement of iron, etc. But the producer of coal has to buy raw material, etc., from them to the amount of £16,000. There remains therefore a debit balance of £4,000, that is, 3,333 $^1/_3$ cwt. of coal. He must therefore, as before, supply 16,666 $^2/_3$+3,333 $^1/_3$ cwt.=20,000 cwt. of coal=two-thirds of the product to the consumers, who would now have to pay £24,000 for it instead of £20,000. In so doing they would have to replace for him not only labour, but also a part of the constant capital.

As regards the consumers, the matter would be very simple. If they wished to consume the same quantity of coal as before, they must pay one-fifth more for it and so must spend one-fifth of their revenue less on other products, if the production costs have remained the same in every branch of production. The difficulty lies only in this: how does the producer of coal pay for the £4,000 of iron, timber, etc., for which their producers do not want coal in exchange? He has sold the 3,333 $^1/_3$ cwt., equal to this £4,000, to the consumers of coal, and has received in exchange commodities of all kinds. But these cannot enter into his consumption or that of his labourers, but must pass into the consumption of the producers of iron, timber, etc., for he must replace in these articles the value of his 3,333 $^1/_3$ cwt. It will be said: it's quite a simple matter. All consumers of coal have to consume $^1/_5$ less of all other commodities, or each of them has to give $^1/_5$ more of his commodities for coal. The producers of timber, iron, etc., consume exactly this $^1/_5$ more. However, it is not *prima facie* evident how the lowered productivity in the ironworks, machine building, timber-felling, etc., is to enable their producers to consume a larger revenue than before, since the price of their articles is supposed to be equal to their values, and, consequently, to have risen only in proportion to the diminished productivity of their labour.

Now it is assumed that iron, timber, machinery have risen in value by three-fifths, by 60 per cent. There are only two causes which can give rise to this. Either the iron, timber, etc., production has become less productive, because the living labour used in it has become less productive, that is, a greater quantity of labour must be used to produce the same product. In this case the producers must use three-fifths more labour than before. The rate of wages has remained the same, because the lowered productivity of labour has only a passing effect on individual products. Therefore the rate of surplus-value also has remained the same. The producer needs 24 days' labour where he needed 15 before; but he pays the labourers, as before, only 10 hours' labour on each of the 24 [working-days], and makes them work 2 [hours] for nothing on each of these days, as previously. If the 15 [labourers] have therefore done 150 hours' labour for themselves and 30 for him; so the 24 work 240 hours for themselves and 48 for him. (Here we don't worry about the rate of profit.) Wages have only fallen in so far as they are spent in iron, timber and machinery, etc., which is not the case. The 24 labourers now consume $^3/_5$ more than the 15 did before. So the coal producers can set aside correspondingly more for them from the value of the 3,333 $^1/_3$ cwt. (i.e., for their master, who pays out the wages).

Or the reduced productivity in the production of iron, timber, etc., arises from the fact that parts of their constant capital, of their means of production, have become dearer. Then the same alternative applies, and finally the reduced productivity must result in the use of a greater quantity of living labour; therefore also in increased wages, which the coal producer has partly received from the consumers in the £4,000.

In the branches of production where more labour is employed, the amount of the surplus-value will have risen because the number of workers employed is greater. On the other hand, the rate of profit will have fallen in so far as all component parts of their constant capital into which their own product enters [have risen]; whether they themselves use a part of their own product as means of production, or, as in the case of coal, their product enters as a means of production into their own means of production. However, if their circulating capital laid out in wages has increased more than the part of the constant capital that they have to replace, their rate of profit will also have risen, and they ||355| will participate in the consumption of a part of the £4,000.

An increase in the value of the constant capital (arising from lowered productivity in the branches of labour which supply it) raises the value of the product into which it enters as constant capital, and reduces the part of the product (in kind) which replaces the newly-added labour, thus making it less productive in so far as this is reckoned in its own product. For the part of the constant capital which is exchanged in kind, the position is the same as it was. The same quantity of iron, timber and coal as before will be exchanged in kind in order to replace the iron, timber and coal that has been used up, and in this transaction the higher prices will balance each other. But the surplus of coal which now forms a part of the constant capital of the coal producer and does not enter into this exchange in kind is, as before, exchanged for revenue (in the case given above, in part not only for wages but also for profit); this revenue, however, instead of going to the former consumers, accrues to the producers in whose spheres of production a greater quantity of labour is used, that is, the number of labourers has increased.

If a branch of industry produces products which enter only into individual consumption, and neither into other industries as means of production (by means of production constant capital is always meant here) nor into their own reproduction (as for example in agriculture, cattle-raising, or the coal industry, into which coal itself enters as auxiliary material), then the annual product of this branch <any possible surplus over the annual prod-

uct making no difference in this connection> must always be paid for out of revenue, wages or profit.

Let us take the case of the linen given earlier.* Three yards of linen consist of: two-thirds constant capital and one-third labour added. One yard of linen therefore represents labour added. If the surplus-value is 25 per cent, then one-fifth of the 1 yard represents the profit, the other four-fifths represent the reproduction of the wages. The manufacturer himself consumes the one-fifth, or what is the same thing, others consume it and pay him the value, which he consumes in their own or in other commodities. <To simplify matters, here the whole profit is—wrongly—considered as revenue.> But he expends the four-fifths of a yard again in wages; his labourers consume them as their revenue either directly or in exchange for other consumable products, whose owners consume the linen.

This is the total part of the 3 yards of linen—the 1 yard—which the linen producers can themselves consume as revenue. The other 2 yards represent the manufacturer's constant capital; they must be reconverted into the conditions of production for linen—yarn, machinery, etc. From the standpoint of the manufacturer, the exchange of the 2 yards of linen is an exchange of constant capital; but he can only exchange it against the revenue of other people. So he pays for the yarn, say, with $^4/_5$ of the 2 yards or $^8/_5$ yards, and for the machinery with $^2/_5$ of a yard. The spinner and machine builder in turn can each consume $^1/_3$ of what they get, that is, the former, out of $^8/_5$ yards, $^8/_{15}$ of a yard, the latter $^2/_{15}$ out of the $^2/_5$ of a [yard]. Added together, $^{10}/_{15}$ or $^2/_3$ of a yard. But $^{20}/_{15}$ or $^4/_3$ yards must replace for them the raw material, flax, iron, coal, etc., and each of these articles in turn consists of one part which represents revenue (labour newly added), and another part which represents constant capital (raw materials and fixed capital, etc.).

The last $^4/_3$ yards, however, can only be consumed as revenue. What therefore ultimately appears as constant capital in yarn and machinery and is used by the spinner and machine builder to replace the flax, iron and coal (except for the part of the iron, coal, etc., which the machine builder replaces with machines) can only represent the part of the flax, iron and coal which forms the revenue of the flax, iron and coal producers, so that there is no constant capital to be replaced in this; that is to say, it must

* See pp. 110 et seqq. of the present volume.—*Ed.*

belong to the part of the product into which, as shown above, no part of the constant capital enters. But these producers consume what is their revenue in iron, coal, flax, etc., in linen or in other consumable products, because their own products do not enter in that form, or only to a small extent, into their individual consumption. Thus a part of the iron, flax, etc., can be exchanged for a product which only enters into individual consumption, that is linen, and in exchange for it replace for the spinner all, and for the machine builder part, of his constant capital; while in turn the spinner and machine builder, with the part of their yarn and machinery that represents revenue, consume linen and thereby replace the weaver's constant capital.

Thus in fact the whole of the linen is resolved into the profits and wages of the weaver, spinner, machine builder, flax-grower and producers of coal and of iron, while at the same time they replace the whole of the constant capital for the linen manufacturer and the spinner. The account would not balance if the final producers of raw materials had to replace their own constant capital by exchange with the linen, since this is an article for individual consumption, which does not enter into any sphere of production as means of production, ||356| as part of the constant capital. The account balances, because the linen bought by the flax-grower, producers of coal and of iron, machine builder, etc., with their own product, replaces for them only the part of their product which consists in revenue for *them*, but in constant capital for those who buy their products. That is only possible because they replace the part of their product which does not consist of revenue and which therefore cannot be exchanged for consumable products, in kind or by the exchange of constant capital for constant capital.

In the example given above it may seem strange that it is assumed that the productivity of labour in a given branch of industry has remained the same, and yet that it has fallen, if the productivity of the living labour employed in this branch of industry is reckoned in its own product. But this is very simply explained.

Suppose the product of a spinner's labour is equal to 5 lbs. of yarn. Assume that he needs for this only 5 lbs. of cotton (that is, there is no waste); and that an lb. of yarn costs 1 shilling (we leave the machinery out of account; that is, we suppose that its value has neither fallen nor risen; for the case we are considering, therefore, its value is equal to nil). [Let] cotton [cost] 8d. an lb. Of the 5s. which the 5 lbs. of yarn costs, 40d. (5×8d.)=3s. 4d. is for the cotton, and 5×4d.=20d.=1s. 8d. is the newly-added labour. Of the total product, therefore, constant capital amounts to 3s. 4d., [that is,] $3^1/_3$ lbs. of yarn, and labour to 1 $^2/_3$ lbs. of yarn. Hence two-thirds of the 5 lbs. of yarn replace constant capital and one-third of the 5 lbs. of yarn, or 1 $^2/_3$ lbs., is the part of the product which pays for the labour. Assume that the price of an lb. of cotton now rises by 50 per cent, from 8d. to 12d., or ls. Then we have for 5 lbs. of yarn, first, 5s. for 5 lbs. of cotton, and ls. 8d. for labour added, whose quantity, and therefore whose value expressed in money, remains the same. Thus the 5 lbs. of yarn now costs 5s. plus ls. 8d.=6s. 8d. Of this 6s. 8d., however, raw material is now 5s. and labour 1s. 8d.

6s. 8d.=80 d., of which 60d. is for raw material and 20d. for labour. Labour now only forms 20d. of the value of the 5 lbs., 80d., or $^1/_4$=25 per cent; previously, 33 $^1/_3$ per cent. On the other hand the raw material is 60d.=$^3/_4$=75 per cent; previously it was only 66 $^2/_3$ per cent. As the 5 lbs. of yarn now costs 80d., 1 lb. costs $^{80}/_5$d.=16d. For his 20d.—the value of the [newly-added] labour—[the spinner] will therefore get $1^1/_4$ lbs. of the 5 lbs. of yarn, and [the other] $3^3/_4$ lbs. [go for] raw material. Previously, $1^2/_3$ lbs. were for labour (profit and wages) and $3^1/_3$ lbs. for constant capital. Reckoned in its own product, therefore, the labour has become less productive, although its productivity has remained the same and only the raw material has got dearer. But it has remained equally productive, because the same labour has transformed 5 lbs. of cotton into 5 lbs. of yarn in the same time, and the actual product of this labour (considered as use-value) is only the *form of yarn* which has been given to the cotton. The 5 lbs. of cotton have been given the form of yarn as before, with the same labour. The actual product, however, consists not only of this form of yarn but also of the raw cotton, the material which has been put into this form, and the value of this material now forms a greater part of the total product than it did before, in proportion to the labour which gives it the form. Consequently the same quantity of spinning labour is paid for in less yarn, or the part of the product which replaces it has become smaller.

So much for that.

[(c) Vulgar Assumptions of Garnier's Polemics against Smith. Garnier's Relapse into Physiocratic Ideas. The View of the Unproductive Labourers' Consumption as the Source of Production—a Step Backwards as Compared with the Physiocrats]

So in the first place Garnier is wrong when he says that the whole capital is in the end always replaced by consumer's revenue, since a part of the capital can be replaced by capital and not by revenue. Secondly, it is in itself a silly statement, since revenue itself, in so far as it is not wages (or wages paid by wages, revenue derived from wages), is profit on capital (or revenue derived from profit on capital). Finally, it is silly to say that the part of capital which does not circulate (in the sense that it is not replaced by consumer's revenue) "yields no profit to its possessor". In fact—conditions of production remaining the same—this part yields no profit (or rather, no surplus-value). But without it capital could in no case produce its profit.

||357| "All that can be deduced from this difference is that, in order to employ *productive* people, what is required is not only the *revenue of the person who enjoys their labour*, but *also a capital which yields profit to intermediaries*, while *to employ non-productive people* the revenue which pays them is most often sufficient" (l. c., p. 175).

This one sentence is such a bundle of nonsense that it makes it clear that Garnier, the translator of Adam Smith, in fact understood nothing of what Adam Smith wrote, and in particular had no conception whatever of the essence of the *Wealth of Nations*—namely, the view that the capitalist mode of production is the most productive mode (which it absolutely is, in comparison with previous forms).

First, it is an extremely silly objection to raise against Smith, who declared that unproductive labour was labour paid directly from revenue, that "to employ *non-productive* people the revenue which pays them is most often sufficient". Now however the antithesis:

"in order to employ *productive* people, what is required is *not only the revenue of the person who enjoys* their labour, but also a *capital which yields profit to intermediaries.*"

(How productive then must agricultural labour be for Monsieur Garnier, which in addition to the revenue which enjoys the product of the land, requires a capital which not only yields profit to intermediaries, but in addition a rent to the landowner!)

In order "to employ these productive people", what is necessary is not first capital that employs them, and secondly revenue that enjoys their labour, but nothing other than capital, which produces the revenue, which enjoys the fruit of their labour. If as a capitalist tailor I lay out £100 in wages, this £100 produces for me say £120. It produces for me a revenue of £20, with which I can then, if I want to, also enjoy tailoring labour in the form of a "frockcoat". If on the other hand I buy clothes for £20 in order to wear them, it is obvious that these clothes have not created the £20 with which I buy them. And the case would be the same if I got a jobbing tailor to come to my house and made him sew coats for me for £20. In the first case I received £20 more than I had before, and in the second case, after the transaction, I have £20 less than I had before. Moreover, I would soon realise that the tailor whom I pay directly from revenue does not make the coat as cheaply as if I bought it from the intermediary.

Garnier imagines that the profit is paid by the consumer. The consumer pays the "value" of the commodity; and although it contains a profit for the capitalist, the commodity is cheaper for him, the consumer, than if he had spent his revenue directly on labour causing it to produce on a small scale for his personal requirements. It is obvious here that Garnier has not the slightest idea of what capital is.

He continues:

"Do not many *unproductive* workers, such as actors, musicians, etc., as a rule only receive their wages through the channel of a manager who draws profits from the capital placed in this kind of enterprise?" (l.c., pp. 175-76).

This observation is correct, but it only shows that a part of the labourers whom Adam Smith in his second definition calls unproductive are productive according to his first definition.

"It follows therefore that in a society in which the *productive* class is very numerous, it must be supposed that a large accumulation of capitals exists in the hands of the intermediaries or entrepreneurs of labour" (l.c., p. 176).

In fact, wage-labour on a mass scale is only another expression for capital on a mass scale.

"It is therefore not, as Smith maintains, the proportion existing between the mass of capitals and that of revenues which will determine the proportion between the *productive* class and the *non-productive* class. This latter proportion seems to depend much more on the customs and habits of the people; on the more or less advanced degree of its industry" (l.c., p. 177).

If productive labourers are such as are paid from capital, and unproductive such as are paid from revenue, the proportion of the productive class to the unproductive is obviously that of capital to revenue. The proportional growth of the two classes, however, will not depend only on the existing proportion of the mass of capitals to the mass of revenues. It will depend on the proportion in which the increasing revenue (profit) is transformed into capital or expended as revenue. Although the bourgeoisie was originally very thrifty, with the growing productivity of capital, i.e., of the labourers, ||358| it imitates the retainer system of the feudal lords. According to the latest report (1861 or 1862)* on the factories, the total number of persons (managers included) employed in the factories properly so called of the United Kingdom was only 775,534,* while the number of female servants in England alone amounted to 1 million. What a convenient arrangement it is that makes a factory girl to sweat twelve hours in a factory, so that the factory proprietor, with a part of her unpaid labour, can take into his personal service her sister as maid, her brother as groom and her cousin as soldier or policeman!

Garnier's last sentence is trite tautology. He makes the proportion between the productive and the unproductive classes depend, not on the proportion of capital and revenue—or rather on the mass of existing commodities which are expended in the form of capital or of revenue—but (?) on the customs and habits of the people, on the degree of development of its industry. In fact, capitalist production first appears at a certain stage of development of industry.

As a Bonapartist senator, Garnier naturally waxes enthusiastic over lackeys and servitors in general: "No class with an equal number of individuals contributes more than domestic servants to the conversion into *capital* of sums originating from *revenue*" (p. 181).

In fact, no class provides a more worthless section of recruits for the petty bourgeoisie. Garnier does not understand how Smith, "a man who has observed things with such sagacity", does not value more highly "this intermediary, placed close to the rich, in order *to gather up* the scraps of revenue which the latter so thoughtlessly dissipates" (l. c., pp. 182, 183). He himself says in this sentence that he merely "gathers up" the scraps of "revenue". But of what does this revenue consist? Of the unpaid labour of the productive labourer.

After all these extremely worthless polemics against Smith, Garnier, relapsing into Physiocracy, declares agricultural labour the only productive labour! And why? Because it "creates another new value, a value which *did not exist* in society, even as an equivalent, at the moment when this labour began to be performed;

* *Return to an Address of the House of Commons*, dated 24 April, 1861 (printed 11 February, 1862).

and it is this value which provides a rent to the owner of the land" (l. c., p. 184).

So what is productive labour? Labour which produces a surplus-value, a new value over and above the equivalent which it receives as wages. Smith is not to blame for Garnier's failing to understand that the exchange *of capital for labour* means *nothing but* the exchange of a commodity of a given value—equal to a given quantity of labour—for a greater quantity of labour than it itself contains, and thus creates "a new value, a value which did not exist in society, even as an equivalent, at the moment when this labour began to be performed". |VIII—358||

* * *

||IX—400| *Monsieur Germain Garnier* had published in Paris *in 1796 Abrégé élémentaire des principes de l'économie politique*. Along with the Physiocratic view that agriculture alone is productive another is to be found (which to a great extent explains his polemic against Adam Smith), namely, that consumption (strongly represented by the "unproductive labourers") is the source of production, and that the volume of the latter is to be measured by the volume of the former. The unproductive labourers satisfy artificial needs and consume material products, and are thus in every way useful. He also polemises, therefore, against economy (thrift). On p. xiii of his preface we find:

"The fortune of an individual is enlarged by saving; the public fortune, *on the contrary*, derives its increase from the increase of consumption."

And on p. 240, in the chapter on public debts:

"The improvement and extension of agriculture and consequently the progress of industry and commerce have *no other cause* than the extension of artificial needs."

From this he concludes that public debts are a good thing, in that they increase these needs.[65] |IX—400||

* * *

||XI—421| S*chmalz*. In his criticism of Smith's distinction between productive labour and unproductive labour this German afterbirth of the Physiocrats says (German edition [it was published *in*] *1818*):

"I observe only ... that Smith's distinction between *productive* and *unproductive* labour should not be considered as essential or very precise, if one has regard to the fact that in general the labour of others never produces anything for us but a saving of time, and that this saving of time is all that forms *its value* and *its price*."*

<There is a confusion here: the value and the price of a thing is not determined by the economy of time effected through the division of labour; but I get more use-value for the same value, labour is more productive, because a greater quantity of products is produced in the same time, however as the echo of the Physiocrats he naturally could not discover value in labour-time itself.>

"The joiner for example who makes a table for me, and the servant who takes my letters to the post, who cleans my clothes or gets for me the things I need, both perform a service of absolutely like nature. Both the one and the other save me the time which I myself would have to use up in doing these things, as also the time I would have to devote to acquire the skill and facility needed for them" (Schmalz, *Économie politique*, traduit par Henri Jouffroy, etc., t. I, 1826, p. 304).

The following remark of this same scribbler Schmalz** is also important for the link with Garnier, for instance his consumption system (and the economic utility of vast expenditure) with the Physiocratic system:

"This system" (Quesnay's) "regards the consumption of artisans, and even of *those who merely consume*, as meritorious, because this consumption, even though in an indirect and mediated way, contributes to the growth of the nation's revenue; since but for *this consumption the consumed products would not have been produced from the land and could not have been added to the revenue of the landowner*" (p. 321)[66]. |IX—421||

[8.] Charles Ganilh [Mercantilist Conception of Exchange and Exchange-Value. Inclusion of All Paid Labour in the Concept of Productive Labour]

||VIII—358| A very inferior and superficial compilation is Charles Ganilh's *Des systèmes d'économie politique*. First edition Paris *1809*, second *1821*. (Quotations from the latter.) His twaddle is directly linked with Garnier, against whom he polemises.

---

* Marx quotes Schmalz from the French translation. See Appendix, p. 436—*Ed.*

** In the manuscript there is a pun upon the name of the author that cannot be translated. Marx calls him Schmalzschmiertopf. (The German noun "Schmalz" means grease, lard, dripping; "Schmiertopf"—grease can, scribbler.)—*Ed.*

<*Canard* in *Principes d'économie politique* defines "*wealth*" [as] "*an accumulation of superfluous labour*".[67] Had he said that it is the labour which is superfluous for keeping the labourer alive as a labourer, the definition would be correct.>

Monsieur Ganilh's starting-point is the elementary fact that the commodity is the element of bourgeois wealth, and therefore labour, in order to produce wealth, must produce commodities, must *sell* itself or its product.

"In the present state of civilisation, labour is only known to us through exchange" (l.c., t. I, p. 79). "Labour without exchange can produce no wealth" (l.c., p. 81).

From this Ganilh jumps straight into the Mercantile system.

Because labour without exchange creates no bourgeois wealth, "wealth comes exclusively from trade" (l.c., p. 84). Or, as he says later: "Exchange or trade alone gives value to things" (l.c., p. 98). On this "principle of the identity of values and wealth ... rests the doctrine of the fruitfulness of general labour" (l.c., p. 93).

Ganilh himself declares ||359| that the "commercial system" which he calls a mere "modification" of the monetary system

"derives private and public wealth from the exchangeable values of labour, whether these values are or are not fixed in material, durable, and permanent objects" (l.c., p. 95).

He thus falls into the Mercantile system, as Garnier fell into the Physiocratic. His trash, if good for nothing else, is consequently not bad as a characterisation of this system and of its views on "surplus-value", especially as he puts forward these views in opposition to Smith, Ricardo, etc.

Wealth is exchangeable value; all labour which produces an exchangeable value or itself has an exchangeable value consequently produces wealth. The only word in which Ganilh shows himself a more profound Mercantilist, is the word *general* labour. The labour of individuals, or rather its product, must take the form of general labour. Only so is it exchange-value, *money*. In fact, Ganilh comes back to the view that wealth is equivalent to money; though no longer only gold and silver, but the commodity itself, in so far as it is *money*. He says: "*Commercial system*, or the exchange of values of *general labour*" (l. c., p. 98). This is nonsense. The product is value as the form of existence, as the incarnation of general labour, but not as "the *value* of general labour", which would be equivalent to the value of value. But let us assume that the commodity is constituted as value, and has even taken on the form of money, is metamorphosed. It is now exchangeable value. But how great is its value? All commodities are exchangeable value. They are not different from each other in this. But what makes the exchangeable value of a definite commodity? Here Ganilh does not get beyond the crudest superficiality. A is of greater exchange-value when it exchanges for more B, C, D, etc.

Ganilh is quite right when he says of Ricardo and most economists that they consider labour without exchange, although their system, like the whole bourgeois system, rests on exchange-value. This however is only due to the fact that to them the *form* of product as commodity seems self-evident, and consequently they examine only the *magnitude of value.* In exchange the products of individuals only manifest themselves as products of general labour by taking the form of *money.* This relativity, however, originates from the fact that they must present themselves as the form of existence of general labour, and can be reduced to it only as relative, merely quantitatively different expressions of social labour. But the exchange itself does not give them their *magnitude of value.* In exchange they appear as general social labour; and the extent to which they can appear as general social labour depends on the extent to which they can present themselves as social labour, that is, on the extent of the commodities for which they can be exchanged, and therefore on the expansion of the market, of trade; on the range of commodities in which they can be expressed as exchange-value. For example, were there only four different branches of production in existence, each of the four producers would produce a great part of his product for himself. If there are thousands, then he can produce his total product as commodities. It can enter entirely into exchange. But Ganilh imagines, with the Mercantilists, that *the magnitude of value is itself the product of exchange*, whereas in fact it is only the form of value or the form of *commodity* which the product receives through exchange.

"Exchange gives *things* a value which they would not have had without it" (p. 102).

If this means that *things*, use-values, only become value, receive this form as relative expressions of social labour, it is a tautology. But if it is intended to mean that through exchange they get a greater value than they would have had without it, it is clearly nonsense, for exchange can only increase A's magnitude of value by reducing that of B. So far as it gives A a greater value than it has before the exchange, it gives B a smaller value. A+B, *therefore, has the same value after the exchange as it had before it.*

"The most useful products may have no value if exchange does not give any to them" (p. 104).

(First, if these things are "products", they are from the start products of labour, not general elemental things provided by nature like air, etc.; if they are "the most useful", they are use-values in the highest sense, use-values that everyone needs; if exchange gives them *no* value, this is only possible if everyone produces them for himself; this however contradicts ||360| the assumption that they are produced for exchange; therefore the whole proposition is nonsense.)

"And the most useless products may have very great value, if exchange is favourable for them" (p. 104).

For Monsieur Ganilh, "exchange" is a mystical being. If the "most useless" products are no use for anything, have no use-value, who will buy them? They must therefore have at least an imaginary "utility" for the buyer. And if he is not a fool, why should he pay more for them? Their dearness must therefore originate in some circumstance which in any case does not arise from their "uselessness". Their "scarcity", rarity? But Ganilh calls them "the most useless *products*". As therefore they are products, why are they not produced in greater quantities, in spite of their great "exchange-value"? If before it was the buyer who was a fool, giving a lot of money for something that had neither a real nor an imaginary use-value for him, now it is the seller, who does not produce these trifles of great exchange-value instead of utilities of small value. That their exchange-value is great in spite of their small use-value (use-value determined by the natural needs of man), must therefore be due to some circumstance that originates not from Lord Exchange, but from the product itself. *Its high exchange-value is therefore not the product of exchange, but only appears in exchange.*

"The exchanged value of things and not their exchangeable value establishes *the real value*, the value which is identical with wealth" (l.c., p. 104).

But exchangeable value is a relation of the thing to other things with which it can be exchanged. <The correct point underlying this statement is: what compels the transformation of the commodity into money is that it has to enter into exchange as an exchange-

able value, but only becomes that as the result of exchange. > On the other hand, the exchanged value of A is a definite quantity of products B, C, D, etc. Therefore (according to Monsieur Ganilh) it is no longer a value, but a thing, without exchange. B, C, D, etc., were not "values". A has become a value through these non-values stepping into its place (as exchanged value). By the mere change of place—after they have come out of exchange and find themselves in the same position as before—these things have become values.

"It is therefore neither the real utility of things, nor their *intrinsic* value, which makes them wealth; it is exchange which fixes and determines their value, and it is this value which identifies them with wealth" (l.c.,p.105).

Lord Exchange fixes and determines something which was there or was not there. If only exchange creates the value of things, then this value, this product of exchange, ceases to exist as soon as exchange itself ceases. Thus what it makes, it equally unmakes. I exchange A for B+C+D. In the act of this exchange A gets value. As soon as the act is past, B+C+D stands on the side where A was, and A on the side where B+C+D was. And in fact each stands on its own, outside Lord Exchange, who only consisted of this change of place. B+C+D is now things, not values. So is A. Or exchange "fixes and determines" in the literal meaning of the word. A dynamometer determines and fixes the degree of strength of my muscles, but it does not make it. In this case value is not produced by exchange.

"There is in truth no wealth for individuals and for peoples, except when each labours for all" (that is to say, when his labour takes the form of *general social labour*, for in any other meaning this would be nonsense; since, except in the form of general social labour, an iron manufacturer does not work for all, but *only* for consumers of iron); "and all for each" (which again is nonsense, if we are dealing with use-value, for the products of all are without exception special products, and each person needs only special products; what this means is therefore only that each special product takes on a form in which *it exists for everyone*; and it only exists in this form, not because as a special product it is distinct from the product of each other person, but because it is identical with it; that is, once more the form of social labour as it exists on the basis of commodity production) (l. c., p. 108).

||361| From this definition—exchange-value is the expression of the labour of the isolated individual as general social labour—

Ganilh falls once more into the crudest conception: that exchange-value is the proportion in which commodity A exchanges against commodity B, C, D, etc. A has great exchange-value if much B, C, D is given for it; but then little A is given for B, C, D. Wealth consists of exchange-value. Exchange-value consists of the relative proportion in which products exchange for each other. The total quantity of products has therefore no exchange-value, since it is not exchanged for anything. Hence, society, whose wealth consists of exchange-values, has no wealth. Consequently it follows not only, as Ganilh himself concludes, that the "national wealth, which is composed of the exchange-values of labour" (p. 108), can never rise and can never fall in exchange-value (therefore there is *no surplus-value*), but that it has no exchange-value whatever, and so is not wealth, since wealth consists only of exchangeable values.

"If the abundance of wheat makes *its value fall*, the farmers will be less rich, because they have less exchange-values to obtain for themselves things that are necessary, useful or pleasant for life; but the consumers of wheat will profit from all that the farmers have lost: the loss of some will be compensated by the gain of others, and the general wealth will undergo no change" (pp. 108-09).

Excuse me. The consumers of wheat eat the wheat and not the exchangeable value of the wheat. They are richer in means of subsistence, but not in exchangeable value. They have exchanged a small amount of their products—which have a high exchange-value because of their relative paucity as compared with the quantity of wheat for which they are exchanged—for the wheat. The farmers have now received the *high exchange-value* and the consumers a good deal of wheat of small exchange-value, so that now the latter are the poor ones and the farmers the rich.

Moreover, the total (the social total of exchange-values) loses its nature of being exchange-value in the same degree as it becomes the total of exchange-values. A, B, C, D, E, F have exchange-value in so far as they are exchanged for each other. When they have been exchanged, they are then all products for their consumers, their purchasers. By exchanging hands they have ceased to be exchange-value. And thereby the wealth of society, which is composed of exchangeable values, has disappeared. The value of A is relative; it is its exchange relation to B, C, etc. A+B has less exchange-value, because its exchange-value now exists only in relation to C, D, E, F. But the total of A, B, C, D, E, F has no exchange-value at all, because it expresses no relation. The total of commodities is not exchanged for other commodities. Therefore the wealth of society, which consists of exchange-values, has no exchange-value and is consequently not wealth.

"Hence it is that it is difficult, and perhaps impossible, for a country to enrich itself by internal commerce. It is not at all the same for peoples who engage in foreign trade" (l.c., p. 109).

This is the old Mercantile system. Value consists in my getting not an equivalent, but more than the equivalent. At the same time, however, for Ganilh there is no equivalent, for this would imply that the value of A and the value of B are determined not by the proportion of A in B or of B in A, but by a third thing in which A and B are identical. But if there is no equivalent, there can also be no excess over the equivalent. I get less gold for iron than iron for gold. Now I have more iron, for which I get less gold. If therefore I gain on the original transaction because less gold is equal to more iron, I now lose just as much because more iron is equal to less gold.

"All labour, whatever be its nature, is productive of wealth provided that it has an exchange-value" (l.c., p. 119). "Exchange pays no regard either to the quantity or to the material nature or to the durability of the products" (l.c., p. 121). "All" (kinds of labour) "are *equally productive* of the *sum* for which they have been exchanged" (pp. 121-22).

First they are equally productive of the *sum*, that is, the *price*, which they have been paid (the *value* of their wages). But Ganilh at once goes another step further. Immaterial labour, he says, produces the material product for which it is exchanged, so that it seems that material labour produces the product of immaterial labour.

||362| "There is no difference between the labour of the workman who makes a chest of drawers for which he gets two bushels of wheat in exchange and the labour of a village fiddler for which he gets two bushels of wheat. In both cases two bushels of wheat are produced: two bushels to pay for the chest of drawers, and two bushels to pay for the pleasure given by the village fiddler. It is true that after the joiner has consumed the two bushels of wheat, a chest of drawers remains, and after the fiddler has consumed the two bushels of wheat, nothing remains; but how many labours reputed productive are in the same case!... it is not by what remains after consumption that one can judge whether a labour is productive or sterile, it is by *the exchange or by the production to which it has given rise*. But since the joiner's labour, as well as the fiddler's labour, is *the cause of the production of two bushels of wheat, both are equally productive of two bushels of wheat*, although the one, after it is finished, does not fix and realise itself in any durable object, and the other fixes and realises itself in a durable object" (l.c., pp. 122-23).

"Adam Smith would like to reduce the number of labourers who are not usefully occupied, in order to multiply that of the labourers who are usefully occupied; but no consideration has been given to the fact that if this desire could be realised all wealth would be impossible, because consumers would be lacking for the producers, and the excess that was not consumed would not be reproduced. The productive classes do not give the products of their labours gratuitously *to the classes whose labours do not yield any material products*" (here he nevertheless himself distinguishes between labours which yield material products and labours which do not); "they give them to them in exchange for the convenience, the pleasures and the enjoyments that they receive from them, and, *in order to give them to them, they are obliged to produce them*. If the material products of labour were not employed to pay for the labours which do not yield material products, they would not have consumers and their *reproduction* would cease. The labours productive of enjoyment *thus contribute to production as efficaciously* as the labour which is considered to be the most productive" (l.c., pp. 123-24).

"Almost always the convenience, the pleasures or the enjoyments which they" (the peoples) "seek *follow* and *do not precede the products which are to pay for them*" (l.c., p. 125). (They seem therefore to be much more effect than cause of the products which are to pay for them). "The position is different when the labours devoted to pleasure, luxury and ostentation *are not wanted by the productive classes*," (thus he himself makes the distinction here) "and they are nevertheless *forced* to pay for them and to cut down their own requirements by this amount. Then it may come about that this forced payment does not bring about an increase in production" (l.c., p. 125). "Apart from this case ... all labour is necessarily productive, and contributes more or less efficaciously to the formation and growth of the public wealth, because *it necessarily calls forth the products which pay for it*" (l.c., p. 126).

<So according to this the "unproductive labours" are productive neither because of their cost, that is, their exchange-value, nor because of the special enjoyment that they produce, that is, their use-value, but because they produce productive labour.>

<If, according to Adam Smith, that labour is productive which is directly exchanged for capital, then we have to consider, apart from the form, also the material components of the capital which is exchanged for labour. It resolves itself into the necessary means of subsistence; that is for the most part into commodities, material things. What the labourer has to pay from these wages to State and Church is a deduction for services which are forced upon him; what he pays out for education is devilishly little, but when he does, his payments are productive, for education produces labour-power; what he pays out for the services of physicians, lawyers, priests, is his misfortune; there are very few unproductive labours or services left on which the labourer's wages are spent, especially as he himself provides his costs of consumption (cooking, keeping his house clean, generally even repairs).>

The following statement of Ganilh's is extremely characteristic:

"If exchange gives to the servant's labour a value of 1,000 francs, while it gives to that of the husbandman or factory worker only a value of 500 francs, one must conclude from this that the servant's labour contributes to the *production of wealth* twice as much as that of the husbandman and the factory worker; and it cannot be otherwise, as long as the labour of servants receives in payment twice as much in material products as the labour of husbandmen and factory workers. How can it be imagined that wealth results from labour which has less exchange-value and which is consequently paid less!" (l.c., pp. 293-94).

||363| If the wages of the factory or agricultural labourer are 500 francs, and the surplus-value (profit and rent) created by him is equal to 40 per cent, his net product would be 200 francs, and five such labourers would be required to produce the wages of 1,000 francs for the servant. If instead of the servant Lord Exchange cared to buy a mistress for 10,000 francs annually, the net product of 50 such productive labourers would be required. And because her unproductive labour brings in for the mistress twenty times as much exchange-value, wages, as the wages of the productive labourer, this person adds twenty times as much to "the production of wealth", and a country produces the more wealth the higher it pays its servants and mistresses. Monsieur Ganilh forgets that only the productivity of manufacturing and agricultural labour, only the surplus created by the productive workers but not paid to them, provides any fund at all for which the unproductive labourers are paid. But he reckons like this: 1,000 francs wage, and the labour of servant or mistress as equivalent for the wage, make together 2,000 francs. The value of servants and mistresses, that is, their production costs, depend entirely on the *net product* of the productive labourers. Indeed, their existence as a special breed of people depends on it. Their price and their value have little in common with each other.

But even assuming that the value (the costs of production) of a servant is twice as great as that of a productive labourer, it must be observed that the productivity of a labourer (like that of a machine) and his value are entirely different things, which are even in inverse proportion to each other. The value that a machine costs is always a minus in relation to its productivity.

"In vain is the objection raised that if the labour of servants is as productive as that of husbandmen and factory workers, there is no reason why the public economy of a country should not be used to maintain them, not only without being squandered but with a constant increase of value. This objection is only specious because it assumes that the fruitfulness of each labour results from its *co-operation in the production of material objects, that material production is constitutive of wealth* and *that production and wealth are completely identical.* It is forgotten that *all production only becomes wealth concurrently with its consumption,** and that exchange determines up to what point it *contributes to the formation of wealth.* If it is remembered that all labours contribute directly or indirectly to the total production of each country, that exchange, in fixing the value of each labour, determines the part that it has had in this production, that *consumption of the production* realises the value that exchange has given it, and that the surplus or deficit of production over consumption determines the state of wealth or poverty of peoples, it will be realised how inconsistent it is *to isolate* each labour, to fix its fertility and its fruitfulness by its *contribution to material production and without any regard to its* ||364| *consumption, which alone gives it a value,* a value without which wealth cannot exist" (l.c., pp. 294-95).

On the one hand the fellow makes wealth depend on the excess of production over consumption, on the other hand he says that only consumption gives value. And a servant who consumes 1,000 francs consequently contributes twice as much to the giving of value as a peasant who consumes 500 francs.

In the first place he admits that these unproductive labours do not directly participate in the formation of material wealth. Smith does not claim more than this. On the other hand he tries to prove that on the contrary they create material wealth in the same measure as, according to his own admission, they do not.

All those who polemise against Adam Smith on the one hand assume a superior attitude to material production, and on the other hand they attempt to justify immaterial production—or even no production, like that of lackeys—as material production. It makes absolutely no difference whether the owner of the net revenue consumes this revenue in lackeys, mistresses or pasties. But it is ludicrous to imagine that the surplus must be consumed by servants and cannot be consumed by productive labourers themselves without the value of the product going to the devil. With Malthus too we find the same view of the necessity of unproductive consumers—which necessity in fact exists when the surplus comes into the hands of idlers. |364||

---

* <And so the same fellow says one page later "that all labour is *productive* of wealth, in proportion to its exchange-value determined by supply and demand" (it *produces* wealth, not in proportion to the exchange-value it produces, but in proportion to its own exchange-value; that is to say, not on the basis of what it produces but of what it costs), "that its respective value only contributes to the accumulation of capitals by *the saving and non-consumption* of the products that this value is entitled to take out of total production".>

[9. Ganilh and Ricardo on Net Revenue. Ganilh as Advocate of a Diminution of the Productive Population; Ricardo as Advocate of the Accumulation of Capital and the Growth of Productive Forces]

||364| *Ganilh* claims to have put forward a theory in his *Théorie de l'économie politique* (a book I don't know) which Ricardo later copied from him.[68] This theory is that wealth depends on net product and not on gross product, and thus on the level of profit and rent. (This is certainly not a discovery of Ganilh's, who distinguishes himself, however, by the way he puts it.)

Surplus-value presents itself (has its real existence) in a surplus-produce in excess of the quantity of products which only replace its original elements, that is, which enter into its production costs and—taking constant and variable capital together—are equal to the total capital advanced to production. The aim of capitalist production is the surplus, not the product. The labourer's necessary labour-time, and therefore also its equivalent in the product with which it is paid for, is only necessary as long as it produces surplus-labour. Otherwise it is *unproductive* for the capitalist.

The surplus-value is equal to the rate of surplus-value $\frac{s}{v}$ multiplied by the number of simultaneous days' labour or the number of employed labourers, that is, by n. So $S=\frac{s}{v}\times n$. This surplus-value can therefore be increased or reduced in two ways. For example, $\frac{s}{\frac{v}{2}}\times n$ is equal to $\frac{2s}{v}\times n=2S$. Here S ||365| has doubled, because the rate has doubled, since $\frac{s}{\frac{v}{2}}$ is $\frac{2s}{v}$, that is, is twice as much as $\frac{s}{v}$. On the other hand, however $\frac{s}{v}\times 2n$ would also be equal to $\frac{2sn}{v}$, that is, also equal to 2S. V, the variable capital, is equal to the price of the single day's labour multiplied by the number of labourers employed. If 800 labourers are employed, each costing £1, then V=£800, that is, £1×800, where $n=800$. Then if the surplus-value is 160, its rate would be $\frac{160}{£1\times 800}=\frac{160}{800}=\frac{16}{80}=\frac{1}{5}=20$ per cent. But the surplus-value itself is $\frac{160}{£1\times 800}\times 800$, that is, $\frac{£S}{£1\times n}\times n$.

With a given length of labour-time, this surplus-value can only be increased by an increase of productivity, or at a given level of productivity, by a lengthening of the labour-time.

But what concerns us here is: $2S = \frac{s}{\frac{v}{2}} \times n$; and $2S = \frac{s}{v} \times 2n$.

The surplus-value (gross amount of surplus-value) remains the same, if the number of labourers is reduced by half—is only n instead of $2n$, but the surplus-labour performed by them each day is twice as much as it was before. On this assumption, therefore, two things would remain the same: first, the total quantity of products produced; secondly, the total quantity of surplus-produce or net product. But the following would have changed: first, the variable capital, or the part of the circulating capital expended in wages, would have fallen by half. The part of the constant capital which consists of raw materials would also remain unchanged, as the same quantity of raw material as before would be worked up, although this would be done by half the labourers employed before. As against this, the part which consists of fixed capital has increased.

If the capital expended in wages was £300 (£1 per labourer), it would now be £150. If that expended in raw materials was £310, it would now be £310. If the value of the machinery was four times as much as the rest of the capital, it would now be £1,600.[69] Therefore if the machinery is worn out in ten years, the machinery entering annually into the product would be £160. We will assume that the capital previously expended annually on instruments was £40, thus only $^1/_4$. Then the account would stand:

	Machinery	Raw material	Wages	Total	Surplus-value	Rate of profit	Total product
Old capital	40	310	300	650	150 or 50%	$23^1/_{13}$%	800
New capital	160	310	150	620	150 or 100%	$24^8/_{31}$%	770

In this case the rate of profit has risen, because the total capital has decreased—the capital expended in wages has fallen by £150, the total value of the fixed capital has only risen by £120, and so in all £30 less than before is expended.

But if the £30 left over is again employed in the same way,

$^{31}/_{62}$ (or $^{1}/_{2}$) in raw material, $^{16}/_{62}$ in machinery and $^{15}/_{62}$ in wages, the result would be:

Machinery	Raw material	Wages	Surplus-value
£7.14.6	£15	£7.5.6	£7.5.6

and taking both together:

	Machinery	Raw material	Wages	Surplus-value	Rate of profit
New capital	£167.14.6	£325	£157.5.6	£157.5.6	24 $^{6}/_{31}$%

Total amount of capital expended: £650 *as before. Total product* £807.5.6.

The total value of the product has risen; the total value of the capital expended has remained the same; and not only the value, but the amount of the total product has risen, since an additional £15 in raw materials has been transformed into the product.

||366| [We find in Ganilh:]

"When a country is deprived of the aid of machines, and its labour is carried out by hand, the labouring classes consume almost the whole of their production. To the degree that industry makes progress, is improved by the division of labour, the skill of the workmen, and the invention of machines, the costs of production diminish, or in other words, a smaller number of labourers is required to obtain a greater production" (l.c., t. I, pp. 211-12).

That is to say, therefore, in the same degree as industry becomes more productive, the production costs of wages are reduced. Fewer labourers are employed in relation to the product, and these therefore also consume a smaller part of the product.

If a labourer without machinery needs 10 hours to produce his own means of subsistence, and if with machinery he only needs 6, then (with 12 hours' labour) in the first case he works 10 for himself and 2 for the capitalist, and the capitalist gets one-sixth of the total product of the 12 hours. In the first case 10 labourers will produce a product for 10 labourers (equal to 100 hours) and 20 [hours] for the capitalist. Of the value of 120, the capitalist gets one-sixth, or 20. In the second case, 5 labourers will produce a product for 5 labourers (equal to 30 hours), and for the capitalist 30 hours. Of the 60 hours the capitalist now gets 30, that is, one half—3 times as much as before. The total surplus-value too would have risen, namely from 20 to 30, by $^1/_3$. When I appropriate one-half of 60 days, this is one-third more than when I appropriate one-sixth of 120 days.

Moreover, the one-half of the total product that the capitalist gets is also greater in quantity than before. For 6 hours now produce as much product as 10 did before; 1 [hour] as much as ten-sixths of an hour [before], or 1 as much as $1^4/_6=1^2/_3$. So the 30 surplus hours contain as much product as did previously 30 $(1+$ $+^2/_3)=30+^{60}/_3=50$. 6 hours produce as much product as 10 did previously, that is, 30—or 5×6—produce as much as 5×10 did before.

The capitalist's surplus-value would therefore have risen and also his surplus-product (if he consumes it himself, or as much of it as he consumes in kind). The surplus-value can even rise without the quantity of the total product being increased. For the increase of surplus-value means that the labourer is able to produce his means of subsistence in less time than before, that therefore the value of the commodities he consumes falls, represents less labour-time, and that therefore a certain value, equal to 6 hours for example, represents a greater quantity of the use-values than before. The labourer receives the same quantity of product as before, but this quantity forms a smaller part of the total product, as its value expresses a smaller part of the fruits of the day's labour. Although an increase in productive power in the branches of industry whose product neither directly nor indirectly enters into the formation of the labourer's means of consumption could not have this result—since increased or reduced productivity in these branches does not affect the relation between the necessary and the surplus-labour—the result for these industries would nevertheless be the same, although it did not originate from a change in their own productivity. The relative value of their products would rise in exactly the same proportion as that of the other commodities had fallen (if their own productivity had remained the same); consequently, a proportionately smaller aliquot part of these products, or a smaller part of the labour-time of the labourer which is materialised in them, would procure for him the same quantity of means of subsistence as before. The surplus-value would therefore rise in these branches of labour just as in the others.

But what will then become of the five displaced labourers?

It will be said that capital has also been released, namely, that which paid the five dismissed workers, who each received 10 hours (for which they worked 12), that is, 50 hours in all, which could previously have paid the wages of five labourers and which [now] that wages have fallen to 6 hours can pay for $^{50}/_{6}=8^{1}/_{2}$ days' labour. Therefore now the capital of 50 [hours'] labour that has been released can employ more labourers than have been dismissed.

But a capital equivalent to the whole 50 hours' labour has not been released. For even assuming that the raw material has become cheaper in the same proportion as the increase in the quantity of it that is worked up in the same labour-time—that is, assuming that the same increase of productivity has taken place in that branch of production—the outlay for the new machinery nevertheless remains. Assuming that this costs exactly 50 hours' labour, it has certainly in no case employed as many labourers as were put off. For this 50 hours' labour was laid out entirely in wages, for 5 labourers. But in the value of the machine, equivalent to 50 hours' labour, both profit and wages are contained, both paid and unpaid labour-time. In addition, constant capital enters into the value of the machine. The number of machine-building labourers [who built the machine] is smaller than the number of labourers discharged; nor are they the same individuals ||367| as those discharged. The greater demand for labourers in machine building can at most affect the future distribution of the number of labourers, so that a larger part of the generation entering the labour-market—a larger part than before—turns to that branch of industry. It does not affect those who have been discharged. Moreover the increase in the annual demand for these is not equal to the new capital expended on machinery. The machine lasts for example for ten years. The constant demand which it creates is therefore equal annually to $^{1}/_{10}$ of the wages contained in it. To this $^{1}/_{10}$ must be added labour for repairs during the 10 years, and the daily consumption of coal, oil and other auxiliary materials; which in all amounts perhaps to another $^{2}/_{10}$.

<If the capital released were equal to 60 hours, these would now represent 10 hours' surplus-labour and only 50 necessary labour. Thus if previously the 60 hours had been expended in wages and 6 labourers had been employed, now it would be only 5.>

<The shifting of labour and capital which increased productivity in a particular branch of industry brings about by means of machinery, etc., is always only prospective. That is to say, *the increase, the new number of labourers entering industry*, is distribut-

ed in a different way; perhaps the children of those who have been thrown out, but not these themselves. They themselves vegetate for a long time in their old trade, which they carry on under the most unfavourable conditions, inasmuch as their necessary labour-time is greater than the socially necessary labour-time; they become paupers, or find employment in branches of industry where a lower grade of labour is employed.>

<A pauper, like a capitalist (*rentier*), lives on the revenue of the country. He does not enter into the production costs of the product, and consequently Monsieur Ganilh would call him a representative of exchangeable value. Ditto, for a criminal who is fed in prison. A large part of the "unproductive labourers", holders of State sinecures, etc., are simply respectable paupers.>

<Assume that the productivity of industry is so advanced that whereas earlier two-thirds of the population were directly engaged in material production, now it is only one-third Previously $^2/_3$ produced means of subsistence for $^3/_3$; now $^1/_3$ produce for $^3/_3$. Previously $^1/_3$ was net revenue (as distinct from the revenue of the labourers), now $^2/_3$. Leaving [class] contradictions out of account, the nation would now use $^1/_3$ of its time for direct production, where previously it needed $^2/_3$. Equally distributed, all [that is, the whole population] would have $^2/_3$ more time for unproductive labour and leisure. But in capitalist production everything seems and in fact is contradictory. The assumption does not imply that the population is stagnant. For if the $^3/_3$ grow, so also do the $^1/_3$; thus, *measured in quantity*, a larger number of people could be employed in productive labour. But relatively, in proportion to the total population, it would always be 50 per cent less than before. Those two-thirds of the population consist partly of the owners of profit and rent, partly of unproductive labourers (who also, owing to competition, are badly paid). The latter help the former to consume the revenue and give them in return an equivalent in services—or impose their services on them, like the political unproductive labourers. It can be supposed that—with the exception of the horde of flunkeys, the soldiers, sailors, police, lower officials and so on, mistresses, grooms, clowns and jugglers—these unproductive labourers will on the whole have a higher level of culture than the unproductive workers had previously, and in particular that ill-paid artists, musicians, lawyers, physicians, scholars, schoolmasters, inventors, etc., will also have increased in number.

Within the productive class itself commercial middlemen will have multiplied, but in particular those engaged in machine construction, railway construction, mining and excavation; moreover, in agriculture labourers engaged in stock-raising will have increased in number, and also those employed in producing chemical and mineral materials for fertilisers, etc. Further, the farmers who grow raw materials for industry will have risen in number, in proportion to those producing means of subsistence; and those who provide fodder for cattle, in proportion to those who produce means of subsistence for people. *As the constant capital grows, so also does the proportionate quantity of the total labour which is engaged in its reproduction.* Nevertheless, the part [of the population] directly producing means of subsistence, although its number declines, ||368| produces more products than before. Its labour is more productive *While for the individual capital the fall in the variable part of the capital as compared with the constant part* takes the direct form of a reduction in the part of the capital expended in wages, for the total capital—in its *reproduction*—this necessarily takes the form that a relatively greater part of the total labour employed is engaged in the reproduction of means of production than is engaged in the production of products themselves—that is, in the reproduction of machinery (including means of communication and transport and buildings), of auxiliary materials (coal, gas, oil, tallow, leather belting, etc) and of plants which form the raw material for industrial products. Relatively to the manufacturing labourers, agricultural labourers will decline in number. Finally the luxury, labourers will increase in number, since the higher revenue will consume more luxury products.>

<The variable capital is resolved into revenue, firstly wages, secondly profit. If therefore capital is conceived as something contrasted with revenue, the constant capital appears to be capital *in the strict sense*: the part of the total product that belongs to production and enters into the costs of production without being individually consumed by anyone (with the exception of draught cattle). This part may originate entirely from profit and wages. In the last analysis, it can never originate from these alone; it is the product of labour, but of labour which regarded the instrument of production itself as revenue, as the savage did the bow. But once transformed into constant capital, this part of the product is no longer resolvable into wages and profit, although its reproduction yields wages and profit. A part of the product belongs to this part. Each subsequent product is the product of this past

labour and of present labour. The latter can only be continued in so far as it returns a part of the total product to production. It must replace the constant capital in kind. If it grows more productive, it replaces the product, but not its value, reducing this value as a result. If it grows less productive, it raises its value. In the first case the aliquot part drawn by past labour from the total product falls; in the second case it rises. In the first case the living labour becomes more productive, in the second, less productive.>

<The factors which reduce the costs of the *constant capital*, also include improved raw materials. For example, it is not possible to make the same quantity of twist in the same time both from good and from bad raw cotton, leaving entirely out of account the relative quantity of waste, etc. Hence the importance of the quality of seed, etc.>

<As an example *combination* where a manufacturer himself makes a part of his former constant capital, or where previously the raw material passed as constant capital out of his sphere of production into a second sphere, and he now himself gives it the second form—this always only amounts to a concentration of profits, as was shown earlier.* *An example of the first*: the linking together of spinning and weaving. *An example of the second*: the mineowners of Birmingham, who took over the *complete* process of making iron, which had formerly been divided between a number of entrepreneurs and owners.>

* * *

Ganilh continues:

"So long as the division of labour is not established in all branches, so long as all classes of the labouring and industrious population have not attained their full development, the invention of machines, and their employment in certain industries, only cause the capitals and labourers displaced by the machines to flow into other employments which can usefully employ them. But it is evident that when all branches of employment have the capital and the labourers they require, every further improvement and every new machine that cuts down labour, necessarily reduces the labouring population: and as this reduction does not diminish production, the part which it leaves available accrues either to the profit of capitals or to the rent of land; and in consequence the natural and necessary effect of machines is to diminish the population of the wage-earning classes who live on the gross product, and to increase the population of the classes which live on the net product" (l.c., p. 212).

---

* See p. 140 of the present volume.—*Ed.*

||369| "*The displacement of the population* of a country, *a necessary consequence of the progress of industry*, is the true cause of the prosperity, the power and the civilisation of modern peoples. The more the lower classes of society decrease in number, the less need it be troubled by the dangers to which the distress, the ignorance, the credulity and the superstition of these unfortunate classes ceaselessly expose it; the more the upper classes multiply, the more subjects the State has at its disposal, the stronger and more powerful it is, the more knowledge, intelligence and civilisation there is in the whole population" (l.c., p. 213).

<*Say* makes the total value of the product resolvable into revenue in the following way: in the Constancio translation of Ricardo's [book *Principles*], Chapter 26, he says in a note:

"The net revenue of an individual consists of *the value of the product* to which he has contributed ... less his disbursements; but as the disbursements that he has made are *portions of revenue* which he has paid to others, *the totality of the value of the product has served to pay revenues*. The total revenue of a nation is composed of its gross product, that is to say, of the gross value of all its products which are distributed among the producers."[70]

The last sentence would be correct if expressed in this way: The total revenue of a nation is composed of that part of its gross product, that is to say, of the gross value of all the products which are distributed as revenues among the producers, that is to say, less that portion of all the products which in each branch of industry had replaced the means of production. But so expressed, the sentence would negate itself.

Say continues:

"This value, after many exchanges, would be entirely consumed in the year which saw its birth, but it would nonetheless be still the revenue of the nation; just as an individual who has 20,000 francs annual revenue has nonetheless 20,000 francs annual revenue, although he consumes it entirely each year. His revenue does not consist only of his savings."

His revenue never consists of his savings, although his savings always consist of his revenues. To prove that a nation can annually consume both its capital and its revenue, Say compares it to an individual who leaves his capital intact and only consumes his revenue each year. If this individual consumed in a single year both his capital of 200,000 francs and the revenue of 20,000, he would have nothing to eat the year after. If the entire capital of a nation, and consequently the entire gross value of its products, consisted of revenues, Say would be right. The individual consumes his 20,000 francs revenue. His 200,000 francs capital, which he does not consume, would be composed of the revenues of other individuals, each of whom consumes his share, and thus, at the end of the year, the whole capital would be consumed. But perhaps it would be reproduced while it is consumed, and thus replaced? But the individual in question reproduces annually his revenue of 20,000 francs, because he has not consumed his capital of 200,000 francs. The others have consumed this capital. Then they have no capital with which to reproduce revenue.>

"Only the *net product*," says Ganilh, "and those who consume it form its" (the State's) "wealth and its power, and contribute to its prosperity, its glory and its grandeur" (l.c., p. 218).

Ganilh further cites Say's notes to Constancio's translation of Ricardo [*Principles*], Chapter XXVI, where Ricardo says that if a country has 12 million [inhabitants], it would be more advantageous for it if 5 million productive labourers labour for the 12 million, than if 7 million productive labourers labour for the 12 million. In the first case the net product consists of the surplus-produce on which the 7 million who are not productive live; in the other, of a surplus-produce for 5 million. Say remarks on this:

"This is quite like the doctrine of the Economists of the eighteenth century,[71] who maintained that manufactures in no way helped towards the wealth of the State, because the *wage-earning class*, consuming a value equal to ||370| that which they produce, contribute nothing to their famous *net product*."

On this, Ganilh observes (pp. 219-20):

"It is not easy to see any connection between the Economists' assertion *that the industrial class consumes a value equal to that which it produces* and the doctrine of Mr. Ricardo, *that the wages of labourers cannot be counted in the revenue of a State*."

Here too Ganilh misses the point. The Economists go wrong in regarding the manufacturers as only *wage-earning classes*. This distinguishes them from Ricardo. They are further wrong in thinking that the *wage-earners* produce what they consume. The correct view, as Ricardo in contrast to them knew very well, is that it is they who produce the net product, but produce it precisely because their consumption, that is to say their wage, is equal not to the time they labour, but to the labour-time that they have put in to produce this wage; that is, that they receive a share of the product only equal to their necessary consumption, or that they receive only as much of their own product as is equivalent to their own necessary consumption. The Economists assumed that the whole industrial class (masters and workmen) was in this position. They considered that only rent bore the character of an excess of production over wages, and consequently that it was the only wealth. But when Ricardo says that profits and rents form this surplus and are consequently the only wealth, in spite of his difference from the Physiocrats, he agrees with them in thinking that only the net product, the product in which the surplus-value exists, forms the national wealth; although he has a better understanding of the nature of this surplus. For him, too, it is only the part of the revenue which is in excess of wages. What distinguishes him from the Economists is not his explanation of the net product, but his explanation of wages, under which category the Economists wrongly also include profits.

Say also remarks in opposition to Ricardo:

"From seven million fully employed labourers there would be more savings than from five million."

Ganilh rightly observes, refuting this:

"That is to suppose that *economies from wages* are preferable to the *economy which results from the reduction of wages*.... It would be too absurd to pay four hundred millions in wages to labourers who give no net product, in order to provide them with the opportunity and the means for making economies on their wages" (l.c., p. 221).

"With every step made by civilisation, labour becomes less burdensome and more productive; the classes condemned to produce and to consume diminish; and the classes which direct labour, which relieve (!), console (!) and enlighten the whole population, multiply, *become more numerous and appropriate to themselves all the benefits which result from the diminution of the costs of labour*, from the abundance of products and the cheapness of consumer goods. In this way, the human race lifts itself up.... Because of this *progressive tendency to the diminution of the lower classes of society and the increase of the upper classes* ... civil society becomes more prosperous, more powerful," etc. (l.c., p. 224). "If ... the number of labourers employed is seven millions, the wages will be fourteen hundred millions; but if the fourteen hundred millions do not yield a larger net product than the thousand millions paid to the five million labourers, *the real economy would be in abolishing the four hundred millions in wages paid to two million labourers who yield no net product*, and not in the savings that these two million labourers could make from the four hundred millions of wages" (l.c., p. 221).

In Chapter XXVI [of his *Principles*] Ricardo observes:

"*Adam Smith* constantly magnifies the advantages which a country derives from a large gross, rather than a large net income.... What would be the advantage resulting to a country from the employment of a great quantity of productive labour, if, whether it employed that quantity or a smaller, its net rent and profits together would be the same?" Whether a nation employs five or seven million productive labourers to produce the net revenue ||371| on which five million others live, "the food and clothing of five millions would be still the net revenue. The employing of a greater number of men would enable us neither to add a man to our army and navy, nor to contribute one guinea more in taxes" (l.c., p. 215).*[72]

This reminds us of the ancient Germans, of whom one part in turn took the field and the other cultivated the field. The smaller the number that was indispensable for cultivating the field, the greater the number who were able to war. It would not have helped them if the number of people had increased by one-third, so that instead of 1,000 they had 1,500, if 1,000 were then required to cultivate the field while previously it was 500. Their disposable forces would have consisted of only 500 men both before and after. If on the other hand the productivity of their labour had increased, so that 250 sufficed to cultivate the field, 750 of the 1,000 could have taken the field, whereas in the opposite case, if the productivity of their labour had fallen, it would be only 500 out of the 1,500.

First it should be noted here that Ricardo means by net revenue or net product not the excess of the total product over the part of it that must be returned to production as means of production, raw materials or instruments. On the contrary, he shares the false view that the gross product consists of gross revenue. By net product or net revenue he means the surplus-value, the excess of the total revenue over the part of it that consists of wages, of the revenue of the labourers. This revenue of the labourer, however, is equal to the variable capital, the part of the circulating capital which he is constantly consuming and constantly reproducing as the part of his production which he himself consumes.

If Ricardo treats the capitalists as not entirely useless, that is to say, as themselves agents of production, and therefore resolves a part of their profit into wages, he has to deduct a part of their revenue from the net revenue and to declare that all these persons only contribute to wealth in so far as their wages form the smallest possible part of their profit. However that may be, at least a part of their time as agents of production belongs, like a fixture, to production itself. And to this extent they cannot be used for other purposes of society or of the State. The more free time their duties as managers of production leave them, the more is their profit independent of their wage. In contrast to these, the capitalists who live only on their interest, and also the landlords who live on rent, are in person entirely at the disposal [of

* Marx here quotes Ricardo from a French translation. See Appendix, pp. 442.—*Ed.*

society and the State], and no part of their income enters into the costs of production—except for that part which is used for the reproduction of their own worthy person. Ricardo should therefore have also desired, in the interests *of the State*, a growth of rent (the pure net revenue) at the cost of profits; but this is not at all his viewpoint. And why not? Because it hinders the accumulation of capitals [or]—what is in part the same thing—because it increases the numher of unproductive labourers at the cost of the productive.

Ricardo fully shares Adam Smith's view of the distinction between productive and unproductive labour, that the former exchanges its labour directly for capital, [the latter] directly for revenue. But he no longer shares Smith's tenderness for and illusion about the productive labourer. It is a misfortune to be a productive labourer. A productive labourer is a labourer who produces wealth *for another*. His existence only has meaning as such an instrument of production for the wealth of others. If therefore the same quantity of wealth for others can be created with a smaller number of productive labourers, then the suppression of these productive labourers is in order. *Vos, non vobis.** Ricardo, incidentally, does not think of this *suppression* as Ganilh does—that through mere suppression the revenue increases and that what was *formerly consumed as variable capital* (that is, in the form of wages) would then be consumed *as revenue*. With the diminution in the number of productive workers also disappears the amount of product which those who have been discharged themselves consumed and themselves produced—their equivalent. Ricardo does not assume, as Ganilh does, that the same quantity of products as before is produced; but the same quantity of net product. If the labourers consumed 200 and their surplus was 100, the total product was 300, and the surplus was one-third=100. If the labourers consume 100 and their surplus is 100 as before, the total product is 200 and the surplus is one-half=100. The total product would have fallen by one-third—by the quantity of products consumed by the 100 dismissed workers, and the net product ||372| [would have] remained *the same*, because $^{200}/_{2}={}^{300}/_{3}$. For Ricardo, therefore, the amount of the gross product does not matter, provided that that portion of the gross product which constitutes the net product remains the same or grows, but in any case does not diminish.

* You work, but not for yourselves (Virgil).—*Ed.*

So he says[73]:

"To an individual with a capital of 20,000 *l.*, whose profits were 2,000 *l.* per annum, it would be a matter quite indifferent whether his capital would employ a hundred or a thousand men, whether the commodity produced sold for 10,000 *l.*, or for 20,000 *l.*, provided, in all cases, his profits were not diminished below 2,000 *l.* Is not the real interest of the nation similar?"*[74] |VIII—372||

* * *

||IX—377| The passage in Ricardo (Chapter XXVI) runs:

"Adam Smith constantly magnifies the advantages which a country derives from a large gross, rather than a large net income" (because, says Adam, "the greater will be the quantity of productive labour which it puts into motion").... "What would be the advantage resulting to a country from the employment of a great quantity of productive labour, if, whether it employed that quantity or a smaller, its net rent and profits together would be the same."

<This therefore means nothing but: if the surplus-value produced by a greater quantity of labour would be the same as that produced by a smaller quantity. That however in turn means nothing but that it is the same thing for a country whether it employs a large number of labourers at a lower rate of surplus or a smaller number at a higher rate. $n \times \frac{1}{2}$ is just as much as $2n \times \frac{1}{4}$, where n represents the number [of labourers] and $\frac{1}{2}$ and $\frac{1}{4}$ the surplus-labour. The "productive labourer" as such is a mere instrument of production for the production of surplus, and if the result is the same a larger number of these "productive labourers" would be a nuisance.>

"To an individual with a capital of 20,000 *l.*, whose profits were 2,000 *l.* per annum, it would be a matter quite indifferent whether his capital would employ a hundred or a thousand men, whether the commodity produced sold for 10,000 *l.* or for 20,000 *l.* provided, in all cases, his profits were not diminished below 2,000 *l.*"

<The meaning of this, as is evident from a later passage, is perfectly banal. For example, a wine-merchant, who makes use of £20,000 and has £12,000 lying in his cellar each year, but sells £8,000 for £10,000, employs few people and makes 10 per cent profit, etc. And then take bankers!>

---

* Marx here quotes Ricardo from a French translation. See Appendix, p. 442.—*Ed.*

"Is not the real interest of the nation similar? *Provided its net real income, its rent and profits be the same, it is of no importance whether the nation consists of ten or of twelve millions of inhabitants.* Its power of supporting fleets and armies, and *all species of unproductive labour*" (this passage shows among other things that Ricardo shared Adam Smith's view of productive and unproductive labour, although he did no longer share Smith's tenderness, based on illusions, for the productive labourer) "must be in proportion to its net, and not in proportion to its gross, income. If five millions of men could produce as much food and clothing as was necessary for ten millions, food and clothing for five millions would be the net revenue. Would it be of any advantage to the country, that *to produce this same net revenue*, seven millions of men should be required, that is to say, that seven millions should be employed to produce food and clothing sufficient for twelve millions? The food and clothing of five millions would be still the net revenue. The employing a greater number of men would enable us neither to add a man to our army and navy, nor to contribute one guinea more in taxes" (Ricardo, *On the Principles of Political Economy and Taxation*, 3rd edition, London, 1821, pp. 415-17).

A country is the richer the smaller its productive population is *relatively* to the total product; just as for the individual capitalist: the fewer labourers he needs to produce the same surplus, so much the better for him. The country is the richer the smaller the productive population in relation to the unproductive, the quantity of products remaining the same. For the relative smallness of the productive population would be only another way of expressing the relative degree of the productivity of labour.

On the one hand it is the tendency of capital to reduce to a dwindling minimum the labour-time necessary for the production of commodities, and therefore also the number of the productive population *in relation to* the amount of the product. On the other hand, however, it* has the opposite tendency to accumulate, to transform profit into capital, to appropriate the greatest possible quantity of the labour of others. It* strives to reduce the norm of necessary labour, but to employ the greatest possible quantity of productive labour at the given norm. The proportion of the products to the population makes no difference in this. Corn and cotton can be changed into wine, diamonds, etc., ||378| or labourers can be employed in productive labour which does not directly add anything to the (consumable) products (such as railway construction, etc.).

If as the result of an invention a capitalist can now only use in his business £10,000 instead of the £20,000 he used previ-

* This refers to the capitalist mode of production.—*Ed.*

ously, because £10,000 is sufficient, and if this sum yields 20 per cent for him instead of 10, that is, as much as the £20,000 brought in before, this would be no reason for him to spend £10,000 as revenue instead of as capital as before. (Actually it is only in the case of State loans that we can speak of a direct transformation of capital into revenue.) He would place it elsewhere—and in addition would capitalise a part of his profit.

Among the economists (including Ricardo in part) we find the same antimony as there is in reality. Machinery displaces labour and increases the net revenue (particularly always what Ricardo here calls net revenue—the quantity of products in which revenue is consumed); it reduces the number of labourers and increases the products (which then are partly consumed by unproductive labourers, partly exchanged abroad, etc.). So this would be desirable. But no. In that case it must be shown that machinery does not deprive the labourers of bread. And how is this to be shown? By the fact that after a shock (to which perhaps the section of the population which is directly affected cannot offer any resistance) machinery once again employs more people than were employed before it was introduced—and therefore once again increases the number of "productive labourers" and restores the former disproportion.

That is in fact what happens. And so in spite of the growing productivity of labour the labouring population could constantly grow not in proportion to the product, which grows with it and faster than it, but proportionately [to the total population], if, for example, capital simultaneously becomes concentrated, and therefore former component parts of the productive classes fall into the ranks of the proletariat. A small part of the latter rises into the middle class. The unproductive classes, however, see to it that there is not too much food available. The constant retransformation of profit into capital always restores the same cycle on a wider basis.

And Ricardo's care for accumulation is even greater than his care for net profit, which he regards with fervent admiration as a means to accumulation. Hence too his contradictory admonitions and consoling remarks to the labourers. They are the people most interested in the accumulation of capital, because it is on this that the demand for them depends. If this demand rises, then the price of labour rises. They must therefore themselves desire the lowering of wages, so that the surplus taken from them, once more filtered through capital, is returned to them for new labour and their wages rise. This rise in wages however is bad, because it restricts accumulation. On the one hand they must not produce children. This brings a fall in the supply of labour, and so its price rises. But this rise diminishes the rate of accumulation, and so diminishes the demand for them and brings down the price of labour. Even quicker than the supply of them falls, capital falls along with it. If they produce children, then they increase their own supply and reduce the price of labour; thus the rate of profit rises, and with it the accumulation of capital. But the labouring population must rise in the same degree as the accumulation of capital; that is to say, the labouring population must be there exactly in the numbers that the capitalist needs—which it does anyway.

Monsieur Ganilh is not altogether consistent in his admiration for the net product. He quotes from Say:

> "I do not doubt at all (...) that in slave labour the excess of the products over consumption is larger than in the labour of a free man.... The worker of the slave has no limit but his capacity.... The slave" (and the free work too) "*labours for an unlimited need: his master's cupidity*" (*Say*, 1re éd., pp. 215, 216).

||379| On this Ganilh observes:

> "The free labourer cannot consume more and produce less than the slave.... All consumption presumes an equivalent produced to pay for it. If the free labourer consumes more than the slave, the products of his labour must be more considerable than those of the slave's labour" (*Ganilh*, t. I, p. 234).

As if the size of the wage depended *only* on the productivity of the labourer, and not, with a given productivity, on the division of the product between labourer and master.

> "I know," he continues, "that it can be said with some reason that the *economies made by the master at the expense of the slave*" (according to this there are after all economies made on the wages of the slave) "serve to augment his personal expenses," etc. "But it is more advantageous to the general wealth that there should be well-being in all classes of society rather than an excessive opulence among a small number of individuals" (pp. 234-35).

How does that tally with the net product? And for that matter Monsieur Ganilh at once retracts his liberal tirades (l. c., pp. 236-37). He wants Nigger-slavery for the colonies. He is only liberal in so far as he does not want to reintroduce it into Europe, having grasped that the free labourers here are slaves, that they only exist to produce net product for capitalists, landlords and their retainers.

"He" (*Quesnay*) "definitely denies that economies made by the wage-earning classes have the faculty to increase capital; and the reason he gives for this is that these classes should not have any means on which to make economics, and that if they had *a surplus, an excess*, this could only be due to an error or to some disorder in the society's economy" (l.c., p. 274).

Ganilh cites in evidence the following passage from Quesnay:

"If the sterile class saves in order to augment its cash ... its labours and its gains will diminish in the same proportion, and it will fall into decay" (*Physiocratie*, p. 321).

The ass! He does not understand Quesnay.

Monsieur Ganilh puts on the keystone in the following paragraph:

"The larger they" (wages) "are, the less is the revenue of the society" (society stands on them, but they do not stand in society), "and all the skill of governments should be applied to reducing the amount [of the wages].... *A task ... worthy of the enlightened century in which we live*" (t. II, p. 24).

Then there are still *Lauderdale* (Brougham's insipit jests are not worth examining after him), (Ferrier?), *Tocqueville*, *Storch*, *Senior*, and *Rossi* to be considered briefly on productive and unproductive labour.

[10.] Exchange of Revenue and Capital [Replacement of the Total Amount of the Annual Product: (a) Exchange of Revenue for Revenue; (b) Exchange of Revenue for Capital; (c) Exchange of Capital for Capital]

{To be distinguished: 1. The part of the *revenue which is transformed into new capital*; that is, the part of the profit which is itself again capitalised. Here we leave this entirely out of account—it belongs to the section on accumulation. 2. The revenue which is exchanged with capital consumed in production, so that by means of this exchange not new capital is formed, but old capital replaced—in a word, the old capital is conserved. In this inquiry, therefore, we can put the part of the revenue which is transformed into new capital as equal to nil, and treat the subject as if all revenue covers either revenue or capital consumed.

The whole amount of the annual product is therefore divided into two parts: one part is consumed as revenue, the other part replaces in kind the constant capital consumed.

Revenue is exchanged for revenue, when for example the producers of linen exchange a portion of that part of their product

—the linen—which represents their profits and wages, their revenue, for corn that represents a portion of the profits and ||380| wages of farmers. Here therefore there is the exchange of linen for corn, those two commodities which both enter into individual consumption—exchange of revenue in the form of linen for revenue in the form of corn. There is absolutely no difficulty in this. If consumable products are produced in proportions corresponding to needs, which means also that the proportionate amounts of social labour required for their production are proportionately distributed <which of course is never exactly the case, there being constant deviations, disproportions, which as such are adjusted; but in such a way that the continuous movement towards adjustment itself presupposes continuous disproportion>, then revenue, for example in the form of linen, exists in the exact quantity in which it is required as an article of consumption, therefore in which it is replaced by the articles of consumption of other producers. What the producer of linen consumes in corn, etc., the farmers and others consume in linen. The part of his product which represents revenue, which he exchanges for other commodities (articles of consumption), is thus taken in exchange as an article of consumption by the producers of these other commodities. What he consumes in the product of others, these others consume in his product.

It may be noted in passing: that no more necessary labour-time is employed on a product than is required by society—that is to say, no more time than on the average is required for the production of this commodity—is the result of capitalist production, which even continuously reduces the minimum of necessary labour-time. But in order to do so, it must constantly produce on a rising scale.

If 1 yard of linen costs only 1 hour and this is the necessary labour-time that society has to use to satisfy its need for 1 yard of linen, it by no means follows from this that if 12 million yards are produced—that is, 12 million hours' labour, or what is the same thing, 1 million days' labour—1 million labourers being employed as linen weavers, society [needs] to employ such a part of its labour-time "necessarily" on the weaving of linen. If the necessary labour-time is given, and therefore also that a certain quantity of linen can be produced in one day, the question arises how many such days are to be used in the production of linen? The labour-time used on the total of particular products, in a year for example, is equal to a definite quantity of this use-value—for example, 1 yard of linen (say equivalent to 1 day's labour)—multiplied by the number of days' labour used in all. The total quantity of labour-time used in a particular branch of production may be under or over the correct proportion to the total available social labour, although each aliquot part of the product contains only the labour-time necessary for its production, or although each aliquot part of the labour-time used was necessary to make the corresponding aliquot part of the total product.

From this standpoint, the necessary labour-time acquires another meaning. The question is, in what quantities the necessary labour-time itself is distributed among the various spheres of production. Competition constantly regulates this distribution, just as it equally constantly disorganises it. If too large a quantity of social labour-time is used in one branch, the equivalent can be paid only, as if the correct quantity had been used. The total product—that is to say, the value of the total product—is in this case therefore not equal to the labour-time contained in it, but is equal to the proportionate labour-time which would have been used had the total product been in proportion to production in the other spheres. But in as much as the price of the total product falls below its value, the price of each aliquot part of it falls. If 6,000 yards of linen instead of 4,000 are produced, and if the value of the 6,000 yards is 12,000 shillings, they are sold for 8,000. The price of each yard is $1\frac{1}{3}$ shillings instead of 2—one-third below its value. It therefore amounts to the same thing as if $\frac{1}{3}$ too much labour-time had been used to produce one yard. Assuming that the commodity has use-value, the fall of its price below its value therefore shows that, although each part of the product has cost only the socially necessary labour-time <here it is assumed that the conditions of production remain unchanged>, a superfluous—more than necessary—total quantity of social labour has been employed in this one branch.

The sinking of the relative value of the commodity as a result of altered conditions of production is something entirely different; ||381| this piece of linen on the market has cost 2s., equal for example to 1 day's labour. But it can be reproduced every day for 1s. Since the value is determined by the socially necessary labour-time, not by the labour-time used by the individual producer, the day that the producer has used for the production of the one yard is now only equal to half the socially determined day. The fall of the price of his yard from 2s. to 1s.—that is, of its price below the value it has *cost* him—shows merely a change in the conditions of production, that is, a change in the necessary labour-time itself. On the other hand, if the production costs of the linen remain the same while those of all other articles rise—with the exception of gold, the material of money; or even [if the rise applies to] certain articles such as wheat, copper, etc., in a word, to articles which do not enter into the component parts of the linen—then one yard of linen would be equal to 2s. as before. Its *price* would not fall, but its relative value expressed in wheat, copper, etc., would have fallen.

Of the part of the revenue in one branch of production (which produces consumable commodities) which is consumed in the revenue of another branch of production, it can be said that the demand is equal to its own supply (in so far as production is kept in the right *proportion*). It is the same as if each branch itself consumed that part of its revenue. Here there is only a formal metamorphosis of the commodity: C—M—C′. Linen—money—wheat.

Both commodities which are exchanged here represent only a part of the new labour added in the year. But in the first place it is clear that this exchange—in which two producers mutually consume a part of their product which represents revenue in each other's commodities—only takes place in those branches of production which produce consumable articles, articles which enter directly into individual consumption, in which consequently revenue can be spent as revenue. Secondly, it is just as clear: that only regarding *this part* of the exchange of products it is true that the producer's supply is equal to the demand for other products which he wishes to consume. Here in fact it is only a question of a simple exchange of commodities. Instead of producing his means of subsistence himself, he produces the means of subsistence for another, who produces his. No relation between revenue and capital enters into this. Revenue in one form of consumable articles is exchanged against revenue in another form of consumable articles, and so in fact consumable articles are exchanged for consumable articles. What determines their process of exchange is not that both are revenue, but that both are consumable articles. Their definite form as revenue does not enter into it at all. It shows itself however in the use-value of the interchangeable commodities, in that both enter into individual consumption; which in turn however means no more than that one part of consumable products is exchanged for another part of consumable products.

The form of revenue can only intervene or make itself manifest where the form of capital confronts it. But even in this case what Say and other vulgar economists assert is not true—that if A cannot sell his linen or can only sell it under its price—that is, the part of his linen which he wishes to consume himself as revenue—then this happens because B, C, etc., have produced too little wheat, meat, etc. It may be because they have not produced enough of these. But it may also be because A has produced too much linen. For assuming that B, C, etc., have enough wheat, etc., to buy all A's linen, they nevertheless do not buy it, because only a definite quantity of linen is *consumed* by them. Or it may also be because A has produced more linen than the part of their revenue which can be spent on clothing materials altogether—that is, absolutely, because each person can expend as revenue only a definite quantity of his own product, and A's production of linen presupposes a greater amount of revenue than in total there is. It is ridiculous, however, when it is only a matter of the exchange of revenue against revenue, to suppose that what is wanted is not the use-value of the product but the quantity of this use-value, thus once again forgetting that *this* exchange concerns only the satisfaction of needs, not, as in exchange-value, the quantity.

But everyone will prefer to have a large rather than a small quantity of an article. If this is supposed to solve the difficulty, then ||382| it is absolutely impossible to understand why the producer of linen, instead of exchanging his linen for other articles of consumption and piling these up *en masse*, does not carry out the simpler process of enjoying a part of his revenue in his superfluous linen. Why does he at all transform his revenue from the form of linen into other forms? Because he has to satisfy other needs than the need for linen. Why does he himself consume only a certain part of the linen? Because only a quantitatively determined part of the linen has use-value for him. The same thing, however, holds for B, C, etc. If B sells wine and C books and D mirrors, each may prefer to consume the surplus of his revenue in his own product—wine, books, mirrors—rather than in linen. Thus it cannot be said that, necessarily, too little wine, books and mirrors have been produced because A cannot transform his revenue in the form of linen (or cannot transform it at its value) into wine, books and mirrors. It is still more ridiculous, however, when this exchange of revenue against revenue—this one section of the exchange of commodities—is passed off as the whole of commodity exchange.

We have thus disposed of one part of the product. A part of the consumable products changes hands between the producers of these consumable products themselves. Each consumes a part of his revenue (profit and wages) in the other's consumable product instead of in his own consumable product, and in fact he can only do this in so far as there is the reciprocal consumption by the other of someone else's consumable product instead of his own. It is the same as if each had consumed that part of his consumable product which represents his own revenue.

For all the rest of the products, however, complicated relations intervene, and it is only here that the commodities exchanged confront each other as revenue and capital, and not only as revenue.

First a distinction has to be made. In all branches of production a part of the total product represents revenue, labour added (during the year), profit and wages. <Rent, interest, etc., are parts of profit; the income of the State good-for-nothings is part of profit and wages; the income of other unproductive labourers is the part of profit and wages which they buy with their unproductive labours—it therefore does not increase the product existing as profit and wages, but only determines how much of it they consume, and how much is consumed by the labourers and capitalists themselves.> But only in one section of the spheres of production can the part of the product representing revenue enter directly in kind into the revenue, or in its *use-value* be consumed as revenue. All products which are *only* means of production cannot be consumed in kind, in their immediate form, as revenue, but only their *value*. This however must be consumed in the branches of production which produce directly consumable articles. A part of the means of production may be immediate articles of consumption—it may be one or the other according to the use made of it, as for example a horse, a cart, etc. A part of the immediate articles of consumption may be means of production, like corn for spirits, wheat for seed, and so on. Almost all articles of consumption can re-enter the production process as excrements of consumption, as for example worn-out and half-rotten rags of linen in the manufacture of paper. But no one produces linen in order that it should become, as rags, the raw material for paper. It only gets this form after the linen weaver's product as such has entered consumption. Only as excrement of this consumption, as residuum and product of the consumption process, can it then go into a new production sphere as means of production. This case, therefore, is not relevant here.

The products therefore—of which the aliquot part that represents revenue can be consumed by their own producers as value, but not as use-value (so that they must sell the part for example of their machines which represents wages and profit in order to consume it, [as they] cannot directly satisfy any individual need with it as a machine)—[these products] can just as little be consumed by the producers of other products; they cannot enter into their individual consumption, and hence cannot form part of the products on which they spend their revenue, since this would be in contradiction to the use-value of these commodities: their use-value by the nature of the case *excludes* individual consumption. The producers of these unconsumable products, therefore, can only consume their *exchange-value*; that is to say, they must first transform them into money in order to retransform this money into consumable commodities. But to whom are they to sell ||383| them? To producers of other individually unconsumable products? Then they would merely have one unconsumable product in the place of the other. It is however presupposed that this part of the product forms their revenue; that they sell these commodities in order to consume their value in consumable products. For that reason they can only sell them to the producers of products that can be consumed individually.

This part of the exchange of commodities represents exchange of one man's capital for another man's revenue, and of one man's revenue for another man's capital. Only one part of the total product of the producer of consumable products represents revenue; the other part represents constant capital. He can neither himself consume the latter, nor can he exchange it for the consumable products made by others. He can neither consume in kind the use-value of this part of the product, nor can he consume its value by exchanging it for other consumable products. He must on the contrary transform it again into the natural elements of his constant capital. He must *consume industrially* this part of his product, that is, use it as means of production.

But in its use-value his product is only capable of entering individual consumption; he cannot therefore transform it again in kind into his own elements of production. Its use-value excludes *industrial consumption.* So he can only industrially consume its *value*, [by selling it] to the producers of those elements of production needed for his product. He can neither consume in kind this part of his product, nor can he consume its value by selling it for other products that can be consumed individually. Just as little as this part of his product can enter into his own revenue, can it be replaced out of the revenue of producers of other individually consumable products; since this would only be possible if he exchanged his product for their product and so *consumed* the value of his product, which cannot happen. But since this part of his product, as well as the other part which he can consume as revenue, by its use-value can only be consumed as revenue, must enter into individual consumption and cannot replace constant capital, it must enter into the revenue of the producers of unconsumable products—it must be exchanged against that part of their products whose value they can consume, or in other words which represents their revenue.

If we look at this exchange from the standpoint of each of the people exchanging, for A, the producer of the consumable product, it represents a transformation of capital into capital. He transforms the part of his total product which is equal to the value of the constant capital it contains back again into the natural form in which it can function as constant capital. Both before and after the exchange it represents, in its value, only constant capital. For B, the producer of the product that cannot be consumed, it is the reverse: the exchange represents merely the transformation of revenue from one form into another. He transforms the part of his total product which forms his revenue —equal to the part of the total product which represents labour newly added, his own labour (capital and labourer)—into the natural form in which only he can consume it as revenue. Both before and after the exchange it represents, in its value, only his revenue.

If we look at the relation from both sides there, A exchanges his constant capital for B's revenue, and B exchanges his revenue for A's constant capital. B's revenue replaces A's constant capital, and A's constant capital replaces B's revenue.

In the exchange itself <irrespective of the purposes of those carrying it out> only commodities confront each other—and a simple exchange of commodities takes place—the relation between which is merely that of commodities, the designations of revenue and capital having no significance here. Only the different *use-value* of these commodities shows that one lot can only serve for industrial consumption, and the other only for individual consumption, can only enter into this consumption. The various practical uses of the various use-values of various commodities, however, concern their consumption and do not affect the process of their exchange as commodities. It is quite a different thing when the capitalist's capital is transformed into wages, and labour is transformed into capital. Here the commodities do not confront each other as simple commodities, but capital as capital. In the exchange we have just been considering sellers and buyers face each other only as sellers and buyers, only as simple commodity owners.

It is further clear that the whole of the product destined for individual consumption or the whole product entering into individual consumption, in so far as it enters into it, can only be exchanged for revenue. The fact that it cannot be industrially consumed means precisely that it can only be consumed as revenue, i.e., only individually. <As noted above, we here abstract from the transformation of profit into capital.>

If A is a producer of a product that can only be individually consumed, let his revenue be equal to one-third of his total product, his constant capital to two-thirds. The assumption implies that he himself consumes the first one-third, whether he ||384| consumes it all himself in kind or only partly or not at all, or whether he consumes its value in other articles of consumption; the sellers of these articles of consumption then consume their own revenue in A's product. So the part of the consumable product which represents the revenue of the producers of consumable products is consumed by them either directly, or indirectly, through exchanging among themselves the products to be consumed by them; in regard to this part, therefore, where *revenue is exchanged for revenue*—here it is the same as if A represented the producers of all consumable products. He himself consumes one-third of this aggregate amount, the aliquot part which represents his revenue. This part, however, represents exactly the quantity of labour which during the year category A has added to its constant capital, and this quantity is equal to the total sum of wages and profits produced by category A during the year.

The other two-thirds of category A's total product are equal to the value of the constant capital, and must therefore be replaced by the product of the annual labour of category B, which produces products that cannot be [individually] consumed and only enter into industrial consumption as means of production in the production process. But as this two-thirds of A's total product, just the same as the first one-third, must enter into individual consumption, it is taken by the producers of category B, in exchange for the part of their product which represents their revenue. Category A has therefore exchanged the constant part of its total product for constant capital in its original natural form, retransforming it into the newly-produced products of category B; but category B has only paid for it with that part of its product which represents its revenue but which it can only consume in the products of A. It has thus in fact paid with its newly-added labour, which is completely represented by the part of B's product that is exchanged for the last two-thirds of A's product. Thus A's total product is exchanged for revenue, or passes entirely into individual consumption. On the other hand (on the assumption that the transformation of revenue into capital is here left out of account, being taken as equal to nil) the *total revenue* of society is expended on product A; for the producers of A consume their revenue in A, and so do the producers of category B. And there is no other category besides these two.

The total product A is consumed, although it contains two-thirds constant capital, which cannot be consumed by the producers of A but must be retransformed into the natural form of their elements of production. The total product A is equal to the total revenue of society. The total revenue of society, however, represents the total labour-time which it has added during the year to the existing constant capital. Now although the total product A consists of newly-added labour only as to one-third, and as to two-thirds of past labour that has to be replaced, it can be bought in its entirety by newly-added labour, because two-thirds of this total annual labour must be consumed not in their own products but in the products of A. A is replaced by two-thirds more newly-added labour than it itself contains, because these two-thirds are labour newly added in B, and B can only consume it individually in A, just as A can only consume the two-thirds industrially in B. Thus the total product of A can in the first place be entirely consumed as revenue, and at the same time its constant capital can be replaced. Or rather it can only be entirely consumed as revenue because two-thirds of it are replaced by the producers of constant capital, who cannot consume in kind the part of their product representing revenue, but are obliged to consume it in A, that is, through exchanging it for two-thirds of A.

We have thus disposed of the final two-thirds of A.

It is clear that it makes no difference if a third category C exists, whose products are consumable both industrially and individually; for example, corn, by men or by cattle or as seed or as bread; vehicles, horses, cattle, etc. In so far as these products enter into individual consumption they must be consumed as revenue, direct or indirect, by their own producers, or by the producers (direct or indirect) of the part of the constant capital contained in them They therefore come under A. In so far as they do not enter into individual consumption, they come under B.

The process of this second kind of exchange, where it is not revenue that is exchanged against revenue but capital against revenue—in which the whole constant capital must in the end be resolved into revenue, that is, into newly-added labour—can be thought of in two ways. Let A's product be for example linen. The two-thirds of the linen which are equal to the constant capital of A (or its value) pay for yarn, machinery and auxiliary materials. But the yarn manufacturer and the manufacturer of machinery ||385| can only consume as much of this product as represents their own revenue. The linen manufacturer pays the whole price of the yarn and machinery with these two-thirds of his product. By so doing he has thus replaced for the spinner and the machinery manufacturer their total product which entered into the linen as constant capital. But this total product is itself equal to the constant capital and revenue—one part being equal to the labour added by the spinner and machinery manufacturer, and another part representing the value of their own means of production, that is, for the spinner flax, oil, machinery, coal, etc., and for the machinery manufacturer coal, iron, machinery, etc. A's constant capital, equal to two-thirds, has thus replaced the total product of the spinner and machinery manufacturer, their constant capital plus the labour newly added by them—their capital plus their revenue. But they can only consume their revenue in A. After deducting the part of the two-thirds of

A which is equal to their revenue, with the rest they pay for their raw materials and machinery. According to our assumption, however, the latter need not replace any constant capital. Only so much of their product can enter into product A—and therefore also into the products which are means of production for A—as A can pay for. But A can only pay with his two-thirds for as much as B can buy with his revenue, that is to say, as much as the product exchanged by B contains revenue, newly-added labour. If the producers of the final elements of production of A had to sell to the spinner a quantity of their product which represented a part of their own constant capital—that is, which represented more than the labour they had added to their constant capital—then they could not accept payment in A, because they cannot consume one part of this product. Consequently what takes place is the opposite.

Let us trace the stages in reverse. Let us assume that the total linen is equal to 12 days. The product of the flax-grower, of the iron manufacturer, etc., is equal to 4 days; this product is sold to the spinner and the machinery manufacturer, who in turn add 4 days to it; these sell it to the weaver, who again adds 4 days. The linen weaver can thus himself consume one-third of his product; 8 days replace his constant capital for him and pay for the product of the spinner and machinery manufacturer; these can consume 4 of the 8 days, and with the other 4 they pay the flax-grower, etc., and thus replace their constant capital; the last-named have only their labour to replace with the last 4 days in linen.

The revenue, although it is assumed to be of the same size—equal to 4 days—in all three cases, is of different proportions in the products of the three classes of producers who participate in producing product A. For the linen weaver, it is one-third of his product, equal to one-third of 12; for the spinner and for the machinery manufacturer it is equal to one-half of his product, equal to one-half of 8; for the flax-grower it is equal to his product, 4. In relation to the total product it is however exactly the same, equal to one-third of 12, that is, 4. But for the weaver, the labour newly added by spinner, machinery manufacturer and flax-grower takes the form of constant capital. For the spinner and machinery manufacturer, the total product represents the labour newly added by themselves and by the flax-grower, the labour-time of the flax-grower appearing as constant capital. For the flax-grower, this phenomenon of constant capital has ceased to exist. Because of this, the spinner for example can use machinery, or constant capital in general, in the same proportions as the weaver. For example, $^1/_3 : ^2/_3$. But in the first place the amount (the total amount) of the capital employed in spinning must be smaller than that used in weaving, since its total product enters as constant capital into weaving. Secondly, if the spinner also has the proportion of $^1/_3 : ^2/_3$, his constant capital would be equal to $^{16}/_3$ his labour added to $^8/_3$; the former equal to $5^1/_3$ days' labour, the latter to $2^2/_3$. In this case there would be proportionately more days' labour contained in the branch which supplies him with flax, etc. He would then have to pay $5^1/_3$ for newly-added labour, instead of 4 days.

It is self-evident that only that part of category A's constant capital has to be replaced by new labour which enters into the process of giving value to A, that is, is consumed by A during the labour-process. The whole of the raw material and the auxiliary materials enter into it, and the wear and tear of the fixed capital. The other part of the fixed capital does not enter into it, and therefore has not got to be replaced.

A large part of the existing constant capital—large as regards the relation of the fixed capital to the total capital—does not therefore require to be replaced annually by new labour. For that reason the (absolute) amount [of the capital to be annually replaced] may be considerable, but nevertheless it is not large in relation to the total (annual) product. This *entire part of the constant capital*, in A and B, which enters into the determination of the rate of profit (with a given surplus-value), does not enter as a determining element into the current reproduction of the fixed capital. The larger this part in relation to the total capital—the greater the scale on which present, already existing, fixed capital is employed in production—the greater the *current volume of reproduction* will be that is used for the replacement of the worn-out fixed capital, but the smaller relatively will be the *proportional* amount, in relation to the total capital.

Let the reproduction period (*the average*) for all kinds of fixed capital be ten years. ||386| Let us assume that the different kinds of fixed capital have a turnover of 20, 17, 15, 12, 11, 10, 8, 6, 4, 3, 2, 1, $^4/_6$ and $^2/_6$ years (14 kinds), so that the fixed capital has an *average* turnover of 10 years.[75]

On the average, therefore, the capital would have to be replaced in 10 years. If the total fixed capital amounted to $^1/_{10}$ of the total capital, then $^1/_{10}$ of this would mean that only $^1/_{100}$ of the total capital would have to be replaced annually.

If it amounted to $^1/_3$, then $^1/_{30}$ of the total capital would have to be replaced annually.

But let us now compare fixed capitals with different reproduction periods—the capital with a 20-year period, for example, in contrast to the capital with a period of $^1/_3$ of a year.

Only $^1/_{20}$ of the fixed capital which is reproduced in 20 years has to be replaced annually. So that if it amounts to $^1/_2$ of the total capital, only $^1/_{40}$ of the total capital has to be replaced annually, and if it amounts even to $^4/_5$ of the total capital, only $^4/_{100}={}^1/_{25}$ of the total capital has to be replaced annually. On the other hand, if the capital which has a reproduction period of $^2/_6$ of a year—that is, turns over three times a year—amounts to only $^1/_{10}$ of the capital, then the fixed capital has to be replaced three times a year, so that $^3/_{10}$ of the capital has to be replaced annually, nearly one-third of the total capital. On the average, the larger the fixed capital in proportion to the total capital, the longer is its *relative* (not absolute) period of reproduction; and the smaller it is, the shorter its *relative* period of reproduction. Implements form a much smaller part of handicraft capital than machinery does of machine-production capital. But handicraft implements wear out much more quickly than machinery.

Although the absolute magnitude of its reproduction—or its wear and tear—grows with the absolute size of the fixed capital, as a rule its proportional magnitude falls, in so far as its period of turnover, its duration, as a rule increases in proportion to its size. This proves among other things that the quantity of labour reproducing machinery or fixed capital is not at all proportional to the labour which originally produced these machines (conditions of production remaining the same), since only the annual wear and tear has to be replaced. If the productivity of labour rises—as it constantly does in this branch of production—the quantity of labour required for the reproduction of this part of the constant capital diminishes still more. However, account has to be taken of the means of consumption daily used by the machine (which however have nothing directly to do with the labour employed in the machine-building industry itself). But machinery, which needs merely coal and a little oil or tallow, lives on an infinitely stricter diet than the labourer—not only the labourer whom it replaces, but the labourer who built the machine itself.

We have now disposed of the product of the entire category A and of a part of category B's product. A is completely consumed: one-third by its own producers, two-thirds by the producers of B, who cannot consume their own revenue in their own product. The two-thirds of A, in which they consume the part of the value of their product which represents revenue, at the same time replace their constant capital in kind for the producers of A, that is, provide them with the commodities which they *consume industrially*. But with the consumption of A's entire product, and with two-thirds of it replaced by B in the form of constant capital, we have also disposed of the *entire* part of the product which represents the labour newly added annually. This labour cannot therefore buy any other part of the total product. In fact, the whole of the labour added annually (leaving out of account the capitalisation of profit) is equal to the *labour contained in A*. For one-third of A which is consumed by its own producers represents the labour newly added by them during the year to the two-thirds of A which represent A's constant capital. They have performed no labour apart from this, which they consume in their own product. And the other two-thirds of A, which are replaced by B's product and consumed by the producers of B, represent all the labour-time which the producers of B have added to their own constant capital. They have added no more in labour, and there is nothing more for them to ||387| consume.

In its *use-value*, product A represents the whole part of the annual total product which enters annually into individual consumption. In its *exchange-value*, it represents the total quantity of labour newly added by the producers during the year.

Thus, however, we have as *residuum* a third part of the total product whose constituent parts, when exchanged, can represent neither the exchange of revenue against revenue nor of capital against revenue and vice versa. This is the part of product B which represents B's constant capital. This part is not included in B's revenue and therefore cannot be replaced by or exchanged against product A, and therefore also cannot enter as a constituent part into A's constant capital. This part is likewise consumed, industrially consumed, to the extent that it enters not only into B's labour-process but also into the formation of value in B. This part, therefore, like all other parts of the total product, must be replaced *in the proportion in which it forms a component part of the total product*, and indeed it must be replaced in kind by *new* products of the same sort. On the other hand, it is not replaced by any new labour. For the total quantity of newly-added labour is equal to the labour-time contained in A, which is completely replaced only by B consuming his revenue in two-thirds of A and supplying to A in exchange all the means of production which are consumed in A and must be replaced. For the first one-third of A, which is consumed by its own producers, consists only—as exchange-value—of the labour newly added by themselves, and it contains no constant capital.

Let us now examine this residuum.

It consists of the constant capital which enters into raw materials, and secondly of the constant capital which enters into the formation of the capital, and thirdly of the constant capital which enters into auxiliary materials.

First, the raw materials. Their constant capital consists in the first place of fixed capital, machinery, instruments of labour and buildings, and perhaps auxiliary materials, which are means of consumption for the machinery employed. In regard to the directly consumable part of the raw materials—such as cattle, corn, grapes, and such like—this difficulty does not arise. In this aspect they belong to class A. This part of the constant capital contained in them enters into the two-thirds of the constant part of A, which is exchanged as capital against the unconsumable products of B or in which B consumes his revenue. This holds good too in general for such raw materials that cannot be immediately consumed as far as they enter in kind into the consumable product itself, however many intermediate stages they may pass through in the processes of production. The part of flax that is transformed into yarn and later into linen enters in its entirety into the consumable product.

But a part of these *vegetative raw materials*, such as timber, flax, hemp, leather and so on, partly enters directly into the components of the fixed capital itself, and partly into the auxiliary materials for the fixed capital. For example, in the form of oil, tallow, etc.

Secondly, however, *seed* [belongs to the constant capital expended for the production of raw materials]. Vegetative materials and animals reproduce themselves. Vegetation and generation. By seed we mean actual seed, and in addition fodder which reverts to the land as dung, pedigree cattle, etc. This large part of the annual product—or of che constant part of the annual product—itself serves directly as material for regeneration, it reproduces itself.

Non-vegetative raw materials. Metals, stones, etc. Their value consists of only two parts, since here there is no seed—which represents the raw materials of agriculture. Their value consists only of added labour and machinery consumed (including the means of consumption for the machinery). In addition therefore to the part of the product which represents newly-added labour and is hence included in the exchange of B for the two-thirds of A, there is nothing to be replaced but the wear and tear of the fixed capital and its means of consumption (such as coal, oil, etc.). But these raw materials form the principal component part of the constant capital, of the fixed capital (machinery and instruments of labour, buildings, etc.). They therefore replace their constant capital in kind by the exchange [of capital against capital].

||388| *Secondly, the fixed capital (machinery, buildings, instruments of labour, containers of all kinds).*

Their constant capital consists of: (1) their raw materials, metals, stones, vegetative raw materials such as timber, leather belting, rope, etc. But though these raw materials form the raw material for them, they themselves enter as instruments of labour into the production of these raw materials. Hence they replace themselves in kind. The iron producer has to replace machinery, the machine builder iron. In quarrying there is wear and tear of machinery, but in factory buildings there is wear and tear of building stone, etc. (2) *The wear and tear of machine-building machinery*, which within a certain period has to be replaced by a new product of the same kind. But the product of the same kind can, of course, replace itself. (3) *The means of consumption for the machine* (auxiliary materials). Machinery consumes coal, but coal consumes machinery, and so on. In the form of containers, tubes, pipes, etc., machinery of all kinds enters into the production of the means of consumption for machinery, as in the case of tallow, soap, gas (for lighting). Therefore also in these cases the products of these spheres enter reciprocally into each other's constant capital, and consequently replace each other in kind.

If beasts of burden are included among machines, what has

to be replaced in their case is fodder and in certain conditions stabling (buildings). But if fodder enters into the production of cattle, so do cattle into the production of fodder.

In the third place, auxiliary materials. Some of these require raw materials, like oil, soap, tallow, gas, etc. On the other hand, in the form of fertilisers, etc., they in turn enter in part into the production of these raw materials. Coal is required for making gas, but gas lighting is used in producing coal, etc. Other *auxiliary materials* consist only of labour added and fixed capital (machinery, containers, etc.). Coal must replace the wear and tear of the steam-engine used to produce it. But the steam-engine consumes coal. Coal itself enters into the means of production of coal. Thus it replaces itself in kind. Transport by rail enters into the production costs of coal, but coal in turn enters into the production costs of the locomotive.

Later on, there is something special to be added about chemical factories, all of which in greater or smaller degree produce auxiliary materials, such as the raw material of containers (for example, glass, porcelain), as well as articles which enter directly into consumption.

All colouring materials are auxiliary materials. But they enter into the product not only as to their value, as for example coal consumed enters into cotton; but they reproduce themselves in the form of the product (its colours).

Auxiliary materials are either *means of consumption for machinery*—in this case either fuel for the prime mover, or means of reducing the friction of the operating machinery, such as tallow, soap, oil, etc.—or they are auxiliary materials for buildings, like cement, etc. Or they are auxiliary materials for carrying on the production process in general, such as lighting, heating, etc. (in this case they are auxiliary materials required by the labourers themselves to enable them to work).

Or *they are auxiliary materials* which enter into the formation of the raw materials as do all types of fertilisers and all chemical products consumed by the raw materials.

Or *they are auxiliary materials* which enter into the finished product—colouring matter, polishing materials, and so on.

The result is therefore:

A replaces his own constant capital, [equal to] two-thirds [of the product], by exchange with that part of B's unconsumable product which represents B's revenue—that is, the labour added in category B during the year. But A does not replace B's constant capital. B for his part must replace this constant capital in kind by new products of the same sort. But B has no labour-time over to replace them with. For all the new labour-time added by him forms his revenue, and is therefore represented by the part of B's product which enters as constant capital into A. How then is B's constant capital replaced?

Partly by his *own reproduction* (vegetative or animal), as in all agriculture and stock-raising; partly by *exchange in kind* of parts of one constant capital for parts of another constant capital, because the product of one sphere enters as raw material or means of production into the other sphere, and vice versa; that is, because the products of the various spheres of production, the ||389| various sorts of constant capital, enter reciprocally in kind into each other's sphere as conditions of production.

The producers of unconsumable products are the producers of constant capital for the producers of consumable products. But at the same time their products serve them reciprocally as elements or factors of their own constant capital. That is to say, they consume each other's products *industrially*.

The whole product A is consumed. Therefore also the whole of the constant capital it contains. The producers of A consume one-third of A, the producers of the unconsumable products B consume two-thirds of A. A's constant capital is replaced by the products of B which form B's revenue. This is in fact the only part of the constant capital that is replaced by *newly-added labour*; and it is replaced by it because the quantity of products B that is the newly-added labour in B, is not consumed by B, but on the contrary is industrially consumed by A, while B consumes individually the two-thirds of A.

Let A be equal to 3 days' labour; his constant capital, on our assumption, is equal to 2 days' labour. B replaces the product of two-thirds of A, and so supplies unconsumable products equal to 2 days' labour. Now 3 days' labour have been consumed, and 2 are left. In other words, the 2 days of past labour in A are replaced by 2 days of newly-added labour in B, but only because the 2 days of newly-added labour in B consume their value in A and not in product B itself.

B's constant capital, in so far as it has entered into the total product B, must likewise be replaced *in kind* by new products of the same sort—that is, by products which are required for *industrial* consumption by B. But it is not replaced by *new* labour-time, although it is replaced by the *products* of the labour-time newly applied during the year.

Let the whole constant capital in B's total product be two-thirds. Then if the newly-added labour (equal to the total wages and profit) is 1, the past labour which served it as material and means of labour is equal to 2. How then are these 2 replaced? The proportion of constant and variable capital may vary considerably within the various spheres of production of B. But on our assumption the average is as $^1/_3 : ^2/_3$, or 1 : 2. Each of the producers of B is now faced by two-thirds of his product, such as coal, iron, flax, machinery, cattle, wheat (i. e., the part of his cattle and wheat that does not enter into consumption), etc.; whose elements of production must be replaced, or which must be reconverted into the natural form of their elements of production. But all these products themselves re-enter industrial consumption. The wheat (as seed) is in turn also its own raw material, and a part of the cattle produced replaces what has been consumed, that is, itself. In these spheres of production of B (agriculture and stock-raising) this part of their product therefore replaces their own constant capital in its natural form. A part of this product, therefore, does not go into circulation (at least need not go into circulation, and can only do so in a formal sense). Others of these products, such as flax, hemp, etc., coal, iron, timber, machinery, in part enter into their own production as means of production, in the same way as seed in agriculture: for example, coal in the production of coal, and machinery in the production of machinery. A part of the product consisting of machinery and coal, and in fact a part of that part of this product which represents its constant capital, thus replaces itself and merely changes its place in the process of production. It changes from a product into its own means of production.

Another part of these and of other products reciprocally enter into each other as elements of production—machinery into iron and timber, timber and iron into machinery, oil into machinery and machinery into oil, coal into iron, iron (tram-rails, etc.) into coal, and so on. In so far as the two-thirds of these products of B are not self-replacing in this way—that is, do not come back in their natural form into their own production, so that a part of B is directly consumed industrially by its own producers, just as a part of A is directly consumed individually by its own producers—the products of the producers of B replace each other reciprocally as means of production. The product of a goes into b's industrial consumption and the product of b into a's industrial consumption; or in a roundabout way, a's product into b's industrial consumption, b's product into that of c, and that of c into that of a. What therefore is consumed as constant capital in one of B's spheres of production is newly produced in another; but what is consumed in the latter is produced in the former. What in one sphere passes from the form of machinery and coal into the form of iron, passes in the other from the form of iron and coal into machinery, and so on.

||390| What has to be done is to replace B's constant capital in its natural form. If we consider B's total product, it represents the entire constant capital in all its natural forms. And where the product of one particular sphere of B cannot replace its own constant capital in kind, purchase and sale, a change of hands, puts everything here in its proper place again.

Here, therefore, there is replacement of constant capital by constant capital; in so far as this does not occur directly and without exchange, here therefore there is *exchange of capital for capital*, that is, of products for products on the basis of their use-value; the products enter reciprocally into their respective production processes, so that each of them is industrially consumed by the producers of the other.

This part of the capital consists neither of profit nor of wages. It contains no newly-added labour. It is not exchanged against revenue. It is neither directly nor indirectly paid for by consumers. It makes no difference whether this reciprocal replacement of capitals is carried through with the aid of merchants (that is, by merchant's capitals) or not.

But since these products are new (machinery, iron, coal, timber, etc., which reciprocally replace each other), since they are the products of the last year's labour—thus the wheat which serves as seed is just as much a product of new labour as the wheat which passes into consumption, etc.—how can it be said that no newly-added labour is contained in these products? And moreover isn't their form striking evidence to the contrary? Even if not in the case of wheat or cattle, surely in the case of a machine its form bears witness to the labour which has transformed it from iron, etc., into a machine, and so forth.

This problem has been solved earlier.* It is not necessary to go into it here again.

<Adam Smith's statement that the trade between dealers and dealers must be equal to the trade between dealers and consumers (by which he means direct, not industrial, consumers, since he himself includes industrial consumers among dealers) is therefore wrong. It is based on his false assertion that the whole product consists of revenue, and in fact only means that the part of the exchange of commodities which is equal to the exchange between capital and revenue is equal to the total exchange of commodities. As the assertion is wrong, the practical applications Tooke made of it for the circulation of money are also wrong (especially the relation between the quantity of money circulating between dealers and the quantity of money circulating between dealers and consumers).

Let us take as the final dealer confronting the consumer the merchant who buys the product of A; this product is bought from him by the revenue of A, equal to one-third of A, and by the revenue of B, equal to two-thirds of A. These replace his merchant's capital for him. The total of their revenues must cover his capital. (The profit which the rascal makes must be accounted for by his retaining a part of A for himself, and selling a smaller part of A for the value of A. Whether the rascal is thought of as a necessary agent of production or as a sybaritic intermediary does not in any way alter the case.) This exchange between dealer in A and consumer of A covers in value the exchange between the dealer in A and all the producers of A, and consequently all dealings between these producers among themselves.

The merchant buys the linen. This is the last dealing between dealer and dealers. The linen weaver buys yarn, machinery, coal, etc. This is the last but one dealing between dealer and dealers. The spinner buys flax, machinery, coal, etc. This is the last dealing but two between dealer and dealers. The flax-grower and machine builder buy iron, machines, etc., and so on. But the dealings between the producers of flax, machinery, iron, coal, [which are carried out] to replace their constant capital, and the value of these dealings, do not enter into the dealings which A's product passes through, whether as the exchange of revenue for revenue, or as the exchange of revenue for constant

* See pp. 107-51 and pp. 187-98 of the present volume.—*Ed.*

capital. These dealings—not those between the producers of B and the producers of A, but those between the producers of B—have not to be replaced by the buyer of A to the seller of A, any more than the value of this part of B enters into the value of A. These dealings too require money, and are carried out through merchants. But the part of the circulation of money which exclusively belongs to this sphere is completely separate from that between dealers and consumers.>

||391| Two questions are still to be solved:

1. In our investigation up to now wages have been treated as revenue, without being distinguished from profit. How far in this connection have we to take account of the fact that wages are at the same time part of the circulating capital of the capitalist?

2. Up to now it has been assumed that the total revenue is spent as revenue. The alteration that comes in when a part of the revenue, of the profit, is capitalised, has therefore to be considered. This in fact comes up in the examination of the process of accumulation—but not in its formal aspect. That a part of the product which represents surplus-value is reconverted, partly into wages and partly into constant capital, presents no difficulty. Here we have to examine how this affects the exchange of commodities under the headings previously considered—under which it can be examined in relation for its holders, that is to say, as exchange of revenue for revenue, exchange of revenue for capital, or finally, exchange of capital for capital.}

<This intermezzo has therefore to be completed in this historico-critical section, as occasion warrants.[76]>

[11.] Ferrier [Protectionist Character of Ferrier's Polemics against Smith's Theory of Productive Labour and the Accumulation of Capital. Smith's Confusion on the Question of Accumulation. The Vulgar Element in Smith's View of "Productive Labourers"]

Ferrier (François-Louis-Auguste) (*Sub-inspector of Customs*): *Du Gouvernement considéré dans ses rapports avec le commerce*, Paris, 1805. (This was the main source for Friedrich List.) This fellow eulogises the *Bonapartist* system of prohibitions, etc. In fact the Government (therefore also State officials—those unproductive labourers) is in his view important, as a manager directly intervening in production. This customs officer is consequently extremely angry with Adam Smith for calling State officials unproductive.

"The principles which Smith *has laid down in regard to the economy of nations* have as their basis a distinction in labour, which he calls productive or unproductive...."

<Because in fact he wants the largest possible part to be spent as capital, i. e., in exchange for productive labour, and the smallest possible part as revenue, in exchange for unproductive labour.>

"This distinction is in essence false. *There is no unproductive labour*" (p. 141). "There is therefore economy and prodigality on the part of nations; but a nation is only prodigal or economic in its relations with *other* peoples, and it is from this standpoint that the question should be considered" (l.c., p. 143).

In a moment we shall quote for comparison the context of the passage from Adam Smith which Ferrier regards with such abomination.

"There is an economy on the part of nations, but it is very different from what Smith recommends.... It consists in not buying foreign products except in so far as a nation can pay for them with its own. It consists sometimes in doing without them altogether" (l.c., pp. 174-75).

<Book I, Chapter VI, (t. I, éd. Garnier, pp. 103-03) *Adam Smith* says at the end of this chapter which deals with the component parts of the price of commodities:

"As in a civilised country there are *but few commodities of which the exchangeable value arises from labour only, rent and profit contributing largely to that of the far greater part of them, so the annual produce of its labour will always be sufficient to purchase or command a much greater quantity of labour than what was employed in raising, preparing, and bringing that produce to market. If the society were annually to employ all the labour which it can annually purchase, as the quantity of labour would increase greatly every year*, so the produce of every succeeding year would be of vastly greater value than that of the foregoing. But there is no country *in which the whole annual produce* is employed in maintaining the industrious. The idle everywhere consume a great part of it; and, according to the different proportions in which it is annually divided between those two different orders of people, its ordinary or average value must either annually increase or diminish, or continue the same from one year to another" [Smith, *Wealth of Nations*, O.U.P. edition, Vol. I, pp. 59-60].

There is confusion of all kinds in this passage, in which Smith is in fact trying to solve the problem of accumulation.

First, once again there is the wrong assumption that the "exchangeable value" of the annual product of labour, and so also "*the annual produce of labour*", resolves itself into wages and profits (including rents). We will not deal again with this nonsense. We only observe: the amount of the annual product—or of the funds, the stocks of commodities which are the annual product of labour—consists for the most part ||392| of commodities in kind which can only enter as elements into constant capital <raw materials, seed, machinery, etc.>, which can *only* be consumed industrially. The very *use-value* of these commodities (and they form the larger part of the commodities entering into constant capital) shows that they are not suitable for individual consumption; that therefore revenue cannot be expended on them, whether it is wages, profit or rent. A part of the raw materials (in so far as it is not required for the reproduction of raw materials themselves, or in so far as it does not enter into the fixed capital as auxiliary material or directly as a component part) will, it is true, later on be given a consumable form, but only through the labour of the current year. As a product of the previous year's labour these raw materials themselves form no part of revenue. It is only the consumable part of the product that can be consumed, can enter into individual consumption and thus form revenue. But even a part of the consumable product cannot be consumed without making reproduction impossible. One part even of the consumable part of commodities therefore must be deducted which must be *consumed industrially*, that is, it must serve as material of labour, as seed, etc., not as means of subsistence, whether for labourers or for capitalists. This part of the product therefore has first to be deducted from Adam Smith's calculation—or rather has to be added to it. *If the productivity of labour remains the same*, then this part of the *product* which does not consist of revenue remains the same from year to year; provided that, with the productivity of labour remaining the same, the same quantity of labour-time as before is employed.

On the assumption therefore that *a greater quantity* of labour than before is used each year, we have to see what happens to the constant capital. In short: in order to employ a greater quantity of labour, it is not enough either that a *greater quantity of labour* should be available, or that a *greater quantity should be paid for*, that is, more should be spent in wages; but the means of labour—raw material and fixed capital—must also be there in order to absorb a greater quantity of labour. Hence this point is still to be discussed *after* the points raised by Adam Smith have been cleared up.

So then, once more [we take] his first sentence:

> "As in a civilised country there are but few commodities of which the exchangeable value *arises from labour only, rent and profit contributing largely* to that of the far greater part of them, *so the annual produce of its labour* will always be sufficient *to purchase or command a much greater quantity of labour* than *what was employed in raising*, preparing, and bringing that produce to market" (in other words, to produce it).

Here different things are obviously mixed up. Not only living labour, living labour employed during the current year, enters into the exchangeable value of the total annual product, but also past labour, product of the labour of past years. Not only labour in living form, but labour in materialised form. The exchangeable value of the product is equal to the total labour-time which it contains, a part of which consisted of living labour and a part of materialised labour.

Let the proportion of the former to the latter be as $^1/_3 : ^2/_3$, or 1 : 2. Then the value of the total product is equal to 3, of which 2 are materialised labour-time and 1 living labour-time. The *value* of the total product can therefore buy more living labour than is contained in it, on the assumption that materialised labour and living labour exchanged for each other as equivalents, that a definite quantity of materialised labour commanded only a quantity of living labour equal to itself. For the product is equal to 3 days' labour; but the living labour-time contained in it is only equal to 1 day's labour. 1 day's living labour sufficed to produce the product (in fact, only to give the final form to its elements). But 3 days' labour is contained in it. Therefore if it was exchanged entirely against living labour-time, if it was employed only "to purchase or command" quantities of living labour, it would be able to command, to purchase, 3 days' labour.

This however is evidently not what Adam Smith has in mind, and would be a quite useless premise for him. What he means is that a large part of the exchangeable value of the product does not resolve itself (or as he *wrongly* expresses it, because of a confusion of ideas noted earlier*) into wages, but into profits and rents, or, as we will say to simplify things, into profits. In other words, the part of the value of the product which is equal to the quantity of labour added during the last year—thus in fact the part of the product which in the proper meaning of the

* See pp. 96-97 of the present volume.—*Ed.*

word is the product of last year's labour—pays first the labourers and secondly enters into the capitalist's revenue, his fund for consumption. This whole part of the total product arises from labour, and indeed exclusively from labour; but it consists of paid and unpaid labour. The wages are equal to the total of the paid labour, the profits ||393| to the total of the unpaid labour. If therefore this total product was expended in wages, it could naturally set in motion a greater quantity of labour than that of which it was the product; and in fact the proportion in which the product can set in motion more labour-time than it itself contains depends exactly on the proportion in which the working-day is divided into paid and unpaid labour-time.

Let us assume that the proportion is such that the labourer produces or reproduces his wages in 6 hours, that is, in half a day. Then the other 6 hours or the other half day forms the surplus. Thus for example of a product which contained 100 days' labour [newly-added labour], equal to £50 (when the day's labour is equal to 10s., making 100 days' labour equal to 1,000s., or £50), there would be £25 for wages and £25 for profit (rent). With the £25—equal to 50 days' labour—100 labourers would have been paid, who would have worked precisely half their labour-time for nothing or for their masters. If therefore the whole product (of the 100 days' labour) were to be expended in wages, then 200 labourers could be set in motion with the £50, each of whom would receive as wages 5s. or half the product of his labour as before. The product of this labour would be equal to £100 (that is, 200 days' labour, equal to 2,000s., or £100), with which 400 labourers (5s. the labourer, making 2,000s.) could be set in motion, whose product would be equal to £200, and so on.

And this is what Adam Smith means by saying that "the annual produce of labour" will always be sufficient "to purchase or command a much greater quantity of labour" than what was employed to produce the product. (If the labourer were paid the whole product of his labour, that is, £50 for 100 days' labour, then the £50 too could only set in motion 100 days' labour.) And so Smith goes on to say:

> "If the society were annually to employ all the labour which it can annually purchase, as the quantity of labour would increase greatly every year, so the produce of every succeeding year would be of vastly greater value than that of the foregoing."

A part of this product however is consumed by the owners of profit and rent; a part by their parasites. The part of the product that can be expended again in (productive) labour is consequently determined by the part of the product which the capitalists, landlords and their parasites (that is the unproductive labourers) do not themselves consume.

But nevertheless there is always a new fund (a new fund of wages) to set in motion, with the previous year's product, a greater quantity of labourers in the current year. And as the value of the annual product is determined by the quantity of labour-time employed, the value of the annual product will grow each year.

Of course it would be of no use to have the fund "*to purchase* or *command*" a "much greater quantity of labour" than in the previous year unless a greater quantity of labour was on the market. It is of no use to me to have more money to buy a commodity, unless more of this commodity is on the market. Let us assume that the £50 set in motion, instead of the 100 as before (who received £25), not 200 but only 150 labourers, while the capitalists themselves consumed £12.10s. instead of £25. The 150 labourers ([receiving] £37.10s.) would perform 150 days' labour, equal to 1,500s. or £75. But if the quantity of labourers available were, as before, only 100, instead of £25 as before, they would receive £37.10s. as wages, though their product [would amount to] only £50 as before. Thus the revenue of the capitalist would have fallen from £25 to £12.10s., because wages had risen by 50 per cent. Adam Smith knows, however, that an increasing quantity of labour will be available. Partly [due to] the annual increase of the population (though this is supposed to be provided for in the old wages), partly unemployed paupers, or half-employed labourers, etc. Then the large numbers of unproductive labourers, part of whom can be transformed into *productive* labourers by a different way of using the surplus-produce. Finally the same number of labourers can perform a *greater quantity* of labour. And whether I pay 125 labourers instead of 100, or whether the 100 work 15 hours a day instead of 12, would be quite the same thing.

It is incidentally an error of Adam Smith's—directly connected with his analysis of the total product into revenue—to say that with the increase of the productive capital—or with the growth of the part of the annual product which is destined for reproduction—the *labour employed* (the living labour, the part of capital expended in wages) must increase in the same proportion.

||394| Thus first Adam Smith has a fund of consumable means of subsistence, which can "purchase or command" a greater quantity of labour this year than the foregoing year; he has more labour; and at the same time more means of subsistence for this labour. Now we must see how this additional quantity of labour is to be realised.>

Had Adam Smith adhered with full consciousness to the analysis of surplus-value which in substance is to be found in his work—which is created only in the exchange of capital against wage-labour—it would have followed that productive labour is only that which is exchanged against capital: never labour which is exchanged with revenue as such. In order for revenue to be exchanged against productive labour, it must first be transformed into capital.

But taking as his starting-point one aspect of the traditional view—that productive labour is labour which directly produces material wealth of any kind—and at the same time combining with this his distinction in so far as it is based on the exchange of either capital for labour or of revenue for labour, with Smith the following became possible: The kind of labour for which capital is exchanged is always productive (it always creates material wealth, etc.). The kind of labour which is exchanged for revenue may be productive or it may not; but the spender of revenue as a rule prefers to set in motion directly unproductive labour rather than productive. One can see how Adam Smith, by this compound of his two distinctions, very much weakens and blunts the principal distinction.

The following quotation shows that Adam Smith does not take the fixation of labour in a purely external sense; among the various component parts of the fixed capital is enumerated:

> "Fourthly, of the acquired and useful abilities of all the inhabitants and members of the society. The acquisition of such talents, by the maintenance of the acquirer during his education, study, or apprenticeship, always costs a real expense, which is a capital fixed and realised, as it were, in his person. Those talents, as they make a part of his fortune, so do they likewise that of the society to which he belongs. The improved dexterity of a workman may be considered in the same light as a machine or instrument of trade which facilitates and abridges labour, and which, though it costs a certain expense, repays that expense with a profit" ([*Wealth of Nations*, O.U.P. edition, Vol. I, p. 308], [Garnier], l.c., t. II. ch. I, pp. 204-05).

The strange origin of accumulation and its necessity:

"In that rude state of society, in which there is no division of labour, in which exchanges are seldom made, and in which every man provides every thing for himself, *it is not necessary that any stock should be accumulated, or stored up beforehand, in order to carry on the business of the society*" (that is, after assuming that there is no society). "Every man endeavours to supply, by his own industry, his own occasional wants, as they occur. When he is hungry, he goes to the forest to hunt"—and so on ([ibid., p.301], [Garnier], l.c., t. II, pp. 191-92) (l. II, *Introduction*). "But when the division of labour has once been thoroughly introduced, the produce of a man's own labour can supply but a very small part of his occasional wants. The far greater part of them are supplied by *the produce of other men's labour*, [which he purchases with the produce], or, what is the same thing, the price of the produce of his own. But this *purchase* cannot be made till such time as *the produce of his own labour* has not only been *completed*, but *sold*."

(Even in the first case he could not eat the hare before he had killed it, and he could not kill it before he had produced for himself the classical "bow" or something similar. The only thing that seems to be added in case II is therefore not the necessity of a stock of any sort, but the "time... *to sell* the produce of his labour".)

"*A stock of goods of different kinds*, therefore, must be *stored up* somewhere, sufficient to maintain him, and to supply him with the materials and tools of his work, till such time at least as both these events can be brought about. A weaver *cannot apply himself entirely* to his peculiar business, unless there is beforehand stored up somewhere, *either in his own possession, or in that of some other persons, a stock* sufficient to maintain him, and to supply him with the materials and tools of his work, till he has not only completed, but sold his web. This *accumulation must* evidently *be previous* to his applying his industry for so long a time to such a peculiar business. ... *The accumulation of s t o c k must*, in the nature of things, *be previous to the division of labour...*" ([ibid., pp. 301-02], [Garnier], l.c., pp. 192-93).

(On the other hand, according to what he has stated at the beginning, it appears that no accumulation of capital takes place *before* the division of labour, just as there is no division of labour before the accumulation of capital.)

He continues:

"... Labour can be more and more subdivided in proportion only as stock is previously more and more accumulated. *The quantity of materials which the same number of people can work up, increases in a great proportion* as labour comes to be more and more subdivided; and as the operations of each workman are gradually reduced to a greater degree of simplicity, a variety of new machines come to be invented for facilitating and |395| abridging those operations. As the division of labour advances, therefore, in order to give constant employment to an equal number of workmen, *an equal stock of provisions, and a greater stock of materials and tools* than what would have been necessary in a ruder state of things, must be *accumulated beforehand*" ([ibid., p. 302], [Garnier], l.c., pp. 193-94). "As *the accumulation of stock is previously necessary* for carrying on this great improvement in the productive powers of labour, so that accumulation naturally leads to this improvement. *The person who employs his stock in maintaining labour*, necessarily wishes to employ it in such a manner as to produce as great a quantity of work as possible. He endeavours, therefore, both to make among his workmen the most proper distribution of employment, and to furnish them with the best machines which he can either invent or afford to purchase. His abilities, in both these respects, are generally in proportion to the extent of his stock, or to the number of people whom it can employ. *The quantity of industry*, therefore, *not only increases in every country with the increase of the stock* which employs it, but, *in consequence of that increase*, the same *quantity of industry produces a much greater quantity of work*" ([ibid., pp. 302-03], [Garnier], l.c., pp. 194-95).

Adam Smith treats the objects which are already in the fund for consumption in exactly the same way as productive and unproductive labour. For instance:

"A dwelling-house, as such, contributes nothing to the revenue of its inhabitant; and though it is, no doubt, extremely useful to him, it is as his clothes and household furniture are useful to him, which, however, make a part of his expense, and not of his revenue" ([ibid., pp. 306-07], [Garnier], l.c., t. II, pp. 201-02). On the other hand, fixed capital includes "all those profitable buildings which are the means of procuring a revenue, not only to their proprietor who lets them for a rent, but to the person who possesses them, and pays that rent for them; such as shops, warehouses, workhouses, farm-houses, with all their necessary buildings, stables, granaries, etc. These are very different from mere dwelling-houses. They are a sort of instruments of trade..." ([ibid., p. 308], [Garnier], l.c., t. II, pp. 203-04).

"... All such improvements in mechanics, as enable the same number of workmen to perform an equal quantity of work with cheaper and simpler machinery than had been usual before, are always regarded as advantageous to every society. A certain quantity of materials, and the labour of a certain number of workmen, which had before been employed in supporting a more complex and expensive machinery, can afterwards be applied to augment the quantity of work which that or any other machinery is useful only for performing" ([ibid., p. 315], [Garnier], l.c., t. II, pp. 216-17).

"... The whole expense of maintaining the *fixed capital* is ... necessarily excluded from the neat revenue of the society" ([ibid., p. 316], [Garnier], l.c., t. II, p. 218). "Every saving, therefore, in the expense of maintaining the *fixed capital*, which does not diminish the productive powers of labour, must increase the fund which puts industry into motion, and consequently the annual produce of land and labour, the real revenue of every society" ([ibid., p. 321], [Garnier], l.c., t. II, pp. 226-27).

Gold and silver money forced to go abroad by bank-notes and by paper money in general—if spent "in purchasing foreign goods for home consumption"—buys either luxury products such as foreign wines, foreign silks, etc., in a word, "goods ... likely to be consumed by *idle people*, who produce nothing... or ... they may purchase *an additional stock of materials, tools, and provisions, in order to maintain and employ an additional number of industrious people, who reproduce, with a profit, the value of their annual consumption*" ([ibid., p. 324], [Garnier], l.c., t. II, pp. 231-32).

The first manner of employment, says Smith, promotes prodigality, "increases expense and consumption, without increasing production, or establishing any permanent fund for supporting that expense, and is in every respect hurtful to the society" ([ibid., p. 324], [Garnier], l.c., t. II, p. 232). On the other hand "employed in the second way, it promotes industry; and though it increases the consumption of the society, it provides a permanent fund for supporting that consumption; *the people who consume reproducing, with a profit, the whole value of their annual consumption*" ([ibid., p. 324], [Garnier], l.c., t. II, p. 232).

"The quantity of industry which any capital can employ, must evidently be equal to the number of workmen whom it can supply with materials, tools, and a maintenance suitable to the nature of the work" ([ibid., p.326], [Garnier], l.c., t. II, p. 235).

‖396| In *Chapter III of Book II* (l. c., t. II, p. 314 sqq.) [we find]:

"Both productive and unproductive labourers, and those who do not labour at all, are all equally maintained by the annual produce of the land and labour of the country. This produce ... must have certain limits. According, therefore, as a smaller or greater proportion of it is in any one year employed in maintaining unproductive hands, the more in the one case, and the less in the other, will remain for the productive, and the next year's produce will be greater or smaller accordingly....

"Though the whole annual produce of the land and labour of every country is ... ultimately destined for supplying the consumption of its inhabitants, and for procuring a revenue to them; *yet when it first* comes either from the ground, or from the hands of the productive labourers, it naturally divides itself into two parts. One of them, and frequently the largest, is, in the first place, destined for *replacing a capital, or for renewing the provisions, materials, and finished work*, which had been withdrawn from a capital; the other for constituting a revenue either to the owner of this capital, as the profit of his stock, or to some other person, as the rent of his land....

"*That part of the annual produce of the land and labour of any country which replaces a capital*, never is immediately employed to maintain any but productive hands. It pays the wages of productive labour only. That which is immediately destined for constituting a revenue... may maintain indifferently either productive or unproductive hands....

"Unproductive labourers, and those who do not labour at all, are all maintained *by revenue*; either, first, by that part of the annual produce which is originally destined for constituting a revenue to some particular persons, either as the rent of land, or as the profits of stock; or, secondly, by that part which, though originally destined for replacing a capital, and for maintaining productive labourers only, yet when it comes into their hands, whatever part of it is over and above their necessary subsistence, may be employed in maintaining indifferently either productive or unproductive hands. Thus ... even the common workman, if his wages are considerable, may maintain a menial servant; or he may sometimes go to a play or a puppet-show, and so contribute his share towards maintaining one set of unproductive labourers; or he may pay some taxes, and thus help to maintain another set ... equally unproductive. No part of the annual produce, however, which had been originally destined to replace a capital, is ever directed towards maintaining unproductive hands, till after it has put into motion its full complement of productive labour.... The workman must have earned his wages by work done, before he can employ any part of them in this manner.... The rent of land and the profits of stock are everywhere... the principal sources from which unproductive hands derive their subsistence." These two sorts of revenue "might both maintain indifferently, either productive or unproductive hands. They seem, however, to have some predilection for the latter....

"The proportion, therefore, between the productive and unproductive hands, depends very much in every country upon the proportion between that part of the annual produce, which, as soon as it comes either from the ground, or from the hands of the productive labourers, is destined for replacing a capital, and that which is destined for constituting a revenue, either as rent or as profit. This proportion is very different in rich from what it is in poor countries" [*Wealth of Nations*, O.U.P. edition, Vol. I, pp. 370-73].

[Adam Smith] then contrasts the "very large, frequently the largest, portion of the produce of the land" which "in the opulent countries of Europe [...] *is destined for replacing the capital of the rich and independent farmer*" with "the prevalency of the feudal government", when "a very small portion of the produce was sufficient to replace the capital employed in cultivation".

It is the same with commerce and manufactures. Large capitals are now employed in them, formerly very small capitals, but they

"yielded very large profits. The rate of interest was nowhere less than ten per cent, and their profits must have been sufficient to afford this great interest. At present, the rate of interest, in the improved parts of Europe, is nowhere higher than six per cent; and in some of the most improved, it is so low as four, three, and two per cent. Though that part of the revenue of the inhabitants which is derived from the profits of stock, is always much greater in rich than in poor countries, it is because the stock is much greater; in proportion to the stock, the profits are generally much less.

"That part of the annual produce, therefore, which, as soon as it comes either from the ground, or from the hands of the productive labourers, is destined for replacing a capital, ||397| is not only much greater in rich than in poor countries, but bears a much greater proportion to that which is immediately destined for constituting a revenue either as rent or as profit. The funds destined for the maintenance of productive labour are not only much greater in the former than in the latter, but bear a much greater proportion to those which, though they may be employed to maintain either productive or unproductive hands, have generally a predilection for the latter."

(Smith falls into the error of identifying the size of the productive capital with the *size of that part of it* which is destined to provide subsistence for productive labour. But in fact large-scale industry, as he knew it, was as yet only in its beginnings.)

"The proportion between those different funds necessarily determines in every country the general character of the inhabitants as to industry or idleness." Thus he says for example: in English and Dutch manufacturing towns "where the inferior ranks of people are chiefly maintained by the employment of capital, they are in general industrious, sober and thriving". On the other hand, in "towns which are principally supported by the [constant or occasional] residence of a court, and in which the inferior ranks of people are chiefly maintained by the spending of revenue, they are in general idle, dissolute, and poor; as at Rome, Versailles",* etc. [ibid., pp. 372-75].

"The proportion between capital and revenue, therefore, seems everywhere to regulate the proportion between industry and idleness. Wherever capital predominates, industry prevails: wherever revenue, idleness. *Every increase or diminution of capital*, therefore, naturally tends to increase or diminish the real quantity of industry, the number of productive hands, and consequently the exchangeable value of the annual produce of the land and labour of the country, the real wealth and revenue of all its inhabitants....

"What is annually saved, is as regularly consumed as what is annually spent, and nearly in the same time, too: but it is consumed by a different set of people." The first portion "by idle guests and menial servants, who leave nothing behind them in return for their consumption". The second [portion] "by labourers [...] who, reproduce, with a profit, the value of their annual consumption.... The consumption is the same, but the consumers are different" [ibid., pp. 377-78].

Hence Smith's homilies (further on [Garnier], l. c., t. II, l. II, ch. III, pp. 328-29 sqq.) on the frugal man, who by his annual savings provides something like a public workhouse for an additional number of productive hands, and thus

"establishes, as it were, a perpetual fund for the maintenance of an equal number in all times to come", while the prodigal diminishes "the funds destined for the employment of productive labour. ... If the quantity of food and clothing, which were thus" (as a result of the prodigal's prodigality) "consumed by unproductive, had been distributed among productive hands, they would have *reproduced, together with a profit*, the full value of their consumption" [ibid., pp. 378-79].

The conclusion of this moral tale is that these (frugality and prodigality) average out among private individuals, that in fact "wisdom" prevails.

"Great nations are never impoverished by private, though they sometimes are by public prodigality and misconduct. The whole, or almost the whole public revenue is, in most countries, employed in maintaining unproductive hands." [These include] the people of the court, the church, fleets and armies, "who in time of peace produce nothing, and in time of

* Marx put the passage in his own words and slightly abbreviated it. —*Ed.*

war acquire nothing which can compensate the expense of maintaining them, even while the war lasts. *Such people, as they themselves produce nothing, are all maintained by the produce of other men's labour.* When multiplied, therefore, to an unnecessary number, they may in a particular year consume so great a share of this produce, as not to leave a sufficiency for maintaining the productive labourers, who should reproduce it next year" [ibid., pp. 382-83].

[In] Chapter IV of Book II [Smith writes]:

"The demand for productive labour, by the increase of the funds which are destined for maintaining it, grows every day greater and greater. Labourers easily find ||398| employment; but the owners of capitals find it difficult to get labourers to employ. Their competition raises the wages of labour, and sinks the profits of stock" ([ibid., p. 395], [Garnier], l.c., t. II, p. 359).

In Chapter V of Book II (p. 369 sqq., t. II) of the "*Different Employments of Capitals*", Smith classifies them according as they employ more or less productive labour, and, consequently, raise "the exchange-value" of the annual product. First *agriculture*. Then *manufacture*. Then *commerce*, and finally *retail trade*. This is the order of precedence in which they set in motion quantities of productive labour. Here too we get a completely new definition of productive labourers:

"The persons whose capitals are employed in any of those four ways, are themselves *productive labourers*. Their labour, when properly directed, fixes and realises itself in the subject or vendible commodity upon which it is bestowed, and generally adds to its price the value at least of their own maintenance and consumption" ([ibid., p. 404], [Garnier], l.c., p. 374).

(On the whole he sees their productivity in the fact that they put into motion productive labour.)

He says of *the farmer*:

"No equal capital puts into motion a greater quantity of *productive labour* than that of the farmer. Not only his labouring servants, but *his labouring cattle are productive labourers*" [ibid., p. 405.].

So in the end the ox too is a productive labourer.

[12.] Earl of Lauderdale [Apologetic Conception of the Ruling Classes as Representatives of the Most Important Kinds of Productive Labour]

Lauderdale (Earl of): *An Inquiry into the Nature and Origin of Public Wealth*, etc., [Edinburgh and] London, 1804. (The French translation: *Recherches sur la nature et l'origine de la richesse publique* etc. par *Lagentie de Lavaïsse*, Paris, 1808.)

Lauderdale's apologetic justification of profit will be examined only later on, in Section III.[77] It regards profit as arising from capitals themselves, because they "*supplant*" labour. They are paid for doing what otherwise, without them, the hand of man would have to do, or could not do at all.

"Now it is apprehended, that in every instance where capital is so employed as to produce a profit, it uniformly arises, either—from its supplanting a portion of labour which would otherwise be performed by the hand of man; or—from its performing a portion of labour, which is beyond the personal exertion of man to accomplish" (French translation, p. 119)* [p. 161].

The "Earl" is a great enemy of Smith's doctrine of accumulation and saving. Also of his distinction between *productive* and *unproductive labourers*; but according to him what Smith calls "productive powers of labour" are only the "productive power of capital". He flatly denies the derivation of surplus-value put forward by Smith, on the following grounds:

"If this, however, was a just and accurate idea of the profit of capital, it would follow that the profit of stock must be derivative, and not an original source of revenue; and capital could not therefore be considered as a source of wealth, its profit being only a transfer from the pocket of the labourer into that of the proprietor of stock" (l.c., pp. 116-17) [p. 157].

It is clear that on these premises he picks on the most superficial points in his polemic against Smith. Thus he says:

"Thus the same labour may appear either productive or unproductive, according to the use subsequently made of the commodity on which it was bestowed. If my cook, for example, makes a tart which I immediately consume, he is considered as an unproductive labourer; and the act of making the tart is unproductive labour; because that service has perished at the moment of its performance; but if the same labour is performed in a pastry cook's shop, it becomes productive labour" (l.c., p. 110) [pp. 149-50].

(*Garnier* has the copyright in this argument, as his edition and notes on Smith appeared in 1802, two years before Lauderdale.)

"This extraordinary distinction, founded on the mere durability of the services performed, classes as unproductive labourers some of those who are occupied in rendering the most important services to society. Thus the sovereign, and all who are employed in the maintenance of religion, the justice, or the defence of the State, as well as those whose skill and care are occupied in superintending the health and education of the society, are alike deemed unproductive labourers" (l.c., pp. 110-11) [p. 151]. (Or, as Adam Smith [Garnier trans.] l. II, ch. III, p. 313) presents the elegant

---

* Marx refers to the French translation from which he takes this and the following passages (see Appendix, p. 450). The page reference in square brackets is to the English edition of 1804.—*Ed.*

sequence: "churchmen, lawyers, physicians, men of letters of all kinds; players, buffoons, musicians, opera-singers, opera-dancers, etc." [*Wealth of Nations*, O.U.P. edition, Vol. I, p. 370].)

"If exchangeable value is to be considered as the basis of wealth,—it is needless to use much argument to explain the errors of this doctrine. ||399| The practice of mankind, in estimating these services, if we can judge by what is paid for them, bears sufficient testimony of its inaccuracy" ([Lauderdale], l.c., p. 111) [pp. 151-52].

Further: "The labour of the manufacturer fixes and realises itself in some vendible commodity.... Neither the *labour performed by the menial servant*, nor that of which the necessity is supplanted by circulating capital," < by this he means *money* > "do naturally stock, or store themselves up in such a manner as to be transferred from one to another for a defined value. The profit of the one and the other alike arises from *saving the labour of the owner* or master. The similarity is indeed such, that it is natural to suppose the same circumstances which led the one to be deemed unproductive, would naturally create the same impression with relation to the other." > And thereupon he quotes Smith, Book II, Chapter II,[78] > (Lauderdale, l.c., pp. 144-45) [pp. 195-97].

* * *

Thus we would have the succession: Ferrier, Garnier, Lauderdale, Ganilh. The latter phrase about the "*saving of labour*" is particularly hard ridden by *Tocqueville*.

[13. Say's Conception of "Immaterial Products". Vindication of an Unrestrained Growth of Unproductive Labour]

After Garnier appeared the inane Jean-Baptiste Say's *Traité d'économie politique*. He reproaches Smith in that "he refuses the name of *products* to the *results* of these activities [e. g., those of the physician, actor, etc.]. He gives the labour spent on them the name *unproductive*" (3me éd., t. I, p. 117).

Smith does not at all deny that these activities produce a "result", a "product" of some kind. He even expressly mentions "the protection, security, and defence of the commonwealth" as "the effect of their labour this year" (the labour of the servants of the public) ([*Wealth of Nations*], O.U.P. edition, Vol. I, pp. 369-70] *Smith*, t. II, éd. Garnier, l. II, ch. III, p. 313).

Say for his part sticks to Smith's secondary definition, that these "services" and their product "generally perish in the very instant of their performance", "in the very instant of their production" (*Smith*, l. c.).

Monsieur Say calls these consumed "services", or their products, results—in a word, their use-value—"immaterial products or values, which are consumed in the instant of their production". Instead of calling them "unproductive", he calls them "productive of immaterial products". He gives them another name. But then he declares further:

"that they do not serve to augment the national capital" (t. I, p. 119). "A nation in which there were a multitude of musicians, priests and officials, might be pleasantly entertained, well educated and governed admirably well, but that would be all. Its capital would not receive any direct increase from all the labour of these industrious men, because their products would be consumed as fast as they were created" (l.c., p. 119).

Thus Monsieur Say declares these labours to be *unproductive* in the most restricted sense used by Smith. But at the same time he wants to appropriate Garnier's "step forward". Hence he invents a new name for unproductive labours. This is his kind of originality, his kind of productivity and way of making discoveries. And with his customary logic, he refutes himself again. He says:

"It is [...] impossible to accept the view of Monsieur Garnier, who concludes from the fact that the labour of physicians, lawyers and other similar persons is productive, that it is as advantageous for a nation to increase it as any other labour" (l.c., p. 120).

And why not, if one kind of labour is as productive as the other, and the increase of productive labour is in general "advantageous for a nation"? Why is it not as advantageous to increase this kind of labour as any other? Because, Say replies with his characteristic profundity, because it is not at all advantageous to increase productive labour of any kind above the need for this labour. But then surely Garnier is right. For it is equally advantageous—that is, equally disadvantageous—to increase the one kind of labours as to increase the other kind above a certain quantity.

"The case is the same," Say continues, "as with physical labour expended on a product beyond what is necessary to make it."

(Not more joiner's labour should be employed to make a table than is necessary for the production of the table. Or to patch up a sick body, not more than is necessary to cure it. So lawyers and physicians should perform only the necessary labour for the production of their immaterial product.)

"The labour which is productive of immaterial products, *like all other labour*, is only productive up to the point at which it increases the utility, and consequently the value" (that is the use-value, but Say mistakes the utility for the exchange-value) "of a product: beyond this point, it is a purely unproductive labour" (l.c., p. 120).

Say's logic is therefore this:

It is *not so useful* for a nation to increase the "producers of immaterial products" as to increase the producers of material products. *Proof*: it is absolutely useless to increase the producers of any kind of product, whether material or immaterial, beyond what is necessary. *Therefore* it is more useful to increase the useless producers of material products than those of immaterial products. It does not follow in both cases that it is useless to increase these producers, but only the producers of a particular kind in their corresponding branch of production.

[According to Say], too many material products cannot ||400| be produced, nor can too many immaterial. But a change is diverting. So different kinds must be produced in both departments. And moreover Monsieur Say teaches: "Sluggishness in the sale of some products arises from the scarcity of some others" (l. c., p. 438).

Therefore there can never be too many tables produced, but at most perhaps too few dishes to be put on the tables. If physicians increase too much in number, what is wrong is not that their services are available in superfluity, but perhaps that the services of other producers of immaterial products are in short supply—for example, prostitutes (see l. c., p. 123, where the industries of street-porters, prostitutes, etc., are grouped together, and where Say ventures to assert that the "apprenticeship" for a prostitute "amounts to nothing").

In the end, the scales come down on the side of the "unproductive labourers". With given conditions of production, it is known exactly how many labourers are needed to make a table, how great the quantity of a particular kind of labour must be in order to make a particular product. With many "immaterial products" this is not the case. The quantity of labour required to achieve a particular result is as conjectural as the result itself. Twenty priests together perhaps bring about the conversion that one fails to make; six physicians consulting together perhaps discover the remedy that one alone cannot find. In a bench of judges perhaps more justice is produced than by a single judge who has no control but himself. The number of soldiers required to protect a country, of police to establish order in it, of officials "to govern it" well, etc.—all these things are problematical and are very often discussed for example in the English Parliament; although how much spinning labour is needed to spin 1,000 lbs. of twist is known very exactly in England. As for other "productive" labourers of this kind, the concept of them includes the fact that the utility which they produce depends only on their number, consists in their number itself. For example, lackeys, who should bear witness to their master's wealth and elegance. The greater the number of them, the greater the effect they are supposed to "produce". Thus Monsieur Say sticks to his point: "unproductive labourers" can never be sufficiently increased in numbers. |400||

[14.] Count Destutt de Tracy [Vulgar Conception of the Origin of Profit. Proclamation of the "Industrial Capitalist" as the Sole Productive Labourer]

||400| Le comte Destutt de Tracy: *Éléments d'idéologie, IVe et Ve parties. Traité de la volonté et de ses effets*, Paris, 1826 ([First edition] 1815).

"All useful labour is really productive, and the whole labouring class of society equally deserves the name *productive*" (p. 87).

But in this productive class he distinguishes "the labouring class which *directly produces* all our wealth" (p. 88)—that is, what Smith calls the productive labourers.

As against these, the *sterile* class consists of the rich, who consume their rent of land or rent on money. They are the *idle class.*

"The real *sterile* class is the class of idlers, who do nothing but live what is called *nobly* on the products of labours performed before them, whether these products are realised in landed property which they farm out, that is to say, which they *lease* to a labourer, or whether they consist in money or goods that they lend for a return, which also means to *lease* them. Those are the real drones of the hive (*fruges consumere nati**)" (p. 87); these idlers "can expend nothing but their *revenue*. If they break into their funds || 401 |, nothing replaces them; and their consumption, increased for the moment, ceases for ever" (p. 237).

"This *revenue* is ... only a deduction from the products of activity of the industrious citizens" (p. 236).

How then does it stand with the labourers whom these idlers directly employ? In so far as they consume commodities, they do not consume actual labour, but the products of the produc-

* Born to consume the fruits (Horace).—*Ed.*

tive labourers. Here therefore we are dealing with labourers for whose labour the idlers directly exchange their revenue, that is, with labourers who draw their wages directly from revenue, not from capital.

"Since the men to whom it" (the revenue) "belongs are idle, it is obvious that they *do not direct any productive labour.* All these labourers whom they pay are intended only to procure some enjoyment for them. No doubt these enjoyments are of different kinds.... The expenditure of all this class of men ... feeds a numerous population whose existence it makes possible, but one whose labour is completely sterile.... Some of it may be more or less fruitful, as for example the construction of a house, the improvement of a landed estate; but these are particular cases when for the time being they cause productive labour to be performed. Apart from these minor exceptions, the whole consumption of this species of capitalists is absolutely pure loss from the standpoint of reproduction, and an equally great diminution of the wealth that has been acquired" (p. 236).

<Real political economy *à la* Smith treats the capitalist only as personified capital, M—C—M, agent of production. But who is to consume the products? The labourers?—but they don't. The capitalist himself? Then he is acting as a big idle consumer and not as a capitalist. The owners of land and money rents? They do not reproduce their consumption, and thereby are of disservice to wealth. Nevertheless, there are also two correct aspects in this contradictory view, which regards the capitalist only as a real amasser of wealth, not an illusory one like the miser proper: (1) capital (and hence the capitalist, its personification) is treated only as an agent for the development of the productive forces and of production; (2) it expresses the standpoint of emerging capitalist society, to which what matters is exchange-value, not use-value; wealth, not enjoyment. The enjoyment of wealth seems to it a superfluous luxury, until it itself learns to combine exploitation and consumption and to subordinate itself to the enjoyment of wealth.>

"To find how these revenues" (on which the idlers live) "have been formed it is always necessary to go back to the *industrial capitalists*" (p. 237, note).

The *industrial capitalists*—the second sort of capitalists—

"include all the entrepreneurs in any industry whatever, that is to say, all the persons who, *having capitals*, ... employ their talent and their labour in turning them to account themselves instead of hiring them to others, and who consequently live neither on wages nor on revenues but on *profits*" (p. 237).

In Destutt it is quite clear—as with Adam Smith before him—that what on the surface is glorification of the productive labourer is in fact only glorification of the *industrial capitalist* in contrast to landlords and such moneyed capitalists as live only on their revenue.

"They have ... in their hands almost all the wealth of society.... It is not only the income from this wealth that they spend annually, but even the fund itself, and sometimes many times in the year, when the course of business is rapid enough to make this possible. For since in their capacity as industrialists they spend only in order that the money shall come back to them with a profit, the more they can do so on this condition, the greater their profits" (pp. 237-38).

As for their personal consumption, it is the same as that of the idle capitalists. But it is

"in total moderate, because industrialists are usually unassuming" (p. 238). But it is different with their industrial consumption, it "is nothing less than final; it returns to them with profits" (l.c.). Their profit must be large enough not only for their "personal consumption, but also" for "the rents for the land and for the money which they hold from the idle capitalists" (p. 238).

Destutt is right on this. Rents of land and interest on money are only "*deductions*" from industrial profit, portions of the latter given by the industrial capitalist from his gross profit to landlords and moneyed capitalists.

"The revenues of the rich idlers are only rents taken from industry; it is industry alone that creates them" (p. 248). The industrial capitalists "rent their" (that is, the idle capitalists') "land, their houses and their money, and they make use of them in such a way as to *draw profits* from them *higher than this rent*" [p. 237]. That is, the rent which they pay to the idlers, which therefore is only a part of this profit. This rent that they thus pay to the idlers is "the sole revenue of these idlers and the sole fund for their annual expenditures" (p. 238).

Up to here, all right. But how then does it stand with the *wage-labourers* (the productive labourers, who are employed by the industrial capitalists)?

"These have no other treasure but their everyday labour. This labour obtains wages for them.... But whence come these wages? It is clear that they come from the properties of those to whom the ||402| wage-labourers *sell their labour*, that is to say, from the funds which are in their possession beforehand, and which are *nothing but the accumulated products of labours previously performed*. It follows from this that the consumption paid for by this wealth is the consumption of the wage-labourers, in the sense that it is they whom it maintains, but at bottom it is *not they who pay it*, or at least they only pay for it *with funds existing beforehand in the hands of those who employ them*. Their consumption should therefore be regarded as having been made by those who hire them. They only receive with one hand and return with the other.... It is therefore necessary to regard not only all that they" (the wage-labourers) "spend but even all that they receive as the real expenditure and *consumption of those who buy their labour.* That is so true that in order to see whether this consumption is more or less destructive of wealth that has been acquired, or even if it tends to increase it ... it is necessary to know *what use the capitalists make of the labour that they buy*" (pp. 234-35).

Very well. And whence come the profits of the entrepreneurs which enable them to pay revenue to themselves and to the idle capitalists, etc.?

"I will be asked how these industrial entrepreneurs can make such large profits, and whence they can draw them? I reply that *it is through their selling everything that they produce at a higher price than it has cost them to produce*" (p. 239).

And to whom do they sell everything at a higher price than it costs them?

"They sell it,

"1. to themselves, for the whole part of their consumption destined for the satisfaction of their needs, which they pay for with a portion of their profits;

"2. to the wage-labourers, both those whom they pay and those paid by the idle capitalists; in this way *they take back from these labourers the total amount of their wages*, apart from any small economies which these may be able to make;

"3. to the idle capitalists, *who pay them with the part of their revenue* which they have not already given to the labourers directly employed by them, so that all the rent which they annually pay to the idle capitalists comes back to them in one or other of these ways" (p. 239).

Let us now have a look at these three categories of sales.

1. The industrial capitalists themselves consume *one part* of their product (or profit). They cannot possibly enrich themselves by swindling themselves and selling their products to themselves at a *dearer price* than they themselves have *paid* for them. Nor can any one of them swindle the others in this way. If A sells his product, which the industrial capitalist B consumes, at too dear a price, then B sells his product, which the industrial capitalist A consumes, at too dear a price. It is the same thing as if A and B had sold their products to each other at their real value. Category 1 shows us how the capitalists spend a part of their profit; it does not show us whence they draw the profit. In any case they make no profit by *selling "to one another"* "everything that they produce *at a higher price* than it has cost to produce".

2. They can likewise draw no profit from the part of the product which they sell to their labourers *above the costs of production*. It is presupposed that the whole consumption of the labourers is in fact "the consumption of those who buy their labour". Moreover Destutt rubs this in by remarking that the capitalists, by selling their products to the wage-labourers (their own and those of the idle capitalists), only "get back their total wages". And in fact not even the total, but after deducting their economies. It is all the same whether they sell the products to them cheap or dear, since they always only get back what they have given them, and, as said above, the wage-labourers only "receive with one hand and return with the other". First the capitalist pays *money* to the labourer as wages. Then he sells him his product "too dear", and by so doing draws the money back again. But as the labourer cannot pay back to the capitalist more money than he has received from him, so the capitalist can *never* sell his products to him *dearer* than he has *paid* him for his labour. He can always only get back from him as much money for the sale of his products as the money he has given him for his labour. Not a farthing more. How then can his money increase through this "circulation"?

||403| In addition to this, there is another absurdity in Destutt. Capitalist C pays the labourer L a weekly wage of £1, and then draws back the £1 for himself again by selling him commodities for £1. By this means, Tracy thinks, he has drawn back to himself the total of the wages paid. But first he gives the labourer £1. And then he gives him commodities for £1. So what in fact he has given him is £2: £1 in commodities and £1 in money. Of this £2, he takes back £1 in the form of money. Therefore in fact he has not drawn back a farthing of the £1 wage. And if he intended to enrich himself by this kind of "drawing back" the wages (instead of by the labourer giving him back in labour what he advanced to him in commodities), he would soon come to his senses.

Here, therefore, the noble Destutt confuses the circulation of money with the real circulation of commodities. Because the capitalist, instead of giving the labourer directly commodities to the value of £1, gives him £1, with which the labourer then decides as he likes which commodities he wants to buy, and returns to the capitalist in the form of money the draft he had given him on his merchandise—after he, the labourer, has appropriated his aliquot share of the merchandise—Destutt imagines that the capitalist "draws back" the wages, because the same piece of money flows back to him. And on the same page Monsieur Destutt remarks that the phenomenon of circulation is "little known" (p. 239). Totally unknown to himself, at any rate. If Destutt had not explained "the drawing back of the total wages" in this peculiar way, the nonsense might at least have been conceivable in a way we shall mention now.

(But before that, a further illustration of his sapience. If I go into a shop and the shopkeeper gives me £1 and I then use this £1 to buy commodities to the value of £1 in his shop, he then draws back the £1 again. No one will assert that he has enriched himself by this operation. Instead of £1 in money and £1 in commodities he now has only £1 in money left. Even if his commodity was only worth 10s. and he sold it to me for £1, in this case too he is 10s. poorer than he was before the sale, even though he has drawn back the whole of one pound sterling.)

If C, the capitalist, gives the labourer £1 wages, and afterwards sells him commodities to the value of 10s. for £1, he would certainly have made a profit of 10s. because he had sold the commodities to the labourer 10s. too dear. But from Monsieur Destutt's point of view even so it could not be understood how any profit from this transaction arises for C. (The profit arises from the fact that he has paid him less wages—in fact has given the labourer a smaller aliquot part of the product in exchange for his labour—than he gives him *nominally*.) If he gave the labourer 10s. and sold his commodity for 10s., he would be just as rich as if he gives him £1 and sells him his 10s. commodity for £1. Moreover, Destutt bases his argument on the assumption of necessary wages. In the best case any profit here would only be explained by the labourer having been cheated over his wages.

This case 2 therefore shows that Destutt has absolutely forgotten what a productive labourer is, and has not the slightest idea of the source of profit. At most it could be said that the capitalist makes a profit by raising the price of the products above their value, in so far as he sells them not to his own wage-labourers but to the wage-labourers of idle capitalists. But since the consumption of unproductive labourers is in fact only a part of the consumption of idle capitalists, we come now to case 3.

3. The industrial capitalist sells his products "too dear", above their value, to the

"idle capitalists, who pay them with the part of their revenue which they have not already given to the labourers directly employed by them, so that all the rent which they annually pay to the idle capitalists comes back to them" (the industrial capitalists) "in one or other of these ways".

Here again there is the childish conception of the rent, etc., coming back, as there was above of the drawing back of the whole of the wages. For example, C pays £100 rent for land and money to I (the idle capitalist). The £100 are means of payment for C. They are means of purchase for I, who with them draws £100 of commodities from C's warehouse. Thus the £100 return to C as the transformed form of his commodity. But he has £100 less in commodities than before. Instead of giving them direct to I, he has given him £100 in money, with which the latter buys £100 of his commodities. But he buys these £100 worth of commodities with C's money, not with his own funds. And Tracy imagines that in this way the rent which C has paid over to I comes back to C. What imbecility! First absurdity.

Secondly, Destutt himself has told us that rent of land and interest on money are only deductions from the industrial capitalist's profit, and therefore only quotas of profit given away to the idler. On the assumption that C drew back this whole quota ||404| to himself by some sort of trick, though not in one or other of the ways described by Tracy—in other words, that capitalist C paid no rent at all, neither to the landlord nor to the moneyed capitalist—he would retain his *whole* profit, but the question is precisely how to explain *whence* he derived the profit, how he has made it, how it arose. As this cannot be explained by his *having* or *retaining* it without giving a quota of it to landlord and moneyed capitalist, just as little can it be explained by the fact that either part or the whole of the quota of profit which he has given away to the idler under one category or another is entirely or partially, in one way or another, dragged back by him from the hand of the idler into his own hand again. Second absurdity!

Let us disregard these absurdities. C has to pay I—the idler—rent to the amount of £100 for the land or the capital that he has rented (loué) from him. He pays the £100 out of his profit (whence the latter arises we do not yet know). Then he sells his products to I, which are consumed either by I directly or through his retainers (the unproductive wage-labourers), and he sells them to him *too dear*, for example, 25 per cent above their value. He sells him products worth £80 for £100. In this transaction C undoubtedly makes a profit of £20. He has given I a draft for £100 worth of commodities. When the latter presents the draft, he gives his commodities only to the value of £80, by fixing the nominal price of his goods 25 per cent above their value. Even if I would be satisfied with consuming commodities worth £80 and paying £100 for them, C's profit could never rise above 25 per cent. The prices and the fraud would be repeated every year. But I wants to consume to the value of £100. If he is a landlord, what is he to do? He mortgages property to C for £25, in exchange for which C gives him commodities worth £20—for he sells his commodities at 25 per cent (one-quarter) above their value. If he is a money-lender, he hands over to C £25 of his capital, in exchange for which C gives him commodities worth £20.

Let us assume that the capital (or value of the land) was lent at 5 per cent. Then it amounted to £2,000. Now it amounts to only £1,975. His rents are now £98$^3/_4$. And so it would go on, with I constantly consuming commodities to the real value of £100, but his rents constantly falling, because in order to have commodities to the value of £100 he must always consume an ever greater part of his capital itself. Thus bit by bit C would get the whole of I's capital into his own hands, and the rents of it together with the capital—that is to say, along with the capital itself he would appropriate that portion of the profit which he makes from borrowed capital. Mr. Destutt evidently has this process in view, for he continues:

"But, I will be told, if that is so and if industrial entrepreneurs in effect *reap each year more than they have sown*, in a very short time they must have attracted to themselves *the whole public fortune*, and soon there would be nothing left in a State but labourers without funds and capitalist entrepreneurs. *That is true*, and things would in fact be so if the entrepreneurs or their heirs did not take the course of resting as they grow wealthy, and did not thus continually go to recruit the class of idle capitalists; and even in spite of this frequent emigration, it still happens that when industry has been at work in a country for some time without too great disturbances, its capitals are always being augmented not only because of the growth of the total wealth, but also in a much greater proportion.... It might be added this effect would be felt even more strongly but for the immense levies that all governments impose each year on the industrious class by means of taxes..." (pp. 240-41).

And Monsieur Destutt is quite right up to a certain point, although not at all in what he wants to explain. In the period of the declining Middle Ages and rising capitalist production the rapid enrichment of the industrial capitalists is in part to be explained by the direct fleecing of the landlords. As the value of money fell, as a result of the discoveries in America, the farmers paid them nominally, but not really, the old rent, while the manufacturers sold them commodities above their value—not only on the basis of the higher value of money. Similarly in all countries, as for example the Asiatic, where the principal revenue of the country is in the hands of landlords, princes, etc., in the form of rent, the manufacturers, *few in number* and therefore not restricted by competition, sell them their commodities at monopoly prices, and in this way appropriate a part of their revenue; they enrich themselves ||405| not only by selling to them "unpaid" labour, but by selling the commodities at over the quantity of labour contained in them. Only Monsieur Destutt is again wrong if he believes that money-lenders let themselves be fleeced in this way. On the contrary, they share, through the high interest they draw, in those high profits, in that fleecing, directly and indirectly.

The following passage shows that this phenomenon was in Monsieur Destutt's mind:

"One has only to see how weak they" (the industrial capitalists) "were throughout all Europe three or four centuries ago, in comparison with the immense wealth of all the powerful men of those days, and how today they have increased and grown in number, while the others have diminished" (l.c., p. 241).

What Monsieur Destutt wanted to explain to us was the *profits* and the *high profits* of industrial capital. He has explained it in two ways. First, because the *money* which these capitalists pay out in the form of wages and rents flows back to them again, since these wages and rents buy products from them. In fact, what this explains is only why they do not pay wages and rents *twice*, first in the form of money, and secondly in the form of commodities to the same amount in money. The second explanation is that they sell their commodities above their price, they sell them *too dear*, first to *themselves*, thus cheating themselves; secondly to the labourers, thus again cheating themselves, as Monsieur Destutt tells us that the consumption of the wage-labourers "must be regarded as the consumption of those who pay them" (p. 235); finally, in the third place, to the *gentlemen living on rents*, whom they fleece, and this would in fact explain why the industrial capitalists always keep for themselves a larger part of their profit, instead of giving it away to the idlers. It would show why *the distribution of the total profit* between the industrial and non-industrial capitalists is increasingly to the advantage of the former at the cost of the latter. It would not help one iota to an understanding of *whence* this *total profit* comes. Let us assume that the industrial capitalists had got the whole of it for themselves, the question remains, where does it come from?

Therefore Destutt has not only given no answer, but he has only revealed that he thinks the reflux of the money is a reflux of the commodity itself. This *reflux of money* means only that the capitalists first pay wages and rents in money, instead of paying them in commodities; that their commodities are bought with this money and hence they have paid in commodities in this roundabout way. This money therefore constantly flows back to them, but only to the extent that commodities to the same money value are definitively taken from them and fall to the share of the consumption of the wage-labourers and drawers of rent.

Monsieur Destutt (in a really French way—similar exclamations of astonishment about himself are to be found in Proudhon) is altogether astonished at the "clarity" which this

> "way of looking at the consumption of our wealth...sheds on the whole progress of society. Whence comes this consistency and this lucidity? From the fact that we have lighted upon the truth. This recalls the effect of those mirrors in which objects are outlined clearly and in their right proportions when one is in the right spot from which to view them, and in which everything appears confused and disjointed when one is too near or too far" (pp. 242-43).

Later, quite incidentally, Monsieur Destutt recalls (from Adam Smith) the real course of things, which however in essence he only repeats as a phrase which he has not understood—as otherwise he (this Member of the Institute of France) would have been unable to shed the streams of light referred to above. Destutt writes (p. 246):

> "Whence come their revenues to these idle men? Is it not from the rent which those who *set their capitals to work* pay to them out of their *profits*, that is to say, those who use their funds *to pay labour which produces more than it costs*, in a word, the men of industry?"

<Aha! So the rents (and also their own profits) which the industrial capitalists pay to the idle capitalists for the funds borrowed from the latter come from their using these funds to pay wages to labour "which *produces more than it costs*"; that is to say, therefore, whose product has more value than is paid to them—in other words, profit comes from what the wage-

labourers produce over and above what they cost; a surplus-product which the industrial capitalist appropriates for himself, and of which he gives away only one part to those receiving rent from land and money.>

Monsieur Destutt concludes from this: not that we must go back to these productive labourers, but that we must go back to the capitalists who set them in motion.

"It is these who really maintain even the labourers employed by the others" (p. 246).

To be sure; inasmuch as they directly exploit labour, and the idle capitalists only do it through their agency. And in this sense it is correct to regard industrial capital as the source of wealth. ||406|

"We must therefore always go back to these" (the industrial capitalists) "in order to find the source of all wealth" (p. 246).

"In the course of time, *wealth has accumulated in greater or less quantity, because the result of previous labours has not been entirely consumed as soon as produced*. Some of the possessors of this wealth are content to draw a rent from it and consume it. These are those whom we have called idle. The other more active ones set to work both their own funds and those which they borrow. They employ them *to pay labour which reproduces them with a profit*."< Hence, therefore, not only the reproduction of this fund, but [the production] of the surplus, which forms *profit*.> "With this profit they pay for their own consumption and defray that of others. By these consumptions themselves" (their own and that of the idlers? Here again the same absurdity) "their funds come back to them somewhat increased, and they start again. That is what constitutes circulation" (pp. 246-47).

The inquiry into the "productive labourer", and the result that only one whose buyer is an industrial capitalist is a productive labourer—one whose labour produces profit for its immediate buyer—led Monsieur Destutt to the conclusion that in fact *the industrial capitalists* are the *sole productive labourers* in the higher meaning of the word.

"They" (the industrial capitalists) "who live on profits maintain all the others and alone augment the public fortune and create all our means of enjoyment. That must be so, *because labour is the source of all wealth* and because they alone give a *useful direction to current labour*, by making a *useful application of accumulated labour*" (p. 242).

That they give "a useful direction to current labour" in fact means only that they employ useful labour, labour which results in use-values. But that they make "useful application of accumulated labour"—if it is not to mean the same thing again, that they make industrial use of accumulated wealth for the production of use-values—means that they make "useful application of accumulated labour" by buying with it more current labour than is contained in it. In the passage just cited Destutt naïvely epitomises the contradictions which make up the essence of capitalist production. Because labour is the source of all wealth, capital is the source of all wealth; the actual propagator of wealth is not he who labours, but he who makes a profit out of another's labour. The productive powers of labour are the productive powers of capital.

"Our faculties are our only original wealth; our labour produces all other wealth, and all labour, properly directed, is productive" (p. 243).

Hence, according to Destutt, it follows as a matter of course that the industrial capitalists "maintain all the others and alone augment the public fortune and create all our means of enjoyment".

Our faculties (*facultés*) are our only original wealth, therefore the faculty of labour is not wealth. Labour produces all other wealth, that means: it produces wealth for all others except for itself, and it itself is not wealth, but only its product is wealth. All properly directed labour is productive; that means: all productive labour, all labour which yields profit to the capitalist, is properly directed.

The following remarks of Destutt—which refer not to the *different classes of consumers*, but to the *different nature of the articles of consumption*—are a very good paraphrase of Adam Smith's views in Book II, Chapter III, at the end of which he inquires into what kind of (unproductive) expenditure, that is to say, of individual consumption, consumption of revenue, is more or less advantageous. He opens this inquiry (Garnier, t. II, p. 345) with the words:

"As frugality increases, and prodigality diminishes, the public capital, so the conduct of those whose expense just equals their revenue, without either accumulating or encroaching, neither increases nor diminishes it. Some modes of expense, however, seem to contribute more to the growth of public opulence than others" [*Wealth of Nations*, O.U.P. edition, Vol. I, pp. 387-88].

Destutt summarises Smith's exposition as follows:

"If consumption is very different according to the kind of consumer, it varies also according to the nature of the things consumed. All indeed represent labour, but its value is fixed more securely in some than in others. As much trouble may have been taken in making a firework as in finding and cutting a diamond, and consequently one may have as much value as the other. But when I have bought, paid for and used both, at the end of half an hour I shall have nothing left of the first, and the second can still be a resource for my grandchildren a century later.... It is the same with what ||407| are called" that is, (by Say) "immaterial products *An invention is of eternal utility*. An intellectual work, a picture also have a utility that is more or less durable, while that of a ball, a concert, a play is instantaneous and disappears immediately. The same can be said of the *personal services* of doctors, lawyers, soldiers, domestic servants, and in general of all who are called *employed persons*. Their utility is that of the moment of need.... The most ruinous consumption is the quickest, because it is that which destroys more labour in the same time, or an equal quantity of labour in less time; in comparison with it, consumption which is slower is a kind of *treasuring up*, since it leaves to times to come the enjoyment of part of the present sacrifices.... Everyone knows that it is more economical to get, *for the same price*, a coat that will last three years than a similar one which will only last three months" (pp. 243-44).

[15. General Nature of the Polemics against Smith's Distinction between Productive and Unproductive Labour. Apologetic Conception of Unproductive Consumption as a Necessary Spur to Production]

Most of the writers who contested Smith's view of productive and unproductive labour regard *consumption* as a necessary spur to production. *For this reason* they regard the *wage-labourers* who live on revenue—the unproductive labourers whose hire does not produce wealth, but is itself a new consumption of wealth—as equally productive *even of material wealth* as the productive labourers, since they widen the field of material consumption and therewith the field of production. This was therefore for the most part apologetics from the standpoint of bourgeois economy, partly for the rich idlers and the "unproductive labourers" whose *services* they consume, partly for "strong governments" whose expenditure is heavy, for the increase of the State debts, for holders of church and State benefices, holders of sinecures, etc. For these "unproductive labourers"—whose services figure in the expenses of the idle rich—all have in common the fact that although they *produce* "*immaterial products*", they consume "*material products*", that is, products of the productive labourers.

Other economists, like Malthus, admit the distinction between productive labourers and unproductive, but prove to the industrial capitalist that the latter are as necessary to him as the former, even for the production of material wealth.

To say that production and consumption are identical or that consumption is the purpose of all production or that production is the pre-condition of all consumption, is of no help in this connection. What—apart from the tendentious purpose—is at the bottom of the whole dispute is rather this:

The labourer's consumption on the average is only equal to his costs of production, it is not equal to his output. He therefore produces the whole surplus for others, and so this whole part of his *production* is *production for others*. Moreover, the industrial capitalist who drives the labourer to this *overproduction* (that is, production over and above his own subsistence needs) and makes use of all expedients to increase it to the greatest extent possible—to increase this relative *overproduction* as distinct from the necessary production—directly appropriates the surplus-product for himself. But as personified capital he produces for the sake of production, he wants to accumulate wealth for the sake of the accumulation of wealth. In so far as he is a mere functionary of capital, that is, an agent of capitalist production, what matters to him is exchange-value and the increase of exchange-value, not use-value and its increase. What he is concerned with is the increase of abstract wealth, the rising appropriation of the labour of others. He is dominated by the same absolute drive to enrich himself as the miser, except that he does not satisfy it in the illusory form of building up a treasure of gold and silver, but in the creation of capital, which is real production. If the labourer's overproduction is *production for others*, the production of the normal capitalist, of the industrial capitalist as he ought to be, is *production for the sake of production*. It is true that the more his wealth grows, the more he falls behind this ideal, and becomes extravagant, even if only to show off his wealth. But he is always enjoying wealth with a guilty conscience, with frugality and thrift at the back of his mind. In spite of all his prodigality he remains, like the miser, essentially avaricious.

When Sismondi says that the development of the productive powers of labour makes it possible for the labourer to obtain ever-increasing enjoyments, but that these very enjoyments, if put at his disposal, would make him unfit for labour (as a wage-labourer)*; it is equally true that the industrial capitalist becomes more or less unable to fulfil his function as soon as he personifies the enjoyment of wealth, as soon as he wants the

* *Sismondi* says: "Because of the progress made by industry and science, each labourer is able to produce each day more, and much more, than he needs to consume. But at the same time as his labour produces wealth, this wealth, if he was called upon to enjoy it, would make him little fitted for labour" (*Nouveaux principes...*, t. I, p. 85).

accumulation of pleasures instead of the pleasure of accumulation.

He is therefore also a producer of *overproduction, production for others*. Over against this overproduction on one side must be placed overconsumption on the other, production for the sake of production must be confronted by consumption for the sake of consumption. What the industrial capitalist has to surrender to landlords, the State, creditors of the State, the church, and so forth, who only consume revenue, ||408| is an absolute diminution of his wealth, but it keeps his lust for enrichment going and thus preserves his capitalist soul. If the landlords, money-lenders, etc., were to consume their revenue also in productive instead of unproductive labour, the purpose would not be achieved. They would become themselves industrial capitalists, instead of representing the function of consumption as such. With regard to this point we shall examine later an extremely comical dispute between a Ricardian and a Malthusian.[79]

Production and consumption are *in their nature* [*an sich*] inseparable. From this it follows that since in the system of capitalist production they are in fact separated, their unity is restored through their opposition—that if A must produce for B, B must consume for A. Just as we find with every individual capitalist that he favours prodigality on the part of those who are co-partners with him in his revenue, so the older Mercantile system as a whole depends on the idea that a nation must be frugal as regards itself, but must produce luxuries for foreign nations to enjoy. The idea here is always: on the one side, production for production, therefore on the other side consumption of foreign production. This idea of the Mercantile system is expressed for example by Dr. Paley, *Moral Philosophy*, Vol. II, Ch. XI:

"... A laborious, frugal people, ministering to the demands of an opulent, luxurious nation." [W. Paley, *Principles of Moral and Political Phylosophy*, Edinburgh, 1788, Vol. II, p. 359.]

"They" (our politicians, Garnier, etc.) says Destutt, "put forward as a general principle that consumption is the cause of production, that therefore it is good for it to be very plentiful. They declare that it is this which constitutes a great difference between public economy and the economy of individuals" (l.c., pp. 249-50).

One more fine phrase:

"*The poor nations* are those where the people are comfortably off; and *the rich nations*, those where the people are generally poor" (l.c., p. 231).

[16.] Henri Storch [Unhistorical Approach to the Problem of the Interaction between Material and Spiritual Production. Conception of "Immaterial Labour" Performed by the Ruling Class]

Henri Storch, *Cours d'économie politique*, etc., edited by Jean-Baptiste Say, Paris, 1823 (Lectures read to Grand Duke Nicholas, concluded in 1815), *Vol. III*.

After Garnier, Storch is in fact the first writer to polemise against Adam Smith's distinction between productive and unproductive labour on a new basis.

He distinguishes the "*internal goods* or the elements of civilisation", with the laws of whose production the "Theory of Civilisation" has to concern itself, from material goods, component parts of material production (l.c., t. III, p. 217).

(On page 136 of t. I [he says]: "It is evident that man only attains to the production of wealth in so far as he is endowed with internal goods, that is to say, in so far as he has developed his physical, intellectual and moral faculties, which implies the means for their development such as *social institutions*, etc. Thus the more civilised a people, the more its national wealth can grow." The reverse is also true.)

Against Smith:

"Smith...excludes from *productive labours* all those which do not contribute *directly* to the production of wealth; but also he only considers the national *wealth*." His error is "not to have distinguished *immaterial* values from *wealth*" (t. III, p. 218).

And that is really all there is to it. The distinction between productive labours and unproductive labours is of decisive importance for what Smith was considering: the production of material wealth, and in fact one definite form of that production, the capitalist mode of production. In spiritual production another kind of labour appears as productive. But Smith does not take it into consideration. Finally, the interaction and the inner connection between the two kinds of production also do not fall within the field he is considering; moreover, they can only lead to something more than empty phrases when material production is examined in its own form. In so far as he speaks of workers who are not directly productive, this is only to the extent that they participate *directly* in the consumption of material wealth but not in its production.

With Storch himself the *theory of civilisation* does not get beyond trivial phrases, although some ingenious observations slip in here and there—for example, that the material division of labour is the pre-condition for the division of intellectual labour. How much it *was inevitable* that Storch could not get beyond trivial phrases, how little he had even *formulated* for himself the task, let alone its solution, is apparent from one *single* circumstance. In order to examine the connection between spiritual ||409| production and material production it is above all necessary to grasp the latter itself not as a general category but in *definite historical* form. Thus for example different kinds of spiritual production correspond to the capitalist mode of production and to the mode of production of the Middle Ages. If material production itself is not conceived in its *specific historical* form, it is impossible to understand what is specific in the spiritual production corresponding to it and the reciprocal influence of one on the other. Otherwise one cannot get beyond inanities. This because of the talk about "civilisation".

Further: from the specific form of material production arises in the first place a specific structure of society, in the second place a specific relation of men to nature. Their State and their spiritual outlook is determined by both. Therefore also the kind of their spiritual production.

Finally, by spiritual production Storch means also all kinds of professional activities of the ruling class, who carry out social functions as a trade. The existence of these strata, like the function they perform, can only be understood from the specific historical structure of their production relations.

Because Storch does not conceive material production itself *historically*—because he conceives it as production of material goods in general, not as a definite historically developed and specific form of this production—he deprives himself of the basis on which alone can be understood partly the ideological component parts of the ruling class, partly the free spiritual production of this particular social formation. He cannot get beyond meaningless general phrases. Consequently, the relation is not so simple as he presupposes. For instance, capitalist production is hostile to certain branches of spiritual production, for example, art and poetry. If this is left out of account, it opens the way to the illusion of the French in the eighteenth century which has been so beautifully satirised by Lessing.[80] Because we are further ahead than the ancients in mechanics, etc., why shouldn't we be able to make an epic too? And the *Henriade*[81] in place of the *Iliad*!

Storch, however, rightly stresses—with special reference to Garnier, who was actually the father of *this* attack on Smith—that Smith's opponents had set about it the wrong way.

"What do his critics do? Far from establishing this distinction" (between immaterial values and wealth), "they succeed in confusing two kinds of value that are so evidently different."

(They assert that the production of spiritual products or the production of services is *material* production.)

"In regarding immaterial labour as *productive*, they assume it is *productive of wealth*" (that is, directly), "that is to say, of material and exchangeable values, while it produces only immaterial and immediate values: they assume that the products of immaterial labour are subject to the same laws as those of material labour: and yet the former are governed by other principles than the latter" (t. III, p. 218).

The following passages from Storch are to be noted as having been copied from him by later authors:

"From the fact that internal goods are in part the product of services, the conclusion has been drawn that they are no more lasting than the services themselves, and that they were necessarily consumed as they were produced" (l.c., t. III. p. 234). "The original" [internal] "goods, far from being destroyed by the use made of them, expand and grow with use, so that even the *consumption* of them augments their value" (l.c., p. 236). "Internal goods are susceptible of being accumulated like wealth, and of forming capitals that can be used in reproduction", etc. (l.c., p. 236). "Material labour must be divided up and its products must be accumulated before the dividing up of immaterial labour can be thought of" (p. 241).

These are nothing but general superficial analogies and relations between spiritual and material wealth. So for example is his observation that undeveloped nations *borrow* their spiritual capitals from abroad, just as materially undeveloped nations borrow their material capitals (l. c., p. 306); and that the division of immaterial labour depends on the demand for it, in a word, on the market, etc. (p. 246).

Here are the passages which have actually been copied:

||410| "The *production* of internal goods, far from diminishing the national wealth by the consumption of material products it requires, is on the contrary a powerful means of increasing it; as the production of wealth, in its turn, is an equally powerful means of increasing civilisation" (l.c., p. 517). "It is the equilibrium of the two kinds of production that causes the advance of national prosperity" (l.c., p. 521).

According to Storch, the physician produces health (but also illness), professors and writers produce enlightenment (but also obscurantism), poets, painters, etc., produce good taste (but also bad taste), moralists, etc., produce morals, preachers religion, the sovereign's labour security, and so on (pp. 347-50). It can just as well be said that illness produces physicians, stupidity produces professors and writers, lack of taste poets and painters, immorality moralists, superstition preachers and general insecurity produces the sovereign. This way of saying in fact that all these activities, these services, produce a real or imaginary use-value is repeated by later writers in order to prove that they are productive workers in Smith's sense, that is to say, that they directly produce not products *suigeneris** but products of material labour and consequently immediate wealth. In Storch there is not yet this nonsense, which for that matter can be reduced to the following:

1. that the various functions in bourgeois society mutually presuppose each other;
2. that the contradictions in material production make necessary a superstructure of ideological strata, whose activity—whether good or bad—is good, because it is necessary;
3. that all functions are in the service of the capitalist, and work out to his "benefit";
4. that even the most sublime spiritual productions should merely be granted recognition, and *apologies* for them made to the bourgeoisie, that they are presented as, and falsely proved to be, direct producers of material wealth.

[17.] Nassau Senior [Proclamation of All Functions Useful to the Bourgeoisie as Productive. Toadyism to the Bourgeoisie and the Bourgeois State]

Nassau William Senior, *Principes fondamentaux de l'économie politique*, traduit par Jean Arrivabene, Paris, 1836. Nassau Senior mounts his high horse:

> "According to Smith, the lawgiver of the Hebrews was an unproductive labourer" (l.c., p. 198).

Was it Moses of Egypt or Moses Mendelssohn? Moses would have been very grateful to Mr. Senior for calling him a "productive labourer" in the Smithian sense. These people are so dominated by their fixed bourgeois ideas that they would think they were insulting Aristotle or Julius Caesar if they called them "unproductive labourers". Aristotle and Caesar would have regarded even the title "labourers" as an insult.

> "Does not the doctor who, by a prescription, heals a sick child and thus assures him many years of life, *produce* a durable result?" (l.c.)

* Of their own peculiar kind.—*Ed.*

Rubbish! If the child dies, the result is no less durable. And if the child is no better after treatment, the doctor's *service* has to be paid for just the same. According to Nassau doctors should only be paid in so far as they cure, and lawyers in so far as they win lawsuits, and soldiers in so far as they are victorious. But now he gets really lofty:

"Did the Dutch produce temporary results by fighting against the tyranny of the Spaniards, or the English by revolting against a tyranny that threatened to be even more terrible?" (l.c., p. 198).

Belletristic trash! Dutch and English revolted at their own cost. No one paid them for labouring "in revolution". But with either productive or unproductive labourers there is always a buyer and seller of labour. Hence what rubbish!

These insipid literary flourishes used by these fellows when they polemise against Smith show only that they are representatives of the "educated capitalist", while Smith was the *interpreter* of the frankly brutal bourgeois upstart. The educated bourgeois and his mouthpiece are both so stupid that they measure the effect of every activity by its ||411| effect on the purse. On the other hand, they are so educated that they *grant recognition* even to functions and activities that have nothing to do with the production of wealth; and indeed they grant them recognition because they too "indirectly" increase, etc., their wealth, in a word, fulfil a "useful" function for wealth.

Man himself is the basis of his material production, as of any other production that he carries on. All circumstances, therefore, which affect man, the *subject* of production, more or less modify all his functions and activities, and therefore too his functions and activities as the creator of material wealth, of commodities. In this respect it can in fact be shown that *all* human relations and functions, however and in whatever form they may appear, influence material production and have a more or less decisive influence on it.

"There are countries where it is quite impossible for people to work the land unless there are soldiers to protect them. Well, according to Smith's classification, the harvest is not produced by the joint labour of the man who guides the plough and of the man at his side with arms in hand: according to him, the ploughman alone is a productive worker, and the soldier's activity is unproductive" (l.c., p. 202).

First, that is not true. Smith would say that the soldier's protective care is productive of defence, but not of the corn. If order was restored in the country, the ploughman would produce the corn just as before, without being compelled to produce the maintenance, and therefore the life, of the soldiers into the bargain. The soldier belongs to the incidental expenses of production, in the same way as a large part of the unproductive labourers who produce nothing themselves, either spiritual or material, but who are useful and necessary only because of the faulty social relations—they owe their existence to social evils.

However, Nassau might say: if a machine is invented that makes nineteen out of twenty labourers superfluous, then these nineteen too are incidental expenses of production. But the soldier can drop out although the *material conditions of production*, the conditions of agriculture as such, remain unchanged. The nineteen labourers can only drop out if the labour of the one remaining labourer becomes twenty times more productive, that is to say, only through a revolution in the actual material conditions of production. Moreover, *Buchanan* already observes:

"If the soldier, for example, be termed a productive labourer because his labour is subservient to production, the productive labourer might, by the same rule, lay claim to military honours; as it is certain that without his assistance no army could ever take the field to fight battles or to gain victories" (David Buchanan, *Observations on the Subjects Treated of in Dr. Smith's Inquiry, etc.*, Edinburgh, 1814, p. 132).

"The wealth of a nation does not depend on a numerical proportion between those who produce *services* and those who produce *values*, but on the proportion between them that is most fitted to render the labour of each more efficacious" (Senior, l.c., p. 204).

Smith never denied this, as he wants to reduce the "necessary unproductive labourers like State officials, lawyers, priests, etc., to the *extent* in which their services are indispensable. And this is in any case the "proportion" in which they make the labour of productive labourers most efficacious. As for the other "unproductive labourers", whose labours are only bought *voluntarily* by anyone in order to enjoy their *services*, that is, as an article of consumption of his own choice, different cases must be distinguished. If the number of these labourers living on revenue is large in proportion to the "productive" labourers, it is, *either*, because the total wealth is small or is of a one-sided character—for example the medieval barons with their retainers. Instead of consuming manufactured goods on any considerable scale, they and their retainers consumed their agricultural products. When instead of these products they began to consume manufactured goods, the retainers had to be set to labour. The number of those living on revenue was only large because a large part of the annual product was not *reproductively* consumed. Along with this, the total population was small. *Or*, the number of those living on revenue is large, because the productivity of the productive labourers is large, and therefore their surplus-produce upon which the retainers feed. In this case the labour of the productive labourers is not productive because there are so many retainers, but on the contrary—there are so many retainers because the labour of the productive labourers is so productive.

Taking two countries with equal populations and an equal development of the productive powers of labour, it would always be true to say, with Adam Smith, that the wealth of the two countries must be measured according to the proportion of productive and of unproductive labourers. For that means only that in the country which has a relatively greater number of productive labourers, a relatively greater amount of the annual revenue is reproductively consumed, and consequently a greater mass of values is produced annually. Therefore Mr. Senior has only paraphrased a statement of ||412| Adam's, instead of counterposing it with a novelty. Moreover, he himself here makes the distinction between the producers of services and the producers of values, and so it is the same with him as with most of those who polemise against the Smithian distinction—they accept and themselves use this distinction, at the same time as they reject it.

It is characteristic that all "unproductive" economists, who achieve nothing in their own speciality, [come out] against the distinction between productive labour and unproductive labour. However, in relation to the bourgeois, it is on the one hand an expression of their servility that they present all functions as serving the production of wealth for him; then on the other hand, they present the bourgeois world as the best of all possible worlds, in which everything is useful, and the bourgeois himself is so educated that he understands this.

In relation to the labourers, [what it expresses is:] it is quite all right that the unproductive ones consume the great mass [of products], since they contribute just as much as the labourers to the production of wealth even though in their own way.

Finally however Nassau blurts out, showing that he has not understood one word of the essential distinction made by Smith:

> "It seems, in truth, that in this case Smith's attention was entirely absorbed by the position of the *great landowners*, the only ones to whom his observations on the unproductive classes can in general be applied. I do not know how otherwise to account for his supposition *that capital is only employed to maintain productive labourers, while unproductive labourers live from revenue*. The greater number of those whom he calls preeminently unproductive—teachers, and those who govern the State—are maintained *at the expense of capital*, that is to say, *by means of what is spent in advance for reproduction*" (l.c., pp. 204-05).

This, in fact, is past all understanding. Mr. Nassau's discovery that State and schoolmasters live at the cost of capital and not at the cost of revenue needs no further commentary. Does Mr. Senior mean by it that they live on profit from capital, and in this sense at the expense of capital? If so, he only forgets that revenue from capital is not capital itself, and that this revenue, the result of capitalist production, is not spent in advance for reproduction, of which on the contrary it is the result. Or does he mean that it is so because certain taxes enter into the production costs of particular commodities? That is, enter into the expenses of certain branches of production? Then he should know that this is only a form of levying taxes on revenue.

With reference to Storch Nassau Senior, the sophist, also remarks:

> "Mr. Storch is doubtless in error when he expressly asserts that these *results*" (health, good taste, etc.) "like other things which have value, form part of the *revenue* of those who possess them, and that they are also exchangeable" (that is, in so far as they can be bought from their produces). "If this was so, if good taste, morality, religion, were really *things* which could be *bought*, wealth would have an importance very different from that given to it by the economists. What we buy is not health, knowledge or piety. The doctor, the priest, the teacher...can only produce the instruments by means of which with greater or less certainty and perfection, these ulterior results will be produced.... If in each particular case the most suitable means to obtain success have been employed, the producer of these *means* has a right to a reward, even when he has not succeeded or when he has not produced the results expected. The exchange is completed as soon as the advice or the lesson has been given and the payment for it has been received" (l.c., pp. 288-89).

Finally, the great Nassau himself adopts the Smithian distinction. For in fact he distinguishes between "productive consumption and unproductive consumption" (p. 206) instead of between productive and unproductive labour. But the object of consumption is either a commodity—which is not referred to here—or direct labour.

Consumption would be productive if it employed labour that either produced labour-power itself (which for example the schoolmaster's or the physician's labour might do) or *reproduced* the value of the commodities with which it was bought. The consumption of labour which accomplished neither the one nor the other of these would be unproductive. And indeed Smith says: the labour which can only be consumed productively (i. e., industrially) I call productive labour, and that which can be consumed unproductively, whose consumption is by its nature not industrial consumption, I call unproductive labour. Mr. Senior has therefore proved his genius by giving things new names.

In general, Nassau copies from Storch.

[18.] Pellegrino Rossi [Disregard of the Social Form of Economic Phenomena. Vulgar Conception of "Labour-Saving" by Unproductive Labourers]

||413| Pellegrino Rossi, *Cours d'économie politique* (année 1836 to 1837), édit. Bruxelles, 1842.

Here is wisdom!

"*The indirect means*" (of production) "include everything that furthers production, everything which tends to remove an obstacle, to make production more active, more speedy, easier." (Earlier, p. 268, he says: "There are direct and indirect means of production. That is to say, there are means which are a cause *sine qua non* of the effect in question, forces which *make* this production. There are others which contribute to production, but do not make it. The former can act even *by themselves*, the latter can only help the former to produce.") "... The whole labour of government is an indirect means of production.... The man who has made this hat must surely recognise that the gendarme who goes by in the street, the judge who sits in his court, the gaoler who takes over a criminal and keeps him in prison, the army which defends the frontier against enemy invasions, contribute to production" (p. 272).

What a pleasure it must be for the hatter, that everyone gets moving so that he can produce and sell this hat! Inasmuch as he makes these gaolers, etc., contribute *indirectly*, not *directly*, to material production, Rossi in fact makes the same distinction as Adam (lecture XII).

In the following lecture XIII, Rossi takes the field particularly against Smith—indeed rather [the same as] his predecessors.

The erroneous distinction between productive labourers and unproductive labourers, he says, arises for three reasons.

1. "Among the *buyers*, some buy products or *labour for their own direct consumption*; others only buy them in order to sell the new products that they obtain by means of the products and the labour that they have acquired."

The determining factor for the former is the *use-value*; for the latter, the exchange-value. But in paying attention only to exchange-value, one falls into Smith's error.

"My servant's labour is unproductive for me: let us admit that for a moment; is it unproductive for *him*?" (l.c., pp. 275-76).

As all capitalist production rests on the direct purchase of labour in order to appropriate a part of it *without purchase* in the process of production; which part however is *sold* in the product—since this is the basis of existence of capital, its very essence—is not the distinction between labour which produces capital and that which does not produce it the basis for an understanding of the process of capitalist production? Smith does not deny that the servant's labour is productive for *him*. Every service is productive for its seller. To swear false oaths is productive for the person who does it for cash. Forging documents is productive for anyone paid to do it. A murder is productive for a man who gets paid for doing it. The trade of sycophant, informer, toady, parasite, lickspittle, is productive for people who do not perform these "services" gratis. Hence they are "productive labourers", producers not only of wealth but of capital. The thief, too, who pays himself—just as the law-courts and the State do—"employs his energy, uses it in a particular way, produces a result which satisfies a human need", i. e., the need of the thief and perhaps also that of his wife and children. Consequently [he is a] productive labourer if it is merely a question of producing a "result" which satisfies a "need", or as in the cases mentioned above, if selling his "services" is enough to make them "productive".

2. "A second error has been not to distinguish between direct production and indirect production." That is why Adam Smith thinks that a magistrate is not productive. But "if production is almost impossible" (without the magistrate's labour) "is it not clear that this labour contributes to it, if not by direct and material co-operation, at least by an indirect action which cannot be left out of account?" (l.c., p. 276).

It is precisely this labour which participates indirectly in production (and it forms only a part of unproductive labour) that we call unproductive labour. Otherwise we would have to say that since the magistrate is absolutely unable to live without the peasant, therefore the peasant is an indirect producer of justice! And so on. Utter nonsense! There is yet another point of view bearing on the division of labour, with which we shall deal later.

[3.] "The three principal facts of the phenomenon of production have not been carefully distinguished: the *force or productive means*, the *application* of this force, the *result*."

We buy a clock at a clockmarker's; we are only interested in the *result* of the labour. The same applies when we buy a coat at the tailor's. But:

"There are still people, men of the old school, who do not understand things in this way. They make a workman come to their home and get him to make such-and-such a piece of clothing, giving him the material and everything he needs for this labour. What is it that these people buy? They buy a force" <but also an application of this force>, "a means to produce results of some kind at their peril and risk.... The object of the contract is the purchase of a force."

(The point here is only that these "men of the old school" make use of a mode of production that has nothing in common with the capitalist mode, and in which all development of labour's productive powers, such as capitalist production brings with it, is impossible. It is characteristic that for Rossi and all the rest of them such a specific distinction is inessential.)

In the case of a servant, "you buy a force", capable of doing "a thousand different things. The results it produces depend on the use that you make of the force" (p. 276).

All this has nothing to do with the matter.

||414| "To buy or to hire...a definite application of this force.... You do not buy a product, you do not buy the result that you have in view." Will the lawyer's pleading win your case? Who knows? "What is certain, what passes between you and your lawyer, is that, for a certain value, he will go on a certain day to a certain place to speak on your behalf, to apply his intellectual powers in your interests" (p. 276).

<One further point on this. In lecture XII, p. 273, Rossi says:

"I am far from seeing producers only in those who pass their lives in making cotton cloth or shoes. I honour labour, whatever it may be...but this respect should not be the exclusive privilege of the *manual labourer*."

Adam Smith does not do this. For him, a person who produces a book, a painting, a musical composition or a statue, is a "productive labourer" in the second sense, although the person who improvises, recites, plays a musical instrument, etc., is not. And Adam Smith treats services, in so far as they directly enter into production, as materialised in the product, both the labour of the manual labourer and that of the manager, clerk, engineer, and even of the scientist in so far as he is an inventor, an indoor or outdoor labourer for the workshop. In dealing with the division of labour, Smith explains how these operations are distributed among different persons; and that the product, the commodity, is the result of their co-operative labour, not of the labour of any individual among them. But the "spiritual" labourers *à la* Rossi are anxious to justify the large share which they draw out of material production.>

After this discourse, Rossi continues:

"Thus in exchange transactions attention is fixed on one or other of the three principal facts of production. But can *these different forms of exchange* deprive certain *products* of the character of *wealth* and deprive the *exertions of a class of producers of the quality of being productive labours*? Clearly, there is no link between these ideas such as would justify a deduction of this kind. Because instead of buying the result, I buy the force necessary to produce it, why *should the action of the force not be productive* and *the product not be wealth*? Take again the example of the tailor. Whether one buys ready-made clothes from a tailor, or whether one gets them from a jobbing tailor who has been given the material and a wage, as far as the results are concerned the two actions are perfectly similar. No one will say that the former is a *productive labour* and the latter an *unproductive labour*; only in the second case the man *who wants a coat* has been his *own entrepreneur*. Well, from the standpoint of productive forces what difference is there between the jobbing tailor you have brought to your home and your domestic servant? None" (l.c., p. 277).

Here we have the quintessence of the whole superwise and would-be profound windbag! When Adam Smith, in his second and more superficial presentation, distinguishes between productive and unproductive labour, according to whether it is or is not directly realised in a vendible commodity for the buyer of the labour, he calls the tailor productive in both cases. But according to his more profound definition the latter is an "unproductive" labourer. Rossi only shows that he "evidently" does not understand Adam Smith.

That the "*forms of exchange*" seem to Rossi to be a matter of complete indifference is just as if a physiologist said that the different forms of life are a matter of complete indifference, that they are all only forms of organic matter. It is precisely these forms that are alone of importance when the question is the specific character of a mode of social production. A coat is a coat. But have it made in the first form of exchange, and you have capitalist production and modern bourgeois society; in the second, and you have a form of handicraft which is compatible even with Asiatic relations or those of the Middle Ages, etc. And these *forms* are decisive for material wealth itself.

A coat is a coat—that is Rossi's wisdom. But in the first case the jobbing tailor produces not only a coat, he produces capital; therefore also profit; he produces his master as a capitalist and himself as a wage-labourer. When I have a coat made for me at home by a jobbing tailor, for me to wear, that no more makes me my own *entrepreneur* (in the sense of an economic category) than it makes the *entrepreneur tailor* an entrepreneur when ||415| he himself wears and consumes a coat made by his workmen. In one case the purchaser of tailoring labour and the jobbing tailor confront each other as mere buyers and sellers. One pays money and the other supplies the commodity into whose use-value my money is transformed. In this transaction there is no difference at all from my buying the coat in a shop. Buyer and seller confront each other simply as such. In the other case, on the contrary, they confront each other as capital and wage-labour. As for the domestic servant, he has the same determinate form as the jobbing tailor No. II, whom I buy for the sake of the use-value of his labour. Both are simply buyers and sellers. But the way in which the use-value is enjoyed in this case in addition bears a patriarchal form of relation, a relation of master and servant, which modifies the relation in its content, though not in its economic form, and makes it distasteful.

For that matter Rossi only repeats in other phrases what Garnier said:

"When Smith wrote that nothing remained of the servant's labour, he was mistaken, to a greater extent, we must say, than an Adam Smith should be mistaken. A manufacturer manages himself a larger manufactory which requires very active and very assiduous supervision.... This man, not wanting to have unproductive labourers around him, has no servants. He is then compelled to *serve himself*.... What becomes of his productive labour during the time that he has to devote to this so-called unproductive labour? Is it not evident that your serving people perform a labour which enables you to apply yourself to a labour more appropriate to your abilities? Then how can it be said that no trace remains of their services? There remains everything that you do and that you could not have done if they had not replaced you in the service of your person and your home" (l.c., p. 277).

This is once more the *labour-saving* idea of Garnier, Lauderdale and Ganilh. According to this, unproductive labours would only be productive in so far as they save labour and leave more time for a person's own labour, whether he is an industrial capitalist or a productive labourer, who can perform a more valuable labour through this replacement by a less valuable labour. A large part of the unproductive labourers who would be excluded by this are menial servants (in so far as they provide only luxury articles), and all unproductive labourers who produce merely enjoyment and whose labour I can only enjoy in so far as I *use just as much time to enjoy it* as its *seller uses to produce it*, to provide it for me. In both cases there can be no talk of "saving" labour. Finally, even really labour-saving personal services would only be productive in so far as their consumer is a producer. If he is an idle capitalist, they only save him the labour of doing anything at all: like a slut having her hair curled or her nails cut instead of doing it herself, or a foxhunter employing a stable-lad instead of being his own stable-lad, or someone who is just a glutton keeping a cook instead of cooking for himself.

Then these labourers would include too those who, according to Storch (l. c.), produce "*leisure*", through which a man gets free time for pleasure, spiritual labour, and so on. The policeman saves me the time of being my own gendarme, the soldier of defending myself, the government official of governing myself, the shoe cleaner of cleaning my shoes myself, the priest the time required for thinking, and so on.

What is correct in this matter is—*the division of labour*. Everyone, apart from his productive labour or the exploitation of productive labour, would have a number of functions to fulfil which would not be productive and would in part enter into the costs of consumption. (The real productive labourers have to bear these consumption costs themselves and to perform their unproductive labour themselves.) If these "services" are pleasant, then sometimes the master performs them for the servant, as the *jus primae noctis** shows, or as is shown by the labour of ruling, etc., which the masters have always taken on themselves. This in no way obliterates the distinction between pro-

* The right of the first night.—*Ed.*

ductive and unproductive labour, but this distinction itself appears as a result of the *division of labour* and thus furthers the general productivity of the labourers by making unproductive labour the exclusive function of one section of labourers and productive labour the exclusive function of another section.

But even the *labour* of a number of menial servants for mere show, to satisfy vanity, "is not unproductive". Why? Because it produces *something*, the satisfaction of vanity, ostentation, the exhibition of wealth (l. c., p. 277). Here once again we meet the nonsense that every kind of services produces something—the courtesan sensual pleasure, the murderer homicide, etc. Moreover Smith said that every form of this trash has its *value*. All that is missing ||416| is that these services are rendered gratis. That is not the point in question. But even if they are rendered gratis, they will not increase (material) wealth by a single farthing.

Then the belletristic piffle:

> "The singer (they claim), when he has finished singing, leaves us nothing.—He leaves us a memory!" (Very fine!) "When you have drunk champagne, what remains?... Whether the consumption does or does not follow closely on the act of production, whether it takes place more or less rapidly, will bring about different economic results, but the fact of consumption, of whatever kind it may be, cannot deprive the product of its character as wealth. There are immaterial products which are of greater durability than certain material products. A palace lasts a long time, but the *Iliad* is a source of even more durable pleasures" (pp. 277-78).

What bosh!

In the sense in which he is here speaking of wealth, as use-value, it is precisely *consumption*, whether slow or rapid (its length depends on its own nature and on the nature of the object), and only consumption, that makes the product wealth at all. Use-value has only value for use, and its existence for use is only existence as an object for consumption, its existence is in consumption. Drinking champagne, although this may produce a "hangover", is as little productive consumption as listening to music, although this may leave behind "a memory". If the music is good and if the listener understands music, the consumption of music is more sublime than the consumption of champagne, although the production of the latter is a "productive labour" and the production of the former is not.

* * *

If we consider all the twaddle against Smith's distinction between productive and unproductive labour, we find that Garnier, and perhaps also Lauderdale and Ganilh (though the latter said nothing new), exhausted [these polemics]. Those who came later (apart from Storch's unsuccessful effort) [produced] merely pretentious literary arguments, learned prattle. Garnier is the economist of the Directory and the Consulate, Ferrier and Ganilh are the economists of the Empire. On the other hand Lauderdale, the Earl, was far more concerned *to make apologies for consumers by presenting them as the producers of "unproductive labour"*. The *glorification* of servility and flunkeyism, of tax-gatherers and parasites, runs through the lot of them. Compared with these, the rough cynical character of classical economy stands out as a critique of existing conditions.

[19. Apologia for the Prodigality of the Rich by the Malthusian Chalmers]

One of the most fanatic Malthusians is the *Reverend Thomas Chalmers*, who thinks that the only means for curing all social ills is the religious education of the labouring class (by which he means ramming down their throats the Malthusian population theory with edifying Christian priestly trimmings); at the same time he is a great defender of all abuses, of wasteful expenditure by the State, of fat livings for the clergy and of wild extravagance on the part of the rich. He laments (p. 260 sqq.) the spirit of the time, the "hard and hunger-bitten economy"; and he wants heavy taxes, a good deal to eat for the "higher" and unproductive workers, clergymen and so on (l. c.). Naturally, he blusters about the Smithian distinction. He devoted a whole chapter to it (Chapter XI) which contains nothing new except that parsimony, etc., only harms "the productive labourers", but whose tendency is exemplified in the following summing up: This "distinction seems to be nugatory [...]; and withal, mischievous in application" (l. c., p. 344). And in what does this mischief consist?

"We have entered at so much length into this argument, because we think *the political economy of our days bears a hard and hostile aspect towards an ecclesiastical establishment*; and we have no doubt, that to this, *the hurtful definition** *of Smith* has largely [...] contributed" (Thomas Chalmers, Professor of Divinity, *On Political Economy, in Connexion with the Moral State and Moral Prospects of Society*, 2nd ed., London, 1832, p. 346).

* In the manuscript: "distinction".—*Ed.*

By the "ecclesiastical establishment" the cleric means his own church, the Church of England as by law "established". Moreover he was one of the fellows who had fostered this "Establishment" upon Ireland. The parson is at least plain spoken.

[20. Concluding Observations on Adam Smith and His Views on Productive and Unproductive Labour]

||417| Before we finish with Adam Smith, we will cite two further passages, the first, in which he gives vent to his hatred of the unproductive government; the second, in which he aims to explain why the advance of industry, etc., presupposes free labour. Concerning *Smith's hatred of the clergy*.[82]

The first passage runs:

"It is the highest impertinence and presumption, therefore, in kings and ministers, to pretend to watch over the economy of private people, and to restrain their expense, either by sumptuary laws, or by prohibiting the importation of foreign luxuries. They are themselves always, and without any exception, the greatest spendthrifts in the society. Let them look well after their own expense, and they may safely trust private people with theirs. If their own extravagance does not ruin the State, that of their subjects never will" ([*Wealth of Nations*], t. II, l. II, ch. III, ed. McCulloch, p. 122).

And once more the following passage—*

"The labour of some of the most respectable orders in the** society is, like that of *mental servants, unproductive of any value*," <it has value, and therefore costs an equivalent, but it produces no value> "and does not fix or realise itself in any permanent subject, or vendible commodity.... The sovereign, for example, with all the officers both of justice and war who serve*** under him, the whole army and navy, are *unproductive labourers*. They are the *servants* of the public, and are maintained by a part of the annual produce of the *industry of other people*.... In the *same class* must be ranked...churchmen, lawyers, physicians, men of letters of all kinds; players, buffoons, musicians, opera-singers, opera-dancers, etc." (l.c., pp. 94-95).

This is the language of the still revolutionary bourgeoisie, which has not yet subjected to itself the whole of society, the State, etc. All these illustrious and time-honoured occupations—sovereign, judge, officer, priest, etc.,—with all the old ideologic-

* See pp. 160, 161 and 264 of the present volume.—*Ed.*

** In the manuscript: "of".—*Ed.*

*** In the manuscript: "are".—*Ed.*

al professions to which they give rise, their men of letters, their teachers and priests, are *from an economic standpoint* put on the same level as the swarm of their own lackeys and jesters maintained by the bourgeoisie and by idle wealth—the landed nobility and idle capitalists. They are mere *servants* of the public, just as the others are their servants. They live on the produce of *other* people's *industry*, therefore they must be reduced to the smallest possible number. State, church, etc., are only justified in so far as they are committees to superintend or administer the common interests of the productive bourgeoisie; and their costs—since by their nature these costs belong to the overhead costs of production—must be reduced to the unavoidable minimum. This view is of historical interest in sharp contrast partly to the standpoint of antiquity, when material productive labour bore the stigma of slavery and was regarded merely as a pedestal for the idle citizen, and partly to the standpoint of the absolute or aristocratic-constitutional monarchy which arose from the disintegration of the Middle Ages—as Montesquieu, still captive to these ideas, so naïvely expressed them in the following passage (*Esprit des lois*, l. VII, ch. IV): "If the rich do not spend much, the poor will perish of hunger".

When on the other hand the bourgeoisie has won the battle, and has partly itself taken over the State, partly made a compromise with its former possessors; and has likewise given recognition to the ideological professions as flesh of its flesh and everywhere transformed them into its functionaries, of like nature to itself; when it itself no longer confronts these as the representative of productive labour, but when the real productive labourers rise against it and moreover tell it that it lives on other people's industry; when it is enlightened enough not to be entirely absorbed in production, but to want also to consume "in an enlightened way"; when the spiritual labours themselves are more and more performed in its *service* and enter into the service of capitalist production—then things take a new turn, and the bourgeoisie tries to justify "economically", from its own standpoint, what at an earlier stage it had criticised and fought against. Its spokesmen and conscience-salvers in this line are the Garniers, etc. In addition to this, these economists, who themselves are priests, professors, etc., are eager to prove their "productive" usefulness, to justify their wages "economically".

||418| The second passage, referring to slavery, runs:

"Such occupations" (as artificer and manufacturer) "were considered" (in several of the ancient states) "as fit only for slaves, and the free citizens of the State were prohibited from exercising them Even in those States where no such prohibition took place, as in Rome and Athens, the great body of the people were in effect excluded from all the trades which are now commonly exercised by the lower sort of the inhabitants of towns. Such trades were, at Athens and Rome, all occupied by the slaves of the rich, who exercised them for the benefit of their masters, whose wealth, power, and protection, made it almost impossible for a poor freeman to find a market for his work, when it came into competition with that of the slaves of the rich. Slaves, however, are very seldom inventive; and all the most important improvements, either in machinery, or in the arrangement and distribution of work, which facilitate and abridge labour have been the discoveries of freemen. Should a slave propose any improvement of this kind, his master would be very apt to consider the proposal as the suggestion of laziness, and of a desire to save his own labour at the master's expense. The poor slave, instead of reward would probably meet with much abuse, perhaps with some punishment. In the manufactures carried on by slaves, therefore, more labour must generally have been employed to execute the same quantity of work, than in those carried on by freemen. The work of the former must, upon that account, generally have been dearer than that of the latter. The Hungarian mines, it is remarked by Mr. Montesquieu, though not richer, have always been wrought with less expense, and therefore with more profit, than the Turkish mines in their neighbourhood. The Turkish mines are wrought by slaves; and the *arms of those slaves are the only machines* which *the Turks* have ever thought of employing. The Hungarian mines are wrought by freemen, who employ a great deal of machinery, by which they facilitate and abridge their own labour. From the very little that is known about the price of manufactures in the times of the Greeks and Romans, it would appear that those of the finer sort were excessively dear" ([*Wealth of Nations*, O.U.P. edition, Vol. II, pp. 305-06] l.c., t. III, l. IV, ch. IX, pp. 549-51, ed. Garnier).

Adam Smith himself says, l. c., t. III, l. IV, ch. I, p. 5[83]:

"Mr. Locke remarks a distinction between money and other movable goods. All other movable goods, he says, are of *so consumable a nature*, that the wealth which consists in them cannot be much depended on.... Money, on the contrary, is a steady friend" and so on [ibid., p. 3].

And again, [Garnier], l. c., pp. 24-25:

"Consumable commodities, it is said, are soon destroyed; whereas gold and silver are of a *more durable nature*, and were it not for this continual exportation, might be accumulated for ages together, to the incredible augmentation of the real wealth of the country" [ibid., p. 14].

The man of the Monetary system raves about gold and silver because they are *money*, the independent, tangible form of existence of exchange-value; and a form of its existence that is indestructible, everlasting—in so far as they are not allowed to become means of circulation, the merely transient form of the exchange-value of commodities. The accumulation of gold and silver, piling it up, hoarding it, is therefore his way of growing rich. And as I showed in the quotation from Petty,[84] other commodities are themselves valued according to the degree in which they are more or less durable, that is, remain exchange-value.

Now *in the first place* Adam Smith repeats this idea of the relatively greater or less durability of commodities in the section where he speaks of consumption which is more or less advantageous for the formation of wealth, according as it is consumption of less or more durable articles of consumption.[85] Here therefore the Monetary system peeps through; and necessarily so, since even in direct consumption there is the mental reservation that the ||419| article of consumption remains *wealth*, a commodity, therefore a unity of use-value and exchange-value; and the latter depends on the degree to which the use-value is durable, that is, on how slowly consumption deprives it of the possibility of being a *commodity* or bearer of exchange-value.

Secondly, in his second distinction between productive and unproductive labour he completely returns—in a wider form—to the distinction made by the Monetary system.

Productive labour "fixes and realises itself in some particular subject or vendible commodity, *which lasts for some time at least after that labour is past*. It is, as it were, a certain quantity of labour stocked and stored up to be employed, if necessary, upon some other occasion"

On the other hand, the unproductive labour's results or services "generally perish in the very instant of their performance, and seldom leave any trace or *value* behind them, for which an equal quantity of service could afterwards be procured" (Vol. II, b. II, ch. III, ed. McCulloch, p. 94).

Thus Smith makes the same difference between commodities and services as the Monetary system did between gold and silver and the other commodities. With Smith too the distinction is made from the point of view of accumulation—no longer however in the form of building a hoard, but in the real form of reproduction. The commodity perishes in consumption, but then it reproduces in turn a commodity of higher value; or, if it is not so used, it is itself value, with which another commodity can be bought. It is the nature of the product of labour that it exists in a more or less durable, and therefore again salable, use-value; in a use-value in which it is a vendible commodity, a bearer of exchange-value, a *commodity*, or, in essence, *money*. The services of unproductive labourers do not again become *money*. I can neither pay debts nor buy commodities nor buy labour which produces surplus-value with the services for which I pay the lawyer, doctor, priest, musician, etc., the statesman or the soldier, etc. They have gone, like perishable articles of consumption.

Thus at bottom Smith says the same thing as the Monetary system. For them, only that labour is productive which produces *money*, gold and silver. For Smith, only that labour is productive which produces *money* for its buyer; although he discerns the money character in all commodities in spite of its mask, while the Monetary system sees it only in the commodity which is the independent existence of exchange-value.

This distinction is founded on the nature of bourgeois production itself, since wealth is not the equivalent of use-value, but only the *commodity* is wealth, use-value as bearer of exchange-value, as money. What the Monetary system did not understand is how this money is made and is multiplied through the consumption of commodities, and not through their transformation into gold and silver—in which they are crystallised as independent exchange-value, in which however they not only lose their use-value, but do not alter the *magnitude of* their *value*.

[CHAPTER V]

NECKER

[ATTEMPT TO PRESENT THE ANTAGONISM OF CLASSES IN CAPITALISM AS THE ANTITHESIS BETWEEN POVERTY AND WEALTH]

Some quotations from Linguet above have already shown that the nature of capitalist production was clear to him [86] nevertheless, Linguet, can be brought in here after Necker. [87]

In his two works *Sur la législation et le commerce des grains* (first published 1775) and *De l'administration des finances de la France*, etc. [published 1784], Necker shows how the development of the productive powers of labour merely results in the worker requiring *less time* for the reproduction of his own wage, and therefore working *more time* for his employer *unpaid*. In dealing with this, he rightly starts from the basis of the *average wage*, the minimum of wages. What he is mainly concerned with, however, is not the transformation of labour itself into capital and the accumulation of capital through this process, but rather the general development of the antithesis between poverty and wealth, between poverty and luxury, because, to the extent that a smaller quantity of labour suffices to produce the necessary means of subsistence, part of the labour becomes more and more superfluous and can therefore be used in the production of luxury articles, in a different sphere of production. Some of these luxury articles are durable; and so they accumulate from century to century in the possession of those who have surplus-labour at their disposal, making the contrast ever deeper.

The important thing is that Necker traces the origin of the wealth of the non-labouring classes ||420|—profit and rent—entirely to surplus-labour. In his treatment of surplus-value, however, what he has in mind is relative surplus-value, resulting not from the lengthening of the total working-day but from the shortening of the *necessary labour-time*. The productive power of labour becomes the productive power of the owner of the conditions of labour. And productive power itself is equivalent to the shortening of the labour-time that is necessary to produce a certain result. The chief passages are the following:

First: *De l'administration des finances de la France*, etc. (*Œuvres*, t. II, Lausanne et Paris, 1789):

"I see one of the classes of society whose wealth must always be pretty nearly the same; I see another of these classes whose wealth necessarily increases: thus luxury, which arises from a relation and a comparison, has had to follow the growth of this disproportion and become more evident as time went on" (l.c., pp. 285-86). (The contrast between *the two classes* as *classes* has already been clearly noticed.) "The class of society whose lot is as it were *fixed* by the effect of social laws is composed of all those who, *living by the labour of their hands*, are subject to the imperative law of the *owners*" (owners of the conditions of production) "and are compelled to content themselves with a *wage proportionate to the simple necessities of life*; competition between them and *the urgency of their needs* bring about their *state of dependence*; these conditions cannot change" (l.c., p. 286).

"*The continual invention of instruments which have simplified all mechanical arts has*, then, *augmented the wealth and the fortunate lot of the owners*; one part of these instruments, *by reducing the costs of working the land, has increased the revenue* of which the owners of such property can dispose; another part of the discoveries of genius has *so greatly facilitated* the labours of industry that the *men who are in the service of the dispensers of the means of subsistence*" (i.e., of the capitalists) "have been able, *in an equal length of time, and for the same reward*, to produce a greater quantity of products of all kinds" (p. 287). "Let us assume that a century ago a hundred thousand workers were required to do what is done today by eighty thousand; the other twenty thousand would have found themselves obliged to take to *other occupations* to obtain wages; and the new products of their manual labour resulting from this would increase the pleasures and the luxuries of the rich" (pp. 287-88).

"For," he continues, "it must not be forgotten that the rewards assigned to all trades which do not require any special talent are always proportionate to the *necessary price of subsistence for each labourer*; thus the *speed of production*, when the knowledge required has become common, *does not accrue to the advantage of the labouring men*, and *the result is only an augmentation of the means* for the satisfaction of the tastes and vanities of those who have at their disposal the products of the land" (l.c., p. 288). "Among the various good things of nature which are fashioned and changed by men's industry there are a large number whose durability greatly exceeds the usual span of life: each generation has inherited a part of the labours of the preceding generation" <he is here only taking into account the accumulation of what Adam Smith calls the consumption fund> "and in all countries there is a continual *accumulation* of a greater quantity of the products of the arts; and as this quantity is always divided among the owners, the disproportion between their possessions and those of the numerous class of citizens has necessarily grown greater and more noticeable" (p. 289). Hence "*the quickening pace of industrial production*, which has multiplied the things of pomp and luxury on earth, *the length of time in which accumulation has grown from this*, and the *laws of property, which have brought these good things into the hands of one class of society alone*... these great sources of luxury would in any case have existed, whatever had been the quantity of coined money" (p. 291).

(The latter argument is directed against those who held that luxury was the result of the growth in the amount of money.)

Secondly: *Sur la législation et le commerce des grains*, etc. (*Œuvres*, t. IV):

"When the artisan or the husbandman *have no reserves left*, they can no longer argue; they must *work today on pain of dying tomorrow*, and in this conflict of interest between ||421| the Owner and Labourer, the one stakes his life and that of his family, and the other a mere delay in the growth of his luxury" (l.c., p. 63).

This contrast between wealth that does not labour and poverty that labours in order to live also gives rise to a contrast of knowledge. Knowledge and labour become separated. The former confronts the latter as capital, or as a luxury article for the rich.

"The faculty of knowing and understanding is a general gift of nature, but it is only developed by education; if properties were equal, everyone *would labour moderately*" (so once again, the quantity of labour-time is the decisive thing), "and *everyone would know a little*, because everyone would have *a portion of time*" (spare time) "left to give to study and reflection; but with the inequality of fortunes, resulting from the social order, *education is prohibited* for all who are born without property; because all sustenance being in the hands of that part of the nation which possesses *money or land*, and no one giving anything for nothing, the man born without any other resource but his strength is obliged to devote it to the service of the Owners from the first moment when his strength develops, and to continue thus all his life, from the moment when the sun rises to the moment when this strength has been worn down and needs to be renewed by sleep" (p. 112). "Lastly, is it not certain that this inequality of knowledge has become necessary for the maintenance of all the social inequalities *which gave rise to it*?" (l.c., p. 113), (cf. pp. 118-19).

Necker ridicules the economic confusion—characteristic of the Physiocrats in relation to the land, and of all subsequent economists in relation to the material elements of capital—which glorifies the owners of the conditions of production, not because they themselves, but these conditions, are necessary for labour and the production of wealth.

"They begin by confusing the importance of the owner (a function so easy to perform) with the importance of the land" (l.c., p. 126). |IX—421||

[CHAPTER VI]

QUESNAY'S TABLEAU ÉCONOMIQUE

(Digression)

[1. Quesnay's Attempt to Show the Process of Reproduction and Circulation of the Total Capital]

|| X — 422 | Tableau économique, according to Quesnay[88]

5,000 millions annual gross product (in pounds of Tours)

In original and annual advances, the farmers lay out	In rents, the landlords receive	The sterile class disposes of a fund of

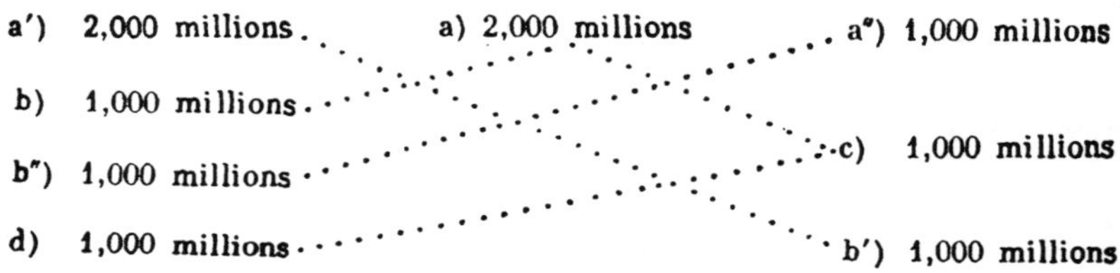

5,000 millions		2,000 millions, of which half remains as a fund belonging to the sterile class

To make the Tableau clearer, I have shown what Quesnay regards each time as the starting-point of a circulation, as a, a', a", the following link in the circulation as b, c, d, and as b', b" respectively.[89]

The first point to note in this Tableau, and the point which must have impressed his contemporaries, is the way in which the money circulation is shown as determined purely by the circulation and reproduction of commodities, in fact by the circulation process of capital.

[2. Circulation between Farmers and Landowners. The Return Circuit of Money to the Farmers, Which Does Not Express Reproduction]

The farmer first pays 2,000 million francs in money to the landlord, the *propriétaire*. With this, the landlord buys from the farmer 1,000 millions worth of means of subsistence. 1,000 millions therefore flow back to the farmer in money, while one-fifth of the gross product is disposed of, passing definitively out of circulation into consumption.

The landlord next buys, with 1,000 millions in money, manufactured commodities, non-agricultural products, to the value of 1,000 millions. With this purchase, a second one-fifth of the (in this case manufactured) products falls out of circulation into consumption. These 1,000 millions in money are now in the hands of the sterile class, who buys with them from the farmer 1,000 millions worth of means of subsistence. Thus the second 1,000 millions which the farmer has paid to the landlord in the form of rent flow back to the farmer. On the other hand, a further one-fifth of the farmer's product has gone to the sterile class, out of circulation into consumption. At the end of this first movement, therefore, we have the 2,000 millions in money back in the hands of the farmer. This money has carried through four different processes of circulation.

First, it served as means of payment for rent. In this function it does not circulate any part of the annual product, but is merely a circulating draft on the part of the gross product which is equal to the rent.

Second, the landlord buys means of subsistence from the farmer, using half the 2,000 millions, that is, 1,000 millions, thus realising his 1,000 millions in means of subsistence. In fact, the farmer merely gets back, in the 1,000 millions in money, half of the draft he has given the landlord for two-fifths of his product. In this transaction the 1,000 millions, since they serve as means of purchase, circulate commodities to that amount, which fall into final consumption. The 1,000 millions here serve the landlord only as *means of purchase*; he reconverts the money into use-value (commodities, which however enter into final consumption, and are bought as use-value).

If we consider purely the isolated act, the money in this transaction plays merely the role which, as means of purchase, it always plays for the seller, namely, being the changed form of his commodity. The landlord has his 1,000 millions in corn, the farmer has converted into money corn to the price of 1,000 millions, he has realised its price. But if we consider this act in connection with the preceding act of circulation, the money here does not appear as a mere metamorphosis of the farmer's commodity, as a golden equivalent of his commodity. The 1,000 millions are in fact only half the 2,000 millions, in money, which the farmer has paid to the ||423| landlord in the form of rent. It is true that he gets 1,000 millions in money for 1,000 millions in commodities, but *in so doing in fact he only buys back the money with which he paid the landlord the rent; that is to say, the landlord buys, with the 1,000 millions which he has received from the farmer, 1,000 millions worth of commodities from the farmer. He pays the farmer* with the money which he has received *from the farmer without any equivalent.*

This flowing back of the money to the farmer, taken in conjunction with the first act, does not at first make it appear to him a mere means of circulation. But then it is different in essence from the flowing back of money to its starting-point when the movement is an expression of a process of reproduction.

For example: the capitalist—or, to leave the characteristics of capitalist reproduction entirely out of account, a producer—lays out £100 for raw material, instruments of labour and means of subsistence for the period of his labour. We will assume that he does not add more labour to the means of production than he had expended on the means of subsistence, the wages that he has paid to himself. If the raw material, etc., equals £80, and tne labour added is equal to £20 (the means of subsistence consumed also being equal to £20), then the product is equal to £100. If he now sells it, the £100 flows back to him in money, and so on. This flowing back of the money to its starting-point here expresses nothing but continuous reproduction. The simple metamorphosis in this case is M—C—M, transformation of money into commodity and retransformation of commodity into money—this mere change of form of money and commodity here representing at the same time the process of reproduction. Money is transformed into commodities, *means of production* and means of subsistence; then these commodities enter as elements into the labour-process and emerge from it as a product. Thus a commodity appears again as a result of the process, that is, when the finished product re-enters the process of circulation, and by so doing again confronts money as a commodity; and finally it is reconverted into money, since the finished commodity can only be exchanged again for its production elements after it has first been transformed into money.

The constant flowing back of the money to its starting-point expresses here not only the formal conversion of money into commodity and commodity into money—as in the simple process of circulation or the mere exchange of goods—*but at the same time the continuous reproduction of the commodity by the same producer*. Exchange-value (money) is converted into commodities which enter into consumption, and are consumed as use-values; they pass however into reproductive or industrial consumption, therefore reproduce the original value and consequently reappear in the *same* amount of money (in the above example, in which the producer labours only for his own maintenance), M—C—M here shows that M is not only formally converted into C, but C is actually consumed as a use-value, falling out of circulation into consumption, but into industrial consumption, so that its value is maintained and reproduced in consumption, and M therefore reappears at the end of the process, being maintained in the movement M—C—M.

In contrast with this, in the case given above, no reproduction process takes place when the money flows back from the landlord to the farmer. It is as if the farmer had given the landlord tokens or tickets for products to the value of 1,000 millions. When the landlord cashes these tokens, they flow back to the farmer and he redeems them. If the landlord had had half the rent paid directly in kind, no circulation of money would have taken place. The whole circulation would have been limited to a simple change of hands, the transfer of the product from the farmer's hand to the landlord's. First the farmer gives the landlord the money instead of the commodity, and then the landlord returns the money to the farmer in order to take the commodity itself. The money serves the farmer as *means of payment* to the landlord; it serves the landlord as *means of purchase* in relation to the farmer. In the first function it moves away from the farmer, in the second it comes back to him.

This type of return flow of the money to the producer must always take place whenever he pays his creditors, instead of a part of his product, its value in money; and everyone who is a co-proprietor of his surplus is in this respect a creditor. For example: all taxes are paid by the producers in money. In this transaction the money is for them means of payment to the State. With this money the State buys commodities from the producers. In the hands of the State it is a means of purchase, and thus returns to the producers in the same measure as they part with their commodities.

This type of return flow—this peculiar flowing back of money that is not determined by reproduction—must take place in all cases where there is exchange of revenue for capital. What makes the money flow back in such cases is not reproduction but consumption. The revenue is paid in money, but it can only be consumed in commodities. The money which is received from the producers as revenue must therefore be paid back to them in order to obtain the same amount of value in commodities, that is, in order to consume the revenue. The money in which revenue is paid—rent for example, or interest or taxes, <the ||424| industrial capitalist pays his revenue to himself in the product, or from the sale of the product that part of it which forms his revenue> —has the general form of means of payment. The person who pays the revenue is supposed to have received from his creditor a part of his own product—for example, in the case of the farmer, the two-fifths of the product which according to Quesnay constitute the rent. He is only its nominal or *de facto* owner.

The part of the farmer's product, therefore, which constitutes his rent, requires for its circulation between farmer and landlord only an amount of money equal to the value of the product, although this value circulates twice. First the farmer pays the rent in money; then with the same money the landlord buys the product. The first is a simple transfer of money, since the money functions only as *means of payment*; the assumption is therefore that the commodity for which it is paid is already in the hands of the payer and does not serve him as a means of purchase; that he receives no equivalent for the money, but on the contrary has this equivalent in advance. In the second transaction, on the other hand, the money functions as means of purchase, means of circulation for commodities. It is as if, with the money in which he pays his rent, the farmer had bought the landlord's share in the product. The landlord, with the same money that he has thus received from the farmer (who however in fact has given it away without any equivalent), buys the product back again from the farmer.

The same sum of money, therefore, which is handed over by the producers to the owners of revenue in the form of means of payment, serves the owners of revenue as means of purchase for the producers' commodities. This twofold change of place of the money—from the hands of the producer into the hands of the owner of revenue, and from the latter's hands back into the hands of the producer—thus expresses only a single change of place on the part of the commodity, that is, from the hands of the producer into the hands of the owner of revenue. Since the producer is supposed to owe a part of his product to the owner of revenue, the money-rent that he pays him is in fact only a retrospective payment for the value of the commodity which has already passed into his possession. The commodity is in his hands; but it does not belong to him. With the money that he pays in the form of revenue, he therefore redeems it making it his property. Therefore the commodity does not change hands. When the money changes hands, this represents only a *change in the title of ownership* of the commodity, which remains in the hands of the producer as before. Hence this twofold change of place of the money with only a single change of hands for the commodity. The money circulates twice, in order to make the commodity circulate once. But it too circulates only once as means of circulation (means of purchase), while the other time it circulates as means of payment; in which type of circulation, as I have shown above, no simultaneous change of place between commodity and money takes place.

In fact, if the farmer has no money in addition to his product, he can only pay for his product after he has first sold his commodity, and it has therefore already passed through its first metamorphosis before he can pay it out as money to the landlord. Even taking this into account, there are more changes of place on the part of the money than on the part of the commodity. First C—M [is carried through]; two-fifths of the commodity is sold and transformed into money. Here there is the simultaneous exchange of commodity and money. Then however this same money, without being exchanged for a commodity, passes from the hands of the farmer into those of the landlord. Here there is a change of place of the money, but no change of place of the commodity. It is the same as if the farmer had a co-partner. He has received the money, but he must share it with his co-partner. Or rather, for the two-fifths it is more as if a servant of the farmer has received the money. This servant must give it to the farmer, he cannot retain it in his own pocket. In this instance the movement of the money from one hand to the other does not express any kind of metamorphosis of the commodity, but is a mere transfer of the money from the hand of its immediate possessor into the hand of its owner. This can therefore be the case when the man who first receives the money is merely an agent for his employer. Then the money is also not a means of payment—there is a simple transfer of it from the hand of the receiver, to whom it does not belong, into the hand of the owner.

This kind of change of place of money has absolutely nothing to do with the metamorphosis of the commodity, any more than has the change of place arising from the mere conversion of one kind of money into another kind. With a means of payment, however, it is always implied that the payer has received a commodity for which he subsequently pays. In the case of the farmer, etc., he has *not received* this commodity; it is in his hands before it is in the landlord's hands, and it is a part of *his* product. But *in law* he becomes its owner only by handing over to the landlord the money received for it. His legal title to the commodity changes; the commodity itself is in his hands both before and after. But first it was in his hands as something *in his possession* but the owner of which was the landlord. It is now in his hands as his own property. The change in the legal form while the commodity remains in the same hands has naturally not caused the commodity itself to change hands.

[3. On the Circulation of Money between Capitalist and Labourer]

[(a) The Absurdity of Speaking of Wages as an Advance by the Capitalist to the Labourer. Bourgeois Conception of Profit as Reward for Risk]

||425| <This also makes it clear how absurd it is to "explain" the profit of the capitalist from the fact that he advances money to the labourer before he has converted the commodity into money.

First: When I buy a commodity for my own consumption I get no "profit" because I am the buyer and the owner of the commodity is the "seller", because my commodity has the form of money and his must first be transformed into money. The capitalist pays for the labour only after he has consumed it, while other commodities are paid for before they are consumed. This arises from the peculiar nature of the commodity which he buys, and which is in fact only delivered after it is consumed. The money here has the form of means of payment. The capitalist has always appropriated to himself the commodity "labour" *before* he pays for it. The fact however that he only buys it in order to make a profit out of the resale of its product is no *reason* for his making this profit. It is a motive. And it would mean nothing but: he makes a profit by buying wage-labour *because* he wants to make a profit out of selling it again.

Secondly: But he does nevertheless advance to the labourer in the form of money the part of the product which is his share as wages, and thus saves the latter himself the trouble and risk and time involved in converting into money the part of the commodity which is due to him as wages. Is the labourer not to pay him for this trouble, this risk, and this time, and on this account to accept less of the product than he would otherwise get?

This would upset the whole relationship between wage-labour and capital, and destroy the economic justification of surplus-value. The result of the process is in fact that the fund from which the capitalist pays the wage-labourer is nothing but the latter's own product, and that therefore capitalist and labourer *actually* share the product in aliquot parts. But this actual result has absolutely nothing to do with the transaction between capital and wage[-labour] (on which rests the economic justification of surplus-value, the justification founded on the laws of commodity exchange itself). What the capitalist buys is the temporary right to dispose of labour-power; he only pays for it when this labour-power has taken effect, materialised itself in a product. Here, as in all cases where money functions as means of payment, purchase and sale precede the real handing over of the money by the buyer. But the labour *belongs* to the capitalist after that transaction, which has been completed before the actual process of production begins. The *commodity* which emerges as product from this process belongs entirely to him. He has produced it with means of production belonging to him and with labour which he has bought and which therefore belongs to him, even though it has not yet been paid for. It is the same as if he had not consumed anyone else's labour in the production of the commodity.

The profit that the capitalist makes, the surplus-value which he realises, springs precisely from the fact that the labourer has sold to him not labour realised in a commodity, but his labour-power itself as a commodity. If he had confronted the capitalist in the first form, as a possessor of commodities, [90] the capitalist would not have been able to make any profit, to realise any surplus-value, since according to the law of value exchange is between equivalents, an equal quantity of labour for an equal quantity of labour. The capitalist's surplus arises precisely from the fact that he buys from the labourer not a commodity but his labour-power itself, and this has less value than the product of this labour-power, or, what is the same thing, realises itself in more materialised labour than is realised in itself. But now, in order to justify profit, its very source is covered up, and the whole transaction from which it springs is repudiated. Because in fact—once the process is continuous—the capitalist only pays the labourer out of his own product, the labourer is only paid with a part of his own product, and the advance is therefore a mere pretence, we are now told that the labourer has sold his share in the product to the capitalist, *before it has been converted into money*. (Perhaps before it was capable of being converted into money, for although the workman's labour had materialised itself in a product, it may be that only one part of the vendible commodity has as yet been realised, for example, [only] part of a house.) So the capitalist is no longer owner of the product, and thereby the whole process through which he has appropriated another's labour *gratis* is invalidated. Now therefore owners of commodities confront each other. The capitalist has money, and the labourer sells him not his labour-power but a commodity, namely, the part of the product in which his own labour is realised.

He [the labourer] will now say to the capitalist: "Of these 5 lbs. of twist, say three-fifths represent constant capital. They belong to you. Two-fifths, that is, 2 lbs., represent my newly-added labour. Therefore you have to pay me the 2 lbs. So pay me the value of 2 lbs." And thereby he would pocket not only the wages but also the profit, in short, a sum of money equal to the quantity of labour newly added by him and materialised in the form of the 2 lbs.

"But," says the capitalist, "have I not advanced the constant capital?"

"Well," says the labourer, "you deduct the 3 lbs. for it, and pay me only 2."

"But," insists the capitalist, "you couldn't materialise your labour, you couldn't spin, without my cotton and my spindles. You must pay extra for that."

"Well," says the labourer, "the cotton would have rotted and the spindles rusted if I hadn't used them for spinning. ||426| The 3 lbs. of yarn which you are deducting do represent, it is true, only the value of your cotton and spindles which were used up, and are therefore contained, in the 5 lbs. of yarn. But it is only my labour that has maintained the value of cotton and spindles unchanged, by using these means of production as means of production. I'm not charging you anything for this value-maintaining power of my labour, because it didn't cost me any extra labour-time beyond the spinning itself, for which I get the 2 lbs. It's natural faculty of my labour which costs me nothing, though it maintains the value of the constant capital. As I don't charge you anything for it, you can't charge me for not being able to spin *without* spindles and cotton. For without spinning, your spindles and cotton wouldn't be worth a brass farthing."

Driven into a corner, the capitalist says: "The 2 lbs. of yarn are in fact worth 2s. They represent that much labour-time of yours. But am I to pay you for them before I have sold them? Perhaps I may not sell them at all. That is risk No. 1. Secondly, perhaps I may sell them at less than their price. That is risk No. 2. And thirdly, in any case it takes time to sell them. Am I to take on both risks on your behalf *without recompense* and lose my time into the bargain? You can't expect something for nothing."

"Wait a bit!" replies the labourer, "what's the relation between us? We face each other *as owners of commodities, you as buyer, we as sellers*, for you want to buy our share in the product, the 2 lbs., and it in fact contains nothing but our own materialised labour-time. Now you assert that we must sell you our commodity *below* its value, so that as a result you would be getting more value in commodity than you now have in money. The value of our commodity is equal to 2s. You want to give only 1s. for it, so that—since 1s. contains as much labour-time as 1 lb. of yarn—you would get from the exchange twice as much value as you give in return. We on the other hand would get, instead of an equivalent, only half an equivalent, an equivalent for only 1 lb. of yarn instead of 2 lbs. And on what do you base this demand, which is contrary to the law of value and the exchange of commodities in proportion to their value? On what? On the fact that you are buyer and we are seller, that our value is in the form of yarn, of a commodity, and your value is in the form of money—that the same value in the form of yarn confronts the same value in the form of money. But, my good friend, that is in fact a mere change of form, which affects the way in which the value is *expressed* but leaves the *amount of value* unaltered. Or do you hold the childish view that every commodity must be sold *under* its price, that is to say, for less than the sum of money which represents its value, because in the form of money it gets an *increased* value? But no, good friend, it does not get any increased value; the magnitude of its value does not change, it merely takes the shape of exchange-value in its pure form.

"Besides, my good friend, think of the troubles you are laying up for yourself by taking this line. For what you assert amounts to this—that the seller must always sell his commodity to the *buyer below* its value. Indeed as far as you are concerned, this was the case earlier when we sold you not a commodity we produced but our labour-power itself. It is true that you bought it at its value, but you bought our actual labour *below* the value in which it is expressed. However that's an unpleasant memory—let's say no more about it. We've got beyond that, thank goodness, since—by your own decision—we are no longer to sell you our labour-power as a commodity, but the commodity itself which is the product of our labour. Let's look at the troubles you're laying up for yourself. The new law you have set up—that the seller pays for the conversion of his commodity into money not with his commodity, through the exchange of his commodity for money, but that he pays for it by selling the commodity *below* its price—this law by which the buyer always fleeces and defrauds the seller must hold good in like measure for every buyer and seller. Let's suppose that we accept your offer—but on the condition that you yourself submit to the law just created by you, namely the law that the seller must surrender to the buyer a part of his commodity *for nothing*, in return for the buyer changing it into money for him. Then you buy our 2 lbs., which are worth 2s., for 1s. and thus make a profit of 1s. or 100 per cent. But now you have 5 lbs. of yarn, of a value of 5s., after you have bought the 2 lbs. belonging to us. Now you think you're going to do a good stroke of business. The 5 lbs. cost you only 4s., and you're going to sell them for 5s. 'Wait a minute!' says *the man who buys from you*, 'your 5 lbs. of yarn is a commodity, and you are a seller. I have the same value in money, and I am a buyer. Consequently, by the law which you recognise I must make 100 per cent profit out of you. You must therefore sell me the 5 lbs. of yarn at 50 per cent below its value, for 2s. 6d. I'll give you then 2s. 6d. and get in exchange a commodity to the value of 5s., and thus make 100 per cent profit out of you, for what's sauce for the goose is sauce for the gander.'

"So you see, my good friend, [continues the worker] where you get with your new law; you would simply have diddled yourself, since although at one moment you are a buyer, the next you're in turn a seller. In this particular case you would lose more as a seller than you gained as a buyer. And don't forget this too—before the 2 lbs. of yarn you want now to buy from us ever existed, didn't you make other purchases in advance, but for which the 5 lbs. of yarn would never have been there at all? ||426a| Didn't you buy cotton and spindles in advance, which are now represented by 3 lbs. of yarn? At that time the cotton jobber in Liverpool and the spindle maker in Oldham faced you as *sellers*, and you faced them as *buyer*; they represented commodity, you money—exactly the same relationship as we have the honour or the misfortune to stand in to each other at this moment. Wouldn't the sharp cotton jobber and your jovial colleague from Oldham have had a good laugh at you, if you had demanded that they hand over to you *for nothing* a part of the cotton and spindles, or what is the same thing, sell you these commodities below their price (and their value), on the ground that you were transforming commodities for them into money but they were transforming money into commodities for you, that they were sellers, you buyer? They risked nothing, for they got ready money, exchange-value in the pure, independent form. You, on the other hand, what a risk you were taking! First you had to make spindles and cotton into yarn, run all the risks of the production process, and then finally the risk of reselling the yarn, changing it back again into money! The risk whether it would sell at its value, or over or under its value. The risk of not selling it at all, of not transforming it back into money; and as to its quality as yarn, you didn't care a straw for it. You did not eat yarn, nor drink it, nor have any use whatever for it except selling it! And in any case the loss of time, in transforming the yarn again into money, and that includes therefore the transformation of spindles and yarn into money. 'Old boy,' your colleagues will reply, 'don't make a fool of yourself. Don't talk nonsense. What the devil do we care what you propose turning our cotton and our spindles to? What use you destine them for! Burn them, hang them, if you like, throw them to the dogs, but pay for them! The idea! We are to make you a present of our goods because you have set up as a cotton spinner, and seem not to feel quite at ease in that line of business, and magnify to yourself its risks and perilous chances! Give up cotton spinning, or don't come into the market with such preposterous ideas!'"

The capitalist, with a supercilious smile, replies to this tirade from the labourers: "Evidently you people are a bit out of your depth. You're talking about things you don't understand. Do you imagine I've paid ready money to the Liverpool ruffian and the chap in Oldham? The devil I did. I've paid them in bills of exchange, and the Liverpool ruffian's cotton was in point of fact spun and sold before his bill fell due. With you it's another affair altogether. You want to get ready money."

"Very well," say the labourers, "and what did the Liverpool ruffian and the Oldham chap do with your bills?"

"What they were doing therewith?" says the capitalist. "Stupid question! They lodged them with their bankers and got them there discounted."

"How much did they pay the banker?"

"Let me see! Money is now very cheap. I think they paid something like 3 per cent discount; that is to say, not 3 per cent on the sum, but they paid so much on the sum for the time the bill was running as would have come up to 3 per cent on the whole matter if the bill had run for a whole year."

"Still better," say the working men. "Pay us 2s., the value of our commodity—or say 12s. as we have dealt today per day, but we will deal per week. But take away from that sum 3 per cent per annum for fourteen days."

"But this bill is too small," says the capitalist, "to be discounted by any banker."

"Well," reply the working men, "we are 100 men. Thus you have to pay to us 1,200 shillings. Give us a bill for them. This makes £60 and is not too small a sum to be discounted; but besides, as you discount it yourself, the sum must not be too small for you, since it is the identical sum whence you pretend to derive your profit on us. The amount deducted wouldn't be worth mentioning. And since we would thus get the major part of our product in its entirety, we would soon reach the point when we didn't need you to discount it for us. Naturally we will not give you longer credit than the fourteen days the stock jobber gives you."

If—turning the actual relationship upside-down—wages are to be derived from the discount on the part of the value of the total product that belongs to the workmen—that is, from the fact that the capitalist pays them this part in advance in *money*—he would have to give them very short-term bills of exchange, such as for example he pays to the cotton jobber, etc. The workman would get the largest share of his product, and the capitalist would soon cease being a capitalist. From being the owner of the product he would become merely the workmen's banker.

Moreover, just as the capitalist takes the risk of selling the commodity below its ||427| value, he equally takes the chance of selling it above its value. The workman will be thrown out onto the street if the product is unsalable; and if it falls for long below the market-price, his wages will be brought down below the average and short time will be worked. It is he, therefore, that runs the greatest risk.

Thirdly: It never enters anyone's head to suggest that the farmer, because he has to pay rent in money, or the industrial capitalist, because he has to pay interest in money—and therefore in order to pay them must first have converted his product into money—is on that account entitled to deduct a part of his rent or his interest. >

[(b) Commodities Which the Labourer Buys from the Capitalist. A Return Flow of the Money Which Does Not Indicate Reproduction]

In that part of the capital which circulates between industrial capitalist and labourer (that is, the part of the circulating capital which is equal to the variable capital), there is also a return flow of the money to its starting-point. The capitalist pays the labourer his wages in money; with this money the labourer buys commodities from the capitalist, and so the money flows back to the capitalist. (In practice, to the capitalist's banker. But the bankers in fact represent, in relation to the individual capitalist, the aggregate capital in so far as it takes the form of *money*.) This return flow of the money does not in itself indicate any reproduction. The capitalist buys labour from the labourer with money; with the same money, the labourer buys commodities from the capitalist. The same money takes the form first of means of purchase for labour, and later on as means of purchase for commodities. That it comes back to the capitalist is due to the fact that at first he is a buyer, and then in turn, in relation to the same parties, he is a seller. He parts with it as a buyer; it returns to him as a seller. The labourer on the contrary is first seller and then buyer, so first he gets the money and then he pays it out, while in relation to him the capitalist first pays it out and then takes it in.

For the capitalist, the movement here is M—C—M. He buys a commodity (labour-power) with money; with the product of this labour-power (a commodity) he buys money; in other words, he sells this product in turn to his former seller, the labourer. For the labourer, on the other hand, the movement of circulation is C—M—C. He sells his commodity (labour-power), and with the money he gets for it he buys back a part of his own product (a commodity). It could indeed be said that the labourer sells a commodity (labour-power) for money, spends this money on commodities, and then sells his labour-power again, so that for him too the movement is M—C—M; and since the money is constantly fluctuating between him and the capitalist, it could equally be said, depending on whether one considers it from the standpoint of the one or of the other, that for him as well as for the capitalist the movement is M—C—M. The capitalist, however, is the buyer. The renewal of the process starts from him, not from the labourer, while the return flow of the money is compulsory, since the labourer must buy means of subsistence. Here, as in all movements where the form of circulation on one side is M—C—M and on the other C—M—C, it is made evident that the aim of the process of exchange on one side is exchange-value, money—and therefore its increase—and on the other side use-value, consumption. This also is the case when the money flows back as in the example first considered, where on the farmer's side the movement is M—C—M, C—M—C on the landlord's side; taking into account the fact that the M with which the landlord buys from the farmer is the money form of the rent, and therefore the result of a movement C—M, the changed form of the part of the product that at bottom belongs to the landlord in kind.

This M—C—M, in so far as it merely expresses, as between labourer and capitalist, the return to the latter of the money laid out by him in wages, in itself does not indicate any reproduction process, but only that the two parties are in turn buyer and seller in relation to each other. Nor does it represent money as capital, in such a way as in M—C—M′, where the second M′ would be a larger sum of money than the first M, so that M represents value (capital) which increases in value. On the contrary, it merely expresses the formal return of *the same* amount of money (often even less) to its starting-point. (By capitalist here, of course, is meant the class of capitalists.) I was therefore wrong in saying in the first Part [91] that the form M—C—M must always be M—C—M′. It may express merely the formal return of the money, as I indicated there already, by showing that the return circuit of the money to the same starting-point arises from the fact that the buyer in turn becomes seller. [92]

It is not *this* return movement of the money that enriches the capitalist. For example, say that he has paid 10s. for wages. The labourer buys goods from him with this 10s. He has given the labourer goods to the value of 10s. for his labour-power. If he had given him means of subsistence in kind to the price of 10s., there would have been no circulation of money, and therefore no return flow of money. This phenomenon of money returning has therefore nothing to do with the enrichment of the capitalist, which only arises from the fact that in the production process itself the capitalist appropriates more labour than he has expended in wages, and that his product is consequently larger than the costs of producing it; while the money that he pays the labourer can in no case be less than the money with which the labourer buys goods from him. This formal return of the money has nothing to do with making a profit, and therefore M here does not signify capital ||428| any more than an increase or replacement of value takes place when money spent in rent, interest or taxes flows back to the payer of rent, interest and taxes.

M—C—M, in so far as it represents the formal return of money to the capitalist, only means that his promissory note issued in money is realised in his own commodity.

As an example of the wrong explanation of this money circuit—this return of money to its starting-point—see Destutt de Tracy above. [93] As a second example, with special reference to the circulation of money between labourer and capitalist, Bray [94] is to be quoted later. Finally, *Proudhon*, [95] in regard to the money-lending capitalist.

This form of return circuit M—C—M is found wherever the buyer becomes in turn seller, and therefore in the movement of all commercial capital, where all dealers buy from each other in order to sell, and sell in order to buy. It is possible that the buyer—M—is unable to sell the commodity, rice for example, at a higher price than he bought it at; he may have to sell it below its price. Thus in such a case a simple return of the money takes place, because the purchase turns into a sale without the M having established itself as value that increases value, that is, as capital.

It is the same for example in the exchange of constant capital. The machine builder buys iron from the producer of iron and sells him machines. In this case the money flows back. It was paid out as means of purchase for the iron. It then serves the iron producer as means of purchase for machines, and so flows back to the machine builder. The latter has got iron for the money he paid out; he has delivered machines for the money he received. The same money has circulated twice its value. For example, the machine builder buys iron with £1,000; with the same £1,000 the iron producer buys machinery. The value of the iron and the machinery together is £2,000. In this way, however, £3,000 must be in motion: £1,000 money, £1,000 machinery and £1,000 iron. If the capitalists made an exchange in kind, the commodities would change hands without a farthing circulating.

It is the same when they have reciprocal accounting and the money serves them as means of payment. If paper money or credit money (bank-notes) circulate, then there is one difference in the transaction. £1,000 still exist in bank-notes, but they have no intrinsic value. In any case here too there are three [times £1,000]: £1,000 iron, £1,000 machinery, £1,000 in bank-notes. But as in the first case these three only exist because the machine builder has had [£1,000] twice—machinery £1,000 and money—in gold and silver or bank-notes—£1,000. In both cases the iron producer returns to him only number two (the money); because the only reason why he received it at all was that the machine builder, as buyer, did not immediately become seller; he did not pay for the first commodity, the iron, in commodities, and so he paid for it in money. When he pays for it in commodities, that is, when he sells commodities to the ironmaster, the latter returns the money to him because payment has not to be made twice, once in money, and the second time in commodities.

In both cases the gold or the bank-note represents the changed form of a commodity previously bought by the machine builder or some other person, or perhaps of a commodity that has been converted into money even though it has not yet been bought (as in the case of revenue), such as the landlord (his forebears, etc.) [96] represents. Here the flowing back of the money only indicates that the person who has paid out the money for commodities, the person who has thrown the money into circulation, pulls back the money out of circulation by the sale of another commodity that he throws into circulation.

The very same £1,000 we are thinking of could in one day pass through forty or fifty hands, from capitalist to capitalist, and [it would] only transfer capital from one to the other. Machinery [goes] to the iron producer, iron to the peasant, grain to the maker of starch or spirits, and so on. In the end it might again come into the hands of the machine builder, and pass from him to the iron producer, and so on, and thus it might circulate a capital of £40,000 or more and might continually flow back to whoever first paid it out. M. Proudhon concludes from this that that part of the profit made on this £40,000 which consists of interest on money, and is therefore paid out by the different capitalists—for example, by the machine builder to the man who lent him £1,000, by the iron producer to the man who lent him £1,000 which he spent long ago for coal, etc., or in wages, etc.—that these £1,000 yield the *total interest* that the £40,000 brings in. So that if the interest was 5 per cent, £2,000 in interest. From which he makes the correct calculation that the £1,000 have brought in 200 per cent. And he is a critic of political economy par excellence!*

But although M—C—M, representing the money circulation between capitalist and labourer, in itself does not imply any act of reproduction, nevertheless this is implied by the continuous repetition of this act, the continuity of the return circuit. There cannot be a buyer continually becoming a seller without the reproduction of the commodity which he sells. In fact, this holds good for everyone except those who live on rent or interest or taxes. But in some cases the return movement M—C—M always takes place if the transaction is to be completed—as in the case of the capitalist in relation to the labourer, or landlord or money-lender (with these latter, there is a simple return of the money). In other cases the act is completed when commodities are bought, when the movement C—M—C has been concluded, as in the case of the labourer. It is this act which he continually renews. His initiative is always as seller, not as buyer. The same holds good for all money circulation ||429| which is merely expenditure of revenue. The capitalist himself, for example, consumes a certain amount each year. He has converted his commodity into money, in order to pay out this money for commodities

* ||437| The passage from Proudhon referred to earlier runs: "The amount of mortgage debts, according to the best-informed writers, is 12 milliards; some put it as high as 16 milliards. The amount of debts on note of hand, at least 6. Limited-liability companies, about 2. The public debt, 8 milliards. Total: 28 milliards. All these debts—note this point—have their source in money lent, or deemed to be lent, at 4, at 5, at 6, at 8, at 12, and up to 15 per cent. I take 6 per cent as the average interest, as far as concerns the first three categories: that would be, then, on 20 milliards, 1,200 millions. Add the interest on the public debt, about 400 millions: in all, 1,600 millions annual interest, for a capital of 1 milliard" (p. 152). That is to say, 160 per cent. For "the amount of ready money, I will not say existing, but circulating in France, including the cash balance of the Bank, does not exceed 1 milliard, according to the most usual estimate" (p. 151). "When the exchange has been completed, the money is once more available, and can therefore give rise to a new loan.... The money-capital, going from exchange to exchange, always returns to its source, and it follows that it can always be reloaned by the same hand and always profits the same person" (pp. 153-54). *Gratuité du crédit. Discussion entre M. Fr. Bastiat et M. Proudhon*, Paris, 1850.[97] |437||

which he wants for his final consumption. Here there is C—M—C, and there is no return of the money to him; but the return is to the seller (the shopkeeper for example), whose capital is replaced by the expenditure of revenue.

Now we have seen that an exchange takes place, a circulation of revenue against revenue. The butcher buys bread from the baker; the baker meat from the butcher; both consume their revenue. They do not pay for the meat that the butcher himself eats or the bread that the baker himself eats. Each of them consumes this part of his revenue in kind. It is however possible that the meat bought by the baker from the butcher replaces not the latter's capital but his revenue—that part of the meat sold by him which not only represents his profit but the part of his profit which he wants to consume himself, as revenue. The bread that the butcher buys from the baker is also an expenditure of his revenue. If the two run accounts with each other, one or the other of them has only to pay the balance. There is no money circulated in respect of the part of their reciprocal purchases and sales which balances out. Let us however assume that the baker has to pay the balance and that this balance represents revenue for the butcher. Then he spends the money from the baker on other articles of consumption. Assuming that this is £10, which he spends with the tailor. If the £10 represents revenue for the tailor, he spends it in a similar way; in turn, he buys bread with it and so on. In this way the money flows back to the baker, no longer however as a replacement of revenue, but as a replacement of capital.

A question that can still be raised is: in M—C—M, as carried through by the capitalist, when it represents self-expanding value, the capitalist draws more money out of circulation than he threw into it. (This was what the miser actually wanted to do but did not succeed in doing. For he does not draw more value in the form of gold and silver out of circulation than he threw into it in the form of commodities. He possesses more value in the form of money, whereas previously he had more value in the form of commodities.) The total production costs of his commodity are £1,000. He sells it for £1,200, because his commodity now contains 20 per cent or one-fifth unpaid labour—labour that he has not paid for but nevertheless sold. How then is it possible for all capitalists, the class of industrial capitalists, continually to draw more money out of circulation than they put into it? First it can be said that on the other hand the capitalist continually puts in more than he draws out. His fixed capital had to be paid for. But he sells it only in the measure that he consumes it, only bit by bit. It always enters only to a much smaller extent into the *value* of the commodity, while it enters in its entirety into the process of producing the commodity. If its circulation is 10 years, only one-tenth of it enters annually into the commodity, and no money circulates in respect of the other nine-tenths, as this nine-tenths does not in any way come into circulation in the form of a commodity. That is the first point.

We will consider this problem later, [98] and meanwhile return to Quesnay.

But first one other point. The return of bank-notes to a bank which discounts bills or makes advances in notes is quite a different phenomenon from the return of money which we have been considering up to now. In this case the transformation of the commodity into money is anticipated. It receives the form of money before it is sold, perhaps before it is produced. Or perhaps it has already been sold (for bills of exchange). *In any case* it has not yet been *paid for*, not yet reconverted into money. This transformation is therefore in any case anticipated. As soon as it is sold (or *deemed* to be sold) the money flows back to the bank, either in its own notes, which thus come back out of circulation, or in notes of other banks, which are then exchanged for its own (between the bankers)—so that then the notes of both are withdrawn from circulation, return to their starting-point—or in gold and silver. If this gold and silver is demanded for bank-notes which are in some third person's hands, the notes come back. If the notes are not converted, a similar quantity of gold and silver is taken out of circulation, and now lies in the bank's reserves instead of the notes.

In all these cases the process is this: the existence of the money (transformation of the commodity into money) was anticipated. As soon as it is actually transformed into money, the transformation into money takes place a second time. This second existence of it as money, however, returns to the starting-point—it cancels out, takes the place of its first existence as money, and comes back out of circulation to the bank. It is perhaps the *same identical* quantity of notes that expressed its first existence which now expresses its second. The bill of exchange for example has been discounted by a yarn manufacturer. He has received the bill of exchange from the weaver. With the £1,000 he pays for coal, raw cotton, etc. The various hands through which these notes pass in payment for their commodities finally spend them on linen, and so the notes come to the weaver, who on the day the bill matures pays the spinner the identical notes, and the spinner in turn takes them back to the bank. It is by no means necessary that the second (posthumous) transformation of the commodity into money—after the transformation in anticipation—||430| should be carried through in different money from the first. And so it seems as if the spinner has in fact got nothing, since he borrowed notes, and the end of the process is that he gets them back again and returns them to the issuer. In fact however these identical notes have served as means of circulation and means of payment during this period, and the spinner has used them in part to pay his debts, and in part to buy goods needed for the reproduction of the yarn, and in this way he has realised a surplus (through the exploitation of his workmen) a part of which he can now pay back to the bank. Likewise in money, since more money has flowed back to him than he had expended, advanced, laid out. How? That again brings us to the question we had meanwhile held over. [99]

[4. Circulation between Farmer and Manufacturer According to the Tableau Économique]

So back to Quesnay. We come now to the third and fourth acts of circulation.

L(the landlord) buys manufactured commodities from S (sterile class, manufacturer)[100] (line a—c in the Tableau [101]) for 1 milliard. Here 1 milliard in money, and commodities to the same amount, circulate. <Because what takes place is a single act of exchange. If L bought from S in instalments and similarly received his rent from F (the farmer) in instalments, the 1 milliard of manufactured commodities could be bought say with 100 millions. For L buys manufactured commodities from S for 100 millions; S buys means of subsistence from F for 100 millions; F pays 100 millions of rent to L; and when this had occurred ten times, ten times 100 millions of commodities would have passed from S to L, and from F to S, and ten times 100 millions from F to L. The whole circulation would then have been carried out with 100 millions. If F however pays the rent in a single payment, a part of the 1 milliard which is now in the possession of S

and of the 1 milliard which is again in F's possession might lie in their money-boxes, and the other part be in circulation. > Commodities to the value of 1 milliard have now passed from S to L; on the other hand, money to the value of 1 milliard has passed from L to S. This is simple circulation. Money and commodities merely change hands in the reverse direction. But in addition to the 1 milliard of means of subsistence which the farmer has sold to L and which have thus gone into consumption, the 1 milliard of manufactured commodities which S has sold to L have also gone into consumption. It must be noted that these existed before the new harvest. (Otherwise L could not buy them with the product of the new harvest.)

S for his part now buys means of subsistence to the value of 1 milliard from F [line c—d in the Tableau]. Now a *second one-fifth of the gross product* has fallen out of circulation and into consumption. As between S and F, the 1 milliard functions as means of circulation. But at the same time two things take place in this transaction which do not take place in the process between S and L. In that process S reconverted into money one part of his product—manufactured goods to the amount of 1 milliard. But in the exchange with F he transforms the money again into means of subsistence (which for Quesnay are equivalent to wages), and in this way replaces the capital which he had expended in wages and consumed. This retransformation of the 1 milliard into means of subsistence expresses, in the case of L, mere consumption, but in the case of S it expresses industrial consumption, reproduction; for he retransforms a part of his commodity into one of the elements in its production—means of subsistence. The one metamorphosis of the commodity, its retransformation from money into commodity, thus in this case expresses at the same time the beginning of its *real*, not merely *formal*, metamorphosis—the beginning of its reproduction, the beginning of its retransformation into its own production elements; in this transaction there is at the same time metamorphosis of the capital. But for L. revenue is merely converted from the form of money into the form of commodity. This implies only consumption.

In the second place, however, since S buys means of subsistence from F for 1 milliard, the second 1 milliard which F paid as money-rent to L returns to F. But it only returns to him because he draws it back out of circulation, buys it back, with an equivalent—1 milliard in commodities. It is the same as if the landlord had bought from him 1 milliard of means of subsistence (in addition to the first milliard); that is to say, as if the landlord had had the second part of his money-rent delivered by the farmer in commodities, and had then exchanged these commodities for commodities from S. S only lifts for L the second part of the 2 milliards in commodities which F has paid to L in money. If payment had been in kind, F would have given L 2 milliards in means of subsistence; L would have consumed 1 milliard of these himself, and exchanged the other 1 milliard in means of subsistence with S, for the latter's manufactured goods. In this case there would only have been: (1) transfer of the 2 milliards in means of subsistence from F to L; (2) a barter transaction between L and S, in which the former exchanges 1 milliard in means of subsistence against 1 milliard in manufactured goods, and vice versa.

But instead of this, four acts have taken place: ||431| (1) transfer of 2 milliards in money from F to L; (2) L buys means of subsistence for 1 milliard from F; the money flows back to F, serving as means of circulation; (3) L buys manufactured goods from S for 1 milliard in money; the money functions as means of circulation; changing hands in the reverse direction to the goods; (4) with the 1 milliard in money, S buys means of subsistence from F; the money functions as means of circulation. For S, it at the same time circulates as capital. It flows back to F because now the second 1 milliard in means of subsistence is lifted—for which the landlord held a note of assignment from him. The money however does not come back to him directly from the landlord, but only after it has served as means of circulation between L and S, and in between, before it lifts the 1 milliard of victuals, has on its passage lifted 1 milliard in manufactures, and transferred them from the manufacturer to the landlord. The conversion of his commodity into money (in the exchange with the landlord) as well as the following conversion of money into victuals (in the exchange with the farmer) are, on the part of S, the metamorphosis of his capital, first into the form of money, and secondly into the form of the constitutive elements necessary to the reproduction of the capital.

The result of the four acts of circulation up to this point is therefore: the landlord has spent his revenue, half on means of subsistence, half on manufactured goods. By these transactions, the 2 milliards he received as rent in the form of money have been spent. Half of it flows back to the farmer from him direct, and half indirect, via S. S however has parted with one part of his finished goods, and has replaced this part with means of subsistence, that is, with an element needed for reproduction. With these processes completed, the circulation is at an end as far as the landlord comes into it. But the following have passed out of circulation into consumption—partly unproductive consumption, partly industrial—(the landlord has partially replaced the capital of S by spending his revenue): (1) 1 milliard of means of subsistence (product of the new harvest); (2) 1 milliard of manufactured goods (product of the previous year's harvest); (3) 1 milliard of means of subsistence which enter into reproduction, that is, into the production of the goods which S next year will have to exchange against half the landlord's rent.

The 2 milliards in money are now again in the hands of the farmer. He then buys goods for 1 milliard from S to replace his annual and original advances, in so far as these consist partly of tools, etc., and partly of manufactured goods which he consumes during the process of production. This is a simple process of circulation. It puts 1 milliard into the hands of S, while the second part of his product existing in the form of a commodity is converted into money. On both sides there is metamorphosis of capital. The farmer's 1 milliard is reconverted into elements of production needed for reproduction. The finished goods of S are reconverted into money; they pass through the *formal* metamorphosis from commodity into money, without which the capital cannot be reconverted into its production elements, and therefore also cannot be reproduced. This is the fifth circulation process. *One milliard of manufactured goods* (product of the previous year's harvest) (a'—b') [102] fall out of circulation into reproductive consumption.

Finally S reconverts the 1 milliard in money, in which form half of his commodities now exist, into the other half of his conditions of production—raw materials, etc. (a''—b''). This is simple circulation. For S, it is at the same time the metamorphosis of his capital into the form suitable for its reproduction; for F, it is the reconversion of his product into money. Now the last one-fifth of the gross product falls out of circulation into consumption.

That is to say: one-fifth goes into reproduction for the farmer, and does not come into circulation; the landlord consumes one-fifth (that makes two-fifths); S gets two-fifths; in all, four-fifths. [103]

Here there is an obvious gap in the explanation. Quesnay seems to reckon like this: F gives L (line a—b) 1 milliard (one-fifth) in means of subsistence. With 1 milliard of his raw materials he replaces S's fund (a″—b″). And 1 milliard in means of subsistence form wages for S, which he adds as value to the commodities and consumes in food while he is doing it (c—d). And 1 milliard remains in reproduction (a′), not entering into circulation. Finally, 1 milliard of the product replaces advances (a′—b′). Only he overlooks the fact that S buys for the 1 milliard in manufactured goods, neither means of subsistence nor raw materials from the farmer, but pays back to him his own money. In fact he sets out from the presupposition that the farmer possesses 2 milliards in money in addition to his gross product, and that this money is the total fund from which the money in circulation is provided.

He also forgets that in addition to the 5 milliards in gross product, a further 2 milliards of gross product exist in manufactured commodities produced before the new harvest. For the 5 milliards represent only the total annual production, ||432| the total crop produced by the farmers, but not the gross product of manufacture, the reproductive elements for which have to be replaced out of this year's harvest.

We thus have: (1) 2 milliards in money in the farmer's hands; (2) 5 milliards in gross product of the land; (3) 2 milliards in manufactured goods. That is, 2 milliards in money, and 7 milliards in product (agricultural and industrial). The circulation process, put briefly, is as follows (F=farmer, L=landlord, S=manufacturer, sterile):

F pays L 2 milliards in money for rent; L buys from F means of subsistence for 1 milliard. So one-fifth of the farmer's gross product is disposed of. At the same time, 1 milliard in money flows back to him. L moreover buys goods from S for 1 milliard. By this transaction, one-half of S's gross product is disposed of. In return for it, he has 1 milliard in money. With this money he buys 1 milliard of means of subsistence from F. By this transaction he replaces one-half of the reproductive elements of his capital. This disposes of another one-fifth of the farmer's gross product. At the same time the farmer finds himself again in possession of the 2 milliards in money, the price of the 2 milliards in means of subsistence which he has sold to L and S. F now buys goods from S for 1 milliard, which replace for him half of his advances. So the other half of the manufacturer's gross product is disposed of. Finally, the latter, S, buys raw materials from the farmer for the last 1 milliard in money; thereby a third one-fifth of the farmer's gross product is disposed of, and the second half of the reproductive elements of the capital of S is replaced; but also 1 milliard flows back to the farmer. The latter finds himself therefore again in possession of the 2 milliards, which is in order, since Quesnay thinks of him as the capitalist, in relation to whom L is merely a receiver of revenue and S merely a wage-earner. If he paid L and S directly in his product, he would not part with any money. If he pays out in money, they buy his product with it, and the money flows back to him. This is the formal return circuit of money to the industrial capitalist, who as buyer opens the whole business and brings it to an end. Moreover, one-fifth of the advances belongs to reproduction. One-fifth of the means of subsistence, however, which has not entered into circulation at all, remains to be disposed of.

[5. Circulation of Commodities and Circulation of Money in the Tableau Économique. Different Cases in Which the Money Flows Back to Its Starting-Point]

S buys from the farmer means of subsistence for 1 milliard and raw materials for 1 milliard; and on the other hand F buys from him only 1 milliard of commodities to replace his advances. So S has to pay a balance of 1 milliard which in the final instance he pays with the 1 milliard he has received from L. Quesnay seems to confuse this *payment* of 1 milliard to F with the *purchase* of F's product to the amount of 1 milliard. Reference must be made to the Abbé Baudeau's explanations on this point.[104]

In fact (on our calculation) the 2 milliards have only served to: (1) pay rent to the amount of 2 milliards in money; (2) circulate 3 milliards of the farmer's gross product (1 milliard means of subsistence to L, 2 milliards means of subsistence and raw materials to S) and to circulate 2 milliards of the gross product of S (1 milliard of it to L, who consumes it, and 1 milliard to F, who consumes it reproductively).

In the last purchase (a″—b″) in which S buys raw materials from F, he pays him back in money.

||433| So once more:

S has received from L 1 milliard in money. With this 1 milliard in money he buys means of subsistence from F to that amount. With the same 1 milliard in money F buys commodities from S. With the same 1 milliard in money S buys raw products from F.

Or, S buys from F raw materials for 1 milliard in money, and means of subsistence for 1 milliard in money. F buys goods from S for 1 milliard [in money]. In this case 1 milliard flows back to S, but only because it was assumed that in addition to the 1 milliard in money he receives from the landlord, and the 1 milliard in goods that he still has to sell, he had over and above this another 1 milliard in money which he himself had thrown into circulation. Instead of 1 milliard circulating the goods between him and the farmer, on this assumption 2 milliards would have been used for it. Then 1 milliard returns to S. For he makes purchases from the farmer for 2 milliards in money. The latter buys 1 milliard from him, for which he pays him back half the money he had received from him.

In the first case S buys in two stages. First he pays out 1 milliard; this flows back to him from F; and then he pays it out once more definitively to F, and so nothing comes back.

In the second case, on the other hand, S makes a single purchase for 2 milliards. If then F makes a return purchase for 1 milliard, this remains with S. The circulation would have used 2 milliards instead of 1 milliard, because in the first case the 1 milliard, by rotating twice, realised 2 milliards in commodities. In the second case 2 milliards, in one rotation, also [realised] 2 milliards in commodities. If the farmer now pays back 1 milliard to S, S has not got more than in the first case. For he has thrown into circulation, in addition to 1 milliard in commodities, also 1 milliard in money from his own fund which existed prior to the circulation process. He has put it out into circulation, and so it flows back to him.

In the first case: S [buys] 1 milliard of commodities from F, for 1 milliard in money; F [buys] 1 milliard in goods from S, [for] 1 milliard in money; S [buys] 1 milliard of commodities from F, [for] 1 milliard in money; so that F keeps 1 milliard.

In the second case: S [buys] 2 milliards of commodities from F, for 2 milliards in money; F [buys] 1 milliard of goods from S, for 1 milliard in money. The farmer, as before, keeps the 1 milliard. S however gets back the 1 milliard of capital advanced by him to circulation, it is thrown back to him by circulation. S buys commodities from F for 2 milliards; F buys goods from S for 1 milliard. Therefore in any event S has to pay a balance of 1 milliard, but not more than this. Since, by way of paying this balance, he had paid F 2 milliards as a result of the particular form of circulation, F pays him back this 1 milliard, while in the first case he does not return any money to him.

In the first case S makes purchases from F for 2 milliards, and F from S for 1 milliard. So in both cases the balance in F's favour is 1 milliard. But this balance is paid to him in such a way that his own money flows back to him, because S first buys 1 milliard from F, then F 1 milliard from S, and finally S 1 milliard from F. In these transactions 1 milliard has circulated 3 milliards. But in the aggregate the value in circulation (if the money is real money) has been 4 milliards, 3 milliards in commodities and 1 milliard in money. The amount of money originally thrown into circulation (to pay F) and circulating was never more than 1 milliard—that is, never more than the balance which S had to pay to F. Because F bought from him to the amount of 1 milliard before he buys from F to the amount of 1 milliard for the second time, S can pay his balance with this 1 milliard.

In the second case S throws 2 milliards into circulation. It is true that with it he buys 2 milliards in commodities from F. These 2 milliards are here required as means of circulation, and are paid out against an equivalent in commodities. But F buys back goods for 1 milliard from S. One milliard therefore returns to S, as the balance which he has to pay to F is only 1 milliard and not 2 milliards. He has now replaced for F 1 milliard in commodities, and so F must pay him back the 1 milliard, which *now* he would have paid him in money for nothing. This case is remarkable enough to spend a moment on it.

There are various possible cases of the circulation assumed above of 3 milliards in commodities, of which 2 milliards are means of subsistence and 1 milliard manufactures; we must however note: *first* that on Quesnay's assumption there is 1 milliard in money in the hands of S and 1 milliard of money in the hands of F at the moment when the circulation between the two of them begins; *secondly*, we will assume by way of illustrating the point that in addition to the 1 milliard which S receives from L, S has in his till another 1 milliard in money.

||434| I. *First*: The case as Quesnay puts it. S buys 1 milliard in commodities from F, for 1 milliard in money; with the 1 milliard in money thus received from S, F buys 1 milliard in commodities from S; finally S, with the 1 milliard in money he has got back in this way, buys 1 milliard of commodities from F. F is therefore left with the 1 milliard in money which to him represents capital (in fact, along with the other 1 milliard in money

which he has got back from L, it forms the revenue with which again next year he pays the rent in money; that is, 2 milliards in money). 1 milliard in money has here circulated three times—from S to F, from F to S, from S to F—and each time in exchange for 1 milliard in commodities, that is, for 3 milliards in all. If the money itself has value, values to a total of 4 milliards are in circulation. Money here functions only as means of circulation; but for F, in whose hands it finally remains, it is transformed into money and possibly into capital.

II. *Secondly*: The money functions merely as means of payment. In this case S, who buys 2 milliards in commodities from F, and F, who buys 1 milliard in commodities from S, settle accounts with each other. At the close of the transaction S has to pay a balance of 1 milliard in money. As in the former case, 1 milliard in money comes into F's money-box, but without having served as means of circulation. The money is a transfer of capital for him, as it only replaces his capital of 1 milliard in commodities. As before, values amounting to 4 milliards are in circulation. But instead of three movements of 1 milliard in money, there has only been one, and the money has only paid for an amount of values in commodity form that is equal to itself. In the former case, it paid for three times as much. What would be saved as compared with case I would be the two superfluous movements of circulation.

III. *Thirdly*: To start with F comes forward as the buyer with the 1 milliard in money (which he has had from L), and buys commodities from S for 1 milliard. Instead of lying fallow with him as a hoard for payment of the next rent, now the 1 milliard circulates. S has now 2 milliards in money (1 milliard from L and 1 milliard from F). With these 2 milliards in money he buys commodities to the amount of 2 milliards from F. Now values to the amount of 5 milliards have been in circulation (3 milliards in commodities, 2 milliards in money). There has been a circulation of 1 milliard in money and 1 milliard in commodities, and a circulation of 2 milliards in money and 2 milliards in commodities. Of these 2 milliards in money, the milliard originating with the farmer circulates twice, the milliard originating with S only once. Now 2 milliards in money return to F, of which however only 1 milliard settles his balance; the other 1 milliard in money, which he himself had thrown into circulation because he took the initiative as buyer, flows back to him through circulation.

IV. *Fourthly*: S buys at once 2 milliards in commodities from

F, with 2 milliards in money (1 milliard from L, and 1 milliard which he puts himself into circulation from his till). F buys back from S 1 milliard in commodities, thus returning to him 1 milliard in money; and F holds, as before, 1 milliard in money to settle the balance between him and S. Values to the amount of 5 milliards have circulated. There are two acts of circulation.

Of the 2 milliards in money which S returns to F, 1 milliard represents the money which F himself threw into circulation, and only 1 milliard the money which S threw into circulation. Here 2 milliards in money instead of 1 milliard in money come back to F, but in fact he gets only 1 milliard, as he himself had thrown the other 1 milliard into circulation. That is, in case III. In case IV 1 milliard in money returns to S, but it is the 1 milliard which he got from his money-box, not from selling his commodities to L, and himself threw into circulation.

In case I and indeed in case II there is never more than 1 milliard in money circulating; but in case I it circulates three times and in case II it only once changes hands; this is merely due to the fact that in case II a high development of credit, and consequently economy in payments, is assumed; while in case I the movement is rapid; however, each time the money functions as means of circulation, and therefore the value at the two poles must each time appear twice, once in money and once in commodity. In case III and IV 2 milliards circulate, instead of 1 milliard as in I and II. This is because on one occasion in both cases (in case III by S as buyer who closes the circulation process, in case IV by S as buyer who opens the circulation process) commodity values to the amount of 2 milliards are at a single stroke thrown into circulation; that is, 2 milliards of commodities enter into circulation in a single act; it is assumed, moreover, that the commodities have to be paid for on the spot and not after the balance has been struck.

The most interesting thing about the movement is however the 1 milliard in money which in case III is left in the hands of the farmer, in case IV in the hands of the manufacturer, although in both cases the balance of 1 milliard is paid to the farmer, and he gets not a farthing more in case III, and not a farthing less in case IV. In these transactions, of course, the exchange is always an exchange of equivalents, and when we speak of a balance we mean only the equivalent value which is paid for in money instead of in commodities.

In case III F throws 1 milliard in money into circulation, and gets in exchange for it from S the equivalent in commodities, or 1 milliard in commodities. But then S buys commodities from him for 2 milliards in money. The first 1 milliard in money which he threw in thus comes back to him, because 1 milliard in commodities has been taken from him in exchange. This 1 milliard in commodities is paid for with the money which he had paid out. He gets the second 1 milliard in money in payment for the second 1 milliard in commodities. This balance is owed to him in money, because he had only bought in all 1 milliard of commodities, and commodities to the value of 2 milliards had been bought from him.

||435| In case IV S throws 2 milliards in money into circulation at once, for which he takes from F commodities for 2 milliards. With the money which S himself had paid him, F in turn buys from S commodities for 1 milliard and so the 1 milliard in money returns to S.

In case IV: S in fact gives F 1 milliard in commodities (the equivalent for 1 milliard in money) and 2 milliards in money, that is, 3 milliards; but S gets from F only 2 milliards in commodities. F has consequently to return to him 1 milliard in money.

In case III: F gives S in commodities the equivalent of 2 milliards in money, and 1 milliard in money. That is, 3 milliards in money. But he gets from S only 1 milliard in commodities, the equivalent of 1 milliard in money. S has consequently to return to him 2 milliards in money; he pays back 1 milliard in the money which F himself threw into circulation, and he himself throws 1 milliard into circulation. He keeps the balance of 1 milliard in money, but cannot keep 2 milliards in money.

In both cases S receives 2 milliards in commodities, and F 1 milliard in commodities plus 1 milliard in money, that is to say, the balance in money. In case III, in addition to this, another 1 milliard comes to F, but this is only the excess of the money which he has thrown into circulation over what he has drawn from circulation in commodities. Similarly with S in case IV.

In both cases S has to pay a balance of 1 milliard in money, because he takes commodities to the value of 2 milliards out of circulation, and puts into it commodities only to the value of 1 milliard. In both cases F has to receive a balance of 1 milliard in money, because he has thrown 2 milliards in commodities into circulation and only drawn from it 1 milliard in commodities; the second 1 milliard must therefore be paid in money to him. In both cases, it is only this 1 milliard in money that can finally change hands. Since however 2 milliards are actually in circulation, this must flow back to the person who put it into circulation; and this holds good whether F, in addition to receiving a balance of 1 milliard out of circulation, has thrown into it another 1 milliard in money; or whether S, who has to pay only a balance of 1 milliard in money, has in addition advanced another 1 milliard in money.

In case III 1 milliard in money comes into circulation in excess of the quantity of money that would under different circumstances be needed for the circulation of this quantity of commodities, because F comes forward as the first buyer, and must therefore throw money into circulation, whatever his ultimate position may be. In case IV, in the same way, 2 milliards in money come into circulation, instead of only 1 milliard as in II, because first S comes forward as buyer at the outset, and secondly buys 2 milliards all at once. In both cases the money that *circulates* between these buyers and sellers can finally only be equal to the balance which one of them has to pay. For the money which S or F has expended in excess of this amount is paid back to him.

Let us assume that F buys commodities from S to the value of 2 milliards. This case, then, would look like this: F gives S 1 milliard in money for commodities. S buys commodities from F to the value of 2 milliards in money, as a result of which the first 1 milliard returns to F and 1 milliard into the bargain. F in turn buys commodities from S for 1 milliard in money, which brings this money back to S. At the end of the process F would have commodities to the amount of 2 milliards and the 1 milliard that he had originally, before the circulation process began; and S commodities for 2 milliards and 1 milliard in money which he too originally had. The 1 milliard in money of F, and the 1 milliard in money of S, would have played their role only as means of circulation and then would have flowed back—as money or in this case also as capital—to both the persons who had advanced them. Had they both used money as means of payment, they would have set off 2 milliards in commodities against 2 milliards in commodities; their accounts would have cancelled out and not a farthing would have circulated between them.

Thus the money which circulates as means of circulation between two persons who confront each other mutually as buyers and sellers returns to its source; there are three cases in which it can circulate.

[*First*:] The commodity values supplied balance each other. In this case the money returns to the person who advanced it to circulation and in this way used his capital to meet the costs of circulation. For example, if F and S each buys commodities for 2 milliards from the other, and S opens the dance, he buys commodities from F for 2 milliards in money. F returns to him the 2 milliards in money, buying with it 2 milliards in commodities from him. Thus S has both before and after the transaction 2 milliards in commodities and 2 milliards in money. Or when, as in the case cited previously, both advance the means of circulation to an equal amount, each gets back what he had advanced to circulation—as above, 1 milliard in money to F and 1 milliard to S.

Secondly: The commodity values exchanged between the two parties do not cancel each other out. There is a balance to be paid in money. If, as above in case I, the circulation of the commodities has taken place in such a way that no more money has entered *into circulation* than is required for the payment of this balance—it being always only this sum that passes to and fro between the two parties—then it comes finally into the hands of the last seller, in whose favour the balance is.

Thirdly: The commodity values exchanged between the two parties are not equal to each other; there is a balance to be paid; but the circulation of the commodities takes place in such a form that more money circulates than is required to settle the balance; in this case the money in excess of this balance returns to the party who has advanced it. In case III to the man who receives the balance, in case IV to the one who has to pay it.

In the second category listed above the money only *returns* when the receiver of the balance is the first buyer, as for example between worker and capitalist. It changes hands, as [in case] II, when the other party comes forward as the first buyer.

||436| <Of course, all this only takes place on the assumption that the definite quantity of commodities is bought and sold between the same persons, so that each of them is alternately buyer and seller in relation to the other one. On the other hand let us assume that the 3 milliards of commodities are equally distributed among the commodity owners. A, A′, A″, the sellers, and they are confronted by the buyers B, B′, B″. If the three purchases take place simultaneously, that is to say, alongside each other, 3 thousand in money[105] must circulate, so that each A is in possession of 1 thousand in money and each B is in possession of 1 thousand in commodities. If the purchases follow each other, succeeding each other in time, the circulation of the same

1 thousand in money can only effect these if the metamorphoses of the commodities are interwoven, that is to say, when some persons function as buyers and sellers, even if not [in relation] to the same persons as in the case above, but as buyer in relation to one person, and as seller in relation to the other. Thus for example: (1) A sells to B for 1 thousand in money; (2) A buys with this 1 thousand from B′; (3) B′ with the 1 thousand in money buys from A′; (4) A′ with the 1 thousand in money from B″; (5) B″ with the 1 thousand in money from A″. The money would have changed hands five times between the six persons; but also commodities to the value of 5 thousand would have circulated. If commodities for 3 thousand are to be circulated, it would be like this: (1) A [buys] from B for 1 thousand in money; (2) B from A′ for 1 thousand in money; (3) A′ from B′ for 1 thousand in money. Three changes of place as between four persons. It is M—C. >

The cases set out above do not contradict the law explained earlier: "that with a given rapidity of circulation of money and a given total sum of prices of commodities the quantity of the circulating medium is determined" (I, p. 85).[106] In example 1 above, 1 thousand in money circulates three times, and in fact it circulates commodities to the amount of 3 thousand. The amount of money in circulation is consequently

$$\frac{3{,}000 \text{ (sum of prices)}}{3 \text{ (velocity)}} \text{ or } \frac{3{,}000 \text{ (sum of prices)}}{3 \text{ cycles}} = 1{,}000 \text{ money.}$$

In case III or IV the total prices of the commodities in circulation are, it is true, equal to 3,000 in money; but the rapidity of circulation is different. 2,000 in money circulates once, that is, 1,000 in money plus 1,000 in money. Of the 2,000, however, 1,000 circulates once more. 2,000 in money circulates two-thirds of the 3,000 in commodities, and half of it, 1,000 in money, circulates another third; one 1,000 in money circulates twice, but another 1,000 in money circulates only once. The twofold circulation of 1,000 in money realises commodities whose prices are equal to 2,000 in money; and the single circulation of 1,000 in money realises commodities whose prices are equal to 1,000 in money—both together, equal to 3,000 in commodities. What then is the rapidity of circulation of the money in relation to the commodities which it circulates in this case? The 2,000 in money makes $1^{1}/_{2}$ cycles (this is the same thing as *first* the total sum circulates once, and then half of it again completes one cycle), that is, $^3/_2$. And in fact:

$$\frac{3{,}000 \text{ (sum of prices)}}{^3/_2 \text{ cycles}} = 2{,}000 \text{ in money.}$$

What is it then that determines the *different rapidity* of circulation of the money in this case?

Both in III and IV the difference arises from the fact that, in contrast to I—where the total amount of prices of the commodities circulating each time is never greater and never smaller than $^1/_3$ of the total prices of the aggregate quantity of commodities which circulate, commodities only to the amount of 1,000 in money circulate at any time—in III and IV, however, commodities for 2,000 circulate once, and commodities for 1,000 circulate once, that is, once two-thirds of the existing quantity of commodities, and once one-third. For the same reason, larger varieties of coin must circulate in wholesale trade than in retail trade.

As I have already observed (I, " [The] Circulation of Money"[107]), the reflux of the money shows in the first place that the *buyer has in turn become seller*; and in fact it makes no difference whether in so doing he sells to the same person from whom he has bought, or not. If however the buying and selling is between the same persons, then the phenomena appear which have been the occasion of so many errors (Destutt de Tracy[108]). The buyer becoming seller shows that new commodities are to be sold. Continuity in the circulation of commodities—tantamount to its constant renewal (I, p. 78[109])—is, therefore, reproduction. The buyer can become in turn seller—as in the case of the manufacturer in relation to the labourer—without this denoting an act of reproduction. It is only the continuity, the repetition of this reflux, in relation to which it can be said that it denotes reproduction.

The reflux of money, when it represents the reconversion of the capital into its money form, necessarily shows the end of one cycle [i.e., turnover] and the beginning again of new reproduction, if the capital as such continues the process. In this case too he [the capitalist], as in all other cases, was the seller, C—M, and then became buyer, M—C; but it is only in M that his capital again possesses the form in which it can be exchanged for its reproductive elements, and here the C represents these reproductive elements. M—C here represents the transformation of the money-capital into productive or industrial capital.

Furthermore, as we have seen, the reflux of the money to its starting-point may show that the money balance in a series of purchases and sales is in favour of the buyer with whom the series of these processes opened. F buys from S for 1,000 in money. S buys from F 2,000 in money. Here the 1,000 in money flows back to F. As for the other 1,000, there is merely a change of place of the money between S and F.

||437| Finally, however, a reflux of the money to its starting-point may take place without indicating payment of a balance, both (1) when the reciprocal payments cancel each other out, and consequently there is no balance to be paid in money; and (2) when the transactions do *not* cancel out, and therefore a balance has to be paid. See the cases analysed above. In all these cases it makes no difference whether for example the same S confronts F; S representing here in relation to F and F to S the total number of those selling to him and buying from him (exactly as in the example where payment of a balance is indicated by the reflux of the money). In all these cases the money flows back to the person who so to speak has advanced it to circulation. It has done its job in circulation, like bank-notes, and comes back to the person who laid it out. *Here it is only means of circulation. The final capitalists settle with each other, and so it comes back to the one who paid it out.*

We have therefore still to deal later on with the question we have held over; the capitalist draws more money out of circulation than he threw into it.[110]

[6. Significance of the Tableau Économique in the History of Political Economy]

Back to Quesnay:

Adam Smith cites with some irony the Marquis de Mirabeau's hyperbolical statement:

> "There have been since the world began three great inventions.... The first is the invention of *writing*.... The second is *the invention* (!) of *money*.... The third is the *economical table*, the result of the other two, which completes them both" ([Smith, *Wealth of Nations*, O.U.P. edition, Vol. II, p. 300], Garnier, t. III, l. IV, ch. IX, p. 540).

But in fact it was an attempt to portray the whole production process of capital as a *process of reproduction*, with circulation merely as the form of this reproductive process; and the circulation of money only as a phase in the circulation of capital; at the same time to include in this reproductive process the origin of revenue, the exchange between capital and revenue, the relation between reproductive consumption and final consumption; and to include in the circulation of capital the circulation between consumers and producers (in fact between capital and revenue); and finally to present the circulation between the two great divisions of productive labour—raw material production and manufacture—as phases of this reproductive process; and all this depicted in a *Tableau* which in fact consists of no more than five lines which link together six points of departure or return—[and this was] in the second third of the eighteenth century, the period when political economy was in its infancy—this was an extremely brilliant conception, incontestably the most brilliant for which political economy had up to then been responsible.

As regards the circulation of capital—its reproductive process, the various forms which it assumes in this process of reproduction, the connection between the circulation of capital and circulation in general (that is, not only the exchange of capital for capital, but of capital for revenue)—Adam Smith in fact only took over the inheritance of the Physiocrats and classified and specified more precisely the separate items in the inventory. But his exposition and interpretation of the movement as a whole was hardly as correct as its presentation in outline in the Tableau économique, in spite of Quesnay's false assumptions.

When moreover Adam Smith says of the Physiocrats: "Their works have certainly been of some service to their country" ([*Wealth of Nations*, O.U.P. edition, Vol. II, p. 299], [Garnier], l. c., p. 538), this is an immoderately moderate statement of the significance for example of Turgot, one of the immediate fathers of the French revolution. |437||

[CHAPTER VII]

LINGUET

[EARLY CRITIQUE OF THE BOURGEOIS-LIBERAL VIEW OF THE "FREEDOM" OF THE LABOURER]

||438| Linguet, *Théorie des lois civiles, etc.*, Londres, 1767.

In accordance with the plan of my work socialist and communist writers are entirely excluded from the historical reviews. These reviews are only intended to show on the one hand in what form the political economists criticised each other, and on the other hand the historically determining forms in which the laws of political economy were first stated and further developed. In dealing with surplus-value I therefore exclude such eighteenth-century writers as Brissot, Godwin and the like, and likewise the nineteenth-century socialists and communists. The few socialist writers whom I shall come to speak of in this survey[111] either themselves adopt the standpoint of bourgeois economy or contest it from its own standpoint.

Linguet however is not a socialist. His polemics against the bourgeois-liberal ideals of the Enlighteners, his contemporaries, against the dominion of the bourgeoisie that was then beginning, are given—half-seriously, half-ironically—a reactionary appearance. He defends Asiatic despotism against the civilised European forms of despotism; thus he defends slavery against wage-labour.

Vol. I. The only statement directed against Montesquieu: *l'esprit des lois, c'est la propriété*,*[112] shows the depth of his outlook.

The only economists whom Linguet found to deal with were the Physiocrats.

The rich have taken possession of all the conditions of production; [hence] the *alienation of the conditions of production*, which in their simplest form are the natural elements themselves.

* The spirit of the laws is property.—*Ed.*

"In our civilised countries, all the elements [of nature] are slaves" ([Linguet, *Théorie des lois civiles...*, Londres, 1767], p. 188).

In order to get hold of some of this wealth appropriated by the rich, it must be purchased with heavy labour, which increases the wealth of these rich persons.

"Thus it is that all captive nature has ceased to offer to these children resources of easy access for the maintenance of their life. Its favours must be paid for by assiduous toil, and its gifts by stubborn labours" [p. 188].

(Here—in the gifts of nature—the Physiocratic view is echoed.)

"The rich man, *who has arrogated to himself the exclusive possession of it*, only at this price consents to restore even the smallest part of it to the community. *In order to be allowed to share in its treasures, it is necessary to labour to increase them*" (p. 189). "One must, then, renounce this chimera of liberty" (p. 190). Laws exist in order to "sanctify a primary usurpation" (of private property), "to prevent new usurpations" (p. 192). "They are, as it were, a conspiracy against the greater part of the human race" [p. 195] (that is, against those who own no property). "It is society which has produced the laws, and not the laws which have produced society" (p. 230). "Property existed before the laws" (p. 236).

Society itself—the fact that man lives in society and not as an independent, self-supporting individual—is the root of property, of the laws based on it and of the inevitable slavery.

On the one hand, there were peaceful and isolated husbandmen and shepherds. On the other hand—

"hunters accustomed to live by blood to gather together in bands the more easily to entrap and fell the beasts on which they fed, and to concert together on the division of the spoils" (p. 279). "It is among the hunters that the first signs of society must have appeared" (p. 278). "*Real society came into being at the expense of the shepherds or husbandmen, and was founded on their subjection*" by a band of hunters who had joined hands (p. 289). All duties of society were resolved into commanding and obeying "This degradation of a part of the human race, after it had produced society, gave birth to laws" (p. 294).

Stripped of the conditions of production, the labourers are compelled by need to labour to increase the wealth of others in order themselves to live.

"It is the impossibility of living by any other means that compels our farm labourers to till the soil whose fruits they will not eat, and our masons to construct buildings in which they will not live. It is want that drags them to those markets where they await masters who will do them the kindness of buying them. *It is want that compels them to go down on their knees to the rich man in order to get from him permission to enrich him*" (p. 274).

"Violence, then, has been the first cause of society, and force the first bond that held it together" (p. 302). "Their" (men's) "first care was doubtless to provide themselves with food...the second must have been to seek to *provide themselves with it without labour*" (pp. 307-08). "They could only achieve this by *appropriating to themselves the fruit of other men's labour*" (p. 308). "The first conquerors only made themselves despots so that they could be idle with impunity, and kings, in order to have something to live on: and this greatly narrows and simplifies ..the idea of domination" (p. 309). "Society is born of violence, and property of usurpation" (p. 347). "As soon as there were masters and slaves, society was formed" (p. 343). "From the beginning, the two ||439| pillars of the civil union were on the one hand the slavery of the greater part of the men, and on the other, the slavery of all the women.... It was at the cost of three-fourths of its members that society assured the happiness, the opulence, the ease of the small number of property-owners whom alone it had in view" (p. 365).

Vol. II: "The question, therefore, is not to examine whether slavery is contrary to nature in itself, but whether it is contrary to the nature of society...it is inseparable from it" (p. 256). "Society and civil servitude were born together" (p. 257). "Permanent slavery...the indestructible foundation of societies" (p. 347).

"Men have only been reduced to depend for their subsistence on the liberality of another man *when the latter by despoiling them has become rich enough* to be able *to return* a small portion to them. His feigned generosity could be no more than a *restitution of some part of the fruits of their labours which he had appropriated*" (p. 242). "*Does not servitude consist* in this obligation to sow without reaping for oneself, to sacrifice one's well-being to that of another, to labour without hope? And did not its real epoch begin from the moment when there were men whom the whip and a few measures of oats when they were brought to the stable could compel to labour? It is only in a fully developed society that food seems to the poor *starveling* a sufficient *equivalent* for his liberty; but in a society in its early stages free men would be struck with horror at this unequal exchange. It could only be proposed for *captives*. Only after they have been deprived of the enjoyment of all their faculties can it" [the exchange] "become a necessity for them" (pp. 244-45).

"*The essence of society...consists in freeing the rich man from labour*, giving him new organs, untiring members, which take upon themselves all the laborious operations *the fruits of which he is to appropriate*. That is the plan which slavery allows him to carry out without embarrassment. He buys men who are to serve him" (p. 461). "In suppressing slavery, no claim was made that either wealth or its advantages were suppressed.... It was therefore necessary that things should remain the same except in name. It has always been necessary for the majority of men to continue to live in the pay of and in dependence on the minority *which has appropriated to itself all wealth*. Slavery has therefore been perpetuated on the earth, but under a sweeter name. Among us now it is adorned with the title of service" (p. 462).

By these servants, Linguet says, he does not mean lackeys and the like:

"The towns and the countryside are peopled by another kind of servant, more widely spread, more useful, more laborious, and known by the name of *journeymen*, *handicraftsmen*, etc. They are not dishonoured by the brilliant colours of luxury; they sigh beneath the loathsome rags which are the *livery* of penury. *They never share in the abundance of which their labour is the source.* Wealth seems to grant them a favour when it kindly accepts the *presents that they make to it.* It is for them to be grateful for *the services which they render to it.* It pours on them the most outrageous contempt while they are clasping its knees imploring *permission to be useful to it.* It has to be pleaded with to grant this, and in *this peculiar exchange of real generosity for an imaginary favour*, arrogance and disdain are *on the side of the receiver*, and servility, anxiety and eagerness *on the side of the giver.* These are the servants who have truly replaced the serfs among us" (pp. 463-64).

"The point that has to be examined is: what effective gain the *suppression of slavery* has brought to them. I say with as much sorrow as frankness: all that they have gained is to be every moment tormented by the fear of death from hunger, a calamity that at least never visited their predecessors in this lowest rank of mankind" (p. 464). "He is free, you say. Ah! That is his misfortune. He is bound to no one; but also no one is bound to him. When he is needed, he is *hired at the cheapest price* possible. The meagre *wage* that he is promised is hardly equal to *the price of his subsistence for the day which he gives in exchange.* He is given *overlookers to compel him to fulfil his task quickly*; he is hard driven; he is goaded on, for fear that a skilfully concealed and only too comprehensible laziness may make him hold back half his strength; for fear that the hope of *remaining employed longer on the same task* may stay his hands and blunt his tools. *The sordid economy that keeps a restless watch on him overwhelms him with reproaches at the slightest respite he seems to allow himself, and claims to have been robbed* if he takes a moment's rest. When he has finished he is dismissed as he was taken on, with the coldest indifference, and without any concern as to whether the twenty or thirty sous that he has just earned for a hard day's labour ||440| will be enough to keep him *if he finds no work the following day*" (pp. 466-67).

"He is free! That is precisely why I pity him. For that reason, he is much less cared for in the labours in which he is used. His life is much more readily hazarded. The slave was precious to his master because of the money he had cost him. But the handicraftsman costs nothing to the rich voluptuary who employs him. Men's blood had some price in the days of slavery. They were worth at least as much as they could be sold for in the market. Since they have no longer been sold they have no real intrinsic value. A pioneer is much less valued in an army than a pack-horse, because the horse is very costly and a pioneer can be had for nothing. The suppression of slavery brought these military calculations into civil life; and *since that epoch there has been no prosperous bourgeois who does not calculate in this way, as heroes do*" (p. 467)

"The day-labourers are born, grow up and are trained for" (are bred for) "the service of wealth without causing it the slightest expense, like the game that it massacres over its estates. It seems as if it really has the secret of which the unfortunate Pompey vainly boasted. Wealth has only to stamp on the ground, and from it emerge legions of hard-working men who contend among themselves for the honour of being at its disposal: if one among this crowd of mercenaries putting up its buildings or keeping its gardens straight disappears, the place that he has left empty is an invisible point which is immediately covered again without any intervention from anyone. A drop of the water of a great river is lost without regret, because new torrents incessantly succeed it. It is the same with labourers; the ease with which they can be replaced fosters the *rich man's*" (this is the form used by Linguet; not yet capitalist) "hard-heartedness towards them" (p. 468).

"These men, it is said, have no master...pure abuse of the word. What does it mean? they have no master—they have one, and the most terrible, the most imperious of masters, that is, *need*. It is this that reduces them to the most cruel dependence. *It is not one man in particular whose orders they must obey, but the orders of all in general.* It is not a single tyrant whose whims they have to humour and whose benevolence they have to court—which would set a limit to their servitude and make it endurable. *They become the valets of anyone who has money*, which gives their slavery an infinite compass and severity. It is said that if they do not get on well with one master they at least have the consolation that they can tell him so and the power to make a change: but the slaves have neither the one nor the other. They are therefore all the more wretched. What sophistry! For bear in mind that the number of *those who make others work* is very small and the number of labourers on the contrary is immense" (pp. 470-71). "What is this apparent liberty which you have bestowed on them reduced to for them? *They live only by hiring out their arms. They must therefore find someone to hire them, or die of hunger. Is that to be free?*" (p. 472).

"What is most terrible is that the very smallness of this pay is another reason for reducing it. The more the day-labourer is driven by want, the cheaper he sells himself. The greater the urgency of his need, the less profitable is his labour. The despots for the moment whom he beseeches with tears to accept his services feel no shame in, as it were, feeling his pulse, to assure themselves that he has enough strength left; they fix the reward that they offer him by the degree of his weakness. The nearer they think he is to death from starvation, the more they deduct from what could keep him from it; and what the savages that they are give him is less to prolong his life than to delay his death" (pp. 482-83). The "independence" (of the day-labourer) "is one of the most baneful scourges that the refinement of modern times has produced. It augments the wealth of the rich and the poverty of the poor. The one saves everything that the other spends. What the latter is forced to economise is not from his superfluity but from what is indispensable to him" (p. 483).

"If today it is so easy to maintain these prodigious armies which join with luxury in order to bring about the extinction of the human race, it is only due to the suppression of slavery.... It is only since there have no longer been slaves that debauchery and beggary make heroes at five sous a day" (pp. 484-85).

"I find this" (Asiatic slavery) "a hundred times more preferable than any other way of existing, for men reduced to having to win their livelihood by daily labour" (p. 496).

"Their" (the slaves' and the labourers') "chains are made of the same material and only differently coloured. Here they are black, and seem heavy: there they look less gloomy and seem hollower: but weigh them impartially and you will find no difference between them; both are equally forged by necessity. They have precisely the same weight, or rather, if they are a few grains more in one case, it is in the one whose external appearance proclaims that it is lighter" (p. 510).

He calls to the men of the French Enlightenment, in regard to the labourers:

"Do you not see that the subjection, the annihilation—since it must be said—of this large part of the flock creates the wealth of the shepherds?... Believe me, in his interest" (the shepherd's), "in yours and even in theirs, leave them" (the sheep) "with the convinction that they have that this cur who yelps at them is stronger by himself than they are all together. Let them flee with stupid fright at the mere sight of his shadow. Everyone benefits from it. It will make it easier for you to gather them in to fleece them for yourself. They are more easily guarded from being devoured by wolves. [441] It is true, only to be eaten by men. But anyway that is their fate from the moment they have entered a stable. Before talking of releasing them from there, start by overthrowing the stable, that is to say, society" (pp. 512-13). |X—441||

ADDENDA

[1. HOBBES ON LABOUR, ON VALUE AND ON THE ECONOMIC ROLE OF SCIENCE]

||XX—1291a| According to Hobbes *science*, not *operative labour*, is the mother of the arts.

"Arts of public use, as fortification, making of engines, and other instruments of war; because they confer to defence, and victory, are power; and though the true mother of them, be *science, namely the mathematics*; yet, because they are brought into the light, by the hand of the artificer, they be esteemed, the midwife passing with the vulgar for the mother, as his issue" (*Leviathan*, in *English Works* of Thomas Hobbes, edit. by Molesworth, London, 1839-44, t. III, p. 75).

The product of mental labour—science—always stands far below its value, because the labour-time needed to reproduce it has no relation at all to the labour-time required for its original production. For example, a schoolboy can learn the binominal theorem in an hour.

Labour power:

"The *value*, or *worth of a man*, is as of all other things, his price; that is to say, so much as would be given *for the use of his power*" (l. c., p. 76). "*A man's labour*" (that is, the use of his labouring power) "also, is a *commodity* exchangeable for benefit, as well as any other *thing*" (l. c., p. 233).

Productive and unproductive labour:

"It is not enough, for a man to *labour* for the maintenance of his life; but also to *fight*, if need be, for the *securing of his labour*. They must either do as the Jews did after their return from captivity, in re-edifying the temple, build with one hand, and hold the sword in the other; or else they must hire others to fight for them" (l. c., p. 333). |XX—1291a||

[2.] HISTORICAL: PETTY

[Negative Attitude to Unproductive Occupations. Germs of the Labour Theory of Value. Attempt to Explain Wages, Rent of Land, the Price of Land and Interest on the Basis of the Theory of Value]

||XXII—1346| Petty, *A Treatise of Taxes, and Contributions*, London, 1667.

Our friend Petty[113] has quite a different "population theory" from Malthus. According to him a check ought to be put upon the "breeding" faculties of parsons, and the "Celibacy" again put upon them.

All this belongs to the [sectional] *productive and unproductive labour* [114]

a) *Parsons*:

"For as much as there be more Males than Females in England...it were good for the Ministers to *return to their Coelibat*; or that none should be Ministers, whilst they were* married.... And then our *unmarried Parson* might live as well *with half*, as now with the whole of his Benefice" (pp. 7-8).

b) *Merchants and Retailers*:

"A large proportion of these also might be retrenched, who *properly and originally earn nothing from the Publick*; being only a kind of *Gamesters, that play with one another* ||1347| *for the labours of the poor*; yielding of themselves no fruit at all, otherwise than as Veins and Arteries, to *distribute* forth and back the blood and nutritive juyces of the Body Politick, namely, the product of Husbandry and Manufacture" (p.10).

c) *Lawyers, physicians, officials, etc.*:

"If the numerous Offices and Fees relating to the *Government, Law*, and *Church*; and if the number of Divines, Lawyers, Physicians Merchants, and Retailers were also lessened, all which do receive *great wages for little work done* to the Publick, with how much greater ease would common expenses be defrayed?" (p.11).

---

* In the manuscript: "are".—*Ed.*

d) *Paupers* (*supernumeraries*):

"Who shall pay these men? I answer, every body.... I think 't is plain, they ought neither to be starved, nor hanged, nor given away" [to another nation] etc. (p. 12). Either they are given "the superfluity", or if there is none, "in case there be *no overplus*...; 't is fit *to retrench a little* from the delicacy of others feeding in quantity or quality" (pp. 12-13). The labour imposed on them (the supernumeraries) may be of any kind; only it must be "without expense of Foreign Commodities"; the important thing is to "keep their minds to discipline and obedience, and their bodies to a patience of more profitable labours when need shall require it" (p. 13). The best "Imployments be" [for them] "The making of Bridges and Cawseys. The working in Mines", etc.* (p. 12).

Population—wealth:

"*Fewness of people, is real poverty*; and a nation wherein are eight Millions of people, are more than twice as rich as the same scope of Land wherein are but four" (p.16).

On (a) above (*Parsons*). Petty handles the priests with exquisite irony:

"Religion best flourisheth when the Priests are most mortified, as... the Law...best flourisheth when Lawyers have least to do" (p. 57). He advises the parsons in any case "*not to breed more Church-men that the Benefices* as they now stand shared out will receive". For example, with 12,000 benefices in England and Wales, "it will not be safe to breed up 24,000 Ministers". For then the 12,000 unprovided for will enter into competition, "which they cannot do more easily, than by persuading the people, that the twelve thousand Incumbents do poyson or starve their Souls" (an allusion to the English religious war) "and misguide them in their way to Heaven" (p. 57).

Origin of surplus-value and how to compute it. His treatment is somewhat confused, but in all the grappling with ideas striking passages can be found here and there.

Petty distinguishes between *natural price*, *political price*, *true price currant* (p. 67). By *natural price* he means in fact *value*, and it is only this that concerns us here, since ||1348| the determination of surplus-value *depends on the determination of value*.

In this treatise he in fact determines the *value of commodities* by the comparative *quantity of labour* they contain.

"But before we talk too much of *Rents*, we should endeavour to explain the misterious nature of them, with reference as well to *Money, the Rent of which we call Usury*; as to that of *Lands and Houses*" (p. 23).

---

* In the manuscript: "Am besten sie zum Bauen van Strassen, Brücken, Bergwerken etc. zu verwenden."—*Ed.*

α) The first question is, what is the *value* of a commodity, or more particularly, of corn?

"If a man can bring to London an ounce of Silver out of the Earth in Peru, *in the same time* that he can produce a Bushel of Corn, then one is the natural price of the other; now if by reason of new and more easie Mines a man can get two ounces of Silver as easily as formerly he did one, then Corn will be as cheap as ten shillings the Bushel, as it was before at five shillings caeteris paribus" (p. 31). "Let the production of a Bushel of [...] Corn be supposed of *equel labour* to *that of producing an ounce of Silver*" (p. 66). This is, in the first place, the "real and not an imaginary way of computing the prices of Commodities" (p. 66).

β) The second point, which has now to be examined, is the *value of labour.*

"The Law...*should allow the Labourer but just wherewithal to live*; for if you allow double, then he works but half so much as he could have done, and otherwise would; *which is a loss to the Publick of the fruit of so much labour*" (p. 64).

The value of labour is therefore determined by the necessary means of subsistence. The labourer is impelled to surplus production and surplus-labour only by being forced to use the whole of the labour-power within his capacity in order to get even as much as he *just needs to live.* However, the cheapness or dearness of his labour is determined by two factors: natural fertility and the standard of expenditure (needs) conditioned by the climate.

"Natural *dearness and cheapness* depends upon the *few or more hands requisite to necessaries of Nature*: As Corn is cheaper where *one man* produces Corn for ten, than where he can do the like but for six; and withal, according as the Climate disposes men to a necessity of spending more or less" (p. 67).

γ) For Petty the *surplus* exists only in two forms: *rent of land* or *rent of money* (usury). The latter he derives from the former. For him, as later for the Physiocrats, the first is the *true form* of surplus-value (but at the same time he explains that corn is intended to cover all necessaries of life, as in the "Lord's Prayer" <Our Father> the word "Bread doth").

In developing his ideas he presents rent (the surplus-value) not only as the excess drawn by the employer beyond the necessary time of labour, but also as the excess of surplus-labour of the producer himself over his wages and the replacement of his own capital.

"Suppose a man could with his own hands plant a certain scope of Land with Corn, that is, could Digg, or Plough; Harrow, Weed, Reap, Carry home,

Thresh, and Winnow so much as the Husbandry of this Land requires; and had withal *Seed* wherewith to sow the same. I say, that when this man *hath subducted his seed out of the proceed of His Harvest*" (that is, in the first place deducted from the product an amount equivalent to the constant capital), ||1349| "and also what himself hath both eaten and given to others in exchange for Clothes, and other Natural necessaries; that the *Remainder of Corn*, is the *natural and true Rent of the Land for that year*; and the *medium of seven years*, or rather of so many years as makes up the Cycle, *within which Dearth and Plenties make their revolution*, doth give the ordinary Rent of the Land in Corn" (pp. 23-24).

In fact for Petty, therefore, since the value of corn is determined by the labour-time contained in it, and the rent is equal to the total product minus wages and seed, rent is equal to the surplus-produce in which the surplus-labour is materialised. Rent here includes profit; the latter is not yet separated from rent. In the same ingenious way Petty goes on to ask:

"But a further, though collateral question may be, *how much English money* this *Corn or Rent is worth*; I answer, *so much as the money* which another single man can save *within the same time*, over and above his expence, if he employed himself wholly to produce and make it; viz. Let another man go travel into a Countrey where is Silver there Dig it, Refine it, bring it to the same place where the other man planted his Corn; Coyn it, etc., the same person, all the while of his working for Silver, gathering also food for his necessary livelihood, and procuring himself covering, etc. I say, the Silver of the one *must be esteemed of equal value with the Corn of the other*: the one, being perhaps twenty Ounces and the other twenty Bushels. From whence it follows that the price of a Bushel of this Corn to be an Ounce of Silver" (p. 24).

The difference in the kind of labour, Petty expressly notes, is here quite immaterial; all that matters is the *labour-time*.

"And forasmuch as possible there may be more Art and Hazard in working about the Silver, then about the* Corn, yet all comes to the same pass; for let a hundred men *work ten years* upon Corn, and *the same number of men the same time*, upon Silver; I say, that the *neat proceed* of the Silver is the *price of the whole neat proceed of the Corn*, and like parts of the one, the price of like parts of the other" (p. 24).

After thus explaining *rent*—which here is equivalent to the total *surplus-value*, profit included—and its expression in money, he then sets out, again in a very brilliant way, to determine the *money value of land*.

"Wherefore we would be glad to find *the natural value of the Fee-simple* of Land, though but no better than we have done that of the *usus fructus*

* In the manuscript: "than upon" instead of "then about the".—*Ed.*

above mentioned.... Having found the *Rent or value of the usus fructus per annum*, the question is, *how many years purchase* (as we usually say) is the *Fee-simple* naturally worth? If we say an infinite number, then an acre of Land would be equal in value to a thousand acres of the same Land; which is absurd, and infinity of Units being equal to an infinity of Thousands: wherefore we must pitch upon some *limited number*, and that I apprehend [...] the number of years, which I conceive one man of fifty years old, another of twenty-eight, and another of seven years old, all being alive together may be thought to live; that is to say, of a Grandfather, Father and Child; few men having reason to take care of more remote Posterity.... Wherefore I pitch the *number of years purchase, that any Land is naturally worth*, to be the ordinary ||1350| extent of three such persons their lives. Now in England we esteem three lives equal to one and twenty years, and consequently the *value of Land*, to be about the *same number of years purchase*" (pp. 25-26).

After resolving rent into *surplus-labour* and consequently *surplus-value*, Petty explains that land is nothing but the capitalised rent, that is to say, a *definite number of years' rent* or the total amount of the rents for a definite number of years.

In fact, rent is *capitalised* or reckoned as the *value of land in this way*:

Let one acre yield an annual rent of £10. If the rate of interest is 5 per cent, then £10 represents the interest on a capital of £200, and, as the interest at 5 per cent replaces the capital in 20 years, the value of the acre would be £200 (20×£10). Capitalisation of rent therefore depends on the rate of interest. If the rate of interest were 10 per cent, it would represent the interest on a capital of £100 or ten years' purchase.

But as Petty starts from the *rent of land* as the general form of surplus-value, which includes profit, he cannot take the rate of interest on capital as something given; on the contrary, he has to deduce it from rent as a *special form* (as Turgot also does—quite consistently from his own standpoint). In what way then is he to determine the number of years—the number of years' rent—which forms the *value of land*? A man is only interested in buying as many yearly rentals as the years during which he has "to take care" of himself and his immediate posterity; that is, as long as an *average man*, grandfather, father and child, lives, and on the "English" reckoning this is twenty-one years. Therefore what lies beyond the twenty-one years' "*usus fructus*" has no value for him. Consequently he pays for the *usus fructus* for twenty-one years, and this constitutes the *value of the land*.

In his ingenious way he gets himself out of the difficulty; but the important thing here is, firstly, that *rent*, as the expression of the total *agricultural surplus-value*, is derived not from the land but from labour, [and is presented as] the surplus of labour in excess of what is necessary for the subsistence of the labourer;

secondly, that the *value of land* is nothing but the rent purchased in advance for a certain number of years—a *transmuted* form of rent itself, in which for example twenty-one years' surplus-value (or labour) appears as the *value of the land*; in a word, *the value of land* is nothing but *capitalised rent*.

Such is Petty's deep insight into the matter. From the standpoint of the *buyer* of rent (i.e., of land) *rent* thus appears merely *as interest on his capital* used to buy it; and in this form rent has become completely unrecognisable and appears as *interest on capital*.

After Petty has thus determined the *value of land* and the *value of the annual rental*, he is able to derive the rent of money or usury as a secondary form.

> "As for *Usury*, the least that can be, is the *Rent of so much Land as the Money lent will buy*, where the Security is undoubted" (p. 28).

Here interest is presented as determined by the *price of rent*, whereas on the contrary the *price of rent* or the *purchase value of land* is determined by interest. But this is quite consistent, as *rent* is presented as the general form of surplus-value and therefore *interest on money* must be derived from it as a secondary form.

Differential rent. Of this too the first notion is to be found in Petty. He derives it not from the *different* fertility of pieces of land of the same size, but from the *different position*, [the different] distance from the market of *pieces of land of equal fertility*, which as we know is one element in differential rent. He says:

> ||1351| "As great need of Money heightens Exchange, so doth great need of Corn raise *the price* of that likewise, and *consequently* of the *Rent of the Land that bears Corn*" (here therefore he says explicitly that the *price* of corn determines rent, it being implicit in the earlier analysis that rent does not determine the *value* of corn) "and *lastly of the Land itself*; as for example, if the Corn which feedeth London, or an Army, be brought forty miles together,* then the *Corn growing within a mile of London*, or the quarters of such Army, *shall have added unto its natural price*, so much as the charge of bringing it thirty nine miles doth amount unto.... Hence it comes to pass, that *Lands intrinsically alike* near populous places, such as where the Perimeter of the Area that feeds them is great, will not only *yield more Rent* for these Reasons, but also more years purchase than in remote places", etc. (p. 29).

* In the manuscript: "thither".—*Ed.*

Petty also mentions the second cause of differential rent—the *differing fertility* of land and therefore the *differing productivity* of labour on equal areas of land:

"*The goodness or badness*, or the value of Land depends *upon the greater or lesser share of the product given for it in proportion to the simple labour bestowed to raise the said Product*" (p. 67).

Petty's exposition of differential rent is therefore *better than that of Adam Smith.* |XXII—1351 ||

* * *

||XXII—1397| [Petty,] *A Treatise of Taxes, and Contributions*, London, 1667. *Supplementary points.*

1. *On the quantity of circulating money* which a nation needs, pp. 16-17.

His view of *total production* is shown by the following passage:

"If there be 1,000 men in a Territory, and if 100 of these can raise necessary food and rayment for the whole 1,000; if 200 more make as much Commodities, as other Nations will give either their Commodities or Money for, and if 400 more be imployed in the Ornaments, pleasure, and magnificence of the whole? if there be 200 Governours, Divines, Lawyers, Physicians, Merchants, and Retailers, making in all 900, the question is", etc. —what happens to the paupers ("supernumeraries") (p. 12).

In his analysis of rent and of its valuation in money, for which he takes as the basis *equal labours* (quantities), Petty remarks:*

"This, I say to be the *Foundation* of *equalising and balancing of values*; yet in the superstructures and practices hereupon, I confess there is much variety and intricacy" (p. 25).

||1398| 2. What he was much preoccupied with is the "*natural Par between Land and Labour*":

"Our Silver and Gold we *call* by several names, as in England by Pounds, Shillings, and Pence: all which may be called and understood by either of the three. But that which I would say upon this matter is, that all things ought to be *valued by two natural Denominations, which is Land and Labour*; that is, we ought to say, a Ship or Garment is worth such a measure of Land, with such another measure of Labour; forasmuch as both Ships and Garments were the *Creatures of Lands* and *mens Labours thereupon*: This being true, we should be glad to find out a *natural Par between Land and Labour*, so as we might express the value by either of them alone, as well

* See pp. 355-56 of the present volume.—*Ed.*

or better than by both, and reduce one into the other, as easily and certainly, as we reduce Pence into Pounds" (p. 25).

For this reason Petty seeks the "*natural values* of the *Fee-Simple* of Land", after he has found the monetary expression of rent.

Running alongside of each other through his work there are three ways of determining value:

a) *The magnitude of value*, determined by equal labour-time, *labour* being here considered *as the source of value*.

b) *Value* as the form of social labour. Hence money is the *true form of value*, although in other passages he knocks down all the illusions of the Monetary system. He is therefore *defining the concept*.

c) Labour as the source of exchange-value is confused with labour as the source of use-value; which presupposes material provided by nature (land). In fact, he "cuts" the "Par" between labour and land by describing the *Fee-simple* of the latter as *capitalised rent*—therefore not treating land as material provided by nature for concrete labour.

3. With reference to the *rate of interest* he says:

"Of the vanity and fruitlessness of making *Civil Positive Laws* against *the Laws of Nature*" (i. e., the laws arising from the nature of bourgeois production) "I have spoken elsewhere" (l.c., p. 29).

4. In regard to *rent*: *surplus-value* consequent on the *greater productivity of labour*:

"If the said Shires by greater labour than now is used, (as by Digging instead of Ploughing, Setting instead of Sowing, picking of choice Seed instead of taking it promiscuously, steeping it instead of using it wholly unprepared, and manuring the ground with Salt instead of rotten Straw, etc.) could be fertilised, then will *the Rent* be as much more advanced, as the *excess of increase exceeds that of the labour*" (p. 32).

([By increase of labour] he means here the *price* or *wages of labour*.)

5. *Raising* [*the value*] *of money* (Chapter XIV).

6. The passage quoted earlier* "if you allow double, then he works but half so much, etc." must be taken to mean: If the labourer received for six hours the value of six hours, then he would

* See p. 356 of the present volume —*Ed.*

receive *double* what he now receives—the value of six for twelve. He would then work only six, "which is a loss to the Publick", etc.

* * *

Petty, *An Essay Concerning the Multiplication of Mankind* (1682). Division of labour (pp. 35-36).

* * *

[Petty, *The*] *Political Anatomy of Ireland* (1672) and *Verbum Sapienti* (London edition 1691).

1. "This brings me to the most important Consideration in *Political Oeconomies*, viz. how to make a *Par and Equation* between Lands and Labour, so as to express the Value of any thing by either alone" (pp. 63-64).

In fact, the task in this connection is only to resolve the *value of land* itself into *labour*.

||1399| 2. This work was written later than the one examined earlier.[115]

"The *days food* of an *adult Man*, at a Medium, and *not the days labour, is the common measure of Value*, and seems to be as regular and constant as the value of fine Silver.... Wherefore I *valued* an Irish Cabbin at the *number of days food, which the Maker spent in building of it*" (p. 65).

This later statement is quite Physiocratic.

"That some Men will eat more than others, is not material, since by a days food we understand $^1/_{100}$ part" [of the food that 100 men] "of all Sorts and Sizes will eat, so as to Live, Labour, and Generate" (p. 64).

But what Petty is searching for here in the *statistics* of Ireland is not the *common* measure of value, but the measure of *value* in the sense that *money* is the measure of value.

3. *Quantity of money and wealth of the nation* (*Verbum Sapienti*, p. 13).

4. *Capital.*

"What we call *the Wealth, Stock, or Provision of the Nation*, being the effect of the *former or past labour*, should not be conceived *to differ from efficiencies in being*" (p. 9).

5. *Productive power of labour.*

"We said, That half the People by a very gentle labour, might much enrich the Kingdom...upon what shall they employ themselves. To which I answer in general, Upon producing Food and Necessaries for the whole People of the Land, *by few hands*; whether by *labouring harder*, or by the *introducing the Compendium, and Facilitations of Art*, which is equivalent to what men vainly hoped from *Polygamy*. For as much as he that can do the Work of five men by one, effects the same as the begetting four adult Workmen" (p. 22). "*Cheapest food*...will be when Food also *is raised, by fewer hands than elsewhere*" (p. 23).

6. Purpose of men and goal (p. 24).

7. *On money, see* also the *Quantulumcunque* (1682). XXII—|1399||

[3.] PETTY, SIR DUDLEY NORTH, LOCKE

||XXII—1397| By comparing North's and Locke's writings with Petty's *Quantulumcunque* (1682), *A Treatise of Taxes, and Contributions* (1662), [and *The Political*] *Anatomy of Ireland* (1672), their indebtedness to Petty can be seen in connection with (1) *lowering of interest*; (2) raising and abasing of money; (3) *North's* calling interest the rent of money, etc.

North and Locke wrote their works[116] at the same time and on the same occasion: *Lowering of Interest* and *Raising of money*. But [they have] opposite views. With Locke it is the "*want of money*" that is responsible for the high rate of interest and in general for the fact that things do not fetch their real prices, and the revenues to be paid out of them. North shows the opposite, that it is not want of money but of capital or revenue. We find in his works the first definite concept of *stock* or *capital*, or rather of *money* as a mere *form of capital*, in so far as it is not means of circulation. In Sir Dudley North's writings we find the first correct conception of interest as opposed to Locke's idea. |XXII—1397||

[4.] LOCKE

[Treatment of Rent and Interest from the Standpoint of the Bourgeois Theory of Natural Law]

||XX—1291a| Taking Locke's general doctrine of labour together with his doctrine of the *origin of interest* and *rent*—for he considers surplus-value only in these specific forms—surplus-value is nothing but *another person's labour*, surplus-labour, which land and capital—the conditions of labour—enable their owners to appropriate. And ownership of a greater quantity of conditions of labour than one person can himself put to use with his own labour is, according to Locke, a *political* invention that contradicts the law of nature on which private property is founded. ||1292a|

<For *Hobbes* too labour is the sole source of all wealth, apart from those gifts of nature which are to be found already in a consumable state. God (nature) "either *freely giveth*, or *for labour selleth* to mankind" (*Leviathan*) [In: *The English Works* of Thomas Hobbes..., now first collected and edited by...Molesworth, Vol. III, London, 1839, p. 232]. But for Hobbes it is the sovereign who distributes property in land at his pleasure.>

The relevant passages [in Locke] are as follows:

"Though the *earth*, and all inferior creatures, be common to all men, yet every man has a property in his own person: this nobody has any right to but himself. The labour of his body, and the work of his hands, we may say, are properly his. Whatsoever then he removes out of the state that nature hath provided, and left it in, he hath mixed his labour with, and joined to it something that is his own, and thereby makes it his property" (*Of* [*Civil*] *Government*, Book II, Chapter V; *Works*, 7th edit., 1768, Vol. II, p. 229).

"His labour hath taken it out of the hands of nature, where it was common, and belonged equally to all her children, and hath thereby appropriated it to himself" (l.c.. p. 230).

"The same law of nature, that does by this means give us property, does also bound that property too.... As much as any one can make use of to any advantage of life before it spoils, so much he may by his labour fix a property in: whatever is beyond this, is more than his share, and belongs to others" (l c.).

"But the chief matter of property being now not *the fruits of the earth*", etc., "but the *earth* itself.... As much land as a man tills, plants, improves, cultivates, and can use the product of, so much is his property. He by his labour does, as it were, enclose it from the common" (l.c.).

"Subduing or cultivating the earth, and having dominion, we see are joined together. The one gave title to the other" (l.c., p. 231).

"The measure of property nature has well set *by the extent of men's labour*, and the conveniences of life: no man's labour could subdue, or appropriate all; nor could his enjoyment consume more than a small part; so that it was impossible for any man, this way, to intrench upon the right of another, or acquire to himself a property, to the prejudice of his neighbour.... This measure did confine every man's possession to a very moderate proportion, and such as he might appropriate to himself, without injury to any body, in the first ages of the world.... And the same measure *may be allowed still* without prejudice to any body, as full as the world seems" (pp. 231-32).

Labour gives things almost all their value <*value* here is equivalent to use-value, and labour is taken as concrete labour, not as a quantum; but the measuring of exchange-value by labour is in reality based on the fact that the labourer creates use-value>. The remainder of use-value which cannot be resolved into labour is the gift of nature, and hence in its essence *common property*. What Locke therefore tries to show is not the contradiction—that property can nevertheless be acquired by other procedures than labour—but how, in spite of the common property in nature, individual property could be created by individual labour.

"*It is labour indeed that put* the difference of value on every thing....* Of the products of the earth useful to the life of man...ninety-nine hundredths are wholly to be put on the account of labour" (p. 234).

"It is labour then which puts the greatest part of the value upon land" (p. 235).

"Though the things of nature are given in common, yet man, by *being master of himself*, and *proprietor of his own person*, and the actions or labour of it, had still in himself the great foundation of property" (p. 235).

One limit to property is therefore *the limit of personal labour*; the other, that a man should not amass more things than he can use. The latter limit however is extended by exchange of perishable products for *money* (apart from other exchanges):

"He might heap as much of these *durable* things as he pleased; the exceeding of the bounds of his just property" <apart from the *limit* of his personal labour> "not lying in the largeness of his possession, but the

* In the manuscript: "puts".—*Ed.*

perishing of any thing uselessly in it. And thus came in the use of money, some lasting thing that men might * keep without spoiling, and that by mutual consent men would take in exchange ||1293a| for the truly useful, but perishable supports of life" (p. 236).

Thus arises the inequality of individual property, though the *limit of personal labour* remains.

"This partage of things in an inequality of private possessions, men have made practicable out of the bounds of society, and without compact; only by putting a value on gold and silver, and tacitly agreeing in the use of money" (p. 237).

We must now compare with this the following passage from Locke's work on interest,[117] not forgetting that according to him natural law makes *personal labour* the limit of property:

"Let us next see how it" (money) "comes to be of the same Nature with Land, by yielding a certain yearly Income, which we call Use or Interest. For Land produces naturally something new and profitable, and of value to Mankind; but money is a barren Thing, and produces nothing, but by Compact, *transfers that Profit, that was the Reward of one Man's Labour, into another Man's Pocket*. That which occasions this, is the unequal Distribution of Money; which Inequality has the same Effect too upon Land, that it has upon Money.... For as the unequal Distribution of Land (you have more than you can, or will manure, and another less) brings you a Tenant for your Land; and the same unequal Distribution of Money... brings me a Tenant for my Money: So *my Money is apt in Trade, by the Industry of the Borrower*, to produce more than 6 per cent, to the Borrower, as well as your Land, *by the Labour of the Tenant*, is apt to produce more Fruits, than his Rent comes to" (*Folio edition of Locke's Works*, 1740, Vol. II [p. 19].[118])

In this passage Locke has in part the polemical interest of showing landed property that its rent is in no way different from usury. Both "transfer that Profit, that** was the Reward of one Man's Labour, into another Man's Pocket" through the unequal distribution of the conditions of production.

Locke's view is all the more important because it was the classical expression of bourgeois society's ideas of right as against feudal society, and moreover his philosophy served as the basis for all the ideas of the whole of subsequent English political economy. |XX—1293a||

* In the manuscript: "which might men".—*Ed.*

** In the manuscript: "which".—*Ed.*

[5.] NORTH

[Money as Capital. The Growth of Trade as the Cause of the Fall in the Rate of Interest]

||XXIII—1418| Sir Dudley North: *Discourses upon Trade, etc.*, London, 1691. (Supplementary notebook C).[119]

This work, like Locke's economic writings, is in direct connection with and directly based on Petty's works.

The work is mainly concerned with *commercial capital*. and so it is not relevant here, though it shows masterly skill in the field with which it deals.

It is particularly remarkable that from the time of the Restoration of Charles II up to the middle of the eighteenth century there were continual complaints from the landlords about the fall in rents (just as the price of wheat continually declined especially from? [120] onwards). Although the industrial capitalist class played a considerable part in the compulsory reduction of the rate of interest (from the time of Culpeper and Sir Josiah Child), the real protogonist of this measure was the *landed interest*. The "*value of land*" and the "raising of it" were proclaimed to be in the national interest. (Just as on the other hand from about 1760 the rise in rents, in the value of land and in the price of corn and provisions, and the complaints of the manufacturers on this score, form the basis of the economic investigations on this subject).

With few exceptions it is the struggle between moneyed interest and landed interest that fills the century from 1650 to 1750, as the nobility, who lived in the grand style, saw with disgust how the usurers had got their hands on them and, with the building up of the modern credit system and the national debt at the end of the seventeenth century, faced them with overwhelming power in the sphere of legislation, etc.

Already *Petty* speaks of the landlords' complaints about the fall in rents and their opposition to the improvements (look up the passage[121]). He defends the usurer as against the landlord and puts rent of money and rent of land on the same footing. *Locke* reduces both to exploitation of labour. He takes the same standpoint as Petty. Both oppose the compulsory regulation of interest. The landed interest had noted that the *value of land* rose when interest fell. At a given level of rent, its *capitalised expression*, i. e., the value of land, falls or rises in inverse relation to the rate of interest.

The third writer to follow this line of Petty's is *Sir Dudley North*, in the work referred to above.

This is the first form in which *capital* starts its revolt against *landed property*, as in fact *usury* was one of the principal agents in the accumulation of capital—i. e., through its co-proprietorship in the landlord's revenues. But industrial and commercial capital go more or less hand in hand with the landlords against this outmoded form of capital.

> "As the Landed Man letts his Land, so these" (who have "*Stock* for Trade [...] who* either have not the skill, or care not for the trouble of managing it in Trade") "lett their *Stock*; this latter is call'd *Interest*, but is only *Rent* for Stock" <here, as also in Petty's writings, it can be seen how rent, to those just emerging from the Middle Ages, ||1419| appears as the primary form of surplus-value> "as the other is for Land. And in several Languages, hiring of Money, and Lands, are Terms of common use; and it is so also in some Countries in England. Thus to be a *Landlord*, or a *Stock-lord* is the same thing, the Landlord hath the advantage only in this: That his Tenant cannot carry away the Land, as the Tenant of the other may the Stock; and therefore Land ought to yield *less profit* than Stock; which is let out at the greater hazard" (p.4).

Interest. North seems to have been the first to have a correct conception of interest, for by *stock*, as will be seen from the passages next quoted, he means not only money, but capital (as indeed even Petty distinguishes between *stock and money*. Locke considered that interest was determined exclusively by the quantity of money; so did Petty. *See the passages in Massie on this.*).

> "If there be more Lenders than Borrowers, Interest will...fall; ...it is not low Interest makes Trade, but *Trade increasing, the Stock of the Nation* makes Interest Low" (p.4).
>
> "Gold and Silver, and, out of them, Money are nothing but the Weights and Measures, by which Traffick is more conveniently carried on, than could be done without them: and also a proper Fund for a *surplusage of Stock to be deposited in*" (p.16).

Price and money. As the price is nothing but the *equivalent*

---

* In the manuscript: "and".—*Ed.*

of the commodity expressed in *money*, and, when we are dealing with a *sale*, the commodity realised in money—that is, it represents the *commodity* as *exchange-value* in order to change it subsequently into a use-value again—it is one of the earliest recognitions of the fact that in this transaction we are dealing with gold and silver only as a *form of existence of the exchange-value* of commodities, as a *phase in their metamorphosis*, not with gold and silver as such. North puts this very felicitously for his time.

"Money being...the Common Measure of Buying and Selling, every body who hath any thing to sell, and cannot procure Chapmen for it, is presently apt to think, that *Want of Money in the Kingdom*, or Country is the cause why his Goods do not go off; and so, want of Money, is the common Cry; which is a great mistake....

"What do these People want, who cry out for Money? I will begin with the *Beggar*...it is not Money, but Bread, and other Neccssaries for Life that he wants...the Farmer complains, for the want of Money...he thinks that were more Money in the Country, he should have a Price for his Goods. Then it seems Money is not his want, but a Price for his Corn, and Cattel, which he would sell, but cannot...why he cannot get a price? ...1 Either there is too much Corn and Cattel in the Country, so that most who come to Market have need of selling, as he hath, and few of buying; Or 2. There wants the usual vent abroad, by Transportation, as in time of War, when Trade is unsafe, or not permitted; Or 3. The Consumption fails, as when men by reason of Poverty, do not spend so much in their Houses as formerly they did; wherefore it is not the increase of specifick Money, which would at all advance the Farmers Goods, but the removal of any of these three Causes, which do truly keep down the Market.

"The Merchant and Shop-keeper want Money in the same manner, that is, they want a Vent for the Goods they deal in, by reason that the Markets fail" (pp.11-12).[122]

Further: *Capital* is *value which produces surplus-value*, *whereas in the building up of a hoard the crystallised form of exchange-value* as such is the aim. One of the earliest discoveries of the classical economists is therefore the antithesis between the *formation of a hoard* and *using money to make profit*, that is to say, the presentation of *money as capital*.

"No Man is richer for having his Estate all in Money, Plate, etc., lying by him, but on the contrary, he is for that reason the poorer. That Man is richest, whose Estate in a *growing condition*, either in Land at Farm, Money at Interest, or Goods in Trade" (p. 11).

<Similarly, John Bellers, *Essays about the Poor, Manufactures, Trade, Plantations, and Immorality, etc.*, London, 1699, says:

"Money neither *increaseth*, nor is useful, but when it's parted with, and as Money is unprofitable to a private Person but as he disposeth of it, for something more valuable, so what Money is more than of absolute necessity for a home Trade, is dead Stock to a Kingdom or Nation and brings no profit to that Country it's kept in" (p.13).>

"Altho' every one desires to have it" (money) "yet none, or very few care for keeping it, but they are forthwith contriving to dispose it; knowing that from all the Money that lies dead, no benefit is to be expected, but it is a certain loss" ([North, l. c.], p. 21).

||1420| *Money as world-money*:

"A Nation in the World, as to Trade, is in all respects like a City in a Kingdom, or Family in a City" (p. 14). "In this course of Trade, Gold and Silver are in no sort different from other Commodities, but are taken from them who have Plenty, and carried to them who want, or desire them" (p.13).

The quantity of money that can circulate is determined by the exchange of commodities.

"If never so much be brought from abroad, or never so much coyned at home, all that is more than what the Commerce of the Nation requires, is *but Bullion*, and will be treated as such; and coyned Money, like wroughs Plate at Second hand, shall sell but for the Intrinsick" (pp.17-18).

Conversion of money into bullion, and vice versa (p.18) (Supplementary notebook C, p. 13). *Valuation and weighing* of money. Oscillatory movement (Supplementary notebook C, p.14).[123]

The usurer and *landed interest* and *trade*:

"The Moneys imployed at Interest in this Nation, are not near the Tenth part; *disposed to Trading People*, wherewith to manage their Trades; but are for the most part lent for the supplying of Luxury, and to support the Expense of Persons, who though great Owners of Lands, yet spend faster than their Lands bring in; and being loath to sell, choose rather to mortgage their Estates" (North, l.c., pp.6-7). |XXIII—1420||

[6. BERKELEY ON INDUSTRY AS THE SOURCE OF WEALTH]

||XIII—670a| "Whether it were not wrong to suppose *land itself* to be *wealth*? And whether the industry of the people is not first to be considered, as that which constitutes wealth, which makes even land and silver to be wealth, neither of which would have any value, but as *means and motives* to industry?" (*The Querist, by Dr. George Berkeley*, London, 1750, Query 38). |XIII—670a||

[7.] HUME AND MASSIE

[(A) MASSIE AND HUME ON INTEREST]

||XX—1293a| *Massie's* anonymous work *An Essay on the Governing Causes of the Natural Rate of Interest* appeared in 1750. The second part of Hume's *Essays*, which contains the [essay] "Of Interest" published 1752, that is, two years later. Massie therefore has priority. Hume attacks Locke, Massie attacks both Petty and Locke, both of whom still held the view that the level of interest depends on the quantity of money, and that in fact the real object of the loan is money (not capital).

Massie laid down more categorically than did Hume, that *interest* is merely a part of profit. Hume is mainly concerned to show that the value of money makes no difference to the rate of interest, since, given the proportion between interest and money-capital—6 per cent for example, that is, £6, rises or falls in value at the same time as the value of the £100 (and, therefore, of one pound sterling) rises or falls, but the proportion 6 is not affected by this.

[(B) HUME. FALL OF PROFIT AND INTEREST DEPENDENT ON THE GROWTH OF TRADE AND INDUSTRY]

Let us start with Hume.

"Every thing in the world is purchased by labour" ([David Hume, "Of Commerce". In:] *Essays,* [*and Treatises on several Subjects,*] Vol. I, Part II, London, 1764, p. 289).

The rate of interest depends on the demand from borrowers and the supply by lenders, that is, on demand and supply, but after that essentially on the level of "profits arising from commerce" (l.c., p.329).

"The greater or less stock of labour and commodities must have a great influence" (upon interest); "since we really and in effect borrow these, when we take money upon interest" (l.c., p.337). "No man will accept of low profits, where he can have high interest; and no man will accept of low interest, where he can have high profits" (l.c., p.335).

High interest and high profit are both the expression "of the small advance of commerce and industry, not of the scarcity of gold and silver" (l.c., p.329). And "low interest" of the opposite.

||1294a| "In a state, therefore, where there is nothing but a landed interest" (or as he says later, "landed gentry and peasants") "the borrowers must be numerous, and interest high" (p.330), because wealth which is only for enjoyment is driven by boredom to seek pleasures, while on the other hand production, except for agriculture, is very limited. The opposite is the case, when commerce has developed. The passion for gain entirely [dominates the] merchant. He "*knows no such pleasure as that of seeing the daily increase of his fortune*". (The passion for exchange-value, abstract wealth, weighs with him far more than that for use-values.)

"And this is the reason why trade encreases frugality, and why, among merchants, there is the same overplus of misers above prodigals, as, among the possessors of land, there is the contrary" (p.333).

<*Unproductive labour:*

"Lawyers and physicians beget no industry; and it is even at the expense of others they acquire their riches; so that they are sure to diminish the possessions of some of their fellow-citizens, as fast as they encrease their own" (pp.333-34).>

"Thus an encrease of commerce [...] raises a great number of lenders, and by that means *produces lowness of interest*" (p.334).

"*Low interest* and *low profits of merchandise* are two events, that mutually forward each other, and *are both originally derived* from that extensive commerce, which produces opulent merchants, and renders the monied interest considerable. Where merchants possess great stocks, whether represented by few or many pieces of metal, it must frequently happen, that, when they either become tired of business, or leave heirs unwilling or unfit to engage in commerce, a great proportion* of these riches naturally seeks an annual and secure revenue The plenty diminishes the price, and makes the lenders accept of a low interest. This consideration obliges many to keep their stock in trade, and rather be content with low profits than dispose of their money at an under value. On the other hand, when commerce has become** extensive, and employs*** large stocks, there must *arise rivalships among the merchants*, which *diminish the profits of trade*, at the same time that they encrease the trade itself. The low profits of merchan-

* In the manuscript: "deal".—*Ed.*

** In the manuscript this is followed by the word: "very".—*Ed.*

*** In the manuscript this is followed by the word: "very".—*Ed.*

dise induce the merchants to accept more willingly of a low interest, when they leave off business, and begin to indulge themselves in ease and indolence. It is *needless*, therefore, to enquire which of these circumstances, to wit,* *low interest or low profits*, is *the cause*, and which *the effect*. They both arise from an extensive commerce, and mutually forward each other.... An extensive commerce, by producing large stocks, diminishes both interest and profits; and is always assisted, in its diminution of the one, by the proportional sinking of the other. I may add, that, as low profits arise from *the encrease of commerce and industry*, they serve in their turn to its farther encrease,** by rendering the commodities cheaper, encouraging the consumption, and heightening the industry. And thus... *interest* is *the**** *barometer of the State*, and *its lowness* is a sign almost infallible of the flourishing of a people" (l.c., pp.334-36).

[(C) MASSIE. INTEREST AS PART OF PROFIT. THE LEVEL OF INTEREST EXPLAINED BY THE RATE OF PROFIT]

[Joseph Massie,] *An Essay on the Governing Causes of the Natural Rate of Interest*; wherein the Sentiments of Sir William Petty and Mr. Locke, on that Head, are considered, London, 1750.

"It appears from these several Extracts,[124] that Mr. Locke attributes the Government of the natural *Rate of Interest* to the Proportion which the Quantity of Money in a Country bears to the Debts of its Inhabitants one amongst another, and to the Trade of it; and that Sir William Petty makes it depend on the Quantity of Money alone; so they only differ in regard to Debts" (pp.14-15). |XX—1294a||

||XXI—1300| Rich people, "instead of employing their Money themselves, [...] let it out to other People for them to make Profit of, reserving for the Owners *a Proportion of the Profits so***** *made*: But when the Riches of a Country are dispersed into so many Hands, and so equally divided, as not to leave many People enough to maintain two Families, by employing it in Trade, *there can be little borrowing*; for 20,000 *l.****** when it belongs to one Man, may be lent, because the Interest of it will keep a Family, but if it belongs to ten Men, it cannot be lent, because the Interest [...] will not keep ten Families" (pp.23-24).

"All Reasoning about natural Interest from *the Rate which the Government pays for Money*, is, and unavoidably must be fallacious; Experience has shown us, they neither have agreed, nor preserved a Correspondence with each other; and Reason tells us they never can; for *the one has its Foundation in Profit*, and *the other in Necessity*; the former of which has Bounds, but the latter none: The Gentleman who borrows Money to improve his Land, and the Merchant or Tradesman who borrow to carry on Trade, have

* In the manuscript: "viz".—*Ed.*

** In the manuscript: "to the farther increase of commerce".—*Ed.*

*** In the manuscript this is followed by the word: "true".—*Ed.*

**** In the manuscript: "to be".—*Ed.*

***** In the manuscript: "2,000£".—*Ed.*

Limits, beyond which they will not go; if they can get 10 per cent by Money, they may give 5 per cent for it; but they will not give 10; whereas he who borrows through Necessity, has nothing else to determine by, and this admits of no Rule at all" (pp.31-32).

"The Equitableness of taking Interest, depends not upon a Man's making or not making *Profit* by what he borrows, but upon its" (the money borrowed) "being capable of producing Profit if rightly employed" (p.49). "If *that which Men pay as Interest* for what they borrow, be *a part of the profits it is capable of producing*, this *Interest* must always be govern'd by those *Profits*" (p.49).

"What Proportion of these Profits do of Right belong to the Borrower, and what to the Lender; and this there is no other Method of determining, than by the Opinions in Borrowers and Lenders in general; for Right and Wrong in this Respect, are only what common Consent makes" (p.49).

"This Rule of *dividing Profits* is not however to be apply'd particularly to every Lender and Borrower, but to Lenders and Borrowers in general ... remarkably great and small Gains are the Rewards of Skill, and the Want of Understanding, which *Lenders have nothing at all to do with*; for as they will not suffer by the one, they ought not to benefit by the other. What has been said of *particular Men in the same Business* is applicable to *particular Sorts of Business*" (p.50).

"The *natural Rate of Interest* is governed by the *Profits of Trade* to Particulars" (p. 51).

Why then was interest 4 per cent instead of 8 as it had been earlier in England?

Because English merchants at that time "get* double the Profits they now make" [p.51].

Why 3 per cent in Holland, 5 and 6 in France, Germany, Portugal, 9 per cent in the West and East Indies, 12 in Turkey?

"One general Answer will do for the whole, which is, that the Profits of Trade in these several Countries differ from the Profits of Trade here, and so much as to produce all those different Rates of Interest" (p.51).

But what is the fall in profit due to?

To competition, foreign and internal, "a Decrease of Trade"** (through foreign competition) "*or to People in Trade lowering the Prices of their Commodities upon each other*...through Necessity to get some Trade, or through Avarice to get most" (pp.52-53).

"The Profits of Trade in general, are governed by the Proportion *which the Number of Traders* bears to the *Quantity of Trade*"*** (p. 55). "In Holland where the Number of People employ'd in Trade, bears the greatest proportion to the whole number of Inhabitants...*Interest is* [...] *lowest*

* In the manuscript: "got".—*Ed.*

** In the manuscript: "by a decrease of foreign trade".—*Ed.*

*** In the manuscript: "Commerce".—*Ed.*

[...] in Turkey, where the Disproportion is still greater, Interest is higher"* (pp.55-56).

||1301| "What governs the *Proportion between Trade and Traders?*" (p. 57). The "Motive** to Trade". "[I.] Natural necessity. [II.] Liberty. [III. The] Preservation of Men's private Rights. [IV.] Publick Safety" (pp. 57-58).

"There are no two Countries which furnish an equal Number of the Necessaries of Life in equal Plenty, and *with the same Quantity of Labour*; [...] Men's Wants increase or diminish with the Severity or Temperateness of the Climate they live in; [...] consequently, the *Proportion of Trade* which the Inhabitants of different Countries are obliged to carry on through Necessity, cannot be the same, nor is it practicable to ascertain the Degree of Variation further than by the Degrees of Heat and Cold; from whence one may make this general Conclusion, that the *Quantity of Labour* required for [the Maintenance of] a certain Number of People is greatest in cold Climates, and least in hot ones; for in the former, Men not only want more Cloaths, but the Earth more cultivating, than in the latter" (p.59). "One kind of Necessity which is peculiar to Holland...arises from the Country being over-peopled; which, with *the great Labour required to fence and drain their*** Land*, makes their Necessity to trade greater than it is in any other Part of the habitable World" (p.60).

[(D) CONCLUSION]

Massie, even more definitely than Hume, presents interest as a mere *part of profit*; both attribute the fall in interest to the accumulation of capitals (Massie [speaks] especially of competition) and the fall in profits resulting from this. Both [say] equally little about the *origin of the Profit of trade* itself. |XXI—1301||

* In the manuscript: "... am grössten, interest am höchsten".—*Ed.*

** In the manuscript: "motives".—*Ed.*

*** In the manuscript: "the".—*Ed.*

[8. ADDENDUM TO THE CHAPTERS ON THE PHYSIOCRATS]

[(A) SUPPLEMENTARY NOTE ON THE TABLEAU ÉCONOMIQUE. QUESNAY'S FALSE ASSUMPTIONS]

||XXIII—1433|

Productive class **Landlords** **Sterile class**

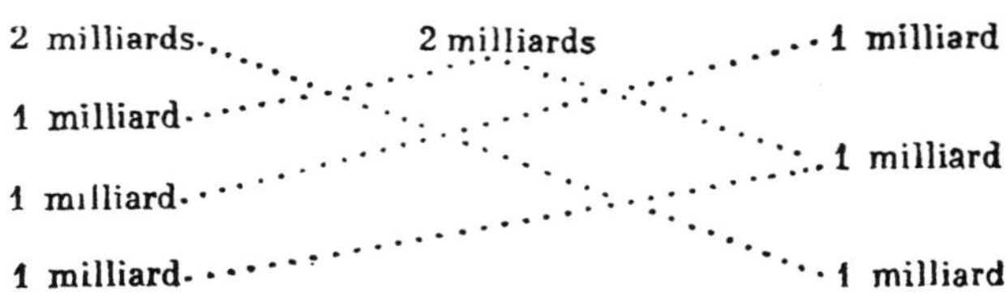

Annual advances
2 milliards
Total 5 milliards

Total 2 milliards

This is the simplest form of the Tableau économique.[125]

1. *Money circulation* (assuming payment is made only annually). The money circulation starts out from the spending class, the landlords who have no *commodities* to sell, who buy without selling.

They buy to the amount of 1 milliard from the productive class, to whom they send back the milliard in money received in payment for rent. (This disposes of one-fifth of the agricultural produce.) They buy to the amount of 1 milliard from the sterile class, who in this way get 1 milliard in money. (This disposes of half the product of manufacture.) With the 1 milliard, the sterile class buy means of subsistence from the productive class; so that 1 milliard in money thus flows back to the latter. (This disposes of a second fifth of the agricultural produce.) With the same milliard in money the productive class buy 1 milliard in manufactured products; this replaces for them one-half of their advances. (This disposes of the second half of the produce of manufacture). The sterile class buy ||1434| raw materials with the same milliard in money. (This disposes of another one-fifth of the agricultural produce.) In this way the [2] milliards in money have flowed back to the productive class.

So what remains is two-fifths of the agricultural produce. One-fifth is consumed in kind, but in what form is the second one-fifth accumulated? That is to be shown later.[126]

2. Even from Ouesnay's point of view, according to which the whole sterile class in fact consist only of wage-labourers, the falsity of the assumptions made is evident from the Tableau itself.

The original advances (fixed capital) made by the productive class are assumed to be five times the size of the annual advances. In the case of the sterile class this item is not mentioned at all —which naturally does not prevent it from existing.

Moreover, it is wrong to say that the reproduction is equal to 5 milliards; the Tableau itself shows it to be 7 milliards; 5 in the case of the productive class and 2 in the case of the sterile class.

[(B) PARTIAL REVERSION OF INDIVIDUAL PHYSIOCRATS TO MERCANTILIST IDEAS. DEMAND OF THE PHYSIOCRATS FOR FREEDOM OF COMPETITION]

The product of the sterile class is equal to 2 milliards. This product consists of 1 milliard in raw materials (which therefore partly enter into the product, and partly replace the wear and tear of the machinery which has entered into the value of the product) and 1 milliard in means of subsistence, which have been consumed in working them up.

They sell this entire product to the landlords and the productive class, in order *firstly* to replace the advance (in raw materials), *secondly* to obtain agricultural means of subsistence. Therefore *not a farthing's worth of the manufactured products* is left for their own consumption, still less for interest or profit. This in fact was noticed by Baudeau (or Le Trosne); he explains it by the sterile class selling their product *above* its *value*, so that what they sell for 2 milliards is equivalent to 2 milliards minus x. Their profit, and even what *they* consume in manufactured goods as necessary means of subsistence, is therefore explained only by the *raising of the price of the commodities above their value.*[127] And here the Physiocrats necessarily fall back on the Mercantile system's *profit upon alienation.*

This is why free competition between the manufacturers is so very essential, so that they do not take too great advantage of the productive class, the agriculturists. On the other hand this free competition is necessary in order that agricultural produce may be sold at a "*good* price", that is, that it may rise *above* its native price by sale abroad—the assumption being a country which exports wheat, etc.

[(C) ORIGINAL FORMULATION OF WHY IT IS IMPOSSIBLE TO INCREASE VALUE IN EXCHANGE]

"Every purchase is a sale, and every sale a purchase" (Quesnay, *Dialogues sur le commerce et sur les travaux des artisans*, etc., éd. Daire[128], p.170). "To buy is to sell, and to sell is to buy" (*Quesnay* in Dupont de Nemours, *Origine, etc.*, 1767, p.392).[129]

"*Price always precedes purchases and sales.* If the competition of sellers and buyers brings about no change in it, it exists as it is through other causes *independent* of trade" (l.c., p.148).[130]

"It is always to be presumed that it" (exchange) "is profitable to both" (contracting parties), "since they mutually procure for themselves the enjoyment of wealth which they could only obtain through exchange. But always there is only exchange of wealth *of a certain value* for other wealth *of equal value*, and consequently *no real increase of wealth*" (this should be: no real increase of value) (l.c., p.197).[131]

Advances and *capital* are explicitly stated to be identical. *Accumulation of capitals* as the principal condition.

"*The increase of capitals* is then *the principal means of augmenting labour*, and of the *greatest benefit to society*", etc. (*Quesnay* in Dupont de Nemours, l.c., p.391).[132] |XXIII—1434||

[9. GLORIFICATION OF THE LANDED ARISTOCRACY BY BUAT, AN EPIGONE OF THE PHYSIOCRATS]

||XXII—1399| Buat (Comte du), *Éléments de la politique, ou Recherche des vrais principes de l'économie sociale*, (6 volumes), London, 1773.

This feeble and diffuse writer, who takes the outward form of Physiocracy for its essence and glorifies the landed aristocracy—and in fact accepts it [Physiocracy] only in so far as it serves this purpose—would not have to be mentioned at all, but for the fact that the brutal characteristics of the bourgeois emerge so sharply in his work; quite as sharply, perhaps, as in Ricardo's writings later. His error in restricting the net product to rent makes no difference to this.

What Buat says is repeated by Ricardo in relation to the net product in general.[133] The labourers belong to the incidental expenses and exist only in order that the owners of the net product may "form society". (See the relevant passages.)[134] The free labourer's lot is conceived as only a changed form of slavery; but this is necessary so that the higher strata may form "society".

< *Arthur Young* too sees the net product, surplus-value, as the purpose of production.[135] >

||1400| In this connection we may recall the passage in Ricardo, directed against Adam Smith, for whom that capital is the most productive which employs the greatest number of labourers.[136] On this, compare Buat—t. VI, pp.51-52, 68-70. Also on the labouring class and slavery—t. II, pp.288, 297, 309; t. III, pp.74, 95-96, 103; t. VI, pp.43, 51; on the necessity for these labourers to work surplus-time, and on the meaning of the *strict nécessaire*—t. VI, pp.52-53.

The one passage to be quoted here—because it deals well with the prattle about the *risk* that the capitalist always runs:

> "They have risked much to gain much? But they have risked men, and goods or money. As for the men, [...] if they have exposed them to manifest peril for the sake of gain, they have done a very wicked act. As for the goods, if there is any merit in producing them, there should be no merit in risking them for the profit of one individual", etc. (t. II, p. 297). |XXII—1400||

[10. POLEMICS AGAINST THE LANDED ARISTOCRACY FROM THE STANDPOINT OF THE PHYSIOCRATS (AN ANONYMOUS ENGLISH AUTHOR)[137]]

||XXIII—1449| *The Essential Principles of the Wealth of Nations, illustrated, in Opposition to some False Doctrines of Dr. Adam Smith, and others*, London, 1797.

This man knew of Anderson, for he prints in his appendix an extract from Anderson's Agricultural Report for the County of Aberdeen.

This is the *only important* English work directly supporting the Physiocratic teaching. William Spence, *Britain Independent of Commerce*, 1807, is a mere caricature. This same fellow in 1814-15 was one of the most fanatic defenders of the landed interest on the basis of Physiocracy—which teaches free trade. The fellow is not to be confused with *Thomas Spence*, the deadly enemy of *Private Property in Land.*

The work [*The Essential Principles*] contains firstly a very excellent and compressed resumé of the Physiocratic doctrine.

He is right in tracing the origin of this view to *Locke* and *Vanderlint*, and he describes the Physiocrats as those who "very systematically, *though not correctly*, illustrated" the doctrine (p. 4). (See also on this p.6; *notebook H*, pp.32-33.)[138]

The summary quoted there brings out very nicely how the *privation theory*—which the later apologists, and partly even Smith, made the basis for the formation of capital—arose precisely from the Physiocratic view that *no surplus-value* is created in industry, etc.:

„The expence laid out in employing and maintaining them" [handicraftsmen, manufacturers[139] and merchants] "does no more than *continue the existence of its own value*, and is therefore unproductive" (because unproductive of surplus-value). "The wealth of society can never in the smallest degree be *augmented* by artificers, manufacturers, or merchants, otherwise than by their *saving and accumulating part of what is intended for their daily subsistence*; consequently it is *by privation or parsimony alone*, that they can add any thing to the general stock" (Senior's theory of abstinence, Adam Smith's theory of savings). "Cultivators, on the contrary, may live up to the whole of their income, and yet at the same time [...] enrich the State; for their industry affords a surplus-produce called rent" (p.6).

"A class of men whose labour though (it produces something) produces no more than what was bestowed, in order to effect that labour, may with the greatest propriety be called an *unproductive class*" (p.10).

Production of surplus-value to be clearly distinguished from its transfer.

"The *augmentation* of revenue" (this is *accumulation*) "is not, but indirectly, the object of the Economists[140]... Their object is the *production and reproduction of* [...] *revenue*" (p.18).

And this is the great merit of Physiocracy. The Physiocrats put themselves the question: how is *surplus-value* (for him [the anonymous writer] it is revenue) produced and reproduced? The question how it is *reproduced on an enlarged scale*, that is, increased, comes up only in the second place. Its *category*, the secret of its production, ||1450| must first be revealed.

Surplus-value and commercial capital.

"When the question is about the *production* of revenue, it is altogether illogical to substitute for that *the transfer of* [...] *revenue*, which *all commercial dealings* are [...] resolvable into" (p.22). "What does the word *commerce* imply but *commutatio mercium**...sometimes more beneficial to the one than the other; but still what the one gains the other loses, and their traffic really *produces no increase*" (p.23). "Should a Jew sell a crown-piece for ten shillings, or a Queen Anne's farthing for a guinea, he would augment his own income, no doubt, but he would not thereby augment the *quantity of the precious metals*; and the nature of the traffic would be the same, whether his virtuoso customer resided in the same street with himself, or in France, or in China" (p.23).

The Physiocrats explain the profit of industry as profit upon alienation (that is, in the Mercantilist way). *This Englishman therefore draws the right conclusion that this profit is only a gain when industrial commodities are sold abroad. From the Mercantilist premise he draws the right Mercantilist conclusion.*

"No man, as a manufacturer, however he may gain himself, adds any thing to the national revenue, if his commodity is sold and consumed at home; for *the buyer precisely loses...what the manufacturer gains*.... There is an *interchange* between the seller and the buyer, but no increase" (p.26).

* Commodity exchange.—*Ed.*

"To supply the want of a surplus...the master-employer takes a profit of 50 per cent upon what he expends in wages, or sixpence in the shilling on each manufacturer's pay; ...and if the manufacture is sold abroad...[this] would be *the national profit"* (p.27) of so and so many "artificers".

Very good presentation of the reasons for Holland's wealth. Fisheries. (He should also have mentioned stock-raising.) Monopoly of the spices of the East. Carrying trade. Lending money abroad. (*Supplementary notebook H*, pp.36-37).[141]

"Manufacturers are [...] a *necessary* class" but not a "*productive class*" (p.35). They "occasion a *commutation* or *transfer* of the revenue previously provided by the cultivator, by giving a *permanency* to that revenue under a new form" (p.38).

There are only four essential classes. Productive class or cultivators. Manufacturers. Defenders. The class of instructors, which he substitutes for the Physiocratic tithe owners or priests, "for every civil society must be fed, [...] clothed, defended and instructed" (pp.50-51).

The mistake of the Economists is that they

"deemed *Receivers of land rents, as mere Receivers of rents, a productive class* in society...they have in some degree compensated for their error by intimating that the Church and King are to be served out of those rents. Dr. Smith...suffering it" (this error of the Economists) "to pervade the *whole of his own* enquiry*," (this is correct) "directs his refutation to the sound part of the Economical system" (p.8).

||1451| The landlords as such are not only not *productive*, but not even an *essential class* of society.

"The *proprietors of land* as mere receivers of land rents are *not an essential class of society.... By separating the rents of lands from the constitutional purpose of the defence of the State*, the receivers of those rents instead of being an essential class, render themselves one of the most unessential and burdensome classes in society" (p.51).

See his further treatment of this, which is very good, [in] *Supplementary notebook H*, pp. 38-39[142]—and this polemic against the receivers of land rent from the standpoint of the Physiocrats, *as the final conclusion from their doctrine, is very important.*

[The author] shows that the real *tax on land* is Turkish (l. c., p. 59).

---

* In the manuscript: "this".—*Ed.*

The *landlord taxes* not only improvements of land, but often the presumption of future improvement (pp. 63-64). Tax on rents (p. 65).

The Physiocratic doctrine *anciently* established in England, Ireland, feudal Europe, Empire of the Mogul (pp. 93-94).

The landlord as tax-imposer (p. 118).

The limitations of Physiocracy break through in the following (lack of *understanding of the division of labour*): Let it be assumed that a clockmaker or calico manufacturer cannot sell his clock or calico. [Then he would be in difficult position. That however shows] "that a manufacturer only enriches himself by being a *seller*" (it shows only that he produces his product as a *commodity* "and that when he ceases to be a *seller*, his *profits*" (and what of the profits of the farmer who is not a *seller*?) "are immediately at a stand, because they are not natural profits, but artificial. The cultivator...*may exist*, and thrive, and multiply, without *selling* any thing" (pp. 38-39). (But then he must also be a manufacturer.)

[Why does the author speak only of a clockmaker or a calico manufacturer? It can equally well be] assumed that a producer of coal, iron, flax, indigo, etc., cannot sell these products, or even that a producer of corn cannot sell his corn. *Béardé de l'Abbaye*, cited above, is very good on this.[143] He [the anonymous author] has to stress production [for] *immediate* consumption as against the *production of commodities*—very much in contradiction with the Physiocratic view that *exchange-value* was the principal thing. But that runs right through the work of this fellow. It is the *bourgeois* view within the pre-bourgeois *way of looking at things*.[144]

[He comes out] against Arthur Young's *high price*, [which the latter regards] as *important for the prosperity of agriculture*; *but this is at the same time polemics against the Physiocrats* (l. c., pp. 65-78 and 118).

Surplus-value cannot be derived from the nominal raising of the price on the part of the seller.

Through "this* augmentation of the *nominal value of the produce... nor are sellers* [...] *enriched*** ... since what they gain as sellers, they precisely expend in quality of buyers" (p. 66).

---

* In the manuscript: "the".—*Ed.*

** In the manuscript: "sellers not enriched".—*Ed.*

This is similar to Vanderlint's arguments:

"While a field admitting cultivation can be found for every idler, let no idler be without a field. Houses of industry are good things; but fields of industry are much better" (p. 47).

[He is] against the farm system, and for long leases, because landownership will otherwise only hinder production and improvements (pp.118-23). (*Irish Right of Tenantry.*)[145] |XXIII—1451||

[11. APOLOGIST CONCEPTION OF THE PRODUCTIVITY OF ALL PROFESSIONS]

||V—182| A philosopher produces ideas, a poet poems, a clergyman sermons, a professor compendia and so on. A criminal produces crimes. If we look a little closer at the connection between this latter branch of production and society as a whole, we shall rid ourselves of many prejudices. The criminal produces not only crimes but also criminal law, and with this also the professor who gives lectures on criminal law and in addition to this the inevitable compendium in which this same professor throws his lectures onto the general market as "commodities". This brings with it augmentation of national wealth, quite apart from the personal enjoyment which—as a competent witness, Herr Professor Roscher, [tells] us—the manuscript of the compendium brings to its originator himself.

The criminal moreover produces the whole of the police and of criminal justice, constables, judges, hangmen, juries, etc.; and all these different lines of business, which form equally many categories of the social division of labour, develop different capacities of the human spirit, create new needs and new ways of satisfying them. Torture alone has given rise to the most ingenious mechanical inventions, and employed many honourable craftsmen in the production of its instruments.

The criminal produces an impression, partly moral and partly tragic, as the case may be, and in this way renders a "service" by arousing the moral and aesthetic feelings of the public. He produces not only compendia on Criminal Law, not only penal codes and along with them legislators in this field, but also art, belles-lettres, novels, and even tragedies, as not only Müllner's *Schuld* and Schiller's *Räuber* show, but also [Sophocles'] *Oedipus* and [Shakespeare's] *Richard the Third*. The criminal breaks the monotony and everyday security of bourgeois life. In this way he keeps it from stagnation, and gives rise to that uneasy tension and agility without which even the spur of competition would get blunted. Thus he gives a stimulus to the productive forces. While crime takes a part of the superfluous population off the labour market and thus reduces competition among the labourers—up to a certain point preventing wages from falling below the minimum—the struggle against crime absorbs another part of this population. Thus the criminal comes in as one of those natural "counterweights" which bring about a correct balance and open up a whole perspective of "useful" occupations.

The effects of the criminal on the development of productive power can be shown in detail. Would locks ever have reached their present degree of excellence had there been no thieves? Would the making of bank-notes have reached its present perfection had there been no ||183| forgers? Would the microscope have found its way into the sphere of ordinary commerce (see Babbage) but for trading frauds? Doesn't practical chemistry owe just as much to adulteration of commodities and the efforts to show it up as to the honest zeal for production? Crime, through its constantly new methods of attack on property, constantly calls into being new methods of defence, and so is as productive as strikes for the invention of machines. And if one leaves the sphere of private crime: would the world-market ever have come into being but for national crime? Indeed, would even the nations have arisen? And hasn't the Tree of Sin been at the same time the Tree of Knowledge ever since the time of Adam?

In his *Fable of the Bees* (1705) Mandeville had already shown that every possible kind of occupation is productive, and had given expression to the line of this whole argument:

> "That what we call Evil in this World, Moral as well as Natural, is the grand Principle that makes us Sociable Creatures, the solid Basis, the *Life and Support of all Trades and Employments* without exception [...] there we must look for the true origin of all Arts and Sciences; and [...] the moment, Evil ceases, the Society must be spoil'd if not totally dissolve'd*" [2nd edition, London, 1723, p. 428].

Only Mandeville was of course infinitely bolder and more honest than the philistine apologists of bourgeois society. |V—183||

* In the manuscript: "destroyed".—*Ed.*

[12.] PRODUCTIVITY OF CAPITAL. PRODUCTIVE AND UNPRODUCTIVE LABOUR

[(A) PRODUCTIVITY OF CAPITAL AS THE CAPITALIST EXPRESSION OF THE PRODUCTIVE POWER OF SOCIAL LABOUR]

||XXI—1317| We have seen not only how capital produces, but how it itself is produced, and how, as an essentially altered relation, it emerges from the process of production and how it is developed in it.[146] On the one hand capital transforms the mode of production; on the other hand this changed form of the mode of production and a particular stage in the development of the material forces of production are the basis and precondition—the premise for its own formation.

Since living labour—through the exchange between capital and labourer—is incorporated in capital, and appears as an activity belonging to capital from the moment that the labour-process begins, all the productive powers of social labour appear as the productive powers of capital, just as the general social form of labour appears in money as the property of a thing. Thus the productive power of social labour and its special forms now appear as productive powers and forms of capital, of *materialised* labour, of the material conditions of labour—which, having assumed this independent form, are personified by the capitalist in relation to living labour. Here we have once more the perversion of the relationship, which we have already, in dealing with money, called *fetishism*.[147]

The capitalist himself only holds power as the *personification of capital*. (In Italian book-keeping this role of his as a *capitalist*, as personified capital, is even always contrasted with him as a mere person, in which capacity he appears only as a personal consumer and debtor of his own capital.)

The *productivity* of capital consists in the first instance—even if one only considers the *formal* subsumption of labour under capital—in the *compulsion to perform surplus-labour*, labour beyond the immediate need; a compulsion which the capitalist mode of production shares with earlier modes of production, but which it exercises and carries into effect in a manner more favourable to production.

Even from the standpoint of this purely formal relation—the *general* form of capitalist production, which is common both to its less developed stage and to its more developed stage—the *means of production*, the material conditions of labour—material of labour, instruments of labour (and means of subsistence) —do not appear as subsumed to the labourer, but the labourer appears as subsumed to them. He does not make use of them, but they make use of him. And it is this that makes them capital. Capital *employs* labour. They are not means for him to produce products, whether in the form of direct means of subsistence, or of means of exchange, commodities. But he is a means for them —partly to maintain their value, partly to create surplus-value, that is, to increase it, absorb surplus-labour.

Already in its simple form this relation is an inversion—personification of the thing and materialisation of the person; for what distinguishes this form from all previous forms is that the capitalist does not rule over the labourer through any personal qualities he may have, but only in so far as he is "capital"; his domination is only that of materialised labour over living labour, of the labourer's product over the labourer himself.

The relation grows still more complicated and apparently more mysterious because, with the development of the specifically capitalist mode of production, it is not only these directly material things <all products of labour; considered as use-values, they are both material conditions of labour and products of labour; considered as exchange-values, they are materialised general labour-time or money> that get up on their hind legs to the labourer and confront him as "capital", but [also] the forms of socially developed labour—co-operation, manufacture (as a form of division of labour), the factory (as a form of social labour organised on machinery as its material basis)—all these appear as *forms of the development of capital*, and therefore the productive powers of labour built up on these forms of social labour—consequently also science and the forces of nature—appear as *productive powers of capital*. In fact, the unity [of labour] in co-operation, the combination [of labour] through the division of labour, the use for productive purposes in machine industry of the forces of nature and science alongside the products of labour—all this confronts the individual labourers themselves as something *extraneous* and *objective*, as a mere form of existence of the means of labour that are independent of them and control them, just as the means of labour themselves [confront them,] in their simple visible form as materials, instruments, etc., as functions of *capital* and consequently of the *capitalist*.

The social forms of their own labour or the forms of their own ||1318| social labour are relations that have been formed quite independently of the individual labourers; the labourers, as subsumed under capital, become elements of these social formations—but these social formations do not belong to them. They therefore confront them as *forms* of capital itself, as combinations belonging to capital, as distinct from their individual labour-power, arising from capital and incorporated in it. And this takes on a form that is all the more real the more on the one hand their labour-power itself becomes so modified by these forms that it is powerless as an independent force, that is to say, *outside* this capitalist relationship, and that its independent capacity to produce is destroyed. And on the other hand, with the development of machinery the conditions of labour seem to dominate labour also technologically while at the same time they replace labour, oppress it, and make it superfluous in its independent forms.

In this process, in which the *social* character of their labour confronts them to a certain degree as *capitalised* (as for example in machinery the visible products of labour appear as dominating labour), the same naturally takes place with the forces of nature and science, the product of general historical development in its abstract quintessence—they confront the labourers as *powers* of capital. They are separate in fact from the skill and knowledge of the individual labourer—and although, in their origin, they too are the product of labour—wherever they enter into the labour-process they appear as *embodied in capital*. The capitalist who makes use of a machine need not understand it. (See Ure.)[148] But science realised *in the machine* appears as *capital* in relation to the labourers. And in fact all these applications of science, natural forces and products of labour on a large scale, these applications founded on *social labour*, themselves appear only as *means for the exploitation* of labour, as means of appropriating surplus-labour, and hence confront labour as *powers* belonging to capital. Capital naturally uses all these means only to exploit labour; but in order to exploit it, it must apply them in production. And so the development of the *social* productive powers of labour and the conditions for this development appear as *acts of capital*, towards which the individual labourer not only maintains a passive attitude, but which take place in opposition to him.

Capital itself has a double character, since it consists of commodities:

1. *Exchange-value* (money); but [it is] *self-expanding value*, value which—because it is *value*—creates value, *grows as value*, receives an increment. This [growth] resolves itself into the exchange of a given quantity of materialised labour for a greater quantity of living labour.

2. *Use-value*; and here it shows itself through its specific relations in the labour-process. But precisely here it is no longer merely material of labour and means of labour to which belongs *labour*, which have absorbed labour, but along with labour [capital includes] also the *social combinations* [of labour] and the development of the means of labour corresponding to these social combinations. Capitalist production first develops on a large scale—tearing them away from the individual independent labourer—both the objective and subjective conditions of the labour-process, but it develops them as powers dominating the *individual labourer* and *extraneous* to him.

Thus capital becomes a very mysterious being. |1318||[149]

||1320| Capital is therefore productive: (1) as a force *compelling* surplus-labour, (2) as the absorber and appropriator (personification) of the productive powers of social labour and of the general social productive forces, such as science.

The question arises, how or for what reason does labour as opposed to capital appear productive or as *productive labour*, since the productive powers of labour are transposed into capital, and the same productive power cannot be counted twice, once as the productive power of labour and the second time as the productive power of capital? <Productive power of labour—productive power of capital. But *labour-power* is productive through the *difference* between its *value* and *the value which it creates.*>

[(B) PRODUCTIVE LABOUR IN THE SYSTEM OF CAPITALIST PRODUCTION]

Only bourgeois narrow-mindedness, which regards the capitalist forms of production as absolute forms—hence as eternal, natural forms of production—can confuse the question of what is *productive labour* from the standpoint of capital with the question of what labour is productive in general, or what is productive labour in general; and consequently fancy itself very wise in giving the answer that all labour which produces anything at all, which has any kind of result, is by that very fact productive labour.

[*Firstly*:] Only labour *which is directly transformed into capital is productive*; that is, only labour which makes variable capital a variable magnitude and consequently [makes the total capital C] equal to $C+\triangle$.[150] If the variable capital before its exchange with labour is equal to x, so that we have the equation $y=x$, then the labour which transforms x into $x+h$, and consequently out of $y=x$ makes $y'=x+h$, is productive labour. This is the *first* point to be elucidated. [That is,] labour which produces surplus-value or serves capital as agency for the creation of surplus-value, and hence for manifesting itself as capital, as self-expanding value.

Secondly: The social and general productive powers of labour are productive powers of capital; but these productive powers relate only to the labour-process, or affect only the use-value. They represent properties inherent in capital as a thing, as its use-value. They do not directly affect *exchange-value*. Whether a hundred work together, or each one of the hundred works by himself, the value of their product is equal to a hundred days' labour, whether represented in a large or small quantity of products; that is to say, the productivity of the labour does not affect the value.

||1321| The varying productivity of labour affects exchange-value only in one way.

If the productivity of labour is increased for example in a single branch of labour—for instance, if weaving with power-looms instead of hand-looms becomes no longer exceptional, and if the weaving of a yard with the power-loom requires only half the labour-time required with the hand-loom, then twelve hours' labour of a hand-loom weaver is no longer represented in a value of twelve hours, but in one of six, since the *necessary* labour-time has now become six hours. The hand-loom weaver's twelve hours now only [represent] six hours of social labour-time, although he still works twelve hours as he did before.

But this is not what we are dealing with here. As against this, take another branch of production, for example type-setting, in which up to now no machinery is used. Twelve hours in this branch produce just as much *value* as twelve hours in branches of production in which machinery, etc., is developed to the utmost. Hence labour as producing *value* always remains the labour of the *individual*, but expressed in the form of *general labour*. Consequently productive labour—as labour producing value—always confronts capital as labour of the individual labour-power, as labour of the *isolated labourer*, whatever social combinations these labourers may enter into in the process of production. While therefore capital, in relation to the labourer, represents the social productive power of labour, the productive labour of the workmen, in relation to capital, always represents only the labour of the *isolated labourer*.

Thirdly: Whereas the extortion of surplus-labour and the appropriation to itself of the social productive powers of labour seem to be a natural property of capital—hence a property springing from its use-value—it seems on the contrary to be a natural property of labour to manifest its own social productive powers as productive powers of capital and its own surplus [-product] as surplus-value, as the self-expansion of capital.

These three points must now be examined, and from them we must deduce the distinction between productive and unproductive labour.

[On (1).] The productivity of capital consists in the fact that it confronts labour as wage-labour, and the productivity of labour consists in the fact that it confronts the means of labour as capital.

We have seen that money is transformed into capital—that is, a certain exchange-value is transformed into self-expanding exchange-value, into value plus surplus-value—through one part of it being converted into commodities which serve labour as means of labour (raw materials, instruments, in short, the material conditions of labour), and another part being used for the purchase of labour-power. However, it is not this first exchange between money and labour-power, or the mere purchase of the latter, which transforms money into capital. This purchase incorporates in the capital the use of the labour-power for a certain time, or makes a certain quantity of living labour one of the modes of existence of capital, so to speak, the entelechy of the capital itself.

In the actual production process the living labour is transformed into capital through the fact that on the one hand it reproduces the wages—that is, the value of the variable capital—and on the other hand it creates surplus-value; and through this process of transformation the whole sum of money is transformed into capital, although the part of it which varies directly is only the part expended in wages. If the value was previously equal to c+v, now it is equal to c+(v+x), which is the same thing as (c+v)+x[151]; or in other words: the original sum of money or magnitude of value has expanded, has shown itself to be value which at the same time maintains itself and also increases.

<This has to be noted: the circumstance that only the *variable part* of the capital produces its increment in no way alters the fact that through this process the whole original value has expanded, has grown greater by a surplus-value, and that therefore the whole original sum of money has been transformed into capital. For the original value was equal to c+v (constant and variable capital). In the process it becomes c+(v+x); the latter is the reproduced part, which has come into existence through the transformation of the living labour into materialised labour—a transformation which is conditioned and initiated through the exchange of v for labour-power, or its transformation into wages. But c+(v+x)=c+v (the original capital)+x. Moreover the transformation of v into v+x, and therefore of (c+v) into (c+v)+x, could only take place through the transformation of a part of the money into c. The one part can only be transformed into *variable* capital through the other part being transformed into constant capital.>

In the actual process of production the labour is *in reality* transformed into capital, but this transformation is conditioned by the original exchange between money and labour-power. It is through this *direct* transformation of labour into *materialised* labour, belonging not to the labourer but to the capitalist, that money is first transformed into capital—including that part of it which has received the form of means of production, or conditions of labour. Up to that point, the money—whether it exists in its own form or in the form of commodities (products) of a kind that can serve as means of production of new commodities—is only *an sich** capital.

* In essence.—*Ed.*

||1322| Only this definite *relation* to labour transforms money or commodities into capital, and that labour is *productive labour* which through this its relation to the conditions of production—to which corresponds a definite conduct in the actual process of production—transforms money or commodities into capital; that is to say, which maintains and increases the value of *materialised* labour rendered independent in relation to labour-power. Productive labour is only a concise term for the whole relationship and the form and manner in which labour-power figures in the capitalist production process. The distinction from *other* kinds of labour is however of the greatest importance, since this distinction expresses precisely the specific form of the labour on which the whole capitalist mode of production and capital itself is based.

Productive labour is therefore—in the system of capitalist production—labour which produces *surplus-value* for its employer, or which transforms the objective conditions of labour into capital and their owner into a capitalist; that is to say, labour which produces its own product as capital.

So when we speak of *productive labour*, we speak of *socially determined* labour, labour which implies a quite specific relation between the buyer and the seller of the labour.

Now although the money which is in the hands of the buyer of labour-power (or the commodities in his possession: [the supply] of means of production and means of subsistence for the labourer) only becomes capital through this process, is only transformed into capital in this process—and therefore these things are not capital before they enter into the process, but are only destined to be capital—they are nevertheless *an sich* capital. They are in their essence capital because of the independent form in which they confront labour-power and labour-power confronts them—a relationship which conditions and ensures the exchange with labour-power and the subsequent process of the actual transformation of labour into capital. They have from the outset the *specific social character* in relation to the labourers which makes them into capital and gives them command over labour. They are therefore *pre-conditions* confronting labour as capital.

Productive labour, therefore, can be so described when it is directly exchanged for *money as capital*, or, which is only a more concise way of putting it, is exchanged directly for *capital*, that is, for money which in its essence is capital, which is destined to function as capital, or confronts labour-power as *capital.* The phrase: labour which is *directly* exchanged for *capital,* implies that labour is exchanged for money as *capital* and actually transforms it into capital. The significance of the *direct nature* of the exchange will be seen more clearly in a moment.

Productive labour is therefore labour which reproduces for the labourer only the previously determined value of his labour-power, but as an activity creating value increases the value of capital; in other words, which confronts the labourer himself with the values it has created in the form of capital.

[(C) TWO ESSENTIALLY DIFFERENT PHASES IN THE EXCHANGE BETWEEN CAPITAL AND LABOUR]

In the exchange between capital and labour, as we saw in examining the production process,[152] two essentially different though interdependent phases have to be distinguished.

First: The first exchange between capital and labour is a *formal process,* in which capital figures as *money* and labour power as *commodity.* From a conceptual or legal standpoint the sale of labour-power takes place in this first process, although the labour is *paid for* only after it has been performed—at the end of the day, of the week, etc. This in no way alters this transaction, in which the labour-power is *sold.* What in this transaction is *directly* sold is not a commodity in which labour has already realised itself, but the *use of the labour-power itself,* and therefore in fact the *labour itself,* since the use of the labour-power is its activity—labour. It is therefore not an exchange of labour mediated through an exchange of commodities. When A sells boots to B, both exchange labour, the first, labour realised in boots, the second, labour realised in money. But in this first exchange, on one side *materialised labour* in its general social form, that is, *money,* is exchanged for *labour which as yet exists only as a power*; and what is brought and sold is the use of this power, that is, the labour itself, although the *value* of the commodity sold is not the value of the labour (a meaningless phrase) but the *value* of the labour-power. What takes place therefore is a direct exchange between *materialised labour* and *labour power,* which in fact resolves itself into living labour; that is, between materialised labour and living labour. The wage—the value of the labour-power—appears, as explained earlier as the direct purchase price, the *price of labour.*[153]

In this first phase the relation between labourer and capitalist is that of seller and buyer of a commodity. The capitalist pays the *value* of the labour-power, that is, the *value* of the commodity which he buys.

At the same time, however, the labour-power is only bought because the labour which it can perform, and undertakes to perform, is more than the labour required for the reproduction of its labour-power; therefore the labour performed by it represents a greater value than the value of the labour-power.

||1323| *Secondly*: The second phase of the *exchange* between capital and labour in fact has nothing to do with the first, and strictly speaking is not an *exchange* at all.

In the first phase there is exchange of money for commodity —exchange of equivalents—and labourer and capitalist confront each other only as owners of commodities. Equivalents are exchanged. (That is to say, it makes no difference to the relation *when* they are exchanged; and whether the price of the labour is *above* or *below* the *value* of the labour-power or is *equal* to it alters nothing in the transaction. It *can* therefore take place in accordance with the general law of commodity exchange.)

In the second phase there is no exchange at all. The owner of money has ceased to be a buyer of commodities and the labourer has ceased to be a seller of commodities. The owner of money now functions as capitalist. He consumes the commodity which he has bought, and the worker supplies it, since the use of his labour-power is his labour itself. Through the earlier transaction the *labour* itself has become part of materialised wealth. The labourer performs it, but it *belongs* to capital and is now only a function of the latter. It is performed therefore directly under the control and direction of capital; and the product in which it is materialised is the new form in which the capital appears, or in which rather it actually *realises* itself as capital. In this process, therefore, labour is directly *materialised*, is transformed *directly* into capital, after it has been *formally* incorporated in capital through the first transaction. And indeed more labour is here transformed into capital than the capital which had earlier been expended on the purchase of labour-power. In this process a part of unpaid labour is appropriated, and only thereby does the money transform itself into capital.

But although in this phase no exchange in fact takes place, the result, abstracting from the means that brought it about, is that in the process—taking both phases together—a certain quantity of materialised labour has exchanged for a greater quantity of living labour. This is expressed in the result of the process by the fact that the labour which has materialised itself in its product is greater in quantity than the labour materialised in the labour-power, and hence greater than the materialised labour paid to the labourer; or in other words by the fact that in the actual process the capitalist gets back not only the part of the capital which he laid out in wages, but a surplus-value which costs him nothing. The *direct* exchange of labour for capital here signifies: (1) the direct transformation of the labour into capital, into a material component part of capital in the production process; (2) the exchange of a certain quantity of materialised labour for the same quantity of living labour [plus] a surplus quantity of living labour which is appropriated *without exchange*.

The statement that *productive labour* is labour which is *directly* exchanged with *capital* embraces all these phases, and is only a derivative formula expressing the fact that it is *labour* which transforms money into capital, which is exchanged with the conditions of production as *capital*, that therefore in its relationship with these conditions of production labour is not faced by them as simple conditions of production, nor does it face the conditions of production as *labour* in general that has no specific social character.

This statement covers: (1) the relation of money and labour-power to each other as commodities, purchase and sale as between the owner of money and the owner of labour-power; (2) the direct subsumption of labour under capital; (3) the real transformation of labour into capital in the production process, or what is the same thing, the creation of surplus-value for capital. *Two kinds of exchange* take place *between labour and capital*. The first expresses merely the purchase of labour-power and therefore in reality of labour and therefore of its product; the second, the direct transformation of *living* labour into capital, in other words the materialisation of living labour as the realisation of capital.

[(D) THE SPECIFIC USE-VALUE OF PRODUCTIVE LABOUR FOR CAPITAL]

The result of the capitalist production process is neither a mere product (use-value) nor a *commodity*, that is, a use-value which has a certain exchange-value. Its result, its product, is the creation of *surplus-value* for capital, and consequently the actual *transformation* of money or commodity into capital—which before the production process they were only in intention, in their essence, in what they were destined to be. In the production process more labour is absorbed than has been bought. This absorption, |1324| this *appropriation* of another's unpaid labour, which is consummated in the production process, is the *direct aim* of the capitalist production process; for what capital as capital (hence the capitalist as capitalist) wants to produce is neither an immediate use-value for individual consumption nor a commodity to be turned first into money and then into a use-value. Its aim is the *accumulation of wealth*, the *self-expansion of value, its increase*; that is to say, the maintenance of the old value and the creation of surplus-value. And it achieves this *specific product* of the capitalist production process only in exchange with labour, which for that reason is called *productive labour*.

Labour which is to produce *commodities* must be useful labour; it must produce a *use-value*, it must manifest itself in a *use-value*. And consequently only labour which manifests itself in *commodities*, that is, in use-values, is labour for which capital is exchanged. This is a self-evident premise. But it is not this concrete character of labour, its use-value as such—that it is for example tailoring labour, cobbling, spinning, weaving, etc. —which forms its specific use-value for capital and consequently stamps it as *productive labour* in the system of capitalist production. What forms its *specific use-value* for capital is not its specific useful character, any more than it is the particular useful properties of the product in which it is materialised. But what forms its specific use-value for capital is its character as the element which creates exchange-value, abstract labour; and in fact not that it represents some particular quantity of this general labour, but that it represents a *greater* quantity than is *contained* in its price, that is to say, in the *value of the labour-power*.

For it [capital], the use-value of labour-power is precisely the excess of the quantity of labour which it performs over the quantity of labour which is materialised in the labour-power itself and hence is required to reproduce it. Naturally, it supplies this quantity of labour *in the determinate form* inherent in it as labour which has a particular utility, such as spinning labour, weaving labour, etc. But this concrete character, which is what enables it to take the form of a commodity, is not its *specific use-value* for capital. Its specific use-value for capital consists in its quantity as labour in general, and in the difference, the excess, of the quantity of labour which it performs *over* the quantity of labour which it costs.

A certain sum of money x becomes capital in that it apppears in its product as x+h; that is to say, in that the quantity of labour contained in it as product is greater than the quantity of labour which it originally contained. And this is the result of the exchange between money and productive labour; in other words, only that labour is *productive* which, exchanged with materialised labour, enables the latter to take the form of an increased quantity of materialised labour.

The capitalist production process, therefore, is not merely the production of commodities. It is a process which absorbs unpaid labour, which makes raw materials and means of labour—the means of production—into means for the absorption of unpaid labour.

It follows from what has been said that the designation of labour as *productive labour* has absolutely nothing to do with the *determinate content* of the labour, its special utility, or the particular use-value in which it manifests itself.

The same kind of labour may be *productive* or *unproductive*.

For example Milton, who wrote *Paradise Lost* for five pounds, was an *unproductive labourer*. On the other hand, the writer who turns out stuff for his publisher in factory style, is a *productive labourer*. Milton produced *Paradise Lost* for the same reason that a silk worm produces silk. It was an activity of *his* nature. Later he sold the product for £5. But the literary proletarian of Leipzig, who fabricates books (for example, Compendia of Economics) under the direction of bis publisher, is a *productive labourer*; for his product is from the outset subsumed under capital, and comes into being only for the purpose of increasing that capital. A singer who sells her song for her own account is an *unproductive labourer*. But the same singer commissioned by an entrepreneur to sing in order to make money for him is a *productive labourer*; for she produces capital.

[(E) UNPRODUCTIVE LABOUR AS LABOUR WHICH PERFORMS SERVICES; PURCHASE OF SERVICES UNDER CONDITIONS OF CAPITALISM. VULGAR CONCEPTION OF THE RELATION BETWEEN CAPITAL AND LABOUR AS AN EXCHANGE OF SERVICES]

||1325| Here different questions must be distinguished.

Whether I buy a pair of trousers or whether I buy cloth and get a tailor to come to my house and pay him for this *service* (that is, his tailoring labour) in converting this cloth into trousers, is a matter of complete indifference to me, if all I am interested in is the trousers. I buy the trousers from the merchant-tailor instead of taking the latter course, because this latter course is more expensive, and the trousers cost less labour and are therefore cheaper when the capitalist tailor produces them than when I get them made by a jobbing tailor. But in both cases I transform the money with which I buy the trousers not into capital but into trousers; and in both cases it is for me only a matter of using the money as mere means of circulation, that is, of transforming it into this particular use-value. Here therefore the money does not function as capital, although in one case it exchanges for a *commodity* and in the other case it buys *labour* itself as a *commodity*. It functions only as money, and more precisely, as means of circulation.

On the other hand the jobbing tailor [who works for me at my home] is *not a productive labourer*, although his labour provides me with the product, the trousers, and him with the price of his labour, the money. It may be that the quantity of labour performed by the jobbing tailor is greater than that contained in the price which he gets from me. And this is even probable, since the price of his labour is determined by the price which the *productive tailor* gets. This however is all the same so far as I am concerned. Once the price has been fixed, it is a matter of complete indifference to me whether he works eight or ten hours. What I am concerned with is only the *use-value*, the trousers; and naturally, whether I buy them one way or the other, I am interested in paying as little as possible for them, but in one case neither less nor more than in the other; in other words, I am interested in *paying only the normal price for them*. This is an *outlay* for my consumption; not an increase but a diminution of my money. It is in no way a means to my enrichment, any more than any other way of spending money for my *personal consumption* is a means to enrichment for me.

One of the savants of Paul de Kock may tell me that without buying trousers, just as without buying bread, I cannot live, and therefore also I cannot *enrich* myself; that the purchase of the trousers is therefore an indirect means, or at least a condition, for my enrichment—in the same way as the circulation of my blood or the process of breathing are conditions for my enrichment. But neither the circulation of my blood nor my breathing in themselves make me any the richer; on the contrary, they both presuppose a costly assimilation of food; if that were not necessary, there would be no poor devils about. The mere *direct* exchange of money for labour therefore does not transform money into capital or labour into productive labour.

What then is the special character of this exchange? How is it different from the exchange of money for productive labour? On the one hand, in that the *money* is spent *as money*, as the independent form of exchange-value, which is to be transformed into a *use-value*, into means of subsistence, into an object for personal consumption. The money therefore does not become capital, but on the contrary, it loses its existence as exchange-value in order to be consumed and expended as use-value. On the other hand, the labour only has any interest for me as a use-value, as a *service* which converts cloth into trousers, as the service which its particular useful character provides for me.

In contrast to this, the service which the same tailor employed by a merchant-tailor renders to this capitalist does not consist at all in the fact that he converts cloth into trousers, but that the necessary labour-time materialised in a pair of trousers is say twelve hours, while the wage that the journeyman tailor gets is equivalent to six hours. The service which he renders the capitalist is therefore that he works six hours for nothing. That this takes place in the form of making trousers only *conceals* the real relationship. As soon as the merchant-tailor can, he therefore tries to transform the trousers again into money, that is, into a form in which the determinate character of tailoring labour has entirely disappeared and in which the service rendered is consequently expressed in the fact that instead of a labour-time of six hours, ||1326| expressed in a certain sum of money. there is now a labour-time of twelve hours, expressed in double that sum of money.

I buy the tailoring labour for the service it renders me as *tailoring labour*, in order to satisfy my need for clothing and consequently to serve one of my *needs*. The merchant-tailor buys it as a means to making two talers out of one. I buy it because it produces a particular use-value, renders me a particular service. He buys it because it produces more exchange-value than it costs, as a mere means for exchanging less labour for more labour.

Where the direct exchange of money for labour takes place without the latter producing capital, where it is therefore *not productive* labour, it is bought as *service*, which in general is nothing but a term for the particular use-value which the labour provides, like any other commodity; it is however a specific term for the particular use-value of labour in so far as it does not render service in the form of a *thing*, but in the form of an *activity*, which however in no way distinguishes it for example from a machine, for instance a clock. *Do ut facias*, *facio ut facias*, *facio ut des*, *do ut des*[154] are here forms that can be used quite indifferently to describe the same relation, while in capitalist production the *do ut facias* expresses a quite specific relation between the material value which is given and the living activity which is appropriated. Because therefore in the purchase of *services* the specific relation between labour and capital is in no way involved, being either completely obliterated or altogether absent, it is naturally the favourite form used by Say, Bastiat and their consorts to express the *relation between capital and labour*.

The question how the *value* of these services is regulated and how this *value* itself is determined by the laws governing wages has nothing to do with the examination of the relation we are considering, and belongs to the chapter on wages.

It follows that the mere exchange of money for labour does not make the latter *productive labour*, and that on the other hand the *content* of this labour at first makes no difference.

The labourer himself can buy labour, that is, commodities, which are provided in the form of services; and the expenditure of his wages on such services is an expenditure which in no way differs from the expenditure of his wages on any other commodities. The service which he buys may be more or less necessary—for example, the service of a physician or of a priest, just as he may buy either bread or gin. As buyer—that is, as representative of money confronting commodity—the labourer is in absolutely the same category as the capitalist where the latter appears only as buyer, that is to say, where there is no more in the transaction than the conversion of money into the form of commodity. How the price of these services is determined, and what relation it has to wages proper, how far it is regulated by the laws of the latter and how far it is not, are questions to be considered in the treatment of wages, and are quite irrelevant for our present inquiry.

If thus the mere exchange of money for labour does not transform the latter into *productive labour*, or, what is the same thing, does not transform the former into capital, so also the *content*, the concrete character, the particular utility of the labour, seems at first to make no difference—as we have just seen, the same labour of the same journeyman tailor is in one case productive, in the other not.

Certain *services*, or the *use-values*, resulting from certain forms of activity or labour are embodied in *commodities*; others on the contrary leave no tangible result *existing apart* from the persons themselves who perform them; in other words, their result is not a *vendible commodity*. For example, the service a singer renders to me satisfies my aesthetic need; but what I enjoy exists only in an activity inseparable from the singer himself, and as soon as his labour, the singing, is at an end, my enjoyment too is at an end. I enjoy the activity itself—its reverberation on my ear. These services themselves, like the commodities which I buy, may be necessary or may only seem necessary—for example, the service of a soldier or physician or lawyer; or they may be services which give me pleasure. But this makes no difference to their economic character. If I am healthy and do not need a doctor or am lucky enough not to have to be involved in a lawsuit, then I avoid paying out money for medical or legal services as I do the plague.

||1328|[155] *Services* may also be forced on me—the *services of officials*, etc.

If I buy the service of a teacher not to develop my faculties but to acquire some skill with which I can earn money—or if others buy this teacher for me—and if I really learn something (which in itself is quite independent of the payment for the service), then these costs of education, just as the costs of my maintenance, belong to the costs of production of my labour-power. But the particular utility of this service *alters nothing in the economic relation*; it is not a relation in which I transform money into capital, or by which the supplier of this service, the teacher, transforms me into *his capitalist*, his master. Consequently it also does not affect the *economic character* of this relation whether the physician cures me, the teacher is successful in teaching me, or the lawyer wins my lawsuit. What is paid for is the performance of the service as such, and by its very nature the result cannot be guaranteed by those rendering the service. A large proportion of *services* belongs to the *costs of consumption* of commodities, as in the case of a cook, a maid, etc.

It is characteristic of all *unproductive labours* that they are at my command—as in the case of the purchase of all other commodities for consumption—only to the same extent as I exploit *productive labourers*. Of all persons, therefore, the *productive labourer* has the least command over the *services* of unproductive labourers. On the other hand, however, my power to employ *productive labourers* by no means grows in the same proportion as I employ *unproductive labourers*, but on the contrary diminishes in the same proportion, although [one has] most to pay for the *compulsory* services (State, taxes).

Productive labourers may themselves in relation to me be *unproductive labourers*. For example, if I have my house re-papered and the paper-hangers are wage-workers of a master who sells me the job, it is just the same for me as if I had bought a house already papered; as if I had expended money for a commodity for my consumption. But for the master who gets these labourers to hang the paper, they are productive labourers, for they produce surplus-value for him. |1328||

* * *

||1333| How very *unproductive*, from the standpoint of capitalist production, the labourer is who indeed produces vendible commodities, but only to the amount equivalent to his own labour-power, and therefore produces no surplus-value for capital—can be seen from the passages in Ricardo saying that the very existence of such people is a nuisance.[156] This is the theory and practice of capital.

"Both the theory relative to capital, and *the practice of stopping labour at that point* where it can produce, in addition to the subsistence of the labourer, a *profit* for* the capitalist, seem opposed to the natural laws which regulate production" (Thomas Hodgskin, *Popular Political Economy*, London, 1827, p. 238). |1333||

* * *

||1336| We have seen: This process of production is not only a process of the production of *commodities*, but a process of the production of *surplus-value*, the absorption of surplus-labour and hence a process of production of capital. The first formal act of exchange between money and labour or capital and labour is only *potentially* the appropriation of someone else's living labour by materialised labour. The actual process of appropriation

* In the manuscript: "to".—*Ed.*

takes place only in the actual production process, behind which lies as a past stage that first formal transaction—in which capitalist and labourer confront each other as *mere owners of commodities*, as buyer and seller. For which reason all vulgar economists —like Bastiat—go no further than that first formal transaction, precisely in order by this trick to get rid of the specific capitalist relation. The distinction is shown in a striking way by the exchange of money for unproductive labour. Here money and labour exchange with each other *only* as commodities. So that instead of this exchange forming capital, it is *expenditure of revenue*. |1336||

[(F) THE LABOUR OF HANDICRAFTSMEN AND PEASANTS IN CAPITALIST SOCIETY]

||1328| What then is the position of independent handicraftsmen or peasants who employ no labourers and therefore do not produce as capitalists? Either, as always in the case of peasants < but for example not in the case of a gardener whom I get to come to my house>, they are *producers of commodities*, and I buy the *commodity* from them—in which case for example it makes no difference that the handicraftsman produces it to order while the peasant produces his supply according to his means. In this capacity they confront me as sellers of commodities, not as sellers of labour, and this relation therefore has nothing to do with the exchange of capital for labour; therefore also it has nothing to do with the distinction between *productive and unproductive labour*, which depends entirely on whether the labour is exchanged for money or for money as money as capital. They therefore belong neither to the category of *productive* nor of *unproductive labourers*, although they are producers of commodities. But their production does not fall under the capitalist mode of production.

It is possible that these producers, working with their own means of production, not only reproduce their labour-power but create surplus-value, while their position enables them to appropriate for themselves their own surplus-labour or a part of it (since a part of it is taken away from them in the form of taxes, etc.). And here we come up against a peculiarity that is characteristic of a society in which one definite mode of production predominates, even though not all productive relations have been subordinated to it. In feudal society, for example (as we can best observe in England because the system of feudalism was introduced here from Normandy ready made and its form was impressed on what was in many respects a different social foundation), relations which were far removed from the nature of feudalism were given a feudal form; for example, simple money relations in which there was no trace of mutual personal service as between lord and vassal. It is for instance a fiction that the small peasant held his land in fief.

It is exactly the same in the capitalist mode of production. The independent peasant or handicraftsman is cut up into two persons*. As owner of the means of production he is capitalist; as labourer he is his own wage-labourer. As capitalist he therefore pays himself his wages and draws his profit on his capital; that is to say, he exploits himself as wage-labourer, and pays himself, in the surplus-value, the tribute that labour owes to capital. Perhaps he also pays himself a third portion as landowner (rent), in exactly the same way, as we shall see later,[157] that the industrial capitalist, when he works with his own ||1329| capital, pays himself interest, regarding this as something which he owes to himself not as industrial capitalist but *qua* capitalist pure and simple.

The *determinate social character* of the means of production in capitalist production—expressing a particular *production relation*—has so grown together with, and in the mode of thought of bourgeois society is so inseparable from, the material existence of these means of production as means of production, that the same determinateness (categorical determinateness) is assumed even where the relation is in direct contradiction to it. The means of production become capital only in so far as they have become separated from labourer and confront labour as an independent power. But in the case referred to the producer—the labourer—is the possessor, the owner, of his means of production. They are therefore not capital, any more than in relation to them he is a wage-labourer. Nevertheless they are looked on as capital, and he himself is split in two, so that *he*, as capitalist, employs himself as wage-labourer.

In fact this way of presenting it, however irrational it may be on first view, is nevertheless so far correct, that in this case the

* "In small enterprises[...] *the employer* is often his *own labourer*" (Storch, [*Cours d'économie politique*], t. I, Petersburg edition, p. 242).

producer in fact creates his own surplus-value <on the assumption that he sells his commodity at its value>, in other words, only his own labour is materialised in the whole product. But that he is able to appropriate *for himself* the whole product of his own labour, and that the excess of the value of his product over the average price for instance of his day's labour is not appropriated by a third person, a *master*, he owes not to his labour—which does not distinguish him from other labourers—but to his ownership of the means of production. It is therefore only through his ownership of these that he takes possession of his own surplus-labour, and thus bears to himself as wage-labourer the relation of being his own capitalist.

Separation appears as the normal relation in this society. Where therefore it does not in fact apply, it is presumed and, as has just been shown, so far correctly; for (as distinct for example from conditions in Ancient Rome or Norway or in the north-west of the United States) in this society *unity* appears as accidental, *separation* as normal; and consequently separation is maintained as the relation even when one person unites the separate functions. Here emerges in a very striking way the fact that the capitalist as such is only a function of capital, the labourer a function of labour-power. For it is also a law that economic development distributes functions among different persons; and the handicraftsman or peasant who produces with his own means of production will either gradually be transformed into a small capitalist who also exploits the labour of others, or he will suffer the loss of his means of production <in the first instance the latter may happen although he remains their *nominal* owner, as in the case of mortgages> and be transformed into a wage-labourer. This is the tendency in the form of society in which the capitalist mode of production predominates.

[(G) SUPPLEMENTARY DEFINITION OF PRODUCTIVE LABOUR AS LABOUR WHICH IS REALISED IN MATERIAL WEALTH]

In considering the essential relations of capitalist production it can therefore be assumed that the entire world of commodities, all spheres of material production—the production of material wealth—are (formally or really) subordinated to the capitalist mode of production <for this is what is happening more and more completely; [since it] is the principal goal, and only if it is realised will the productive powers of labour be developed to

their highest point>. On this premise—which expresses the limit [of the process] and which is therefore constantly coming closer to an exact presentation of reality—all labourers engaged in the production of commodities are wage-labourers, and the means of production in all these spheres confront them as capital. It can then be said to be a characteristic of *productive labourers*, that is, labourers producing capital, that their labour realises itself in *commodities*, in material wealth. And so *productive labour*, along with its determining characteristic—which takes no account whatever of the *content of labour* and is entirely independent of that content—would be given a second, different and subsidiary definition.

[(H) MANIFESTATIONS OF CAPITALISM IN THE SPHERE OF IMMATERIAL PRODUCTION]

Non-material production, even when it is carried on purely for exchange, that is, when it produces *commodities*, may be of two kinds:

1. It results in *commodities*, use-values, which have a form different from and independent of producers and consumers; these commodities may therefore exist during an interval between production and consumption and may in this interval circulate as *vendible commodities*, such as books, paintings, in a word, all artistic products which are distinct from the artistic performance of the artist performing them. Here capitalist production is applicable only to a very restricted extent: as for example when a writer of a joint work—say an encyclopaedia—exploits a number of others as hacks. ||1330| In this sphere for the most part a *transitional form* to *capitalist production* remains in existence, in which the various scientific or artistic producers, handicraftsmen or experts work for the collective trading capital of the book-trade—a relation that has nothing to do with the capitalist mode of production proper and even formally has not yet been brought under its sway. The fact that the exploitation of labour is at its highest precisely in these transitional forms in no way alters the case.

2. The production cannot be separated from the act of producing, as is the case with all performing artists, orators, actors, teachers, physicians, priests, etc. Here too the capitalist mode of production is met with only to a small extent, and from the

nature of the case can only be applied in a few spheres. For example, teachers in educational establishments may be mere wage-labourers for the entrepreneur of the establishment; many such educational factories exist in England. Although in relation to the pupils these teachers are not *productive labourers*, they are productive labourers in relation to their employer. He exchanges his capital for their labour-power, and enriches himself through this process. It is the same with enterprises such as theatres, places of entertainment, etc. In such cases the actor's relation to the public is that of an artist, but in relation to his employer he is a *productive labourer*. All these manifestations of capitalist production in this sphere are so insignificant compared with the totality of production that they can be left entirely out of account.

[(I) THE PROBLEM OF PRODUCTIVE LABOUR FROM THE STANDPOINT OF THE TOTAL PROCESS OF MATERIAL PRODUCTION]

With the development of the specifically capitalist mode of production, in which many labourers work together in the production of the same commodity, the direct relation which their labour bears to the object produced naturally varies greatly. For example the unskilled labourers in a factory [158] referred to earlier have nothing directly to do with the working up of the raw material. The workmen who function as overseers of those directly engaged in working up the raw material are one step further away; the works engineer has yet another relation and in the main works only with his brain, and so on. But the *totality of these labourers*, who possess labour-power of different value (although all the employed maintain much the same level) produce the result, which, considered as the *result* of the labour-process pure and simple, is expressed in a *commodity* or *material product;* and all together, as a workshop, they are the living production machine of these *products*—just as, taking the production process as a whole, they exchange their labour for capital and reproduce the capitalists' money as capital, that is to say, as value producing surplus-value, as self-expanding value.

It is indeed the characteristic feature of the capitalist mode of production that it separates the various kinds of labour from each other, therefore also mental and manual labour—or kinds of labour in which one or the other predominates—and distributes them among different people. This however does not prevent the material product from being the *common product* of these persons, or their common product embodied in material wealth; any more than on the other hand it prevents or in any way alters the relation of each one of these persons to capital being that of wage-labourer and in this pre-eminent sense being that of a *productive labourer*. All these persons are not only *directly* engaged in the production of material wealth, but they exchange their labour *directly* for money as capital, and consequently directly reproduce, in addition to their wages, a surplus-value for the capitalist. Their labour consists of paid labour plus unpaid surplus-labour.

[(J) THE TRANSPORT INDUSTRY AS A BRANCH OF MATERIAL PRODUCTION. PRODUCTIVE LABOUR IN THE TRANSPORT INDUSTRY]

In addition to extractive industry, agriculture and manufacture, there exists yet a fourth sphere of material production, which also passes through the various stages of handicraft industry, manufacture and mechanical industry; this is the *transport industry*, transporting either people or commodities. The relation of *productive labour*—that is, of the wage-labourer—to capital is here exactly the same as in the other spheres of material production. Moreover, here a material change is effected in the object of labour—a *spatial* change, a change of place. In the case of the transport of people this takes the form only of a *service* rendered to them by the entrepreneur. But the relation between buyer and seller of this *service* has nothing to do with the relation of the productive labourer to capital, any more than has the relation between the buyer and seller of yarn.

If on the other hand we consider the process in relation to commodities, ||1331| in this case there certainly takes place, in the labour-process, a change in the object of labour, the *commodity*. Its spatial existence is altered, and along with this goes a change in its use-value, since the location of this use-value is changed. Its exchange-value increases in the same measure as this change in use-value requires labour—an amount of labour which is determined partly by the wear and tear of the constant capital, that is, the total materialised labour which enters into the commodity, and partly by the quantity of living labour, as in the process of increasing the value of all other commodities.

When the commodity has reached its destination, this change which has taken place in its use-value has vanished, and is now only expressed in its higher exchange-value, in the enhanced price of the commodity. And although in this case the real labour has left no trace behind it in the use-value, it is nevertheless realised in the exchange-value of this material product; and so it is true also of this industry as of other spheres of material production that the labour incorporates itself in the *commodity*, even though it has left no visible trace in the use-value of the commodity.

* * *

Here we have been dealing only with *productive capital*, that is, capital employed in the *direct process of production*. We come later to capital in the *process of circulation*. And only after that, in considering the special form assumed by capital as *merchant's capital*, can the question be answered as to how far the labourers employed by it are productive or unproductive.[159] |XXI—1331||

[13. DRAFT PLANS FOR PARTS I AND III OF *CAPITAL* [160]]

[(A) PLAN FOR PART I OR SECTION I OF *CAPITAL*]

||XVIII—1140| The first section[161] "*Production Process of Capital*" to be divided in the following way:

1. Introduction. Commodity. Money.
2. Transformation of money into capital.
3. Absolute surplus-value. (a) Labour-process and the process of producing surplus-value. (b) Constant capital and variable capital. (c) Absolute surplus-value. (d) Struggle for the normal working-day. (e) Simultaneous working-days (number of simultaneously employed labourers). Amount of surplus-value and rate of surplus-value (magnitude and height?).
4. Relative surplus-value. (a) Simple co-operation. (b) Division of labour. (c) Machinery. etc.
5. Combination of absolute and relative surplus-value. Relation (proportion) between wage-labour and surplus-value. Formal and real subsumption of labour under capital. Productivity of capital. Productive and unproductive labour.
6. Reconversion of surplus-value into capital. Primitive accumulation. Wakefield's colonial theory.
7. Result of the production process.

(Either under 6 or under 7 the change in the form of the law of appropriation can be shown.)

8. Theories of surplus-value.
9. Theories of productive and unproductive labour. |XVIII—1140||

[(B) PLAN FOR PART III OR SECTION III OF *CAPITAL*]

||XVIII—1139| The third section "*Capital and Profit*" to be divided in the following way:

1. Conversion of surplus-value into profit. Rate of profit as distinguished from rate of surplus-value.

2. Conversion of profit into average profit. Formation of the general rate of profit. Transformation of values into prices of production.

3. Adam Smith's and Ricardo's theories on profit and prices of production.

4. Rent (illustration of the difference between value and price of production).

5. History of the so-called Ricardian law of rent.

6. Law of the fall of the rate of profit. Adam Smith, Ricardo, Carey.

7. Theories of profit.

(Query: whether Sismondi and Malthus should also be included in the *Theories of Surplus-Value.*)

8. Division of profit into industrial profit and interest. Merchant's capital. Money-capital.

9. Revenue and its sources. The question of the relation between the processes of production and distribution also to be included here.

10. Reflux movements of money in the process of capitalist production as a whole.

11. Vulgar economy.

12. Conclusion. Capital and wage-labour. |XVIII—1139||.

[(C) PLAN FOR CHAPTER II[162] OF PART III OF *CAPITAL*]

||XVIII—1109| In the second chapter of Part III, on "*Capital and Profit*", where the formation of the general rate of profit is dealt with, the following must be considered:

1. Different organic composition of capitals, partly conditioned by the difference between variable and constant capital in so far as this arises from the *stage of production*—the absolute *quantitative* relations between machinery and raw materials on the one hand, and the quantity of labour which sets them in motion. These differences relate to the labour-process. The differences between fixed and circulating capital arising from the circulation process have also to be considered—differences which lead to variations in the increase of value, in a given period of time, as between different spheres.

2. Differences in the relative value of the parts of different capitals which do not arise from their organic composition. These arise from the difference of value particularly of the raw mate-

rials, even assuming that the raw materials absorb an equal quantity of labour in two different spheres.

3. The result of those differences is diversity of the rates of profit in different spheres of capitalist production. It is true only for capitals of equal composition, etc., that the rate of profit is the same and the quantity of profit is in proportion to the size of the capital employed.

4. For the total capital, however, what has been explained in Chapter I holds good. In capitalist production each capital is assumed to be a unit, an aliquot part of the total capital. Formation of the general rate of profit (competition).

5. Transformation of values into prices of production. Difference between value, cost-price, and production price.

6. To take up also the Ricardian point: the influence of general variations in wages on the general rate of profit and hence on prices of production. |XVIII—1109||

APPENDICES

QUOTATIONS IN FRENCH, GERMAN AND ITALIAN*

48 „Durch die Landwirtschaft...ein Wert — in der Bodenrente — erzeugt, welcher in den Gewerben und im Handel nicht vorkommt; ein Wert, welcher übrigbleibt, wenn aller aufgewendete Arbeitslohn und alle verwendete Kapitalrente ersetzt sind." (Karl Arnd, *Die naturgemässe Volkswirtschaft*, etc., Hanau, 1845, S. 461-62.)

54 „...la classe productive, la classe des propriétaires, et la classe stérile... tous les citoyens occupés à d'autres services et à d'autres travaux que ceux de l'agriculture..." (François Quesnay, *Analyse du Tableau économique*. In: *Physiocrates*...par M. Eugène Daire. Première partie, Paris, 1846, p. 58.)

54 „Son travail, dans l'ordre des travaux partagés entre les différents membres de la Société, conserve la même primauté ..qu'avait, entre les différents travaux qu'il était obligé dans l'état solitaire de consacrer à ses besoins de toute espèce, le travail qui subvenait à sa nourriture. Ce n'est pas ici une primauté d'honneur ou de dignité ; elle est de nécessité *physique*... Ce que son travail fait produire à la terre au-delà de ses besoins personnels est l'unique fonds des salaires que reçoivent tous les autres membres de la société en échange de leur travail. Ceux-ci, en se servant du prix de cet échange pour acheter à leur tour les denrées du laboureur, ne lui rendent exactement que ce qu'ils ont reçu. C'est une différence essentielle entre ces deux genres de travaux..." (Turgot, *Réflexions sur la formation et la distribution des richesses* (1766). In : *Œuvres de Turgot*. Nouvelle édition par M. Eugène Daire. Tome premier, Paris, 1844, pp. 9-10).

55 „Dès que le travail du laboureur *produit au-delà* de ses besoins, il peut, avec ce superflu *que la nature lui accorde en pur don* au-delà du salaire de ses peines, acheter le travail des autres membres de la société. Ceux-ci en le lui vendant ne gagnent que leur vie ; mais le laboureur recueille, outre sa subsistance, une richesse indépendante et disponible, *qu'il n'a point achetée et qu'il vend.* Il est donc l'unique source des richesses qui par leur circulation animent tous les travaux de la société, *parce qu'il est le seul dont le travail produise au-delà du salaire du travail.*" (ibidem, p.11.)

---

* See Publisher's Note.—*Ed.*

56 „Dans les premiers temps le propriétaire n'a pas dû être distingué du cultivateur...dans ce premier temps, tout homme laborieux, trouvant autant de terre qu'il en voulait, ne pouvait être tenté de *labourer pour autrui*... Mais à la fin toute terre trouva son maître, et ceux qui ne purent avoir des propriétés n'eurent d'abord d'autre ressource que celle *d'échanger le travail de leurs bras* dans les emplois de la *classe stipendiée* contre le superflu des denrées du propriétaire cultivateur." (ibidem, p. 12.)

56 „...payer des hommes pour cultiver sa terre, et pour des hommes qui vivent de salaires, autant valait les gagner à ce métier qu'à tout autre. *La propriété dut donc être séparée du travail de la culture, et bientôt elle le fut*... Les propriétaires commencent à...se décharger du travail de la culture sur des cultivateurs salariés." (ibidem, p.13.)

56 „Le simple ouvrier, qui n'a que ses bras et son industrie, n'a rien qu'autant qu'il parvient à vendre à d'autres sa peine... En tout genre de travail il doit arriver et il arrive en effet que le salaire de l'ouvrier se borne à ce qui lui est nécessaire pour lui procurer sa subsistance." (ibidem, p.10.)

56 „...le produit de la terre se divise en deux parts : l'une comprend la subsistance et les profits du laboureur, qui sont la récompense de son travail et la condition sous laquelle il se charge de cultiver le champ du propriétaire ; ce qui reste est cette partie indépendante et disponible que la *terre donne en pur don à celui qui la cultive* au-delà de ses avances et du salaire de ses peines, et c'est la part du propriétaire ou le revenu avec lequel celui-ci peut vivre sans travail et qu'il porte où il veut." (ibidem, p.14.)

57 „...ce qui lui est nécessaire pour lui procurer sa subsistance." (ibidem, p.10.)

57 „...le *cultivateur* produit *son propre salaire*, et en outre le revenu qui sert à salarier toute la classe des artisans et autres stipendiés... *Le propriétaire n'a rien que par le travail du cultivateur*; il reçoit de lui sa subsistance et ce avec quoi il paye les travaux des autres stipendiés... le cultivateur n'a besoin du propriétaire qu'en vertu des conventions et des lois..." (ibidem, p.15.)

57 „...Fermage ou louage des terres...méthode * [...] la plus avantageuse de toutes, mais elle suppose un pays déjà riche." (ibidem, p.21.)

58 „Dans quelque métier que ce soit, il faut d'avance que l'ouvrier ait des outils, qu'il ait une suffisante quantité des matières qui sont l'objet de son travail; il faut qu'il subsiste en attendant la vente de ses ouvrages." (ibidem, p.34.)

58 „...elle [...] a donné le premier fonds des avances antérieures à toute culture".** (ibidem, p.34.)

58 „...laitages, [...] laines, [...] cuirs et autres matières qui, avec le bois pris dans les forêts, ont été le premier fonds des ouvrages d'industrie." (ibidem, p.34.)

---

* In the manuscript: „la méthode" —*Ed.*

** In the manuscript: „toutes cultures".—*Ed.*

58 „...*Lorsqu'une* grande partie de la société *n'eut que ses bras pour vivre*, il fallut que ceux qui vivaient ainsi de salaires commençassent par avoir *quelque chose d'avance*, soit pour se procurer les matières sur lesquelles ils travaillaient, soit pour vivre en attendant le payement de leur salaire." (ibidem, pp.37-38.)

58 „...valeurs mobilaires accumulées..." (ibidem, p. 38.)

59 „...que lui aurait valu son argent s'il l'avait employé en acquisition de fonds ; ...car, sans doute, à profit égal, il aurait préféré vivre, sans aucune peine, du revenu d'une terre qu'il aurait pu acquérir avec le même capital." (ibidem, p.39.)

59 „...en entrepreneurs capitalistes et simples ouvriers." (ibidem, p. 39.)

59 „Tout cela doit être prélevé sur le prix des productions de la terre; le *surplus* sert au cultivateur à payer au propriétaire la permission que celui-ci lui a donnée de se servir de son champ pour y établir son entreprise. C'est le prix du fermage, le revenu du propriétaire, le *produit net*, car tout ce que la terre produit jusqu'à la concurrence de la rentrée des avances de toute espèce et des profits de celui qui les fait, ne peut être regardé comme un revenu, mais seulement comme *rentrée des frais de culture*, attendu que si le cultivateur ne les retirait pas, il se garderait bien d'employer ses richesses et sa peine à cultiver le champ d'autrui." (ibidem, p.40.)

59 „...quoique les capitaux se forment en partie de l'épargne des profits des classes laborieuses, cependant, comme ces profits viennent toujours de la terre, puisque tous sont payés ou sur le revenu, ou sur les frais qui servent à produire le revenu, il est évident que les capitaux viennent de la terre tout comme le revenu, ou plutôt qu'ils ne sont que l'accumulation de la partie des valeurs produites par la terre que les propriétaires du revenu ou ceux qui le partagent peuvent mettre en réserve chaque année, sans l'employer à leurs besoins." (ibidem, p.66.)

60 „Tale *moltiplicazione di materia* non si ha certamente nè mai aver potrassi dalle arti, ma sola forma, sola modificazione: non si ha dunque produzione dalle arti. Ma le arti, mi si replica, danno la forma alla materia, dunque esse son produttive; imperocchè è questa una produzione se non di materia, di forma. Va bene, io nol contrasto; ma *questa non è produzione di ricchezze, ella non è anzi altro che un dispendio*... La politica economia propone e cerca produzione fisica e reale, la quale si ha dalla sola agricultura, giacchè questa sola moltiplica le materie ed i prodotti che dan le ricchezze... Le arti comprano dall'agricoltura le materie prime per lavorarle. Questo lavoro altro non fa, come è già detto, che dare una forma a quelle materie prime, ma non le accresce però nè le moltiplica.

Date al cuoco una misura di piselli che ve gli apresti pel pranzo, egli ben cotti e ben conditi ve li manda in tavola, ma nella stessa misura in cui gli ha ricevuti; date al contrario quella misura all' ortolano acciò li confidi alla terra, egli vi riporta a suo tempo il quadruplo almeno della misura ricevuta. Ecco la vera e sola produzione.

...il valore alle cose lo danno i bisogni degli uomini. Dunque il valore o l'aumento del valore delle derrate non è l'effetto de' lavori delle arti, ma delle spese de' lavoranti.

...qualunque manifattura di moda appena è comparsa, di subito si estende e dentro e fuori del paese; ed ecco che *ben presto* la concorrenza di altri artefici, di altri mercanti riduce il prezzo al suo giusto livello, che è quello...del valore delle materie prime e della sussistenza de' lavoranti." (Ferdinando Paoletti, *I veri mezzi di render felici le società*. In: *Scrittori Classici Italiani di Economia Politica*. Parte moderna. Tomo XX, Milano, 1804, pp.196, 197, 198, 204-05.)

62 „...il est le seul dont le travail produise *au dela du salaire du travail*." (Turgot, *Réflexions sur la formation et la distribution des richesses* (1766). In: *Œuvres de Turgot*. Nouvelle édition par M Eugène Daire. Tome premier, Paris, 1844, p.11.)

62 „...Le cultivateur fait naître, au-delà de cette rétribution, le revenu du propriétaire; et l'artisan ne fait aucun revenu, ni pour lui, ni pour d'autres." (ibidem, p.16.)

62 „...tout ce que la terre produit jusqu'à la concurrence de la rentrée des avances de toute espèce et des profits de celui qui les fait, *ne peut être regardé comme un revenu*, mais seulement comme rentrée *des frais de culture...*" (ibidem, p.40)

62 „Le travail appliqué à la culture de la terre produisait non seulement de quoi s'alimenter lui-même pendant toute la durée de l'ouvrage, mais encore *un excédant de valeur* qui pouvait s'ajouter à la masse des richesses déjà existantes: ils appelèrent cet excédant le *produit net*. Le produit net devait nécessairement appartenir au propriétaire de la terre et constituait entre ses mains un revenu pleinement disponible. Quel était donc le produit net des autres industries ?... Manufacturiers, commerçants, ouvriers, tous étaient les commis, les *salariés* de l'agriculture, souveraine créatrice et dispensatrice de tous les biens. Les produits du travail de ceux-là ne représentaient, dans le système des *économistes*, que l'équivalent de leurs consommations pendant l'ouvrage, en sorte qu'après le travail achevé, la somme totale des richesses se trouvait absolument la même qu'auparavant, *à moins que les ouvriers ou les maîtres n'eussent mis en réserve*, c'est-à-dire *é p a r g n é**, *ce qu'ils avaient le droit de consommer*. Ainsi donc, le travail appliqué à la terre était le seul productif de la richesse, et celui des autres industries était considéré comme *stérile*, parce *qu'il n'en résultait aucune augmentation du capital général*." (Adolphe Blanqui, *Histoire de l'économie politique...*, Bruxelles, 1839, p.139.)

62 „... : pour avoir de l'argent, il faut l'acheter; et après cet achat, on n'est pas plus riche qu'on l'étoit auparavant; on n'a fait que recevoir en argent une valeur égale à celle qu'on a donnée en marchandises." ([Mercier de la Rivière] *L'Ordre naturel et essentiel des sociétés politiques*. Tome second, Londres et Paris, 1767, p.338.)

63 „ Le travail des artisans et manufacturiers n'ouvrant aucune source nouvelle des richesses, *ne peut être profitable que par des échanges avan-*

* Words and passages which Marx translated into German are indicated by spaced type.—*Ed.*

tageux, et n'a qu'une valeur purement relative, valeur qui ne se répétera plus quand il n'y aura plus occasion de *gagner sur les échanges...*" (Adam Smith, *Recherches sur la nature et les causes de la richesse des nations*. Traduction nouvelle...par Germain Garnier, t. V, Paris, 1802, p.266.)

63 „Le travail des artisans et manufacturiers ne pouvant ajouter à la masse générale des richesses de la société que les épargnes faites par les salariés et les capitalistes, il peut bien, par cette voie, tendre à enrichir la société..." (ibidem, p. 266.)

63 „Les ouvriers de la culture enrichissent l'Etat par le produit même de leur travail: les ouvriers des manufactures et du commerce, au contraire, ne sauraient l'enrichir autrement que par des *épargnes sur leur propre consommation.* Cette assertion des économistes est une conséquence de la distinction qu'ils ont établie, et paraît aussi incontestable. En effet, le travail des artisans et manufacturiers ne peut ajouter autre chose à la valeur de la matière, que la valeur de leur propre travail, c'est-à-dire, celle des salaires et profits que ce travail a dû gagner, au taux courant actuel des uns et des autres, dans le pays. Or, ces salaires, quels qu'ils soient, faibles ou forts, sont la récompense du travail; c'est ce que l'ouvrier a droit de consommer et ce qu'il est présumé de consommer; car c'est en consommant seulement qu'il peut jouir du fruit de son travail, et cette jouissance est tout ce qui constitue réellement sa récompense. *Pareillement les profits, quels qu'ils soient, faibles ou forts*, sont aussi réputés être la consommation journalière et successive du capitaliste, qui est naturellement présumé de proportionner ses jouissances au revenu que lui donne son capital. Ainsi, à moins que l'ouvrier ne se retranche une partie de l'aisance à laquelle il a droit, d'après le taux courant du salaire attribué *à son travail*; à moins que le capitaliste ne se soumette à épargner une partie du revenu que lui rend son capital, l'un et l'autre consommeront, à mesure que l'ouvrage s'achèvera, toute la valeur résultante de ce même ouvrage. La masse totale des richesses de la société sera donc, après leur travail fait, la même qu'elle était auparavant, *à moins qu'ils n'aient épargné* une partie de ce qu'ils* avaient droit de consommer, de ce qu'ils pouvaient consommer sans être taxés de dissipation; dans lequel cas, la masse totale des richesses de la société aurait été grossie *de toute la valeur de ces épargnes*. Il est donc juste de dire que les agents des manufactures et du commerce ne peuvent *ajouter à la masse totale des richesses existantes dans la société, que par leurs privations seulement.*" (ibidem, pp. 263-64.)

64 „Enfin, si les économistes ont soutenu [...] l'industrie manufacturière et commerçante ne pouvait ajouter à la richesse nationale que par des privations seulement, Smith a dit également que l'industrie s'exercerait en vain, et que le capital d'un pays ne serait jamais plus grand si l'économie ne l'augmentait par ses épargnes." (ibidem, p.270).

64 „Smith est donc parfaitement d'accord avec les économistes..." (ibidem, p.270.)

64 „De toutes les valeurs [...] écloses sous l'atmosphère embrasée du *système*, il ne restait plus rien que la ruine, la désolation et la banqueroute.

* In the manuscript: „de qu'ils".—*Ed.*

La *propriété foncière* seule n'avait pas péri dans cette tourmente." (Adolphe Blanqui, *Histoire de l'économie politique...*, Bruxelles, 1839, p. 138.)

64 „Elle s'était même améliorée en changeant de mains, et en se *subdivisant sur une vaste échelle*, pour la *première fois*, peut-être, depuis la féodalité." (ibidem, p.138).

64 „Les mutations innombrables qui s'effectuèrent sous l'influence du système, commencèrent le morcellement de la propriété... La propriété foncière sortit pour la première fois de l'état de torpeur où l'avait si longtemps maintenue le système féodal. Ce fut un véritable réveil pour l'agriculture... Elle venait de passer du régime de la main-morte à celui de la circulation." (ibidem, pp. 137-38.)

64 „...fermage ou louage des terres... Cette dernière méthode est la plus avantageuse de toutes, mais elle suppose un pays déjà riche." (Turgot, *Réflexions sur la formation et la distribution des richesses* (1766). In: *Œuvres de Turgot.* Nouvelle édition par M. Eugène Daire. Tome premier, Paris, 1844, p.21.)

65 „Que les terres employées à la culture des grains soient réunies, autant qu'il est possible, en grandes fermes exploitées par de riches laboureurs; car il y a moins de dépense pour l'entretien et la réparation des bâtiments, et à proportion beaucoup moins de frais, et beaucoup plus de produit net dans les grandes entreprises d'agriculture, que dans les petites." (François Quesnay, *Maximes générales du gouvernement économique d'un royaume agricole.* In: *Physiocrates...* par M. Eugène Daire. Première partie, Paris, 1846, pp.96-97.)

65 „Toute épargne faite à profit dans les travaux qui peuvent s'exécuter par le moyen des animaux, des machines, des rivières, etc., revient à l'avantage de la population..." (ibidem, p.97.)

65 „Modérez votre enthousiasme, aveugles admirateurs des faux produits de l'industrie: avant de crier miracle, ouvrez les yeux, et voyez combien sont pauvres, du moins mal-aisés, ces mêmes fabricants * qui ont l'art de changer 20 sous en une valeur de 1000 écus: *au profit de qui passe donc cette multiplication énorme de valeurs? Quoi, ceux par les mains ** desquels elle s'opère, ne connoissent pas l'aisance!* ah, défiez-vous de ce contraste..." ([Mercier de la Rivière] *L'Ordre naturel et essentiel des sociétés politiques.* Tome second, Londres et Paris, 1767, p.407.)

65 „ Que l'autorité [...] soit unique... Le système des contreforces dans un gouvernement est une opinion funeste qui ne laisse apercevoir que la discorde entre les grands et l'accablement des petits." (François Quesnay, *Maximes générales du gouvernement économique d'un royaume agricole.* In: *Physiocrates...* par M. Eugène Daire. Première partie, Paris, 1846, p.81.)

65 „...que l'homme [...] est destiné à vivre en société, est *** destiné à vivre sous le despotisme." ([Mercier de la Rivière] *L'Ordre naturel et*

---

* In the manuscript: „ouvriers".—*Ed.*

** In the manuscript: „la main".—*Ed.*

*** In the manuscript: „il est".—*Ed.*

essentiel des sociétés politiques. Tome premier, Londres et Paris, 1767, p.281.)

67 „...si la nature lui paie aussi *un intérêt double de l'intérêt légal*, par quelle raison plausible prétendrait-on l'en priver?" (Schmalz, *Economie politique, Ouvrage traduit de l'allemand par Henri Jouffroy*, t. 1, Paris, 1826, p.90.)

67 „Le terme moyen du salaire d'une profession est égal au terme moyen de ce que consomme un homme de cette profession pendant le temps de son travail." (ibidem, p.120.)

67 „...*la rente foncière* est le seul et unique élément du revenu national; et que l'intérêt des capitaux placés et le salaire de tous les genres de travaux ne font que faire passer et circuler le produit de cette rente foncière dans toutes les mains." (ibidem, pp.309-10.)

67 „...la disposition du sol, sa faculté, sa capacité pour la reproduction annuelle de la rente foncière, est tout ce qui constitue la richesse nationale." (ibidem, p.310.)

67 „Si l'on remonte jusqu'au fondement, jusqu'aux premiers éléments de la *valeur* de tous les objets, quels qu'ils soient, on est forcé de reconnaître que cette valeur n'est autre chose que celle des simples productions de la nature; c'est-à-dire que, quoique le travail ait donné une valeur nouvelle à ces objets et haussé leur prix, cette nouvelle valeur, ou ces prix, ne se compose cependant que de l'ensemble des valeurs réunies de tous les produits naturels, qui, en raison de la nouvelle forme que le travailleur a donnée, ont été anéantis, consommés, ou employés par l'ouvrier, d'une manière quelconque." (ibidem, p.313.)

67 „...ce genre de travail étant le seul qui contribue à produire de *nouveaux corps*, il est aussi le seul qui puisse, jusqu'à un certain point, être considéré comme productif. Quant aux travaux d'apprêt ou d'industrie... ils donnent simplement une forme nouvelle à des corps que la nature a produits." (ibidem, pp.15-16.)

67 „ Tutti i fenomeni dell' universo, sieno essi prodotti dalla mano dell'uomo, ovvero dalle universali leggi della fisica, non ci danno idea di attuale *creazione*, ma unicamente di una *modificazione* della materia. *Accostare e separare* sono gli unici elementi che l'ingegno umano ritrova analizzando l' idea della *riproduzione*; e tanto è *riproduzione di valore* e di *ricchezza* se la terra, l'aria e l' acqua ne' campi si trasmutino in grano, come se colla mano dell'uomo il glutine di un insetto si trasmuti in velluto, ovvero alcuni pezzetti di metallo si organizzino a formare una ripetizione." (Pietro Verri, *Meditazioni Sulla Economia Politica.* In: *Scrittori Classici Italiani di Economia Politica.* Parte moderna. Tomo XV, Milano, 1804, pp.21-22.)

68 „...la classe dei manufattori [...] sterile, [...] perchè *il valore della manifattura*, secondo essi, è *una quantità eguale alla materia prima*, più gli *alimenti che consumarono gli artigiani nel fabbricarla.*" (ibidem, p. 25.)

68 „... questo dimostra che l'artigiano, nel prezzo che riceve, non solamente ottiene il *rifacimento della consumazione fatta, ma ne ottiene una*

*porzione di più, a questa porzione è una nuova * quantità di valore creata* nella massa dell'annua riproduzione" (ibidem, p.26.)

68 „La riproduzione di valore è [...] quella quantità di prezzo che ha la derrata o manifattura, *oltre il valor primo* della materia e la consumazione fattavi per formarla. Nell' agricoltura si detraggono la semente e la consumazione del contadino: nelle manifattura ugualmente si detraggono la materia prima e la consumazione dell'artigiano, e tanto annualmente si crea un *valore di riproduzione, quanto importa questa quantità restante.*" (ibidem, pp.26-27.)

69 „ Il faut de toute nécessité qu'un homme vive de son travail, et que son salaire suffise au moins à sa subsistance; il faut même quelque chose de plus dans la plupart des circonstances, autrement il lui serait impossible d'élever une famille, et alors la race de ces ouvriers ne pourrait pas durer au-delà de la première génération." (Adam Smith, *Recherches sur la nature et les causes de la richesse des nations.* Traduction nouvelle... par Germain Garnier, t. I, Paris, 1802, p.136.)

71 „Il en coûtait une bien plus grande quantité de travail pour mettre la marchandise au marché; ainsi, quand elle y était venue, il fallait bien qu'elle achetât ou qu'elle obtînt en échange le prix d'une plus grande quantité de travail." (Adam Smith, *Recherches sur la nature et les causes de la richesse des nations.* Traduction nouvelle...par Germain Garnier, t. II, Paris, 1802, p.156.)

73 „Le même auteur ajoute que le travail d'un esclave bien constitué est estimé valoir le double de sa subsistance, et il pense que celui de l'ouvrier le plus faible ne peut pas valoir moins que celui d'un esclave bien constitué." (ibidem, p.137.)

74 „Que l'échange du drap contre la toile soit accompli, les producteurs du drap participeront à la toile dans une proportion égale à celle dans laquelle ils avaient auparavant participé au drap." (Karl Marx, *Misère de la Philosophie. Réponse à la Philosophie de la misère de M. Proudhon*, Paris et Bruxelles, 1847, p.29.)

75 „Un homme est riche ou pauvre, suivant les moyens qu'il a de se procurer les besoins, les aisances et les agrémens de la vie. Mais la division une fois établie dans toutes les branches du travail, il n'y a qu'une partie extrêmement petite de toutes ces choses qu'un homme puisse se procurer directement par son travail, et s'est du *travail d'autrui* qu'il lui faut attendre la très-majeure partie de toutes ces jouissances; ainsi il sera riche ou pauvre, *selon la quantité de travail qu'il pourra commander ou qu'il sera en état d'acheter. Ainsi la valeur d'une denrée quelconque* pour celui qui la possède, et qui n'entend pas en user ou la consommer lui-même, mais qui a intention *de l'échanger pour autre chose, est égale à la quantité du travail que cette denrée le met en état d'acheter ou de commander.* Le travail est donc la mesure *réelle* de la *valeur échangeable*, de toute marchandise." (Adam Smith, *Recherches sur la nature et les causes de la richesse des nations.* Traduction nouvelle... par Germain Garnier, t. I, Paris, 1802, pp.59-60.)

---

* In the manuscript: „porzione à vera nova".—*Ed.*

75 „*Elles* contiennent *la valeur d'une certaine quantité de travail que nous échangeons pour ce* qui *est supposé alors contenir la valeur d'une quantité égale de travail*... Ce n'est point avec de l'or ou de l'argent, c'est avec du travail que toutes les richesses du monde ont été achetées originairement; et leur valeur pour ceux qui les possèdent et qui cherchent à les échanger contre de nouvelles productions, est précisément égale à la quantité de travail qu'elles le mettent en état d'acheter ou de commander." (ibidem, pp.60-61.)

75 „Comme dit M. Hobbes, *richesse* veut dire *pouvoir*; mais celui qui acquiert une grande fortune ou qui l'a par héritage, n'acquiert par là nécessairement aucun pouvoir politique, soit civil, soit militaire... Le genre de pouvoir que cette possession lui transmet immédiatement et directement, c'est le pouvoir d'acheter; c'est un droit de commandement sur *tout le travail d'autrui, ou sur tout le produit de ce travail existant alors au marché*." (ibidem, p.61.)

75 „Elles * contiennent la valeur d'une certaine quantité de travail que nous échangeons pour ce qui est supposé alors contenir *la valeur d'une quantité égale de travail*." (ibidem, p.60.)

76 „Sa fortune est plus ou moins grande exactement en proportion de l'étendue de ce pouvoir, en proportion de la quantité du travail d'autrui, qu'elle le met en état de commander, ou *ce qui est la même chose, du produit du travail d'autrui*, qu'elle le met en état d'acheter." (ibidem, p.61.)

76 „Elles contiennent la valeur d'une certaine quantité du travail que nous échangeons pour ce qui est supposé alors [...] la valeur *d'une quantité égale* de travail." (ibidem, p.60.)

77 „Ainsi le travail, ne variant jamais dans sa *valeur propre*, est la seule mesure réelle et définitive qui puisse servir, dans tous les temps et dans tous les lieux, à apprécier et à comparer la valeur de toutes les marchandises." (ibidem, p.66.)

78 „Dans ce premier état informe de la société, qui *précède l'accumulation des capitaux et la propriété des terres*, la seule circonstance qui puisse fournir quelque règle pour les échanges, c'est, à ce qu'il semble, *la quantité du travail nécessaire pour acquérir les différents objets d'échange*... Il est naturel que ce qui est ordinairement le produit de deux jours ou de deux heures de travail, vaille le double de ce qui est ordinairement le produit d'un jour ou d une heure de travail." (ibidem, pp.94-95.)

78 „Dans cet état de choses, le produit de travail appartient tout entier à l'ouvrier, et la quantité du travail communément employée à acquérir ou à produire un objet échangeable est la seule circonstance qui puisse régler la quantité de travail que cet objet devrait communément acheter, commander ou obtenir en échange." (ibidem, p.96.)

78 „Aussitôt qu'il y aura *provisions accumulées dans les mains de quelques particuliers*, certains d'entre eux emploieront naturellement ces provisions à mettre en œuvre des gens d'industrieux, auxquels ils fourniront

* In the manuscript: „Les marchandises".—*Ed.*

des matériaux et des subsistances, *afin de faire un profit sur la vente de l'ouvrage, ou sur ce que le travail de ces ouvriers ajoute de valeur aux matériaux.*" (ibidem, p.96.)

78 „ ... *Afin de faire un profit sur la vente de l'ouvrage*, ou sur ce que le travail de ces ouvriers ajoute de valeur aux matériaux. " (ibidem, p. 96).

79 „ Quand *l'ouvrage fini* est échangé, ou contre de l'argent, *ou contre du travail*, ou contre d'autres marchandises, il faut bien qu'en outre de ce qui pourrait suffire à payer le prix des matériaux et les salaires des ouvriers, il *y ait encore quelque chose de donné* pour les profits de l'entrepreneur de l'ouvrage, qui hasarde ses provisions dans cette affaire. " (ibidem, p. 96.)

79 „ Ainsi la *valeur que les ouvriers ajoutent à la matière* se résout *alors en deux parties, dont l'une paie leurs salaires* et *l'autre paie les profits que fait l'entrepreneur sur la somme des fonds qui lui ont servi à avancer ces salaires* et la matière à travailler." (ibidem, pp. 96-97.)

80 „ Quand l'ouvrage fini est échangé, ou contre de l'argent, *ou contre du travail*, ou contre d'autres marchandises... " (ibidem, p. 96.)

81 „ Les profits des fonds, dira-t-on peut-être, ne sont autre chose qu'un nom différent donné aux salaires d'une espèce particulière de travail, le travail d'inspection et * de direction. " (ibidem, p. 97.)

81 „ Dans cet état de choses donc, le produit du travail n'appartient pas toujours tout entier à l'ouvrier. Il faut le plus souvent que celui-ci le partage avec le *propriétaire de capital* qui le fait travailler. Ce n'est plus alors la quantité de travail mise communément à acquérir ou à produire quelque marchandise, qui est la seule circonstance qui puisse régler la quantité de travail que cette marchandise devra communément acheter, commander ou obtenir en échange. Il est clair qu'il sera encore dû une *quantité additionnelle* pour le profit du capital qui a avancé les salaires de ce travail et qui en a fourni les matériaux. " (ibidem, p. 99.)

82 „ Dès l'instant que le sol d'un pays est divisé en autant de propriétés privées, les propriétaires, comme *tous les autres hommes*, aiment à recueillir où ils n'ont pas semé, et ils demandent une *rente*, même pour le produit naturel de la terre... il faut qu'il cède au propriétaire du sol *une portion de ce qu'il recueille ou de ce qu'il produit par son travail.* Cette portion ou, ce qui revient au même, le prix de cette portion constitue la *rente de la terre...* " (ibidem, pp. 99-100.)

82 „ ... *intérêt* [...] *l'argent* ** *est toujours un revenu secondaire* qui, s'il ne se prend pas sur le *profit* que procure l'usage de l'argent, doit être payé par quelqu'autre source de revenu, à moins que l'emprunteur ne soit un dissipateur qui contracte une seconde dette pour payer l'intérêt de la première. " (ibidem, pp. 105-06.)

84 „ Tous les impôts et tous les revenus qui sont fondés sur les impôts, les appointements, pensions et annuités de toute sorte, sont, en dernière analyse, dérivés de l'une ou de l'autre de ces trois sources primitives de

* In the manuscript: „ou".—*Ed.*
** In the manuscript: „d'argent".—*Ed* .

revenu, et sont payés, soit immédiatement, soit médiatement, ou avec des salaires de travail, ou avec des profits de capitaux, ou avec des rentes de terres. " (Adam Smith. *Recherches sur la nature et les causes de la richesse des nations*. Traduction nouvelle... par Germain Garnier, t. I, Paris, 1802, p. 106.)

89 „ Ainsi la valeur que les ouvriers *ajoutent* à la matière se résout alors en deux parties, dont l'une paie leurs salaires et l'autre paie les profits que fait l'entrepreneur sur la somme des fonds qui lui ont servi à avancer ces salaires et la matière à travailler. Il n'aurait pas d'intérêt à employer ces ouvriers, s'il n'attendait pas de la vente de leur ouvrage quelque chose de plus que ce qu'il fallait pour lui remplacer ses fonds, et il n'aurait pas d'intérêt à employer une grosse somme de fonds plutôt qu'une petite, si ses profits ne gardaient pas quelque proportion avec l'étendue des fonds employés. ". (Adam Smith, *Recherches sur la nature et les causes de la richesse des nations*. Traduction nouvelle... par Germain Garnier, t. I, Paris, 1802, pp. 96-97.)

90 „ ... sur la somme des fonds qui [...] ont servi à avancer ces salaires et la matière à travailler." (ibidem, p. 97.)

90 „ ... n'aurait pas d'intérêt à employer ces ouvriers, s'il n'attendait pas de la vente de leur ouvrage *quelque chose de plus* que ce qu'il fallait pour lui remplacer ses fonds... " (ibidem, p. 97.)

91 „Ils sont cependant d'une nature absolument différente des salaires ; ils se règlent sur des principes entièrement différens, et ne gardent aucune proportion avec la quantité et la nature de ce prétendu travail d'inspection et de direction. *Ils se règlent en entier sur la valeur du capital employé*, et ils sont plus ou moins forts, à proportion de l'étendue des fonds. Par exemple, supposons qu'en un lieu particulier où les *profits des fonds* employés dans les manufactures *sont communément de dix pour cent par an*, il y ait deux différentes manufactures, chacune desquelles emploie vingt ouvriers, à raison de 15 livres par chacun, ou bien fait une dépense de 300 livres par an pour chaque atelier ; supposons encore que les matériaux grossiers qu'on travaille annuellement dans l'une, coûtent seulement 700 livres, tandis que dans l'autre on travaille des matières plus précieuses qui coûtent 7000 livres, le capital employé annuellement dans l'une sera, dans ce cas, de 1000 liv. seulement, tandis que celui employé dans l'autre montera à 7300 liv. Ainsi, au taux de dix pour cent, l'entrepreneur de l'une comptera sur un profit annuel d'environ 100 liv. seulement, tandis que l'entrepreneur de l'autre s'attendra à un bénéfice d'environ 730 liv. Mais malgré cette différence énorme dans leurs profits, il se peut que leur travail d'inspection et de direction soit tout à fait le même ou très approchant. " (ibidem, pp. 97-98.)

93 „Il y a plus d'un siècle que M. Locke établit à-peu-près la même opinion ..., l'argent est une chose stérile qui ne produit rien: tout le service qu'on en retire, c'est qu'il transporte, par un accord mutuel, le profit qui a salarié le travail d'un homme dans la poche d'un autre. Si cette idée du bénéfice des capitaux était rigoureusement juste, il s'ensuivrait qu'il serait, non une source première de revenu, mais

u n e s o u r c e d é r i v é e ; et l'on ne pourrait considérer les capitaux comme un des principes de la richesse, leur profit n'étant qu'un transport de la poche du travailleur dans celle du capitaliste. " (Comte de Lauderdale, *Recherches sur la nature et l'origine de la richesse publique*... Traduit de l'anglais par E. Lagentie de Lavaïsse, Paris, 1808, pp. 116-117.)

93 „ *Salaire, profit et rente* sont les *trois sources primitives* de tout revenu, *aussi bien que de toute valeur échangeable.* " (Adam Smith, *Recherches sur la nature et les causes de la richesse des nations.* Traduction nouvelle... par Germain Garnier, t. I, Paris, 1802, p. 105.)

94 „ Ainsi dans le *prix* des marchandises, les *profits* des fonds ou capitaux sont une *source de valeur* entièrement *différente* des salaires [...], et réglée sur des principes tout-à-fait différens. " (ibidem, p. 99.)

97 „ La rente fait... partie du prix des denrées, mais tout autrement que les profits et les gages *. Suivant que ceux-ci sont hauts ou bas, ils sont la *cause* du haut ou *du bas prix du blé, et la rente haute ou basse en est le résultat.* " (Adam Smith; quoted from : Charles Ganilh, *Des Systèmes d'économie politique*..., t. II, Paris, 1821, p. 3.)

98 „ Ces trois parties semblent constituer immédiatement ou en définitif la *totalité* du prix du blé. " (Adam Smith, *Recherches sur la nature et les causes de la richesse des nations.* Traduction nouvelle... par Germain Garnier, t, I, Paris, 1802, p. 101.)

98 „ On pourrait peut-être penser qu'il faut y ajouter une *quatrième partie*, nécessaire pour remplacer le capital du fermier ou pour compenser le dépérissement et l'user de ses chevaux de labour et autres instruments d'agriculture. Mais il faut considérer que le prix de tout instrument de labourage, tel qu'un cheval de charrue, est lui-même formé de ces mêmes trois parties ; la rente de la terre sur laquelle il a été élevé, le travail de ceux qui l'ont nourri et soigné, et les profits d'un fermier qui a fait les avances tant de cette rente que des salaires de ce travail. " (ibidem, p. 101.)

98 „ Ainsi quoique le prix du blé doive payer aussi bien le prix principal du cheval que son entretien, la *totalité* du prix de ce blé se résout toujours, soit immédiatement, soit en dernière analyse, dans ces mêmes trois parties, rente, travail et profit. " (ibidem, pp. 101-102.)

99 „ On a fait voir... *que le prix de la plupart des marchandises* se résout en trois parties, dont l'une paie les salaires du travail, l'autre les profits du capital, et la troisième la rente de la terre... " (ibidem, t. II, p. 212.)

100 „ On a observé que puisqu'il en était ainsi pour toute marchandise quelconque prise séparément, il fallait nécessairement qu'il en fût du même pour les marchandises qui composent la *totalité* du produit de la terre et du travail d'un pays, prises en masse. La *somme totale du prix ou de la valeur échangeable* de ce produit annuel doit se résoudre de même en ces trois parties et se distribuer entre les différents habitants du pays, ou

* In the manuscript: „salaires".—*Ed.*

comme salaires de leur travail, ou comme profits de leur capital, ou comme rentes de leur terre. " (ibidem, p. 213.)

100 „ Mais quoique la valeur totale du produit annuel des terres et du travail d'un pays soit ainsi partagée entre les différens habitans et leur constitue un revenu, cependant, de même que dans le revenu d'un domaine particulier, nous distinguons le *revenu brut* et le *revenu net*, nous pouvons aussi faire une pareille distinction à l'égard du revenu *de tous les habitans* d'un grand pays." (ibidem, p. 213.)

101 „ Le *revenu brut* d'un domaine particulier comprend généralement tout ce que débourse le fermier ; le *revenu net* est ce qui reste franc et quitte de *toutes charges au propriétaire*, après la déduction des frais de régie, des réparations et tous autres *prélèvements nécessaires*, ou bien ce qu'il peut, sans nuire à sa fortune, placer dans le fonds qu'il destine à servir immédiatement à sa consommation, c'est-à-dire, dépenser pour sa table...*
Sa richesse réelle n'est pas en proportion de son revenu *brut*, mais bien de son revenu *net*. " (ibidem, pp. 213-14.)

101 „ Le revenu *brut* de tous les habitans d'un grand pays comprend la *masse totale* du produit annuel de leur terre et de leur travail ; leur revenu *net* est ce qui leur reste franc et quitte, déduction faite de ce qu'il faut pour entretenir premièrement leur *capital fixe* ; secondement, leur *capital circulant* ; ou bien ce qu'ils peuvent placer, sans empiéter sur leur capital, dans leur *fonds de consommation*..." (ibidem, p. 214.)

101 „ Il est évident qu'il faut retrancher du revenu *net* de la société, toute la dépense d'entretien du *capital fixe*. Ni *les matières nécessaires* pour la conservation des machines utiles, des instruments de métier, bâtimens d'exploitations, etc. ni le *produit du travail nécessaire* pour façonner ces matières dans la forme convenable, ne peuvent jamais faire partie de ce revenu *net*. Le *prix de ce travail*, à la vérité, peut bien en faire partie, puisque les ouvriers qui y sont employés, peuvent placer *la valeur entière de leurs salaires* dans leurs *fonds de consommation*. Mais la différence, c'est que, dans les autres sortes de travail, *et le prix et le produit vont l'une et l'autre à ce fonds* ; le prix va à celui des ouvriers et le produit à celui d'autres personnes dont la subsistance, les aisances et les amusemens se trouvent augmentés par le travail de ces ouvriers. " (ibidem, pp. 214-15.)

102 „ ... ne peuvent jamais faire partie de ce revenu *net*. " (ibidem, p. 215.)

102 „ ... les machines et instrumens de métier, etc. qui composent le *capital fixe*, soit d'un individu, soit d'une société, ne font partie *ni du revenu brut ni du revenu net* de l'un ou de l'autre, de même *l'argent*... " (ibidem, p. 220.)

103 „ A considérer une nation en masse, elle n'a point de produit net ; car les *produits* n'ayant qu'une valeur égale aux *frais* de leur production, lorsqu'on retranche ces *frais*, on retranche toute la *valeur* des *produits*... Le *revenu annuel* est le *revenu brut*. " (Jean-Baptiste Say, *Traité d'économie politique*... Troisième édition, t. II, Paris, 1817, p. 469.)

* In the manuscript: „etc."—*Ed.*

103 „ Il est [...] clair que la valeur du produit annuel se distribue partie en capitaux et partie en profits, et que chacune de ces portions *de la valeur du produit annuel va régulièrement acheter les produits dont la nation a besoin*, tant pour entretenir son capital que pour renouveler son fonds consommable. " (Henri Storch, *Cours d'économie politique...*, t. V: „ Considération sur la nature du revenu national ", Paris, 1824, pp. 134-35.)

104 „ Qu'on se représente donc une famille qui suffit par son propre travail à tous ses besoins, comme il y en a tant d'exemples [dans l'intérieur de la Russie] *... si le revenu d'une pareille famille est égal au produit brut résultant de ses terres, de son capital et de son industrie? Peut-elle habiter ses granges ou ses étables, manger ses semailles et ses fourrages, s'habiller de ses bestiaux de labour, se divertir de ses instruments aratoires? D'après la thèse de M. Say, il faudrait affirmer toutes ces questions." (ibidem, pp. 135-36.)

104 „ M. Say [...] regarde le produit brut comme le revenu de la société; et il en conclut que la société peut consommer une valeur égale à ce produit... " (ibidem, p. 145.)

104 „ Le revenu (net) d'une nation n'est pas l'excédant des valeurs produites sur la *totalité des valeurs consommées* (comme l'auteur ** le représente), mais seulement sur les *valeurs consommées pour produire*... si une nation consomme dans son *** année tout cet excédant, elle consomme tout son revenu (net). " (ibidem, p. 146.)

104 „ Si l'on admet que le revenu d'une nation est égal à son produit brut, c'est-à-dire qu'il n'y a point de *capital* à en déduire, il faut aussi admettre qu'elle peut dépenser improductivement la valeur entière de son produit annuel sans faire le moindre tort à son revenu futur. " (ibidem, p. 147.)

104 „ *...les produits qui constituent le capital d'une nation ne sont point consommables.* " (ibidem, p. 150.)

125 „ On peut regarder la circulation d'un pays comme divisée en deux branches différentes; la circulation qui se fait entre commerçans seulement, et la circulation entre les commerçans et les consommateurs. Quoique les mêmes pièces de monnaie, soit papier, soit métal, puissent être employées tantôt dans l'une de ces deux branches de circulation, et tantôt dans l'autre, cependant comme ces deux branches marchent constamment en même tems, chacune d'elles exige un certain fonds de monnaie, d'une espèce ou de l'autre, pour la faire marcher. *La valeur des marchandises qui circulent entre les différens commerçans, ne peut jamais excéder la valeur de celles qui circulent entre les commerçans et les consommateurs; tout ce qui est acheté par les gens de commerce étant en définitif destiné à être vendu aux consommateurs.* " (Adam Smith, *Recherches sur la nature et les causes de la richesse des nations*. Traduction nouvelle... par Germain Garnier, t. II, Paris, 1802, pp. 292-93.)

150 „ Pour achever d'entendre cette matière des revenus, il faut considérer

* In the manuscript: „in Rußland".—*Ed.*

** In the manuscript: „Say".—*Ed.*

*** In the manuscript: „une".—*Ed.*

que la valeur toute entière d'un produit se partage en revenus à diverses personnes ; car la valeur *totale* de chaque produit se compose des profits des propriétaires fonciers, des capitalistes et des industrieux qui ont contribué à lui donner l'existence. C'est ce qui fait que le revenu de la société est égal à la *valeur brute* qui a été produite, et non, comme l'imaginait la secte des économistes, au *produit net* des terres... S'il n'y avait de revenus dans une nation que l'excédent des valeurs produites sur les valeurs consommées, il résulterait de là une conséquence véritablement absurde : c'est qu'une nation qui aurait consommé dans son année autant de valeurs qu'elle en aurait produit, n'aurait point [...] de revenu. " (Jean-Baptiste Say, *Traité d'économie politique*... Troisième édition. t. II, Paris, 1817, pp. 63-64.)

162 „ Premièrement, on convient que cette classe *reproduit annuellement la valeur* de sa propre consommation annuelle, *et continue au moins l'existence du fonds ou capital qui la tient employée et la fait subsister*... A la vérité, les fermiers et les ouvriers de la campagne, outre le capital qui les fait travailler et subsister, reproduisent encore annuellement un *produit net*, une rente franche et quitte au propriétaire... le travail des fermiers et ouvriers de la campagne est assurément plus productif que celui des marchands, des artisans et des manufacturiers. Avec cela, la supériorité du produit de l'une de ces classes ne fait pas que l'autre soit *stérile et non productive*. " (Adam Smith, *Recherches sur la nature et les causes de la richesse des nations*. Traduction nouvelle... par Germain Garnier, t. III, Paris, 1802, p. 530.)

163 „ Secondement, sous ce même rapport, il paraît aussi tout-à-fait impropre de considérer des artisans, manufacturiers et marchands sous le même point de vue que de simples domestiques. *Le travail d'un domestique ne continue pas l'existence du fonds qui lui fournit son emploi et sa subsistance. Ce domestique est employé et entretenu finalement aux dépens de son maître*, et *le travail qu'il fait n'est pas de nature a pouvoir rembourser cette dépense*. Son ouvrage consiste en *services* qui, *en général, périssent et disparaissent à l'instant même où ils sont rendus*, qui *ne se fixent ni ne se réalisent en aucune marchandise qui puisse se vendre et remplacer la valeur de leur subsistance et de leurs salaires*. Au contraire, le travail des artisans, marchands et manufacturiers *se fixe et se réalise naturellement en une chose vénale et échangeable*. C'est sous ce rapport que, dans le chapitre où je traite du *travail productif* et du *travail non productif*, j'ai classé les artisans, les manufacturiers et les marchands parmi les ouvriers *productifs*, et les domestiques parmi les ouvriers *stériles* et *non productifs*. " (ibidem, p. 531.)

164 „ ... *en une chose vénale et échangeable... en aucune* * *marchandise qui puisse se vendre et remplacer la valeur de leur subsistance et de leurs salaires*. " (ibidem, p. 531.)

168 „ Troisièmement, dans toutes les suppositions, il semble impropre de dire que le travail des artisans, manufacturiers et marchands n'augmente pas le *revenu réel* de la société. Quand même nous supposerions, par exemple, comme on le fait dans ce système, que la valeur de ce que consomme cette classe dans un jour, un mois, une année, est précisément égale à ce qu'elle produit dans ce jour, dans ce mois, dans cette année, cependant il ne

* In the manuscript: „une".—*Ed.*

s'ensuivrait nullement de là que son travail n'ajoutât rien au revenu réel de la société, à la valeur réelle du produit annuel des terres et du travail du pays. Par exemple, un artisan qui, dans les six mois que suivent la moisson, exécute pour la valeur de 10 livres d'ouvrage, quand même il aurait consommé pendant le même tems pour la valeur de 10 livres de blé et d'autres denrées nécessaires à la vie, néanmoins, dans la réalité, il ajoute une valeur de 10 livres au produit annuel des terres et du travail de la société. Pendant qu'il a consommé une demi-année de revenu valant 10 livres, en blé et autres denrées de première nécessité, il a en même tems produit une valeur égale en ouvrage, laquelle peut acheter pour lui ou pour quelque autre personne une pareille demi-année de revenu. Par conséquent la valeur de ce qui a été tant consommé que produit pendant ces six mois, est égale non à 10, mais à 20 livres. Il est possible, à la vérité, que de cette valeur il n'en ait jamais existé, dans un seul instant, plus de 10 livres en valeur à la fois. Mais si les 10 livres vallant, en blé et autres denrées de nécessité qui ont été consommées par cet artisan, eussent été consommées par un soldat ou par un domestique, la valeur de la portion existante du produit annuel, au bout de ces six mois, aurait été de 10 livres moindre de ce qu'elle s'est trouvée être, en conséquence du travail de l'ouvrier. Ainsi, quand même on supposerait que la valeur produite par l'artisan n'est jamais, à quelque moment que ce soit, plus grande que la valeur par lui consommée, cependant la valeur totale des marchandises actuellement existantes dans le marché, à quelque moment qu'on la prenne, se trouve être, en conséquence de ce qu'il produit, plus grande qu'elle ne l'aurait été sans lui." (Adam Smith, *Recherches sur la nature et les causes de la richesse des nations.* Traduction nouvelle... par Germain Garnier, t. III, Paris, 1802, pp. 531-33.)

169 „ Quand les champions de ce système avancent que la *consommation* des artisans, manufacturiers et marchands est *égale à la valeur de ce qu'ils produisent*, vraisemblablement ils n'entendent pas dire autre chose, sinon que le *revenu de ces ouvriers* ou le *fonds destiné à leur subsistance est égal à cette valeur:*" (ibidem, p. 533.)

169 „ Le produit annuel des terres et du travail d'une société ne peut recevoir d'augmentation que de deux manières ; ou bien *premièrement*, par un *perfectionnement survenu dans les facultés productives du travail utile* actuellement en activité dans cette société : ou bien, *secondement*, *par une augmentation survenue dans la quantité de ce travail.* Pour qu'il survienne quelque perfectionnement ou accroissement de puissance dans les facultés productives du travail utile, il faut, *ou* que *l'habileté de l'ouvrier se perfectionne, ou que l'on perfectionne les machines avec lesquelles il travaille... L'augmentation dans la quantité de travail utile* actuellement employé dans une société, dépend uniquement *de l'augmentation du capital qui le tient en activité* ; et, à son tour, *l'augmentation de ce capital doit être précisément égale au montant des épargnes* que font sur leurs revenus, ou les personnes qui dirigent et administrent ce capital, ou quelques autres personnes qui le leur prêtent." (ibidem, pp. 534-35.)

170 „ Le commerce qui s'établit entre ces deux différentes classes du peuple, consiste, en dernier résultat, dans l'échange d'une certaine quantité

de produit brut, contre une certaine quantité de produit manufacturé. Par conséquent, plus celui-ci est cher, plus l'autre sera à bon marché ; et tout ce qui tend dans un pays à élever le prix du produit manufacturé, tend à abaisser celui du produit brut de la terre, et par-là à décourager l'agriculture." (ibidem, p. 554.)

173 „ ...la richesse des nations comme ne consistant pas dans ces richesses non consommables d'or et d'argent, mais dans les biens consommables reproduits annuellement par le travail de la société..." (Adam Smith, *Recherches sur la nature et les causes de la richesse des nations*. Traduction nouvelle ... par Germain Garnier, t. III, Paris, 1802, p. 538).

174 „ En réservant exclusivement la qualité de *richesses* aux valeurs fixées dans des substances matérielles, il raya du livre de la production cette masse illimitée de valeurs immatérielles, filles du *capital moral* des nations civilisées..." (Adolphe Blanqui, *Histoire de l'économie politique...*, Bruxelles, 1839, p. 152.)

177 „ ...l'une échange toujours son travail contre le capital d'une nation, l'autre l'échange toujours contre une partie du revenu national." (J.-C.-L. Simonde de Sismondi, *Nouveaux principes d'économie politique...*, t. I, Paris, 1827, p. 148.)

177 „Quoique l'ouvrier, par son travail journalier, ait produit beaucoup plus que sa dépense journalière, il est rare qu'après avoir partagé avec le propriétaire de terre et le capitaliste il lui reste grand-chose au-delà du strict nécessaire." (ibidem., p. 87.)

181 „ Supposons [...] qu'un homme plante en * blé, avec ses mains, une certaine étendue de terre, c'est-à-dire, laboure, sème, herse, récolte, engrange, vanne, en un mot, fasse tout ce que la culture exige, je dis que, quand cet homme a retiré sa semence et tout ce qu'il a mangé ou donné à d'autres en échange de ses vêtemens et de ses autres besoins naturels, ce qui reste de blé est la véritable rente de la terre pour cette année ; et le *médium* de sept années, ou plutôt du nombre d'années dans lesquelles la cherté et l'abondance font leur révolution, donne la rente ordinaire de la terre cultivée en blé. Mais une question, ultérieure et collatérale peut être, combien d'argent vaut ce blé ou cette rente ? Je réponds qu'il en vaut autant qu'il en resteroit à un autre individu qui emploieroit *le mieux son temps* pour aller dans le pays de mines, pour en extraire le minerai, pour le raffiner, le convertir en monnoie et le rapporter au même lieu où l'autre individu a semé et recueilli son blé. La somme restante à cet individu, après le prélèvement de toutes ses dépenses, seroit parfaitement égale en valeur à celle du blé qui resteroit au cultivateur." (William Petty, *A Treatise of Taxes, and Contribution...* London, 1662, pp. 23-24 ; quoted from Charles Ganilh, *Des Systèmes d'économie politique...*, t. II, Paris, 1821, pp. 36-37.)

183 „ ...travail [...] productif... celui qui se réalise sur un objet, celui qui laisse après soi des traces de son opération et dont le produit peut être la matière d'une vente ou d'un échange." (Adam Smith, *Recherches*

* In the manuscript: „du". — *Ed.*

sur la nature et les causes de la richesse des nations. Traduction nouvelle... par Germain Garnier, t. V, Paris, 1802, p. 169.)

183 „ Cette distinction est fausse, en ce qu'elle porte sur une différence qui n'existe pas. *Tout travail est productif* dans le sens dans lequel l'auteur entend ce mot productif. Le travail de l'une comme de l'autre de ces deux classes est également productif de quelque joüissance, commodité ou utilité pour la personne qui le paie, sans quoi ce travail ne trouverait pas de salaire." (ibidem, p. 171.)

183 „ Le domestique qui est à mon service, qui allume mon feu, qui me coëfe, qui néttoie et entretient mes habits et mes meubles, qui prépare mes alimens, etc. rend des *services absolument du même genre* que la blanchisseuse ou la lingère, qui néttoie et entretient le linge de ses pratiques ; ...que le traiteur, rôtisseur ou cabaretier, qui fait son métier de préparer des alimens aux personnes auxquelles il convient mieux de venir manger chez lui ; que le barbier, le coëfeur ... qui rendent des services immédiats ; que le maçon enfin, le couvreur, le menuisier, le vitrier, le fumiste... etc. et cette foule d'ouvriers employés aux bâtimens, qui viennent lorsqu'ils sont appelés pour faire des raccommodages et réparations, et dont le bénéfice annuel consiste autant en ouvrages de simple réparation et entretien, qu'en constructions nouvelles." (ibidem, pp. 171-72.)

184 „ Ce genre de travail consiste moins à produire qu'à conserver ; il a moins pour but d'ajouter à la valeur des sujets auxquels il s'applique, que de prévenir leur dépérissement. Tous ces travailleurs, y compris le domestique, *épargnent à celui qui les paie, le travail d'entretenir sa propre chose...*" (ibidem, p. 172.)

184 „ ...c'est pour cela et pour cela seul le plus souvent qu'ils travaillent ; ainsi, ou ils sont tous *productifs*, ou aucun d'eux n'est productif." (ibidem, p. 172.)

184 „ ... le travail d'un commis-inspecteur ou directeur d'une entreprise particulière de commerce ou de manufacture, est comme *non productif*, celui de l'administrateur, qui veillant à l'entretien des routes publiques, des canaux navigables, des ports, des monnaies et autres grands instrumens destinés à animer l'activité du commerce, veillant à la sûreté des transports et des communications, à l'exécution des conventions, etc. peut, à juste titre, être regardé comme le *commis-inspecteur de la grande manufacture sociale*? C'est un travail absolument de même nature, quoique dans des proportions plus vastes." (ibidem, pp. 172-73.)

185 „ ... le parfumeur, q u i ... mon odorat ... charmer mon oreille..." (ibidem, p. 173.)

185 „ ... luthier, le facteur d'orgues, le marchant de musique, le machiniste..." (ibidem, p. 173.)

185 „ Les uns et les autres ont, pour dernier terme de *leur travail, une consommation du même genre.* Si la fin que se proposent les uns, ne mérite pas d'être comptée au nombre *des produits* du travail de la société, pourquoi traiterait-on plus favorablement ce qui n'est autre chose qu'un *moyen pour arriver à cette fin*?" (ibidem, p. 173.)

186 „ La seule différence générale qu'on puisse, à ce qu'il semble, observer entre [...] deux classes imaginées par Smith, c'est que dans ceux de la classe qu'il nomme *productive*, il y a ou il *peut toujours y avoir quelque personne intermédiaire entre le travailleur de la chose et celui qui la consomme* ; au lieu que, dans celle qu'il nomme *non productive*, il *ne peut y avoir aucun intermédiaire*, et que la relation est *nécessairement directe et immédiate entre le salarié et le consommateur*. Il est évident qu'il y a *nécessairement* une relation directe et immédiate entre celui qui use de l'expérience du médecin, de l'habilité du chirurgien, du savoir de l'avocat, du talent du musicien ou de l'acteur, ou enfin des services du domestique, et entre chacun de ses différens salariés au moment de leur travail ; tandis que dans les professions qui composent l'autre classe, *la chose à consommer étant matérielle et palpable, elle peut être l'objet de plusieurs échanges intermédiaires* avant d'arriver de la personne qui travaille, à celle qui consomme." (ibidem, p. 174.)

187 „ ... encore faudrait-il déduire toujours de sa classe *productive* tous les ouvriers dont le travail consiste purement à nettoyer, entretenir, conserver ou réparer des choses finies, et ne fournit pas par conséquent de produit nouveau dans la circulation." (ibidem, p. 175.)

187 „ C'est par [...] suite de cette différence que la classe *non productive*, ainsi que Smith l'a observé, ne subsiste que de revenus. En effet, cette classe n'admettant aucun intermédiaire entr'elle et celui qui consomme ses produits, c'est-à-dire, celui qui jouit de son travail, elle est immédiatement payée par le consommateur ; or, *celui-ci ne paie qu'avec des revenus*. Au contraire, les ouvriers de la classe productive étant, pour l'ordinaire, payés par un *intermédiaire qui se propose de faire un profit sur leur travail, sont le plus souvent payés par un capital*. Mais ce capital est toujours en définitif remplacé par le revenu d'un consommateur, sans quoi il ne circulerait point et dès-lors ne rendrait aucun profit à son possesseur." (ibidem, p. 175.)

199 „ Tout ce qu'on peut conclure de cette différence, c'est que, pour employer les gens *productifs*, il faut non seulement le *revenu de celui qui jouit de leur travail*, mais *encore* un *capital qui donne des profits aux intermédiaires*, au lieu que pour *employer les gens non productifs*, il suffit le plus souvent du revenu qui les paie..." (ibidem, p. 175.)

199 „ ... que pour employer les gens *non productifs*, il suffit le plus souvent du revenu qui les paie..." (ibidem, p. 175.)

199 „ ... pour employer les gens *productifs*, il faut non-seulement *le revenu* de celui qui *jouit* de leur travail, mais encore un *capital* qui *donne des profits aux intermédiaires*..." (ibidem, p. 175.)

200 „ ... encore beaucoup d'ouvriers *non productifs*, tels que les comédiens, musiciens, etc. ne reçoivent-ils leurs salaires le plus souvent que par le canal d'un directeur qui tire des profits du capital placé dans ce genre d'entreprise ?" (ibidem, p. 175-76.)

200 „ Il s'ensuit donc que, dans une société où la classe *productive* est très-multipliée, on doit supposer qu'il existe une grande accumulation de capitaux dans les mains des intermédiaires ou entrepreneurs de travail." (ibidem, p. 176.)

200 „ Ce n'est donc pas, comme le prétend Smith, la proportion existante entre la masse des capitaux et celle des revenus, qui déterminera la proportion entre la classe *productive* et la classe *non productive*. Cette dernière proportion semble dépendre bien d'avantage des mœurs et des habitudes du peuple ; du degré plus ou moins avancé de son industrie." (ibidem, p. 177.)

201 „ ... à nombre égal d'individus, aucune classe ne contribue plus que celle des domestiques, à convertir en *capitaux* des sommes procédant de *revenus*." (ibidem, p. 181.)

201 „ ... un homme qui a observé avec autant de sagacité..." (ibidem, p. 182.)

201 „ ... cet intermédiaire placé près du riche, pour *recueillir* les débris du revenu que celui-ci dissipe avec tant d'insouciance..." (ibidem, p. 183.)

201 „ ... crée encore une valeur nouvelle, une valeur qui *n'existait pas* dans la société, même en équivalent, au moment où ce travail a commencé son opération ; et c'est cette valeur qui fournit une rente au propriétaire du sol." (ibidem, p. 184.)

201 „ ... crée [...] une valeur nouvelle... qui n'existait pas dans la société, même en équivalent, au moment où ce travail a commencé son opération..." (ibidem, p. 184.)

202 „ La fortune d'un individu se grossit par l'épargne ; la fortune publique *au contraire*, reçoit son accroissement de l'augmentation des consommations." ([Germain Garnier] *Abrégé élémentaire des principes de l'économie politique*, Paris, 1796, p. XIII ; quoted from : Destutt de Tracy, *Eléments d'idéologie*, IV et V parties. Traité de la volonté et de ses effets, Paris, 1826, p. 250.)

202 „ L'amendement et l'extension de la culture et par suite des progrès de l'industrie et du commerce n'ont pas *d'autre cause* que l'extension des besoins artificiels. ([Germain Garnier] *Abrégé élémentaire des principes de l'économie politique*, Paris, 1796, p. 240 ; quoted from : Destutt de Tracy, *Eléments d'idéologie*, IV et V parties. Traité de la volonté et de ses effets, Paris, 1826, p. 251.)

203 „ Je remarque seulement... que l'on ne devra pas considérer comme essentielle et très-exacte la distinction de Smith entre le travail *productif* et le travail *improductif*, si l'on fait attention que le travail d'autrui en général ne produit jamais pour nous qu'une économie de temps, et que cette économie de temps est tout ce qui constitue *sa valeur* et *son prix*." (Schmalz, *Économie politique*, Ouvrage traduit de l'allemand par Henri Jouffroy, t. I, Paris, 1826, p. 304.)

203 „ Le menuisier, par exemple, qui me fait une table, et le domestique qui porte mes lettres à la poste, qui bat mes habits ou qui cherche pour moi les choses qui me sont nécessaires, me rendent l'un et l'autre un service absolument de même nature ; l'un et l'autre m'épargne et le temps que je serais obligé d'employer moi-même à ces occupations, et celui qu'il m'aurait fallu consacrer à acquérir l'aptitude et les talents qu'elles exigent." (ibidem, p. 304.)

203 „ ... ce système fait aux artisans et même aux *simples consommateurs*

un mérite de leurs consommations ; par le motif, que ces consommations contribuent, quoique d'une manière indirecte et médiate, à augmenter le revenu national, puisque, sans *ces consommations, les objets consommés n'auraient pas été produits par le sol* et *n'auraient pu être ajoutés au revenu du propriétaire foncier*." (ibidem, p. 321.)

204 „ ... *la richesse, une accumulation de travail superflu*." (Nicolas-François Canard, *Principes d'économie politique*, Paris, 1801, p. 4 ; quoted from Charles Ganilh, *Des Systèmes d'économie politique...*, t. I, Paris, 1821, p. 75.)

204 „ Dans l'état actuel de la civilisation, le travail ne nous est connu que par l'échange..." (Charles Ganilh, *Des Systèmes d'économie politique...*, t. I, Paris, 1821, p. 79.)

204 „ ... le travail sans échange ne peut produire aucune richesse." (ibidem, p. 81.)

204 „ La richesse dérive exclusivement du commerce." (ibidem, p. 84.)

204 „ ... l'échange ou le commerce donne seul la valeur aux choses..." (ibidem, p. 98.)

204 „ ... principe de l'identité des valeurs et de la richesse... repose la doctrine de la fécondité du travail général..." (ibidem, p. 93.)

204 „ ... fait dériver la richesse particulière et générale des valeurs échangeables du travail, soit que ces valeurs soient ou non fixées dans des objets matériels durables et permanens. (ibidem, p. 95.)

204 „ ... *système commercial*, ou l'échange des valeurs *du travail général*." (ibidem, p. 98.)

205 „ ... l'échange donne aux *choses* une valeur qu'elles n'auroient pas eue sans lui..." (ibidem, p. 102.)

206 „ Les produits les plus utiles peuvent n'avoir aucune valeur si l'échange ne leur en donne point..." (ibidem, p. 104.)

206 „ ... et les produits les plus inutiles peuvent avoir une très-grande valeur si l'échange leur est favorable." (ibidem, p. 104.)

206 „ ... la valeur échangée des choses et non leur valeur échangeable constitue la *véritable valeur*, celle qui est identique avec la richesse..." (ibidem, p. 104.)

207 „ Ce n'est donc ni l'utilité réelle des choses, ni leur valeur *intrinsèque* qui en font des richesses ; c'est l'échange qui fixe et détermine leur valeur, et c'est cette valeur qui les identifie avec la richesse." (ibidem, p. 105.)

207 „ Il n'y a véritablement des richesses pour les particuliers et pour les peuples que lorsque chacun travaille pour tous et tous pour chacun..." (ibidem, p. 108.)

208 „ ... richesse nationale, qui se compose des valeurs échangeables du travail..." (ibidem, p. 108.)

208 „ Si l'abondance du blé en fait *baisser la valeur*, les cultivateurs seront moins riches, parce qu'ils ont moins de valeurs d'échange pour se pro-

curer les choses nécessaires, utiles ou agréables à la vie ; mais les consommateurs du blé profiteront de tout ce que les cultivateurs auront perdu : la perte des uns sera compensée par le gain des autres, et la richesse générale n'éprouvera point de variation." (ibidem, pp. 108-09.)

209 „ De là vient qu'il est difficile, et peut-être impossible à un pays de s'enrichir par le commerce intérieur. Il n'en est pas tout-à-fait de même des peuples qui se livrent au commerce avec l'étranger." (ibidem, p. 109.)

209 „ ...tout travail, quelle que soit sa nature, est productif de la richesse, pourvu qu'il ait une valeur d'échange." (ibidem, p. 119.)

209 „ L'échange n'a aucun égard, ni à la quantité, ni à la matérialité, ni à la permanence des produits..." (ibidem, p. 121.)

209 „ ... tous sont *également productifs* de la *somme* contre laquelle ils ont été échangés." (ibidem, pp. 121-22.)

209 „ Il n'y a aucune différence entre le travail de l'ouvrier qui fait une commode dont l'échange lui produit un septier de blé, et le travail de ménétrier qui lui produit un septier de blé. Des deux côtés il y a un septier de blé produit pour payer la commode, et un septier de blé produit pour payer le plaisir procuré par le ménétrier. A la vérité, après la consommation du septier de blé par le menuisier, il reste une commode, et après la consommation du septier de blé par le ménétrier, il ne reste rien ; mais combien de travaux réputés productifs sont dans le même cas ... ce n'est pas par ce qui reste après la consommation qu'on peut juger si un travail est productif ou stérile, c'est par *l'échange ou par la production qu'il a fait naître*. Or, comme le travail du ménétrier est, aussi bien que le travail du menuisier, *la cause de la production d'un septier de blé, tous deux sont également productifs d'un septier de blé*, quoique l'un, après qu'il est fini, ne se fixe et ne se réalise dans aucun objet permanent, et que l'autre se fixe et se réalise dans un objet permanent." (ibidem, pp. 122-23.)

210 „ ... Adam Smith voudroit réduire le nombre des travailleurs qui ne s'occupent pas utilement, pour multiplier celui des travailleurs qui s'occupent utilement ; mais on n'a pas fait attention que si ce désir pouvoit se réaliser, toute richesse seroit impossible, parce que les consommateurs manqueroient aux producteurs, et que les excédans non consommés ne seroient pas reproduits. Les classes productives ne donnent pas gratuitement les produits de leurs travaux *aux classes dont les travaux ne donnent aucuns produits matériels* ; elles les leur donnent en échange des commodités, des plaisirs ou des jouissances qu'elles en reçoivent, et, *pour les leur donner, elles sont obligées de les produire*. Si les produits matériels du travail n'étoient pas employés à salarier les travaux qui ne donnent point de produits matériels, ils n'auroient pas de consommateurs et leur *reproduction* cesseroit. Les travaux productifs d'agrément *concourent donc aussi efficacement à la production* que le travail réputé le plus productif." (ibidem, pp. 123-24.)

210 „ Presque toujours les commodités, les plaisirs ou les agrémens qu'ils recherchent, *suivent* et *ne devancent pas les produits qui doivent les acquitter...*" (ibidem, p. 125.)

210 „ Il en est autrement lorsque les travaux consacrés au plaisir, au luxe et au faste, *ne sont pas demandés par les classes productives*, et que cependant elles sont *forcées* de les salarier et de prendre ce salaire sur leurs besoins. Alors il peut arriver que ce salaire forcé ne fasse pas naître un surcroît de productions..." (ibidem, p. 125.)

210 „ Hors ce cas... tout travail est nécessairement productif, et contribue plus ou moins efficacement à la formation et à l'accroissement des richesses générales, parce qu'*il fait naître nécessairement les produits qui les salarient*." (ibidem, p. 126.)

211 „ Si l'échange donne au travail du domestique une valeur de 1000 francs, quand il ne donne à celui du cultivateur et du manufacturier qu'une valeur de 500 francs, il faut en conclure que le travail du domestique contribue à la *production de la richesse* deux fois autant que celui du cultivateur et du manufacturier ; et cela ne peut pas être autrement, tant que le travail des domestiques reçoit en paiement deux fois autant de produits matériels que le travail des cultivateurs et des manufacturiers. Le moyen de concevoir que la richesse provient du travail qui a le moins de valeur d'échange et qui par conséquent est le moins payé " (ibidem, pp. 293-94.)

211 „ Vainement objecte-t-on que si le travail des domestiques est aussi productif que celui des cultivateurs et des manufacturiers, on ne voit pas pourquoi les économies générales d'un pays ne seroient pas employées à leur entretien non-seulement sans être dissipées, mais avec une augmentation constante de valeur. Cette objection * n'est spécieuse que parce qu'elle suppose que la fécondité de chaque travail résulte de sa *coopération à la production des objets matériels*, *que la production matérielle est constitutive de la richesse*, et *que production et richesse sont parfaitement identiques*. On oublie que *toute production n'est richesse que jusqu'à concurrence de sa consommation*, et que l'échange détermine jusqu'à quel point elle *contribue à la formation de la richesse*. Si l'on se rappeloit que tous les travaux concourent directement ou indirectement à la production totale de chaque pays, que l'échange, en fixant la valeur de chaque travail détermine la part qu'il a eue à la production, *que la consommation de la production* réalise la valeur que lui a donnée l'échange, et que l'excédant ou le déficit de la production sur la consommation détermine l'état de la richesse ou de la misère des peuples, on sentiroit combien il est inconséquent, *d'isoler* chaque travail, de fixer sa fertilité et sa fécondité par son *concours à la production matérielle et sans aucun égard à sa consommation, qui seule lui donne une valeur*, valeur sans laquelle la richesse ne peut exister " (ibidem, pp. 294-95.)

212 „ ... que tout travail est *productif* de la richesse, dans la proportion de sa valeur d'échange déterminée par l'offre et la demande, que sa valeur respective ne concourt à l'accumulation des capitaux que par l'*économie et la non-consommation* des produits que ces valeurs autorisent à prendre dans la production générale. " (ibidem, p 296.)

---

* In the manuscript: „observation".—*Ed.*

215 „ Quand un pays est privé du secours des machines, et que son travail se fait à force de bras, les classes laborieuses consomment la presque totalité de leurs productions. A mesure que l'industrie fait des progrès, qu'elle se perfectionne par la division du travail, par l'habilité des ouvriers, par l'invention des machines, les frais de la production diminuent, ou, en d'autres termes, il faut un moindre nombre d'ouvriers pour obtenir une plus grande production. " (ibidem, pp. 211-12.)

220 „ Tant que la division du travail n'est pas établie dans toutes ses branches, tant que toutes les classes de la population laborieuse et industrieuse n'ont pas atteint le terme de leur complément, l'invention des machines, et leur emploi dans certaines industries, ne font que refluer les capitaux et les ouvriers déplacés par les machines, dans d'autres travaux qui peuvent les employer utilement. Mais il est évident que quand tous les travaux ont le capital et les ouvriers qui leur sont nécessaires, tout perfectionnement ultérieur, toute machine nouvelle qui abrègent le travail, réduisent nécessairement la population laborieuse ; et comme sa réduction ne diminue point la production, la part qu'elle laisse disponible accroît ou au profit des capitaux, ou à la rente de la terre ; et par conséquent l'effet naturel et nécessaire des machines est de diminuer la population des classes salariées qui vivent du produit brut, et d'augmenter la population des classes qui vivent du produit net. " (ibidem, p. 212.)

221 „ *Le déplacement de la population d'un pays, effet nécessaire des progrès de l'industrie*, est la véritable cause de la prospérité, de la puissance et de la civilisation des peuples modernes. Plus les classes intérieures de la société décroissent en nombre, moins elle doit s'inquiéter des dangers auxquels l'exposent sans cesse les besoins, l'ignorance, la crédulité et la superstition de ces classes infortunées ; plus les classes supérieures se multiplient, plus l'état a de sujets à sa disposition, plus il est fort et puissant, plus il y a dans toute la population de lumières, de raison et de civilisation. " (ibidem, p. 213.)

221 „ Le revenu net d'un particulier se compose de *la valeur du produit* auquel il a concouru... moins ses déboursés ; mais comme les déboursés qu'il a faits sont *des portions de revenu* qu'il a payées à d'autres, *la totalité de la valeur du produit a servi à payer des revenus*. Le revenu total d'une nation se compose de son produit brut, c'est-à-dire, de la valeur brute de tous ses produits qui se distribue entre les producteurs. " (J.-B. Say in : David Ricardo, *Des principes de l'économie politique, et de l'impôt*. Traduit... par F. S. Constancio ... avec des notes... par Jean-Baptiste Say, t. II. Paris, 1819, p. 218 ; quoted from : Charles Ganilh, *Des Systèmes d'économie politique...*, t. I, Paris, 1821, p. 216.)

221 „ Cette valeur, après plusieurs échanges, se consommeroit tout entière dans l'année qui l'a vue naître, qu'elle n'en seroit pas moins encore le revenu de la nation ; de même qu'un particulier qui a 20 000 fr. de revenu annuel, n'a pas moins 20 000 fr. de revenu annuel, quoiqu'il le mange tout entier chaque année. Son revenu ne se compose pas seulement de ses épargnes. " (J.-B. Say in : David Ricardo, *Des Principes de l'économie politique, et de l'impôt*. Traduit... par F. S. Constancio... avec des notes... par Jean-Baptiste Say, t. II, Paris. 1819, p.

218-19 ; quoted from : Charles Ganilh, *Des Systèmes d'économie politique...*, t. I, Paris, 1821, p. 216.)

222 „ Le seul *produit net* et ceux qui le consomment composent sa richesse et sa puissance, et concourent à sa prospérité, à sa gloire et à sa grandeur. " (Charles Ganilh, *Des Systèmes d'économie politique...*, t. I, Paris, 1821, p. 218.)

222 „Cela ressemble tout-à-fait à la doctrine des économistes du dix-huitième siècle, qui prétendoient que les manufactures ne servoient nullement à la richesse de l'état, parce que la *classe salariée*, consommant une valeur égale à celle qu'elle produisoit, ne contribuoit en rien à leur fameux produit net. " (J.-B. Say in : David Ricardo, *Des Principes de l'économie politique, et de l'impôt.* Traduit... par F. S. Constancio... avec des notes... par Jean-Baptiste Say, t. II, Paris, 1819, p. 222 ; Quoted from : Charles Ganilh, *Des Systèmes d'économie politique* ..., t. I, Paris, 1821, p. 219.)

222 „ Il n'est pas facile d'apercevoir quelque rapport entre l'assertion des économistes, *que la classe industrieuse consommoit une valeur égale à celle qu'elle produisoit*, et la doctrine de M. Ricardo, *que le salaire des ouvriers ne peut [...] être compté dans le revenu d'un état.* " (Charles Ganilh, *Des Systèmes d'économie politique....* t. I, Paris, 1821, pp. 219-20.)

223 „ Sur sept millions d'ouvriers tous occupés, il y aura plus d'épargnes que sur cinq millions. " (J.-B. Say in : David Ricardo *Des Principes de l'économie politique, et de l'impôt.* Traduit... par F. S. Constancio... avec des notes... par Jean-Baptiste Say, t. II, Paris, 1819, p. 223 ; quoted from : Charles Ganilh, *Des Systèmes d'économie politique...*, t. I, Paris, 1821, p. 220.)

223 „ ... c'est supposer que les économies sur les salaires sont préférables à l'économie qui résulte de la supression des salaires... seroit par trop absurde de payer quatre cent millions de salaires à des ouvriers qui ne donnent aucun produit net, afin de leur procurer l'occasion et le moyen de faire des économies sur leur salaire. " (Charles Ganilh, *Des Systèmes d'économie politique*, t. I, Paris, 1821, p. 221.)

223 „ ... à chaque pas que fait la civilisation, le travail devient moins pénible et plus productif ; les classes condamnées à produire et à consommer diminuent ; et les classes qui dirigent le travail, qui soulagent, consolent et éclairent toute la population, se multiplient, *deviennent plus nombreuses, et s'approprient tous les bien faits qui résultent de la diminution des frais du travail*, de l'abondance des productions et du bon marché des consommations. Dans cette direction, l'espèce humaine s'élève... dans cette *tendance progressive de la diminution des classes inférieures de la société* et *de l'accroissement des classes supérieures...* la société civile devient plus prospère, plus [...] puissante..." (ibidem, p. 224.)

223 „ Si... le nombre des ouvriers employés est de sept millions, les salaires seront de quatorze cents millions ; mais si les quatorze cents millions [...] ne donnent pas un plus grand produit net que le milliard payé aux cinq millions d'ouvriers, *la véritable économie seroit dans la sup-*

pression des quatre cents millions de salaires à deux millions d'ouvriers. qui ne donnent aucun produit net, et non dans les épargnes que les deux millions d'ouvriers peuvent faire sur les quatre cents millions de salaire." (ibidem, p. 221.)

223 „ *Adam Smith* [...] exagère toujours les avantages qu'un pays tire d'un gros revenu brut comparés à ceux d'un gros revenu net... quel avantage résultera-t-il pour un pays de l'emploi d'une grande quantité de travail productif, si, soit qu'il emploie cette quantité ou une moindre [...], son revenu et ses profits doivent rester les mêmes ? (David Ricardo, *Des Principes de l'économie politique, et de l'impôt*. Traduit... par F. S. Constancio ... avec des notes ... par Jean-Baptiste Say, t. II, Paris, 1819, pp. 218-20 ; quoted from : Charles Ganilh, *Des Systèmes d'économie politique...*, t. I, Paris, 1821, pp. 213-14.)

223 „ ... la nourriture et l'habillement de ces cinq millions seroient toujours le revenu net. L'emploi d'un plus grand nombre d'hommes ne nous mettroit en état ni d'ajouter un homme à notre armée ou à notre marine, ni de fournir une guinée de plus aux impôts. " (David Ricardo, *Des Principes de l'économie politique, et de l'impôt*. Traduit ... par F. S. Constancio ... avec des notes... par Jean-Baptiste Say, t. II, Paris, 1819, pp. 221-22 ; quoted from : Charles Ganilh, *Des Systèmes d'économie politique...*, t. I, Paris, 1821, p. 215.)

226 „ ... il seroit tout-à-fait indifférent pour une personne qui, sur un capital de 20 000 liv., feroit 2 000 liv. par an de profit, que son capital employât cent hommes ou mille, et que ses produits se vendissent 10 000 liv. ou 20 000 liv., pourvu que dans tous les cas ses produits * ne baissassent point au-dessous de 2 000 liv. " (David Ricardo, *Des Principes de l'économie politique, et de l'impôt*. Traduit ... par F. S. Constancio ... avec des notes ... par Jean-Baptiste Say. t. II, Paris, 1819, p. 220-21 ; quoted from : Charles Ganilh, *Des Systèmes d'économie politique...*, Paris, 1821, p. 214.)

229 „ Je ne doute aucunement** [...] que dans le travail de l'esclave, l'excédent des produits sur les consommations ne soit plus grand que dans le travail de l'homme libre. Le travail du premier*** n'a de bornes que le pouvoir de ses facultés ... L'esclave *travaille pour un besoin illimité : la cupidité de son maître...*" (Jean-Baptiste Say, *Traité d'économie politique...*, t. I, Paris, 1803, pp. 215-16.)

229 „ L'ouvrier libre ne peut dépenser plus et produire moins que l'esclave... Toute dépense suppose un équivalent produit pour la payer. Si l'ouvrier libre dépense plus que l'esclave, les produits de son travail doivent être plus considérables que ceux du travail de l'esclave." (Charles Ganilh, *Des Systèmes d'économie politique...*, t. I, Paris, 1821, p. 234.)

229 „ Je sais qu'on peut dire avec quelque raison, que les *économies que le maître fait sur les dépenses de l'esclave* servent à augmenter ses dépen-

* In Ganilh's book the word „produits" is substituted for the word „profits" used by Constancio in his translation of Ricardo's work.—*Ed.*

** In the manuscript: „nullement".—*Ed.*

*** In the manuscript, the words „du premier" are replaced by „de l'esclave".—*Ed.*

ses personnelles... Mais il est plus avantageux à la richesse générale qu'il y ait de l'aisance dans toutes les classes de la société qu'une excessive opulence parmi un petit nombre d'individus." (ibidem, pp. 234-35.)

230 „ ... il refuse positivement aux économies des classes salariées la faculté d'accroître les capitaux ; et la raison qu'il en donne, c'est que ces classes ne doivent avoir aucun moyen de faire des économies, et que si elles avoient *un surplus*, *un excédent*, il ne pourroit provenir que d'une erreur ou d'un désordre dans l'économie sociale." (ibidem, p. 274.)

230 „ Si la classe stérile épargne pour augmenter son numéraire..., ses travaux et ses gains diminueront dans la même proportion, et elle tombera dans le dépérissement." (ibidem, pp. 274-75, footnote ; Ganilh quotes Quesnay from the volume : *Physiocratie*..., publié par Du Pont, Leyde et Paris, 1767, p. 321.)

230 „ ... plus ils sont considérables, moindre est le revenu de la société, et [...] toute l'habilité des gouvernemens doit s'appliquer à en réduire la masse... *Tâche... digne du siècle éclairé dans lequel nous vivons.*" (Charles Ganilh, *Des Systèmes d'économie politique*..., t. II, Paris, 1821, p. 24.)

253 „ Les principes que Smith *a posés sur l'économie des nations*, ont pour fondement une distinction [...] d a n s l e t r a v a i l q u'i l a p p e l l e p r o d u c t i f o u i m p r o d u c t i f..." (F.-L.-A. Ferrier, *Du Gouvernement considéré dans ses rapports avec le commerce*, Paris, 1805, p. 141.)

253 „ Cette distinction est essentiellement fausse. *Il n'y a point de travail improductif.*" (ibidem, p. 141).

253 „ Il y a donc une économie et une prodigalité des nations; mais une nation n'est prodigue ou économe que dans ses relations avec les *autres* peuples, et c'était ainsi que la question devait être envisagée." (ibidem, p. 143.)

253 „ ... i l e x i s t a i t une économie des nations, mais t r è s d i f f é r e n t e d e c e l l e q u e S m i t h l e u r c o n s e i l l e... c o n s i s t e à n'acheter de productions étrangères qu'autant qu'elle en peut payer avec les siennes. Elle consiste quelquefois à s'en passer absolument." (ibidem, pp. 174-75.)

253 „ Des parties constituantes du prix des marchandises." (Adam Smith, *Recherches sur la nature et les causes de la richesse des nations*. Traduction nouvelle... par Germain Garnier, t. I, Paris, 1802, p. 94.)

253 „ Comme dans un pays civilisé il n'y a que *très peu de marchandises dont toute la valeur échangeable procède du travail seulement*, et que, dans la *très majeure partie d'entr'elles, la rente et le profit y contribuent pour de fortes portions*, il en résulte que *le produit annuel du travail de ce pays suffira toujours pour acheter et commander une quantité de travail beaucoup plus grande que celle qu'il a fallu employer pour faire croître ce produit, le préparer et l'amener au marché. Si la société employait annuellement tout le travail qu'elle est en état d'acheter an-*

nuellement, comme la quantité de ce travail augmenterait considérablement chaque année, il s'ensuivrait que le produit de chacune des années subséquentes serait d'une valeur incomparablement plus grande que celui de la précédente. Mais il n'y a aucun pays *dont tout le produit annuel* soit employé à entretenir des travailleurs. Partout les oisifs en consomment une grande partie ; et selon les différentes proportions dans lesquelles ce produit se partage entre ces deux différentes classes de gens, sa valeur ordinaire ou moyenne doit nécessairement ou augmenter ou décroître, ou demeurer la même d'une année à l'autre." (ibidem, pp. 108-09.)

255 „ Comme dans un pays civilisé il n'y a que très peu de marchandises dont toute la valeur échangeable *procède du travail seulement,* et que, dans la très majeure partie d'entr'elles, *la rente et le profit y contribuent pour de fortes portions,* il en résulte *que le produit annuel de travail de ce pays* suffira toujours *pour acheter et commander une quantité de travail* beaucoup plus grande que celle *qu'il a fallu employer pour faire croître ce produit,* le préparer et l'amener au marché." (ibidem, pp. 108-09.)

256 „ Si la société employait annuellement tout le travail qu'elle est en état d'acheter annuellement, comme la quantité de ce travail augmenterait considérablement chaque année, il s'ensuivrait que le produit de chacune des années subséquentes serait d'une valeur incomparablement plus grande que celui de la précédente." (ibidem, p. 109.)

258 „ 4°. Les talens utiles acquis par les habitans ou membres de la société. L'acquisition de ces talens coûte toujours une dépense réelle à cause de l'entretien de celui qui les acquiert, pendant le tems de son éducation, de son apprentissage ou de ses études, et cette dépense est un capital fixé et réalisé pour ainsi dire dans sa personne. Si ces talens composent une partie de sa fortune, ils composent pareillement une partie de la fortune de la société à laquelle il appartient. La dextérité perfectionnée, dans un ouvrier, peut être considérée sous le même point de vue qu'une machine ou un instrument de métier qui facilite et abrège le travail, et qui, malgré la dépense qu'il a coûté, restitue cette dépense avec un profit." (ibidem, t. II, pp. 204-05.)

259 „ Quand la société est encore dans cet état d'enfance où il n'y a aucune division de travail, où il ne se fait presque point d'échanges, et où chaque individu pourvoit par ses mains à ses besoins, *il n'est pas nécessaire qu'il y ait aucun fonds accumulé ou amassé d'avance pour faire aller les affaires de la société.* Chaque homme cherche, dans sa propre industrie, les moyens de satisfaire aux besoins du moment, à mesure qu'ils se font sentir. Quand la faim le presse, il s'en va chasser dans la forêt..." (ibidem, pp. 191-92.)

259 „ Mais quand une fois la division du travail est généralement établie, un homme ne peut plus appliquer son travail personnel qu'à une bien petite partie des besoins qui lui surviennent. Il pourvoit à la très majeure partie de ces besoins avec *des choses produites par le travail d'autrui* [...] ou, ce qui revient au même, avec le prix de ce produit. Or, cet *achat* ne peut se faire à moins qu'il n'ait eu le tems, non-seulement

d'achever tout-à-fait, mais encore *de vendre le produit de son travail.*" (ibidem, p. 192.)

259 „ ... le tems ... *de vendre* le produit de son travail." (ibidem, p. 192.)

259 „ Il faut donc qu'au moins, jusqu'à ce qu'il ait pu venir à bout de ces deux choses, il existe quelque part *un fonds de denrées de différentes espèces, amassé d'avance* pour le faire subsister et lui fournir en outre la matière et les instrumens nécessaires à son ouvrage. Un tisserand *ne peut pas vaquer entièrement* à sa besogne particulière s'il n'y a quelque * part, *soit en sa possession, soit en celle d'un tiers, une provision* fait par avance, où il trouve de quoi subsister et de quoi se fournir des outils de son métier et de la matière de son ouvrage, jusqu'à ce que sa toile puisse être non-seulement achevée, mais encore vendue. Il est évident qu'il faut que l'*accumulation précède* le moment où il pourra appliquer son industrie à entreprendre et achever cette besogne... dans la nature des choses, *l'accumulation d'un capital est un préalable nécessaire à la division du travail...*" (ibidem, pp. 192-93.)

259 „ ... le travail ne peut recevoir de subdivisions ultérieures qu'à proportion que les capitaux se sont préalablement accumulés de plus en plus. A mesure que le travail vient à se subdiviser, *la quantité de matières qu'un même nombre de personnes peut mettre en œuvre augmente dans une grande proportion* ; et comme la tâche de chaque ouvrier se trouve successivement réduite à un plus grand degré de simplicité, il arrive qu'on invente une foule de nouvelles machines pour faciliter et abréger ces tâches. A mesure donc que la division de travail va en s'étendant, il faut, pour qu'un même nombre d'ouvriers soit constamment occupé, qu'on *accumule d'avance une égale provision de vivres et une provision de matières et d'outils plus forte* que celle qui aurait été nécessaire dans un état de choses moins avancé." (ibidem, pp. 193-94.)

260 „ De même que le travail ne peut acquérir cette grande extension de puissance productive *sans une accumulation préalable des capitaux*, de même l'accumulation des capitaux amène naturellement cette extension. *La personne qui emploie son capital à faire travailler*, cherche nécessairement à l'employer de manière à ce qu'il fasse produire la plus grande quantité possible d'ouvrage : elle tâche donc à la fois d'établir entre ses ouvriers la distribution de travaux la plus convenable, et de les fournir des meilleures machines qu'elle puisse imaginer ou qu'elle soit à même de se procurer. Ses moyens pour réussir dans ces deux objets, sont proportionnées en général à l'étendue de son capital ou au nombre de gens que ce capital peut tenir occupés. Ainsi non-seulement *la quantité d'industrie augmente dans un pays à mesure de l'accroissement du capital* qui la met en activité, mais encore, *par une suite de cet accroissement*, la même *quantité d'industrie produit une beaucoup plus grande quantité d'ouvrage.*" (ibidem, pp. 194-95.)

260 „ Une maison servant de logement ne contribue en rien, sous ce rapport au revenu de celui qui l'occupe ; et quoique, sans contredit, elle lui soit extrêmement utile, elle l'est comme ses habits et ses meubles

---

* In the manuscript: „a pas quelque".—*Ed.*

de ménage, qui lui sont aussi très-utiles, mais qui pourtant font une partie de sa dépense et non pas de son revenu." (ibidem, pp. 201-02.)

260 „ ... Tous les bâtimens destinés à un objet utile, et qui sont des moyens de revenu, non-seulement pour le propriétaire qui en retire un loyer en les louant, mais même pour la personne qui les tient et qui en paie le loyer ; tels que les boutiques, les magasins, les ateliers, les bâtimens d'une ferme, avec toutes leurs dépendances nécessaires, étables, granges, etc. Ces bâtimens sont fort différens des maisons purement habitables : ce sont des espèces d'instrumens de métier..." (ibidem, pp. 203-04.)

260 „ ... on regarde toujours comme un grand avantage pour une société tous les nouveaux procédés en mécanique, qui mettent un même nombre d'ouvriers en état de faire la même quantité d'ouvrage avec des machines plus simples et moins coûteuses que celles dont on faisait usage précédemment. Il se trouve alors une certaine quantité de matériaux et un certain nombre d'ouvriers qui avaient été employés auparavant à entretenir des machines plus compliquées et plus dispendieuses, et qui maintenant peuvent l'être à augmenter la quantité de l'ouvrage pour lequel ces machines ou toutes autres ont été faites." (ibidem, pp. 216-17.)

260 „ ... la dépense d'entretien du *capital fixe* se trouve... nécessairement retranchée du revenu net de la société..." (ibidem, p. 218.)

260 „ ... toute épargne dans la dépense d'entretien du *capital fixe*, qui ne diminue pas dans le travail la puissance productive, doit augmenter le fonds qui met l'industrie en activité, et par conséquent accroître le produit annuel de la terre et du travail, revenu réel de toute société." (ibidem, pp. 226-27.)

260 „ ... à acheter des marchandises étrangères pour la consommation intérieure..." (ibidem, p. 231.)

260 „ ... marchandises ... à être consommées *par des gens oisifs* qui ne produisent rien ... ou bien... ils achèteront *un fonds additionnel de matières, d'outils et de vivres, dans la vue d'entretenir et d'employer un nombre additionnel de ces gens industrieux qui reproduisent, avec un profit, la valeur de leur consommation annuelle.*" (ibidem, pp. 231-32.)

261 „ ... augmente la dépense et la consommation sans rien ajouter à la production, ou sans établir un fonds permanent propre à entretenir cette dépense, et sous tous les rapports il tourne au préjudice de la société." (ibidem, p. 232.)

261 „ Employé de la seconde manière, il agrandit d'autant les bornes de l'industrie ; et quoiqu'il augmente la consommation de la société, il ouvre une source permanente pour fournir à cette consommation, *les gens qui consomment reproduisant avec un profit la valeur entière de leur consommation annuelle.*" (ibidem, p. 232.)

261 „ La quantité d'industrie que peut mettre en œuvre un capital, doit évidemment être égale au nombre d'ouvriers auxquels il peut fournir des matériaux, des outils et une subsistance convenable à la nature de l'ouvrage." (ibidem, p. 235.)

261 „ Les travailleurs productifs et les non-productifs, et ceux qui ne travaillent pas du tout, sont tous également entretenus par le produit annuel de la terre et du travail de pays. Ce produit... a nécessairement ses bornes. Suivant donc que, dans une année, une portion plus ou moins grande de ce produit est employée à entretenir des gens non-productifs, plus ou moins grande sera la portion qui restera pour les gens productifs, et plus ou moins grand sera par concéquent le produit de l'année subséquente...

Quoique la totalité du produit annuel des terres et du travail d'un pays soit ... destinée en definitif à fournir à la consommation de ses habitans et à leur procurer un revenu, *cependant, à l'instant* qu'il sort de la terre ou des mains des ouvriers productifs, il se divise naturellement en deux parties. L'une d'elles, et c'est souvent la plus forte, est, en premier lieu, destinée *à remplacer un capital ou à renouveler la portion de vivres, de matières ou d'ouvrage fait* qui a été retirée d'un capital ; l'autre est destinée à former un revenu, ou au maître de ce capital, comme profit, ou à quelqu'autre personne, comme rente de sa terre...

Cette partie du produit annuel de la terre et du travail d'un pays qui remplace un capital, n'est jamais immédiatement employée à entretenir d'autres salariés que des salariés productifs ; elle ne paie des salaires qu'au travail productif seulement. Celle qui est destinée à former immédiatement un revenu... peut indifféremment entretenir des salariés productifs ou des salariés non-productifs...

Les travailleurs non-productifs et les gens qui ne travaillent pas du tout, sont tous entretenus *par un revenu* : soit, en premier lieu, par cette partie du produit annuel, qui est, dès l'origine, destinée à former un revenu à quelques personnes particulières, ou comme rente de terre, ou comme profit de capital ; soit, en second lieu, par cette autre partie qui, bien qu'elle soit destinée à remplacer un capital et à n'entretenir que des ouvriers productifs, néanmoins, quand elle est une fois venue dans les mains de ceux-ci, pour tout ce qui excède leur subsistance nécessaire, peut être employée indifféremment à l'entretien de gens qui produisent ou de gens qui ne produisent pas. Ainsi, le simple ouvrier, si ses salaires sont forts, peut ... entretenir un domestique à son service personnel, ou bien il peut aller quelquefois à la comédie ou aux marionettes, et par-là contribuer pour sa part à l'entretien d'une classe de travailleurs non-productifs, ou enfin il peut payer quelque impôt, et par-là concourir à l'entretien d'une autre classe ... également non-productive. Néanmoins, de cette partie du produit de la terre, destinée originairement à remplacer un capital, il n'en passe jamais aucune portion à l'entretien de salariés non-productifs, qu'après avoir mis en activité sa mesure complète de travail productif... Il faut que l'ouvrier ait pleinement gagné son salaire par de l'ouvrage fait, avant qu'il puisse en dépenser la moindre chose en travail non-productif... La rente de la terre et les profits des capitaux sont ... partout les principales sources où les salariés non-productifs puisent leur subsistance ... L'un et l'autre de ces revenus peuvent indifféremment entretenir des salariés productifs et des salariés non-productifs ; ils semblent pourtant avoir toujours pour les derniers quelque prédilection ...

Ainsi, ce qui contribue beaucoup à déterminer dans tout pays la proportion entre les gens productifs et les gens non-productifs, c'est principalement la proportion qui s'y trouve entre cette partie du produit annuel, qui, au sortir même de la terre ou des mains des ouvriers qui l'ont produite, est destinée à remplacer un capital, et cette autre partie qui est destinée à former un revenu, soit comme rente, soit comme profit. Or, cette proportion est très différente, dans les pays riches, de ce qu'elle est dans les pays pauvres." (ibidem, pp. 314-18, passim.)

262 „... très-forte partie * [...] souvent la plus forte du produit de la terre..." (ibidem, p. 318.)

262 „... nations opulentes de l'Europe, [...] *est destinée à remplacer le capital d'un fermier riche et indépendant* [...] empire du gouvernement féodal, une très petite portion du produit était suffisante pour remplacer le capital employé à la culture." (ibidem, pp. 318-19.)

262 „... rendissent de très gros profits. Nulle part l'intérêt n'était au-dessous de 10 pour 100, et il fallait bien que les profits des fonds pussent suffire à payer un intérêt aussi fort. *À présent dans les pays de l'Europe qui ont fait quelques progrès vers l'opulence, le taux de l'intérêt n'est nulle part plus haut que 6 pour 100, et dans quelques-uns des plus riches,* il est même *tombé jusqu'à 4,3 et 2 pour 100.* Si cette partie du revenu des habitants, qui provient de profits, est toujours beaucoup plus grande dans les pays riches que dans les pays pauvres, c'est parce que le capital y est beaucoup plus considérable ; mais les profits y sont en général dans une proportion beaucoup moindre, relativement au capital.

Ainsi cette partie du produit annuel qui, au sortir de la terre ou des mains des ouvriers productifs, est destinée à remplacer un capital, est non-seulement beaucoup plus grande dans les pays riches que dans les pays pauvres, mais encore elle s'y trouve dans une proportion bien plus forte, relativement à la partie destinée immédiatement à former un revenu, soit comme rente, soit comme profit. Le fonds qui est destiné à fournir de la subsistance au travail productif est non-seulement bien plus abondant dans les premiers de ces pays, qu'il ne l'est dans les autres, mais il est encore dans une plus grande proportion, relativement au fonds qui, pouvant être employé à entretenir des salariés productifs aussi bien que des salariés non-productifs, a néanmoins toujours en général plus de tendance à aller à ceux-ci." (ibidem, pp. 320-21.)

263 „La proportion qui se trouve entre ces deux différentes espèces de fonds, détermine nécessairement dans un pays le caractère général des habitants, quant à leur penchant à l'industrie ou à la paresse." (ibidem, pp. 321-22.)

263 „*Dans les villes manufacturières* [...] *où* les classes inférieures du peuple *subsistent principalement par des capitaux employeés*, il est *en général* laborieux, frugal et économe, comme dans beaucoup de villes d'*Angleterre* et [la plupart des celles de la] *Hollande*. Mais dans [...] *villes* [qui se soutiennent principalement par la] résidence [permanente ou temporaire d'une] *cour, et dans lesquelles* les classes inférieures du peuple tirent surtout leur subsistance de dépen-

* In the manuscript: „portion".—*Ed.*

ses de revenu, il est en général paresseux, débauché et pauvre, comme a Rome, Versailles...

C'est donc la proportion existante entre la somme des capitaux et celle des revenus qui détermine partout la proportion dans laquelle se trouveront l'industrie et la fainéantise : partout où les capitaux l'emportent, c'est l'industrie qui domine ; partout où ce sont les revenus, la fainéantise prévaut. Ainsi *toute augmentation ou diminution dans la masse des capitaux* tend naturellement à augmenter ou à diminuer réellement la somme de l'industrie, le nombre des gens productifs, et. par conséquent, la valeur échangeable du produit annuel des terres et du travail du pays, la richesse et le revenu réel de tous ses habitans...

Ce qui est annuellement épargné, est aussi régulièrement consommé que ce qui est annuellement dépensé, et il l'est aussi presque dans le même tems ; mais il est consommé par une autre classe de gens. [...] portion de [...] revenu... par des bouches inutiles et par des domestiques, qui ne laissent rien après eux en retour de leur consommation ... par des ouvriers [...] qui reproduisent avec profit la valeur de leur consommation annuelle... La consommation est la même, mais les consommateurs sont différens. (ibidem, pp. 322-28, passim.)

263 „ ... et établit en quelque sorte un fonds pour l'entretien à perpétuité d'un même nombre de gens productifs." (ibidem, p. 328.)

263 „ ... la masse des fonds destinés à employer le travail productif ... si cette quantité de vivres et d'habits ainsi consommés par des gens non-productifs, eût été distribuée entre des gens productifs, ceux-ci auraient *reproduit, avec encore un profit*, la valeur entière de leur consommation..." (ibidem, pp. 329-30.)

263 „ ... grandes nations ne s'appauvrissent jamais par la prodigalité et la mauvaise conduite des particuliers, mais quelquefois bien par celle de leur gouvernement. Dans la plupart des pays, la totalité ou la presque totalité de revenu public est employée à entretenir des gens non-productifs. [Tels sont les gens qui composent une cour nombreuse et brillante, un grand établissement ecclésiastique, de grandes flottes et de grandes armées] qui ne produisent rien en tems de paix, et qui, en tems de guerre, ne gagnent rien qui puisse compenser la dépense que coûte leur entretien, même pendant la durée de la guerre. *Les gens de cette espèce* ne produisant *rien par eux-mêmes, sont tous entretenus par le produit du travail d'autrui*. Ainsi, quand ils sont multipliés au-delà du nombre nécessaire, ils peuvent, dans une année, consommer une si grande part de ce produit, qu'ils n'en laissent pas assez de reste pour l'entretien des ouvriers productifs, qui devraient le reproduire pour l'année suivante." (ibidem, p. 336.)

264 „ Le fonds destiné à l'entretien du travail productif grossissant de jour en jour, la demande qu'on fait de ce travail devient aussi de jour en jour plus grande : les ouvriers trouvent aisément de l'emploi, mais les possesseurs de capitaux ont de la difficulté à trouver des ouvriers à employer. La concurrence des capitalistes fait hausser les salaires du travail et fait baisser les profits." (ibidem, p. 359.)

264 „ *Des différens emplois des capitaux.*" (ibidem, p. 369.)

264 „ Les personnes dont les capitaux sont employés de l'une de ces quatre manières, sont elles-mêmes des *ouvriers productifs*. Leur travail, quand il est convenablement dirigé, se fixe et se réalise dans le sujet ou la chose vénale sur laquelle il est appliqué, et en général il ajoute au prix de cette chose la valeur au moins de leur subsistance et consommation personnelle" (ibidem, p. 374.)

264 „ ... aucun capital, à somme égale, ne met en activité plus de *travail productif* que celui du fermier. Ce sont non seulement ses valets de ferme, mais *ses bestiaux de labour et de charroi qui sont autant d'ouvriers productifs.*" (ibidem, p. 376.)

265 „ On conçoit maintenant que le profit des capitaux provient toujours, ou de ce qu'ils suppléent à une portion de travail que l'homme devrait faire de ses mains ; ou de ce qu'ils accomplissent une portion de travail au-dessus des efforts personnels de l'homme, et qu'il ne saurait exécuter lui-même." (Comte de Lauderdale, *Recherches sur la nature et l'origine de la richesse publique*... Traduit de l'anglais par E. Lagentie de Lavaïsse, Paris, 1808, p. 119.)

265 „ Si cette idée du bénéfice des capitaux était rigoureusement juste, il s'ensuivrait qu'il serait, non une source première de revenu, mais une source dérivée ; et l'on ne pourrait considérer les capitaux comme un des principes de la richesse, leur profit n'étant qu'un transport de la poche du travailleur dans celle du capitaliste." (ibidem, pp. 116-17.)

265 „ Ainsi le même travail paraîtra ou productif ou non-productif, selon l'emploi subséquent de l'objet auquel on l'a appliqué. Si mon cuisinier, par exemple, fait une tarte que je mange sur-le-champ, c'est un ouvrier non-productif, et sa besogne un travail également stérile, parce que ce service a péri aussitôt qu'il a été rendu. Mais ce même travail se fait-il dans la boutique d'un pâtissier, dès-lors il devient productif..." (ibidem, p. 110.)

265 „ Cette distinction extraordinaire, fondée sur la simple durée des services, range parmi les travailleurs non-productifs, des personnes occupées aux plus importantes fonctions de la société. Le souverain, les ministres de la religion, les magistrats, les défenseurs de l'Etat, tous ces hommes, sans excepter ceux dont l'habileté... conserve la santé ou forme l'éducation des citoyens, tous ces hommes sont réputés travailleurs non-productifs." (ibidem, pp. 110-11.)

266 „ ... les ecclésiastiques, les gens de loi, les médecins et les gens de lettres de toute espèce, ainsi que les comédiens, les farceurs, les musiciens, les chanteurs, les danseurs de l'opéra, etc." (Adam Smith, *Recherches sur la nature et les causes de la richesse des nations*. Traduction nouvelle ... par Germain Garnier, t. II, Paris, 1802, p. 313.)

266 „ Si l'on veut que la valeur vénale soit la base de la richesse, il est inutile d'entrer dans de longs raisonnemens pour démontrer les erreurs de cette doctrine. Rien n'en prouve mieux la fausseté que l'estime que les hommes font de ces services, à en juger par le prix qu'ils y mettent." (Comte de Lauderdale, *Recherches sur la nature et l'origine de la richesse publique*... Traduit de l'anglais par E. Lagentie de Lavaïsse, Paris, 1808, p. 111.)

266 „Le travail du manufacturier se fixe et se réalise en quelque production commerçable... Ni le *travail du domestique*, ni celui du capital circulant ne forment naturellement une accumulation, un fonds qui puisse se transmettre pour une valeur déterminée. Le profit qu'ils donnent provient également de ce qu'ils *épargnent le travail du maître* ou du possesseur. Ils ont des effets tellement semblables, que ce qui a fait juger l'un non-productif, a dû donner de l'autre la même opinion." (ibidem, pp. 144-45.)

266 „... refuse aux *résultats* de ces industries le nom de *produits*. Il donne au travail auquel elles se livrent le nom d'*improductif*..." (Jean-Baptiste Say, *Traité d'économie politique*... Troisième édition, t. I, Paris, 1817, p. 117.)

266 „La protection, la tranquillité, la défense de la chose publique [...] résultat du travail d'une année..." (Adam Smith, *Recherches sur la nature et les causes de la richesse des nations*. Traduction nouvelle ... par Germain Garnier, t. II, Paris, 1802, p. 313.)

266 „En général, ses services périssent à l'instant même où il les rend ..."* (ibidem, p. 312.)

267 „Des produits immatériels, ou des valeurs qui sont consommées au moment de leur production." (Jean-Baptiste Say, *Traité d'économie politique*... Troisième édition, t. I, Paris, 1817, p. 116.)

267 „... qu'ils ne servent point à augmenter le capital national. Une nation où il se trouverait une foule de musiciens, de prêtres, d'employés, pourrait être une nation fort divertie, bien endoctrinée, et admirablement bien administrée, mais voilà tout. Son capital ne recevrait de tout le travail de ces hommes industrieux aucun accroissement direct, parce que leurs produits seraient consommés à mesure qu'ils seraient créés." (ibidem, p. 119.)

267 „Il est [...] impossible d'admettre l'opinion de M. Garnier, qui conclut de ce que le travail des médecins, des gens de loi et autres personnes semblables, est productif, qu'il est aussi avantageux à une nation de la multiplier que tout autre." (ibidem, p. 120.)

267 „Il en est de cela comme de la main-d'œuvre qu'on répandrait sur un produit, par-delà ce qui est nécessaire pour l'exécuter." (ibidem, p. 120.)

267 „Le travail productif de produits immatériels n'est productif, *comme tout autre travail*, que jusqu'au point où il augmente l'utilité, et par-là la valeur d'un produit : au-delà de ce point, c'est un travail purement improductif." (ibidem, p. 120.)

268 „Le défaut d'écoulement de plusieurs produits vient de la rareté de plusieurs autres." (ibidem, p. 438.)

269 „... tout travail utile est réellement productif, et [...] toute la classe laborieuse de la société mérite également le nom de *productive*." (Destutt

---

* This quotation is rendered in the manuscript in the following way: „... ouvrage—en général—s'évanouissent, perissent à l'instant même où ils sont rendus, au moment même de leur production."—*Ed.*

de Tracy, *Eléments d'idéologie*, IVe et V[e] parties. Traité de la volonté et de ses effets, Paris, 1826, p. 87.)

269 „ ... la classe laborieuse et *directement productive* de toutes nos richesses..." (ibidem, p. 88.)

269 „ La vraie classe *stérile* est celle des oisifs, qui ne font rien que vivre ce que l'on appelle *noblement*, du produit de travaux exécutés avant eux, soit que ces produits soient réalisés en fonds de terre qu'ils afferment, c'est-à-dire qu'ils *louent* à un travailleur, soit qu'ils consistent en argent ou effets qu'ils prêtent moyennant rétribution, ce qui est encore *louer*. Ceux-là sont les vrais frelons de la ruche (fruges consumere nati)... (ibidem, p. 87.)

269 „ ... ne peuvent dépenser que leur *revenu*. S'ils entament leurs fonds rien ne les remplace ; et leur consommation momentanément exagérée cesse pour toujours." (ibidem, p. 237.)

269 „ Ce *revenu* n'est ... qu'un prélèvement qui se fait sur les produits de l'activité des citoyens industrieux..." (ibidem, p 236.)

270 „ ... puisque les hommes à qui il appartient sont oisifs, il est manifeste qu'ils *ne dirigent aucun travail productif*. Tous les travailleurs qu'ils soldent sont uniquement destinés à leur procurer des jouissances. Sans doute ces jouissances sont de différens genres... les dépenses de toute cette classe d'hommes ... alimentent une nombreuse population qu'elles font subsister, mais dont le travail est complètement stérile... quelques-unes qui soient * plus ou moins fructueuses, comme par exemple, la construction d'une maison [...], l'amélioration d'un fonds de terre ; mais ce sont des cas particuliers qui font ** [...] momentanément [...] *** du travail productif. A ces légères exceptions-là près, toute la consommation de cette espèce de capitalistes est absolument en pure perte sous le rapport de la reproduction, et autant de diminué sur les richesses acquises." (ibidem, p. 236.)

270 „ ... pour trouver la formation de ces revenus il faut toujours remonter jusqu'à des *capitalistes industrieux*." (ibidem, p. 237, note.)

270 „ ... comprend tous les entrepreneurs d'une industrie quelconque, c'est-à-dire tous les hommes qui *ayant des capitaux* [...] emploient leur talent et leur travail à les faire valoir eux-mêmes au lieu de les louer à d'autres, et qui par conséquent ne vivent ni de salaires ni de revenus mais de *profits*." (ibidem, p. 237.)

271 „ Ils ont ... entre les mains presque toutes les richesses de la société ... ce n'est pas seulement la rente de ces richesses qu'ils dépensent annuellement, mais bien le fonds lui-même, et quelquefois plusieurs fois dans l'année, quand la marche du commerce est assez rapide pour que cela se puisse. Car comme en leur qualité d'hommes industrieux ils ne font aucune dépense que pour qu'elle leur rentre avec profit, plus

* In the manuscript: „Einige dieser dépenses können".—*Ed.*

** In the manuscript: „Aber dies Ausnahmen, wodurch sie werden". —*Ed.*

*** In the manuscript: „directeurs".—*Ed.*

ils en peuvent faire qui remplisse cette condition, plus leurs bénéfices sont grands." (ibidem, pp. 237-38.)

271 „ Au total [...] médiocre, car les hommes industrieux sont ordinairement modestes ... n'est rien moins que définitive ; elle leur rentre avec profits ... consommation personelle [...], mais encore ... la rente des terres et de l'argent qu'ils tiennent des capitalistes oisifs ..." (ibidem, p. 238.)

271 „ ... les revenus des riches oisifs ne sont que des rentes prélevées sur l'industrie ; c'est l'industrie seule qui les fait naître." (ibidem, p. 248.)

271 „ ... prennent à rente leurs terres, leurs maisons et leur argent, et ils s'en servent de manière à en *tirer des profits supérieurs à cette rente.*" (ibidem, p. 237.)

271 „ ... le seul revenu de ces oisifs et le seul fonds de leurs dépenses annuelles." (ibidem, p. 238.)

271 „ Ceux-là n'ont d'autre trésor que leur travail de tous les jours. Ce travail leur procure des salaires ... Mais sur quoi sont pris ces salaires ? il est évident que c'est sur les propriétés de ceux à qui les salariés *vendent leur travail*, c'est-à-dire, sur des fonds qui sont d'avance en leur possession, et qui ne sont *autre chose que les produits accumulés de travaux antérieurement exécutés.* Il suit de là que la consommation que paient ces richesses est bien la consommation des salariés, en ce sens que ce sont eux qu'elle substante, mais qu'au fond ce ne sont *pas eux qui la paient*, ou du moins qu'ils ne la paient qu'*avec les fonds existant d'avance entre les mains de ceux qui les emploient* [...]. Leur consommation doit donc être regardée comme faite par ceux qui les soudoient [...]. Ils ne font que recevoir d'une main et rendre de l'autre ... il faut [...] considérer non seulement tout ce qu'ils dépensent mais même la totalité de ce qu'ils reçoivent, comme la dépense réelle et la *consommation propre de ceux qui achètent leur travail.* Cela est si vrai que pour voir si cette consommation est plus ou moins destructive de la richesse acquise, ou même si elle tend à l'augmenter ... tout dépend de savoir *quel usage font capitalistes du travail qu'ils achètent.*" (ibidem, pp. 234-35.)

272 „ On me demandera comment ces entrepreneurs d'industrie peuvent faire de si grands profits, et de qui ils peuvent les tirer ? Je réponds que *c'est en vendant tout ce qu'ils produisent plus cher que cela ne leur a coûté à produire...*" (ibidem, p. 239.)

272 „ ... ils le vendent : 1° à eux-mêmes pour toute la partie de leur consommation destinée à la satisfaction de leurs besoins, laquelle ils paient avec une portion de leurs profits ; 2° aux salariés, tant ceux qu'ils soldent que ceux que soldent les capitalistes oisifs, *desquels salariés ils retirent* par ce moyen *la totalité de leurs salaires*, à cela près de petites économies qu'ils peuvent faire ; 3° aux capitalistes oisifs *qui les paient avec la partie de leur revenu* qu'ils n'ont pas déjà donnée aux salariés qu'ils emploient directement, en sorte que toute la rente qu'ils leur desservent annuellement leur revient par un de ces côtés ou par l'autre." (ibidem, p. 239.)

272 „... *vendant* * tout ce qu'ils produisent *plus cher* que cela ne leur a coûté à produire..." (ibidem, p. 139.)

273 „... la consommation propre de ceux qui achètent leur travail." (ibidem, p. 235.)

273 „... retirent [...] la totalité de leurs salaires..." (ibidem, p.239.)

273 „ Ils** ne font que recevoir d'une main et rendre de l'autre." (ibidem, p. 235.)

275 „... capitalistes oisifs qui les paient avec la partie*** de leur revenu qu'ils n'ont pas déjà donnée aux salariés qu'ils emploient directement, en sorte que toute la rente qu'ils leur desservent annuellement leur revient par un de ces côtés ou pas l'autre." (ibidem, p. 239.)

276 „ Mais, me dira-t-on, si cela est et si les entrepreneurs d'industrie recueillent en effet *chaque année plus qu'ils n'ont semé*, ils devraient en très peu de temps avoir attiré à eux *toute la fortune publique*, et bientôt il ne devrait plus rester dans un état que des salariés sans avances et des capitalistes entrepreneurs. *Cela est vrai*, et les choses seraient ainsi effectivement, si les entrepreneurs ou leurs héritiers ne prenaient le parti de se reposer à mesure qu'ils se sont enrichis, et n'allaient ainsi continuellement recruter la classe des capitalistes oisifs ; et même malgré cette émigration fréquente, il arrive encore que quand l'industrie a agi pendant quelques temps dans un pays sans de trop grandes perturbations, ses capitaux se sont toujours augmentés non-seulement en raison de l'accroissement de la richesse totale, mais encore dans une bien plus grande proportion... On pourrait ajouter que cet effet serait bien plus sensible encore sans les prélèvements immenses que tous les gouvernemens font chaque année sur la classe industrieuse par la voie des impôts..." (ibidem, pp. 240-41.)

277 „... il n'y a qu'à voir dans toute l'Europe combien ils étaient faibles il y a trois ou quatres siècles, en comparaison des richesses immenses de tous les hommes puissans, et combien ils sont aujourd'hui multipliés et accrus, tandis que les autres sont diminués." (ibidem, p. 241.)

277 „... doit [...] être regardée comme faite par ceux qui les soudoient." (ibidem, p. 235.)

278 „... clarté ... manière de considérer la consommation de nos richesses ... répand sur toute la marche de la société. D'où vient cet accord et cette lucidité ? de ce que nous avons rencontré la vérité. Cela rappelle l'effet de ces miroirs où les objets se peignent nettement et dans leur justes proportions quand on est placé dans le **** vrai point de vue, et où tout paraît confus et désuni quand on est trop près ou trop loin." (ibidem, pp. 242-43.)

278 „ D'où viennent à ces hommes oisifs leurs revenus ? N'est-ce pas de la rente que leur paient sur leurs *profits* ceux qui *font travailler leurs*

* In the manuscript this is followed by the words: „à eux-mêmes".—*Ed.*
** In the manuscript: „salariés".—*Ed.*
*** In the manuscript: „portion".—*Ed.*
**** In the manuscript: „leur".—*Ed.*

capitaux, c'est-à-dire, ceux qui avec leurs fonds *salarient du travail qui produit plus qu'il ne coûte*, en un mot, les hommes industrieux ?" (ibidem, p. 246.)

279 „ Ce sont ceux-là [...] nourissent réellement même les salariés qu'emploient les autres." (ibidem, p. 246.)

279 „ C'est donc toujours jusqu'à ceux-là qu'il faut remonter pour trouver la source de toute richesse." (ibidem., p. 246.)

279 „ Avec le temps, des *richesses se sont accumulées en plus ou moins grande quantité, parce que le résultat des travaux antérieurs n'a pas été entièrement consommé aussitôt que produit.* Des possesseurs de ces richesses, les uns se contentent d'en tirer une rente et de la manger. Ce sont ceux que nous avons appelés oisifs. Les autres plus actifs font travailler leurs propres fonds et ceux qu'ils louent. Ils les emploient *à solder du travail qui les reproduit avec profit.* Avec ce profit ils paient leur propre consommation et défraient celle des autres. Par ces consommations-là, même leurs fonds leur reviennent un peu accrus, et ils recommencent. Voilà ce qui constitue la circulation." (ibidem, pp. 246-47.)

279 „ ... ceux qui vivent de profits [...] alimentent tous les autres et [...] seuls augmentent la fortune publique et créent tous nos moyens de jouissance. Cela doit être *puisque le travail est la source de toute richesse*, et puisqu'eux seuls donnent une *direction utile au travail actuel*, en faisant un *usage utile du travail accumulé.*" (ibidem, p. 242.)

279 „ ... une direction utile au travail actuel ... un usage utile du travail accumulé. " (ibidem, p. 242.)

280 „ ... nos facultés sont notre seule richesse originaire [...] notre travail [...] produit toutes les autres, et [...] tout travail bien dirigé est productif... " (ibidem, p. 243.)

280 „ ... alimentent tous les autres, et qui seuls augmentent la fortune publique et créent tous nos moyens de jouissance. " (ibidem, p. 242.)

280 „ Si l'économie augmente la masse générale des capitaux et si la prodigalité la diminue, la conduite de ceux qui dépensent tout juste leur revenu, sans rien amasser ni sans entamer leurs fonds, ne l'augmente ni ne la diminue. Avec cela il y a certaines manières de dépenser, qui semblent contribuer plus que d'autres à l'accroissement de l'opulence générale. " (Adam Smith, *Recherches sur la nature et les causes de la richesse des nations*. Traduction nouvelle... par Germain Garnier, t. II, Paris, 1802, p. 345.)

280 „ Si la consommation est fort différente suivant l'espèce de consommateur, elle varie aussi suivant la nature des choses consommées. Toutes représentent bien du travail, mais sa valeur est fixée plus solidement dans les unes que dans les autres. On peut avoir pris autant de peine pour fabriquer un feu d'artifice que pour trouver et tailler un diamant, et, par conséquent, l'un peut avoir autant de valeur que l'autre. Mais quand j'aurai acheté, payé et employé l'un et l'autre, au bout d'une demi-heure il ne me restera rien du premier, et le second pourra être encore la ressource de mes petits-enfans dans un siècle... Il en est de même de ce que l'on appelle les produits immatériels. *Une découverte est d'une utilité éternelle.* Un ouvrage d'esprit, un tableau sont encore

d'une utilité plus ou moins durable, tandis que celle d'un bal, d'un concert, d'un spectacle est instantanée et disparaît aussitôt. On en peut dire autant des *services personnels* des médecins, des avocats, des soldats, des domestiques, et généralement de tout ce que l'on appelle des *employés*. Leur utilité est celle du moment du besoin... la consommation la plus ruineuse est la plus prompte, puisque c'est celle qui détruit le plus de travail dans le même temps, ou une égale quantité de travail en moins de temps ; en comparaison de celle-là, celle qui est plus lente est une espèce de *thésaurisation* puisqu'elle laisse à des temps à venir la jouissance d'une partie des sacrifices actuels... chacun sait qu'il est plus économique d'avoir *pour le même prix* un habit qui dure trois ans que d'en avoir un pareil qui ne dure que trois mois. " (Destutt de Tracy, *Eléments d'idéologie*, IVe et V^e^ parties. Traité de la volonté et de ses effets, Paris, 1826, pp. 243-44.)

282 „ En raison des progrès de l'industrie et de ceux de la science, [...] chaque ouvrier peut produire chaque jour plus et beaucoup plus qu'il n'a besoin de consommer. Mais en même temps que son travail produit la richesse, la richesse, s'il était appelé à en jouir, le rendrait peu propre au travail... " (J.-C.-L. Simonde de Sismondi, *Nouveaux principes d'économie politique...*, t. I, Paris, 1827, p. 85.)

283 „ ... un peuple frugal et laborieux emploie son activité à satisfaire aux demandes d'une nation, riche et adonnée au luxe. " (William Paley, *Principes de philosophie morale et politique*, traduit de l'anglais ... par J.-L.-S. Vincent, t. II, Paris, 1817.)

283 „ Ils posent en principe général que la consommation est la cause de la production, [...] qu'ainsi il est bon qu'elle soit [très] forte. Ils affirment que c'est là ce qui met une grande différence entre l'économie publique et l'économie privée". (Destutt de Tracy, *Eléments d'idéologie*, IVe et V^e^ parties. Traité de la volonté et de ses effets, Paris, 1826, pp. 249-50.)

283 „ ... *les nations pauvres*, c'est là où le peuple est à son aise ; et *les nations riches*, c'est là où il est ordinairement pauvre. " (ibidem, p. 231.)

284 „ ... *biens internes* ou les éléments de la civilisation... " (Henri Storch, *Cours d'économie politique...* par J.-B. Say, t. III, Paris, 1823, p. 217.)

284 „ Il est évident que l'homme ne parvient jamais à produire des richesses qu'autant qu'il est pourvu des biens internes, c'est-à-dire, qu'autant qu'il a développé ses facultés physiques, intellectuelles et morales, ce qui suppose les moyens de leur développement, tels que les *institutions sociales*, etc. Ainsi, plus un peuple est civilisé, plus sa richesse nationale peut s'accroître " (ibidem, t. I, p. 136.)

284 „ Smith ... exclut des *travaux productifs* tous ceux qui ne coopèrent pas *directement* à la production des richesses ; mais aussi il ne considère que la *richesse* nationale ... n'avoir pas distingué les valeurs *immatérielles des richesses.*" (ibidem, t. III, p. 218.)

286 „ ... que font ces critiques ? * Loin d'établir cette distinction, ils achè-

---

* In the manuscript: „Was machen Smiths Kritiker?"—*Ed.*

vent de confondre des deux espèces de valeurs si évidemment différentes. " (ibidem, p. 218.)

286 „ En regardant le travail immatériel comme *productif*, ils le supposent *productif en richesses*, c'est-à-dire en valeurs matérielles et échangeables : et il ne l'est qu'en valeurs immatérielles et directes : ils admettent * que les produits du travail immatériel sont soumis aux mêmes lois que ceux du travail matériel : et cependant les premiers se régissent par d'autres principes que les seconds. " (ibidem, p. 218.)

286 „ De ce que les biens internes sont en partie le produit des services, on en a conclu qu'ils n'avaient pas plus de durée que les services mêmes, et qu'ils étaient nécessairement consommés à mesure qu'ils étaient produits. " (ibidem, p. 234.)

286 „ ... les biens primitifs, loin d'être détruits par l'usage qu'on en fait, s'étendent et s'accroissent par l'exercice, de sorte que *la consommation* même en augmente la valeur. " (ibidem, p. 236.)

286 „ ... les biens internes sont susceptibles d'être accumulés comme les richesses, et de former des capitaux qu'on peut employer à la reproduction... " (ibidem, p. 236.)

286 „ ... l'industrie doit être divisée et ses produits doivent être accumulés avant qu'on puisse songer à diviser le travail immatériel. " (ibidem, p. 241.)

286 „ ... la *production* des biens internes, loin de diminuer la richesse nationale par la consommation des produits matériels qu'elle exige, est au contraire un puissant moyen de l'augmenter ; comme la production des richesses, à son tour, est un moyen également puissant d'augmenter la civilisation. " (ibidem, p. 517.)

286 „ ... c'est l'équilibre des deux genres de production qui fait avancer la prospérité nationale. " (ibidem, p. 521.)

287 „ Selon Smith, le législateur des Hébreux fut un travailleur improductif. " (N.-W. Senior, *Principes fondamentaux de l'économie politique...* tirés ... par le c-te Jean Arrivabene, Paris, 1836, p. 198.)

287 „ ... le médecin qui, par une ordonnance, guérit un enfant malade et lui assure ainsi la vie pour de longues années, ne *produit*-il pas un résultat durable ? " (ibidem, p. 198.)

288 „ Les Hollandais, en s'opposant à la tyrannie des Espagnols, ou les Anglais se révoltant contre une tyrannie qui menaçait d'être encore plus terrible, ont-ils produit des résultats temporaires ? " (ibidem, p. 198.)

288 „ Il y a des pays où on ne peut absolument pas cultiver la terre, si on n'est pas protégé par des soldats. Eh bien! suivant la classification de Smith, la récolte n'est pas produite par l'association du travail de l'homme qui conduit la charrue et de celui qui se tient à son côté l'arme à la main : selon lui, le laboureur seul est un travailleur productif, et le soin du soldat est improductif. " (ibidem, p. 202.)

* In the manuscript: „soumettent".—*Ed.*

289 „ La richesse d'une nation ne dépend pas d'une proportion numérique entre ceux qui produisent des *services* et ceux qui produisent des *valeurs*, mais de cette proportion entre eux qui est la plus propre à rendre plus efficace le travail de chacun. " (N.-W. Senior, *Principes fondamentaux de l'économie politique* ...tirés ... par le c-te Jean Arrivabene, Paris, 1836, p. 204.)

291 „ Il semble, en vérité, que dans ce cas-ci l'attention de Smith a été adsorbée tout entière par la condition des *grands propriétaires*, les seuls auxquels ses observations sur les classes improductives puissent généralement être appliquées. Je ne sais me rendre autrement compte de sa supposition, *que le capital n'est employé qu'à entretenir les travailleurs productifs, tandis que les improductifs vivent du revenu*. Le plus grand nombre de ceux qu'il appelle par excellence improductifs, les précepteurs, ceux qui gouvernent l'Etat, sont entretenus *aux dépens du capital*, c'est-à-dire, *au moyen de ce qui est dépensé d'avance pour la reproduction*... " (ibidem, pp. 204-05.)

291 „ M. Storch [...] se trompe, sans aucun doute, lorsqu'il établit formellement que ces *résultats* font partie du *revenu* de ceux qui les possèdent, comme les autres objets qui ont de la valeur, et qu'ils sont de même échangeables. S'il en était ainsi, si le goût, la moralité, la religion, étaient réellement des *objets* que l'on pût *acheter*, la richesse aurait une importance bien autre que celle que les économistes ... lui donnent. Ce que nous achetons, ce n'est point la santé, le savoir ou la piété. Le médecin, le prêtre, l'instituteur ... ne peuvent produire que les instrumens au moyen desquels, avec plus ou moins de certitude et de perfection, ces résultats ultérieurs seront produits ... si dans chaque cas particulier les moyens les plus propres pour obtenir du succès ont été employés, le producteur de ces *moyens* a droit à une récompense, lors même qu'il n'aurait pas réussi ou qu'il n'aurait pas produit les résultats auxquels on s'attendait. L'échange est complet aussitôt que le conseil ou la leçon a été donnée et qu'on en a reçu le salaire. " (ibidem, pp. 288-89.)

291 „ ... la consommation productive et la consommation improductive. " (ibidem, p 206.)

292 „ *Les moyens indirects* [...] est tout ce qui favorise la production, tout ce qui tend à faire disparaître un obstacle, à la rendre plus active, plus prompte, plus facile. " (P. Rossi, *Cours d'économie politique* ..., Bruxelles, 1842, p. 272.)

292 „ Il y a des moyens de production directs et des moyens indirects. C'est dire qu'il est des moyens qui sont une cause *sine qua non* de l'effet dont il s'agit, des forces qui *font* cette production. Il y en a d'autres qui contribuent à la production, mais ne la feraient pas. Les premiers peuvent agir même *seuls*, les autres ne peuvent qu'aider les premiers à produire. " (ibidem, p. 268.)

292 „ ... tout le travail gouvernemental est un moyen indirect de production ... Il faut bien que celui qui a fabriqué ce chapeau reconnaisse que le gendarme qui passe dans la rue, que le juge qui siège dans son tribunal, que le geôlier qui reçoit un malfaiteur et le garde en prison, que

l'armée qui défend la frontière contre les invasions de l'ennemi contribuent à la production. " (ibidem, p. 272.)

293 „ Parmi les *acheteurs*, les uns achètent des produits ou du *travail pour les consommer eux-mêmes directement* ; d'autres ne les achètent que pour vendre les nouveaux produits qu'ils obtiennent au moyen des produits et du travail qu'ils ont acquis. " (ibidem, pp. 275-76.)

293 „ Le travail de mon domestique est improductif pour moi : admettons-le pour un instant ; est-il improductif pour lui ? " (ibidem, p. 276.)

293 „ ... emploie une force, [...] l'applique selon un certain mode, [...] produit un résultat qui satisfait un besoin de l'homme. " (ibidem, p. 275.)

293 „ Une seconde [...] erreur a été de ne pas distinguer la production directe et la production indirecte..: " (ibidem, p. 276.)

293 „ Si elle * est presque impossible, n'est-il pas évident que ce travail y contribue, si ce n'est par un concours direct et matériel, du moins par une action indirecte dont on ne peut pas ne pas tenir compte ? " (ibidem, p. 276.)

294 „ On n'a pas soigneusement distingué les trois faits principaux du phénomène de la production : la *force ou moyen productif*, *l'application* de cette force, le *résultat*. " (ibidem, p. 276.)

294 „ Il se trouve encore des personnes, gens de la vieille roche, qui n'entendent pas les choses ainsi. Ils font venir chez eux un ouvrier et lui donnent à faire telle ou telle pièce d'habillement, en lui fournissant l'étoffe et tout ce qui est nécessaire à ce travail. Qu'achètent-ils, ceux-là ? Ils achètent une force, un moyen qui produira des résultats quelconques à leurs périls et risques ... l'objet du contrat, c'est l'achat d'une force. " (ibidem, p. 276.)

294 „ ... vous engagez un domestique, vous louez un homme, vous achetez une force. Que fera cet homme ? Il fera mille choses diverses [...] résultats de son travail, ils dépendront de l'usage que vous ferez de cette force. " (ibidem, p. 276**.)

294 „ ... acheter ou de louer ... une application déterminée de cette *** force ... vous n'achetez pas [...] un produit, vous n'achetez pas le résultat que vous avez en vue. Le plaidoyer fera-t-il gagner votre procès? Qui le sait?**** Ce qu'il y a de certain, ce qui se passe entre vous et votre avocat, c'est que, pour une certaine valeur, il ira tel jour, en tel endroit, porter la parole pour vous, faire, dans votre intérêt, une application de ses forces intellectuelles... " (ibidem, p. 276.)

294 „ ... je suis loin de ne voir des producteurs que dans ceux qui passent

* In the manuscript: „Si la production".—*Ed.*

** Marx puts the passage in his own words summarising the idea developed by Rossi.—*Ed.*

*** In the manuscript: „d'une".—*Ed.*

**** In the manuscript: „Das Plädoyer des Advokaten mag mich den Prozen gewinnen machen oder nicht".—*Ed.*

leur vie à faire de la toile de coton ou des souliers. J'honore le travail quel qu'il soit ... mais ce respect ne doit pas être le privilège exclusif du *travailleur manuel.* " (ibidem, p. 273.)

295 „ C'est ainsi que dans les échanges on fixe son attention sur l'un ou [...] l'autre des trois faits principaux de la production. *Mais ces diverses formes de l'échange* peuvent-t-elles enlever à certains *produits* le caractère de *richesse* et aux *efforts d'une classe de producteurs la qualité de travaux productifs*? Evidemment, il n'est entre ces idées aucune liaison propre à légitimer une pareille déduction. Parce qu'au lieu d'acheter le résultat, j'achète la force nécessaire pour le produire, *l'action de* [...] *force ne sera* [...] *productive* et le *produit ne sera pas richesse*? Reprenons l'exemple du tailleur. Qu'on achète d'un tailleur des vêtements tous confectionnés, ou qu'on les obtienne d'un ouvrier tailleur auquel on fournit la matière et un salaire, toujours est-il que, quant aux résultats, les deux faits sont parfaitement semblables. Nul ne dira que le premier est un *travail productif* et le second un *travail improductif*; seulement, dans le second cas, celui *qui désirait un habit* a été son *propre entrepreneur.* Or, entre l'ouvrier tailleur que vous avez pris chez vous et votre domestique, quelle différence y a-t-il sous le rapport des forces productives ? Aucune. " (ibidem, p. 277.)

296 „ Quand Smith a dit qu'il ne restait rien du travail du domestique, il s'est trompé, disons-le, au-delà de ce qu'il était permis à Adam Smith de se tromper. Un fabricant dirige lui-même une vaste manufacture qui exige une surveillance très active et très laborieuse ... Ce même homme, ne voulant pas autour de lui des ouvriers improductifs, n'a point de domestiques. Il est donc forcé de se *servir lui-meme* ... que devient son travail productif pendant le temps qu'il doit consacrer à ce prétendu travail improductif ? N'est-il pas évident que vos gens font un ouvrage qui vous donne les moyens de vous livrer à un travail plus approprié à vos facultés ? Dès lors, comment dire qu'il ne reste pas de traces de leur service ? il reste tout ce que vous faites et que vous ne pourriez pas faire si vous n'étiez pas remplacé par eux dans le service de votre personne et de votre maison. " (ibidem, p. 277.)

298 „ Le chanteur (on insiste), quand il a fini de chanter, ne nous laisse rien.—Il nous laisse un souvenir! Quand vous avez bu du vin de Champagne, que reste-t-il ? ... Que la consommation suive ou non de près le fait de la production, qu'elle s'accomplisse plus ou moins rapidement, les résultats économiques pourront être divers, mais le fait de la consommation, quel qu'il soit ne peut ôter au produit la qualité de richesse. Il est des produits immatériels qui sont de plus longue durée que certains produits matériels. Un palais dure longtemps, mais l'*Iliade* est une source des plaisirs encore plus durables. " (ibidem, pp. 277-78.)

301 „ Si les riches n'y dépensent pas beaucoup, les pauvres mourront de faim. " (Charles-Louis de Montesquieu, *De l'esprit des lois*, t. IV, Paris, 1820, p. 200.)

302 „ De telles occupations étaient censées ne convenir qu'à des esclaves, et on défendait aux citoyens de s'y adonner. Dans les Etats même où cette défense n'eût pas lieu, tels que Athènes et Rome, le peuple était, par le fait, exclu de tous les métiers qui sont maintenant exercés, pour

l'ordinaire, par la dernière classe des habitants des villes. Ces métiers, à Rome et à Athènes, étaient remplis par les esclaves des riches, qui les exerçaient pour le compte de leurs maîtres, et la richesse, la puissance et la protection de ceux-ci mettaient le pauvre libre, presque dans l'impossibilité de trouver le débit de son ouvrage, quand cet ouvrage venait en concurrence avec celui des esclaves du riche. Mais les esclaves sont rarement inventifs et les procédés les plus avantageux à l'industrie, ceux qui facilitent et abrègent le travail, soit en fait de machines, soit en fait d'arrangement et de distribution de tâches, ont tous été inventés par des hommes libres. Si même un esclave s'avisait de proposer quelque moyen de ce genre, le maître serait [...] disposé à regarder sa proposition comme suggérée par la paresse et par un désir d'épargner sa peine aux dépens du maître. Le pauvre esclave, au lieu de récompense, n'aurait vraisemblablement qu'une fort mauvaise réception à attendre, peut-être même quelque châtiment. Par conséquent, dans les manufactures qui vont par le moyen d'esclaves, il faut, en général, employer plus de travail pour exécuter la même quantité d'ouvrage, que dans celles qui vont par le moyen d'hommes libres. Par cette raison, l'ouvrage des manufactures de cette première espèce a dû, en général, être plus cher que celui des autres. M. de Montesquieu observe que les mines de la Hongrie, sans être plus riches que les mines de la Turquie de leur voisinage, ont toujours été exploitées à moins de frais, et par conséquent avec plus de profit. Les mines de la Turquie sont exploitées par des esclaves, et les *bras de ces esclaves sont les seules machines que les Turcs* se soient jamais avisés d'y employer. Les mines de la Hongrie sont exploitées par des hommes libres qui font usage d'une grande quantité de machines pour faciliter et abreger leur travail. D'après le peu que nous connaissons des prix des ouvrages de manufactures dans le tems des Grecs et des Romains, il paraît que ceux du genre le plus fin étaient d'une cherté excessive. " (Adam Smith, *Recherches sur la nature et les causes de la richesse des nations.* Traduction nouvelle ... par Germain Garnier, t. III, Paris, 1802, pp. 549-51.)

302 „ M. Loche observe qu'il y a une distinction à faire entre l'argent et les autres bien-meubles. Tous les autres bien-meubles, dit-il, sont d'une *nature si périssable*, qu'il y a peu de fonds à faire sur la richesse qui consiste dans ce genre de biens ... L'argent, au contraire, est un ami solide... " (ibidem, p. 5.)

302 „ Les marchandises consommables, dit-on, sont bientôt détruites, tandis que l'or et l'argent sont d'une *nature plus durable*, et que sans l'exportation continuelle qu'on en fait, ces métaux pourraient s'accumuler pendant plusieurs siècles de suite, de manière à augmenter incroyablement la richesse réelle d'un pays. " (ibidem. pp. 24-25.)

306 „ Je vois une des classes de la société, dont la fortune doit toujours être à peu près la même ; j'en apperçois une autre dont la richesse augmente nécessairement : ainsi, le luxe, qui naît d'un rapport et d'une comparaison, a dû suivre le cours de ces disproportions, et devenir plus apparent avec la succession des années. " (Necker, *De l'administration des finances de la France.* In : *Œuvres de Necker*, t. II, Lausanne et Paris, 1789, pp. 285-86.)

306 „ La classe de la société dont le sort se trouve comme *fixé* par l'effet

des loix sociales, est composée de tous ceux qui, *vivant du travail de leurs mains*, reçoivent impérieusement la loi des *propriétaires*, et sont forcés de se contenter d'un *salaire proportionné aux simples nécessités de la vie*: leur concurrence et *l'urgence de leurs besoins*, constituent leur *état de dépendance* ; ces circonstances ne peuvent point changer. " (ibidem, p. 286.)

306 „ *L'invention successive des instrumens* qui ont *simplifié tous les arts méchaniques* a donc *augmenté les richesses et le lot fortune* * *des propriétaires* ; une partie de ces instruments, *en diminuant les frais d'exploitation des fonds de terre*, a rendu *plus considérable le revenu* dont les possesseurs de ces biens peuvent disposer ; et une autre partie des découvertes du génie a *tellement facilité* [...] les travaux de l'industrie, que les *hommes, au service des dispensateurs des subsistances*, ont pu *dans un espace de tems égal*, et *pour la même rétribution*, fabriquer une plus grande quantité d'ouvrages de toute espèce. " (ibidem, p. 287.)

306 „ Supposons que dans le siècle dernier, il fallut cent mille ouvriers, pour exécuter ce qui se fait aujourd'hui avec quatre-vingt mille ; les autres vingt mille se trouveroient dans la nécessité de s'adonner à des *occupations différentes*, pour obtenir des salaires ; et les nouveaux ouvrages de main-d'œuvre qui en résulteroient accroîtroient les jouissances et le luxe des riches... " (ibidem, pp. 287-88.)

306 „ ... car il ne faut point ** perdre de vue, que les rétributions assignées à tous les métiers qui n'exigent point un talent distingué, sont toujours proportionnées, au *prix de la subsistance nécessaire* à chaque ouvrier ; ainsi *la rapidité de l'exécution*, quand la science en est devenue commune, *ne tourne point à l'avantage des hommes de travail*, et il *n'en résulte qu'une augmentation des moyens*, pour satisfaire les goûts et les vanités de ceux qui disposent des productions de la terre. " (ibidem, p. 288.)

306 „ Entre les différents biens de la nature que l'industrie des hommes façonne et modifie, il en est un grand nombre, dont la durée excède de beaucoup le terme commun de la vie : chaque génération a hérité d'une partie des travaux de la génération qui l'a précédée, et il s'est *accumulé* successivement, dans tous les pays, une plus grande quantité des productions des arts ; et comme cette quantité est toujours répartie entre les mains des propriétaires, la disproportion entre leurs jouissances et celle de la classe nombreuse des citoyens a dû nécessairement être plus considérable et plus remarquée. " (ibidem, p. 289.)

306 „ ... *l'accélération des travaux de l'industrie*, qui a multiplié sur la terre les objets de faste et de somptuosité, *le tems qui en a grossi l'accumulation, et les loix de la propriété, qui ont rassemblé ces biens dans une seule classe de la société* ... ces grandes sources du luxe eussent également existé, quelle qu'eût été la somme de numéraire ... " (ibidem, p. 291.)

307 „ ... dès que l'Artisan ou l'homme de campagne *n'ont plus de réserve*, ils ne peuvent plus disputer ; il faut qu'ils *travaillent aujourd'hui sous peine de mourir demain*, et dans ce combat d'intérêts entre le Pro-

---

* In the manuscript: „et la fortune" instead of „et le lot fortune".—*Ed.*

** In the manuscript: „pas".—*Ed.*

priétaire et l'Ouvrier, l'un met au jeu sa vie et celle de sa famille, et l'autre un simple retard dans l'accroissement de son luxe. " (Necker, *Sur la législation et le commerce des grains* (1775). In : *Œuvres de Necker*, t. IV, Lausanne et Paris, 1786, p. 63.)

307 „ La faculté de savoir et d'entendre est un don général de la Nature, mais il n'est développé que par l'instruction ; si les propriétés étoient égales, *chacun travailleroit modérément*, et *chacun sauroit un peu*, parce qu'il resteroit à chacun une *portion de tems* à donner à l'étude et à la pensée ; mais dans l'inégalité des fortunes *, effet de l'ordre social, *l'instruction est interdite à* tous les hommes nés sans propriétés ; car toutes les subsistances étant entre les mains de la partie de la Nation qui possède *l'argent ou les terres*, et personne ne donnant rien pour rien ; l'homme né sans autre ressource ** que sa force, est obligé de la consacrer au service des Propriétaires, dès le premier moment où elle se développe, et de continuer ainsi toute sa vie, depuis l'instant où le Soleil se lève jusqu'à celui où cette force abattue a besoin d'être renouvelée par le sommeil. " (ibidem, p. 112.)

307 „ Est-il bien sûr enfin que cette inégalité de connoissance ne soit pas devenue nécessaire au maintien de toutes les inégalités sociales *qui l'on fait naître* ?" (ibidem, p. 113.)

307 „ On commence par confondre l'importance du Propriétaire (fonction si facile à remplir) avec l'importance de la terre ... " (ibidem, p. 126.)

325 „ La somme des créances hypothécaires, d'après les auteurs les mieux informés, est de 12 milliards, quelques-uns la portent à 16 milliards [...]. Celle de créances chirographaires, au moins 6. La commandite, environ 2 [...], la dette publique, 8 milliards. Total 28 milliards [...]. Toutes ces dettes, notez ce point, proviennent d'argent prêté, ou censé l'avoir été, qui à 4 [...], à 5 [...], à 6 [...], à 8 [...], à 12, et jusqu'à 15 ***. Je prends pour moyenne de l'intérêt, en ce qui concerne les trois premières catégories, 6 pour 100 **** : soit donc, sur 20 milliards, 1200 millions.—Ajoutez l'intérêt de la dette publique, environ 400 millions : en tout, 1600 millions d'intérêt annuel, pour un capital de 1 milliard. " ([Bastiat et Proudhon] *Gratuité du crédit. Discussion entre M. Fr. Bastiat et M. Proudhon*, Paris, 1850, p. 152.)

325 „ La somme de numéraire, je ne dirai pás existant, mais circulant en France, y compris l'encaisse de la Banque, ne dépasse pas, suivant l'évaluation la plus commune, 1 milliard ". (ibidem, p. 151.)

325 „ L'échange conclu, l'argent redevient disponible, capable, par conséquent, de donner lieu à une nouvelle location ... le capital-argent, d'échange en échange, revient toujours à sa source, il s'ensuit que la relocation, toujours faite par la même main, profite toujours au même personnage. " (ibidem, pp. 153-54.)

---

* In the manuscript: „de la fortune".—*Ed.*

** In the manuscript: „reserve".—*Ed.*

*** In the manuscript: „15%".—*Ed.*

**** In the manuscript: „6%" instead of „6 pour 100".—*Ed.*

343 „ Depuis l'origine du Monde il y eu trois grandes découvertes ... La première, c'est l'invention de *l'écriture* ... La seconde est *l'invention de la monnaie* ... La troisième est *le Tableau économique*, le résultat des deux autres, qui en est le complément ... " (Victor de Riqueti Mirabeau, *Tableau économique avec ses explications* (1760) ; quoted from : Adam Smith, *Recherches sur la nature et les causes de la richesse des nations*. Traduction nouvelle ... par Germain Garnier, t. III, Paris, 1802, p. 540.)

344 „ Leurs travaux ont certainement rendu quelques services à leur pays ... " (Adam Smith, *Recherches sur la nature et les causes de la richesse des nations*. Traduction nouvelle ... par Germain Garnier, t. III, Paris, 1802, p. 538.)

346 „ Dans nos pays policés *, tous les élémens sont esclaves. " ([Linguet] *Théorie des loix civiles* ..., t. I, Londres, 1767, p. 188.)

346 „ C'est ainsi que toute la nature captive a cessé d'offrir à ces enfans des ressources faciles pour le soutien de leur vie. Il faut payer ses bienfaits par des fatigues assidues, et ses présens par des travaux opiniâtres. " (ibidem, p. 188.)

346 „ Le riche *qui s'en est attribué la possession exclusive*, ne consent qu'à ce prix à en remettre en commun la plus petite portion. *Pour être admis à partager ses trésors, il faut s'employer à les augmenter*. "(ibidem, p. 189.)

346 „ Il faut donc renoncer à ces chimères de liberté ... " (ibidem, p. 190.)

346 „ ... consacrer une première usurpation pour en prévenir de nouvelles. " (ibidem, p. 192.)

346 „ elles sont, en quelque sorte, une conspiration contre la plus nombreuse partie du genre humain. " (ibidem, p. 195.)

346 „ ... c'est la société qui a produit les loix, et non les loix qui ont produit la société. " (ibidem, p. 230.)

346 „ ... la propriété leur soit** antérieure. " (ibidem, p. 236.)

346 „ ... des chasseurs accoutumés à vivre de sang, à se réunir par bandes, pour surprendre et terrasser plus aisément les bêtes dont ils se nourrissoient, et à se concerter pour en partager les dépouilles. " (ibidem, p. 279.)

346 „ ... c'est chez les chasseurs qu'a dû se montrer la première apparence de société " (ibidem, p. 278.)

346 „ ... *la vraie société s'est formée aux dépens des pasteurs ou agriculteurs, et été fondée sur leur assujettissement*. " (ibidem, p. 289.)

346 „ ... cette dégradation d'une partie du genre humain, après avoir occasionné la société, a donné naissance aux loix. " (ibidem, p. 294.)

346 „ C'est l'impossibilité de vivre autrement, qui force nos journaliers à remuer la terre dont ils ne mangeront pas les fruits, et nos maçons à élever des édifices où ils ne logeront pas. C'est la misère qui les traîne sur ces marchés, où ils attendent des maîtres qui veuillent bien leur faire la grâce de les acheter. *C'est elle qui les réduit à se mettre aux ge-*

---

* In the manuscript: „civilisés".—*Ed.*

** In the manuscript: „est".—*Ed.*

noux du riche, pour obtenir de lui la permission de l'enrichir. " (ibidem, p. 274.)

346 „ La violence a donc été la première occasion de la société, et la force son premier lien. " (ibidem, p. 302.)

347 „ Leur premier soin a été sans doute de se pourvoir de nourriture ... le second a dû être de chercher *à s'en pourvoir sans travail.* " (ibidem, pp. 307-08.)

347 „ Or ils n'ont pu y parvenir qu'en *s'appropriant le fruit du travail étranger.* " (ibidem, p. 308.)

347 „ Les premiers Conquérans [...] ne se faisoient despotes que pour être inpunément paresseux, et Rois, que pour avoir de quoi vivre : ce qui rétrécit et simplifie beaucoup ... l'idée de la domination. " (ibidem, p. 309.)

347 „ ... la société est née de la violence, et la propriété de l'usurpation. " (ibidem, p. 347.)

347 „ ... dès qu'il y eut des maîtres et des esclaves, la société fut formée ... " (ibidem, p. 343.)

347 „ ... dès l'origine, les deux soutiens de l'union civile furent d'une part l'esclavage de la plus grande partie des hommes, et de l'autre, celui de toutes les femmes... Ce fut aux dépens des trois quarts de ses membres que la société assura le bonheur, l'opulence, le repos du petit nombre de propriétaires qu'elle avoit seuls en vue. " (ibidem, p. 365.)

347 „ Il ne s'agit donc pas d'examiner si l'esclavage est contre la nature en elle-même, mais s'il est contre la nature de la société ... il en est inséparable. " (ibidem, p. 256.)

347 „La société et la servitude civile sont nées ensemble." (ibidem, p. 257.)

347 „ L'esclavage durable ... le fondement indestructible des sociétés." (ibidem, p. 347.)

347 „ Il n'y a eu des hommes réduits à tenir leur subsistance de la libéralité d'un autre homme que *quand celui-ci a été assez riche de leurs dépouilles* pour pouvoir leur en *rendre* une petite portion. Sa prétendue générosité n'a pu être qu'une *restitution de quelque partie des fruits de leurs travaux qu'il s'était appropriés.* " (ibidem, p. 242.)

347 „ N'est-ce pas dans cette obligation de semer sans recueillir pour soi, de sacrifier son bien-être à celui d'un autre, de travailler sans espérance, que *consiste la servitude.* Sa véritable époque n'est-elle pas l'instant où il y eut des hommes que l'on put contraindre au travail à coups de fouet, sauf à leur donner quelques mesures d'avoine en les ramenant à l'écurie. C'est dans une société perfectionnée que les aliments paraissent au pauvre *affamé* un *équivalent* suffisant de sa liberté, mais dans une société qui commence cet échange inégal ferait horreur à des hommes libres. Ce n'est qu'à de *captifs* qu'on peut le proposer. Ce n'est qu'après leur avoir ôté la jouissance de toutes leurs facultés qu'on peut le leur rendre nécessaire." (ibidem, pp. 244-45.)

347 „ *L'essence de la société ... est d'exempter le riche du travail* ; c'est de lui donner des nouveaux organes, des membres infatigables qui prennent sur eux toutes les opérations laborieuses *dont il doit s'approprier le fruit.* Voilà le plan que l'esclavage lui permettait d'exécuter sans embarras. Il achetait les hommes qui devaient le servir." (ibidem, p. 461.)

347 „ En supprimant la servitude, on n'a prétendu supprimer ni l'opulence ni ses avantages... il a [...] fallu que les choses restassent, au nom près, dans le même état. Il a toujours fallu que la plus grande partie des hommes continuât de vivre à la solde et dans la dépendance de la plus petite *qui s'est approprié tous les biens.* La servitude s'est donc perpétuée sur la terre, mais sous un nom plus doux. Elle s'est décorée parmi nous du titre de domesticité." (ibidem, p. 462.)

347 „ Les villes et les campagnes sont peuplées d'une autre espèce de domestiques plus répandus, plus utiles, plus laborieux, et connus sous le nom de *journaliers, manouvriers,* etc. Ils ne sont point déshonorés par les couleurs brillantes du luxe ; ils gémissent sous les haillons dégoûtants qui font la *livrée* de l'indigence. *Ils n'ont jamais de part à l'abondance dont leur travail est la source.* La richesse semble leur faire grâce quand elle veut bien agréer les *présents qu'ils lui font.* C'est à eux d'être reconnaissants *des services qu'ils lui rendent.* Elle leur prodigue le mépris le plus outrageant dans le temps où ils embrassent les genoux pour obtenir la *permission de lui être utiles.* Elle se fait prier pour l'accorder, et *dans cet échange singulier d'une prodigalité réelle contre une bienfaisance imaginaire,* la fierté, le dédain sont *du côté de celui qui reçoit,* et la bassesse, l'inquiétude, l'empressement *du côté de celui qui donne.* Ce sont là les domestiques qui ont vraiment remplacé les serfs parmi nous..." (ibidem, pp. 463-464.)

348 „ Il s'agit d'examiner quel est le gain effectif que lui a procuré la *suppression de l'esclavage.* Je le dis avec autant de douleur que de franchise : tout ce qu'ils ont gagné, c'est d'être à chaque instant * tourmentés par la crainte de mourir de faim, malheur dont étoient du moins exempts leurs prédécesseurs dans ce dernier rang de l'humanité." (ibidem, p. 464.)

348 „ Il est libre, dites vous. Eh! voilà son malheur. Il ne tient à personne : mais aussi personne ne tient à lui. Quand on en a besoin, on le *loue au meilleur marché* que l'on peut. La faible *solde* qu'on lui promet égale à peine *le prix de sa subsistance pour la journée qu'il fournit en échange.* On lui donne des *surveillans pour l'obliger à remplir promptement sa tâche* ; on le presse ; on l'aiguillonne de peur qu'une paresse industrieuse et excusable ne lui fasse cacher la moitié de sa vigueur ; on craint que l'espoir de *rester plus long-tems occupé au même ouvrage* n'arrête ses bras et n'émousse ses outils. *L'économie sordide qui le suit des yeux avec inquiétude l'accable de reproches au moindre relache qu'il paroît se donner,* et s'il prend un instant de repos, *elle prétend qu'il la vole.* A-t-il fini, on le renvoie comme on l'a pris, avec la plus froide indifférence, et sans s'embarrasser si les vingt ou trente sols qu'il vient de gagner par une journée pénible suffiront à sa subsistance, *en cas qu'il ne trouve pas à travailler le jour d'après.* " (ibidem, pp. 466-467.)

* In the manuscript: „moment".—*Ed.*

348 „ Il est libre ! C'est précisément de quoi je le plains. On l'en ménage beaucoup moins dans les travaux dans lesquels * on l'applique. On en est plus hardi à prodiguer sa vie. L'esolave étoit précieux à son maître en raison de l'argent qu'il lui avoit coûté. Mais le manouvrier ne coûte rien au riche voluptueux qui l'occupe. Du tems de la servitude, le sang des hommes avoit quelque prix. Ils valoient du moins la somme qu'on les vendoit au marché. Depuis qu'on ne les vend plus ils n'ont réellement aucune valeur intrinsèque. Dans une armée on estime bien moins un pionnier qu'un cheval de caisson, parce que le cheval est fort cher et qu'on a le pionnier pour rien. La suppression de l'esclavage a fait passer ces calculs de la guerre dans la vie commune ; *et depuis cette époque il n'y a point de bourgeois à son aise qui ne suppute en ce genre comme le font les héros.*" (ibidem, p. 467.)

348 „ Les journaliers naissent, croissent et s'élèvent pour le service de l'opulence sans lui causer le moindre frais, comme le gibier qu'elle massacre sur ses domaines. Il semble qu'elle ait réellement le secret dont se vantoit sans raison le malheureux Pompée. En frappant du pied la terre, elle en fait sortir des légions d'hommes laborieux qui se disputent l'honneur d'être à ses ordres : en disparoit-il quelqu'un parmi cette foule de mercenaires qui élèvent ses bâtiments, ou alignent ses jardins, la place qu'il a laissée vacante est un point invisible qui est sur le champ recouvert sans que personne s'en mêle. On perd sans regret une goutte de l'eau d'une grande rivière, parce qu'il en survient sans cesse de nouveaux flots. Il en est de même des manouvriers ; la facilité de les remplacer nourrit l'insensibilité du *riche* à leur égard. " (ibidem, p. 468.)

349 „ Ceux-ci, dit-on, n'ont point de maître ... pur abus du mot. Qu'est-ce à dire ? Ils n'ont point de maître : ils en ont un et le plus terrible, le plus impérieux des maîtres, c'est le *besoin*. Celui-là les asservit à la plus cruelle dépendance. *Ils ne sont pas aux ordres d'un homme en particulier, mais a ceux de tous en général.* Ce n'est point d'un seul tyran qu'ils ont à flatter les caprices, et à rechercher la bienveillance, ce qui borneroit la servitude, et la rendroit supportable. C'est *de quiconque a de l'argent qu'ils deviennent les valets*, ce qui donne à leur esclavage une étendue et une rigueur infinie. S'ils ne se trouvent pas bien d'un maître, dit-on, ils ont au moins la consolation de le lui dire, et le pouvoir d'en changer : les esclaves n'ont ni l'un ni l'autre. Ils sont donc plus malheureux. Quel sophisme ! songez-donc que le nombre de ceux *qui font travailler* est très petit et que celui des travailleurs au contraire est immense. " (ibidem, pp. 470-71.)

349 „ A quoi se réduit pour eux cette liberté apparente dont vous les avez investis ? ils ne *subsistent que du loyer de leurs bras. Il fout donc trouver à qui les louer ou mourir de faim. Est-ce là être libre* ? " (ibidem, p. 472.)

349 „ ... ce qu'il y a de plus terrible, c'est que la modicité même de cette paie est encore une raison pour la diminuer. Plus le journalier est pressé par le besoin, plus il se vend à bon marché. Plus sa nécessité est urgente, moins son travail est fructeux. Les despotes momentanés qu'il conjure en pleurant d'accepter ses services, ne rougissent pas de lui tâter, pour

---

* In the manuscript: „auxquels".—*Ed.*

ainsi dire, le pouls, afin de s'assurer de ce qu'il lui reste encore de forces ; c'est sur le degré de sa défaillance qu'ils règlent la rétribution qu'ils offrent. Plus ils le sentent près de périr d'inanition, plus ils retranchent de ce qui peut l'en préserver : et les barbares qu'ils sont lui donnent bien moins de quoi prolonger la vie que de quoi retarder la mort. " (ibidem, pp. 482-83.)

349 „ ... indépendance ... est un des plus funestes fléaux qu'ait produits le raffinement des tems modernes. Il augmente l'opulence du riche, et l'indigence du pauvre. L'un épargne tout ce que l'autre dépense. Ce n'est pas sur son superflu que celui-ci est forcé d'économiser, c'est sur son nécessaire. " (ibidem, p. 483.)

349 „ ... si l'on trouve aujourd'hui tant de facilités à entretenir ces prodigieuses armées qui se joignent au luxe pour achever d'exterminer la race humaine, on n'en est redevable qu'à la suppression de l'esclavage ... Ce n'est que depuis qu'il n'y a plus d'esclaves que la débauche et la mendicité forment des héros à cinq sols par jour. " (ibidem, pp. 484-85.)

349 „ C'est celle que je trouve cent fois préférable à toute autre façon d'être, pour les hommes réduits à gagner leur vie par un travail journalier. " (ibidem, p. 496.)

349 „ Leurs chaînes, tissues de la même matière, ne sont que diversement coloriées. Ici elles sont noires, et semblent massives, là elles ont une apparence moins triste, et paraissent plus évidées : pesez-les cependant avec impartialité, vous n'y trouverez aucune différence ; les unes et les autres sont également fabriquées par la nécessité. Elles ont précisément le même poids, ou plutôt s'il y a quelques grains de plus d'un côté, c'est de celui qui annonce à l'extérieur plus de légèreté. " (ibidem, p. 510.)

350 „ Ne voyez-vous pas que l'obéissance, l'anéantissement, puisqu'il faut le dire, de cette nombreuse partie du troupeau fait l'opulence des bergers ? ... Croyez-moi, pour son intérêt, pour le vôtre, et même pour le leur, laissez-les dans la persuasion où elles sont, que ce roquet qui les aboie, a plus de force à lui seul, qu'elles toutes ensemble. Laissez-les fuir stupidement au simple aspect de son ombre. Tout le monde y gagne. Vous en avez plus de facilité à les rassembler, pour vous approprier leurs toisons. Elles sont plus aisément garanties d'être dévorées par les loups. Ce n'est il est vrai, que pour être mangées par les hommes. Mais enfin, c'est là leur sort du moment qu'elles sont entrées dans une étable. Avant que de parler de les y soustraire, commencez par renverser l'étable, c'est-à-dire la société. " (ibidem, pp. 512-13.)

380 „ ... tout achat est vente, et [...] toute vente est achat. " (François Quesnay, *Dialogues sur le commerce et sur les travaux des artisans*. In : *Physiocrates* ... par M. Eugène Daire. Première partie, Paris, 1846, p. 170.)

380 „ Acheter c'est vendre, et vendre c'est acheter. " (Dupont de Nemours, *Maximes du docteur Quesnay* ... In : *Physiocrates* ... par M. Eugène Daire. Première partie, Paris, 1846, p. 392.)

380 „ ... le *prix précède toujours les achats et les ventes*. Si la concurrence des vendeurs et d'acheteurs n'y apporte pas de changement, il existe

tel qu'il est par d'autres causes *indépendantes* du commerce. " (François Quesnay, *Dialogues sur le commerce et sur les travaux des artisans*. In : *Physiocrates* ... par M. Eugène Daire. Première partie, Paris, 1846, p. 148.)

380 „ ... il est toujours à présumer qu'il est profitable à tous deux ; car de part et d'autre ils se procurent la jouissance de richesses qu'ils ne peuvent obtenir que par l'échange. Mais toujours n'y a-t-il qu'échange de richesses *d'une valeur* pour d'autres richesses de *valeur égale*, et par conséquent *point d'augmentation réelle de richesses*. " (ibidem, p. 197.)

380 „ *L'augmentation des capitaux* est donc *le principal moyen d'accroître* le travail, et *le plus grand intérêt de la société*. " (Dupont de Nemours, *Maximes du docteur Quesnay* ... In : *Physiocrates* ... par M. Eugène Daire. Première partie, Paris, 1846, p. 391)

381 „ ... ils ont risqué beaucoup pour gagner beaucoup ? Mais ils ont risqué des hommes, et des denrées ou de l'argent. Pour les hommes [...] s'ils les ont exposés à un péril évident, pour gagner, ils ont fait une très-vilaine action. Pour les denrées, si c'est un mérite d'en produire, [...] ce ne doit être un mérite de les risquer pour le profit d'un seul homme. ([du Buat-Nançay] *Eléments de la politique* ... t. II, Londres, 1773, p. 297.)

408 „ ... dans les petites entreprises ... l'*entrepreneur* est souvent son *propre ouvrier*. " (Henri Storch, *Cours d'économie politique* ..., t. 1, St-Pétersbourg, 1815, p. 242.)

NOTES

1 Marx wrote this table of contents of the manuscript *Theorien über den Mehrwert* (*Theories of Surplus-Value*) on the covers of notebooks VI to XV. In some of these notebooks he wrote the table of contents before he wrote the text itself, as can be seen from the corrections and deletions which he made to the contents table after the corresponding notebook had been filled with the text. In notebook XIV he did not make the table of contents outlined on the cover correspond with the actual content of the notebook; it represents the plan which he carried out in notebooks XIV, XV and XVIII. p. 37

2 Before the heading *Theorien über den Mehrwert* Marx put the Arabic figure 5. It indicates the fifth, concluding section of the first chapter of the analysis of capital which Marx had in mind to publish as the direct sequel to the first part of *Zur Kritik der politischen Ökonomie* (*A Contribution to the Critique of Political Economy*) dealing with commodity and money. This fifth section was preceded by three sections, in notebooks I to V, which in the main had been written: (1) Transformation of money into capital; (2) Absolute surplus-value; and (3) Relative surplus-value. In notebook V, page 184 of the manuscript, Marx noted that "after relative surplus-value, absolute and relative surplus-value to be considered in their combination". This analysis was to form the fourth section, which however was not written at that time. Marx passed on directly from the third section to the fifth, *Theories of Surplus-Value*. p. 37

3 This in fact turned out not to be the "Conclusion" but only the "Continuation" of the section on Smith. The conclusion of this section comes in the following notebook, IX. p. 37

4 The chapter on the "Adversaries of the Economists" begins only in notebook XIV; its continuation is given in the first half of notebook XV. p. 38

5 The extracts from Bray's book *Labour's Wrongs and Labour's Remedy; or, the Age of Might and the Age of Right*, Leeds-Manchester, 1839, are in notebook X with some comments by Marx. p. 38

6 The chapters on Ramsay, Cherbuliez and Richard Jones are contained in notebook XVIII of the manuscript. p. 39

7 Marx deals with revenue and its sources in the second half of notebook XV, in this connection laying bare the class and gnosiological roots of

vulgar political economy. Marx had intended this "Episode" (i.e. excursus) for the third part of *Capital*, as is shown by the plan he worked out in January 1863 for this part, according to which the ninth chapter was to be headed "Revenue and Its Sources" (see p. 415 of the present volume). p. 39

8 The section on Ravenstone begins on page 861 of the preceding (XIV) notebook. Before this section in notebook XIV there is a section marked No. 1 on the anonymous pamphlet *The Source and Remedy of the National Difficulties, deduced from Principles of Political Economy in a Letter to Lord John Russell*, London, 1821. p. 39

9 The end of the section on Hodgskin is in notebook XVIII (pages 1084 to 1086 of the manuscript). p. 39

10 Marx gives the analysis of vulgar political economy in notebook XV, in connection with his elaboration of the question of revenue and its sources. On page 935 of this notebook he refers to the "section on the vulgar economists" as a chapter of his work which he had not yet written, in which he would "return" to the polemic between Proudhon and Bastiat which he mentions in passing. This reference shows that Marx intended to devote a special chapter to the critique of vulgar political economy, which however he did not write. In notebook XVIII, in which the analysis of Hodgskin's views is complete, Marx observes: "His" (Hodgskin's) "polemics against...the savings theory...to be dealt with in the chapter on the vulgar economists" (page 1086 of the manuscript). This also is evidence of Marx's intention, in the further course of his work, to write a special chapter on vulgar political economy. In the plan for the third part of *Capital* which he drew up in January 1863, the chapter before the last, Chapter XI, is headed "Vulgar Economy" (see p. 415 of the present volume). p. 39

11 On the cover of notebook XV, where Marx had noted the contents of this notebook, he wrote down some of the headings in the margin or at the top of the page. The present edition puts these headings in the text of the list of contents in the order that corresponds with the actual contents of the notebook. p. 39

12 By Chapter III ("third chapter") Marx here means Part III of his inquiry into "capital in general". This chapter is called "The Production Process of Capital, Circulation Process of Capital, Unity of the Two or Capital and Profit". Later Marx used "Section III" instead of "Chapter III" (see for example notebook IX, page 398, and notebook XI, page 526). Still later he began to call this Chapter III "Third Book" (for example in the letter to Engels of July 31, 1865). In notebook XVI Marx sketched out the beginning of the analysis of "capital in general" contained in "Chapter III".

As can be seen from the draft plan of this "Chapter III" or "Part III" (see pp. 414-15 of the present volume), Marx intended to give there a separate historical excursus on theories of profit. But in the course of his work on *Theories of Surplus-Value* he brought into this historical-critical inquiry a basic critical analysis also of the views of various bourgeois economists on profit. For that reason he gave in *Theories of Surplus-Value* the further, more comprehensive exposure of the theoretical errors arising from the confusion of surplus value with profit. p. 40

[13] In the manuscript of 1861-63 Marx uses almost all through the term "Arbeitsvermögen" instead of "Arbeitskraft". In Volume I of *Capital* he uses both these terms as expressing the same idea; "Unter *Arbeitskraft* oder *Arbeitsvermögen* verstehen wir den Inbegriff der physischen und geistigen Fähigkeiten, die in der Leiblichkeit, der lebendigen Persönlichkeit eines Menschen existieren und die er in Bewegung setzt, so oft er Gebrauchswerte irgend einer Art produziert" (Karl Marx, *Das Kapital*, I. Band, Berlin 1955, S. 175). The English translation of this passage reads: "By *labour power* or *capacity for labour* is to be understood the aggregate of those mental and physical capabilities existing in a human being, which he exercises whenever he produces a use-value of any description" (Karl Marx, *Capital*, Vol. I, Moscow, 1959, p. 167.)

The English expression "capacity for labour" does not adequately express the full meaning of the term "Arbeitsvermögen". Throughout this volume it has therefore been rendered as "labour-power", as has also the term "Arbeitskraft". p. 43

[14] What is meant is the second chapter of the examination of "capital in general", which finally grew into the second volume of *Capital*. Chapter X, Volume II of *Capital* ("Theories of Fixed and Circulating Capital. The Physiocrats and Adam Smith") contains the analysis of the views of the Physiocrats on fixed and circulating capital. And in the section on "The Reproduction and Circulation of the Aggregate Social Capital", there is a special paragraph on the Physiocrats in Chapter XIX ("Former Presentations of the Subject"). p. 44

[15] Marx means pages 58-60 in notebook II of his manuscript (the section "Transformation of Money into Capital", paragraph "The Two Component Parts of the Transformation Process"). p. 45

[16] Marx means notebook III of his manuscript, pages 105-06, where he incidentally mentions also the Physiocrats (section "Absolute Surplus-Value", paragraph "Character of Surplus-Labour"). p. 48

[17] The Physiocrats were called Economists in France of the second half of the 18th century and the first half of the 19th. p. 62

[18] Volume V of Germain Garnier's French translation of Adam Smith's work *An Inquiry into the Nature and Causes of the Wealth of Nations* (1802 edition) contains "Translator's Notes" by Garnier. p. 63

[19] Mirabeau the Elder was called during his lifetime "l'ami des hommes" (the friend of the people) after the title of one of his works. p. 66

[20] In the manuscript this paragraph is three paragraphs further down (on the same page 241). It is separated from the text that precedes and follows it—since it is not directly linked with either the preceding or the following paragraph—by horizontal lines. In this edition it has therefore been placed at the end of page 240 of the manuscript, where by its content it directly belongs. p. 66

[21] See present volume, page 44 and Note 14 referring to it. In notebook X, in *Theories of Surplus-Value*, where there is a long "excursus" under the heading "Quesnay's Tableau économique" (see pp. 308-44 of the present volume), Marx comes back to the Physiocrats. p. 66

22 The representatives of liberal-democratic ideas in the first decades of the nineteenth century were called *demagogues* by the authorities in Germany. In 1819, a special commission was set up in Mainz to investigate the "intrigues of the demagogues" in all German States. p. 67

23 Schmalz's book was originally published in Berlin in 1818, under the title *Staatswirthschaftslehre in Briefen an einen deutschen Erbprinzen, Erster und zweiter Theil.* p. 67

24 Marx makes a critical analysis of the Physiocratic element in Smith's views on rent in notebook XII, pages 628-32 of the manuscript, in the chapter "Adam Smith's Theory of Rent". Cf. present volume, Chapter II "The Physiocrats", pp.60-63. p. 70

25 Marx means his work *Zur Kritik der politischen Ökonomie, Erstes Heft* (Ausgabe Berlin, 1951, S. 57-58). p. 70

26 The reference is to Ricardo's work *On the Principles of Political Economy, and Taxation*, Chapter I, Section I. p. 71

27 In notebooks XIII and XIV, in the chapter "Malthus" (pages 753-81 of the manuscript), Marx criticises in detail Malthus's views on value and surplus-value (pages 753-67). p. 73

28 Marx quotes from the first edition of his *Misère de la Philosophie. Réponse à la Philosophie de la misère de M. Proudhon*, Paris et Bruxelles, 1847. (Cf. K. Marx. *The Poverty of Philosophy*, Moscow, p.57). p. 74

29 Marx refers to one of his notebooks in which he recorded excerpts from the books and papers which he read. On page 173 of the seventh book of excerpts (judging from the extracts from newspapers contained in this part of the notebook, p.173 was written in January 1860) Marx noted down passages from Chapter VI of Book I of Smith's *An Inquiry into the Nature and Causes of the Wealth of Nations* and made critical comments on them, in which he shows the absurdity of attempting to deduce profit from "entrepreneur's risk". As for the "chapter on the apologetic accounts of profit", Marx intended to write it as Part III of his inquiry into "capital in general". In notebook XIV of the 1861-63 manuscript (page 777) Marx similarly calls this still unwritten section "The Apologetic Account of the Relation between Capital and Wage-Labour".

The bourgeois conception of profit as "premium on risk" is also subjected to a critique in notebook X of Marx's manuscript of 1861-63, in the analysis of Quesnay's Tableau économique (see pp. 314-21 of the present volume). p. 79

30 The apologetic conception of the entrepreneur's revenue as wages received by the capitalist for the "labour of superintendence and management" is criticised by Marx in the section on Ramsay (notebook XVIII) and in the excursus "Revenue and Its Sources. Vulgar Political Economy" (notebook XV). See also *Capital*, Vol. I, Moscov, 1959, Chapter XIII, pp.330-32, and Vol. III, Moscow, 1959, Chapter XXIII, pp.374-82. p. 81

31 Marx discusses the "antediluvian forms" of capital in the excursus "Revenue and Its Sources. Vulgar Political Economy" (notebook XV, pages 899-901). See also *Capital*, Volume III, Chapter XXXVI, "Pre-capitalist Relationships". p. 83

32 See Note 27. p. 88

33 See Note 12. In the course of his further work on *Theories of Surplus-Value* Marx criticised also the Ricardians' conceptions of profit. In notebook XIV of the 1861-63 manuscript, in the chapter "Dissolution of the Ricardian School", Marx dwells particularly on the scholastic methods by means of which James Mill, a disciple of Ricardo, attempted to solve the contradictions in Ricardo's theory of profit, and also on John Stuart Mill's fruitless efforts to deduce Ricardo's thesis on the inverse proportionality between the rate of profit and the level of wages directly from the theory of value. p. 89

34 The term "*average price*" ("Durchschnittspreis") is here used by Marx to denote the same concept as the term "price of production", i. e., the cost of production (c+v) plus the average profit. Marx examines the correlation between the value of the commodities and their "average price" in Part II of *Theories of Surplus-Value*: in the chapter on Rodbertus and the chapter "Ricardo's and Adam Smith's Theory of Cost-Price". The very term "average price" indicates that Marx has in mind "the average market-price over a lengthy period of time, or the centre towards which the market-price gravitates", as Marx explains on page 605 of his manuscript (in the chapter "Ricardo's Theory of Rent [Conclusion]"). p. 95

35 The term "*cost-price*" ("Kostenpreis" or "Kostpreis") is used by Marx in three different ways, in the sense of: (1) the cost of production to the capitalist (c+v), (2) "the immanent cost of production" of the commodity (c+v+s), which is identical with the value of the commodity, and (3) the price of production (c+v+average profit). In this passage the term is used in the second sense, i. e., the immanent cost of production. Marx uses the term "cost-price" in the third sense, that of the price of production or "average price", in Part II of *Theories of Surplus-Value*. There Marx treats these terms as identical. For instance, on page 529 of the manuscript Marx writes: "...average prices or—let us say—*cost-prices* which differ from the values themselves and which are not directly determined by the values of the commodities but by the capital advanced in them plus the average profit." And on page 624 Marx states: "...the price which is necessary for the supply of the commodity, which is necessary for it to be produced at all, for it to appear as a commodity on the market, is of course its *price of production* or *cost-price*."

In Part III of *Theories of Surplus-Value* the term "Kostenpreis" is sometimes used by Marx in the sense of price of production (in these cases it has been rendered as "cost-price"), and sometimes in the sense of the cost of production to the capitalist, i.e., c+v (where this has seemed to be the case it has been rendered as "cost of production").

The use of the term "Kostenpreis" in three different ways is due to the fact that in political economy the word "Kosten" ("costs") has been used for three concepts as Marx especially emphasises in Part III of *Theories of Surplus-Value* (pages 788-90 and 928 of the manuscript of 1861-63), namely to denote: (1) the amount advanced by the capitalist, (2) the value of the advanced capital plus the average profit, and (3) the real—or immanent—cost of production of the commodity itself.

In addition to these three meanings, which occur in the works of the classics of bourgeois political economy, the term "cost of production" has a fourth, vulgar meaning, and in this sense it has been used by J. B. Say, who defines "the costs of production" as the amount "which is paid for the productive services of labour, capital and land" (J. B. Say, *Traité d'économie politique*. Seconde édition. Tome II, Paris, 1814, p.453). Marx emphatically rejects this vulgar conception of "costs of production" (see, for example, pages 506 and 693-94 of the manuscript in Part II of *Theories of Surplus-Value*). p. 96

36 In the lengthy section on Ricardo, which fills notebooks XI, XII and XIII of Marx's manuscript, there is a chapter "Ricardo's and Adam Smith's Theory of Cost-Price (Refutation)", in which Marx returns to the analysis of the Smithian conception of "natural price" (notebook XI, pages 549-60). p. 97

37 In notebook XII, page 620 in the chapter "Adam Smith's Theory of Rent", Marx gives a critical analysis of Smith's thesis that rent enters into the composition of the price of production in a different way from profit and wages. Marx takes the quotation from Smith's *An Inquiry into the Nature and Causes of the Wealth of Nations* as given by Ganilh in *Des systèmes d'économie politique* (Paris, 1821, t. II, p.3). p. 97

38 See Note 12. p. 105

39 Marx formulates the problem posed here in the following way in Volume III of *Capital*, Chapter XLIX: "Thus, how is it possible for the labourer with his wages, the capitalist with his profit, the landlord with his rent, to be able to buy commodities, each of which contains not only one of these constituent elements, but all three of them; and how is it possible for the sum of the values of wages, profit and rent, that is, the three sources of revenue together, to be able to buy the commodities which go to make up the total consumption of the recipients of these incomes—commodities containing an additional component of value, namely constant capital, outside these three components of value? How should they buy a value of four with a value of three?" (*Capital*, Vol. III, Moscow, 1959, pp. 821-22.)

Immediately following this, Marx writes: "We presented our analysis in Book II, Part III". (ibid.) The reference is to the part "The Reproduction and Circulation of the Aggregate Social Capital" (*Capital*, Vol. II, Moscow, 1957, pp.351-523). p. 107

40 The words (*Forcade, Proudhon*) have been added by Marx in pencil.

In Volume III of *Capital*, Chapter XLIX, Note 53, Marx criticises Proudhon's "ignorant formulation": "l'ouvrier ne peut pas racheter son propre produit (the labourer cannot buy back his own product), because the interest which is added to the prix-de-revient (cost-price) is contained in the product." He also shows there the shallowness of the attempt made by the vulgar economist Forcade to solve the problem "by means of a meaningless phrase: the growth of capital". Marx pillories this attempt as a typical example of "the optimism of bourgeois thoughtlessness" (*Capital*, Vol. III, Moscow, 1959, p.822). p. 112

41 While keeping the above figures, Marx altered the letters denoting the spheres of production (except A) in what follows. Instead of B and C he now uses B^1—B^2 (or B^{1-2}); instead of D, E, F, G, H, I, C^1—C^6 (or C^{1-6}); instead of K^1—K^{18}, D^1—D^{18} (or D^{1-18}); instead of L^1—L^{54}, E^1—E^{54} (or E^{1-54}); instead of M^1—M^{162}, F^1—F^{162} (or F^{1-162}): instead of N^1—N^{486}, G^1—G^{486} (or G^{1-486}). p. 118

42 Here Marx uses "B" and "C" in the same sense as up to page 118 (see Note 41). Here he has in mind two spheres of production, in each of which the newly-added labour amounts to one day's labour. The total newly-added labour in spheres A, B and C is equal to three days' labour, that is, equal to the labour materialised in the product of sphere A. p. 123

43 Here the letters "B" and "C" are no longer used by Marx to denote two spheres of production, for the product of two spheres only amounts to 6 days' labour while Marx speaks of 18 days' labour. On the other hand, Marx does not use the letters in the sense of B^1—B^2 and C^1—C^6 (since B^1—B^2, as used by Marx, stands for a group of two spheres of production and C^1—C^6 for a group consisting of six spheres of production; the aggregate product of these eight spheres comes to 24 days' labour). Apparently here Marx has in mind a group comprising six spheres of production—corresponding to "C" in the table (see p. 122 of the present volume)—the total product of which amounts to 18 days' labour and can, therefore, be exchanged for the newly-added labour of D^1—D^{18}, which also equals 18 days' labour. p. 123

44 The insertions in square brackets follow from the whole line of Marx's thought. On his reckoning, in each following group the number of spheres of production is double the total number of all preceding spheres. Thus in the group D^{1-18}, embracing eighteen spheres of production there are twice as many spheres as in all the preceding groups (A=one sphere, B^{1-2}=two spheres, C^{1-6}=six spheres, in all nine spheres). That is why, after D^{1-18}, Marx puts in brackets: 2×9. p. 123

45 Marx quotes Smith here in the Garnier translation. The explanation of the term "dealers", to which Marx refers in brackets, comes from Garnier. p. 125

46 Marx makes critical comments on this erroneous thesis of Smith and Tooke further on, on pages 141-42, 251-52.

In Volume II of *Capital*, Chapter XX, Marx shows that the view held by Smith and Tooke "that the money required for the circulation of the yearly revenue must also suffice for the circulation of the entire annual product", is closely linked with Smith's dogma which reduces the total value of the social product to revenues (*Capital*, Vol. II, Moscow, 1957, pp.473-76). See also *Capital*, Vol. III, Moscow, 1959, Chapter XLIX, pp.821-22. p. 125

47 According to the previous calculation $5^1/_3$ yards of linen represent the total constant capital of the spinner and the loom manufacturer. Therefore what must be taken as the starting-point for determining the flax-grower's share is not $5^1/_3$ yards, but a smaller quantity of linen. In what follows Marx corrects this inaccuracy and assumes that the spinner's constant capital represents only four yards of linen in all. p. 128

48 Marx here criticises the Smithian thesis which Tooke adopted that "the value of the goods circulated between the different dealers never can exceed the value of those circulated between the dealers and the consumers" (see p.125 of the present volume). p. 142

49 Marx means his explanation that here he leaves entirely out of account "the part of the profit which is transformed into new capital" (see p.141 of the present volume). p. 143

[50] See *Capital,* Vol. II, Moscow, 1957, Chapter XX, pp.422-25. p. 147

[51] Marx criticises the bourgeois conception according to which all that "is capital to one is revenue to another, and vice versa" in *Capital,* Vol. II, Moscow, 1957, pp. 439-42. See also pp.378-84, 389-91 in that volume, and Vol. III, Moscow, 1959, pp.820-21. p. 147

[52] The fragment in these brackets is on page 304 of the manuscript, which belongs to the fourth chapter. In accordance with a note by Marx at the beginning of this fragment, "To p. 300", it was put into the third chapter. On page 300 of the manuscript there is a fragment on Say, beginning with the words: "In addition to the foregoing". Comparison of these fragments shows the following: the fragment on page 304 ends with the words: "how can the value of the product sold..." The end of the fragment on Say contains the answer to this question: "The revenue, which consists only of added labour, is able to pay for this product, which consists partly of added and partly of pre-existing labour...." The fragment on p. 304 has accordingly been put before the fragment on Say, which comes at the end of Section 10 of the third chapter. p. 150

[53] See Note 17. p. 150

[54] Marx here means the vicious circle in the Smithian conception of the "natural rate" of wages which he dealt with also previously (see p.95 of the present volume). p. 150

[55] See *Zur Kritik der politischen Ökonomie. Erstes Heft.* Berlin 1951, S. 62 ff. p. 151

[56] In this edition the fragment which states the general character of the contradictions in Smith's work is put as a closing note at the end of the third chapter. This corresponds to the position it occupies in Marx's manuscript; for immediately after this fragment come the opening lines of the next chapter. p. 151

[57] On bankers and their parasitic role in capitalist society see *Capital,* Vol. III, Moscow, 1959, pp. 466-67, 494, 498-500 and 531-33. p. 164

[58] Marx speaks of the concentration of capital as the primary condition for the increase in the productivity of labour in notebook IV, pp. 171-72 of the manuscript (section "Relative Surplus-Value", paragraph "Division of Labour"). p. 170

[59] Marx means his work *Zur Kritik der politischen Ökonomie. Erstes Heft;* the quotation from Petty referred to is on p. 137 of the German edition (Berlin, 1951). p. 174

[60] The reference is to a satire by the English writer Mandeville: *The Fable of the Bees: or Private Vices, Publick Benefits,* which was first published in 1705. p. 176

[61] The translation of this passage in the text was brought into conformity with what Marx says on D'Avenant in his book of excerpts, from which all quotations from D'Avenant's works are taken (the cover of the notebook bears the note in Marx's hand: "Manchester, July 1845"). p. 179

[62] Marx quotes here William Petty's *A Treatise of Taxes, and Contributions* from Charles Ganilh's *Des systèmes d'économie politique,* t. II, Paris,

1821, pp. 36-37, where this passage is given in Ganilh's French translation. The text of the French translation of the passage cited is somewhat different from the text of the English original, which Marx quotes in English in notebook XXII of his manuscript (see p.357 of the present volume). p. 182

63 After this quotation from Garnier, in the manuscript come a lengthy excursus on John Stuart Mill (pages 319-45), a small note on Malthus (pages 345-46) and a short note on Petty (pages 346-47). The excursus on John Stuart Mill begins with the words: "Before dealing with Garnier, something (by way of a digression) on the above mentioned *Mill junior*. What is to be said here really belongs later in this section, where Ricardian theory of surplus-value is to be discussed; therefore not here, where we are still concerned with Adam Smith." In the table of contents of notebook XIV (see p.38 of the present volume) and also in the text itself of this notebook there is the section on John Stuart Mill, in the chapter "Dissolution of the Ricardian School". For these reasons the excursus on John Stuart Mill has been put in the chapter mentioned, which belongs to Part III of the *Theories*. The note on Malthus was put in the chapter on Malthus, and the excursus on Petty higher up (see this volume, pp.180-81). After all these digressions the manuscript says (notebook VIII, page 347): "We come back to productive and unproductive labour. *Garnier*. See notebook VII, page 319." And then follows the analysis of Garnier's views (see pp.183-202 of the present volume). p. 183

64 Up to here Marx used the letter x to indicate the product considered as use-value, and the letter z the value of the product. From this passage on he changes the letters, using x for the value and z for the use-value. In the present edition the lettering as first used by Marx is retained, so that from here on the letters x and z are transposed, and thus keep their meaning unchanged. p. 188

65 This paragraph, which is supplementary to the section on Germain Garnier, is taken from notebook IX, where it comes between the section on Say and that on Destutt de Tracy. Garnier's book *Abrégé élémentaire des principes de l'économie politique* is quoted by Marx from Destutt de Tracy's *Élements d'idéologie*, IV-e et V-e parties, pp.250-51. p. 202

66 The four paragraphs under the common heading "Schmalz" are a postscript right at the end of notebook IX. By their content they supplement the additional note on Garnier, which is in the same notebook, page 400 (see pp.202-03 of the present volume). p. 203

67 Marx quotes Canard's definition of wealth from Ganilh's *Des systèmes d'économie politique*, t. I, Paris, 1821, p. 75. In Canard's book the definition is on p. 4. p. 204

68 This assertion of Ganilh's is in the first volume of his work *Des systèmes d'économie politique*, Paris, 1821, p.213. p. 213

69 Accurately speaking the value of the machine—on the assumption that it is four times the size of the rest of the capital, which is £460 (150+ +310)—must come to £1,840. But this figure would greatly complicate the calculation. To simplify it Marx takes the round figure of £1,600. p. 214

[70] Marx here quotes Say's note to Chapter XXVI of Ricardo's *Principles* from Ganilh's book (tome I, p.216). p. 221

[71] See Note 17. p. 222

[72] Marx refers here to the page of the first volume of Ganilh's book, from which he takes the quotation from Chapter XXVI of Ricardo's *Principles* in the French translation by Constancio. A little later, on page 377 of the manuscript, Marx again quotes the same passage from Ricardo's *Principles*, but this time in English (from the third edition) and more fully (see p.227 of the present volume). p. 224

[73] Marx gives the quotation from Chapter XXVI of Ricardo's *Principles* first in French, in Constancio's translation (from Ganilh's book, t.I, p.214) and shortly after in the English original (from the third edition, p.416). p. 226

[74] In the manuscript following this there are $4^1/_2$ pages (372-76) crossed out in pencil, in which Marx makes a detailed analysis of the figures given in Ricardo's example of the "person with a capital of £20,000". Marx shows that these figures are nonsensical. In the first case the owner of a capital of £20,000 employs a hundred men and sells the goods produced for £10,000. In the second case he employs a thousand men and sells the goods produced for £20,000. Ricardo asserts that in both cases the profit on the £20,000 capital could be the same—£2,000. Marx makes detailed calculations which show that this result, on the assumptions made, is impossible. Then he puts forward the following thesis: "The *assumptions* in the illustrations must not be contradictory. They must therefore be so formulated that they are *real* assumptions, *real* hypotheses, not assumed absurdities, not hypothetical unrealities and nonsensicalities" (page 373). Ricardo's example is also unsatisfactory because only the number of employed men is given, but not the amount of the gross product produced in the two cases. In order to make a deeper analysis of both cases Marx selects more appropriate figures for the number of men and the amount of products produced, with corresponding calculations. But when he comes to working out the quantity of products which the workmen in each of these two cases receive as wages, he notices an error in his calculations and decides not to go on with them. The passage crossed out in the manuscript (page 376) ends with the words: "This calculation must be abandoned. No point in wasting time on working out Ricardo's nonsense." p. 226

[75] Marx takes the round figure 10 in order not to complicate the subsequent calculations. From the figures given in the text (110 years as the total of the turnover periods for fourteen different sorts of fixed capital), the average turnover period of the fixed capital (assuming that all the various sorts are of the same magnitude) would work out not at 10, but at only 7.86 years. p. 242

[76] Marx returns to some of the questions touched on in this "intermezzo" in notebook X of his manuscript, in connection with the analysis of Quesnay's Tableau économique (see present volume, Chapter VI). But he gives a detailed and systematic reply to the last two questions raised in Volume II of *Capital* (especially in Chapter XX, Section X, "Capital

and Revenue: Variable Capital and Wages", and in Chapter XXI, "Accumulation and Reproduction on an Extended Scale"). p. 252

77 See Note 12. p. 265

78 The reference is to the following passage: "The gold and silver money which circulates in any country, and by means of which the produce of its land and labour is annually circulated and distributed to the proper consumers, is, in the same manner as the ready money of the dealer, all dead stock. It is a very valuable part of the capital of the country, which produces nothing to the country". (Adam Smith, *The Wealth of Nations*, Oxford University Press, 1928, Vol. I, p.357.) p. 266

79 In notebook XIV (this belongs to Part III of the present edition), after analysing the views of Malthus, Marx examines two anonymous works, one of which attacks Malthus from the Ricardian standpoint, while the other defends Malthus's views against the Ricardians. The first is called *An Inquiry into those Principles, respecting the Nature of Demand and the Necessity of Consumption, lately advocated by Mr. Malthus, from which it is concluded, that Taxation and the Maintenance of Unproductive Consumers can be conducive to the Progress of Wealth*, London, 1821 (see Index of Authorities). The second is called *Outlines of Political Economy, being a plain and short View of the Laws relating to the Production, Distribution and Consumption of Wealth* ..., London, 1832. p. 283

80 Marx means the polemic against Voltaire in Lessing's *Hamburgische Dramaturgie* (1767-68). p. 285

81 *Henriade*—an epic poem of Voltaire's on the French King Henri IV; the first edition appeared in 1723. p. 285

82 On Smith's hostile attitude to the clergy see *Capital*, Vol. I, Moscow, 1959, Chapter XXV, note 2, pp.616-18. p. 300

83 In this chapter Smith examines the general theoretical ideas of Mercantilism. p. 302

84 Marx means the subsection "Hoarding" in *A Contribution to the Critique of Political Economy*, where he quotes from Petty's *Political Arithmetick*. Marx also refers to the same excerpt above (p.174 of the present volume), where he brings out Smith's partial return to the ideas of the Mercantilists. p. 303

85 Marx means the last six paragraphs of Book II, Chapter III, of Smith's work *An Inquiry into the Nature and Causes of the Wealth of Nations*, in which the author examines what kind of expenditure of revenue would contribute in greater measure to the growth of social wealth, and what kind would contribute less. Smith assumes that this depends on the different nature of the articles of consumption, on the degree of their permanence. Marx mentions this view of Smith's on pp. 280-81 of the present volume, in the section on Destutt de Tracy. p. 303

86 In notebook V, page 181 of the manuscript (Chapter I, Section III "Relative Surplus-Value", paragraph "Division of Labour"), Marx gives the following quotation from Linguet :

"The sordid economy that keeps a restless watch on him" (day labourer) "overwhelms him with reproaches at the slightest respite he seems to allow himself, and claims to have been robbed if he takes a moment's rest" (S. N. Linguet, *Théorie des lois civiles*, tome II, Londres, 1767, p.466).

Marx cites the same passage in notebook X, page 439 of the manuscript, in the chapter on Linguet (see p. 348 of the present volume). In Vol. I of *Capital* (Moscow, 1959, Chapter X, p. 233, footnote 4) he gives the excerpt in shortened form. p. 305

87 Marx puts the chapter on Linguet only after the one on Necker—disregarding the fact that Linguet's work *Théorie des lois civiles* (1767), according to its date of publication, preceded the two works of Necker considered here, namely, *Sur la législation et le commerce des grains* (1775) and *De l'administration des finances de la France* (1784). The reason for putting them in this order is that in its grasp of the character of capitalist production Linguet's work is on a higher level than Necker's two books. p. 305

88 Marx here uses the outline of the Tableau économique from Schmalz's book *Économie politique. Ouvrage traduit de l'allemand par Henri Jouffroy*, tome I, Paris, 1826, p.329.

Marx gives a critique of Schmalz's views in notebook VI, pages 241-42 (see pp. 67-68 of the present volume).

Supplementary notes on Schmalz, with excerpts from his book, come at the end of notebook IX, page 421 (see pp.202-03 of the present volume). On the following page of the manuscript (notebook X, page 422) Marx passes over to the "Digression" devoted to the critical analysis of Quesnay's Tableau économique, which he here uses as it is in Schmalz's book.

It is noteworthy that in the whole "Digression" (pages 422-37 of the manuscript) Marx gives almost no extracts from the works of the authors he mentions. Only on the last page (page 437) does he give excerpts from Smith and an extract from Proudhon, saying that they belong to that passage in the manuscript (page 428) which deals with Proudhon (the Proudhon extract has accordingly been put in the present volume on p. 325). All this leads to the conclusion that when he was writing his "Digression" Marx did not have by him the works of Quesnay and of the other authors mentioned. It is very probable that he wrote almost the whole of the "Digression" (up to the quotations from Smith and Proudhon given on page 437) in April 1862, during his stay in Manchester.

In the supplementary notes on the Physiocrats in notebook XXIII, pages 1433-34, Marx uses the Tableau économique in the form in which Quesnay gives it in his *Analyse du Tableau économique* (see p. 378 of the present volume). He gives the Tableau in the same form also in his letter to Engels of 6 July, 1863 (see Marx-Engels, *Selected Correspondence*, Moscow, pp.174-78). p. 308

89 The letters used here by Marx (with the corresponding signs) give the Tableau a clarity that is lacking both in Schmalz and in Quesnay.

The identification of each line by two letters (a-b, a-c, c-d, etc.) makes it possible to determine its direction, that is, from which class to which class the line leads (the direction is shown by the alphabetical sequence of the letters: a-b, a-c, c-d, etc.). Thus the line a-b shows that the circulation between the class of landlords and the "productive class" (farmers) has as its starting-point the class of landlords (who buy food from the farmers).

The denotation of each line by two letters also expresses the movement of money and the movement of goods. Thus the line a-b shows the movement of money (the class of landlords pays one milliard in money to the productive class); but the same line, considered in its reverse direction (b-a) shows the movement of commodities (the productive class hands over foodstuff to the class of landlords to the amount of one milliard).

The broken line a-b-c-d is made up of the following links: (1) the section a-b, which shows the circulation between the landlords and the productive class (the landlords buy one milliard of foodstuff from the farmers); (2) the section a-c, which shows the circulation between the landlords and the sterile class (manufacturers)—the landlords buy manufactured goods from the manufacturers to the amount of one milliard; (3) the section c-d, which shows the circulation between the sterile class and the productive class (the manufacturers buy food from the farmers to the amount of one milliard).

The line a′-b′ shows the circulation between the productive class and the sterile class (the farmers buy one milliard of manufactured goods from the manufacturers).

The line a″-b″ shows the closing circulation between the sterile class and the productive class (the manufacturers buy from the farmers one milliard of raw materials required for the production of their manufactures). p. 308

90 Marx here contrasts the labourer, whose sole commodity is his labour-power, with the "possessor of commodities in the first form", that is, a possessor of commodities who has for sale "commodities as distinct from labour-power itself" (cf. pp. 167 and 171 of the present volume). p. 315

91 Marx means the first two paragraphs of the section "Money" ("Geld") in *Zur Kritik der politischen Ökonomie. Erstes Heft.* (Berlin, 1951, S.129-30). p. 322

92 Marx means the following passage from *A Contribution to the Critique of Political Economy*: "The money which they have spent as buyers gets back into their hands as soon as they appear again as vendors of commodities. The constant renewal of the circulation of commodities finds its reflection in the continual circulation over the entire surface of bourgeois society of a quantity of money which, passing from hand to hand, describes at the same time a number of different small cycles starting from numberless points and returning each to its own starting-points, to repeat the same movement over again" (Berlin, 1951, S. 102). p. 322

93 See pp. 269-81 of the present volume; cf. also *Capital*, Vol. II, Chapter XX, Section XIII, "Destutt de Tracy's Theory of Reproduction". p. 323

94 The section on Bray is in notebook X, pages 441-44 of the manuscript. It is unfinished; Bray's views on the circulation of money between workmen and capitalists are not touched on in it.

On Bray's views on the nature and role of money, cf. Marx's manuscript of 1847 *Arbeitslohn* (Wages) (in Marx-Engels *Kleine ökonomische Schriften*, Berlin, 1955, S. 228-29); Marx, *Grundrisse der Kritik der politischen Ökonomie* (Berlin, 1953), S. 55, 690, 754; Marx's letter to Engels of April 2, 1858 (Marx-Engels, *Selected Correspondence*, Moscow, p.127); Marx, *Zur Kritik der politischen Ökonomie. Erstes Heft* (Berlin, 1951, S. 86-87). p. 323

95 Subsequently, in notebook X, pages 428 and 437 of the manuscript, Marx gives a short characterisation of Proudhon's views on this question (see pp. 324-25 of the present volume). p. 323

96 The words in brackets indicate ideas which Marx intended to develop later. In all probability he had in mind Quesnay's apologist conception of private property in land. According to this conception, the right of landowners to their land is founded on the fact that their forebears had made the virgin land suitable for cultivation. In Chapter X of Part II of *Anti-Dühring*, which Marx wrote, he characterised this idea of the Physiocrats in the following way: "...by 'natural law' their" (the landlords') "proper function consists precisely in 'provision for the good management and expenditure for the maintenance of their patrimony in good repair', or...in making the *avances foncières*, that is, outlays for the preparation of the soil and provision of all equipment needed by the farms, which enable the farmer to devote his whole capital exclusively to the business of actual cultivation" (F. Engels, *Anti-Dühring*, Moscow, 1959, p. 341). p. 324

97 In notebook XV, pages 935-37 of the manuscript, Marx criticises Proudhon's vulgar view on the role of money-capital and the nature of interest, as expounded by Proudhon in *Gratuité du crédit*. See also *Capital*, Vol. III, Moscow, 1959, pp.339-41. p. 325

98 Marx made a comprehensive study of this problem in *Capital*, Vol. II, in Chapters XVII, XX (sections V and XII), and XXI (section I, subsection 1, "The Formation of a Hoard"). p. 327

99 See Note 98. p. 328

100 Here Marx uses, for the three classes of Quesnay, the following letters: L=*classe des propriétaires* (landlords); S=*classe stérile* (manufacturers, the sterile class); F=*fermiers, classe productive* (farmers, the productive class). p. 328

101 See Note 89. p. 328

102 See Note 89. p. 331

103 Marx assumes here and in his further account that according to Quesnay only one-fifth of the gross agricultural product does not enter into circulation, but is used by the "productive class" in natural form.

In notebook XXIII, pages 1433-34 of the manuscript, Marx returns to this point, and also in Chapter X of Part II of *Anti-Dühring*, written by him. There he defines his interpretation of Quesnay's views on the replacement of circulating capital in agriculture: "The whole gross product, of a value of five milliards, is therefore in the hands of the productive class, that is, in the first place the farmers, who have produced it by advancing an annual working capital of two milliards, which corresponds to an invested capital of ten milliards. The agricultural products

—foodstuffs, raw materials, etc.—which are required for the replacement of the working capital, including therefore the maintenance of all persons directly engaged in agriculture, are taken *in natura* from the total harvest and expended for the purpose of new agricultural production. Since, as we have seen, constant prices and simple reproduction on a given scale are assumed, the money value of the portion which is thus taken from the gross product is equal to two milliard *livres*. This portion, therefore, does not enter into general circulation. For, as we have noted, circulation which takes place only *within* a particular class, and not between one class and another, is excluded from the Tableau" (F. Engels, *Anti-Dühring*, Moscow, 1959, pp.337-38). p. 331

104 Marx means Baudeau's commentary *Explication du Tableau économique* (contained in *Physiocrates. Avec une introduction et des commentaires* par M. Eugène Daire, Deuxième partie, Paris, 1846, pp. 822-67). p. 333

105 Instead of the *thousand million* livres of Tours which are used in Quesnay's Tableau économique, Marx here speaks simply of *thousand* money units, which in no way alters the essence of the matter. p. 340

106 What is meant is *Zur Kritik der politischen Ökonomie. Erstes Heft* (Berlin, 1951, S. 110). p. 341

107 See *Zur Kritik der politischen Ökonomie. Erstes Heft.* (Berlin, 1951, S. 101-02, 305). p. 342

108 See Note 93. p. 342

109 See *Zur Kritik der politischen Ökonomie. Erstes Heft.* (Berlin, 1951, S. 100-01.) p. 342

110 See Note 98. p. 343

111 In notebooks XIV and XV (pages 852-90 of the manuscript) there is a chapter on the proletarian opposition to the Economists—opponents who base their views on Ricardo's theory. The unfinished section on Bray in notebook X (pages 441-44) and the end of the section on Hodgskin in notebook XVIII (pages 1084-86) also belong to this chapter. p. 345

112 See Linguet, *Théorie des lois civiles, ou Principes fondamentaux de la société*, tome I, Londres, 1767, p. 236. Marx puts the passage "Leur esprit est de consacrer la propriété" in his own words. p. 345

113 Marx spoke earlier of some of Petty's views, in the chapter "Theories of Productive and Unproductive Labour" in the part which deals with early attempts to distinguish between productive and unproductive labour (see pp. 179-81 of the present volume). p. 354

114 What is meant is the last or ninth section of Part I of *Capital*, as projected by Marx in the plan outlined in notebook XVIII, page 1140 (see the plan for Part I of *Capital*, on p. 414 of the present volume). p. 354

115 What is meant is Petty's work *A Treatise of Taxes, and Contributions*, first published in 1662. p. 362

116 The reference is to North's book *Discourses upon Trade*, and Locke's work *Some Considerations of the Consequences of the Lowering of Interest, and Raising the Value of Money*. Both were written in 1691, and published in London, the former in 1691 and the latter in 1692. p. 364

117 This work is called *Some Considerations of the Consequences of the Lowering of Interest, and Raising the Value of Money* (see also Note 116). p. 367

118 Marx quotes Locke here from Massie's book *An Essay on the Governing Causes of the Natural Rate of Interest*, London, 1750, pp. 10-11. In the 1768 edition of Locke's works this passage is in Vol. II, p. 24. p. 367

119 Marx here means one of his "supplementary notebooks" to the 1861-63 manuscript, in which in the spring of 1863, as he wrote to Engels on May 29, 1863, he had made extracts of "all kinds of literary historical material in connection with the part of Political Economy I have been working at". (Marx-Engels, *Briefe über "Das Kapital"*, Berlin, 1954, S. 118.) Supplementary notebooks A, B, C, D, E, F, G, H have survived. In supplementary notebook C the extracts from North's works are on pages 12-14. p. 368

120 Originally, "from 1688" was here in the manuscript, but then Marx struck the figure 1688, and put a question mark. In notebook XI, pages 507-08, he gives dates for the movement of the price of wheat. Between 1641 and 1649 the average price of wheat was 60s. $5^2/_3$ d. per quarter; but in the second half of the seventeenth century it fell to 44s. $2^1/_5$ d., and in the first half of the eighteenth century to 35s. $9^{29}/_{50}$ d. p. 368

121 Marx evidently means the passage from Chapter IV of Petty's treatise *Political Arithmetick* (1676), which he cites in the section on Rodbertus (notebook XI, page 494 of the manuscript). Cf. *Capital*, Vol. III, Moscow, 1959, p. 644: "In Petty's and D'Avenant's time, farmers and landowners complained about improvements and the bringing into cultivation of new land; the rent on better lands decreased...." p. 369

122 This quotation (beginning with the words "I will begin with the *Beggar*") is taken from supplementary notebook C, pages 12-13, in accordance with a note of Marx's on page 1419 of the manuscript (notebook XXIII). p. 370

123 In supplementary notebook C, page 14, Marx gives extracts from North's works in which the latter speaks of the "ebbing and flowing" in the money circulation of a country. Marx uses one of these quotations in Vol. I of *Capital* (Moscow, 1959, p.134, footnote 1). p. 371

124 Before this passage Massie gives extracts from Petty's *Political Arithmetick* and from Locke's *Some Considerations of the Consequences of the Lowering of Interest, and Raising the Value of Money.* p. 375

125 Marx puts here (with some abbreviations) the Tableau économique in the form given by Quesnay in the *Analyse du Tableau économique* (in: *Physiocrates*, par M. Eugène Daire, Première partie, Paris, 1846, p. 65). p. 378

126 See Note 103. p. 379

127 The Physiocrat Baudeau develops this point of view in his *Explication du Tableau économique* (Chapter III, paragraph 12; in: *Physiocrates*, par M. Eugène Daire, Deuxième partie, Paris, 1846, pp. 852-54). p. 380

128 Two dialogues of Quesnay's—"Du Commerce. Premier dialogue entre M. H. et M. N." and "Sur les travaux des artisans. Second dialogue"—are put together under this title in *Physiocrates*, Première partie, Paris,

1846, published by Daire. The passage cited by Marx is taken from the first dialogue. p. 380

129 This quotation from Quesnay is not in the actual text of Dupont de Nemours' book *De l'origine et des progrès d'une science nouvelle*, but in his *Maximes du docteur Quesnay, ou Résumé de ses principes d'économie sociale*" which by its contents is linked with that book; they are both in *Physiocrates*... par M. Eugène Daire, Première partie, Paris, 1846. The page number given by Marx refers to this edition. p. 380

130 The extract is taken from Quesnay's "Du Commerce. Premier dialogue entre M.H. et M.N.". p. 380

131 From the dialogue "Sur les travaux des artisans". p. 380

132 From the *Maximes du docteur Quesnay*. p. 380

133 Marx means Chapter XXVI ("On Gross and Net Revenue") in Ricardo's *Principles of Political Economy*. p. 381

134 Marx means his extracts from Buat's work in supplementary notebook A (see Note 119), pages 27-32. Further on, Marx's references to the pages of the supplementary notebook are replaced by references to the pages of Buat's work itself. p. 381

135 On Arthur Young as the "fanatical upholder of surplus-produce" see Vol. I of *Capital* (Moscow, 1959, p. 230, footnote 1). p. 381

136 See Note 133. p. 381

137 It was later ascertained that the author of this anonymous treatise analysed here by Marx was a certain John Gray, the dates of whose birth and death are not known. In 1802 this author published in London one more book on income tax. p. 382

138 Marx means his supplementary notebook H (see Note 119). In the next paragraph, Marx gives almost all the extracts from page 6 of anonymous work, which are on pages 32-33 of supplementary notebook H. p. 382

139 By "manufacturers" the anonymous English author means both the labourers in manufacture (whom he sometimes calls "labouring manufacturers") and the entrepreneurs in manufacture (who sometimes figure in his writings under the term "masters employers"). As used by this author the term "artificers" includes both the wage-labourers and also the handicraftsmen in the strict sense of the word. p. 382

140 See Note 17. p. 383

141 On pages 36-37 of supplementary notebook H there are extracts from pp. 31-33 of the anonymous work. p. 384

142 On pages 38-39 of supplementary notebook H there are extracts from pp. 51-54 of the anonymous work. In what follows, the references by Marx to the pages of supplementary notebook H have been replaced by references to the pages of the anonymous work. p. 384

143 On page 1446 of the manuscript (notebook XXIII) Marx mentions the book directed against the Physiocrats by Béardé de l'Abbaye, *Recherches sur les moyens de supprimer les impôts*, Amsterdam, 1770. Extracts from this book are on pages 10-11 of supplementary notebook H. p. 385

144 In this paragraph the order of the separate interpolations by Marx, which he put into the text of the extract from the anonymous author's book (pp. 38-39), has been somewhat altered. Marx gives the extract in shortened form. The words omitted have been replaced from the book cited, *The Essential Principles of the Wealth of Nations*, London, 1797, inasmuch as without them Marx's criticism of the considerations advanced in the anonymous work cannot be fully understood. p. 385

145 On the "Irish Right of Tenantry" see Marx's article in the *New York Daily Tribune* of July 11, 1853 (in Marx-Engels, *Werke*, Bd. 9, Dietz Verlag, Berlin, 1960, S. 157-63). p. 386

146 Marx means the section "Formal and Real Subsumption of Labour under Capital. Transitional Forms" (notebook XXI, pages 1306-16), which directly precedes the section "Productivity of Capital. Productive and Unproductive Labour". On the formal and real subsumption of labour under capital, see *Capital*, Vol. I, Moscow, 1959, pp. 509-10 and 736-38. p. 389

147 In *A Contribution to the Critique of Political Economy* (1859) Marx had already shown that in bourgeois society the mystification of social relations appears particularly strikingly in money, that the crystallisation of wealth as a fetish in the form of precious metals is a characteristic of bourgeois production (see Berlin edition, 1951, pp. 45-46 and 167). Marx makes an analysis of the process of fetishisation of bourgeois social relations in notebook XV, pages 891-99 and 910-19 of the manuscript. p. 389

148 Marx writes in Vol. I of *Capital*, "Science, generally speaking, costs the capitalist nothing, a fact that by no means hinders him from exploiting it. The science of others is as much annexed by capital as the labour of others. Capitalistic appropriation and personal appropriation, whether of science or of material wealth, are, however, totally different things. Dr. Ure himself deplores the gross ignorance of mechanical science existing among his dear machinery-exploiting manufacturers..." (K. Marx, *Capital*, Vol. I, Moscow, 1959, pp. 386-87, footnote 2). p. 391

149 Marx cut out from notebook XXI page 1318 of the 1861-63 manuscript (except for the last nine lines) and fastened it on to page 490 of the manuscript of the penultimate variant of Vol. I of *Capital* (the sixth chapter of this variant, which has been preserved, was published in Russian in Marx-Engels Archives, Vol. II (VII), 1933). Marx intended to use the further text (pages 1318, 1319 and the first half of 1320) for the section on profit, as is evident from his twice repeated note "Profit" in the margin of the manuscript (at the end of page 1318 and beginning of page 1320). p. 392

150 Marx here uses the Greek letter Δ (delta) which is used in mathematics to denote an increment, as the symbol of surplus-value. Later in the text he uses the letter h in the same sense. p. 393

151 Here and also further on Marx uses the letter x as the symbol of surplus-value. p. 395

152 Marx means the section "Exchange with Labour. Labour Process. The Production of Surplus-Value" (notebook I, pages 15-53 of the manuscript),

in which there is the subsection "Unity of Labour Process and Process of Producing Surplus-Value (Capitalist Production Process)" (pages 49-53 of the manuscript). p. 397

153 The reference here is to the subsections "Value of Labour-Power. Minimum of Wages or Average Wages" (notebook I, pages 21-25), and "Exchange between Money and Labour-Power" (ibid., pp. 25-34). Marx deals with the "price of labour" in notebook XXI, pages 1312-14 of the manuscript. p. 397

154 The four formulas for contractual relations according to Roman law: I give, that you may do; I do, that you may do; I do, that you may give; I give, that you may give. Cf. *Capital*, Vol. I, Moscow, 1959, p.540. p. 404

155 In numbering the pages of the manuscript, Marx wrote here 1328 instead of 1327. p. 405

156 See Note 133. p. 406

157 See *Capital*, Vol. III, Moscow, 1959, pp. 363-74. p. 408

158 In the same notebook XXI, page 1308 of the manuscript, Marx wrote of the labour of a factory handy man. p. 411

159 See *Capital*, Vol. II, Moscow, 1957, Chapter VI, and Vol. III, Moscow, 1959, Chapter XVII. p. 413

160 Marx wrote these draft plans in January 1863. They are in notebook XVIII of the 1861-63 manuscript, in the chapters on Cherbuliez and Richard Jones (they are separated from the text of these chapters by heavy square brackets). p. 414

161 Marx at first called the three theoretical parts of *Capital* "Chapters", then "Sections", and finally "Books". Cf. Note 12. p. 414

162 At the time when this plan was written out the first chapter of Part III of *Capital* had already been written in draft in notebook XVI of the 1861-63 manuscript; its heading there was "Surplus-Value and Profit". p. 415

INDEX OF AUTHORITIES

A

ARND, Karl. *Die naturgemässe Volkswirtschaft, gegenüber dem Monopoliengeiste und dem Communismus, mit einem Rückblicke auf die einschlagende Literatur*, Hanau, 1845.—48.

B

BARTON, John. *Observations on the Circumstances which Influence the Condition of the Labouring Classes of Society*, London, 1817. —154-55.

BASTIAT, Frédéric et Pierre-Joseph Proudhon. *Gratuité du crédit. Discussion entre M. Fr. Bastiat et. M. Proudhon*, Paris, 1850.—325.

BAUDEAU, l'abbé Nicolas. *Explication du Tableau économique, à Madame de***, par l'auteur des Ephémérides* (1776). In: *Physiocrates.* Avec une introduction et des commentaires par M. Eugène Daire. Deuxième partie Paris, 1846.—333, 379.

BELLERS, John. *Essays about the Poor, Manufactures, Trade, Plantations, and Immorality, and of the Excellency and Divinity of Inward Light Demonstrated from the Attributes of God, and the Nature of Man's Soul, as well as from the Testimony of the Holy Scriptures*, London, 1699.—370-71.

BERKLEY (BERKELEY). George. *The Querist, containing several Queries proposed to the Consideration of the Public*, London, 1750. (The first edition appeared 1735 to 1737 in Dublin.)—372.

BLANQUI, Jérome-Adolphe. *Histoire de l'économie politique en Europe depuis les anciens jusqu'à nos jours, suivie d'une bibliographie raisonnée des principaux ouvrages d'économie politique*, Bruxelles, 1839.—62, 64, 174.

BUAT-NANÇAY, Louis-Gabriel, comte du. *Éléments de la politique, ou Recherche des vrais principes de l'économie sociale.* Tomes I-VI, Londres, 1773.—381.

BUCHANAN, David. *Observations on the Subjects treated of in Dr. Smith's Inquiry into the Nature and Causes of the Wealth of Nations*, Edinburgh, 1814.—289.

C

CANARD, Nicolas-François. *Principes d'économie politique*, Paris, 1801.—204.

CANTILLON, Richard de. *Essai sur la nature du commerce en général.* Traduit de l'anglais, Londres, 1755.—73.

CHALMERS, Thomas. *On Political Economy, in Connexion with the Moral State and Moral Prospects of Society.* Second edition. Glasgow, Edinburgh, Dublin and London, 1832. (The first edition was published in the same year.) —299.

Considerations on the East India Trade. See NORTH Dudley, *Considerations upon the East India Trade.*

D

DAIRE, Louis-François-Eugène. *Introduction sur la doctrine des physiocrates.* In: *Physiocrates.* Avec une introduction et des commentaires par M. Eugène Daire. Première partie, Paris, 1846.—53.

D'AVENANT, Charles. *Discourses on the Publick Revenues, and on the Trade of England.* In two Parts. Viz. I. Of the Use of Political Arithmetick, in all Considerations about the Revenues and Trade. II. On Credit, and the Means and Methods by which it may be restored. III. On the Management of the King's Revenues. IV. Whither to Farm the Revenues, may not, in this Juncture, be most for the Publick Service? V. On the Publick Debts and Engagements. By the Author of *The Essay on Ways and Means,* London, 1698.—178-79.

D'AVENANT, Charles. *An Essay on the East India Trade* (1697). In: *Discourses on the Publick Revenues, and on the Trade of England.* Part II. London 1698. —178-79.

D'AVENANT, Charles. *An Essay upon the Probable Methods of Making a People Gainers in the Ballance of Trade.* Treating of these Heads, viz. Of the People of England. Of the Land of England, and its Products. Of our Payments to the Publick, and in what manner the Ballance of Trade may be thereby affected. That a Country cannot increase in Wealth and Power but by private Men doing their Duty to the Publick, and but by a steady Course of Honesty and Wisdom, in such are trusted with the Administration of Affairs. By the Author of *The Essay on Ways and Means,* London, 1699.—178.

DESTUTT DE TRACY, Antoine Louis Claude, le comte. *Éléments d'idéologie,* IV-e et V-e parties. Traité de la volonté et de ses effets. Paris, 1826. (The first edition appeared in 1815; in 1823 Part IV was published in Paris under the title *Traité de l'économie politique.*)—269-81, 283.

DUPONT DE NEMOURS, Pierre-Samuel. *De l'origine et des progrès d'une science nouvelle* (1767). In: *Physiocrates.* Avec une introduction et des commentaires par M. Eugène Daire. Première partie, Paris, 1846.—380.

DUPONT DE NEMOURS. Pierre-Samuel. *Maximes du docteur Quesnay, ou Résumé de ses principes d'économie sociale.* In: *Physiocrates.* Avec une introduction et des commentaires par M. Eugène Daire. Première partie, Paris, 1846.—380.

E

An Essay on the East India Trade. See D'AVENANT, Charles, *An Essay on the East India Trade.*

The Essential Principles of the Wealth of Nations, illustrated, in Opposition to some False Doctrines of Dr. Adam Smith, and others, London, 1797.—382-86.

F

FERRIER, François-Louis-Auguste. *Du Gouvernement considéré dans ses rapports avec le commerce*, Paris, 1805.—252-53.

G

GANILH, Charles. *Des systèmes d'économie politique, de la valeur comparative de leurs doctrines, et de celle qui paraît la plus favorable aux progrès de la rechesse*. Seconde édition. Tome I et II. Paris, 1821. (The first edition was published in Paris in 1809.)—203-12, 215, 220-23, 229-30.

GANILH, Charles. *La théorie de l'économie politique*. Tome I et II. Paris. 1815.—213.

GARNIER, Germain. *Abrégé élémentaire des principes de l'économie politique*, Paris, 1796.—202.

GARNIER, Germain. *Notes du traducteur*. In: Adam Smith. *Recherches sur la nature et les causes de la richesse des nations*. Traduction nouvelle, avec des notes et observations; par Germain Garnier. Tome cinquième. Paris, 1802.—63-64, 183-87, 198-202, 265.

H

HOBBES. Thomas. *Leviathan: or the Matter, Form and Power of a Commonwealth, Ecclesiastical and Civil* (1651). In: *The English Works of Thomas Hobbes of Malmesbury*, now first collected and edited by Sir William Molesworth, Bart. Vol. III, London, 1839.—353, 365.

HODGSKIN, Thomas. *Popular Political Economy*. Four Lectures delivered at the London Mechanics' Institution, London, 1827.—88, 406.

HUME,David. *Of Commerce* (1752), In: HUME, David, *Essays and Treatises on several Subjects*. In two volumes. Vol. I, containing Essays, moral, political and literary. A new edition. London, 1764.—373.

HUME, David. *Of Interest* (1752). In: HUME, David, *Essays and Treatises on several Subjects*. In two volumes, Vol. I, containing Essays, moral, political and literary. A new edition. London, 1764.—373-75.

I

An Inquiry into those Principles, respecting the Nature of Demand and the Necessity of Consumption, lately advocated by Mr. Malthus, from which it is concluded, that Taxation and the Maintenance of Unproductive Consumers can be conducive to the Progress of Wealth, London, 1821.—61, 283.

J

JONES, Richard. *An Essay on the Distribution of Wealth, and on the Sources of Taxation*, Part I: Rent. London, 1831.—48.

K

KING, Gregory. *Natural and political Observations and Conclusions upon the State and the Condition of England*, 1696.—178.

L

LAUDERDALE, James Maitland, the Earl of. *An Inquiry into the Nature and Origin of Public Wealth, and into the Means and Causes of its Increase*, Edinburgh and London, 1804.—93, 264-65.

LAUDERDALE, James Maitland, le comte de. *Recherches sur la nature et l'origine de la richesse publique, et sur les moyens et les causes qui concourent à son accroissement.* Traduit de l'anglais par E. Lagentie de Lavaïsse, Paris, 1808.—93, 264-66.

LINGUET, Simon-Nicolas-Henri, *Théorie des lois civiles, ou Principes fondamentaux de la société.* Tome premier et second, Londres, 1767.—345-50.

LOCKE, John. *Some Considerations of the Consequences of the Lowering of Interest, and Raising the Value of Money* (1691). In: *The Works of John Locke.* Folio edition. Vol. II, London, 1740.—367.

LOCKE, John. *Two Treatises of Government* (1690). In: *The Works of John Locke*, in four volumes. The 7th edition. Vol. II, London, 1768.—365-67.

M

MALTHUS, Thomas Robert. *Definitions in Political Economy*, preceded by an Inquiry into the Rules which ought to guide Political Economists in the Definition and Use of their Terms; with Remarks on the Deviation from these Rules in their Writings. A new edition with a preface, notes, and supplementary remarks by John Cazenove, London, 1853.—74.

MANDEVILLE, Bernard de. *The Fable of the Bees: or Private Vices, Publick Benefits.* 5th edition, London, 1728; the second edition, London, 1723. (The first edition was published in 1705.)—176, 388.

MARX, Karl. *Misère de la Philosophie. Réponse à la philosophie de la misère de M. Proudhon.* Paris et Bruxelles, 1847.—74.

MARX, Karl. *Zur Kritik der politischen Oekonomie*, Erstes Heft, Berlin, 1859.—70, 151, 174, 303, 322, 341, 342, 389.

MASSIE, Joseph. *An Essay on the Governing Causes of the Natural Rate of Interest; wherein the Sentiments of Sir William Petty and Mr. Locke, on that Head, are considered*, London, 1750.—373, 375-77.

MERCIER DE LA RIVIERE, Paul-Pierre. *L'ordre naturel et essentiel des sociétés politiques.* Tome premier et second. Londres et Paris, 1767—62, 65.

MILL, John Stuart, *Essays on some Unsettled Questions of Political Economy*, London, 1844—182.

MIRABEAU, Victor Riqueti, marquis de. *Tableau économique avec ses explications.* In: *L'ami des hommes, ou Traité de la population*, t. VIII, 1760.—343.

MONTESQUIEU, Charles-Louis de. *De l'esprit des lois* (1748). Tomes I-IV. Paris, 1820.—304.

N

NECKER, Jacques. *De l'administration des finances de la France* (1784). In: *Œuvres de Necker.* Tome deuxième. Lausanne et Paris, 1789.—305-307.

NECKER, Jacques, *Sur la législation et le commerce des grains*, (1775). In: *Œuvres de Necker.* Tome quatrième. Lausanne, 1786, —305, 307.

NORTH, Sir Dudley. *Considerations upon the East India Trade*, London, 1701.—179.

NORTH, Sir Dudley. *Discourses upon Trade; principally directed to the Cases of the Interest, Coynage, Clipping, Increase of Money*, London, 1691.—368-71.

P

PALEY, William. *The Principles of Moral and Political Philosophy*, London, 1785.—283.
PALEY, William. *Principes de philosophie morale et politique*, traduits de l'anglais sur la 19-e édition par J.-L.-S. Vincent. Deux volumes. Paris, 1817.—283.
PAOLETTI, Ferdinando. *I veri mezzi di render felici le società* (1722). In: *Scrittori Classici Italiani di Economia Politica*. Parte moderna. Tomo XX. Milano, 1804.—60.
PETTY, William. *An Essay Concerning the Multiplication of Mankind* (1682). In: PETTY, William. *Several Essays in Political Arithmetick*: The Titles of which follow in the Ensuing Pages. Political Arithmetick, or a Discourse concerning the Extent and Value of Lands, People, Buildings; Husbandry, Manufactures, Commerce, Fishery, Artizans, Seamen, Soldiers, Publick Revenues, Interest, Taxes, Superlucration, Registries, Banks; Valuation of Men, Increasing of Seamen, of Militia's, Harbours, Situation, Shipping, Power at Sea, etc. As the same relates to every Countrey in general, but more particularly to the Territories of His Majesty of Great Britain, and his Neighbours of Holland, Zealand, and France, London, 1699.—362.
PETTY, William. *The Political Anatomy of Ireland* (1672). With the Establishment for that Kingdom when the late Duke of Ormond was Lord Lieutenant. Taken from the Records. To which is added Verbum Sapienti; or an Account of the Wealth and Expenses of England, and the Method of raising Taxes in the most Equal manner, Shewing also, That the Nation can bear the Charge of Four Millions per Annum, when the occasions of the Government require it. London, 1691.—362-63, 364.
PETTY, William. *Political Arithmetick* (1676). In: PETTY, William. *Several Essays in Political Arithmetick*. London, 1699.—174, 180, 181.
PETTY, William. *Quantulumcunque concerning Money*, 1682. To the Lord Marquess of Halyfax, London, 1695.—363, 364.
PETTY, William. *A Treatise of Taxes, and Contributions*. Shewing the Nature and Measures of Crown-Lands, Assessments, Customs, Poll-Moneys, Lotteries, Benevolence, Penalties, Monopolies, Offices, Tythes, Raising of Coins, Harth-Money, Excise, etc. With several intersperst Discourses and Digressions concerning Warrs, The Church, Universities, Rents and Purchases, Usury and Exchange, Banks and Lombards, Registries for Conveyances, Beggars, Ensurance, Exportation of Money, Wool, Free Ports, Coins, Housing, Liberty of Conscience, etc. The same being frequently applied to the State and Affairs of Ireland, and is now thought seasonable for the present Affairs of England, London, 1662.—181-82, 364.
Idem, London, 1667.—354-62.
Idem, London, 1679.—181.
PETTY, William. *Verbum Sapienti*. (1665). In: PETTY, William. *The Political Anatomy of Ireland*, London, 1691.—362.
Physiocrates. Quesnay, Dupont

de Nemours, Mercier de la Rivière, l'abbé Baudeau, Le Trosne. Avec une introduction sur la doctrine des Physiocrates, des commentaires et des notices historiques, par M. Eugène Daire, Première et deuxième partie. Paris, 1846. See BAUDEAU, *Explication du Tableau économique...*; DAIRE, *Introduction sur la doctrine des physiocrates...*; DUPONT DE NEMOURS, *De l'origine...*; DUPONT DE NEMOURS, *Maximes du docteur Quesnay...*; QUESNAY, *Analyse du Tableau économique*; QUESNAY, *Dialogues...*; QUESNAY, *Maximes...*

Physiocratie, ou Constitution naturelle du gouvernement le plus avantageux au genre humain. Recueil [d'œuvres de Quesnay] publié part Du Pont. Leyde et Paris, 1767.—230.

PROUDHON, Pierre-Joseph. *Système des contradictions économiques, ou Philosophie de la misère.* Deux volumes, Paris, 1846.—64.

PROUDHON, Pierre-Joseph. *Gratuité du crédit.* See BASTIAT, Frédéric et Pierre-Joseph Proudhon. *Gratuité du crédit. Discussion entre M. Fr. Bastiat et M. Proudhon.*

Q

QUESNAY, François. *Analyse du Tableau économique* (1766). In: *Physiocrates.* Avec une introduction et des commentaires par M. Eugène Daire. Première partie, Paris, 1846.—54, 378.

QUESNAY, François. *Dialogues sur le commerce et sur les travaux des artisans* (1766); *Du Commerce. Premier dialogue entre M. H. et M. N.*; *Sur les travaux des artisans. Second dialogue.* In: *Physiocrates.* Avec une introduction et des commentaires par M. Eugène Daire. Première partie, Paris, 1846.—380.

QUESNAY, François. *Maximes générales du gouvernement économique d'un royaume agricole* (1758). In: *Physiocrates.* Avec une introduction et des commentaires par M. Eugène Daire. Première partie, Paris, 1846.—64-65.

R

RAMSAY, George. *An Essay on the Distribution of Wealth,* Edinburgh, 1836.—104-105, 107-108.

Return to an Address of the Honourable The House of Commons, dated 24 April 1861. Ordered, by The House of Commons, to be printed, 11 February 1862.—201.

RICARDO, David. *On the Principles of Political Economy, and Taxation,* 2nd edition. London, 1819. (The first edition was published in London in 1817.)—60.

Idem. Third edition, London, 1821.—177, 226-27, 381.

RICARDO, David. *Des Principes de l'économie politique et de l'impôt.* Traduit de l'anglais par F. S. Constancio. D. M. etc.; avec des notes explicatives et critiques, par M. Jean-Baptiste Say. Tome premier et second, Paris, 1819.—221, 222, 224, 226.

ROSSI, Pellegrino Luigi Edoardo. *Cours d'économie politique.* Année 1836-1837 (Contenant les deux volumes de l'édition de Paris). Bruxelles, 1842.—292-98.

S

SAY, Jean-Baptiste. *Traité d'économie politique, ou simple Exposition de la manière dont se forment, se distribuent, et se consomment les richesses.* Tome premier et second, Paris, 1803.—229, 266.

Idem. Troisième édition. Tome premier et second, Paris, 1817.—103, 150, 266-69.

SCHMALZ, Theodor Anton Heinrich. *Économie politique.* Ouvrage traduit de l'allemand par Henri Jouffroy. Tome I et II. Paris, 1826.—67, 202-203.

SENIOR, Nassau William. *Principes fondamentaux de l'économie politique, tirés de leçons édites et inédites de Mr. N. W. Senior, professeur émérite d'économie politique à l'université d'Oxford, par le c-te Jean Arrivabene,* Paris, 1836.—287-89, 290-92.

SISMONDI, Jean-Charles-Léonard Simonde de. *Nouveaux principes d'économie politique, ou De la richesse dans ses rapports avec la population.* Seconde édition. Tome premier et second, Paris, 1827. (The first edition was published in Paris in 1819).—177, 282.

SMITH, Adam. *An Inquiry into the Nature and Causes of the Wealth of Nations.* Two vols. London, 1776.—43, 61, 87-88, 97, 199.

SMITH, Adam. *An Inquiry into the Nature and Causes of the Wealth of Nations.* With a Life of the Author, and introductory Discourse, Notes and supplemental Dissertations. By J. R. McCulloch. In four volumes. Edinburgh, 1828—69-70, 83, 84-85, 155-56, 159-60, 161, 300, 303.

SMITH, Adam. *Recherches sur la nature et les causes de la richesse des nations.* Traduction nouvelle, avec des notes et observations; par Germain Garnier. Tomes I-VI, Paris, 1802.—69, 71, 73-77, 78-79, 81-83, 84, 89-90, 91, 93, 94, 97-102, 125, 162-63, 168-70, 173, 253-64, 265-66, 280, 302, 343.

SPENCE, William. *Britain independent of Commerce; or Proofs deduced from an Investigation into the true Causes of the Wealth of Nations, that our Riches, Prosperity and Power are derived from Sources inherent in ourselves, and would not be affected even though our Commerce were annihilated.* London, 1807.—382.

STEUART, Sir James. *An Inquiry into the Principles of Political Economy: Being an Essay on the Science of Domestic Policy in Free Nations.* In which are particularly considered, Population, Agriculture, Trade, Industry, Money, Coin, Interest, Circulation, Banks, Exchange, Public credit, and Taxes. In two volumes. London, 1767.—43.

STEUART, Sir James. *An Inquiry into the Principles of Political Economy: Being an Essay on the Science of Domestic Policy in Free Nations....* In: *The Works, political, metaphysical, and chronological, of the late Sir James Steuart, of Coltness, Bart.* Now first collected by General Sir James Steuart, Bart., his son, from his father's corrected copies, to which are subjoined anecdotes of the Author. In six volumes. London, 1805.—41-43.

Idem. Vol. III. London, 1805.—43.

STORCH, Henri. *Considérations sur la nature du revenu national* (tome V du *Cours d'économie politique*), Paris, 1824.—103-104.

STORCH, Henri. *Cours d'économie politique, ou Exposition des principes qui déterminent la prospérité des nations.* Tomes I-VI, St. Petersbourg, 1815.—408.

STORCH, Henri. *Cours d'économie politique, ou Exposition des principes qui déterminent la pros-*

périté des nations. Avec des notes explicatives et critiques par J.-B. Say, Tomes I-IV, Paris, 1823.—284-87.

T

TURGOT, Anne-Robert-Jacques. *Réflexions sur la formation et la distribution des richesses* (1766). In: Œ*uvres de Turgot.* Nouvelle édition par M. Eugène Daire. Tome premier, Paris, 1844.—43, 54-59, 62, 64.

V

VERRI, Pietro. *Meditazioni sulla Economia politica* (1771). In: *Scrittori Classici Italiani di Economia Politica.* Parte moderna. Tomo XV. Milano, 1804.—60, 67-68.

NAME INDEX

A

Anderson, James (1739-1808)—English bourgeois economist who set forth the principal features of the theory of differential rent.—382.

Anne (1665-1714)—Queen of Great Britain and Ireland (1702-14).—383.

Aristotle (384-322 B.C.)—great philosopher of antiquity, vacillated between materialism and idealism, ideologist of the slave-holding class; advocate of the natural slave economy, was the first to analyse value.—287.

Arnd, Karl (1788-1877)—German bourgeois economist, representative of vulgar political economy.—48.

Arrivabene, Jean (1787-1881)—Italian political emigrant, economist; translator of Senior's works into French.—287.

B

Babbage, Charles (1792-1871)—English mathematician and mechanist, bourgeois economist.—388.

Barton, John (end of the 18th-beginning of the 19th century)—English economist, representative of classical bourgeois political economy.—38, 155.

Bastiat, Frédéric (1801-1850)—French vulgar economist; propagated the theory that harmony of class interests exists in bourgeois society.—325, 404, 407.

Baudeau, Nicolas (1730-1792)—French abbé, economist, representative of the Physiocratic school.—333, 379.

Béardé de l'Abbaye (1704-1771)—French economist and agronomist.—385.

Bellers, John (1654-1725)—English economist, stressed the part labour played in the creation of wealth; author of several utopian projects of social reforms.—370.

Berkeley, George (1685-1753)—English reactionary philosopher, prominent representative of subjective idealism, bishop; opponent of Mercantilism; considered labour to be the main source of wealth; representative of the nominalistic theory of money.—372.

Blanqui, Jérôme Adolphe (1798-1854)—French bourgeois economist, wrote a history of political economic doctrines, representative of vulgar political economy.—62, 64, 174.

Boisguillebert, Pierre (1646-1714)—French economist, founder of classical bourgeois political economy in France, precursor of the Physiocrats.—50.

Bray, John Francis (1809-1897)—English economist, utopian socialist, follower of Robert Owen; developed the theory of "labour money".—37, 38, 323.

Brissot, Jean Pierre (1754-1793)—prominent figure in the French bourgeois revolution of the end of the 18th century, member of the Jacobins' Club at the beginning of the revolution, later became the leader and theoretician of the Girondists.—345.

Brougham, Henry Peter, Baron (1778-1868)—English lawyer and man of letters; in the 1820s and 1830s, active member of the Whig Party, Lord Chancellor (1830-34). —176, 230.

Buat-Nançay, Louis-Gabriel, comte du (1731-1787)—French historian and economist, follower of the Physiocrats.—381.

Buchanan, David (1779—1848)—English publicist and bourgeois economist, follower and commentator of Adam Smith.—49, 289.

C

Caesar (Gaius Julius) (c. 100-44 B.C.)—famous Roman soldier and statesman. —287.

Canard, Nicolas-Francois (1750-1833) — French economist and mathematician.—204.

Cantillon, Richard (1680-1734)—English economist, forerunner of the Physiocrats.—73.

Carey, Henry Charles (1793-1879)—American vulgar economist, author of the reactionary theory of the harmony of class interests in capitalist society.—175, 415.

Cazenove, John (19th century)—English vulgar economist, follower of Malthus.—74.

Chalmers, Thomas (1780-1847)—English Protestant theologian and bourgeois economist, follower of Malthus. —299.

Charles II (1630-1685)—King of Great Britain and Ireland (1660-85)—368.

Cherbuliez, Antoine Elisée (1797-1869)—Swiss economist, Sismondi's follower who combined Sismondi's theory with some elements from Ricardo's theory.—38.

Child, Sir Josiah (1630-1699)—English economist, Mercantilist, banker and merchant.—368.

Colbert, Jean Baptiste (1619-1683)—French statesman, Controller-General of Finance, pursued a Mercantilist policy to strengthen the absolute monarchy.—59, 66.

Constancio, Francisco Solano (1772-1846)—Portuguese doctor, diplomat and writer; translated the works of English economists into French.—221, 222.

Culpeper, Sir Thomas (1578-1662)—English bourgeois economist, adherent of Mercantilism.—368.

Custodi, Pietro (1771-1842)—Italian economist, published the works of Italian economists written between the end of the 16th century and the beginning of the 19th.—60, 67.

D

Daire, Louis-François-Eugène (1798-1847)—French bourgeois economist, publisher of works on political economy.—53, 54, 380.

D'Avenant, Charles (1656-1714)—English economist and statistician, Mercantilist.—178, 179.

Destutt de Tracy, Antoine-Louis Claude, comte (1754-1836)—French vulgar economist, sensationalist philosopher; protagonist of constitutional monarchy.—184, 269, 271, 272, 280, 283, 323, 342.

Dupont de Nemours, Pierre-Samuel (1739-1817)—French statesman and economist, Physiocrat.—380.

E

Epicurus (c. 341-c. 270 B.C.)—outstanding materialist philosopher of ancient Greece, atheist.—66.

F

Ferrier, François-Louis-Auguste (1777-1861)—French vulgar economist, follower of the Mercantilists.—230, 252-53, 266.
Forcade, Eugène (1820-1869)—French bourgeois writer; vulgar economist.—112.

G

Ganilh, Charles (1758-1836)—French bourgeois politician; vulgar economist, follower of the Mercantilists.—158, 203-209, 211, 212, 215, 218, 220, 222-23, 225, 229-30, 266, 297, 299.
Garnier, Germain (1754-1821)—French economist and politician, monarchist; follower of the Physiocratic school; translator and critic of Adam Smith.—63-64, 73, 78-79, 83, 99-100, 168-70, 176, 183, 185-87, 198-203, 253, 258-61, 265-66, 267, 280, 284, 285, 297, 299, 301, 302, 344.
Godwin, William (1756-1836)—English petty-bourgeois novelist and writer on political subjects; rationalist, one of the founders of anarchism.—345.

H

Hobbes, Thomas (1588-1679)—outstanding English philosopher, representative of mechanistic materialism; Hobbes's social and political views were strongly anti-democratic.—75, 353, 354, 365.
Hodgskin, Thomas (1787-1869)—English economist and journalist; defended the interests of the proletariat and criticised capitalism from the standpoint of utopian socialism, drew socialist conclusions on the basis of Ricardo's theory.—39, 88, 406.
Homer—semi-legendary epic poet of ancient Greece, author of *Iliad* and *Odyssey*.—285, 298.
Horace (Quintus Horatius Flaccus) (65-8 B.C.)—outstanding Roman poet.—176, 269.
Hume, David (1711-1776)—English philosopher, subjective idealist, agnostic; bourgeois historian and economist, opponent of Mercantilism, one of the early representatives of the quantitative theory of money.—373, 377.

J

Jones, Richard (1790-1855)—English economist, one of the last representatives of classical bourgeois political economy.—39, 48.
Jouffroy, Henri—author and translator of several works on political economy and law published in the 1820s and 1840s; of French descent.—67, 203.

K

King, Gregory (1648-1712)—English statistician.—178.
Kock, Charles-Paul de (c. 1794-1871)—French bourgeois writer, author of light frivolous novels.—402.

L

Lagentie de Lavaïsse—translated Lauderdale's book *An Inquiry into the Nature and Origin of Public Wealth...* into French.—92.

Lauderdale, James Maitland, Earl of (1759-1839)—Scottish bourgeois politician and economist; criticised Smith's theory from the standpoint of vulgar political economy.—92-93, 176, 230, 264-66, 297, 299.

Law, John (1671-1729)—Scottish bourgeois economist and financier, Minister of Finance of France (1719-20); notorious for his speculative enterprises—connected with the issuing of bank-notes—which ended in a complete failure.—59, 64.

Lessing, Gotthold Ephraim (1729-1781)—great German writer, critic and philosopher, one of the outstanding representatives of the Enlightenment of the 18th century—285.

Le Trosne, Guilleaume François (1728-1780)—French bourgeois economist, Physiocrat.—379.

Linguet, Simon Nicolas Henri (1736-1794)—French lawyer, publicist, historian and economist; criticised the Physiocrats and bourgeois liberalism from the standpoint of feudal absolutism; he made, however, profound critical observations about bourgeois freedom and property.—37, 305, 344-47, 349-50.

List, Friedrich (1789-1846)—German vulgar economist, advocate of extreme protectionism.—252.

Locke, John (1632-1704)—outstanding English dualist philosopher, sensualist; bourgeois economist, vacillated between the nominalistic and metal theory of money.—93, 302, 365-67, 368-69, 373, 375, 382.

Luther, Martin (1483-1546)—prominent figure of the Reformation, founder of Protestantism (Lutheranism) in Germany; ideologist of the German burghers; during the Peasant War in 1525 sided with the princes against the insurgent peasants and the urban poor.—39.

M

McCulloch, John Ramsay (1789-1864)—English bourgeois economist, vulgariser of Ricardo's economic theory, ardent apologist of capitalism.—38, 69, 83, 85, 156, 179, 300, 303.

Malthus, Thomas Robert (1766-1834)—English priest, economist, ideologist of the bourgeoisified landed aristocracy, apologist of capitalism, propounded a misanthropic theory of population—38, 73, 74, 88, 154, 157, 176, 212, 281, 299, 354, 415.

Mandeville, Bernard (1670-1733)—English writer and economist.—388.

Massie, Joseph (d. 1784)—English economist, representative of classical bourgeois political economy.—369, 373, 375, 377.

Mendelssohn, Moses (1729-1786)—German reactionary bourgeois philosopher, deist.—287.

Mercier de la Rivière, Paul Pierre (1720-1793)—French bourgeois economist, Physiocrat.—62, 65.

Mill, James (1773-1836)—Scottish bourgeois economist and philosopher; vulgarised Ricardo's theory but at the same time he arrived at some radical conclusions based on this theory.—38.

Mill, John Stuart (1806-1873)—Scottish bourgeois economist and positivist philosopher, follower of the classical school of political economy, son of James Mill.—38, 182.

Milton, John (1608-1674)—great English poet and writer, took part in the English Revolution of the 17th century.—401.

Mirabeau, Victor Riqueti, marquis de (1715-1789)—French economist, Physiocrat; father of Honoré Gabriel Mirabeau, a prominent figure in the French bourgeois revolution of the end of the 18th century.—47, 50, 66, 343.

Molesworth, William (1810-1855)—English politician, published the works of Hobbes.—353.

Montesquieu, Charles-Louis de Secondat, Baron de la Brede et de (1689-1755)—outstanding French bourgeois sociologist, economist and writer, representative of the 18th-century bourgeois Enlightenment; advocate of the quantitative theory of money.—301, 302, 345.

Müllner, Amadeus Gottfried Adolf (1774-1829)—German writer and critic.—387.

N

Napoleon I (Bonaparte) (1769-1821)—Emperor of the French (1804-14 and 1815).—252.

Necker, Jacques (1732-1804)—French politician and economist; was several times appointed Director General of Finance in 1770s and 1780s, attempted to introduce certain reforms on the eve of the bourgeois revolution.—37, 305-07.

Nicholas I (1796-1855)—Tsar of Russia (1825-55).—284.

North, Sir Dudley (1641-1691)—English economist, one of the first representatives of classical bourgeois political economy.—364, 368-71.

P

Paley, William (1743-1805)—English theologian, philosopher and economist.—283.

Paoletti, Ferdinando (1717-1801)—Italian clergyman; Physiocrat.—60.

Petty, William (1623-1687)—outstanding English economist and statistician, founder of classical school of bourgeois political economy in Britain.—174, 178-82, 303, 354-62, 364, 368, 369, 373, 375.

Pompey (Gnaeus Pompeius Magnus) (106-48 B.C.)—Roman general and statesman.—348.

Prevost, Guilleaume (1799-1883)—Swiss bourgeois economist, vulgariser of Ricardo's theory—38.

Proudhon, Pierre-Joseph (1809-1865)—French publicist, economist and sociologist, ideologist of the petty bourgeoisie, one of the founders of anarchism.—64, 112, 278, 323, 324.

Q

Quesnay, François (1694-1774)—great French economist, physician, founder of the Physiocratic school.—37, 50, 54, 64-65, 203, 230, 308, 312, 327, 328, 329, 332-33, 335, 343-44, 378-80.

R

Ramsay, Sir George (1800-1871)—English economist, one of the last representatives of the classical school of bourgeois political economy.—38, 103-106, 107.

Ravenstone, Piercy (d. 1830)—English economist, follower of Ricardo, defended the interests of the proletariat, opponent of Malthusianism.—39.

Ricardo, David (1772-1823)—English economist, leading representative of classical bourgeois political economy.—38, 52, 61, 71, 73, 81, 82, 88, 89, 92, 97, 98, 104, 105, 151, 176-77, 204, 205, 221-28, 381, 406, 415, 416.

Rodbertus-Jagetzow, Johann Karl (1805-1875)—German vulgar economist and politician, ideologist of the Prussian bourgeoisified landed aristocracy, advocate of the reactionary Prussian "state socialism".—38.

Roederer, Pierre-Louis, comte (1754-1835)—French bourgeois politician.—66.

Roscher, Wilhelm Georg Friedrich (1817-1894)—German vulgar economist, professor at Leipzig University, founder of the so-called historical school in political economy.—387.

Rossi, Pellegrino Luigi Edoardo (1787-1848)—Italian vulgar economist, lawyer and politician; lived in France for a long time.—176, 230, 292, 294-96.

S

Say, Jean-Baptiste (1767-1832)—French bourgeois economist, representative of vulgar political economy.—103-104, 150, 176, 221-23, 229, 234, 266-69, 281, 284, 404.

Schiller, Friedrich (1759-1805)—great German writer.—387.

Schmalz, Theodor Anton Heinrich (1760-1831)—German lawyer and economist, follower of the Physiocrats, extreme reactionary.—67, 202-03.

Senior, Nassau William (1790-1864)—English vulgar economist; apologist of capitalism, opposed the reduction of working hours.—176, 230, 287, 289-92, 383.

Shakespeare, William (1564-1616)—great English writer.— 375.

Sismondi, Jean-Charles-Léonard Simonde de (1773-1842)—Swiss economist, petty-bourgeois critic of capitalism, prominent representative of economic romanticism.—177, 282, 415.

Smith, Adam (1723-1790)—Scottish economist, one of the great representatives of the classical school of bourgeois political economy.—37, 38, 43, 44, 47, 49, 60, 61, 63, 69-104, 106, 150-51, 152-57, 159-64, 167-77, 182-87, 199-204, 210, 212, 223, 225, 226, 251, 253-58, 260, 262-67, 269-71, 278, 281, 283-85, 287-93, 295-96, 298-300, 302-304, 306, 343-44, 360, 381, 382, 384, 415.

Sophocles (c. 497-c. 406 B.C.)—famous dramatist of ancient Greece, author of classic tragedies.—387.

Spence, Thomas (1750-1814)—English utopian socialist, advocated the abolition of private property in land and establishment of agrarian socialism.—382.

Spence, William (1783-1860)—English entomologist, and economist.—382.

Steuart, Sir James (1712-1780)—English bourgeois economist, one of the last representatives of Mercantilism.— 37, 41-43, 48, 50, 79.

Stirling, Patrick James (1809-1891)—English vulgar economist.—38.

Storch, Andrei (Henri, Heinrich) *Karlovich* (1766-1835)—Russian economist, statistician and historian, member of the St. Petersburg Academy of Sciences, follower of classical bourgeois political economy.—113, 174, 176, 230, 284-86, 291, 292, 297, 299, 408.

T

Tocqueville, Alexis Charles Henri Maurice Clérel de (1805-1859)—French bourgeois historian and politician, legitimist and advocate of constitutional monarchy.—230, 266.

Tooke, Thomas (1774-1858)—English bourgeois economist, belonged to the classical school of political economy, criticised Ricardo's theory of money; author of the voluminous work *History of Prices*.—125, 251.

Torrens, Robert (1780-1864)—English bourgeois economist; vulgariser of Ricardo's economic principles; denied that the labour theory of value can be applied to the capitalist mode of production.—38.

Turgot, Anne-Robert-Jacques (1727-1781)—French economist and statesman; outstanding representative of the Physiocratic school; Controller-General of Finance (1774-76)—43, 47, 50, 54-55, 57-58, 62, 65, 66-67, 344, 358.

U

Ure, Andrew (1778-1857)—English chemist and vulgar economist, wrote several works on economic aspects of industry.—391.

V

Vanderlint, Jacob (d. 1740)—English economist, precursor of the Physiocrats, one of the early representatives of the quantitative theory of money.—382, 386.

Verri, Pietro (1728-1797)—Italian bourgeois economist, one of the first to criticise the theory of the Physiocrats.—60, 67-68.

Virgil (Publius Vergilius Maro) (70-19 B.C.)—great Roman poet. —225.

Voltaire, François Marie (real name: Arouet) (1694-1778)—French deist philosopher, satirist, prominent representative of 18th-century bourgeois Enlightenment, fought against absolutism and Catholicism.—285.

W

Wakefield, Edward Gibbon (1796-1862)—English statesman and economist who put forward the reactionary colonisation theory. —38, 414.

Y

Young, Arthur (1741-1820)—English agronomist and bourgeois economist.—381, 385.